European
erotic romance

MANCHESTER
1824
Manchester University Press

The
Manchester
Spenser

The Manchester Spenser is a monograph and text series devoted to historical and textual approaches to Edmund Spenser – to his life, times, places, works and contemporaries.

A growing body of work in Spenser and Renaissance studies, fresh with confidence and curiosity and based on solid historical research, is being written in response to a general sense that our ability to interpret texts is becoming limited without the excavation of further knowledge. So the importance of research in nearby disciplines is quickly being recognised, and interest renewed: history, archaeology, religious or theological history, book history, translation, lexicography, commentary and glossary – these require treatment for and by students of Spenser.

The Manchester Spenser, to feed, foster and build on these refreshed attitudes, aims to publish reference tools, critical, historical, biographical and archaeological monographs on or related to Spenser, from several disciplines, and to publish editions of primary sources and classroom texts of a more wide-ranging scope.

The Manchester Spenser consists of work with stamina, high standards of scholarship and research, adroit handling of evidence, rigour of argument, exposition and documentation. The series will encourage and assist research into, and develop the readership of, one of the richest and most complex writers of the early modern period.

General Editor J. B. Lethbridge
Editorial Board Helen Cooper, Thomas Herron, Carol V. Kaske,
James C. Nohrnberg & Brian Vickers

Also available
Shakespeare and Spenser: Attractive opposites   J. B. Lethbridge (ed.)

European erotic romance

Philhellene Protestantism,
Renaissance translation
and English literary politics

VICTOR SKRETKOWICZ

Manchester University Press
Manchester and New York
distributed in the United States exclusively by Palgrave Macmillan

Published by Manchester University Press
Oxford Road, Manchester M13 9NR, UK
and Room 400, 175 Fifth Avenue, New York, NY 10010, USA
www.manchesteruniversitypress.co.uk

Distributed in the United States exclusively by
Palgrave Macmillan, 175 Fifth Avenue, New York,
NY 10010, USA

Distributed in Canada exclusively by
UBC Press, University of British Columbia, 2029 West Mall,
Vancouver, BC, Canada V6T 1Z2

British Library Cataloguing-in-Publication Data
A catalogue record for this book is available from the British Library

Library of Congress Cataloging-in-Publication Data applied for

ISBN 978 0 7190 7970 2 *hardback*

First published 2010

Typeset in Minion by
Koinonia, Manchester
Printed in Great Britain by
MPG Books Group, UK

Contents

Acknowledgements

This book owes its beginnings to Neil Keeble and its ending to Julian Lethbridge, who kindly helped with its final preparation. Colleagues in The International Sidney Society, The Spenser Society, The Society for Renaissance Studies and The International Society for the History of Rhetoric have commented on many of the issues, raised in conference presentations. Their assistance has shaped this study into what, I hope, they and their students will find a novel and rewarding approach to a complex body of work.

Of the many librarians who have assisted me, those on whom I have most frequently called are in the National Library of Scotland, and the universities of Dundee, St Andrews, Edinburgh and Manchester. I am grateful to the University of California Press and the Renaissance English Text Society for permission to quote from their publications. The Carnegie Trust for the Universities of Scotland provided a research grant and the University of Dundee research leave.

Work on this project spans four decades. Those who encouraged it and have now departed include, in alphabetical order, Ephim Fogel, Charles Levy, John Norton-Smith, William Ringler, Jean Robertson and Gerald Rubio. I owe special thanks for their help and support to Gavin Alexander, Ronald Asher, Joseph Black, Jean Brink, Arthur Kinney, Roger Kuin, Mary Ellen Lamb, James Stewart and Robert Stillman, as well as the readers for the Manchester University Press. Those who have contributed in many ways include Christine Backler, Iain Barclay, Paul Hegarty, Shirley Hill, Jeanette Hunter, Lorraine Jones, Preethi Kay, Andy McMahon, Christine Pinder, Robin Rae and Gavin Skretkowicz.

During preparation of this work, my wife Carole endured Sidney's *New Arcadia*, Nightingale's *Notes on Nursing*, the *Dictionary of the Older Scottish Tongue* and the Internet *Dictionary of the Scots Language*. I have depended throughout on her devotion and sound advice. She is the true heroine of *European erotic romance*.

Victor Skretkowicz
University of Dundee

Victor Skretkowicz died when his book was in production. He did, however, revise the complex MS twice, once in response to reader reports and again because of his own dissatisfactions. Apart from the robust revisions and sharp-eyed proof reading, Victor carried on a rewarding and very full email correspondence with me. Latterly, due to the severe conditions of his illness, he could communicate only via computer. The inspiration I take from him cannot be fully expressed. Never did he relax his standards, only under pressure did he allow others to help with bibliography and indices. Any errors that remain are mine.

J. B. Lethbridge, Series Editor

Introduction

The ancient 'love-and-adventure' – or 'ideal' – prose romances[1] that inspire the erotic romances of Sir Philip Sidney, William Shakespeare and Lady Mary Sidney Wroth were written in Greek between the first and fourth centuries AD. While modern scholars know of 'over twenty' novels of this type, no more than five survive complete. Of these, only the three by Longus, Achilles Tatius and Heliodorus received wide circulation during the Renaissance. Relatively late manifestations of the European philhellene ('lovers of ancient Greece') revival of Greco-Roman letters, they were published and translated during the sixteenth and early seventeenth centuries. These works gave readers their first experience of the long-forgotten art of writing rhetorically complex, extended prose fiction in which the trials of love, resolved in the denouement, mask an implicit moral and political allegory.

Inevitably, coming during the Reformation, Counter-Reformation and the Catholic Reformation, this cultural phenomenon was not without its religious and political dimensions. If 'France in the sixteenth century displaced Italy as the pre-eminent centre of Hellenic studies in western Europe',[2] rivalling, among others, Rome and the Vatican, Florence, Venice and Padua, its hegemony was challenged by French Protestant scholars in Geneva and elsewhere.[3] Opposed to the Church of Rome and what they interpreted as its tyranny, and its support for tyrannical monarchy, these Calvinist religious exiles regarded themselves as true Christians. Of republican orientation, they were determined to demonstrate that they

1 B. P. Reardon, 'Introduction', in *Collected Ancient Greek Novels*, ed. by B. P. Reardon (Berkeley: University of California Press, 1989), pp. 2–3. Unless otherwise noted, quotations from Longus, Achilles Tatius and Heliodorus are from this edition, cited as 'Reardon'.
2 G. N. Sandy, 'Resources for the Study of Ancient Greek in France', in *The Classical Heritage in France*, ed. by G. N. Sandy (Leiden: E. J. Brill, 2002), pp. 47–78 (p. 48).
3 Cf. P. Conner, *Huguenot Heartland: Montauban and Southern French Calvinism during the Wars of Religion* (Aldershot: Ashgate, 2002).

were intellectually, morally, ethically, spiritually and politically superior to those of Roman persuasion.

Erotic romance played its part in this complicated drama. Heliodorus first appeared from Protestant presses in Basel: 1534 in Greek; 1552 in Latin. The earliest complete Latin text of Achilles Tatius came out of Basel in 1554; the Greek in 1601 from Heidelberg. These editions both precede and overlap with Bishop Jacques Amyot's French translations of Heliodorus (1547 (i.e., 1548); corrected 1559), Longus (1559), his monumental Plutarch's *Lives* (1559), and François de Belleforest's translation of Achilles Tatius (1568).

On the Continent, both sides of the religious and political divide use prefatory dedications, and addresses to the reader, to politicise their publications. More subtly, Calvinist-inspired translators painstakingly distinguish their work from fashionable courtly expansions, like Amyot's and Belleforest's, by making a concerted effort to represent their authors without textual embellishment or rhetorical ornamentation. Associating scholarly integrity with political and religious propaganda, they use the medium of print to create intellectual and spiritual bonds among disparate Protestant communities of quasi-republican inclination.

The cumulative effects on content and style of these varying approaches to translation manifest themselves through detailed comparison of passages. How translation theory and practice affect the representation of the text, and attempt to guide reader response, is the thrust of the following chapters on Longus, Achilles Tatius and Heliodorus.

The three principal English exponents of rhetorically conscious Greco-Roman erotic romance were all witnesses to, and participants in, this war of rhetorical styles. It had been engendered by the preceding generation, and they were fully aware of its political and religious overtones. All three were born during the reign of Elizabeth I, when the bulk of literary output was patronised by first- and second-generation Protestants of more or less Anglican or Calvinist disposition. Neither Sidney, Shakespeare nor Sidney Wroth, working in cadenced prose and dramatic verse, schematically shuns extremes of plainness and ornament. Rather, each studiously engages with the Renaissance politicisation of Greco-Roman models through negative portrayal of national and domestic tyranny, at times associating rhetorical with political style.

Amyot's translations and prefatory remarks may have established a precedent for French writers to address their readers, emphasising the eloquence, morality and instruction contained in their fiction.[4] The

---

4 L. Plazenet, *L'ébahissement et la délectation. Réception comparée et poétiques du roman*

fashion was emulated in England, especially following the ascendancy in 1625 of Charles I and the French Henriette-Marie. Nonetheless, the earlier politicisation of stylised erotic romance by Sidney, Shakespeare and Sidney Wroth challenges the notion that 'the idea of an aesthetic vocation of the genre has no impact before the translation of French heroic novels'.[5]

The Calvinist emphasis on style as an identifier of political sympathies contrasts with the focus on 'rhetoric' as encoded diction, particularly when used in meaningful clusters. Blair Worden, in *The Sound of Virtue: Philip Sidney's Arcadia and Elizabethan Politics* (New Haven: Yale University Press, 1996), traces this practice among the coterie of philhellene Protestants associated with the Sidney circle, whom he terms 'forward Protestants'. Similarly David Norbrook, in *Writing the English Republic: Poetry, Rhetoric and Politics, 1627–1660* (Cambridge: Cambridge University Press, 1999), notes how, from the second decade of the seventeenth century onwards, many writers of political polemic and its literary representations employed a hitherto undreamed-of directness of expression.

In some measure both of these observations could apply to the potentially elitist, politically charged vocabulary used by Sidney, Shakespeare and Sidney Wroth. However, as the following chapters illustrate, through consciously imitating and adapting the plots, structures, characters and literary styles of their Greco-Roman literary precedents, these three demonstrate a potent rhetorical commitment to the evolving philhellene Protestant movement in England. In the larger social context, they politicise erotic romance by promoting tolerant pan-European Protestantism, destruction of tyrants and the establishment of a notional English 'republicanism' through elected, or chosen, consultative monarchy. On a deeply personal level, they portray selfless dedication to Christian stoicism and reverential respect for romantic love, and make a special effort to represent female dignity in the face of male tyranny.

Aim and structure

The aim of this book is to enhance the understanding of the erotic romances of Sidney, Shakespeare, and Sidney Wroth by setting them within an integrated political, rhetorical, and aesthetic context. It demonstrates more

---

grec en France et en Angleterre aux XVIe et XVIIe siècles (Paris: Honoré Champion Éditeur, 1997), pp. 679–80.

5 L. Plazenet, *L'ébahissement et la délectation. Réception comparée et poétiques du roman grec en France aux XVIe et XVIIe siècles*, p. 680, 'L'idée d'une vocation esthétique du genre n'a pas d'impact avant la traduction des romans héroïques français'.

cohesive interrelationships during the Renaissance than was possible in Margaret Ann Doody's wide-ranging *The True Story of the Novel* (New Brunswick, NJ: Rutgers University Press, 1996). To achieve this, it sets out on a fresh trajectory, applying the interdisciplinary approach encouraged by fellow members of The Society for Renaissance Studies, The International Sidney Society, The International Society for the History of Rhetoric, The Society for Emblem Studies and The Bibliographical Society. Close readings integrate studies in the classics, culture, history, language, literature, politics, religion, rhetoric and translation.

Because of the complexities relating to the 'discovery', translation and publication of the Greek texts, the study of the artistry and politics of European erotic romance is best approached through a series of stepping-stones. This book is therefore in two parts, with each chapter divided into shorter digestible units.

Part One begins with a brief chapter on the nature of ancient and Renaissance Greco-Roman romance. It contains introductory notes on the rhetorical exercises of Aphthonius; on Philostratus, ecphrasis and artistic style; on Theophrastan and Plutarchan characterisation; and on the implicit links between philhellenism and allegorical politicisation. It then devotes one chapter each to the Continental editions, and their English derivatives, of the sixteenth- and earlier seventeenth-century translations of Longus, Achilles Tatius and Heliodorus. The order in which they are encountered is more or less chronological, and coincides with the degree of the complexity of their narratives and rhetorical programmes.[6] These chapters investigate how Renaissance translators alter rhetorical styles, and even contents, to accord with contemporary taste, political agendas and the restrictions of censorship. To assist readers unfamiliar with these works, plot outlines are introduced through close comparison of passages selected to follow the events of the narrative. Particular attention is paid to differences between the French courtly style of Amyot and Belleforest and the more literal translations of their English counterparts.

In Chapter 2, these aspects of Jacques Amyot's version of Longus, *Les amours pastorales de Daphnis et Chloe*, are examined alongside Angel Day's *Daphnis and Chloe Excellently describing the weight of affection, the simplicitie of loue, the purport of honest meaning, the resolution of men, and disposition of Fate, finished in a Pastorall, and interlaced with the praises of a most peerlesse Princesse, wonderfull in Maiestie, and rare*

---

6 B. P. Reardon, 'Introduction', in *Collected Ancient Greek Novels*, ed. by B. P. Reardon, pp. 5–6.

in perfection, celebrated within the same Pastorall, and therefore termed by the name of The Shepheards Holidaie (1587), and George Thornley's *Daphnis and Chloe. A Most Sweet, and Pleasant Pastorall Romance for Young Ladies* (1657).

Chapter 3, on Achilles Tatius, explores relationships among Ludovico Annibale della Croce's *De Clitophontis & Leucippes amorib[us]* (1554), François de Belleforest's *Les amours de Clitophon et de Leucippe* (1568), William Burton's *The Most Delectable and Plesaunt History of Clitiphon and Leucippe* (1597) and Anthony Hodges's *The Loves of Clitophon and Leucippe. A most elegant History* (1638).

Central to Chapter 4 are the principal translations of Heliodorus: Amyot's *L'histoire aethiopique de Heliodorus, contenant dix livres traitant des loyales et pudiques amours de Theagenes thessalien et Chariclea aethiopie[n]ne* (1547 (i.e., 1548)); Stanislaus Warschewiczki's *Heliodori Aethiopicae Historiae libri decem* (1552); Thomas Underdowne's *An Aethiopian Historie written in Greeke by Heliodorus: very wittie and pleasaunt* (1569); and William L'Isle's *The Faire Aethiopian* (1631). Brief accounts are also given of three fragmentary translations and adaptations: James Sanford's *The Amorous and Tragicall Tales of Plutarch. Wherevnto is annexed the Hystorie of Cariclea & Theagenes, and the sayings of the Greeke Philosophers.* (1567); Abraham Fraunce's 'The beginning of Heliodorus his Aethiopical History' (1591); and John Gough's *The Strange Discovery* (1640).

An appreciation of the individuality of each translation, and its political and cultural context, involves critical analyses of illustrative passages, often comparing Latin, French and English. Valuable perspective on the early translations is offered through the modern English versions in Reardon's *Collected Ancient Greek Novels*.

Part Two examines Sidney's, Shakespeare's and Sidney Wroth's politicised adaptations of their Greco-Roman precursors. Chapter 5 considers the three texts of Sidney's *Arcadia*, probably written between 1577 and 1584, as a political romance sharing many of the thematic and rhetorical concerns of the ancients. Sidney died on 17 October 1586, a month before his thirty-second birthday, of wounds received fighting against Spanish occupational forces subduing the Protestant revolt in the Netherlands. Sidney is the earliest major English author to use erotic romance to illustrate the practical impact of European philhellene Protestant political theory. He uniquely portrays himself as a Samothean, a descendant of Noah, lamenting the decayed state of relationships between rulers and their subjects. One of the work's principal themes is how conflicting self-interest motivates individuals of varying psychological disposition to act against notions of orderly behaviour. 'Dramatised' in the manner of Heliodorus, Sidney studies the influence this has on the state.

Chapter 6 focuses on a narrow range of Shakespeare's plays: *Julius Caesar* (1599), *Antony and Cleopatra* (1606), *Coriolanus* (1608), *The Winter's Tale* (1609–10) and *Cymbeline* (1609–10). The Roman plays, derived from Amyot's and North's translations of Plutarch's *Lives*, are linked through theme and rhetorical styles to the philhellene Protestant programmes of political and social reform. Political allegory and stylistic symbolism characterise the evolutionary series of Garnier's *Marc-Antoine* (1578), Mary Sidney Herbert's *Antonius* (1592), Samuel Daniel's *Cleopatra* (1594) and Fulke Greville's *Antony and Cleopatra*. Here Sidney Herbert and Daniel especially anticipate James I's connecting plainness with good governance in his first speech to Parliament in 1603. To an extent, this rhetorical convention becomes the basis of Shakespeare's stylistic border-line between Egypt and Rome in *Antony and Cleopatra*.

Shakespeare uses rhetorical distinctions to represent factional and cultural differences in the late Elizabethan *Julius Caesar*, though the anti-romances *Antony and Cleopatra* and *The Winter's Tale* are coloured by moralisation of rhetoric. This somewhat refines the broad notion that, during the Elizabethan-Jacobean period, structures of Roman rhetoric permeate virtually all levels of sophisticated English discourse.[7] It also reflects the rhetorical-political distinctions that come to divide moderate philhellene Protestants from those of a more Puritan disposition, and which provide Shakespeare with the rationale for royal compliment in *The Winter's Tale* and *Cymbeline*.

Chapter 7 identifies Mary Sidney Wroth's masque-like prose allegory, *The Countess of Montgomery's Urania*, as philhellene Protestant political propaganda. Its complex rhetorical programme is complicated by a knack of obfuscation, in the manner of Fulke Greville, when addressing delicate personal matters or court intrigue. For *Urania* is, par excellence, a brilliant *tour de force* in ambiguous autobiography, panegyric and utter condemnation of political and familial tyrants of both sexes. Written between 1618 and 1626 under the guise of erotic romance, Sidney Wroth's work adopts an implicit anti-Spanish stance inherited from the Sidneys and Herberts. Opposing conciliatory royal and courtly opinion, this niece of Philip Sidney and Mary Sidney Herbert, and daughter of their brother Robert Sidney, adapts erotic romance to present an idealised vision of a

---

7 P. Mack, *Elizabethan Rhetoric: Theory and Practice* (Cambridge: Cambridge University Press, 2002).

Protestant Europe. It will be united through intermarriage, and be under the leadership of her first cousin and lover, William Herbert.

Chapter 8 concludes this study with a review of the semiotic qualities of the genre, as perceived during the sixteenth and seventeenth centuries. How the erotic romances gain social and political significance is the subject of this book, which begins with an introduction to the nature of these long and complex works.

Part one

Greco-Roman romance in the Renaissance

1

The nature of erotic romance

Greco-Roman Romance of the Second Sophistic and the Renaissance

Erotic romance, Middle Eastern in its provincial origins but European in its flavour, achieved a spectacular flourishing between 1579 and 1626 in the writings of Sir Philip Sidney (1554–1586), William Shakespeare (1564–1616) and Mary Sidney Wroth (1587–1651/53). The romances of arguably the most rhetorically sophisticated and politically aware authors of the age represent the ultimate English response to lengthy, complex and rhetorically artistic Greco-Roman prose fiction.

The ancient romances available to Sidney, Shakespeare and Sidney Wroth were Longus's *Daphnis and Chloe* (?AD 200), Achilles Tatius's *Leukippe and Kleitophon* (late second century AD) and Heliodorus's *An Ethiopian Story* (third century or late fourth century AD).[1] These authors were Greek-speaking rhetoricians during the period known as the 'Second Sophistic',[2] when itinerant 'sophists',[3] learned teachers of rhetoric, revived the rhetorical and philosophical traditions of the ancient city-state of Athens – the Athens of Socrates (469–399 BC), Plato (?429–347 BC) and Aristotle (384–322 BC).

The writings of Longus, Achilles Tatius, and Heliodorus 'are marked by acute self-awareness, unrepentant artificiality, the pursuit of stylistic effect and a withdrawal into the past and the imagination'.[4] These qualities,

---

1 This dating follows B. P. Reardon, 'Introduction', in *Collected Ancient Greek Novels*, ed. by B. P. Reardon (Berkeley: University of California Press, 1989), p. 5.
2 See G. Anderson, *The Second Sophistic: A Cultural Phenomenon in the Roman Empire* (London: Routledge, 1993); G. A. Kennedy, *A New History of Classical Rhetoric* (Princeton: Princeton University Press, 1994), pp. 230–2; and L. Pernot, *La rhétorique dans l'antiquité* (Paris: Le Livre de Poche, Librairie Générale Française, 2000), pp. 244–57.
3 See J. Walker, *Rhetoric and Poetics in Antiquity* (Oxford: Oxford University Press, 2000), pp. 27–8.
4 J. R. Morgan, 'Introduction', in *Greek Fiction: The Greek Novel in Context*, ed. by J. R. Morgan and R. Stoneman (London: Routledge, 1994), p. 5.

combined with promoting high ethical and moral standards, encourage description of early Greek prose fiction both as 'sophistic romances' and as 'sophistic novels'. While 'no Greek generic term was ever proposed for this kind of literature before the nineteenth century',[5] B. P. Reardon's argument, that Greek prose romances are 'sufficiently similar to what we call novels to justify the use of the term',[6] is supported by a growing body of publications.[7] Further, H. Hofmann includes Latin translations of 'the Greek novels' within the corpus of 'Latin fiction in the Early Modern period'.[8]

It is typical of the rhetorical blueprint of ancient novels that central story-lines unfold gradually, are frequently interrupted and suspended by artfully contrived digressions, and have happy romantic endings. The theme of abandoned babies fostered as foundlings is fundamental to *Daphnis and Chloe* and *An Ethiopian Story*, as well as to Shakespeare's *The Winter's Tale* and Sidney Wroth's *Urania*. Each of these texts contains episodes that depend on miraculous recognitions that effect a reversal in fortunes, anticipating 'cliff-hanging', albeit confident and optimistic, resolutions. Vehicles of plot-change include oracles, chance, coincidence, dream-vision and supernatural intervention.

Such highly integrated narrative structures form a stark contrast to the sequences of quasi-realistic tales that predominate in late medieval and early Renaissance prose fiction, as in Boccaccio's *Decameron*. During the sixteenth and seventeenth centuries, and later, each of these individual stories might be described by the term 'novel'.[9] This distinguished them from more loosely structured fiction in the medieval chivalric mode,

5 R. Beaton, *The medieval Greek Romance* (Cambridge: Cambridge University Press, 1989), p. 1.
6 B. P. Reardon, 'Introduction', in *Collected Ancient Greek Novels*, ed. by B. P. Reardon, p. 1.
7 F. A. Todd, *Some Ancient Novels* (London: Oxford University Press, 1940); A. Heiserman, *The Novel Before the Novel* (Chicago: University of Chicago Press, 1977); T. Hägg, *The Novel in Antiquity* (Oxford: Basil Blackwell, 1983); M. A. Doody, *The True Story of the Novel* (New Brunswick, NJ: Rutgers University Press, 1996; London: Fontana Press, 1998); N. J. Lowe, *The Classical Plot and the Invention of Western Narrative* (Cambridge: Cambridge University Press, 2000), pp. 222–58; K. Haynes, *Fashioning the Feminine in the Greek Novel* (London: Routledge, 2003); *The Search for the Ancient Novel*, ed. by J. Tatum (Baltimore: Johns Hopkins University Press, 1994); *Greek Fiction: The Greek Novel in Context*, ed. by J. R. Morgan and R. Stoneman (London: Routledge, 1994); *The Novel in the Ancient World*, ed. by G. Schmeling (Leiden: E. J. Brill, 1996); *The Ancient Novel and Beyond*, ed. by S. Panayotakis, M. Zimmerman and W. Keulen (Leiden: Brill, 2003).
8 H. Hofmann, 'Introduction', in *Latin Fiction: The Latin Novel in Context*, ed. by H. Hofmann (London: Routledge, 1999), pp. 9–10.
9 Cf. *Oxford English Dictionary* (hereafter *O.E.D.*), 'novel' n.4.a, citing examples from c. 1500 to 1957, six from before 1700.

such as Malory's *Morte d'Arthur*, known from the fourteenth century as 'romance'.[10] More familiarly, predominant usage from the fourth decade of the seventeenth century onwards identifies the novel with sustained prose fiction representing a degree of reality.[11] Romance, whether in prose, verse or drama, is associated with improbable erotic plots.[12]

Aphthonius, Philostratus, ecphrasis and artistic style

In their erotic romances, Longus, Achilles Tatius and Heliodorus adhere to the earlier 'basic structure' and literary qualities of the 'love-and-adventure' novel.[13] They decorously employ a 'studied *Künstsprache*, artistic prose', characterised as 'reactionary in word and thought, artistic but at the same time artificial'.[14] Exhibitions of verbal artificiality reappear in stylised Renaissance adaptations. In addition to speeches, these occur in descriptions of characters, symbolic gardens, buildings, statues, allegorical paintings and emblematic devices or *imprese* related to costume. The extensive narrative significance with which Sidney endows these in the *Old Arcadia* and *New Arcadia* adds a cryptic oracular dimension that is without precedent,[15] and places an enormous interpretative burden on the reader. The complex allegories of Shakespeare and Sidney Wroth may appear to utilise elaborate description more transparently, but all three of these English Renaissance writers remain indebted to the rhetorical practices of the Second Sophistic.

Readily available during the Renaissance was Aphthonius's *Progymnasmata*, the popular students' guide to the forms of artful discourse practised by rhetoricians of the Second Sophistic. This condensed summary, compiled by a fourth-century sophist, provides examples of the content, structure and attributes of fourteen types of subject-based orations.[16] It is

10 Cf. *O.E.D.*, 'romance' n.II.2. The mosaic rather than integrated structure of *Morte d'Arthur* prompted Isaac D'Israeli to describe it as 'that tessellated compilement' (*Amenities of Literature* (1841), cited in *O.E.D.*, 'compilement' n.2.a).
11 Cf. *O.E.D.*, 'novel' n.4.b.
12 Cf. *O.E.D.*, 'novel' n.3.a; 'romance' n.II.3.
13 B. P. Reardon, 'Introduction', in *Collected Ancient Greek Novels*, ed. by B. P. Reardon, p. 122.
14 T. Hägg, *The Novel in Antiquity*, pp. 106–7.
15 Sir P. Sidney, *The Countess of Pembroke's Arcadia (The Old Arcadia)*, ed. by J. Robertson (Oxford: Clarendon Press, 1973), hereafter referred to as *OA*, and Sir P. Sidney, *The Countess of Pembroke's Arcadia (The New Arcadia)*, ed. by V. Skretkowicz (Oxford: Clarendon Press, 1987), hereafter cited in the text as *NA*.
16 See Aphthonius, *Progymnasmata*, trans. by G. A. Kennedy, in *Progymnasmata: Greek Textbooks of Prose Composition and Rhetoric*, ed. and trans. by G. A. Kennedy (Atlanta: Society of Biblical Literature, 2003), pp. 96–127; Aphthonius, *Progymnasmata*, trans. by

concise, meant to be copied, remained in use for centuries, and became a prescribed text in various English schools from at least 1523.[17]

Aphthonius's *Progymnasmata* was first printed in 1507, and frequently reprinted in Greek and in Latin translation. In Richard Pynson's Latin edition (London, *c.* 1520), with comments by Gentian Hervet or Hervetus (1499–1584), it occupies only 43 pages.[18] The massively expanded 1542 Latin edition, by the Lutheran Reinhard Lorich or Lorichius (*c.* 1500–64), based on translations by Rodolphus Agricola and Joannes Maria Catanaeus, was reprinted hundreds of times. Lorich provides the opinions of ancient rhetors, and adds many model orations. Twelve editions of 231 leaves (463 pages) were published in London and Cambridge between 1572 and 1636.[19]

Lorich's edition formed the basis of the 62–leaf (121–page) partial translation, reduction and adaptation by Richard Reynolds or Reynoldes,[20] *A booke called the Foundacion of Rhetorike, because all other partes of Rhetorike are grounded thereupon, euery parte sette forthe in an Oracion vpon questions, verie profitable to bee knowen and redde: Made by Richard Rainolde Maister of Arte, of the Uniuersitie of Cambridge* (1563). Such wide variation in the representation of Greco-roman texts is not unusual, largely being determined by the political impetus leading to their production. Reynolds contributes to the philhellene Protestant cultural revolution in England, dedicating his volume to Robert Dudley, master of the horse, arch-Elizabethan philhellene Protestant and Philip Sidney's uncle. Typical of an author seeking patronage in the Dudley camp of monarchomachists (royalists dedicated to fighting against tyrannical monarchy), Reynolds overtly politicises his work in a sympathetic manner. Aphthonius, who illustrates his seventh type, 'commonplace', with a denunciation of tyrants, invites domestication. Substituting many of his own illustrations, Reynolds repeatedly emphasises the benefits of responsible

M. Heath, published at www.leeds.ac.uk/classics/resources/rhetoric/prog-aph.htm. See the summary in G. A. Kennedy, *A New History of Classical Rhetoric*, pp. 203–7.

17 See P. Mack, *Elizabethan Rhetoric: Theory and Practice* (Cambridge: Cambridge University Press, 2004), pp. 13, 27; T. W. Baldwin, *William Shakespeare's Small Latine & Lesse Greeke*, 2 vols (Urbana: University of Illinois Press, 1944), ii.28; and D. L. Clark, 'The Rise and Fall of Progymnasmata in Sixteenth and Seventeenth Century Grammar Schools', *Speech Monographs*, xix (1952), 259–63.

18 *Aphthonii sophistae praeexercitamenta interprete viro doctissimo* (1520?).

19 *Aphthonii sophistae Progymnasmata, partim a Rodolpho Agricola, partim a Ioanne Maria Catanaeo Latinitate donata: cum luculentis & vtilibus in eadem Scholijs Reinhardi Lorichij Hadamarij. Ad rhetorices candidatos, Tetrastichon eiusdem* (1572).

20 See L. D. Green, 'Reynolds, Richard (*c.*1530–1606)', *Oxford Dictionary of National Biography* (Oxford: Oxford University Press, 2004). Citations are from the Internet edition.

monarchy at the head of a commonwealth in which all ranks of society are interdependent. His monarchomachism is most obvious in his 'narracion historicall', a critique of the usurper and 'cruell tiraunt', Richard III (D1–D2).

Aphthonius taught the inter-related subjects of character depiction and description under the headings of ἠθοποιία (*'Ethopoeia*, or personification')[21] and ἔκφρασις (*'Ekphrasis*, or description'). Ethopoeia is vital to the creation of dialogue-based erotic romance, as it deals with the representation of speech and reported speech. It includes προσωποπιία, prosopopoeia, where, as Reynolds puts it, 'speache is feigned to bee giuen' (N2), even by invented characters. These speeches reveal a person's ethical and moral attributes, particularly at times of crisis. By contrast, ecphrasis deals with physical appearance and its interpretation. Omitting plants from Aphthonius's list of suitable topics for ecphrasis, Reynolds includes descriptions of 'the person, thynges or actes, tymes, places, brute beastes' (N3v).

No text could better illustrate training in ecphrasis than Philostratus the elder's Εἰκόνες (*Icones* or *Imagines*), a collection of brief descriptive essays published in Greek (1503), Latin (1521) and French (Paris, 1578).[22] Born about AD 190, Philostratus, the elder, was a sophist or teacher in Naples, 'a city in Italy settled by men of the Greek race and people of culture, and therefore Greek in their enthusiasm for discussion'.[23] He composed his series of short rhetorical exercises to provide his students with models of how to describe scenes from nature.

As one of his aims is to teach the art of ecphrasis, literally 'speaking out', Philostratus incorporates scenes purporting to represent stories, paintings and sculpture. He does this to demonstrate how the written word can emulate and heighten visual impressions, rivalling the art of the painter. He also awakens a critical awareness to extended meaning, metaphor and allegory, 'to interpret paintings and to appreciate what

---

21 G. A. Kennedy, *A New History of Classical Rhetoric*, pp. 205–6.
22 It was first published in print by Aldus Manutius in his edition of Lucian of Samosata, Τάδε ἔνεστιν ἐν τῷδε τῷ βιβλίῳ. Λουκιανου. Φιλοστρατου εἰκόνες [...] (Venice, 1503); next in *Stephani Nigri Elegantissime è graeco authorum subditorum traslationes. uidelicet. Philostrati Icones. Pythagorae Carmen aureum Athenaei Collectanea Musonij philosophi Tyrij De principe optimo Isocratis de regis muneribus orno. & alia multa scitu digniss. & rara inuentu, quae uersa pagina lector bone lubens, & gaudens inuenies* (Milan, 1521); and finally in *Les images ou tableaux de platte-peinture de Philostrate Lemnien sophiste grec. Mis en françois par Blaise de Vigenere. Avec des argumens & annotations sur chacun d'iceux* (Paris, 1578).
23 Philostratus, the elder, 'Introduction' to Book I, in Philostratus, *Imagines*; Callistratus, *Descriptions*, trans. by A. Fairbanks (London: William Heinemann Ltd, 1960), p. 5.

is esteemed in them'.[24] Consequently, his description of a gathering of cupids opens with an explanation of their significance:

> See, Cupids are gathering apples; and if there are many of them, do not be surprised. For they are children of the Nymphs and govern all mortal kind, and they are many because of the many things men love; and they say it is heavenly love which manages the affairs of the gods in heaven. Do you catch aught of the fragrance hovering over the garden, or are your senses dull? But listen carefully; for along with my description of the garden the fragrance of the apples also will come to you. (I.6)

The clarity of this ecphrastic style masks its complexity. Like other teachers of rhetoric during the Second Sophistic, including Longus, Achilles Tatius and Heliodorus, Philostratus the elder writes in a consciously exemplary style that his students should emulate. Around AD 300, his grandson, Philostratus, the younger, in the 'Prooemium' to his continuation of *Εἰκόνες*, describes the essays as being written 'in very pure Attic Greek and with extreme beauty and force'.[25] This observation, and Fairbanks's critique of the style of *Εἰκόνες*, could equally apply to *Daphnis and Chloe*, *Leukippe and Kleitophon* and *An Ethiopian Story*:

> a simplicity more studied or more often interrupted by grandiloquent and complicated passages would be difficult to imagine. The loose nominatives, the choppy phrases, the frequent parentheses are apparently intended to give the illusion of a casual conversation [...] the figures of speech, the paradoxical expressions and the tricks of phrase-making, often become quite laboured [...] almost buried under the mass of literary allusion and quotation [...] Such is the acquaintance with the classics which was demanded both of the sophist and of his hearers.[26]

Nor would Fairbanks's assessment be out of place in a discussion of the rhetorical artistry of the demanding erotic romances of Sidney, Shakespeare and Sidney Wroth.

Characterisation: Theophrastus and Plutarch

In biography-centred European erotic romance, as in the Greek 'love and adventure' novels, ecphrasis combines flexibly with ethopoeia in the portrayal of characters. In orations describing people, according to

---

24 Philostratus, the elder, 'Introduction' to Book I, in Philostratus, *Imagines*; Callistratus, *Descriptions*, trans. by A. Fairbanks, p. 8.
25 Philostratus, the younger, 'Prooemium', in Philostratus, *Imagines*; Callistratus, *Descriptions*, trans. by A. Fairbanks, p. 283.
26 A. Fairbanks, 'Introduction' to Philostratus, *Imagines*, pp. xxiii–xxiv.

Aphthonius, 'A summis ad ima vsque ire oportebit, id est, a capite ad pedes' – 'one should go from the highest to the lowest, from the head to the feet'.[27] Reynolds's representation of Richard III provides a variant Renaissance model. Beginning with an evil deed, Reynolds accentuates size and shape before facial features, eliding a moral interpretation of the physical into a holistic psychological profile:

> Richard duke of Glocester, after the death of Edward the fowerth his brother king of England, vsurped the croune, moste traiterouslie and wickedlie: this kyng Richard was small of stature, deformed, and ill shaped, his shoulders beared not equalitie, a pulyng face, yet of countenaunce and looke cruell, malicious, deceiptfull, bityng and chawing his nether lippe: of minde vnquiet, pregnaunt of witte, quicke and liuely, a worde and a blowe, wilie, deceiptfull, proude, arrogant in life and cogitacion bloodie. (D1)

Reynolds's portrait would not be out of place in an Elizabethan translation of a Greco-Roman erotic romance, or in a Renaissance representation of the genre. In these works, physical and moral properties are described as characters are introduced into the plot. Their emotions and psychological turmoil are carefully documented when tested by abandonment, alienation, shipwreck, kidnapping, enforced imprisonment, combat and sexual compromise.

While creating feeling, thinking women and men, and treating them as historical realities possessed of extraordinary fidelity to love, Longus, Achilles Tatius, Heliodorus and their Renaissance successors combine the principles of characterisation practised by Aphthonius with those of Theophrastus and Plutarch. During the third century BC, Aristotle's student and successor, the philosopher and botanist Theophrastus (c. 372–c. 287 BC), compiled his Χαρακτῆρες or *Characters*, a collection of short essays illustrating the extremes of flawed personality. The essays that survive are satirical, 'descriptive sketches of types exhibiting deviations from proper norms of behaviour'.[28] These 'types' are closely related to allegorical representations of greed, promiscuity, bullying, arrogance or even naivety which are found in ancient Greek drama.

Theophrastus's method of describing archetypal characters through extended caricature became increasingly influential during the Renaissance. The earliest edition, in Greek and Latin, contained fifteen 'charac-

---

27 *Aphthonii sophistae Progymnasmata, partim a Rodolpho Agricola, partim a Ioanne Maria Catanaeo Latinitate donata: cum luculentis & vtilibus in eadem Scholijs Reinhardi Lorichij Hadamarij* (1572), Aa8.
28 J. J. Keaney, 'Theophrastus', in *The Oxford Classical Dictionary*, ed. by N. G. L. Hammond and H. H. Scullard, 2nd edn (Oxford: Clarendon Press, 1970), pp. 1058–9 (p. 1058).

ters'. This was published in Protestant Nuremberg in 1527, the year Rome was sacked by the armies of the Holy Roman Emperor, Charles V.[29] The editor, Bilibald or Willibald Pirkheimer (1470–1530), a friend of Albrecht Dürer, used a manuscript lent by John Francis Picus (*c.* 1469–1533),[30] nephew of John Picus, the neoplatonist Pico della Mirandula (1463–94). In 1552, Giovanni Battista Camozzi or Camotius (*d.* 1581) included twenty-three 'characters' in volume six of his Aldine edition of Aristotle.[31] Isaac Casaubon's 1599 edition contained twenty-eight *Characters*,[32] the maxmum available to Renaissance readers.[33]

Theophrastus may lie behind the method of listing personality traits, but that the idealised characters of erotic romance are neither caricatures nor wooden reflects the influence of Plutarch's *Lives*. This work provides semi-fictional biographical accounts of twenty-three pairs, plus four individual *Lives* of Greek and Roman leaders. Nineteen of the concluding summaries that emphasise their differences survive.

Plutarch, an ardent Greek nationalist who taught moral philosophy and Greek rhetoric, lived from *c.* AD 45 till after 120, and was a priest at Delphi from about 90. Although his subjects were long dead – many by hundreds of years – Plutarch represents lengthy orations in direct speech, which he reconstructs or invents using προσωποποιία (prosopopoeia). His practice is typical of Greek historical method, for which 'The real presentational parallel is the modern novel, and it is unsurprising that modern narratological techniques, forged for analysing novelistic fiction, are proving so fruitful when applied to ancient historiographic texts'.[34]

Plutarch's biographies remain credible despite his moralistic interventions, skewing of history and fictive interpretations. This is because he reports his sources (often from memory), and writes in a lucid, factual

29　Θεοφράστου Χαρακτήρες. *Cum interpretatione Latina, per Bilibaldu[m] Pirkeymheru[m], iam recens aedita* (Norembergae, 1527).
30　T. F. Dibden, *An Introduction to the Knowledge of Rare and Valuable Editions of the Greek and Latin Classics*, 4th edn, 2 vols (1827), ii.499–500.
31　Ἀριστοτελους πασαν λογικην […] *Aristotelis omnem logicam, rhetoricam et poeticam disciplinam continens*, ed. by Ioannes Baptista Camotius, 6 vols (Venetiis, 1551–53 [i.e., 1551–52]).
32　Θεοφράστου ηθικοι Χαρακτήρες, *sive Descriptiones morum, Graece Isaacus Casaubonus recensuit, in Latinum sermonem vertit, et libro commentario illustravit* (Lugduni [i.e., Lyon], 1599).
33　Thirty were published in the Parma, 1786, edition. See Theophrastus, *Characters*, ed. by J. Diggle, Cambridge Classical Texts and Commentaries, 43 (Cambridge: Cambridge University Press, 2004), p. 52; *Théophraste, Caractères*, ed. by O. Navarre, 2nd edn (Paris, 1931), p. 25.
34　C. Pelling, *Literary Texts and the Greek Historian* (London: Routledge, 2000), p. 8.

style.[35] Nonetheless, while he provides intimate detail, including family background, education, preferred life style and love affairs, an imaginary idealism colours his characterisation. He holistically interrelates morality and personality, linking political achievements, shortcomings, and even style of speech and writing, to morality: 'Plutarch had a clear moral purpose here: to provide exemplars for himself and his readers, both to imitate if good and to avoid if bad'.[36] The effect is to create characters possessing exaggerated perfections and faults, but who, like those in the later erotic romance, remain pre-eminently human rather than Theophrastan types:

> Plutarch was writing for a varied audience, including Philhellene Romans of great political power and Greeks so unfamiliar with Rome that they needed basic Roman institutions explained. The one thing Plutarch assumed was a readiness to enter imaginatively into the ethical issues which his *Lives* raised. For Plutarch is a moralist. He hopes that his writings, when properly read, will improve his audience's ethical behaviour and understanding. But he does not reduce his heroes to one-dimensional embodiments of virtues and vice.[37]

During the fifteenth and sixteenth centuries, printed editions of the *Lives* were published in Latin (Rome, c. 1470); Italian (Aquila, 1482 – twenty-six *Lives*; Venice, 1525 – full text); Spanish (Seville, 1491); Greek (Florence, 1517);[38] German (Augsburg, 1534 – eight *Lives;* Colmar, 1541 – full text); French (Paris, 1559); and English (London, 1579).[39] Plutarch's biographical analyses provided fresh insights into the human frailties of the military and political leaders who shaped early modern Europe. The Genevan Calvinist response by Simon Goulart (1575–1628) was to anno-tate the *Lives* as Christian allegories from which moral lessons should be drawn. Equally important, Plutarch gave Renaissance creators of fictional characters a model for a relatively plain, unadorned prose style through which they could convey the impression of telling the truth.

It was not so much Plutarch as the ancient novels that provided Renais-sance authors with models of chaste 'young, wellborn, and handsome' heroes and heroines, and complex plots wherein 'marriage is disrupted

35 Cf. C. Pelling, *Literary Texts and the Greek Historian*, pp. 44–60.
36 M. J. Edwards, *Plutarch: The Lives of Pompey, Caesar and Cicero*[.] *A Companion to the Penguin Translation* (London: Bristol Classical Press, 1991; repr. 2003), p. 1.
37 C. Pelling, *Literary Texts and the Greek Historian*, p. 46.
38 *Του σοφωτατου Πλουταρχου Παραλληλον. Βιοι Ρωμαιων και Ελληνω.* […] *Sapientis-simi Plutarchi paralellum. Vitae Romanorum et Graecorum. Quadriginta novem. Ed. pr.* (Florence, 1517).
39 The editions are listed in A. M. Woodward, 'Greek History at the Renaissance', *Journal of Hellenic Studies*, lxiii (1943), 1–14 (p. 14).

or temporarily prevented' by separation, travel and misfortune.[40] Sidney, Shakespeare and Sidney Wroth were clearly struck by their encounters with vivacious, intelligent, eloquent, educated, ethically sound and morally pure women, as well as appallingly wicked ones, upon whom they modelled heroines and harridans of their own creation. With the examples of Chloe, Leukippe and Charikleia before them, it is no coincidence that the most stylistically aware authors of the Renaissance created the '"strong" or transgressive women' that Lorna Hutson investigates in *The Usurer's Daughter*.[41] But rather than finding inspiration, as Hutson suggests, among Bandello's followers,[42] it is more probable that the development of literature addressed to women in the 1570s, and the growth of writing by women, stemmed from the recent publication of the Greco-Roman romances.

Evidence that the novels of the early Christian era, the Second Sophistic, were written for a female, as well as male, readership is collected by Margaret Anne Doody in *The True Story of the Novel*. There she argues that 'The low, the uneducated – the impotent – *women*: these unenviable and even despised groups keep turning up as the putative readers of antique novels'.[43] It would be unexpected if women were not naturally drawn towards these same novels when they circulated throughout Europe during the sixteenth century. Proof that this occurred comes from the publisher of the second, unauthorised edition of Amyot's translation of the popular *L'histoire aethiopique de Heliodorus* (1549), who added a prefatory address 'Aux Dames Françoyses'.[44] In England, Sidney dedicated his *Arcadia* 'To my dear lady and sister the Countess of Pembroke'. And, especially in the more personal *Old Arcadia*, he speaks directly through his narrator to female readers:

> I might entertain you, fair ladies, a great while, if I should make as many interruptions in the repeating as she did in the singing. For no verse did pass out of her mouth but that it was waited on with such abundance of sighs […] that, though the words were few, yet the time was long she employed in uttering them. (*OA*, p. 29)

40 *Collected Ancient Greek Novels*, edited by B. P. Reardon, p. 2.
41 L. Hutson, *The Usurer's Daughter: Male Friendship and Fictions of Women in Sixteenth-Century England* (London: Routledge, 1994), p. 7.
42 L. Hutson, *The Usurer's Daughter*, p. 94.
43 M. A. Doody, *The True Story of the Novel*, p. 21; cf. H. Morales, *Vision and Narrative in Achilles Tatius' Leucippe and Clitophon* (Cambridge: Cambridge University Press, 2004), pp. 2–4.
44 L. Plazenet, 'Jacques Amyot and the Greek Novel: The Invention of the French Novel', in *The Classical Heritage in France*, ed. by G. N. Sandy (Leiden: Brill, 2002), pp. 237–80 (p. 242).

The publication of the Greco-Roman erotic romances, rather than directly challenging chivalric fiction,[45] coincides with the Renaissance eroticisation of heroic literature. Sidney, Shakespeare and Sidney Wroth blend love and knighthood in proportion to the scenic action. In these authors, erotic romance is not tied to form. Sidney seems determined to include every possibility. Like the Spanish chivalric pastoral romance *Diana* by Jorge de Montemayor, the *Old Arcadia* contains poems and songs; but it is structured like a five-act drama with substantial interludes, 'eclogues', in the manner of Sannazaro's prose and verse *Arcadia*. The revised *New Arcadia* includes poems and songs, but follows the epic form, beginning in the middle like *An Ethiopian Story*, which also served Cervantes as the structural model of *Persiles and Sigismunda*. Shakespeare's *The Winter's Tale* is a drama in verse, with song and prose, while Sidney Wroth's *Urania* incorporates verse and songs within its prose, and in addition possesses qualities of the Jacobean masque.

This variety of forms encouraged uncertainty during the earlier seventeenth century about how to label erotic prose fiction in the Greco-Roman mode. Bourdelotius, in his 1619 reprint of Warschewiczki's 1552 Latin translation of Heliodorus, describes *An Ethiopian Story* as an 'Amatoria', a love story. In *A Dedication to Sir Philip Sidney* (1604–14), Fulke Greville initially refers to Sidney's *Arcadia* by the Italian term *romanzas*, which his friend John Florio, in *Queen Anna's New World of Words* (1611), spells 'romanzi', and embracingly defines as 'romants, fabulous tales, faigned stories in rime of errand Knights'. While Greville replaced *romanzas* after 1610 with a Latinate plural *romantiae*, an editor anglicised to *romanties* in the printed version, *The Life of the Renowned Sir Philip Sidney* (1652).[46]

But where Greville is complimentary, and may describe fiction, or, less likely, simply literature in the vernacular,[47] Mary Sidney Wroth invokes 'romance' before 1626 to denigrate morally reprehensible and rhetori-

---

45 L. Plazenet, 'Jacques Amyot and the Greek Novel: The Invention of the French Novel', pp. 238–9.

46 *A Dedication to Sir Philip Sidney*, in *The Prose Works of Fulke Greville, Lord Brooke*, ed. by J. Gouws (Oxford: Clarendon Press, 1986), pp. xxii–xxiv, 8, which modernises the text as 'romances'. In *A Defence of Ryme* (1603), dedicated to William Herbert, son of his patron Mary Sidney Herbert, Countess of Pembroke, Samuel Daniel, a friend of Greville and Florio, writes of 'Romance […] songs the *Bards* & *Druydes* about Rymes vsed & therof were caled *Remensi*, as some Italians hold' (*A Panegyrike Congratulatory Deliuered to the Kings most excellent maiesty at Burleigh Harrington in Rutlandshire. By Samuel Daniel. Also certaine Epistles. With a Defence of Ryme, heeretofore written, and now published by the Author* (1603), G4.

47 E. R. Curtius, *European Literature and the Latin Middle Ages*, trans. by W. R. Trask (Princeton: Princeton University Press, 1953; repr. London: Routledge and Kegan Paul, 1979), p. 32.

cally unsophisticated fictional writing. In the Second Part of *Urania*, she condemns an old man whose 'blassphemous swearing and curses' form 'the greatest part of his discourse', because 'for learning, ore reading above a Romancie, hee never troubled him self withall'.[48] Yet, while admitting the shortcomings of 'lying Romances',[49] Edward Gayton notes that the innkeeper in Cervantes's *Don Quixote* (1605–15) improved his temperament by reading them:

> Mine Host hath another benefit by his books, or his wife rather, for it seems he was a fiery cholerick man, and the book was her security, as long as he was reading, shee was at quiet; a very good recipe for either sex that are troubled with the Alarum of the tongue. Romances may be very well read by women in such cases, and not as *Maritornes* the fousty slattern made use of them to defile her braines with the conceit of embracing a Knight under an Orange Tree, what a Lemman should he have of her? (Cc1v)

Philhellenism and the allegorical politicisation of erotic romance

Sidney Wroth defines the moral and ethical qualities of characters by what they read or how they act. This typifies the allegorical schema intrinsic to artfully written erotic romance, both during the Renaissance in England and in Greco-Roman prose romance. The practice of coupling surface with deeper meanings has its roots in the schools of rhetoric in ancient Greece. There 'Hyponoiac, allegorical reading consisted, in effect, of working back through the mythical and tropical declensions of the poetic *logos* to the underlying code, which only philosophical discourse could articulate and explain'.[50] Six hundred years later, coinciding with the advent of erotic romance, 'extremes of allegorical fantasia [...] had a well-established tradition in grammatical hermeneutics and the grammatical *paideia*'.[51] Neoplatonists of the time fostered the development of keys to decode divine wisdom in Homer's poems.[52] By contrast, sceptics such as Plutarch,[53] and those exceptional sophists whose rhetorically exemplary romances survive, aspired to train their readers away from

48 *The Second Part of The Countess of Montgomery's Urania*, ed. by J. A. Roberts, S. Gossett and J. Mueller, medieval and Renaissance Texts and Studies, vol. 211; Renaissance English Text Society, 7th ser. xxiv (Tempe, AZ: Arizona Centre for medieval and Renaissance Studies, 1999), ii.213.
49 E. Gayton, *Pleasant Notes Upon Don Quixot* (1654), D3.
50 J. Walker, *Rhetoric and Poetics in Antiquity*, p. 294.
51 J. Walker, *Rhetoric and Poetics in Antiquity*, p. 295.
52 J. Walker, *Rhetoric and Poetics in Antiquity*, p. 297.
53 J. Walker, *Rhetoric and Poetics in Antiquity*, pp. 297–302, discusses Plutarch's 'How the Young Man Should Study Poetry'.

the false allure of what they deemed to be poetic sorcery. It is a comparatively transparent nuancing that gives their writing an added dimension, encouraging erotic romance to be read as allegory. The genre itself came to stand for what it contained: stoicism, virtuous behaviour, and personal and political freedom.

As discussed in Chapters 2 and 4, Amyot follows Plutarch's critical approach by stressing the exemplary moral and ethical allegories offered by the characters in *An Ethiopian Story*. His positive avoidance of metaphysical and philosophical suggestion corresponds to the Renaissance shift from 'the medieval notion of Apuleius', the author of the Latin novel *The Golden Ass*, 'as pre-eminently a philosopher' to viewing him primarily 'as a literary artist and shaper of fictions'.[54] These perspectives were often blended. But in his much reprinted *Commentarii a Philippo Beroaldo conditi in asinum Lucii Apulei* (Bologna, 1500), Filippo Beroaldo takes a radically advanced stand: 'I [...] will not seek allegories, but rather the historical significance, and [...] the interpretation of the unknown things and of the words, so as not to appear to be a bad philosopher, rather than a commentator'.[55]

Amyot and other Renaissance commentators take this lighter approach towards the Greco-Roman romances. They view Hydaspes in *An Ethiopian Story* as a model of kingship, but avoid the potential religious and political significance of Heliodorus's use of the myth of Perseus and Andromeda. Yet the early history of philhellenism and its links with administrative and rhetorical reform offers the potential for politicised interpretation. During the centuries following the 'Romans' brutal crushing of all vestiges of Greek independence in the middle of the second century BC', functional classical Greek declined under pressure from more popular, comparatively 'affected, "Asian" rhetoric'.[56] When 'the back-to-the-classics "Atticist" reaction of the first century BC set in',[57] the growing momentum of the philhellene movement reversed this trend. New, plainer styles derived from philosophically based ancient Attic developed, and characterise writing during the Second Sophistic. As in Plutarch, Aphthonius and the Philostratii, these styles were associated with freedom, good education and wise government. They resurrected

54 R. H. F. Carver, 'The Rediscovery of the Latin Novels', in *Latin Fiction: The Latin Novel in Context*, ed. by H. Hofmann (London: Routledge, 1999), pp. 253–68 (p. 263).
55 C. Moreschini, 'Towards a History of the Exegesis of Apuleius: The Case of the "Tale of Cupid and Psyche"', trans. by C. Stevenson, in *Latin Fiction: The Latin Novel in Context*, ed. by H. Hofmann (London: Routledge, 1999), pp. 215–28 (p. 224), citing Beroaldo's note to IV.28.
56 See T. Hägg, *The Novel in Antiquity*, pp. 104–6.
57 J. Walker, *Rhetoric and Poetics in Antiquity*, pp. 59, 65–70.

ideals of the democratic city-state, and of the cultural sophistication associated with the glorious pre-Roman period of Greece. Roman loan-words for 'ruler', 'imperator' and 'princeps', were replaced by Greek-based diction such as 'basilius' – literally 'king', but designating all forms of sovereign power in Greek civilisation.[58]

Rehabilitation of Greek political diction in the provinces provided a platform for sedition.[59] Motivated as much by political expediency as by philhellene antiquarianism, Roman leaders ensured that they made themselves thoroughly bilingual. Plutarch notes that Antony 'delighted to be called a Philhellene, and still more to be addressed as Philathenian'.[60] Greek sophists flourished. Cicero recalls that, as a student, he practised his declamations in Greek because 'the foremost teachers, knowing only Greek, could not, unless I used Greek, correct my faults nor convey their instruction'.[61] One hundred and fifty years later, towards the end of the first century AD, Plutarch encouraged and reaped the benefits of bilingual Roman education. He laments in his 'Life' of Demosthenes that as a rhetorician teaching

> in Rome and various parts of Italy I had no leisure to practise myself in the Roman language, owing to my public duties and the number of my pupils in philosophy. It was therefore […] when I was well on in years that I began to study Roman literature. […] But to appreciate the beauty and quickness of the Roman style, the figures of speech, the rhythm, and the other embellishments of language, while I think it a graceful accomplishment and one not without its pleasures, still, the careful practice necessary for attaining this is not easy for one like me, but appropriate for those who have more leisure.[62]

Some decades later, Plutarch's descendant Apuleius, the rhetorician and author of *The Golden Ass*, moved to Rome. He had been schooled in Athens, and while still young taught himself 'the full perfection of the Latin tongue' in Rome. He used both languages professionally.[63]

58 L. Pernot, 'La rhétorique de l'Empire ou comment la rhétorique grecque a inventé l'Empire romain', *Rhetorica*, xvi (1998), 131–48, esp. p. 141.
59 L. Pernot, 'La rhétorique de l'Empire ou comment la rhétorique grecque a inventé l'Empire romain', p. 138.
60 'Antony', in *Plutarch's Lives*, trans. by B. Perrin, 11 vols (London: William Heinemann, 1914–26), ix.185–7. For a transcription of this text, see: http://penelope.uchicago.edu/Thayer/E/Roman/Texts/Plutarch/Lives/Antony*.html.
61 Cicero, *Brutus*, in *Brutus [and] Orator*, trans. by G. L. Hendrickson and H. M. Hubbell (London: William Heinemann Ltd, 1952), xc.310.
62 Plutarch, 'Demosthenes', in *Plutarch's Lives*, trans. by B. Perrin, 11 vols (London: William Heinemann, 1914–26), vii.5. For a transcription of this text, see: http://penelope.uchicago.edu/Thayer/E/Roman/Texts/Plutarch/Lives/Demosthenes*.html.
63 Apuleius, *The Golden Ass* [,] *Being the Metamorphoses of Lucius Apuleius* [,] *with an*

The sixteenth-century Greco-Roman literary revival in England owes much to Renaissance European philhellenism, and brings with it similar political connotations. In France, as in England, philhellenism becomes associated in the court with linguistic and political nationalism. François I patronised the translation of Plutarch's *Lives*, a task completed by the royal tutor, Jacques Amyot. And, to a certain extent, the elegant neo-classical style that Amyot imposed on Heliodorus, Longus and Plutarch is carried into English adaptations of these writers.

Philhellenism was encouraged throughout the Protestant world by Erasmus, and later by Calvin and his followers.[64] French scholars and publishers based in Geneva produced annotated editions of Greco-Roman texts, through which they publicised the virtues of a Calvinist Christian republic. In Elizabethan and Jacobean England, philhellenism manifests itself through writings strongly associated with supporters of the tolerant French Huguenots and Dutch Reformed Protestants, struggling for survival under regimes subservient to the interests of Rome.

As the following chapters show, none could escape the impact on London of the huge influx of Protestant refugees from France and the Low Countries, who from 1567 and for decades thereafter fled daily massacres of untold thousands.[65] The official protection they received is reflected in Thomas Kyd's arrest and torture on 12 May 1593 on charges related to the posting of 'divers lewd and mutinous libels ... set uppon the wall of the Dutch Churchyard'. A surviving anonymous example in verse alludes to Marlowe's *Tamburlaine*, and issues dire threats to the swarms of immigrant labourers who live in densely packed houses, and take jobs away from native Londoners.[66]

More than twenty years earlier, Thomas Bette's pro-Huguenot broadside, *A Newe Ballade Intituled, Agaynst Rebellious and false Rumours. To the newe tune of the Black Almaine, vpon Scissillia* (1570), anticipated the threat from Catholic extremists, and from Spain in particular, that dictated English policy for generations to come:

English Translation by W. Adlington (1566), rev. by S. Gaselee (London: William Heinemann, 1922), pp. 3–4; cf. G. Sandy, 'Apuleius's *Golden Ass*: From Miletus to Egypt', in *Latin Fiction: The Latin Novel in Context*, ed. by H. Hofmann, pp. 81–102 (pp. 81–2).

64 Cf. S. Goldhill, *Who Needs Greek: Contests in the Cultural History of Hellenism* (Cambridge: Cambridge University Press, 2002), pp. 14–59.

65 L. Forster, *Janus Gruter's English Years: Studies in the Continuity of Dutch Literature in Exile in Elizabethan England* (Leiden: Leiden University Press, 1967), pp. 3–4, notes Dutch communities, besides London, at Norwich, King's Lynn, Yarmouth, Thetford, Colchester, Ipswich, Halstead; Sandwich, Maidstone and Dover.

66 A. Freeman, 'Marlowe, Kyd, and the Dutch Church Libel', *English Literary Renaissance*, iii (1973), 44–52.

Experiaunce well may showe,
What numbers here doth flowe.
Of Flemmings fled from Tirantes hand,
Which dayly commeth to this land:
Whose harts in wrath full long hath boyld
And eake there Countrye cleane dispoyld.
    Which thing may warne vs well I saye
    Least that we feele the lyke decaye.[67]

The trials of faith experienced by exiled Dutch and French Protestants resembles the stoicism exhibited by wronged and displaced characters in erotic romance, suffering at the hands of repressive tyrants.

As is clear from Fulke Greville's *Dedication to Sir Philip Sidney*,[68] in response to the Pope and his Spanish allies taking the Netherlands by force, exerting control over the king of France and plotting the deaths of Elizabeth I and James I, English philhellenes long maintained an ardent anti-Spanish policy. Many Huguenot supporters, such as the interrelated Sidney, Herbert (Pembroke), Gamage, Stradling and Devereux (Essex) families, cherished their Norman and Gallic origins. Their spiritual roots lay in the ancient Christian church before it became perverted by Papal politics. A generation earlier, they had all been Roman Catholics, and some still were. Formal religious differences did not, however, prevent many from being friends, colleagues and ardent nationalists. Donne, Southampton and even Shakespeare, all with Catholic backgrounds, were directly or indirectly associated with Essex, a militant advocate of anti-Roman policy.[69]

By inviting the quasi-republican philhellenes into the centre of his court, James I strengthened royal control over their aspirations; and by the time Charles I succeeded to the throne in 1625, the movement had lost its impetus. Coincidentally, the understanding of how to read allegory and symbolism as used by authors of erotic romance simultaneously faded. By the late 1630s, young Oxford scholars lacked the reading techniques to understand either Heliodorus or Sidney in depth. They would have fared little better with Shakespeare, or their near contemporary Mary Sidney

67 Sidney's perspective on Elizabeth's sending forces into the Protestant United Provinces is investigated in V. Skretkowicz, '"O pugnam infaustam": Sidney's Transformations and the Last of the Samotheans', *Sidney Journal*, xxii (2004 [published 2006]), 1–24.
68 Cf. V. Skretkowicz, 'Greville, Politics, and the Rhetorics of *A Dedication to Sir Philip Sidney*', in *Fulke Greville: A Special Double Number*, ed. by M. C. Hansen and M. Woodcock, *Sidney Journal*, xix (2001 [published 2002]), 97–123.
69 P. E. J. Hammer, *The Polarisation of Elizabethan Politics: the Political Career of Robert Devereux, 2nd Earl of Essex, 1587–1597* (Cambridge: Cambridge University Press, 1999), pp. 174–8, 291.

Wroth, in whose hands Longus's pastoral romance *Daphnis and Chloe* becomes transformed into a stylised vehicle of Protestant political and social engagement.

2

Longus's *Daphnis and Chloe*

The novel as ecphrasis

Unlike Sidney Wroth's huge and complex *Urania*, *Daphnis and Chloe* contains a relatively short, chronological exploration of innocent love. Longus's romance is best known as the model for stories in which infants are abandoned by parents of social or political prominence, found by rustic shepherds and reared in pastoral surroundings. They fall in love, endure separation, reunite with their natural father and mother, and marry. *Daphnis and Chloe* may serve readers 'as preparatory education for the inescapable experience of love', though the ease with which characters cope with learning of their abandonment underscores 'the factual unreality of the story'.[1]

If Heliodorus develops the plot-line of discovery, identification and denouement in his 'life' of Charikleia, Longus doubles and complicates this conventional motif by paralleling and intertwining the biographies of Daphnis and Chloe. He supports the artificiality of this structure with a quasi-allegorical plot that carefully blurs distinctions between natural and supernatural, profane and divine. Daphnis and Chloe inhabit an otherworldly universe that corresponds with the artificiality of their own characters, and the thoughts, sayings and doings of those they encounter. Their lives progress through a series of psychological developments and calamitous events calculated to demonstrate the benefits of human virtue, and the rewards of faith in the divine.

The autobiographical opening, 'When I was hunting in Lesbos', inspires confidence in the author-narrator's veracity, as he draws readers into his tale. The sequence of events and narrative strategy are set out in the Prologue. There the narrator comes across a painting 'in a grove that

---

1 J. R. Morgan, 'Daphnis and Chloe: Love's Own Sweet Story', in *Greek Fiction: The Greek Novel in Context*, ed. by J. R. Morgan and R. Stoneman (London: Routledge, 1994), pp. 64–79, citing pp. 65, 75, 74.

was sacred to the Nymphs', and frequented by pilgrims. The painting is composed of vignettes: 'women giving birth, others dressing the babies, babies exposed, animals suckling them, shepherds adopting them, young people pledging love, a pirates' raid, an enemy attack – and more, much more, all of it romantic' (Prologue; Reardon, pp. 288–9). The narrator finds a local interpreter, whose report forms the four Books of the novel. The list of events in the picture functions as a table of contents, the entire novel becoming an ecphrasis – a description of the picture, fleshed out with speaking parts.[2]

Amyot, translation and the kings of France

The survival of many sixteenth-century Greek manuscripts of Longus, as well as the manuscript of the Italian translation by Annibale Caro (1507–66), which he ceased working on by 1538, indicates serious engagement with Longus.[3] But the wider Renaissance history of *Daphnis and Chloe* begins with the anonymous publication of Jacques Amyot's translation, *Les amours pastorales de Daphnis et Chloe, escriptes premierement en grec par Longus et puis traduictes en François* (Paris: Vincent Sertenas, 1559).[4] Amyot based this on the manuscript that Jerome Fondulo probably had made in Rome just before François I ordered him, in 1529 or 1539, to send his books to France.[5] Amyot

2 Reardon, B. P., ed., *Collected Ancient Greek Novels* (Berkeley, CA: University of California Press. 1989), p. 289, note 1. Cf. S. Bartsch, *Decoding the Ancient Novel: The Reader and the Role of Description in Heliodorus and Achilles Tatius* (Princeton: Princeton University Press, 1989).
3 On Caro, see M. D. Reeve, 'Fulvio Orsini and Longus', *The Journal of Hellenic Studies*, xcix (1979), 165–7 (p. 167). R. F. Hardin, *Love in a Green Shade: Idyllic Romances Ancient to Modern* (Lincoln: University of Nebraska Press, 2000), p. 246, records that G. B. Manzini, in *Gli amore innocenti di Dafni, e della Cloe* (Bologna, 1643), published Caro's translation as his own. H. Hofmann, 'Introduction' to *Latin Fiction: The Latin Novel in Context*, ed. by H. Hofmann (London: Routledge, 1999), p. 8, notes that Caro was later acknowledged in Italian editions. *Gli Amori pastorali di Dafni e di Cloe*, trans. by A. Caro, was published in Parma (1784) and Florence (1786) and London (1786).
4 See F. Lestringant, 'Les amours pastorales de Daphnis et Chloé: fortunes d'une traduction de J. Amyot', in *Fortunes de Jacques Amyot: Actes du colloque international (Melun 18–20 avril 1985)*, ed. by M. Balard (Paris: A.-G. Nizet, 1986), pp. 237–57. References are to Longus, *Les amours pastorales de Daphnis et Chloé, traduit du grec ancien par Jacques Amyot*, avant-propos de Sabine Wespieser, Les Belles Infidèles (Arles: Actes Sud, 1988).
5 The evidence is summarised in L. Plazenet, 'Jacques Amyot and the Greek Novel: The Invention of the French Novel', in *The Classical Heritage in France*, ed. by G. N. Sandy (Leiden: E. J. Brill, 2002), pp. 237–80 (pp. 251–2). On Bibliothèque Nationale MS Parisinus Graecus 2895, see M. D. Reeve, 'Fulvio Orsini and Longus', *The Journal of Hellenic Studies*, xcix (1979), 165–7 (p. 166); cf. *Achilles Tatius. Leucippe and Clitophon*, ed. by E. Vilborg (Stockholm: Almquist and Wiksell, 1955), pp. xxi, lxxv.

invented the title.[6] His addition of 'amours' associates the work with his
– also anonymous – translation of *Heliodorus, L'histoire aethiopique de
Heliodorus, contenant dix livres traitant des loyales et pudiques amours de
Theagenes thessalien et Chariclea aethiopie[n]ne, nouuellement traduite de
grec en françoys* [trans. by Jacques Amyot] (Paris: [par Estienne Groul-
leau], 1547 [i.e., 1548]).[7]

Amyot (1513–93) held the posts of Professor of Latin and Greek at the
University of Bourges, royal tutor to Charles IX, Abbot of Bellozane, then
Abbot of Saincte Corneille de Compiègne. In 1570 he became Bishop of
Auxerre as well as Grand Almoner in the court of the king of France. His
translation of Plutarch's essay 'Of Intemperate Speech or Garrulitie' won
the attention of François I (1494–1547), who appointed him to succeed
Georges de Selve, Bishop of Lavaur and ambassador, as translator of
Plutarch's *Lives*.[8]

Amyot benefited from the Gallican independence from Rome of the
French monarchy and its control over an autonomous Catholic church.[9] It
is not without significance that Amyot's early books compliment the royal
family at times of death and renewal. François I died on 31 March 1547;
Amyot's anonymous translation of Heliodorus's *An Ethiopian Story*, dated
1547 on the title-page, was published the following February. This was at
the end of 1547 by the Old Style calendar, or 1548 New Style.[10] The new
king was Henri II (1519–59); his Florentine queen consort, Catherine de
Médicis (1519 to January 1589). When Henri II was killed in a jousting
accident, on 30 June 1559, the throne passed to his son, François II (1544–
60), who in 1558 had married Mary Stuart, Queen of Scots. In addition to
Les amours pastorales de Daphnis et Chloe, done between 1553 and 1559,[11]

---

6 See L. Plazenet, 'Jacques Amyot and the Greek Novel: The Invention of the French
   Novel', p. 247.
7 For details of the dates and publishing history of Amyot's translations of Heliodorus
   and Longus, see L. Plazenet, 'Jacques Amyot and the Greek Novel: The Invention of the
   French Novel', pp. 240–7, 273.
8 R. Sturel, *Jacques Amyot, traducteur des Vies Parallèles de Plutarque* (Paris: H. Champion,
   1908), pp. 37–8. De Selve, whose eight 'Lives' were published in 1543, is believed to
   be portrayed with Jean de Dinteville in Holbein's *The Ambassadors*; cf. J. North, *The
   Ambassador's Secret: Holbein and the World of the Renaissance* (London: Hambledon
   and London, 2002).
9 On ecclesiastical Gallicanism and royal Gallicanism, see T. I. Crimando, 'Two French
   Views of the Council of Trent', *The Sixteenth Century Journal*, xix, no. 2 (1988),
   169–86 (pp. 170–4).
10 R. Sturel, *Jacques Amyot, traducteur*, p. 51. The evidence is reviewed in L. Plazenet,
   'Jacques Amyot and the Greek Novel: The Invention of the French Novel', pp. 240–1.
11 L. Plazenet, 'Jacques Amyot and the Greek Novel: The Invention of the French Novel',
   p. 252.

in 1559 Amyot published the revised edition of Heliodorus and his massive Plutarch, *Les vies des hommes illustres Grecs, & Romains*, later translated by Thomas North as *The Lives of the Noble Grecians and Romanes* (1579). But even in this magisterial work, it is only in closing his dedication to Henri II that the cautious Amyot discloses his name.

François II died on 5 December 1560, to be succeeded by his brother, Amyot's pupil, Charles IX (1550–74). On 26 November 1570, Charles IX married Elisabeth of Austria, daughter of Maximilian II, the Holy Roman Emperor, and the Infanta Maria of Spain. In 1572, Amyot published his translation of Plutarch's essays, *Les Oeuvres morales & meslees de Plutarque. Translatees du Grec en François par Messire Iacques Amyot* (Paris, 1572), of which Philemon Holland used a later edition when independently translating *The Morals* (1603) from the Greek.

During the summer of 1572, Paris was the venue for two internationally attended events. Both were witnessed by the seventeen-year-old Philip Sidney. On Sunday 15 June, Amyot officiated at a service to mark the ratification of the Treaty of Blois.[12] Charles IX became so enchanted with Sidney that on 9 August he created him a gentleman of his bedchamber, with the title Baron de Sidenay.[13] Then, on 18 August 1572, Charles gave his sister Marguerite de Valois in marriage to the Huguenot leader, Henri III of Navarre. Disaster struck when on 24 August, Charles, his mother, his brother – who on 30 May 1574 would succeed him as Henri III of France (1551–89) and their fanatical Papist cousin Henri, Duc de Guise, initiated the infamous St Bartholomew's Day massacre of the Huguenots. The ensuing years of Protestant persecution encouraged English military intervention, supported by the literary endeavours of philhellene Protestants such as Philip Sidney and his sister, Mary Sidney Herbert, Countess of Pembroke.

Reading, Education and Translation

Amyot's philhellenism and translations are inseparable from his nationalism and his vocation as priest and teacher. Longus writes that Daphnis and Chloe were taught 'to read and write and to do everything that was regarded as elegant in the country' (1.8; Reardon, p. 291). As, with very few exceptions, Greek was not taught in any depth in French (or English)

---

12 J. M. Osborn, *Young Philip Sidney 1572–1577* (New Haven: Yale University Press, 1972), pp. 39–40.
13 A. Stewart, *Philip Sidney: A Double Life* (London: Chatto & Windus, 2000), p. 81.

schools during the Renaissance,[14] Amyot intended his translations to offer educational, social, political and rhetorical models.[15]

Amyot had no doubts that the erotic romances of the Second Sophistic, appropriately translated, were suited to his didactic purpose. In 1599, when Amyot published his Longus and the corrected edition of Heliodorus, he returned to the partnership of printer-publishers, Longis, Groulleau and Sertenas.[16] Whilst Amyot may have been hard pressed to find another publisher, Plazenet argues that Amyot used Vincent Sertenas, 'who had published the *Amadis*' and the 1548 Heliodorus, precisely so that the erotic romances 'would unambiguously appear as entertaining works belonging to French "belles-lettres"'.[17] Yet in the 1548 and 1559 Translator's Proem – 'Pröesme du Translateur' – to Heliodorus, he particularly commends the philosophical content, rhetorical artifice, moral characterisation and artful structure of *An Ethiopian Story*.

In this Proem, Amyot puts his own gloss on the enduring debate among Greek philosophers, about whether poetry was fit 'to remain a suitable part of the grammatical curriculum'.[18] His starting point is the influential, pseudo-Plutarchan first essay in Plutarch's *Morals*, 'The Education of Children', which John Lyly adapts in *Euphues: The Anatomy of Wit* (1578), and which parallels Plutarch's 'How the Young Man Should Study Poetry'. Amyot's message, expressed in his characteristically expansive prose style, is clear, even in a literal translation.[19] 'A certain great philosopher', Amyot writes, 'wisely admonishes nurses not to tell their little children all kinds of tales indiscriminately, taking care that their minds should not drink deeply of folly from the beginning, and do not grasp some vicious impression. Further, it seems to me that one could

14 See J. W. Binns, *Intellectual Culture in Elizabethan and Jacobean England: The Latin Writings of the Age* (Leeds: Francis Cairns, 1990), pp. 216–18.

15 J. Amyot, *Projet d'Eloquence Royale*, ed. by P.-J. Salazar (Paris: Les Belles Lettres, 1992); see G. P. Norton, 'Amyot et la rhétorique: La revalorisation du pouvoir dans le *Projet de l'éloquence royale*', in *Fortunes de Jacques Amyot: Actes du colloque international (Melun 18–20 avril 1985)*, ed. by M. Balard (Paris: A.-G. Nizet, 1986), pp. 191–205.

16 L. Plazenet, 'Jacques Amyot and the Greek Novel: The Invention of the French Novel', p. 246.

17 L. Plazenet, 'Jacques Amyot and the Greek Novel: The Invention of the French Novel', p. 260.

18 J. Walker, *Rhetoric and Poetics in Antiquity* (Oxford: Oxford University Press, 2000), p. 293.

19 Quotations are from *L'histoire aethiopique de Heliodorus, contenant dix livres, traitant des loyales et pudiques amours de Theagenes Thessalien, & Chariclea Aethiopienne. Traduite de Grec en François, & de nouueau reueüe et corrigée sur un ancien exemplaire escript à la main, par le translateur, ou est declaré au vray qui en a esté le premier autheur* (Paris: Vincent Sertenas, 1559).

with good cause counsel people who are already at the age of respon-
sibility not to amuse themselves in reading all sorts of books of fiction
without using their judgement, lest their minds little by little grow accus-
tomed to liking falschood, and feed on vainglory.[20] 'All such mendacious
writings' – 'tous escritz mensongers' – ought to be condemned (¶2). In
contrast, Heliodorus offers no 'model for doing evil' – 'exemple de mal
faire' (¶2v).

Of particular relevance to *Daphnis and Chloe*, Amyot also idealises
the chaste behaviour of Heliodorus's central characters. His subtitle,
traitant des loyales et pudiques amours – 'treating the loyal and chaste
loves' of Theagenes and Charikleia – makes this abundantly clear.[21]
Heliodorus certainly exemplified the physical boundaries on courtship
behaviour encouraged by Renaissance Christian neoplatonists. In Baldas-
sare Castiglione's internationally popular *Il Libro del Cortegiano* (1528)
– *The Book of the Courtier* – Pietro Bembo teaches that sex should be
limited to kissing, by which lovers' souls pass into one another's bodies.[22]
Amyot recognised that Longus offers similar lessons in maintaining
chaste behaviour between his principal characters. He even emphasises
Daphnis's mental chastity during and following Lycaenion's instruction in
sexual intercourse, a virtue strengthened in Amyot's text.

In addition to this tendency to accentuate morality, Amyot was instru-
mental in politicising European erotic romance. He cultivated a belief
in the ancient Greek cultural roots of France, in the manner of Henri
Estienne in *Traicte de la conformité du language François auec le Grec*
(*c.* 1565).[23] In 1579, Henri III commissioned Estienne, Philip Sidney's
Huguenot friend, scholar, publisher and manuscript collector, to come

---

20 'vn certain grand Philosophe amonneste sagement les nourrices, de ne conter indif-
    feremment toutes sortes de fables à leurs petitz enfantz, de peur que leurs ames des le
    commencement ne s'abreuuent de folie, & ne prennent quelque vicieuse impression:
    aussi me semble il, que lon pourroit auecques bo[n]ne cause conseiller aux personnes ia
    paruenues en aage de cognoissance, de ne s'amuser à lire sans iuge[m]ment toutes sortes
    de liures fabuleux: de peur que leurs ente[n]deme[n]s ne s'acoustument petit à petit à
    aymer mensonge, & à se paistre de vanité' (¶2).
21 See V. Skretkowicz, 'Sidney and Amyot: Heliodorus in the Structure and Ethos of the
    New Arcadia', *Review of English Studies*, n.s., xxvii (1976), 170–4.
22 The first English edition was *The Courtyer of Count Baldessar Castilio diuided into
    foure bookes. Very necessary and profitatable [sic] for yonge Gentilmen and Gentilwomen
    abiding in Court, Palaice or Place, done into Englyshe by Thomas Hoby* (1561). There
    was a French translation at least as early as *Les quatres livres du courtisan* (1537); see B.
    Castiglione, *The Book of the Courtier*, trans. by Sir Thomas Hoby (London: J. M. Dent,
    1959), pp. 303–24.
23 H. Estienne, *Conformité du Langage Français avec le Grec*, nouvelle ed. par L. Feugère
    (Paris, 1853; repr. Geneva: Slatkine Reprints, 1970).

to court to write his *Projet de l'oeuvre intitulé de la précellence du langage françois.*[24] In the same year Amyot, who in his youth had studied with Estienne in the Collège des Lecteurs Royaux,[25] wrote the *Projet d'eloquence royale.* Estienne calls on the king to develop a royal style, and to speak 'royalement'; Amyot urges his pupil to adopt a Greco-Roman style that will be clear, slightly ornate and distinctively 'royal'.[26]

In the spirit of this rhetorical programme, Amyot's translations take French to new levels of elegance. He adds evocative adverbs and picturesque adjectives; intensifiers; superlatives; and, most significantly, glosses in the form of explanatory phrases. These are often accentuated through alliteration, internal rhyme and parallel clauses. The result is a heavily balanced, rhythmic musical symmetry 'linked to the elegant euphony recommended in the *Projet d'eloquence royale*',[27] but which is noticeably absent from the Greek originals.[28]

Amyot's rhetorical model for *Les amours pastorales de Daphnis et Chloe* was his own 1548 translation of Heliodorus's *An Ethiopian Story*. But in all of his translations he followed the prevalent trend in France of the expansive, elaborative representation of Greek and Latin literary texts,[29] as practised by his mentor, Guillaume Bochetel. In their 1544 collaborative verse translation of Euripides' *Hecuba,* they expand 1300 lines to 1774. Similarly, in *Les Troades* (1542) Amyot turns Euripides' 1330 lines into 2461, and in *Iphigénie en Aulis* (1545–47) he expands 1630 lines into 3109.[30] Although Montaigne, who lacked Greek, was openly besotted

24 H. Estienne, *Projet de l'oeuvre intitulé de la précellence du langage françois,* ed. by E. Huguet (Paris: Armand Colin, 1896).
25 A. Billault, 'Plutarch's *Lives*', in *The Classical Heritage in France,* ed. by G. N. Sandy (Leiden: E. J. Brill, 2002), pp. 219–35 (p. 221).
26 Cf. M. Fumaroli, *L'âge de l'éloquence: Rhétorique et 'res literaria' de la Renaissance au seuil de l'époque classique* (Geneva: Librairie Droz, 1980), pp. 495–6.
27 L. Plazenet, 'Jacques Amyot and the Greek Novel: The Invention of the French Novel', p. 278.
28 R. Aulotte, *Amyot et Plutarque: La tradition des moralia au XVIe siècle* (Geneva: Librairie Droz, 1965), pp. 146–53; 284–95; R. Sturel, *Jacques Amyot, traducteur,* pp. 189–267, 424–5.
29 See V. Worth-Stylianou, 'Translations from Latin into French in the Renaissance', in *The Classical Heritage in France,* ed. by G. N. Sandy (Leiden: E. J. Brill, 2002), pp. 137–64, especially pp. 152–62, 'Examples of the Evolution of Translations *c.* 1500–1630', focusing on the increased length of translations of Virgil's *Aeneid;* and G. Jondorf, 'Drama', in *The Classical Heritage in France,* pp. 453–70 (p. 456), noting that, in his 1556 translation of Seneca's *Agamemnon,* Jacques Toutain expands Eurybates' speech in Act 3, on Agamemnon's return from Troy, from 158 lines to 202. It occupies 366 lines in John Studley's English version of 1566 (D5–E4).
30 Euripide, *Les Troades – Iphigénie en Aulis, traductions inédites de Jacques Amyot,* ed. by L. de Nardis (Naples: Bibliopolis, 1996), pp. 17, 27; cf. L. Plazenet, 'Jacques Amyot and the Greek Novel: The Invention of the French Novel', p. 260.

with the language and style of Amyot's translations of Plutarch,[31] Paul-
Louis Courier de Méré (1772–1825) justifiably complains that *Les vies des
hommes illustres* is three times longer than the original.[32] Courier, who
from 1803 onwards published editorially modified versions of Amyot's
Les amours pastorales de Daphnis et Chloe, accuses him of 'speaking
Italian in French', pandering to Catherine de Médicis' Florentine taste by
using words of Italian origin and writing four lines of French for four
words of Greek.[33]

Only those with access to a manuscript of Longus could be aware of
Amyot's rhetorical embellishments, for the earliest Greek edition was
published in Florence in 1598. This was edited by Raphael Columbani
or Columbanius with the assistance of Henry Cuffe, secretary to Robert
Devereaux, second Earl of Essex, and the antiquarian Fulvio Orsini
(1529–1600), who owned three manuscripts.[34]

Amyot, working from manuscript, was not an unfaithful translator.
Glosses and paraphrases throughout his text typify his efforts to clarify the
Greek. While preparing *Daphnis et Chloe*, he undertook further manu-
script research for the 1559 revised Heliodorus, on the whole confirming
his hypothetical emendations.[35] He may at this time have consulted the
manuscript of Longus written, and bequeathed to the Vatican Library,
by Fulvio Orsini.[36] Certainly he scrupulously added a note to indicate

31 A. Billaut, 'Plutarch's *Lives*', in *The Classical Heritage in France*, ed. by G. N. Sandy, pp.
     219–35 (pp. 226–31).
32 *Les pastorales de Longus, ou Daphnis Et Chloé, Traduction de Messire Jacques Amyot, en
     son vivant Évêque d'Auxerre et Grand-Aumonier de France; Revue, Corrigée, Completée,
     De Nouveau Refaite en Grande Partie Par Paul-Louis Courier, Vigneron, Membre de
     la Légion-D'Honneur, Ci-devant Canonnier à Cheval, Aujourd'hui en Prison à Sainte-
     Pélagie*. Cinquième Édition [first edn Paris, 1803] (Paris, 1821), p. 247, 'Son Plutarque
     est trois fois plus long que l'original'.
33 *Les pastorales de Longus, ou Daphnis Et Chloé*, p. 242.
34 Λόγγου ποιμενικῶν, τῶν κατὰ Δάφνιν καὶ Χλόην βιβλία τέτταρα. *Longi pastoralium, de
     Daphnide & Chloë libri quatuor* (Florence, 1598); see P. E. J. Hammer, 'Cuffe, Henry
     (1562/3–1601)', *Oxford Dictionary of National Biography* (Oxford: Oxford Univer-
     sity Press, 2004), and M. D. Reeve, 'Fulvio Orsini and Longus', *The Journal of Hellenic
     Studies*, xcix (1979), 165–7.
35 L. Plazenet, 'Jacques Amyot and the Greek Novel: The Invention of the French Novel',
     pp. 254–6, gives examples. Amyot's fastidiousness as a translator is the theme of G. N.
     Sandy, 'Jacques Amyot and the Manuscript Tradition of Heliodorus' *Aethiopica*', *Revue
     d'Histoire des Textes*, xiv-xv (1984–85), 1–22.
36 On Vaticanus Graecus MS 1347, see M. D. Reeve, 'Fulvio Orsini and Longus'; cf. J. M.
     Edmonds, 'Introduction', in *Daphnis & Chloe by Longus, With the English Translation of
     George Thornley*, rev. and augmented by J. M. Edmonds; *The Love Romances of Parthe-
     nius and Other Fragments*, trans. by S. Gaselee (London: Heinemann, 1916), pp. xiii-xv;
     Longus, *Pastorales (Daphnis et Chloé)*, ed. and trans. by G. Dalmeyda, 2nd edn (Paris:
     Société D'Édition 'Les Belles Lettres', 1960), p. xlv; and *Achilles Tatius. Leucippe and
     Clitophon*, ed. by E. Vilborg, p. xxv.

the absence of a passage (1.12–1.17) in the First Book: 'En cet endroit y a une grande omission de l'original' (p. 28) – 'in this place there is a great omission from the original'. This 'great lacuna', as it is known, occurs in all seven sixteenth century manuscripts with textual authority. Courier transcribed the missing text in 1807 from the thirteenth-century manuscript in Florence that also contains a fragment of Achilles Tatius, plus full texts of Chariton and Xenophon of Ephesus.[37] That he then obliterated it with a blot of ink caused an international incident. The passage first appeared in his 1810 edition.

Translating Erotic Romance

The earliest English representation of Longus is *Daphnis and Chloe Excellently describing the weight of affection, the simplicitie of loue, the purport of honest meaning, the resolution of men, and disposition of Fate, finished in a Pastorall, and interlaced with the praises of a most peerlesse Princesse, wonderfull in Maiestie, and rare in perfection, celebrated within the same Pastorall, and therefore termed by the name of The Shepheards Holidaie. By Angell Daye* (1587). In 1586, Angel Day had dedicated *The English Secretorie* to Edward de Vere, seventeenth Earl of Oxford, who for years had been selling off lands to meet his debts. Changing patron, Day dedicates *Daphnis and Chloe* to Sir Christopher Hatton's cousin and heir, Sir William Hatton, also known as Sir William Newport. Sir Christopher Hatton (1540 to November 1591) held the office of vice-chamberlain from 1577 till 1587. On being appointed Lord Chancellor in April 1587, he was succeeded by the Earl of Southampton's stepfather, Sir Thomas Heneage. William Hatton was married to Elizabeth, daughter of Thomas Cecil, who was the first (and prodigal) son of William Cecil, Lord Burghley. On 16 February 1587, William Hatton marched in Philip Sidney's funeral; on 18 November, he was one of the knights in the Accession Day tilts celebrated in Day's 'Pastorall'.

Angel Day's omissions, stylistic alterations and additions to the text transform Longus's novel into a substantial politicised romance. For *The Shepheards Holidaie* is the sole surviving record of a masque-like drama and jousts that appears to have been performed before Elizabeth I on Accession Day, 1587. Further, through the characters of Daphnis and Chloe, Day appears to idealise the courtship of a young couple seeking royal approval for their marriage.

---

37 Biblioteca Laurenziana [Florence] MS Laurentianus conv. sopp. 627; cf. *Achilles Tatius. Leucippe and Clitophon*, ed. by E. Vilborg, p. xix.

This unusual approach to translation demonstrates the art of adapting Greco-Roman erotic romance into panegyric, and of transforming a politically anodyne text into one charged with courtly resonance. Day's translation frames and sets the pastoral tone of his additions, and provides them with a narrative context. But the interpolation of such a substantial amount of original material not only shifts the focus of the plot. It also dictates the content of many of the less noticeable alterations to Amyot's version of Longus.

The first complete English translation of Longus is George Thornley's *Daphnis and Chloe. A Most Sweet, and Pleasant Pastorall Romance for Young Ladies* (1657). Thornley, a physician and 'contemporary of Milton's at Christ's College, Cambridge',[38] and able to follow both languages in Jungermann's 1605 Greek and Latin edition, often places 'a Greek loan word alongside an English equivalent, thereby glossing within the text'.[39] He also 'moves the story toward the character-centred fiction of the later seventeenth century' by 'expanding descriptive phrases that heighten the sense of place or character'.[40]

Thornley reinvents Longus in a rollicking, waggish manner. The freedom of his translation and informality of his tone go far beyond those of other translators, both reflecting and feeding the growth of libertinism during the atrocities of the civil wars. His colloquialism and overtly sexual emphasis liberate Longus from the 'royal' stylistic mannerisms and moral constraints imposed by Amyot. They also signal Thornley's royalist opposition to Oliver Cromwell.

During the reign of Charles I, from 1625 until his execution as a tyrant on 30 January 1649, sentimental French romance grew in popularity. While Puritanism encouraged plainness in style, the subject matter and rhetorical decoration of ancient erotic romance proved attractive to royalist supporters, evidenced by Anthony Hodges's *The Loves of Clitophon and Leucippe. A most elegant History, written in Greeke by Achilles Tatius: And now Englished* (1638). By contrast, John Milton (1608–74), who rejected limited monarchy for republicanism, took 'particular, indeed pedantic, care to restore specifically republican forms of language'.[41] In *Paradise*

38 R. F. Hardin, *Love in a Green Shade: Idyllic Romances Ancient to Modern* (Lincoln: University of Nebraska Press, 2000), p. 60.
39 R. F. Hardin, 'A Romance for Young Ladies: George Thornley's Translation of *Daphnis and Chloe*', *Classical and Modern Literature*, xv (1994), pp. 45–56 (pp. 48–9). Hardin compares Thornley's elaborations with the conservative translation by P. Turner, *Daphnis and Chloe*, rev. edn (Harmondsworth: Penguin, 1968).
40 R. F. Hardin, *Love in a Green Shade: Idyllic Romances Ancient to Modern*, p. 59.
41 D. Norbrook, *Writing the English Republic: Poetry, Rhetoric and Politics, 1627–1660* (Cambridge: Cambridge University Press, 1999), p. 209.

Lost (ten books, 1667; twelve in 1674), the brilliant but wrong-headed
Satan uses a parodic royal style in opposition to the studied plainness
of God and the Son. Ironically, in 1657, when Thornley demonstrated
through his irreverent *Daphnis and Chloe* that he was no strait-laced
pedantic republican, Cromwell was offered (and refused) the crown.

Thornley's robust, cavalier attitude to translation is evident from the
outset. His style forms a studied contrast to the measured plainness
Longus uses to introduce the erotic intention of his romance. Longus
boasts that his novel will 'cure the sick, comfort the distressed, stir
the memory of those who have loved, and educate those who haven't'
(Prologue; Reardon, p. 289). In Thornley's exaggerated verbiage, readers
should expect '*A Perpetuall Oblation to Love; an Everlasting Anathêma,
Sacred to Pan, and the Nymphs; and A Delightful Possession, even for all
men*. For this will cure him that is sick; and rouze him that is in dumps;
one that has loved, it will remember of it; one that has not, it will instruct'
(D3).

Daphnis and Chloe consists of a series of lessons in erotic love. The
narrative begins when the goatherd Lamon discovers a baby boy being
nursed by one of his goats. With the foundling are 'a purple cloak with
a gold clasp, and a dagger with an ivory handle' (1.2; Reardon, p. 290).
Lamon and his wife, Myrtale, name him Daphnis. Two years later, Lamon's
neighbour, the shepherd Dryas, finds one of his ewes feeding an infant
girl. This overt cross-reference to the introductory picture immediately
endows her with special significance and divine protection. She is in a
cave sacred to the Nymphs, containing statues of Nymphs and a flowing
spring. Beside her, Dryas sees 'a belt threaded with gold, gilded sandals,
and golden anklets' (1.5; Reardon, p. 291). He prays and takes the baby
to his wife, Nape. They name her Chloe, and bring her up as their own.
Within a few lines of text, Daphnis is fifteen and Chloe thirteen. The
process of educating them begins when Lamon and Dryas simultane-
ously dream they 'were handing Daphnis and Chloe over to' Eros (1.7;
Reardon, p. 291).

Through a series of vignettes, Longus's novel describes the evolu-
tion of Daphnis and Chloe's education in the theory and practice of the
science of Eros. The first demonstrates the awakening of an awareness
of sexual attraction. Close comparison of passages illustrates how differ-
ently Renaissance translators respond to the text. Chasing a dominant
billy-goat, Daphnis tumbles down 24 feet into a deep wolf-trap. Chloe
seeks help from a cowherd, Dorcon. Unable to find a long enough rope,
Chloe 'took off her breast band and gave it to the cowherd to let down'

(1.12; Reardon, p. 293). In Amyot's expansive paraphrase, 'breast band' becomes 'hair-lace': 'le cordon dont les tresses de ses cheveux étaint liées, pour en tendre un des bouts à Daphnis' (p. 28) – 'the cord with which the tresses of her hair were tied, in order to offer one end of it to Daphnis'. Whether prudishness or ambiguity in his original influences Amyot's translation, his choice of words colours Day's ecphrastic rendering. Day, whose details may represent Chloe's coiffure in an actual dramatisation of the text, amplifies Amyot's rhythmic parallel clauses into a rambling periodic sentence, more than quadruple in length:

> *Chloe* with great desire vntressed quickly her golden wirie lockes, and with the silkin twine that bound vp the same, eftsones dobled togethers in manie co[m]passes, supplied what wanted to the former shortnesse, by fastning it to the cordes end that by the Cowherds meanes, they had there already prepared. And this done, ioyning both their aides together, they did so much *Daphnis* without great hurt, was goten forth again. (B2)

Thornley, working from Jungermann's Greek and Latin edition, avoids the potential ambiguity by having Chloe provide both: '*Chloe* in a tearing haste, pulls off her hair-lace and her fillet, gives him them to let down' (E2v). Here Thornley's 'fillet' stands for 'breast-band', and is analogous to Phineas Fletcher's usage in *The Purple Island* (1633), 'Her daintie breasts, like to an Aprill rose / From green-silk fillets yet not all unbound / Began their little rising heads disclose'.[42]

Longus (and Thornley) presents Chloe naked from the waist upwards, intertwining with Dorcon as they bend over the wolf-trap to rescue Daphnis. Dorcon falls 'immediately in love with Chloe', becoming Daphnis's rival. They stage a verbal 'beauty contest' (1.15; Reardon, p. 295). The winner will kiss Chloe, who acts as judge. Each praises himself, then criticises his rival. When Chloe 'leapt up and kissed' Daphnis, he reacts 'as though he had been stung' (1.17; Reardon, p. 296). There is further nudity when Chloe helps Daphnis bathe at the spring in the Nymph's shrine, and persuades him to bathe again the next day. The soliloquy in which she describes her pangs of love is her only significant speech in the novel (1.14).

This scene with Chloe's sexual awakening falls within 'the great lacuna' (1.12–1.17), and was unavailable in print prior to Courier's 1810 edition. Neither Amyot, Angel Day nor Thornley could have been aware of the rhetorical parallelism of its sequel. Dorcon is attacked by pirates, who steal his cows and kidnap Daphnis. Still in love with Chloe, Dorcon

---

42 P. Fletcher, *The Purple Island*, 10.37, S4v (p.144), cited in *O.E.D.*, under 2a.

persuades her to take up his pipes and play the tune to which his cows are trained to come. Dorcon dies. The cows overturn the pirate ship, freeing Daphnis to return to Chloe, who for the first time bathes in front of him. Daphnis in turn learns about love's agonies (1.30–32).

Longus's simple but effective step-by-step rhetorical presentation next recontextualises the independent emotional experiences of his central characters within a metaphysical setting. In Book 2, Daphnis and Chloe both recognise sexual desire but remain at a loss how to express it. They celebrate the harvest festival of Dionysus. Philetas, a retired herdsman and devotee of Pan, recounts a visionary conversation he held with Eros in his garden. Longus stops the action to focus on this ecphrastic account:

> each season it grows everything that the season brings. In spring, there are roses, lilies, hyacinths, and violets, both light and dark; in summer there are poppies, pears, and all sorts of apples; at this time of year there are vines, figs, pomegranates, and green myrtle berries. (2.3; Reardon, p. 304)

Amyot omits hyacinths, but treats this list conservatively. Perhaps representing the Accession Day setting, Day transforms Philetas's comparatively modest Greco-Roman garden into one mimicking the extravagant horticultural display of a southern English great house:

> For the spring time, I haue roses, violets, flouredelis, hearbs, and other deuises of sundry sorts: for the summer, peares, apples, cherries, plummes, berries, and fruites of all kinde of pleasure. Now for this season of autumne haue I also, grapes, figs, nuts, orenges, pomegranats, mirtles, and twentie other like pleasures. (E3)

The supernatural overtones of Philetas's vision integrate seamlessly into Longus's idealised shadow of a naturalistic world. Selected by Eros to teach Daphnis and Chloe the mystic rite of procreation, Philetas reduces all to a formula of utmost simplicity: 'There is no medicine for Love, no potion, no drug, no spell to mutter, except a kiss and an embrace and lying down together with naked bodies' (2.7; Reardon, p. 306). His advice becomes a thematic touchstone. Amyot's version, and Thornley's, is direct and concise: 'Car il n'y a médecine quelconque, qu'on la mange ou qu'on la boive, ni espèce aucune de charme qui puisse guérir le mal d'amour, sinon le baiser, embrasser et coucher ensemble nue à nu' (p. 52) – 'For there is no med'cine for Love, neither meat, nor drink, nor any Charm, but only Kissing, and Embracing, and lying naked together' (G7v). Day's expansive translation buries Amyot's simplicity under a plethora of subordinate clauses. But rather than a moral stricture, his added allusion to the wedding night suggests the pre-nuptial nature of the 1587 Accession Day celebrations:

I neuer could finde anie remedie whereby to lessen the vehement and ardent flames that fretted within me, saue onely the last and finall conclusion of all manner of affection, which was the sole and onely linke whereby enchained eache to other, my long beloued *Amarillis* did at the last embrace me. In the enioying whereof I founde that kisses gaue ease to sighes, liking to longing, and bedding eache with other after mariage concluded, the some of all our determined affection. (F1v)

Book 2 closes with two episodes that symbiotically conflate the natural with the supernatural. Violence breaks out when Daphnis's goats eat a rope with which Methymnean hunters have tied their boat to shore. He is cleared at a trial presided over by his mentor, Philetas, opening the way for Longus to demonstrate the supernatural impact of Pan on the action.

The Methymneans kidnap Chloe from the Nymph's cave, the same cave where she was discovered as an infant. In a mystical intervention implying his divine patronage, Pan secures her release, and Daphnis demonstrates his expertise on the pipes. He and Chloe act out the story of Pan's love for Syrinx, who turned into a reed. Philetas bestows his own pipes on Daphnis, acknowledging Daphnis's affinity with Pan. Daphnis gives up his child's pipes 'as an offering to Pan' (2.38; Reardon, p. 317), and Chloe persuades him to swear by Pan that he will never leave her. Through the improbable character of Philetas, Longus establishes their worthiness of Pan's protection, completing this stage of their rite of passage.

Angel Day, *The Shepheards Holidaie* and Accession Day, 1587

Longus structures the sexual awakening of his characters around the 'rhythms of the natural year',[43] presenting himself with the opportunity to intertwine the rituals of personal and divine love. In Book 3, deep snow drives everyone indoors. Contriving to trap birds on a pair of myrtle trees at Dryas's farm, Daphnis finds himself invited to stay the night: 'they were going to make a sacrifice to Dionysus the next day' (3.9; Reardon, p. 321). In the morning, they 'sacrificed a year-old ram to Dionysus' (3.10; Reardon, p. 321). Sitting down to dinner, they offer Dionysus 'the first drops from the mixing bowl, they put garlands of ivy on their heads and ate their meal. When it was time, they shouted "Iacchus" and "Evohe" and sent Daphnis on his way' (3.11; Reardon, p. 322).

43 J. R. Morgan, '*Daphnis and Chloe*: Love's Own Sweet Story', in *Greek Fiction: The Greek Novel in Context*, ed. by J. R. Morgan and R. Stoneman (London: Routledge, 1994), p. 70.

Amyot simplifies this passing reference to the cult of Dionysus, 'et bien chanté les louanges de Bacchus' (p. 90) – 'and sung well the praises of Bacchus'. At this point, however, Angel Day abandons Amyot to insert *The Shepheards Holidaie*. He amplifies Amyot's religious ceremony into an extravagant pageant-masque in prose and verse, celebrating the cult of Elizabeth on Accession Day, 1587:[44]

> The next day calling them foorth to the celebration of a certaine yearly feast, euermore with great and most religious deuotion honoured among all the sheepeheards from the highest vnto the lowest of that Island, and all the territories therevnto adioyning [...] the custome and occasion whereof grew thus. There was at that present a *Princesse* by lineall dissent sprong from out the auncient and most renowmed race of their worthiest Kinges [...] Their Queene was then, and so alwaies continued a virgin [...]. (I4–I4v)

Amyot's *Les amours pastorales de Daphnis et Chloe* provides Day with the underlying narrative to his royal panegyric. In 1587, Day's 'certaine yearly feast', the Accession Day festival held on 17 November to mark Elizabeth's accession to the throne took place at the Westminster home of Charles Howard (1536–1624), Baron Howard of Effingham.[45] Charles Howard was the cousin both of the Queen and of Robert Sidney's wife, Barbara Gamage. In 1585, when he became Lord Admiral, Howard resigned the position of Lord Chamberlain. In 1587, he was placed in charge of preparing the army and navy for war against Spain. On 23 October 1597, he became Earl of Nottingham.[46] Howard's wife, Katherine Carey, was first cousin to Lettice Knollys Devereux, mother of Robert Devereux, second Earl of Essex.[47] Her father Henry Carey (1524?–96), first Lord Hunsdon, who succeeded Howard as Lord Chamberlain, was responsible for overseeing the 1587 Accession Day pageant.

Philip Gawdy (1562–1617),[48] who waited on the Queen during the festivities, sent a brief report to his father Bassingbourne Gawdy (*c.*1532–90) on 19 November. In it, he noted that the Queen did not arrive at

---

44 Cf. R. Strong, *The Cult of Elizabeth: Elizabethan Portraiture and Pageantry* (London: Thames and Hudson, 1977).

45 Cf. J. McDermott, 'Howard, Charles, Second Baron Howard of Effingham and First Earl of Nottingham (1536–1624)', *Oxford Dictionary of National Biography* (Oxford: Oxford University Press, 2004).

46 P. E. J. Hammer, *The Polarisation of Elizabethan Politics: The Political Career of Robert Devereux, 2nd Earl of Essex, 1587–1597* (Cambridge: Cambridge University Press, 1999), p. 386.

47 P. E. J. Hammer, *The Polarisation of Elizabethan Politics*, pp. 283–4.

48 See J. Rowe, 'Gawdy Family (*per. c.* 1500–1723)', *Oxford Dictionary of National Biography* (Oxford: Oxford University Press, 2004).

Howard's till Friday 17 November. The Accession Day jousts were held at the Whitehall tiltyard on Saturday the 18th, the day *The Shepheards Holidaie*, in the absence of contradictory evidence, could plausibly be inferred to have been performed. On Monday 20th, the Queen dined with Sir Francis Walsingham. She returned at night, dining with Howard on Tuesday 21 November. She then left for Ely House, the home of Sir Christopher Hatton, where she remained until 6 December.[49]

Day's dedication to Sir William Hatton draws particular attention to *The Shepheards Holidaie*:

> Nowe, if the course of the week-daies pastimes of these SHEPEHEARDS seeme happelie to mislike you, turn then I pray to their HOLIDAIE, where (how rudelie so euer handled) yet the Maiesty of her, who is without compar-ison, being there in most especially honoured, shunneth not the fauour of anie sweete conceipte to haue the same recommended. (Prelim., 2v)

Participants in *The Shepheards Holidaie* dressed as shepherds and shep-herdesses. Of 'the greatest and mightiest of all the Shepeheardes' at this gathering, the 'youthfull and gallantest troppe of them richly trimmed on horse-backe and on foot, exercised in her honer diuers and sundrye feates of actiuitie' (K1). The principal tilter was the precocious Robert Devereux, second Earl of Essex (1566–1601). His appointment on 18 June 1587 as master of the horse, succeeding his stepfather Robert Dudley, Earl of Leicester, established 'his domination of royal tournaments'.[50] The tilt-yard pageantry within Carey's programme would have been organised by the Queen's champion Sir Henry Lee (1533–1611), who would retire on Accession Day 1590.[51] On this occasion, Essex was forced to undergo a symbolic initiation, jousting first against Lee, and then against Elizabeth's next champion, George Clifford (1558–1605), third Earl of Cumber-land.[52]

After the jousts and other demonstrations of military prowess by armed courtiers disguised as shepherds,

49 E. K. Chambers, *The Elizabethan Stage*, 4 vols (Oxford: Clarendon Press, 1923), iv.102–3; *Letters of Philip Gawdy of West Harling, Norfolk, and of London to various members of his family 1579–1616*, ed. by I. H. Jeayes (London: Roxburghe Club, 1906), pp. 25–6.
50 P. E. J. Hammer, *The Polarisation of Elizabethan Politics*, pp. 60, 297, glosses over this event, p. 68, which is not discussed in S. W. May, *The Elizabethan Courtier Poets* (Columbia: University of Missouri Press, 1991).
51 E. Fernie, 'Lee, Sir Henry (1533–1611)', *Oxford Dictionary of National Biography* (Oxford: Oxford University Press, 2004).
52 The Tilt List, College of Arms MS. M 4 and 14, f. 35, is cited in R. Strong, *The Cult of Eliz-abeth*, p. 207. It is reproduced in A. Young, *Tudor and Jacobean Tournaments* (London: George Philip, 1987), p. 56, superseding F. A. Yates, 'Accession Day Tilts', *Journal of the Warburg and Courtauld Institutes*, xx (1957), 4–25 (p. 18).

they altogether came to a publike place, to that sole end and purpose, specially of long time reserued, where reuelling and sporting themselues vniuersally in all kinde of shepherds, pastimes & dances, they sing before *Pan* and the *Nymphs* […] reuerencing also with like regarde the *Paragon* [i.e., 'Eliza'], whome they honor. (K1)

This 'publike place' may be the Banqueting House at Whitehall, or grounds adjacent to it, where temporary pavilions could be erected.

The characters in the '*Holiday* of the *Shepeheards*', an interlude in the day's sports, include 'the good *Meliboeus* and *Faustus*, the yong and gallant *Thyrsis, Philetas,* and *Tytirus*', and Meliboeus's daughters, Licoria and Phoenicia (K1). Faustus has no speaking part, and Philetas only plays his pipes, but the others all recite poems in praise of the Queen. Of these figures, only Pan's expert musician Philetas, and his son Tityrus, appear in Longus's text. Day also scripts less formal parts, including poems, for the characters acting Daphnis and Chloe, who break out of their narrative roles to participate in the closing dance of the satyrs and shepherdesses.

The Shepheards Holidaie, court drama, and court poets

Day presupposes that his audience and the participants in this masque – the Queen and the court – are conversant with both Amyot's French translation and Sidney's *Old Arcadia*. Day knew the *Old Arcadia* well, mentioning it in his elegiac *Upon the life and death of the most worthy and thrice renowmed knight, Sir Philip Sidney*, entered in the Stationers' Register on 22 February 1587, and dedicated to Walsingham (*OA*, p. xxxix n.). Like *Daphnis and Chloe*, this was published by the Huguenot printer William Waldegrave, who in 1588–89 covertly printed several of the infamous tracts of 'Martin Marprelate', vituperative attacks against the anti-Puritan bishops.

Like Sidney in the First Eclogues of the *Old Arcadia* (*OA*, pp. 57–8), Day uses erotic prose romance to record a courtly pastoral entertainment containing a satyr's dance. More significantly, he uses the first sentence of *Daphnis and Chloe* to pay tribute to his literary mentor through a stylistic echo. Where Sidney begins, 'Arcadia among all the provinces of Greece was ever had in singular reputation, partly for the sweetness of the air and other natural benefits […]' (*OA*, p. 4), Day opens, 'Mitelene among all the notable cities of Greece, is for the delicacie and strength of the same, not the least in bewtie and greatnes of all others to be commended' (A1).

No other version of Longus even begins to approach the style and diction of Sidney's rhythmic opening. Amyot reads, 'Mitylène est une

forte ville dans l'île de Metelin, belle et grande [...]' (p. 19) – 'Myteline
is a strong city in the island of Metelin [i.e., Lesbos] beautiful and large'.
And Thornley translates, '*Mitylene* is a City in *Lesbos*, and by ancient
Titles of honour, it is the Great, and Fair *Mitylene*' (D3). From the
outset, then, Day's *Daphnis and Chloe* compliments Sidney's political and
cultural successors. His particular target is the highest ranked tilter in *The
Shepheards Holidaie*, Essex, and his new wife, Sidney's widow, Frances
Walsingham Sidney.

In response to Elizabethan decorum, Day largely transforms Longus's
eroticism into a musical celebration of courtship. He changes Amyot's
text from the outset. And he omits the Prologue, shifting attention away
from Longus's well-known ecphrastic catalogue of events towards *The
Shepheards Holidaie* in the third Book. Day expects his readers to recog-
nise that, in place of Longus's overt allusions to sex, he adds lengthy solil-
oquies for Daphnis on the frustrations of love. In imitation of Sidney's
Old Arcadia (1577–81), and anticipating Shakespeare's *As You Like It*
(1598–1600), he introduces songs and verse lamentations into the prose
of the first two books, as well as in *The Shepheards Holidaie*. In the cave
of the nymphs, Day's Lamon and Dryas write their supplication to Cupid
in the form of a quatrain. Daphnis is given six poems in various forms in
Books 1 and 2, and Book 1 closes with a dialogue in verse sung in turns
by Daphnis and Chloe.

The pageantry opens with a compliment to Meliboeus, an aged and
faithful courtier with a conventional pastoral name. He is probably the
host, Charles Howard, whom Day identifies as a known court poet: '*Meli-
boeus* (greatlie deuoted to the seruices of this *Nymphe*) had not omitted at
many other times before that to pen diuers ditties aduauncing the most
singuler partes, that in this Paragon were ordinarilie appearing' (L2). The
'graue old' Meliboeus plays his harp, and 'deliuered vnto them in song'
(K2) a long poem on the subject of princely virtue, particularly Eliza-
beth's. His song includes an allusion to Elizabeth as the huntress Diana,
goddess of chastity:[53]

> such as haunt with siluer bowe the chace,
> Thy virgin steppes ful meekely do embrace
> [...]
> For if I should thy soueraignetie descriue,

---

53 See F. A. Yates, *Astraea: The Imperial Theme in the Sixteenth Century* (London: Routledge
    & Kegan Paul, 1975; repr. Harmondsworth: Peregrine Books, 1977), p. 29; P. Berry, *Of
    Chastity and Power: Elizabethan Literature and the Unmarried Queen* (London: Rout-
    ledge, 1989).

These 29. yeares for to contriue,
Thy royall state and glory passing great,
Thy wondrous acts if here I should repeat,
Th'unspotted honor of thy princely race,
[…]
So sacred *Queene* so fittes the noble name.
                              (L1–L1v)

In a contrived response, 'the whole companie clapping their handes, highlie commended these hys Metaphoricall allutions' (L2). They then call on Meliboeus's 'two daughters yet virgins' to sing – perhaps Howard's daughters, Elizabeth, who married Sir Robert Southwell, and Frances, who married Henry Fitzgerald, twelfth Earl of Kildare.[54] Their song is an early example of a female vocal contribution to court entertainment. Licoria, who learned to play the harp from Meliboeus, performs first alone, then with Phoenicia.

Next to perform is Tytirus, 'auncient' and 'mellowed in yeares' (L3v), who chants his poetic wish for Elizabeth's continuing reign. Old Tityrus is 'a bacheler', probably Sir Christopher Hatton, at whose Ely House Elizabeth would stay for the two weeks immediately following these celebrations.

The final singer in *The Shepheards Holidaie* is Thyrsis, 'a youthfull impe seemely in shape' (L4v), whose 'more then common inclination to the highest exploits' and ancient lineage wins the admiration of all. Thyrsis, who in his poem vows to devote his 'actiue forces' (M1) to her majesty's service, is undoubtedly Essex. Essex first appeared in an Accession Day tilt on 17 November 1586,[55] one month to the day after Philip Sidney's death. Sidney's body ceremoniously arrived at Tower Hill aboard 'The Black Pinnace' on 5 November,[56] and the 1586 Accession Day tilt organised by Lee accordingly included 'A remembrance of Sir Philip Sidney Knight'. Latin verses were spoken Sidney's closest friends (possibly Fulke Greville and Edward Dyer), and verses were set on a 'mourning horse', whose rider was symbolically absent.[57]

---

54 S. Adams, 'Howard, Katherine, Countess of Nottingham (1545x50–1603)', *Oxford Dictionary of National Biography* (Oxford: Oxford University Press, 2004).

55 On Essex's tiltyard career, see R. C. McCoy, '"A dangerous Image": The Earl of Essex and Elizabethan Chivalry', *Journal of medieval and Renaissance Studies*, xiii (1983), 313–29 (p. 317).

56 M. W. Wallace, *The Life of Sir Philip Sidney* (Cambridge: Cambridge University Press, 1915), p. 392.

57 See E. K. Chambers, *Sir Henry Lee: An Elizabethan Portrait* (Oxford: Clarendon Press, 1936), p. 272, cited in F. A. Yates, *Astraea: The Imperial Theme in the Sixteenth Century*, p. 102.

Sidney's father-in-law, Sir Frances Walsingham, ran himself into debt funding Sidney's extravagant funeral, held on 16 February 1587, and depicted processing towards St Paul's in engravings by Sidney's protégé, Thomas Lant.[58] While Essex's marriage to Sidney's widow Frances did not become public until October 1590, already in June 1587 the recusant Dr William Gifford reported that Walsingham had 'married his daughter Lady Sidney to' Essex to secure money to help settle Sidney's estate.[59]

Essex's success in supplanting Sidney as a chivalric hero is confirmed by George Peele's *An eclogue Gratulatorie. Entituled: to the honorable shepherd of Albions arcadia: Robert earle of Essex* (1589). In the Accession Day tilt of 1590, Essex devised a funereal pageant, appearing in sable and riding in a chariot drawn by coal-black horses. In *Polyhymnia* (1590), Peele connects this with his continued mourning for Sidney, though it is as likely that Essex presented an overdue public tribute to his late father-in-law, Walsingham.[60] The financially ruined Secretary of State, Huguenot sympathiser and Protestant spy-master had died on 6 April 1590, and was interred the following night in St Paul's, privately, as he had requested.

According to Day's record of the events on Accession Day, 1587, on completion of the tilts and the day's 'other braue feates and exercises' (M1), the entire company turned to

> feasting, reuelling, and dauncing, where-in *Philetas* occupied his pipe whilest *Daphnis* and the other youthfull heards-men, sported in the coun-terfeite disguisings of sundry shapes of *Satyres*, to the accompaning where-of *Chloe* and the rest of the shepeheards daughters stood foorth, and by them were in diuers straunge gestures sued vnto and entreated. (M1v)

During the recognition scene in Book 4, Day introduces Daphnis and Chloe's ages. At this point in the text, none are given by either Longus or Amyot. Daphnis's foster-father declares that it is 'nowe eighteene yeares since I found him' (O2), and Chloe's foster-father says he found her 'about sixteene yeeres since' (O4v). Day consciously alters the time scheme of the

---

58 *Sequitur celebritas et pompa funeris* [...] (1587); cf. M. W. Wallace, *The Life of Sir Philip Sidney*, pp. 394–6; S. Bos, M. Lange-Meyers and J. Six, 'Sidney's Funeral Portrayed', in *Sir Philip Sidney: 1586 and the Creation of a Legend*, ed. by J. van Dorsten, D. Baker-Smith and A. F. Kinney (Leiden: E. J. Brill, 1986), pp. 38–61. Lant's engraving is in K. Duncan-Jones, *Sir Philip Sidney, Courtier Poet* (London: Hamish Hamilton, 1991), pp. 308–39; see H. R. Woudhuysen, *Sir Philip Sidney and the Circulation of Manuscripts, 1558–1640* (Oxford: Clarendon Press, 1996), pp. 216–17.

59 C. Read, *Mr Secretary Walsingham and the Policy of Queen Elizabeth*, 3 vols (Oxford: Clarendon Press, 1925; repr. New York: AMS Press, 1978), iii.170, note 2; see H. R. Woudhuysen, *Sir Philip Sidney and the Circulation of Manuscripts*, p. 375.

60 Cf. H. A. Lloyd, *The Rouen Campaign 1590–1592* (Oxford: Clarendon Press, 1973), p. 34.

romance, about which Longus is particularly clear. Day correctly records in Book 1 (A5v) that Daphnis and Chloe are fifteen and thirteen, when 'It was the beginning of spring' (1.9; Reardon, p. 292). Longus then catalogues the changing seasons, placing the recognition scene and denouement eighteen months later.[61] Day extends this to three years, possibly to make Daphnis and Chloe's ages agree with those of the characters who act out their courtship and marriage. Given that the speaking parts of Meliboeus, Licoria and Phoenicia are probably played by Charles Howard and two of his daughters, then Chloe could well be Howard's third daughter Margaret, and Daphnis her fiancé, Richard Leveson (1570–1605),[62] later vice-admiral. They were married either at these celebrations, or very shortly thereafter, by a licence dated 13 December 1587.[63]

As some of the characters in *The Shepheards Holidaie* can be identified as courtiers, it is far more likely that the speakers themselves, rather than Day, composed the variously structured poems they recite. Day may have had access to their texts through a book, of which no copy survives, sent by Philip Gawdy to his father on 24 November 1587. Gawdy describes a book that 'was gyven me that day that they rann at tilt. Divers of them being gyven to most of the lordes, and gentlemen about the Court, and one especially to the Quene.'[64] Gawdy's reference has led to the belief that books describing events, participants and scenic devices were prepared by the office of the Master of Revels for distribution at Elizabethan or Stuart tournaments.[65] But, as not a single example from over half a century survives, the odds are that Gawdy benefited from a unique gesture. Day's *Daphnis and Chloe*, of which only one copy survives, appears to incorporate and reproduce the bulk of Gawdy's otherwise unknown book, reporting the events and characters' speeches as they happened.

---

61 An allegorical schema relating the advancing seasons to Daphnis and Chloe's maturing is in H. H. O. Chalk, 'Eros and the Lesbian Pastorals of Longus', *Journal of Hellenic Studies*, lxxx (1960), 32–51 (see pp. 39–43), summarised in N. J. Lowe, *The Classical Plot and the Invention of Western Narrative* (Cambridge: Cambridge University Press, 2000), p. 242.

62 R. Wisker, 'Leveson, Sir Richard (*c.* 1570–1605)', *Oxford Dictionary of National Biography* (Oxford: Oxford University Press, 2004).

63 J. K. Laughton, 'Leveson, Sir Richard (1570–1605)', in *The Compact Edition of the Dictionary of National Biography*, 2 vols (Oxford: Oxford University Press, 1975).

64 *Letters of Philip Gawdy of West Harling, Norfolk, and of London to various members of his family 1579–1616*, p. 25.

65 A. Young, *Tudor and Jacobean Tournaments*, p. 56.

Translating Eros: Amyot, Day and Thornley

In Book 3, Angel Day substitutes *The Shepheards Holidaie* for Longus's description of Daphnis and Chloe's sexual development. Winter ends, spring arrives. Newborn lambs suck at their mothers' teats. The other ewes are chased by the rams,

> until each got his ewe in position and mounted her. The he-goats were even more passionate in chasing the she-goats and jumping on them [...] Even old men would have been excited to desire by such sights. But Daphnis and Chloe, blooming with youthful energy, who had long since been searching for love, were inflamed by what they heard and felt faint at what they saw and looked for something more than kissing and embracing for themselves – especially Daphnis. He had been wasting his youth in the winter, sitting at home doing nothing, and now he was hot for kisses, eager for embraces, more vigorous and ready for anything. (3.13; Reardon, p. 323)

Amyot enhances Longus's sexual innuendo, exaggerating Daphnis's desire through a series of puns: 'Mêmement Daphnis, lequel étant devenu gras et en bon poinct, pour n'avoir bougé tout le long de l'hiver de la maison à ne rien faire, frissait après le baiser, et était gros (comme l'on dit) d'embrasser [...]' (p. 92) – 'Daphnis likewise having grown fat and in good condition, for not having gone out of the house all winter to do anything, burned to kiss, and was enlarged [or 'with child'], as they say, to embrace'. The sober Courier condemns such prurient adventurism during translation: 'Amyot ne manque guèrre l'occasion de présenter quelqu'image grossière' (p. 272); 'Grossière sottise' (p. 279) – 'Amyot barely misses the opportunity of presenting some gross image', 'Crude stupidity'.

The special strength of *Daphnis and Chloe* lies in its portrayal of guileless sexual naivety. Longus's suffering adolescents retain their virginity solely because no one has taught them the rudiments of making love. Despite years of watching the mating habits of their sheep and goats, they remain singularly unobservant and insensitive to the mechanics of sexual intercourse. Grasping the general principles of physical proximity and lively action, Daphnis proposes taking their clothes off and lying together, as recommended by the sage Philetas. But he is easily dissuaded, as he has no answer to Chloe's question: 'She asked what more there was than kissing and embracing and actually lying down, and what he proposed to do when they were lying down naked together' (3.14; Reardon, p. 323).

Thornley renders Chloe's question as, 'what he could do by lying naked upon a naked Girle?' (M1). While Thornley's alterations are frequently motivated by mischief, this reading demonstrates fidelity to his text, only slightly accentuating Longus's titillating double reference to nakedness. Amyot correctly translates this as 'nue à nu', repeating his rendering of Philetas's instructions. Thornley's 'upon a naked Girle' also comes directly from Amyot, who adds zest to Chloe's question by putting it into direct speech, and introducing a light-hearted pun, 'Et qu'y a-t-il plus à coucher nue à nu par-dessus [literally 'on top of'] le baiser et l'embrasser qu'à coucher tout vêtu?' (p. 92) – 'And what more is there in lying naked together, in addition to kissing and hugging, than there is in lying completely dressed?' Thornley is all too eager to decode Amyot for his readership of young ladies.

In response to Chloe's argument that 'these hairy animals are much more well covered than I am even in my clothes' (3.14; Reardon, p. 323), they conduct a woefully unsuccessful experiment fully dressed: 'he made her stand up and clung to her from behind, copying the he-goats. He felt more puzzled and sat down and wept at the thought that he was more stupid than the rams at making love' (3.14; Reardon, pp. 323–4). Thornley's light-hearted nuancing manifests itself in Daphnis's dissatisfaction: 'finding a meer frustration there, he sate up, and lamented to himself, that he was more unskilfull then a very Tup in the practice of the mystery and the Art of Love' (M1v). But having emulated the sheep and the goats, they quickly reach the limits of their sexual knowledge, leaving Daphnis in tears.

Cultural conventions handed down by experienced elders guide them through the rites of Dionysus, but Philetas's cryptic instructions on love-making open the way for Longus to introduce a shallowly developed Theophrastan character type to make up this earthly deficit. Enter the predatory Lycaenion ('she-wolf'), a pretty town girl who by implication is unsympathetic to the comprehensive unity of the natural and divine. Married to the ageing farmer Chromis, Lycaenion seizes her chance to relieve her frustration by seducing Daphnis: 'She wanted to acquire him as a lover' (3.15; Reardon, p. 324). Amyot uses a well-known provocative pun in 'eut envie de s'accointer de luy' (p. 93), 'she desired to acquaint herself with him'. In Middle and Renaissance English, 'acquaint' was in common use, compactly implying both motion 'towards' and 'a woman's quaint or privities'.[66] Compare Alice's 'count', representing 'cown', the unladylike French version of 'gown', in Shakespeare's *Henry V* (III.iv.46), and the title and innuendo-laden dialogue of Wycherley's *The Country Wife* (1675). There Sir Jasper Fidget asks the appositely named Horner, 'Won't

66 *O.E.D.*

you be acquainted with her Sir? [...] Pray salute [i.e., 'sault', 'leap on'] my Wife, my Lady, Sir [...] Not know my Wife, Sir?'[67]

Lycaenion contrives a ruse to lure Daphnis into a secluded wood, pretending to need his help to rescue the best of her geese. It has been snatched, she claims, by an eagle:

> As it was so heavy to carry, he couldn't carry it right up to his usual high rock over there but fell down into the wood down here, still holding it [...] come into the wood with me (I'm frightened to go by myself), rescue my goose, and don't let my flock lose one of its number. Perhaps you'll be able to kill the eagle too, and he'll stop snatching off so many of your lambs and kids. (3.16; Reardon, p. 324)

Amyot turns Lycaenion's geese into young goslings, 'oisons'. The French practice of using the feminine for eagles in 'une aigle' (p. 94) enhances Longus's portrait of a predatory female, adding an erotic ambiguity to the metaphor: 'je te prie [...] que tu y viennes avec moi pour m'aider à le recouvrer, car j'ai peur d'y entrer toute seule. Ne veuille souffrir que mon compte soit imparfait; à l'aventure pourras-tu bien tuer l'aigle même, et par ainsi elle ne ravira plus vos peitits agneaux, ni vos chevreaux' (p. 95) – 'I beg you to come with me to help me to recover it, for I am afraid to enter there all alone. Do not allow my count to be imperfect; by chance you might even kill the eagle itself, and by that act she will not ravish your little lambs nor your kids any more'. Amyot's text reads like a passage from a French farce, or a dictionary of courtly erotic language: 'come with me', 'help me', 'recover it', 'enter there', 'my count to be imperfect', 'suffer', and 'kill'. The eagle's desisting from ravishing lambs and kids after her death becomes Lycaenion's promise of future abstinence, in return for present sexual gratification.

It is typical of the Amyot paradox that he should indulge in this risqué innuendo to compensate for his omission, immediately following, of Lycaenion's schooling Daphnis in the art of sexual penetration and female orgasm. Courier notes of this brief suppressed passage that 'Ce qui suit n'a point été traduit par Amyot' – 'what follows was not translated by Amyot'.[68] In terms of the Renaissance understanding of Longus, Amyot's omission is more significant than 'the great lacuna'. Lycaenion teaches Daphnis 'the skill that would make him able to do what he wanted to Chloe' (3.18; Reardon, p. 325), anticipating the celebration of sexual fulfilment in the

---

67 *The Plays of William Wycherley*, ed. by A. Friedman (Oxford: Clarendon Press, 1979), I.i.66–73.
68 *Les pastorales de Longus, ou Daphnis Et Chloé*, p. 278.

final lines of the novel. Lycaenion entices him with the promise that 'This isn't just kissing and embracing and doing what the rams and he-goats do. It is a kind of leaping that is sweeter than theirs, for it takes longer and gives a longer pleasure' (3.17; Reardon, p. 325). Typically, Thornley employs rustic diction, coupled with inventive additions, to undermine Longus's intended plainness: 'But those are not Kisses, nor Embracing, nor yet such things as thou seest the Rams, and the he-goats do. There are other leaps, there are other friskins then those, and far sweeter then them: For unto these there appertains a much longer duration of pleasure' (M3v).

George Thornley's itch

If Amyot and Day believe that Daphnis's introduction to sex might not be properly edifying for young readers, George Thornley experiences no such qualms. Longus's explicit description of Daphnis's arousal, 'he was capable of action and was swollen with desire' (3.18; Reardon, p. 325), seems to embarrass Thornley into paraphrase and euphemism. Plainness, however, never deserts him, even in his overstated and evasive rendering of the culmination of Lycaenion's lesson: 'As now he was sitting, and kissing, and lay down with her; She, when she saw him itching to be at her, lifted him up from the reclination on his side, and slipping under, not without art, directed him to her *Fancie*, the place so long desired and sought' (M4–M4v). The *O.E.D.* cites 'reclination' from this passage, but offers no assistance with '*Fancie*, the place so long desired and sought', Thornley's translation of (ζητουμένην ὁδòν), 'the road he had been searching for' (3.18; Reardon, p. 325).

Daphnis suffers no guilt because he has no concept of having betrayed Chloe. Partly out of clinical interest, but principally to heighten suspense, Longus stops the action to discuss post-coital bleeding in virgins. After his schooling, Lycaenion has to restrain Daphnis from rushing to show Chloe what he has learned. She issues a chill warning that stops him in his tracks: 'if Chloe has this sort of wrestling match with you, she will cry out and weep and will lie there, bleeding heavily' (3.19; Reardon, p. 325). Amyot emphsises her virginity in an interpolation: 'elle sentira du mal pour la première fois, elle criera [...]' (p. 96). Despite Lycaenion's reassurance, 'don't be afraid of the blood' (3.19; Reardon, p. 325), fear of blood becomes Daphnis's sole motivation for sexual abstinence: 'Having only just learned about the blood, he was frightened of it and thought it was only from a wound that blood came. So he decided to take only his usual pleasures with her' (3.20; Reardon, pp. 325–6).

Longus suspends Daphnis's anxiety and sexual fulfilment indefinitely, developing a series of episodes that threaten to separate him from Chloe. But Thornley's rendering of this pivotal moment ends in travesty. Where Amyot's text contains the chilling addition from the manuscript tradition, 'elle [...] saignera comme qui l'aurait tuée' (p. 96), 'she will bleed as if she had been slaughtered', Thornley revels in adding metaphors of sadistic mutilation. Two vigorous male pastimes provide analogues to violent penetration, jousting with lances and pig-sticking: 'But if thou strive with *Chloe* in this list, she will squeak, and cry out, and bleed as if she were stickt' (M5). Longus reassures; Amyot terrifies. Thornley treats female readers with disdain.

Thornley's translation reflects the diminution in censorship that occurs during the 1640s. His forthrightness does not please everyone, as is evidenced by James Wright's poem in Thornley's volume, 'Upon the Translator' (A8). Wright compares Lesbos with England, and Myteline with London: 'Both Citties speak one Language, and our stock / Of sheep first sure were brought from *Chloes* Flock'. But he objects to Thornley's handling of this passage, which, for modesty's sake, he would have preferred to read in Greek:

> Only I with *Lycaenium* and her Goose
> Had still spoke Greek; and not her selfe prov'd loose,
> And publike too: For sure a dimme eye may,
> See through her thick dark Grove too much of day.

In spite of lapses in decorum, Wright compliments Thornley for his accuracy: 'The Book thee Scholar speaks, the Grove a man'.

Thornley outlines some of the principles behind his translation in his Epistle. He denigrates stylistic affectation, while promising a further publication 'if I find, that this book lyes nearer to you, then the other Romances do, those of the affected, twirling tongue' (A4). He rationalises his choice of rustic language on nationalistic grounds. Thus, his address 'To the Criticall Reader' anticipates 'a Snapdragon Objection from a Poetaster': 'These Books (sayes he) are handsome in the Greek, but in our Saxon (make the best) it cannot be'. Thornley's retort invokes two English precedents for use of dialect: 'Our Pastorall Doricque (Sir) has shewn it self in verse, and prose, fine as *Arcadian* Holy-dayes' (A6–A6v). He could not be more correct, compactly referring to the eclogues in Sidney's *Old Arcadia* (incorporated with variations into the 'complete' 1593 and subsequent editions), and to Angel Day's *The Shepheards Holidaie*.

Angel Day and Dionysophanes' garden

Longus closes Book 3 with Daphnis and Chloe engaged to be married in the autumn. As the *Daphnis and Chloe* pageant on Accession Day 1587 comes to an end, Angel Day concludes Book 3 with the sun setting on the final dance in *The Shepheards Holidaie*. Further celebrations are deferred till the following year, 'wherewith, as they that euer wished happinesse, long life, health, hie estate and vnmatchable prosperitie, vnto hir for whom they liued, making a great shout in conclusion, each one seuered themselues therevpon, and so for the present departed' (M1v). Day makes up for his many omissions, which include Lycaenion's seduction of Daphnis, by transferring the remaining episodes of Book 3 into his Book 4.

Time almost stands still in Book 4. Like the final chapter of a mystery novel, it opens with a seemingly irrelevant event that initiates the unravelling of the tale. The landowner, Dionysophanes, 'Dionysus made manifest',[69] intends to inspect the farm managed for him by Daphnis's stepfather, Lamon: 'One of Lamon's fellow slaves arrived from Mytilene and brought the news that their master would be coming there just before the grape harvest' (4.1; Reardon, p. 333). Dionysophanes is coming to check for damage done by the Methymneans. The episode carefully links the past to the present, and anticipates the ending, as Dionysophanes will shortly recognise that he is Daphnis's natural father (4.13; Reardon, p. 338, and note).[70]

Anticipating this visit, Lamon clears the springs and tidies the farmyard. Longus creates this opportunity to remind readers of earlier instances of religious devotion, focusing on the enclosed garden. This contains 'a temple and altar to Dionysus', a tribute to Dionysophanes' namesake (4.3; Reardon, p. 333). Reiterating the theme of universal integration, Longus's idealised ecphrasis portrays a symbiotic relationship among the plants. It illustrates both the harmonious perfection of nature and Lamon's achievement in applying art to show nature at its best. Longus, followed by Amyot, locates the garden 'on elevated ground', and provides dimensions – 200 by 100 yards. Its trees, 'apple, myrtle, pear, pomegranate, fig, and olive', are reminiscent of those in old Philetas's garden in Book 2, and symbolise love and fertility (4.2; Reardon, p. 333). Amyot adds oranges (p. 114). Apple and pear trees support an enormous vine laden with grapes, 'as if it was competing with their fruit'. Ivy, whose ripening

---

69 Reardon, p. 338, n.68.
70 See R. L. Hunter, *A Study of Daphnis and Chloe* (Cambridge: Cambridge University Press, 1983), p. 38.

berries resemble grapes, overgrows the nearby forest trees: both ivy and grapes are sacred to Dionysus.

Nature parallels human endeavours. The trees stand like an artfully built wall, but are themselves fenced in. Below, the trunks grow separately; above, the branches intertwine: 'This was the work of nature, but it also seemed to be the work of art' (4.2; Reardon, p. 333). Wild and cultivated flowers mingle in beds.

Day noticeably reduces Amyot's embroidered description of the garden to only a few lines, missing out every reference to flowers. He virtually repeats the phrasing he uses for Philetas's garden:

> The shew of this place was a thing of most excellent pleasure, as well of the scituation, prospects, plentie and varietie of deuises, as also for diuersitie of trees, and all kinds of fruits [...] a thing rare and wonderfull. The trees hung yet laden with all kinde of fruites, plums, apples, peares, mirtes, granades, orinyes, limons, figs, oliues, and twentie other pleasing conceits. (N2v)

Thornley, however, renders Longus's text clearly:

> Nor were there wanting to these, borders and banks of various flowers; some the Earth's own Voluntiers; some the structure of the Artist's hand. The Roses, Hyacinths, and Lillies, were set, and planted by the hand: The Violet, the Daffodill [i.e., narcissi], and Anagall [i.e., pimpernels], the Earth gave up of her own good will. (O6v)

Dionysus' temple occupies the physical and symbolic centre of the garden. Ivy grows around the altar, and grape vines 'surrounded the temple' (4.3; Reardon, p. 334). Pictures of Satyrs treading grapes, of bacchants dancing, and of Pan sitting on a rock playing the pan-pipes, emphasise the festive and devotional ambiance. Paintings in the temple describe episodes in Dionysus' life. The first, showing his mother Semele giving birth, echoes the first scene of the painting in the Prologue, 'women giving birth', and projects beyond the end of the novel to the birth of Daphnis and Chloe's children (4.39).

Angel Day glosses over the description of Dionysus' temple. His omitting the paintings in the Prologue, as well as these in the temple of Dionysus, which foreshadow narrative themes, suggests he had never seen Sidney's *New Arcadia* (1582–84; published 1590). For had he known the descriptions of Kalander's picture gallery, where ecphrasis becomes a method of introducing themes into the narrative, he would have recognised that Sidney was signalling his debt to Longus. He would also have appreciated the skill with which Sidney interweaves this tribute with one to Achilles Tatius, in borrowing the double perspective of Kalander's reflecting fountain from *Leukippe and Kleitophon*.[71]

If Longus uses Dionysophanes' garden to symbolise the ideal harmony that shapes his plot, it now becomes a locus to represent conflicts of erotic passion. Lampis, a cowherd rejected by Chloe, seeks to ruin Daphnis's chance of securing Dionysophanes' permission to marry her. He calculatedly vandalises Lamon's garden, heralding a sequence of disasters that is finally rectified in the closing stages of the romance.

Terrified of being caught, Lampis attacks only the flowers; it would make too much noise to hack at the trees. Amyot is explicit: 'Or s'il se fût mis à couper les arbres, il eut pu être surpris, par le son de la cognée' (p. 118) – 'for if he should cut the trees, he might be given away by the noise of his axe'. After attacking the flowers, 'il se retira secrètement, sans que personne l'aperçût' – 'he secretly withdrew, without anyone noticing'. This emphasis on silence is accentuated by Thornley, who adds 'unheard' to his colloquial translation:

> There was one *Lampis* an untoward, blustering, fierce Herdsman [...] To cut the Trees he durst not attempt, lest so he should be taken by the noyse. Wherefore he thinks to ruine the flowers; and when 'twas night, gets over the hedge, and some he pull'd up by the roots, of some he graspt and tore the stems; the rest he trod down like a Boare, and so escap't unheard, unseen. (P2–P2v)

Subverting Longus's intention, Day exaggerates the noise and the scale of the damage. He introduces vigorous assonances and alliterations, elevating Longus's tranquil passage in 4.7 into a violent focal point:

> a cow-heard, a stubborne and a knurleheaded knaue, whose name was Lapes [...] this false and villanous churle, woond himselfe secretly into the garden, and there moiled and spoiled, with hookes, with hatchets, and other cutting instruments, the most part of the hedgerows, vines, fruites, and trees of all the hearberie and garden – which being doone he returned himselfe secretly againe, without being perceiued of any man. (N2v-N3)

Day changes Lamon's garden from one on a second-century Lesbian estate to one typical of a southern English Renaissance great house. Longus's Lamon goes into shock on discovering the damage to his beds of roses, violets, hyacinths and narcissi. Day contrives to make Daphnis return later from the hills, making him particularly horrified at the 'great disgrace most vile and detestable hauocke and wracke doone and committed on

---

71 Sir P. Sidney, *The Countess of Pembroke's Arcadia (The New Arcadia)*, ed. by V. Skretkowicz (Oxford: Clarendon Press, 1987), pp. 14–15.

all partes of the hearberie' (N3v), the medieval and Renaissance term for a garden where medicinal plants are grown.

In Longus, Dionysophanes' son Astylus arrives early and generously offers to say that his horses got loose and trampled the flowers (4.10). In Day, he evasively 'promised, that at his fathers comming, hee woulde endeuour to make some preatye excuse of the matter, and for to take the cause and choice occasion thereof wholly vppon him-selfe' (N4). Then, after Day's Lamon repairs what he can, Dionysophanes inspects 'his herberies, his gardens, walks, and other fine and pleasant deuises' (N4v). Day's restraint suggests he may be indicating an affinity with a real garden, and that the recognition scene that immediately follows is an extension of *The Shepheards Holidaie*. If so, the final stages of the narrative may have been adapted for performance in the grounds of Charles Howard's home.

The end: nothing but shepherds' games

In the first stage of the recognition scene, Lamon discloses how he first came across Daphnis being cared for by a nanny-goat, and Dionysophanes recognises that this is the child he abandoned. Longus presents this as though it were the inevitable outcome of a series of haphazard events. The day after Lampis wrecks the garden, and two days before Dionysophanes' visit, Dionysophanes' wealthy son Astylus arrives for a country holiday, bringing a 'hanger-on' called Gnathon.

Although incidental to the plot, Gnathon becomes the catalyst for its resolution. A Theophrastan satirical type, he is a glutton, a drunkard and a lecher: 'He was nothing but a mouth and a stomach and what lies underneath the stomach' (4.11; Reardon, p. 337). Amyot, who omits these general references to Gnathon's sexual activity, does not shy away from the key issue that 'He had homosexual inclinations', and 'decided to make advances, thinking it would be easy to win over Daphnis, who was a goatherd' (4.11; Reardon, p. 337). Amyot translates, 'Car outre ce qu'il était de nature vicieux, aimant les garçons, il vit en Daphnis une beauté si exquise qu'à peine en eût-il su trouver de pareille en la ville, si proposa en lui-même de l'accointer, espérant facilement en venir à bout' (p. 122) – 'Because in addition he was of a depraved nature, loving boys, he saw in Daphnis such an exquisite handsomeness that he hardly ever found equalled in the city, so proposed to acquaint himself with him, hoping easily to achieve his aim'. Once again Amyot indulges in playful erotic puns: 'accointer' implies Gnathon's sexual intentionality, as it had

Lycaenion's, and 'venir à bout', 'come to the point', is no more subtle.

Longus relates Daphnis's rejection of homosexual relations to the underlying motif of procreation. Gnathon ambushes Daphnis one evening as he drives his herd home:

> Gnathon ran up to Daphnis, kissed him first, and then tried to talk him into letting himself be used as he-goats use the she-goats. Daphnis slowly realised what he meant and said that it was all right for he-goats to mount she-goats, but that nobody had ever seen a he-goat mounting a he-goat or a ram mounting a ram instead of an ewe or cocks mounting cocks instead of hens. Gnathon then got ready to take him by force and was putting his hands on him, but Daphnis pushed him away and threw him to the ground (the man was drunk and could hardly stand up). (4.12; Reardon, 337)

Both Amyot and Thornley work from the Greek, and both retain the spirit of Longus's text. Thornley regards Gnathon's homosexuality as a fact of nature: 'from the beginning he was struck with Paederastie (the Love of boys) by the Terrestriall gods' (P5v). This puts a different colouring on Daphnis's appeal to natural law: 'That the he-goats rid the shees, That was very right indeed: but that a he-goat rid a he, that was never yet seen; nor the Rams, instead of the Ewes, to ride Rams; nor Cocks tread Cocks instead of Hens' (P6v). Thornley also increases Gnathon's physical contact with Daphnis: 'he ran at him, and lolled [*i.e.*, leaned] upon him; and when he had kist him o're and o're, he shuffled himself odly-behind him, as if he meant to attempt something like the he-goats with the She's' (P6).[72]

Angel Day, working from Amyot's text, introduces radical changes. He sanitises this account of Gnathon's attempt to rape Daphnis, and omits Daphnis's witty riposte:

> Nowe *Gnatho* this parasite being a right belli-god, a villaine by nature [...] beganne as an vnnaturall beast, so against nature become wanton ouer him. The paunch-filled rascall [...] mouing to the goat-heard manie questions, & perceiuing his simplicity and vnacquainted disposition to villanous purposes, one time by watching his goings and co[m]mings wold haue found means in forcible maner to abuse him. (N4)

Far more important, Day insists that, because Daphnis is the child of a nobleman, he is virtuous by nature. This concept, which recurs in Shakespeare's *As You Like It* and *Cymbeline*, skews the text to anticipate the revelation of Daphnis's origins:

---

72 Cf. R. F. Hardin, 'A Romance for Young Ladies: George Thornley's Translation of *Daphnis and Chloe*', p. 52.

But the insinuat condition by nature and his former birth, planted in the imboldned spirits of the yoong youth, with a maner of sweltring kind of disdaine. shooke the raskall off, and that so rudelie, as his pampered drunken carcas squatted against the ground with the pezant and unweldie burden thereof. (N4v)

When Dionysophanes and his wife Cleariste arrive to inspect the estates, Dionysophanes promises to make Lamon a free man. Longus employs a theatrical metaphor to emphasise the artifice of the scene, as Daphnis demonstrates his skill in controlling goats with the pan-pipes: 'Daphnis made them all sit down like the audience in a theatre' (4.15; Reardon, p. 338). The drama unfolds as simple country propriety asserts itself over civic insensitivity. Gnathon begs Astylus to secure Daphnis for him; Dionysophanes gives Daphnis to Astylus as his slave (in Thornley, '*Gnatho*'s Pathic-boy' (Q2v)). In response, the horrified Lamon reveals Daphnis's wealthy parentage:

> I am not Daphnis's father [...] I found him exposed [...] It isn't that I think it's beneath him to become the slave of Astylus, a fine servant for a fine gentleman. But I can't let him become the object of Gnathon's drunken lust – for Gnathon's keen to take him to Mytilene to do the job of a woman. (4.19; Reardon, p. 341)

Thornley balks at this final clause, ducking the issue in 'I cannot endure to have him now exposed to be injuriously and basely used by the drunken Glutton *Gnatho*; and, as it were, be made a slave to such a drivell' (Q5). Amyot follows Longus closely, but Day, working from Amyot's text, refocuses Lamon's address to Dionysophanes, implying that both Astylus and Gnathon conspire to victimise Daphnis:

> I am not (sir) discontented [...] that a woorthie and noble Maister, might also enioy of him by this meanes, a free and noble seruaunt, but that by pretext thereof, and vnder colour to drawe him hence to an other place, whereby in most vile and insufferable manner to abuse the woorthinesse of his shape against nature [...] also to become a vessell to his filthinesse, euen the grosse villanie of this parasiticall gester: this *Gnatho* heere present, who vpon a beastlie and wicked conceipt to accomplish the same, hath onelie suggested this motion [...]. (O1v-O2)

Longus's Lamon announces at the beginning of this speech that he found and fostered Daphnis. Day's Lamon keeps this information till the end, where he adds details of Daphnis's age and good breeding: 'but beeing nowe eighteene yeares since I found him [...] howe vnseeming it is, that so gentle a nature shoulde become the subiect and spoile of so base and seruile a condition' (O2).

Dionysophanes recognises the 'purple cloak, a gold clasp, and a dagger with an ivory handle' that Lamon produces (4.21; Reardon, p. 341). He admits he had a nurse leave Daphnis in the fields: 'I married when I was quite young'. Having two sons and a daughter, 'I thought I had a big enough family [...] I exposed him, putting these objects out with him not as tokens of his identity but as funeral ornaments'. Thornley reports this callously: 'I married a Wife [...] when I was yet very young [...] I thought there was enow of the breed, and therefore I exposed this boy, who was born after the rest, and set him out with those Toyes, not for the monuments of his Stock, but for Sepulchral ornaments' (Q7v-Q8).

Amyot alters Longus's closing paradox, creating two parallel clauses in Ciceronian style: 'non pas en intention de le retrouver et le reconnaître un temps à venir' – 'not with the intention of getting him back and recognising him some time in the future', and 'mais afin que celui qui le trouverait eût de quoi l'ensevelir' (p. 133) – 'so that whoever might find him had something to bury him in'. But Day changes Dionysophanes' direct speech into the third person, and then frames a number of excuses to portray him as an unfortunate victim of straitened financial circumstances:

> he declared, that in the beginning of his marriage when as yet he had not attempted the fortune of the worlde, and seeing children to increase vpon him [...] the fourth child which was this Daphnis newlie receiued, because the possessions left him by his frends were few, & his stocke but small, he greeuing with the great charge, concluded with himself by the consent of his wife, to take this last of all, and with such things as were found about it, to commit the same to the guidance of Fate & her sisters [...] in mind that neuer againe he should heare tell of it.[73]

Families without inherited wealth, living through the hyper-inflation and high unemployment that affected England at the end of the sixteenth century, would recognise the hardship of having to support an extra child. But Day at least substitutes an element of optimism for Longus's acceptance that abandoned babies face inevitable death.

Longus focuses on Daphnis's new identity as Astylus's brother, briefly minimising Chloe's stature in the narrative. An enormous social gap, misunderstandings and violence threaten to split them apart. While Daphnis is sacrificing to the gods, Chloe suffers from depression: 'Daphnis

73 *Daphnis and Chloe: The Elizabethan Version From Amyot's Translation by Angel Day*, ed. by J. Jacobs (London: David Nutt, 1890), p. 148, cited where sigs. O2v-O3 (4.21–4) are lacking in the University Microfilms/Early English Books Online reproduction.

has forgotten me completely. He's dreaming about a rich marriage' (4.27, Reardon, p. 344). Then, when Daphnis learns she has been carried off by the cowherd Lampis, who now believes her free to marry, consciousness of his new status paralyses him: 'he didn't dare speak to his father; nor could he bear it either' (4.28; Reardon, p. 344). Gnathon, anxious to ingratiate himself to Daphnis, leads a rescue party.

Day acknowledges Daphnis's aloofness, but credits him with surreptitiously organising a posse: 'but the yoonge goteheard conferring nowe the state and reputation of his freends, durst not be acknowne publikelie of the action, but called foorth some of the house' (O3v). Day also exaggerates brutal instincts in Gnathon (4.29), who 'rescuing *Chloe* againe lambskind the rude lobkins welfauoredlie' (O4) – that is, 'gave the farmers a thorough beating'.

In Longus's drama of double abandonment, one recognition becomes a catalyst for the other. Both combine rural honesty with appreciation of the advantages of wealth. The next day, Chloe's stepfather Dryas speaks hopefully to Dionysophanes:

> 'Like Lamon, I'm compelled to say things that have been kept secret till now. I am not the father of Chloe here [...] she may turn out to be a match for Daphnis [...]' [...] When he saw the tokens that Dryas had brought, the golden sandals, the anklets, the belt, he called Chloe to him. (4.30–1; Reardon, p. 345)

Avoiding dialogue, Day's narrative has a blandness that might come from describing a mimed performance. Dryas 'made known vnto them the finding of *Chloe* [...] he shewed also the call, mantle, slippers and other attire and iewels he found with hir: and those with hir, recommended eftsoones to their patronage, loue, care, and common defense' (O4).

Because Day's Daphnis and Chloe are real young people closely associated with the court, he skirts around the next issue in Longus's text. Social status carries exclusions with it, and Dionysophanes will not accede to Daphnis and Chloe's marriage until he has ascertained 'if Chloe was a virgin. Daphnis swore that nothing more had taken place between them than kissing and vows' (4.31; Reardon, p. 345). Thornley's looser construction parallels the Greek: '*Dionysophanes* taking *Daphnis* aside, askt him, if *Chloe* were a maid; And he swearing, that nothing had past betwixt them, but only kissing, embraceing, and Oathes' (R5). Amyot elaborates by stating that Daphnis and Chloe have already agreed a legally binding *de praesenti* contract of marriage. Dionysophanes 'lui demanda si elle était encore pucelle' (p. 139) – 'asked him if she was still a virgin'. Daphnis swears 'qu'elle ne lui avait rien été de plus près que du baiser' – 'that she had never been closer to him than kissing', adding the qualification, 'et du serment par lequel ils avaient promis marriage l'un à l'autre' – 'and no further than the oath by which they had promised marriage to one another'.

While Day retains Amyot's legitimisation of this marriage, he entirely suppresses the question of Chloe's virginity: 'they accepted hir immedi-atlie as thir daughter in law, and confirmed the liking, wherewith before he had receiued hir as his wife'. (O4v). Day seems to understand that this was neither a tactful question to raise at a celebration honouring the Virgin Queen, nor one calculated to endear him to his new patron, Hatton.

Following rural festivities, Dionysophanes takes the wedding party into the city, hoping to discover Chloe's parents. In a dream, Love instructs Dionysophanes to throw a party for 'all the best of the Mytileneans' (4.34; Reardon, p. 346), where he is to circulate Chloe's tokens for identification. The oldest guest of all, Megacles, recognises them and reveals why he abandoned her in the much frequented cave of the Nymphs:

> I had very little money to live on; for what I did have, I spent on public services, paying for dramatic choruses and warships. At that time, a little daughter was born to me. Shrinking from bringing this child up in poverty, I fitted her up with these tokens and exposed her, knowing that many people are eager to become parents even by this means. So the child was exposed in the cave of the Nymphs […] I haven't had the good luck to have any more children, even a daughter. In fact, the gods seem to make fun of me, sending me dreams at night that show a sheep making me father! (4.35; Reardon, p. 347)

Whereas Amyot (p. 143) follows Longus in every detail, Day omits the country celebrations, Dionysophanes' dream and his party, simplifying to 'the woorthiest of the citie and their wiues visited *Dionysophanes*' (O4v). Significant changes to Megacles' tale correspond with the political inflexion of Day's interventions. Charles Howard, in addition to his three daughters, had two sons. By November 1587, he had gone into debt on the Queen's behalf, sponsored an acting company and had begun refurbishing the army and navy.

Day purges embarrassing references to debt incurred on behalf of the state, making Megacles a shipping merchant. He reiterates that Chloe is sixteen, likely to be the age of the real Chloe of *The Shepheards Holidaie*, and sustains the illusion of reality by cutting out Megacles' dreams 'that show a sheep making me father':

Megacles a wealthie noble citizen [...] said: It is now about sixteene yeeres
since, that by reason of my great charge bestowed in trauell, and sundrie
losses hapned vnto me by seas, I had then a daughter borne vnto me by my
wife *Rhode*, and forsomuch as my estate was at that instaut [*sic*] so weake
[...] and yeelded me also some dispaire how, or by what meanes I might
afterwards liue hauing so manie children: in great agonie of minde I tooke
the infant and gaue it in like manner as thou *Dionysophanes* to one of my
seruants, with apparell, iewelles, and other things about it, and willed him,
in some conuenient place to bestowe the same. (O4v–O5)

In Day's restructured sequence of events, Megacles has not yet seen Chloe's
tokens. By deferring his emotional outburst and increasing his despair,
Day accentuates the sense of relief offered by the denouement. Chloe is
brought in, Megacles approves of the marriage, and on the instant gives
her all his possessions, reserving only enough to reward 'those that so
charily had vnto that estate conducted hir' (P1v).

In Longus, the party returns to Lamon's house in the country for a
wedding of 'pastoral character' (4.37; Reardon, p. 347), Amyot's 'des
noces pastorales' (p. 144). But Day's *Daphnis and Chloe* has now served
its purpose as a combined royal compliment and marriage pageant, and
he brings the proceedings to an abrupt conclusion: 'The citizens all there-
abouts [...] praied *Himenaeus* to giue vnto them, a happie, fruitfull, and
gladsome continuance: whereby were finished in most honourable, and
sumptuous maner, to the reioycing of al the beholders, the finall determi-
nation of all these pastorall amours' (P1v). By contrast, Longus's tale ends
with the young couple actively consummating their marriage.

In a novel where the action follows a trajectory subservient to the
interests of Dionysus and Pan, and characterisation is flattened to accen-
tuate moral allegory, it is inevitable that Chloe's virginity becomes a factor
in Daphnis being granted permission to marry her. Longus accordingly
delays their sexual union until the closing lines. A superb rhetorical tacti-
cian, he precedes this with a reassuring glimpse into the future. Daphnis
and Chloe will become the parents of Philopoemen, 'aimant des bergers'
(p. 146) – 'carer of shepherds', and Agele, 'prenant plaisir des troupeaux'
– 'taking pleasure in flocks'. Only then does he return to their wedding
night, couching it in evasive paraphrase reflecting on Philetas's ethereal,
and Lycaenion's practical, advice:

Daphnis and Chloe lay down naked together, embraced and kissed, and
had even less sleep that night than the owls. Daphnis did some of the things
Lycaenion taught him; and then, for the first time, Chloe found out that

what they had done in the woods had been nothing but shepherds' games. (4.40; Reardon, p. 348)

Reversing Longus's 'embrace and kiss', Amyot has the newly-weds exchange kisses in a mutual embrace: 'ils s'entrebaisèrent et s'entre-embrassèrent'. (p. 146) Thornley's additional verbs prolong the action and imitate the rhythmic action of coition: '*Daphnis* and *Chloe* lying naked together, began to clip, and kisse, and twine, and strive with one another, sleeping no more then birds of the night' (S3).[74] Amyot imposes a note of modesty, providing them with bedding: 'Daphnis et Chloé se couchèrent entre deux draps' – 'Daphnis and Chloe went to bed between two sheets', where Chloe 'understood well' that what they had previously done in the woods and meadows 'n'étaient que jeux de petits enfants' – 'was nothing but little children's games'. A textual quibble in the manuscript tradition lies behind Amyot's 'children's games' (as opposed to 'shepherds' games') and Thornley's 'sweetest Sports of Shepherds' (S3). Angel Day, the tone of whose *Daphnis and Chloe* is governed by the Elizabethan cult of chastity, and perhaps also the live representation of a wedding day, stops the action before the marriage can be consummated.

Conclusion

In 1657, George Thornley made a concerted effort to represent Longus's complete ecphrastic novel in 'Saxon' English. Anti-Puritan diction, tinged with risqué innuendo in keeping with his cavalier, royalist support, colours his expansive rendering. A century earlier, in 1559, Bishop Jacques Amyot turned *Daphnis and Chloe* into a fetchingly erotic representation of adolescent purity. By reconstructing Amyot's text, and embedding in it the *Daphnis and Chloe* pageant of Accession Day, 1587, Angel Day abandons any attempt at literal translation in order to create a unique record of an important Elizabethan court entertainment. It is hardly surprising that Amyot, a royal tutor preoccupied with teaching morality, omits from his repertoire of Greek translations the next work to be considered. For Achilles Tatius's *Leukippe and Kleitophon* satirises prudishness, and far more openly represents heterosexuality and homosexuality.

---

74 Cf. R. F. Hardin, 'A Romance for Young Ladies: George Thornley's Translation of *Daphnis and Chloe*', p. 55.

3

Achilles Tatius's *Leukippe* and *Kleitophon*

Rhetorics of love

Far from being an idealised pastoral, *Leukippe and Kleitophon* differs from Longus's *Daphnis and Chloe* in structure, in rhetorical complexity and in the range of the issues it addresses. These include perspectives on the significance of female chastity, the denial of the rights of women to self-expression and self-fulfilment, male self-interest, and the rewards of stoicism and self-discipline.

Achilles Tatius takes his characters through a range of adventures as they move around the eastern Mediterranean. He focuses on how the lives of his hero and heroine are influenced by erotically driven men and women. *Daphnis and Chloe* gains strength by delicately drawing back from the threshold of sexual fulfilment until its closing lines. By contrast, in *Leukippe and Kleitophon*, highly charged emotional circumstances repeatedly test the fidelity and chastity of the two central figures. But as Achilles Tatius's writing is characterised by paradox, any implicit allegorical interpretations, but especially the Renaissance notion of exemplary morality, are prone to instability. For rather than being interpreted as a betrayal of Leukippe, Kleitophon's having sex with Melite is represented as the pleasurable fulfilling of a moral obligation. Their tender relationship also serves as a foil to the violent sadism of Melite's husband, Thersandros, who abuses Leukippe in an opposing strand of the plot.

Unlike the otherworldly pastoral of *Daphnis and Chloe*, Achilles Tatius's *Leukippe and Kleitophon* is a sexually explicit and ostensibly very human study of the harsh effects of misfortune and interruption on the course of true love. A provocative story with strongly delineated characters, it touches many a raw nerve through its candid representation of the psychological effects of absence and death. Its depiction of the warmth, and also the cruelty, of homoerotic and heterosexual love, and the politics of power in these relationships, provides Renaissance translators with the substance that they craved in erotic romance. Their prefaces, dedications, diction, style, additions, omissions and alterations, including bowdlerisation, demonstrate how readily this text could be adapted to serve their social, political and cultural agendas. The most ecphrastic and rhetorically artificial of the Greco-Roman erotic romances, in France it joined the courtly band of stylised nationalist works inspired by Amyot's Heliodorus. In England, it first played its part in late Elizabethan philhel-lene Protestant propaganda. Later, reflecting the French taste of the Caro-line court, it was altered in style and content into a portrayal of exemplary innocence.

European dissemination

The rhetorical artistry of *Leukippe and Kleitophon* and the ease by which, with the change of a few words, it could be turned into a moral alle-gory, was recognised long before the Renaissance. An epigram ascribed to Photius, the learned ninth-century Patriarch of Constantinople, speaks allegorically of Clitophon's tale of 'The most virtuous life of Leucippe' which 'joins in marriage those who loved wisely'.[1] Better known, however, is Photius's praise of the style, and 'moral disapproval'.[2] For Photius laments that 'Achilles Tatius pushes his obscenity to impudence':

> It is a dramatic work, introducing some unseemly love episodes. The diction and composition are excellent, the style distinct, and the figures of speech [...] well adapted to the purpose [...] But the obscenity and impu-rity of sentiment impair his judgment, are prejudicial to seriousness, and make the story disgusting to read or something to be avoided altogether. Except for the names of the characters and his abominable indecency, the story, in method of treatment and invention, has a great resemblance to the *Aethiopika* of Heliodorus.[3]

No doubt the disreputability of this novel helped to promote its relatively wide dissemination during the Renaissance. Of the twelve full-text and three nearly complete extant manuscripts, ten, including those commis-sioned by Fulvio Orsini and Henri Estienne, were made in the sixteenth

---

1 H. Morales, *Vision and Narrative in Achilles Tatius' Leucippe and Clitophon* (Cambridge: Cambridge University Press, 2004), p. 227.
2 B. P. Reardon, 'Achilles Tatius and Ego-Narrative', in *Greek Fiction: The Greek Novel in Context*, ed. by J. R. Morgan and R. Stoneman (London: Routledge, 1994), pp. 80–96 (p. 80).
3 Photius, *The Library of Photius*, ed. by J. H. Freese (London: Society for Promoting Christian Knowledge, 1920), pp. 87, 94; see www.tertullian.org/fathers/photius_03bibliotheca. htm.

century.[4] One from the renowned collection of Niccolo Ridolfi, and which also contains the text of *Daphnis and Chloe*, was owned by Catherine de Médicis.[5]

The earliest European publication of Achilles Tatius was Ludovico Annibale della Croce's Latin translation of Books 5–8, *Narrationis Amatoriae Fragmentum* (Lyon, 1544). The manuscript behind this text probably belonged to Don Diego Hurtado de Mendoza, Imperial ambassador in Venice, to whom della Croce (1499–1577) dedicated his volume. The manuscript was destroyed in 1671 without 'notes of the readings', though it 'may well have been fragmentary'.[6] It is therefore not possible to determine whether the manuscript or, more likely, the translator suppresses Kleitophon's intimacy with Melite in 5.27. Della Croce's text was anonymously translated into French by P. de Vienne as *Les devis amoureux* by 'l'Amoureux de Vertu' (Paris, 1545). An Italian translation by Ludovico Dolce was entitled *Amorosi Ragionamente. Dialogo Nel Qvale si Racconta Vn Compassionevole Amore Di Dve Amanti* (Venice, 1546).[7]

The first 'full' eight book edition was Francesco Angelo Coccio's anonymous and much reprinted Italian translation, *Dell'amore di Leucippe et di Clitophonte* (Venice, 1550/51), a relatively straightforward representation of the Greek. In his dedication to 'Signor Siluestro Gigli dignissimo Decano di Lucca' (*2), Coccio relates the Byzantine Suda's brief observations on Achilles Tatius, latterly a Christian (5v). He then purports to cite Photius when praising the author's artful but clear style and comparing him with Heliodorus (*5v). But although the text quoted by Coccio edits out every one of Photius's negative comments,[8] and may well be from a

4 *Achilles Tatius. Leucippe and Clitophon*, ed. by E. Vilborg (Stockholm: Almquist and Wiksell, 1955), pp. xviii–xxx.
5 Bibliothèque Nationale MS Parisinus Graecus 2913; cf. *Achilles Tatius. Leucippe and Clitophon*, ed. by E. Vilborg, p. xxii.
6 *Achilles Tatius. Leucippe and Clitophon*, ed. by E. Vilborg, pp. xxxi–xxxii, lxxv.
7 This summary incorporates details from *Achilles Tatius. Leucippe and Clitophon*, ed. by E. Vilborg, pp. vii–ix; L. Plazenet, *L'ébahissement et la délectation. Réception comparée et poétiques du roman grec en France et en Angleterre aux XVIe et XVIIe siècles* (Paris: Honoré Champion Éditeur, 1997), pp. 121–2, 687ff.; and H. Hofmann, 'Introduction', in *Latin Fiction: The Latin Novel in Context*, ed. by H. Hofmann (London: Routledge, 1999), p. 8.
8 The pagination of the 1550/1551 copy in The John Rylands University Library, University of Manchester (Christie 22 c 6), differs slightly from the 1560 edition cited in M. A. Doody, *The True Story of the Novel* (New Brunswick, NJ: Rutgers University Press, 1996; repr. London: Fontana Press, 1998), pp. 247, 513–14. J. de Perrot, 'Robert Greene and the Italian Translation of *Achilles Tatius*', *Modern Language Notes*, xxix (1914), 63, compares the ecphrasis on Europa, cited in S. L. Wolff, *The Greek Romances in Elizabethan Prose Fiction* (New York: Columbia University Press, 1912), p. 399, to verify Robert Greene's paraphrase of Coccio's translation in *Morando* (1584), B2v–B3.

secondary source, Coccio's altogether positive notice supports his subsequent gloss on erotic fictions as neoplatonic allegories of love.[9]

Coccio's edition preceded by up to four years the publication of Della Croce's internationally known *Achillis Statii Alexandrini De Clitophontis & Leucippes amorib[us]. Libri VIII. E Graecis Latini facti a L. Annibale Cruceio.* Della Croce's text was published by Herwagen's press in Protestant Basel (Basileae: per Ioannem Heruagium, 1554), which in 1534 had also published the earliest edition of Heliodorus, in Greek. Della Croce dedicates his volume from Milan, 12 January 1552, to Petro Francisco [i.e., Pierfrancesco] Pallavicino, bishop of Aleria. Describing his translation policy as between literal and free, he says he does not refer here to hypothetical emendations where his manuscript contains corruptions or deletions – 'Omitto, graeci exemplaris deprauatione coactum fuisse me aliquando diuinare, ac nonnulla ex ingenio emendare' (A2v). Nonetheless, this exemplar, found in Rome in 1552/53,[10] is far more complete than the one he had previously used, which contained no indication of the author – 'absque auctoris nomine' (A2), or title. This Latin translation, which appeared with variant readings, was popular enough in England to merit being reprinted in Cambridge, probably in 1589.[11]

Della Croce restructures Achilles Tatius's artful plainness into Ciceronian rhythms and sound patterns, though without the expansion favoured by translators into French. Although it is unlikely to be intended, he frequently alters or destroys the meaning. Perhaps responding to the expectations of medieval and Renaissance heroic literature, he goes against the entire extant manuscript tradition in giving Kleitophon precedence over Leukippe in the title. This is the order retained in the derivative French and English translations.

In 1601, the first Greek edition, printed with Greek text facing Latin, was produced by the Heidelberg printing house of the late scholar-publisher Hieronymus Commelinus.[12] The Greek half-title places Leukippe's name before Kleitophon's (a1–a1v), while the parallel Latin retains della Croce's

---

9 See M. A. Doody, *The True Story of the Novel*, p. 247.
10 Vaticanus Graeci 114; cf. *Achilles Tatius. Leucippe and Clitophon*, ed. by E. Vilborg, p. lxxvi; and see della Croce's dedicaton to Petro Francisco Pallavicino, Bishop of Aleria, Corsica, dated 12 January 1552/3 (A3).
11 Achilles Tatius, *Achillis Statii Alexandrini De Clitophontis & Leucippes amorib[us]. Libri VIII. E Graecis Latini facti à L. Annibale Cruceio.* (Cambridge, [1589]). Unless specified, quotations are from this edition.
12 *De Clitophontis et Leucippes amoribus lib. VIII. Longi sophistae de Daphnidis et Chloes amoribus lib. IV. Parthenii Nicaeensis de amatoriis affectibus lib. I. Omnia nunc primum simul edita Graece ac Latine*, ed. by J. and N. Bonnvitius (Heidelberg, 1601). It was reprinted in 1604 and 1606, the edition cited.

reversed order, and reprints his translation. Commelinus had published an authoritative Greek text of Heliodorus in 1596. He probably died in 1598. His nearly completed Achilles Tatius was based on a manuscript in the Palatine Library (A2),[13] a sixteenth-century copy of the thirteenth-century manuscript in Venice.[14] While in Venice, Henri Estienne had a copy of this made for himself, and 'we cannot exclude the possibility' that the Palatine manuscript and one other 'were made on Stephanus's initiative'.[15]

Commelinus's edition was published by his nephews, Juda and Nicolaus Bonnvitius (also known as 'Bonnuitius' and 'Bonutius')[16] in a composite volume containing Achilles Tatius, Longus (facing a metrical rendering by Laurentius Gambara (1506–96)) and Parthenius. It was dedicated to the Antwerp-born Protestant scholar Jan de Gruytere (Janus Gruterus, 1560–1627), known as Gruter in England.[17] Gruter, whose family fled the Duke of Alba's punitive regime in 1567, grew up in Norwich and attended Cambridge and Leyden universities.[18] A philhellene Protestant poet, academic classicist and historian, he held chairs in the Reformed Protestant centres of Wittenberg (1591–92), then Rostock,[19] and from 1593 at Heidelberg. The move from Wittenberg was occasioned by Elector John Sigismund's imposition of Lutheranism, 'In Dutch exile circles [...] often felt to be more dangerous enemies even than the Catholics'.[20] In 1602 he was appointed librarian of Heidelberg's Bibliotheca Palatina.[21] In common with Philip and Robert Sidney, Gruter numbered among his friends Janus Dousa and Daniel Rogers.[22]

13 Biblioteca Apostolica Vaticana MS Palatinus Graecus 52; cf. *Achilles Tatius. Leucippe and Clitophon*, ed. by E. Vilborg, pp. xxiii, lxxviii.

14 Biblioteca Nazionale di San Marco MS Marcianus Graecus 409; cf. *Achilles Tatius. Leucippe and Clitophon*, ed. by E. Vilborg, pp. xxviii, lxxv.

15 Cf. *Achilles Tatius. Leucippe and Clitophon*, ed. by E. Vilborg, p. lxxv.

16 *Achilles Tatius. Leucippe and Clitophon*, ed. by E. Vilborg, p. lxxviii.

17 L. Forster, *Janus Gruter's English years: Studies in the Continuity of Dutch Literature in Exile in Elizabethan England* (Leiden: Leiden University Press, 1967), p. ix.

18 L. Forster, *Janus Gruter's English Years: Studies in the Continuity of Dutch Literature in Exile in Elizabethan England* (Leiden: Leiden University Press, 1967), pp. 2–5. Forster, p. 21, demonstrates that Gruter's mother was from Antwerp rather than English, as is often reported. In addition to the languages of the Low Countries, which included Spanish, she knew Greek, Latin, French, Italian and English (pp. 36, 38).

19 Press release, University of Heidelberg: www.uni-heidelberg.de/presse/news/2210 gelehrten.html.

20 L. Forster, *Janus Gruter's English Years*, p. 5.

21 L. Forster, *Janus Gruter's English Years*, p. 141.

22 J. van Dorsten, *Poets, Patrons, and Professors: Sir Philip Sidney, Daniel Rogers, and the Leiden Humanists* (Leiden: Leiden University Press, 1962), p. 109; R. Kuin and A. L. Prescott, 'Versifying Connections: Daniel Rogers and the Sidneys', *Sidney Journal*, xviii, no. 2 (2000), 1–35.

Belleforest's French

The earliest full-text edition in French, *Les amours de Clitophon et de Leucippe* (Paris, 1568), is an anonymous translation of della Croce's Latin. The subtitle emphasises that the work is very useful and enjoyable, and that it clarifies philosophical points as well as ancient histories do: *Oeuure tresvtile & delectable, où sont deduits & esclarcis plusieurs poincts, tant des histoires anciennes que de toutes les parties de la Philosophie*. The French translator is only identified in subsequent editions as 'B. Comingeois', that is, François de Belleforest. The exclusive 'privilege' to print this work, which contains only translations of della Croce's dedication and text, was granted to Pierre l'Huillier of Paris on 16 November 1568.

Achilles Tatius had previously been represented in French through Jacques de Roquemaure or Rochemaure's last four books, *Les quatre derniers livres des propos amoureux contenans le discours des amours et mariage du seigneur Clitophont et de damoiselle Leucippe* (Lyon, 1556), and a near translation and adaptation by Jean Hérembert, Sieur de la Rivière, *Les advantureuses et fortunées Amours de Pandion et de Yonice. Tirées des anciens autheurs Grecz* (1599).[23] The second full translation, *Les Amours de Clytophon, et de Leucippe* (Paris, 1635), was by I[ean] B[audoin], who in 1624–25 published his translation of Sidney's *Arcadia*.

Following Amyot's precedent, Belleforest's translation provided the linguistically nationalistic French court with a text in its preferred Greco-Roman style. In 1568, Belleforest (1530–83) was appointed historiographer to Amyot's pupil, Charles IX, to whom he dedicated *L'Histoire des Neuf Rois Charles de France* (1568). In this dedication, Belleforest reveals his consciousness of the current interest in developing a French royal diction and style. *L'Histoire* is written 'in your tongue, which being the most perfect, sweet and elegant one could know, almost equalling Greek, and the Latin aspired to by all nations'.[24] This same year, Belleforest published the second and third volumes of the immensely successful translation of Bandello, *Histoires Tragiques*, and his Achilles

23 L. Plazenet, *L'ébahissement et la délectation. Réception comparée et poétiques du roman grec en France et en Angleterre aux XVIe et XVIIe siècles*, pp. 19, 130, citing G. Sandy, 'Classical Forerunners of the Theory and Practice of Prose Romance in France. Studies in the Narrative Form of Minor French Romances of the Sixteenth and Seventeenth Centuries', *Antike und Abendland*, cxviii (1982), 169–91 (pp. 176–9).

24 'en vostre langue. Laquelle estant des plus parfaictes, douces, et eloquentes que l'on scache, esgallant presque le Grec, et le Latin souhaitée de toutes nations' (aijr-aijv), cited in M. Simonin, *Vivre de sa plume au XVIe siècle ou la carrière de François de Belleforest* (Geneva: Droz, 1992), p. 89.

Tatius, begun in 1567.[25] Like Amyot and other translators into French, Belleforest expands his text considerably through stylistic and verbal embellishment.

Burton and the English philhellenes

Without revealing his source text, in 1597 the twenty-year-old William Burton (1575–1645)[26] published his translation of della Croce's Latin as *The Most Delectable and pleasaunt History of Clitiphon and Leucippe: Written first in Greeke, by Achilles Statius, an Alexandrian: and now newly translated into English, By W. B.* [i.e. William Barton] (1597).[27] William is the elder brother of Robert (1577–1640), the author of *The Anatomy of Melancholy* (1621). The copy of the 1601 Greek and Latin Commelinus edition of Achilles Tatius that William gave to Robert, formerly in Christ Church College, Oxford, is now in the Durham University library. William Burton shares the Elizabethan penchant for titivating his text in a 'free rendering',[28] though in the restrained mode of English philhellene Protestant translators, and in contrast with the French, he attempts to represent the stylistic spirit of the Latin. Even so, his 'Most Delectable and pleasaunt History' consciously understates Achilles Tatius's vivid cocktail of thematic adventure, eroticism, elation and suspense, expressed through vibrant, paradox-laden, rhetorical artistry.

Burton dedicates his *Clitiphon and Leucippe* to Shakespeare's patron, Henry Wriothesley (1573–1624), third Earl of Southampton, who in 1597 was closely involved with the philhellene Protestant Essex-Sidney circle.[29] In a culture where idleness was deemed to be ungodly, Burton translates

25 M. Simonin, *Vivre de sa plume au XVIe siècle ou la carrière de François de Belleforest*, pp. 87–8.

26 See R. Cust, 'Burton, William (1575–1645)', *Oxford Dictionary of National Biography* (Oxford: Oxford University Press, 2004).

27 Gaselee's conjecture that Burton consulted a text in Italian is based solely on the enigmatic reading 'with *Stella*' (M3) as a translation of 'filis', 'with threads'; cf. *The Loves of Clitophon and Leucippe*[,] *Translated from the Greek of Achilles Tatius by William Burton* [,] *Reprinted for the first time from a copy now unique printed by Thomas Creede in 1597* (Oxford: Basil Blackwell Publisher to the Shakespeare Head Press of Stratford-upon-Avon, 1923), p. xx. This is more probably a compositor's misconstruction of an English word, possibly of 'fillet', meaning 'thread' (*O.E.D.* 4), or an Italian-based neologism such as 'filosella', 'a mixture of silk and wool', of which the earliest example in *O.E.D.* is from 1611.

28 *The Loves of Clitophon and Leucippe*, ed. by S. Gaselee and H. F. B. Brett-Smith (Oxford: Basil Blackwell, 1923), p. xxviii.

29 P. E. J. Hammer, *The Polarisation of Elizabethan Politics: The Political Career of Robert Devereux, 2nd Earl of Essex, 1587–1597* (Cambridge: Cambridge University Press, 1999), p. 286.

this work so 'that amo[n]gst so many multitudes of writers, which euery day doo publish and set foorth new workes, I alone might not be idle' (A3v). His medium is translation rather than original composition, for 'neither is euerie mans Muse alike, to flie aloft'.

Burton is nearly as exacting as Amyot and Sidney about the need for poetry to exhibit didactic qualities. In his note 'To the Curteous Reader', he energetically recommends *Leukippe and Kleitophon* as an instructive moral tonic:

> a worke most rare and delectable: of the reading of which, I may verily say (as *Fulgentius* saith in his *Mythiologickes*) the morall dooth yeelde vnfained profit:[30] whose copious eloquence, pleasant & delightful stile, I leaue to the gentle Readers to commend: to whome I may say (as *Crucius* saith vppon *Heliodorus*) there is none who is learned, and desirous of good instructions, which once hauing begun to read him, can lay him aside, vntill he haue perused him ouer. (A4)

Burton's closing remark is a quotation from 'De Heliodoro Iudicium', a short essay preceding the 1596 Commelinus edition of Heliodorus: 'Hinc nemo, qui modo φιλήκοος [*sic*] est, [...] si semel id legere coeperit, de manibus deponere potest, antequam absoluerit.'[31] His allusion to the prolific philhellene diarist Martin Kraus (Martinus Crusius or Crucius, 1526–1607) associates his translation with Protestant philhellene educational practice.

Kraus was Professor of Greek and Latin in Tübingen and a leading Lutheran theologian. 'De Heliodoro Iudicium' reprints critical observations from his earlier *Martini Crusii Aethiopicae Heliodori Historiae Epitome* (Francofurti: Johann Wechel, 1584), a reduction of Obsopoeus's 1534 Greek text for use in teaching.[32] Kraus follows the Italian critical

---

30 On Fulgentius as the general inspiration behind the Renaissance practice of reading moral allegory into literary works, see C. Moreschini, 'Towards a History of the Exegesis of Apuleius: The Case of the "Tale of Cupid and Psyche"', trans. by C. Stevenson, in *Latin Fiction: The Latin Novel in Context*, ed. by H. Hofmann (London: Routledge, 1999), pp. 215–28 (pp. 223–6).

31 Ἡλιοδώρου Αἰθιωπικων Βιβλια δεκα. *Heliodori Aethiopicorum Libri X. Collatione MSS. Bibliothecae Palatinae & aliorum, emendati & multis in locis aucti, Hieronymi Commelini opera.* (Heidelberg, 1596), ¶5v.

32 H. Hofmann, 'Introduction', in *Latin Fiction: The Latin Novel in Context*, ed. by H. Hofmann, p. 9, citing G. Berger, 'Rhetorik und Leserlenkung in der Aithiopika-Epitome des Martin Crusius', in *Acta Conventus Neo-Latini Guelpherbytani. Proceedings of the Sixth International Congress of Neo-Latin Studies*, ed. by S. P. Revard, F. Rädle and M. A. Di Cesare (Binghamton, NY: Medieval and Renaissance Studies, 1988), pp. 481–90. The literary import of Crusius's Preface is discussed by M. A. Doody, *The True Story of the Novel*, pp. 244–6. For a full bibliography, see *Die griechischen Handschriften der Universtätsbibliothek Tübingen: Sonderband Martin Crusius: Handschriftenverzeichnis*

tradition in accepting that poetry need not be in verse. He emphasises that poetry is identifiable by its creative achievement: 'Mon [i.e., Non] enim ex metro potius, quam fictione, Poema spectari conuenit' (¶3v),[33] which includes allegorical moral exempla. Burton applies these qualities to *Leukippe and Kleitophon*, 'a delightful poeme, although in prose: which doth consist in the fiction, not in the meeter; although seeming full of prolixitie, yet with delight auoyding satietie' (A3v). Burton also had access to similar notions in Sidney's *Defence of Poetry*, written about 1581 and published in 1595: 'it is not rhyming and versing that maketh a poet', but 'that feigning notable images of virtues, vices, or what else, with that delightful teaching, which must be the right describing note to know a poet by'.[34]

Given Leukippe's sexual precocity, and her subsequent self-denial, Burton rightly ignores Crusius's blaming Charikleia for the self-interest that jeopardises her and Theagenes' lives (¶4).[35] But his reconciliation of *Leukippe and Kleitophon* with *An Ethiopian Story* illustrates the ease with which erotic romance found acceptance within the prevailing Protestant aesthetic. Like Sidney in the *Arcadia*, and Spenser in *The Faerie Queene*, Burton is relatively unconstrained by the strictures of puritan repression. Heliodorus treats sex and sexual fantasies as pleasurable agonies, albeit in poor taste. Achilles Tatius not only represents them as wholesome when accompanied by love, but, within the spectacular and varied events of Kleitophon's story, also imbues them with erotic emotion and sensuality. Burton's translation mutes, rather than eradicates, such forthrightness. His aim in emphasising Leukippe's chastity is to cast her as an icon of model behaviour.

Hodges, erotic arousal and Sidney's *Arcadia*

Forty years after Burton, Anthony Hodges translated della Croce far more literally. Nonetheless, Hodges reduces Achilles Tatius's literary pyrotechnics to a relatively cautious and tasteful romance, *The Loves of Clitophon and Leucippe. A most elegant History, written in Greeke by Achilles Tatius:*

---

und Bibliographie, ed. by T. Wilhelmi (Wiesbaden: O. Harrassowitz, 2002).

33 Emended from *Martini Crusii Aethiopicae Heliodori Historiae Epitome* (Francofurti: Johann Wechel, 1584), p. 5, 'Non enim ex metro potius, quam fictione, Poëma spectari conuenit', cited by M. A. Doody, *The True Story of the Novel*, p. 513.

34 Sir P. Sidney, *A Defence of Poetry*, in *Miscellaneous Prose of Sir Philip Sidney*, ed. by K. Duncan-Jones and J. van Dorsten (Oxford: Clarendon Press, 1973), pp. 81–2.

35 Kraus's observations are discussed by M. A. Doody, *The True Story of the Novel*, pp. 245, 513.

And now Englished (1638). Commendatory verses in Hodges's volume indicate that he and his Oxford companions idolised Sidney and associated *Leukippe and Kleitophon* both generically and stylistically with *Arcadia*. 'A. H.' compliments Hodges: 'still / *Sydney's* soule liues in you', and with boyish fantasy twists the notion of protective patronage into a suggestive metaphor:

> Since then you are so happy in your charmes,
> Goe on, let Ladies laps shield safe from harmes
> Your innocent *Booke*, let it their fondling be,
> And 'tice their tempers into extasie.
> So let them freely in their rosie bowres,
> Crop th'early fruit of your not serious houres.
>
>   (a3v–a4)

George Thornley may have drawn on A. H.'s poem when penning his strikingly similar Epistle Dedicatory, 'To Young Beauties', prefixed to his *Daphnis and Chloe* (1657). Hodges and Thornley, both born in 1614, reflect their generation's libertine tendency to interpret sophistic erotic romance as adolescent voyeurism.

Among Hodges's friends who contributed verse to his volume were Francis Rous (1615–43), son of the Puritan writer of the same name (1579–1659), and the young royalist poet Richard Lovelace (1618–58). In his address 'To the Ladies', Lovelace encourages readers to 'breathe', or relax, by reading *The Loves of Clitophon and Leucippe*: 'Faire ones, breathe: a while lay by / Blessed *Sidney's Arcady*' (A5v). This book is short, a 'Little *Love's* Epitome', much easier than the massive 'complete' form of Sidney's *Arcadia*, first published in 1593. To Lovelace, who in 1638 was only twenty, Sidney's tales of princes and princesses falling in love made the *Arcadia* suitable reading for girls, along with Heliodorus's *An Ethiopian Story* and Honoré d'Urfé's *L'Astrée* (1607–27), of which a partial translation, *The history of Astrea the first part*, was published in 1620. Lovelace idealises a female readership that purportedly amalgamates characteristics of erotic romance heroines: 'Brave *Pamela's* majestie, / And her sweet Sisters [i.e., Philoclea's] modestie', Charikleia's divinity, Astrée's idealism, and Leukippe's chastity (A5v–A6).

In 'The Translator to the Reader', Hodges defends cutting Kleitophon and Menelaos's debate on the superiority of heterosexual or homosexual intercourse, and bowdlerising Kleitophon's intercourse with Melite: 'I have so refined the author, that the modestest matron may looke in his face and not blush' (A3v). He also avoids attracting the censor's attention. Aware of 'the censure of the Patriarch of *Constantinople*', Photius, whose *Bibliotheca* was available to Hodges in the Jesuit Andreas Schottus's edition (Augustae Vindelicorum [*i.e.*, Augsburg], 1606), he omits ('spared to English') passages he knows would draw criticism 'of some of these times' (A3v).

The distinctive representations of *Leukippe and Kleitophon* by della Croce, Belleforest, Burton and Hodges demonstrate that each has his preferred method for dealing with morality, rhetorical display and textual fidelity. Belleforest, like Amyot, expands and elaborates to satisfy the rhythmic Greco-Roman taste of the French court. Twenty-nine years later, and thirty-nine years into Elizabeth's reign, Burton adds a festive atmosphere to this most playful of the sophistic romances. Although Hodges is aware that there is a disparity between Greek and English concepts of elegance, he nonetheless refrains from rhetorical embellishment. He explains this policy in an adaptation of della Croce's dedication:

> I present him not here clad in the ragges of mine own phancie, nor yet in language rackt and disjoynted out of its proper idiom; but I have observed a medium betwixt both: I could with some unnecessary paines have given it a flourish, but I preferred the fidelity of the Translation before the Ornament. (A3v)

Hodges appears to equate the literary and linguistic qualities of della Croce's Latin with those of the Greek text, and admits he finds it difficult 'to maintaine the elegancy of a Greeke author in our language' (A3). Citing '*Longus* the Sophist', among others, 'were they Englisht, they would bee as little esteemed of, as the Latine translation of *Plato*, or that of my Author done by *Hanniball Cruceius*' (A3–A3v). Hodges's genteel paraphrases, seeming to reflect the controlled, decorous and reactionary neoclassicism required by Charles I's censors, remain closer to the Latin than Burton's. But through a naive ignorance even of the quasi-allegorical process used by Amyot or Sidney, they distort the didactic properties so greatly valued by the Elizabethan and Jacobean courts.

Translating the opening

The Renaissance approach to Achilles Tatius's introductory passage provides ample evidence of textual and stylistic variation. *Leukippe and Kleitophon*, a reported ego-narrative in eight books,[36] opens with

---

36 B. P. Reardon, 'Achilles Tatius and Ego-Narrative', in *Greek Fiction: The Greek Novel in Context*, ed. by J. R. Morgan and R. Stoneman, pp. 81–2.

a brief, factual preamble. This establishes the veracity and location of the first narrator, a stranger who meets Kleitophon. Thereafter, Kleitophon engages in 'the longest first-person narrative extant in Greek'. This doubling of 'narrator and hero' in a fictional autobiography is unique in Greek letters.[37] That Achilles Tatius gradually evolves Kleitophon's role into that of omniscient narrator may be taken either as a structural anomaly or as a gifted, persuasive rhetor's lesson in how to stretch the credible limits of near-plausibility.[38]

The initial narrator is a traveller and sightseer in Sidon, now Sayda in Lebanon, where his ship harbours during a storm: 'Sidon is a city beside the sea. The sea is the Assyrian; the city is the metropolis of Phoenicia; its people are the forefathers of Thebes' (1.1; Reardon, p. 175). Renaissance translators stamp their individual tastes on this apparently simple list. The rhetorical crispness of these four elements remains visible in della Croce's compressed version, in which the character in the shape of a semi-colon merely indicates abbreviation: 'Sidon Phoeniciae princeps ciuitas, Thebanorumq[ue]; generis origo, in Assyrii maris litore posita est' (A4). Imposing French courtly style, Belleforest adds parallel descriptors to create an elegantly rhythmic neoclassical opening: 'Sidon cité principale, & chef du païs de Phenisse, ayant sa source & co[m]mencement de peuple de ceux de Thebes, est assise sur la mer d'Assyrie' (A1). Burton translates with characteristic verve: 'In the shore of the *Assyrian* sea, is scituated *Sydon,* chiefe Citie of *Phaenicia,* and the original of ye famous race of the *Thebans*' (B1); and Hodges with the caution that permeates his work: '*Sidon* the chiefe Citie of *Phoenicia,* and which gave the first originall to the *Thebans,* is situated on the shore of the *Assyrian* Sea' (B1). If Achilles Tatius intended his reference to Phoenicia, Kleitophon's homeland, to signal a 'Phoenician tale', a type of spectacularly lurid narrative,[39] there is no indication that Renaissance readers recognised this signpost.

Once he has identified his location, the narrator relates his actions on disembarking: 'Arriving at this port after a violent storm, in thanks for my safe arrival I offered a sacrifice to the Phoenician's great goddess, who in Sidon is known as Astarte' (1.1; Reardon, p. 176). Astarte is also associated in Sidon with Aphrodite, goddess of love.[40] Where Achilles Tatius

---

37 N. J. Lowe, *The Classical Plot and the Invention of Western Narrative* (Cambridge: Cambridge University Press, 2000), p. 246, with the exception of 'the very different case of Plato's *Republic*'.

38 B. P. Reardon, 'Achilles Tatius and Ego-Narrative', pp. 84–5.

39 H. Morales, *Vision and Narrative in Achilles Tatius' Leucippe and Clitophon*, pp. 49–50.

40 H. Morales, *Vision and Narrative in Achilles Tatius' Leucippe and Clitophon*, pp. 42–3.

identifies Astarte for a Greek readership unfamiliar with Phoenicia,[41] della Croce glosses for his Renaissance audience, adding an explanatory relative clause that exists in two versions. The 1601 Bonnvitius/Bonutii edition of della Croce's text contains a further description, 'almost all the Latins call her Venus', in 'Phoenicum deae (Sidonij Astarten, Venerum Latinorum plerique vocant)' (A2).

This extended variant was available to Belleforest, in '& quelques Latins luy ont mis Venus à no[m]' (A1v), and Burton, who adapts it into a lengthy periodic sentence. Here it closes neatly in parallel clauses, the first for Astarte, the second for Venus: 'Thither when out of the maine sea by force of a mightie tempest I was brought, for the safe arriuall (as the custome was) I sacrificed to the Goddesse of the *Phaenicians*, which the *Sydonyans* do call *Astarte*; but the most of the *Latines* do call her *Venus*' (B1). Burton's almost metric rhythms provide a forward, thrusting movement. By contrast, the edition published in Cambridge around 1589 reads 'Phoenicum Deae Veneri (Astarten Sidonii vocant)' – 'the Phoenicians' Goddess Venus (whom Sidonians call Astarte)' (A4).[42] And this variant text lies behind Hodges's construction, 'Whither by the violence of the tempest being cast, I sacrificed to the Goddesse *Venus*, whom the *Sydonians* call *Astarte* (which solemnity is usually performed by those who have escaped the danger of the Seas)' (B1v).

The traveller's account of a tour of Sidon's 'memorial offerings' focuses solely on a picture depicting the rape of Europa. In Greco-Roman mythology, Europa comes from the royal family of Tyre, around twenty miles south of Sidon. Seduced by Zeus in the form of a beautiful bull, the picture shows her riding on his back as he swims across the sea to Crete. As instructed by the Delphic oracle, her brother, Cadmus, Zeus follows a heifer. Where it lies down, he begins the settlement which becomes the city of Thebes, north-west of Athens.

Europa: An ecphrasis

Longus opens *Daphnis and Chloe* with an obviously artful description of a painting. In a work renowned for its ecphrases, Achilles Tatius rapidly moves his narrator away from the factual account of the harbour towards

---

41　J. J. Winkler, trans. *Leukippe and Kleitophon*, in Reardon, p. 176, n.3.

42　The conjectural introduction of 'Aphrodite' into the text by J. Diggle, 'A Note on Achilles Tatius', *Classical Review*, xxii, no. 1 (1972), 7, accepted by H. Morales, *Vision and Narrative in Achilles Tatius' Leucippe and Clitophon*, p. 42, coincides with the point at which della Croce (or his source) introduced 'Veneri' into the text.

his own version of an ecphrastic introduction: 'Then touring the rest of the city to see its memorial offerings, I saw a votive painting whose scene was set on land and sea alike: the picture was of Europa; the sea was Phoenicia's; the land was Sidon' (1.1; Reardon, p. 176).[43] The narrator's curt style reinforces the connection between this picture and his earlier observation on Thebes, contrasting with the blatantly artificial style and substance of the forthcoming treatment of the painting.

Hodges translates della Croce's flowing Latin quite succinctly:[44] 'then viewing other parts of the City, and seeing the donaries which hung up in the Temples of their gods, I chanc'd to cast mine eye on a picture, wherein was most curiously represented the Sea and the Land, the fable also of *Europa*: the sea I descried to be the *Phoenicians*, the land the *Sidonians'* (B1v). Typical of translators during the later sixteenth century, Belleforest and Burton independently make a travesty of this deliberate brevity, inventing supplementary details. The catalyst for this radical change is della Croce's blurring the differences between the stranger's stark opening preamble and Kleitophon's stylistically rich narration. Both translators transform the plain prefatory passage into a rambling travelogue, their additions conforming to the mellifluous Ciceronian taste of the period.

Belleforest's explanatory and stylistic embellishments form a stately rhythm:

> Apres cecy comme ie visitasse les autres lieux de la cité, & contemplasse les dons & presents faits aux dieux, pendus en la voute de leurs temples, i'aduisay vn tableau painct lequel contenoit la mer, la terre, & auec ce la fable du rauissement d'Europé: & la mer de Phoenisse qui faisoit ente[n]dre que c'estoit la figure du païs Sydonien. (A1v)

Burton's interpolation on the city's geography and architecture creates an idealised impression of ancient Phoenicia, about which Achilles Tatius, keeping irrelevance to a minimum, says nothing:

> Then walked I round about many partes of the citie, viewing the lofty situation, the famous edifices, and sumptuous buildings, admiring also the magnificences of their temples, wherein when I had sufficiently gazed on their offerings to their gods hung at their tabernacles, I by chance espied a faire large picture, wherin was drawe[n] the sea & land, & the whole history

---

43 See S. Bartsch, *Decoding the Ancient Novel: The Reader and the Role of Description in Heliodorus and Achilles Tatius* (Princeton: Princeton University Press, 1989), pp. 40–79.
44 'Deinceps cu[m] alia ciuitatis loca perlustrarem, ac in deorum templis munera tholis suspensa contemplarer, tabula animaduerti pictam, terram ac mare, nec non Europae fabulam continentem: ac mare Phoenicum, Sidoniorum terra esse dignoscebatur' (A4).

of *Europe*: the sea was called ye *Phaenician* sea, but ye land was called ye *Sydonian*. (B1–B1v)

The ecphrasis on the painting of Europa is a stylistic bridge in which the factual plainness of the opening mutates into Achilles Tatius's character-istically dense programme of paradoxes. The composition of the painting is presented in two stages, in which details of the landscape contrast with what is happening on the sea:

> On the land were represented a meadow and a chorus of maidens, on the sea swam a bull, and on his back was seated a beautiful maiden, sailing on the bull towards Crete. The meadow was in full flower [...] At the far end of the meadow, where the land jutted out into the sea, the artist had placed the maidens [...] The sea itself was dichromatic [...] A bull was painted in midsea [...] The maiden sat on his back. (1.1; Reardon, p. 176)

But Achilles Tatius also uses the painting as a symbol of his own rhetorical process. He stresses the artistry with which the painter integrates his scene into an organic whole, echoing his own approach to the elements of his novel. The narrator methodically pores over the details in the painted landscape, beginning with the meadow. A literal rendering shows how Achilles Tatius idealises the harmonious interrela-tionship of the painting's elements: 'The meadow was thick with all kinds of flowers, and among them was planted a thicket of trees and shrubs, the trees growing so close that their foliage touched: and the branches, intertwining their leaves, thus made a kind of continuous roof over the flowers beneath'.[45]

Burton, who begins with della Croce's similarly close translation,[46] transforms the scene into a picture of an Elizabethan summer lodge: 'whose boughs & leaues did so naturally (as it were) imbrace & tie one another, as that they did serue for vse of a house' (B1v). But the prosopo-peia that Hodges introduces in 'the meadow seemed to smile, [...] whose boughes and leaves with their mutuall embracements were so wel knit and united, that they served for an arbour' (B1v), gives his translation a nationalistic gloss. For in it, he depends heavily on Sidney's reworking of this passage in the *New Arcadia*, 'a fine, close arbour [...] of trees whose branches so lovingly interlaced one the other that it could resist the

---

45 *Achilles Tatius*, with an English translation by S. Gaselee, M.A., rev. by E. H. Warm-ington (London: William Heinemann, 1969), 1.1, hereafter referred to as Gaselee.

46 'Pratum multa florum varietate distinctum, arborumque & fruticum copia intersitum erat: quarum rami atque frondes mutuo complexu ita sese nectebant, vt tecti vsum floribus praestarent' (A4v).

strongest violence of eyesight'.[47] In turn, Sidney's rendering, coupled with his description of Kalander's garden, 'beds of flowers, which being under the trees, the trees were to them a pavilion' (*NA*, p. 14), relates closely to Belleforest's 'les rameaux, & feillages desquels s'entrelaçoie[n]t de telle sorte qu'ils seruoyent de toict, & pauillon aux fleurs' (A1v).

The narrator's rhetorical artistry parallels the skill with which the painter harmonises light, shadow and objects. As in Lamon's garden in Book 4 of *Daphnis and Chloe*, there is a conscious elision of the boundaries between the wild harmony of trees and plants, and attentive landscape gardening. Hodges, in 'under the trees were planted beds of Roses, Daffadillies, and Myrtles' (B2), puts this as clearly as della Croce.[48] A spring, spreading naturally from the exact centre of the garden, is being channelled at that very moment. Achilles Tatius gives this rhetorical immediacy: 'An irrigator bent down over one rivulet with hoe in hand, depicted in the very act of making a channel for the stream' (1.1; Reardon, p. 176), della Croce's 'nec deerat qui sumpto ligone riuulo imminens, aquae viam patefaceret' (A4v). Belleforest gives a faithful rendering in 'des siegez plantes par ordre faits de Narcisse Murtes & Roses: […] encore n'estoit point esloigné de là vn hom[m]e lequel auec vne besche departoit ce ruisseau en canaux, & faisoit voye à l'eau decoulante' (A1v–A2).

Hodges in 1638 reduces the description of the creation of the irrigation channel to generalisations: 'nor was there one wanting who with a spade digged a passage, through which the water might the more easily diffuse it self' (B2). But Burton in 1597 expands the text in the manner of Angel Day, to represent an Elizabethan great house garden, complete with lavender (spike) and furniture: 'this groue was co[m]passed round with reeds, and set throughout with sweete and odoriferous plants, as myrrhe, roses, spike, daffadill, whereunder were made pleasant seats to rest vpon'. Here 'seats to rest vpon' is a mistranslation of della Croce's 'puluini' (A4v), which Hodges correctly interprets as 'beds', as in 'flower beds'.[49] Without textual precedent, Burton also adds two gardeners to the staff, changing the entire scale of the picture: 'neither were they wanting who had the ouersight of it: for one was weeding & picking the beds, another pruning the trees, an other standing ouer the riuer with a spade in his hand, did open the course of the water' (B1v). The garden, like

---

47 Sir P. Sidney, *The Countess of Pembroke's Arcadia (The New Arcadia)*, ed. by V. Skretkowicz (Oxford: Clarendon Press, 1987), p. 69, hereafter referred to as *NA*.
48 'sub plantis narcisso, rosa, myrtoque ordinatim sati puluini cernebantur' (A4v).
49 Other examples of mistranslation are described in *The Loves of Clitophon and Leucippe*, ed. by S. Gaselee and H. F. B. Brett-Smith, pp. xxix–xxxi.

the splendours of the city, grows to grand proportions. Like Angel Day, who localises and familiarises Philetas' and Dionysophanes' gardens in *Daphnis and Chloe*, Burton adapts *Leukippe and Kleitophon* for a wealth-admiring patron, Southampton, and a philhellene Protestant readership in the Sidney–Devereux circle.

In an ecphrastic description of what can be seen through her tightly belted diaphanous garment, Achilles Tatius presents an erotic view of Europa's body: 'navel well recessed, stomach flat, waist narrow, but with a narrowness that widened downwards towards the hips. Breasts gently nudging forward: a circumambient sash pressed chiton to breasts, so that it took on the body's form like a mirror' (1.1; Reardon, p. 177). Both courtly taste for embellishment, and awareness that the treatment of this early passage sets the moral tone for readers, influences translation practice.

Burton's version of della Croce (A4v-A5) is remarkably disciplined. Burton remains disengaged in 'her breast to her priuy parts [pectus ad pudenda] was attired with a vaile of lawne, [...] she had a deepe nauill [profundus vmbilicus], a plaine smooth belly [& planus venter], narrow flanke [& angusta ilia], round buttocks [verum amplos in lumbos]' (B2). By contrast, Belleforest adds a note of moralistic condemnation in 'couuert iusques aux parties ho[n]teuses' – 'covered to her shameful parts'. He further embellishes with personification in 'le no[m]bril s'aprofondissant en ce[n]tre' – 'the navel deepening itself in the centre'; beautification in 'le ve[n]tre sansplissure' – 'the unwrinkled belly' and 'la foys du corps ge[n]te & estroite' – 'the liver of the body handsome and narrow'. And he exhibits a Rubens-like admiration for a well-fed woman: 'les ha[n]ches massiues, grosses & refaites' – 'massive, fat and well-conditioned haunches' (A2v).

Where Burton opens the next section with an attempt at close trans-lation, 'her tender brests seemed to swel [papillae modice tumebant]', Belleforest employs a standard Renaissance erotic metaphor to turn them into small delightful mountains: 'les teti[n]s luy enfloye[n]t vn peu faisa[n]ts vne agreable colline' (A2v). Burton then abandons his text, substituting, 'throgh the midle of which went down a faire narrow way most pleasant & delightfull to the beholders' (B2). Here Burton appears to respond to the popularity of Sidney's *Arcadia* among his readers: 'Betwixt these two [breasts] a way doth lie [...] This leads into the joyous field [...] Waist it is called, for it doth waste / Men's lives until it be embraced' (*NA*, p. 192).

The mirror image that concludes this passage, della Croce's 'quae corporis speculum erat' (A5), alludes back to the garden. Whilst suggestive

of the illusions that govern much of the plot, the image promotes the
notion of comprehensive harmony, both metaphysically and in literary
structure. Belleforest represents it in 'le vray miroir pour faire remarquer
les beautez & perfections du corps' (A2v). Burton omits it, indicating his
insensitivity to the novel's rhetorical programme of doubles.[50] Extraor-
dinarily, Hodges preserves the mirror-image, but removes every trace
of Europa's body, describing only the transparent texture of her upper
garment. After this bowdlerisation, his elegance of expression barely
suggests the passage's complexity: 'The virgins upper parts were covered
with a white vesture, the rest with a purple robe, yet so, as one might
discerne each part through her garments, which being girt about her,
were truly no other than the looking-glasse of her whole body' (B2v).

Europa and apparent cyclic form

Despite the mannered lack of closure that consciously avoids returning
to the traveller-narrator, Achilles Tatius designs this ecphrasis to create
the impression of cyclic rhetorical completeness. In the picture's fore-
ground, the open curvature of the colonnade that 'enclosed the meadow
on every side' (1.1; Reardon, p. 176). is paired with a corresponding arc,
described by Europa's posture and her veil. She rides sideways on the
swimming bull, 'with her feet together towards the right' (1.1; Reardon,
p. 176). Her arms are 'outstretched, one to the horn and one towards
the tail; connecting them from either side was her veil, which fluttered
behind her in a long arc above her head' (1.1; Reardon, p. 177). (In della
Croce's Latin, her head-scarf, 'capitis tegmen', billows around her shoul-
ders, 'circum humeros effusum' (A5).) It is simple enough to visualise this
circular pattern.

Achilles Tatius's two comments on the artist's technical manipulation
of the design and content suggest parallels with the strategic develop-
ment of events in the narrative. The first identifies irregularity within the
artistic scheme. The narrator observes how the artist invents and accentu-
ates the loose and unrestrained pattern of Europa's encircling veil: 'The
bosomy folds of this garment billowed out in all directions, puffed full
by a wind of the artist's own making' (1.1; Reardon, p. 177). Second, the
proliferation of erotic events, and the multiplicity of their forms within
the narrative, are immediately signalled by pointing out the artist's care to
describe concurrent motions: 'Around the bull dolphins danced and Loves

---

50 Cf. H. Morales, *Vision and Narrative in Achilles Tatius' Leucippe and Clitophon*, p. 42.

cavorted: you would have said their very movements were visibly drawn'
(1.1; Reardon, p. 177). The traveller's 'special attention' to that portion of
the picture showing 'Eros leading the bull' draws the reader's focus away
from that patterned circle and towards the starting point of the narrative
proper, an incidental remark to a stranger about the power of love. Kleito-
phon's reply, which comprises all rest of the novel, completes its own cycle
through a convoluted progression of events.

In representing the rhetorical features of his romance as a painting,
Achilles Tatius offers a unique perspective on the properties of ecphrasis
as a narrative device. For however brief a glimpse he provides of the
painter's hand, the controlled artifice that permeates his writing remains
constantly in evidence. While this self-conscious rhetorical artistry
conveys itself to the minds of the Renaissance translators and adapters,
they nonetheless de-emphasise the author's stress on the painter's active
engagement with his subject. Della Croce, for example, conveys the
idea of the wind as an artistic creation, 'cuius sinum depictus ventus ita
implebat' (A5). But his Latin also implies the simpler descriptive 'painted',
as in Belleforest's interjection, 'là painct' (A3). This becomes conflated
with 'delphini assultabant, [...] quorum quidem motus etiam illic pictos
esse diceres' (A5v), in Belleforest's 'Les Daufins y estoyent effigiez, iusques
à y representer leurs mouueme[n]ts' (A3). The result of della Croce's
compactness is that Burton simply cannot see in his source the signifi-
cance of the initial reference to painting:

> a scarf cast ouer her shoulders, was held on fast against the force of the
> wind, which did so beat on her bosom, that euery where it seemed to swell
> [...] Round about the bull Dolphins floted about, and sported at their loues
> in such sort, as that you would thinke, you saw their verie motions drawne.
> (B2)

Hodges's garbled version of della Croce's text simply reinforces the fact
that the Latin contains impossible ambiguities. In Hodges, the painter
becomes the first in the history of art to invent pictorial representation of
the wind. And the dolphins' activities become no more than static repre-
sentations:

> the winde, never till nowe painted, getting into her veile, made it swel
> like the sailes of a ship. About the Bull were many Dolphins skipping and
> playing, whose wanton gestures you would sweare to bee no others than
> were there painted. (B2v)

Hodges's fear of the censor lends his text an aura of gossamer-like abstrac-
tion. Nor is he well trained in rhetoric and stylistics, a reflection on his

schooling and university studies. For the subtleties of how style, content, structure, symbol and characterisation are interdependent in this work completely evade him.

Kleitophon and characterisation

The narrator's description of the picture ends in three lines on 'Eros, a tiny child', who exerts the power of erotic love. This completes the contrived transition in genre from traveller's diary to erotic romance. The description prompts a brief self-analysis, followed by the first vocalised speech of the novel: 'I devoted my special attention to this figure of Eros leading the bull, for I have long been fascinated by passion, and exclaimed, "To think that a child can have such power over heaven and earth and sea."' His words invite a reply from 'a young man standing nearby'. It is the narrator-in-waiting, the principal character, Kleitophon, who remarks, 'How well I know it – for all the indignities Love has made *me* suffer' (1.2; Reardon, p. 177).

The traveller and Kleitophon exchange three brief remarks in direct speech. The identity of the speakers is clear from the context, though the speeches are unattributed in the text. The traveller then describes how he leads his new acquaintance into a grove, where they sit on a bench by a stream. Commenting on the idyllic setting, the traveller invites Kleitophon to begin: 'I said, "See, here we have the perfect spot […] for your tales of love"' (1.2; Reardon, p. 177).

Unfortunately, for Renaissance readers, the balanced rhythmic structures and verbal repetitions of della Croce's Ciceronian register flattens and obscures the stylistic and tonal distinctions of this opening. The result is that the traveller's preamble sounds much the same as the rest of the novel. Further, by adding speech identifiers throughout, della Croce (A5v-A6) transforms and dramatises the dialogue leading into Kleitophon's story. This colours both Belleforest's (A3–A3v) and Burton's understanding of the work (B2–B2v). Compare:

della Croce: 'Ego igitur […] ita mecum loquebar'
Belleforest: '& parloy en moy mesme en ceste sorte'
Burton: 'I spake thus to myselfe'

della Croce: 'adolescens […] inquit, ego […] testis esse possum'
Belleforest: 'respondit vn adolescent […], Ie peux (dit-il) estre tesmoin de pareille chose'
Burton: 'a yong man […] sayd […] I can testifie'

della Croce: 'Tum ego',
Belleforest: 'Auquel ie dis'
Burton: 'The[n] said I'

della Croce: 'Tum ille'
Belleforest: 'Lors il respond'
Burton: 'Then answered he'

della Croce: 'Tum ego [...] tempus est, inquam, initium narrandi vt facias'
Belleforest: 'respons-ie lors [...] Il est te[m]ps (dis-ie) que tu co[m]mences à discourir tes malheurs'
Burton: 'Then said I [...] Then (said I) "now is it time that you begin to declare your hard mishaps"'.

Hodges, by combining indirect and direct speech, even further reduces the stylistic differences that separate discreet rhetorical components of the novel, as in

> All other parts of the picture I much commending [...] burst out into this admiration; See how a little infant ha's the command of sea, of earth, and of heaven it selfe! Which speech of mine a young man that was there present, hearing, said hee found what I, spake to be true. (B3)

By designating speakers in the preamble to Kleitophon's lengthy mono-logue, della Croce creates a rhetorically artificial bridge between the traveller's opening ecphrasis and Kleitophon's factual introduction. A spurious poetic consistency conceals the abrupt tonal change dividing the two structural parts. This blurs the calculated stylistic disjunction between the enigmatic artificiality of the allegorical picture, and the comparative though mannered plainness of its purportedly true sequel.

Characterisation is cunningly influenced by the development of Kleito-phon's role as narrator and rhetor. His autobiography is a master-class in rhetorical display. It provides the medium through which the rhetor manipulates his reader into experiencing the full gamut of conflicting emotions – laughter, sorrow, surprise, delight, pathos, concern, horror and finally relief. Kleitophon's revelations about the power of love continue uninterrupted through to the end, which, temporally, precedes the first narrator's arrival in Sidon.

Achilles Tatius's technique requires that Kleitophon's artistic function as storyteller should, from time to time, be clearly visible as a rhetorical device controlled by the author. His presentation is transparently arti-ficial, contrived to create suspense. For though the latest actions in the story are recent and still fresh in his memory, Kleitophon begins at the very beginning, with his own birth, and remains detached from future events. As the opening narrative, which begins *in medias res*, gives ground to a sequel beginning *ab ovo*, notions of idealised characterisation are, perforce, subject to the forces of dramatic irony.

Kleitophon's monologue begins, like the novel and the first narrator, with a string of historical-sounding facts: 'I was born at Tyre in Phoenicia. My name is Kleitophon. My father and his brother are named […]' (1.3; Reardon, p. 178). While this allusion to his Phoenician origins encourages associations with proverbial national characteristics such as exaggeration and lying,[51] its implications tie in neatly with the rhetorical posturing of illusion that pervades the novel.

Kleitophon's opening is reshaped by della Croce's staccato-like compression: 'genitis mihi origo e Phoenicia est, patria Tyrus, nomen Clitophon, pater Hippias, patris frater Sostratus, quod quidem ad patrem attinet: nam matres du[a]e fuere, Sostrati Byzantia, Hippiae Tyria' (A6). Belleforest introduces elegantly rhythmic parallel clauses. His addition of explanatory minutiae, and the change from 'my father's brother' to 'my uncle on my father's side', substantially enlarges his text:

> La source de mes ancestres est Phenisse, & Tyr, cité de ma naissance, i'ay
> à nom Clitophon, mon père Hippie & mon oncle de père s'apelle Sostrate,
> & voila qua[n]t au costé paternel: or estoyent ils freres de diuerses meres,
> estant Sostrate fils de'vne Bisantine & Hippie d'vne natiue de Tyr. (A3v)

Burton, like Belleforest, adds verbs: 'My Country is *Phaenicia*, borne in *Tyrus*; my name is *Clitophon*, my father called *Hippias*, my fathers brother in lawe is called *Sostratus*'. But where della Croce at least squeezes in their relationship, translated by Winkler as 'they had the same father, but my uncle's mother was a lady of Byzantium, and my father's mother was from Tyre' (1.3; Reardon, p. 178), Burton botches this in 'for my father had two wiues' (B2v). Hodges avoids the difficulty by radically simplifying familial relationships: 'I am by birth, saith he, a *Phoenician*, my Countrey is *Tyre*, my name *Clitophon*, my Father *Hippias*, my uncle *Sostratus*' (B3v).

Burton's alteration anticipates Kleitophon's saying that his mother died during his infancy, and that his father took a second wife with whom he had Kalligone. Hippias would have engaged Kalligone to Kleitophon had not the fates decided otherwise – in della Croce, 'sed pote[n]tiora hominibus fata mihi aliam seruabant' (A6). Burton expands, 'but the destinies which are more mighty the[n] mortal man, had appointed the

---

51 H. Morales, *Vision and Narrative in Achilles Tatius' Leucippe and Clitophon*, pp. 55–6.

contrary, and reserued another for that end' (B2v), as does Hodges: 'but
the Fates, whose power is able easily to over master the decrees of men,
reserved another for me' (B3v). Both of these admirers of *Arcadia* would
have known that Sidney alludes to this passage when Pyrocles, describing
the ill-fated Zelmane to Philoclea, confesses that 'if my stars had not
wholly reserved me for you, there else perhaps I might have loved' (*NA*,
p. 268). Sidney's expression 'reserved me' could suggest he may have
remembered Belleforest's translation, 'Mais les destinées plus puissantes
que ne sont les desseins des hommes m'en reseruoyent vn autre'.(A4).

Kleitophon's factual-sounding introduction may paradoxically be the
prelude to a tissue of lies, part-lies, exaggerations and truths. Reliable or
not as a narrator, he remains the sole authority for information about
himself, Leukippe and every other character and event. Given the artifice
of the immediately preceding preamble, one could anticipate a degree of
contrasting idealising and demonising of other characters throughout his
reminiscences. Kleitophon's self-portrait is fantastic and scarcely cred-
ible. And yet, like the audience of a stage performance, readers eagerly
share the traveller's experience of listening to a brilliantly constructed
monologue.

By the time Leukippe's turn comes for self-identification, in Book 6,
Kleitophon's narration bears the hallmarks of quasi-fictional historical
writing. He gives Leukippe's formulaic speech an aura of truth, reporting
it as a contemplative soliloquy overheard by Thersandros and Sosthenes:

> if Thersandros comes inquiring, what am I to say? [...] 'I am the daughter
> of a Byzantine general, and wife of one of the leading men of Tyre. I am
> not Thessalian, and my name is not Lakaina. This is an insult imposed by
> pirates who robbed me even of my name. My husband is Kleitophon; my
> country, Byzantium; Sostratos is my father, and Pantheia my mother'. (6.16;
> Reardon, pp. 256–7)[52]

But the entire scene, as plausible as any in Plutarch, contains only a
rhetorically contrived reconstruction of events. For even while Kleito-
phon assumes the posture of a reliable, well-informed reporter, he adds
an intrusive gloss on Leukippe's opening apostrophe, 'O Kleitophon'. His
observation, '(She repeated this [i.e., ἔλεγε = 'song'] a lot)' (6.16; Reardon,
p. 256), reminds readers that his narrative, a multi-layered προσωποποιία

---

52 'Sed quidnam Thersandro, si forte rursum interrogaturus adsit, respondebo? [...]
Byzantiorum exercitus ducis filiam & Tyrii adolscentis viri primarii vxorem esse scias.
Ego nec Thessala sum, nec Lacaenae mihi est nomen. piratica haec contumelia est, per
quam nomen etiam mihi ademptum fuit. coniux mihi est Clitophon, patria Byzantium,
pater Sostratus, mater Panthia' (M3v).

or prosopopoeia, contains a sophisticated and edited version of what actually occurred. (Della Croce alters the emphasis by having Leukippe repeat only Kleitophon's name, in 'nominis' (M3). His change persists in Belleforest's 'nom' (O4v), Burton's 'that name' (Q2v) and Hodges's 'that name' (N4v).) Such overt emphasising of Kleitophon's role in the way information is presented heightens appreciation of his character as an accomplished rhetor and author. He can be seen adding suspense before this episode in his ecphrasis on a tear as it appears in a 'dull, unlovely eye' and a 'sweet eye' (6.7; Reardon, p. 252); and after this episode in a digressive discourse on the difference between anger and love (6.19; Reardon, p. 258).

Kleitophon's symbolic dream

The closely integrated, cyclic plot progresses resolutely from its inauspicious beginning towards an ending steeped in romantic – and romance – synthesis. Kleitophon and Leukippe marry in Byzantium, and set off for Tyre. Two days later, they find Kleitophon's father, Hippias, preparing for his daughter Kalligone's wedding (8.17–18; Reardon, pp. 282–4). Kleitophon's remarks about his half-sister, Kalligone, therefore frame his entire narrative. The tranquility of these closing scenes contrasts with the ominously destabilising opening, where Kleitophon announces to the traveller-narrator, 'My father decided that Kalligone and I should marry, but the powers above were reserving someone else to be my wife' (1.3; Reardon, p. 178).

Readers are given no help in understanding the clever ambiguity of Kleitophon's perspective. Achilles Tatius creates unexpected tension, suppressing the insights and interpretations that might be anticipated from a narrator whose gripping tale is rooted in personal experience. Kleitophon's detached naivety is a rhetorical trick, inviting readers to share his sense of surprise, as he relives his adventures in chronological sequence. His hindsight, expressed as narrative foresight, prompts the sentencious observation, 'Often the celestial powers delight to whisper to us at night about what the future holds [...] that we may bear it more lightly when it comes' (1.3; Reardon, p. 178). But the ironic inadequacy of such an anodyne commonplace is finally revealed by the shocking horror of Kleitophon's symbolic nightmare. He is nineteen, and considering his forthcoming wedding to Kalligone:

> In a dream I saw my sister's body and mine grown together into a single
> body from the navel down and separating into two above. Over me there

> hovered a huge, fearsome woman [...] eyes shot with blood, rough cheeks,
> snakes for hair, a sickle in her right hand, a torch in her left. In a wild attack
> she aimed her sickle at our groin where the two bodies joined, and severed
> the girl from me [...] I decided to tell no one. (1.3; Reardon, p. 178)

Kleitophon's dream, a rhetorical enigma introduced to foreshadow the
plot, is badly mangled by Renaissance translators. Della Croce, followed
by both Burton and Hodges, seems to have found its imagery distastefully
incestuous. His solution is to join Kalligone to Kleitophon the other way
around, at the top, so that their sexual organs maintain a modest distance,
and to remove their familial relationship: 'visus sum ita cum virgine coni-
ungi, vt a capite ad vmbilicum vsque duo corpora essemus, deinceps vero
in vnu[m] coaluissemus' (A6v). Belleforest is more explicit about their
blood tie – 'joined to the virgin my sister' – in his extended 'que i'estoy
telleme[n]t coulé, & ioint à la pucelle ma soeur, que de la teste iusques
au nombril nous estio[n]s, & faisions deux corps, mais de là en auant ce
n'estoit qu'vne mesme chose tant bien nous estions lacez ensemble' (A4).
Della Croce's interpreting '*παρθένῳ*' as 'virgine', however, causes Burton
to introduce vagueness: 'me thought that I was so ioyned together with a
mayde, that from the nauill to the heade we were but one body, and then
after wee grew all into one' (B3).

Hodges reinvents Kleitophon's dream. The conjoined twin image dis-
appears, and the vision turns into a self-censoring, neoplatonic erotic
fantasy:

> I dreamt that I was love with a virgin, and so intimately knit unto her by
> the bond of affection, that wee seemed both of us to have but one soule;
> with her as I was sporting, me thoughts there appeared unto us a woman
> of a most horrid aspect, [...] in her right hand a sickle, with which she gave
> such a stroke that shee parted us as we were embracing. (B4)

Hodges omits and changes details. His use of 'sporting [...] embracing'
suggests that he reads della Croce's 'cum virgine coniungi' in the spirit
of propriety governing Amyot's *Daphnis and Chloe*. This downplaying of
sexual innuendo, a taste possibly imported from France with Henriette-
Marie (Henrietta Maria), indicates the extent to which Hodges fails to
communicate the novel's symbolism. Here, instead of having a joined
body that is chopped asunder, Hodges's Kleitophon and his unknown
virgin suffer only the indignity of separation.

Had Hodges been able to interpret Parthenia's tournament device
in Sidney's *New Arcadia*, it is unlikely he would have reduced Achilles
Tatius's symbolism of marital bonding to such misleading simplicity.

For Sidney adapts this symbol of joined twins to represent the idealised marriage between Parthenia and Argalus, 'each making one life double because they made a double life one' (*NA*, p. 372). Argalus is killed in combat by Amphialus, whom Parthenia then challenges, disguised as the Knight of the Tomb. Sidney's version of the joined twins symbolism clearly indicates her suicidal intention: 'In his shield for impresa he had a beautiful child, but having two heads – whereon, the one showed that it was already dead; the other alive, but in that case necessarily looking for death. The word was "No way to be rid from death, but by death"' (*NA*, pp. 395–6). The last of the royal tournaments, in which costumes and representational props conveyed these sorts of multiple allegorical dimensions, was held in 1625.[53] Writing thirteen years later, Hodges lacks experience of these forms of artistic complexity. Unable to decipher the narrative purpose of Achilles Tatius's and Sidney's symbolism, he struggles to make it acceptable to his refined, though intellectually lax, Caroline audience.

Sidney's examples of court pageantry, political responsibility and monarchomachia – war against tyrants have no relevance to Hodges and Lovelace. That they had lost the ability to read Sidney can be attributed to Charles I's stifling of political debate. The four parliaments that met between June 1625 and March 1629 so strongly opposed the King that for the next eleven years, till April 1640, he refused to summon one. By 1638, other politicised allegories, such as Spenser's *Faerie Queene* (1590–96), and Shakespeare's *The Winter's Tale* and *Cymbeline*, first published in the 1623 folio, must also have seemed irrelevant, old-fashioned and obscure. Shakespeare's editors were certainly aware that a radical cultural shift had occurred, warning their readers, 'Reade him, therefore; and againe, and againe: And if then you doe not like him, surely you are in some manifest danger, not to vnderstand him. and so we leaue you to other of his Friends, whom if you need, can bee your guides' (A3).

The frenzied detail of Kleitophon's dream makes the turning point that follows barely noticeable. Leucippe and her mother, Pantheia, the wife of Kleitophon's father's half-brother, Sostratos, travel to Tyre from Byzantium. They are evacuees, fleeing the perils of a war between Byzantium and Thrace, and come to stay in Kleitophon's father's house (1.3; Reardon, p. 178). Sidney bonds his central plot to this episode: Musidorus and Pyrocles are brought up together while Musidorus's father engages in conquering Thrace and setting up court in its principal city, Byzantium.[54]

53 A. Young, *Tudor and Jacobean Tournaments* (London: George Philip, 1987), p. 41.
54 *OA*, p. 10; *NA*, pp. 162, 164.

Achilles Tatius brings his central characters together when the wealthy Byzantine youth, Kallisthenes, who has never seen Leukippe, convinces himself he loves her, and kidnaps Kalligone in error. Kleitophon can only watch as his intended is taken aboard Kallisthenes' ship. His self-centred report to the traveller-narrator contains an implied interpretation of his dream: 'I felt a great relief at my wedding being thus all unexpectedly made impossible, and yet at the same time I was of course much distressed' (Gaselee, 2.18).

The beginning of Leukippe and Kleitophon's relationship is rapid and intense. On the day Leukippe arrives, Kleitophon sits across from her at dinner, and falls immediately in love: 'Such beauty I had seen once before, and that was in a painting of Selene on a bull' (1.4; Reardon, p. 179).[55] 'Europa' rather than 'Selene' in della Croce's 'sedentis in tauri tergo Europae mihi venit in mentem' (A7) represents the minority manuscript tradition, adapted by Belleforest as 'il me souueint d'Europe seant sur la croppe du toreau' (A5), Burton in 'I remembred *Europa*, sayling vpon the backe of the Bull' (B3), and Hodges in the condensed 'I straightway thought on Europa' (B4v). Notwithstanding that 'Europa' may now generally be preferred by editors over 'Selene' 'to make it *fit*', and that the scribe who created the 'Europa' archetype may have emended to create 'literary consistency',[56] della Croce ensured that Renaissance readers experienced the kind of rhetorical patterning that Achilles Tatius excels at, and which they expected him to provide.

Kleinias on love, sex and marriage

Four days later, Kleitophon seeks his cousin Kleinias's advice on courting a virgin. Achilles Tatius's Kleinias is a homosexual misogynist. But, unlike Longus's bestial Gnathon, he is thoughtful, caring and saddened by the experience of lost love. Kleinias's parents are dead. He is two years older than Kleitophon, and 'already an initiate in the rites of love' (1.7; Reardon, p. 180). Kleinias advocates delicacy in wooing the sexually inexperienced Leukippe. He understands intimate matters to be issues of sensitivity that transcend sexuality, and that they are psychologically and physically interrelated.

55 Cf. H. Morales, *Vision and Narrative in Achilles Tatius' Leucippe and Clitophon*, p. 38, reads Burton and Hodges as independent translations rather than representing della Croce's text.

56 H. Morales, *Vision and Narrative in Achilles Tatius' Leucippe and Clitophon*, pp. 39–40, where the case is exaggerated by having all 'the scribes who penned the manuscript family β' emend to 'Europa' (p. 40). They simply followed a single archetype.

There is a marked difference between Burton's, Belleforest's and Hodges's versions. Burton correctly has Kleinias equate the sexual feelings of adolescent boys and girls, presenting him as universally knowledgeable about love. Burton translates della Croce:[57]

> take heed of vnchast and immodest dealings: but vse the matter so with silence, as that by your action they might conceiue your meaning. For yong men and maids are affected with like modesty: and although they be desirous of copulation, yet they wold not seeme to haue any talke concerning such matters, for why they thinke dishonestie in the words, but they who haue bin well experienced in mens matters, holde it no disgrace to talke more amply of such a subiect. (C2v)

Belleforest's initial focus is on secrecy in addition to silence, emulating the courtly love convention: 'Et premierement don[n]e toy bie[n] garde de ne req[ue]rir point vne fille d'auoir affaire à elle, mais fais de sorte que le tout se passe & face secreteme[n]t sans mot dire' (B3v). In keeping with this shift towards chaste respect for the beloved, he omits the references to 'young men' and sexual desire. Instead, Belleforest turns this passage into a warning to virgins, in keeping with the didactic role assigned to erotic romance by Amyot. Belleforest focuses on the danger posed to those who naively believe that male villainy lies in words alone, rather than in deeds:

> Car ceste gra[n]de ieunesse est voilée d'vne gra[n]de ho[n]te, telleme[n]t que encore q[ue] les filles souhaite[n]t le plaisir & deduit amoureux, si est ce que elles ne veulent qu'on leur parle de ce que volontiers elles endurent, pensans que la vilennie consiste és seules parolles, & et non au fait. (B3v)

Finally, he reassures gentlemen courtiers that even experienced women are also quite happy just to talk: 'Mais celles qui ont gousté les embrassemens des hommes, elles se plaisent aussi d'en ouyr parler' (B3v).

Far from adapting Achilles Tatius into a Renaissance courtesy book, Hodges removes the reference to young men. Seemingly seeking the approval of fellow collegiate wags, through the addition of risqué colloquialism, he represents female sexual drive as morally opprobrious:

> be sure you talke not obscenely to her, but dispatch your love with silence, for women though they be most lascivious and wanton, yet in this they

---

57 'virginem in primis ne de stupro appelles, caueto: sed vt negocium re ipsa conficiatur, silentio curato: pari enim verecundia pueri sunt, & puellae. ac quanquam venereorum cupiditate teneantur, non tamen de iis quae perpetiuntnr [*sic*] sermonem secum haberi volunt, turpitudinem in verbis collocatam existimantes. quae viros expertae sunt, verbis etiam delectantur' (B4).

are modest, detesting to heare that spoken, which they make no bones of doing, accounting the words more filthie than the deed. Those that have made shipwrack of their virginitie will suffer you to talke more freely [...]. (C1v)

Achilles Tatius contains this dialogue between Kleitophon and Kleinias within yet another frame, or verbal parenthisis. Through it, he contrasts Kleitophon's adoration of Leukippe and his desire for pre-marital sex with the forbidding constraints of a marriage based on an exchange of wealth. This is what Pantheia envisages for Leukippe. The frame opens when Kleinias's lover, Charikles, rushes in to announce that his father has arranged a marriage for him with a rich but ugly girl. His misogynist remark enjoys a varied fortune: 'an ugly maiden [...] A wife is a troublesome thing, even a pretty one; but if she also has the bad luck to be ugly, the disaster is doubled' (1.7; Reardon, p. 181). Compare della Croce's compact 'eamque deformem, [...] nam cum magnum malum sit formosa mulier, qui poterit deformis non duplo maius esse?' (B1v) with Belleforest's literal translation, 'fort laide [...] Car co[m]me ainsi soit que c'est vn malheur que d'auoir femme tant soit elle belle, co[m]me ne redoublera le desastre sur celuy qui l'aura laide?' (A7v–A8). Burton's English is expansive: 'she is hard fauoured, and deformed too [...] for since a faire wife is a great trouble, how can it otherwise be, but that an ill fauored one must needs be twice worse' (B4v). But in Hodges's jaunty but evasive and paraphrastic version, this becomes, 'such a blouze that I shall bee tormented with her above measure; if a handsome woman bee an evil intolerable, what is an ill favoured one' (B6v).[58]

Achilles Tatius closes this opening frame with a shock. Determined to enjoy what freedom remains to him, Charikles takes his first ride on a horse that Kleinias has given him (1.7–8). Burton turns the unadorned 'equum' – Belleforest's 'vn cheual' (A7) – into 'a goodly faire gelding' (B4v); Hodges, 'a most gallant horse' (B6v). Charikles parts company with Kleinias with the self-assured, albeit fatalistic, quip, 'The gods and I will look after this. The wedding is still some days off, and much can happen in a single night' (1.8; Reardon, p. 182). Kleitophon and Kleinias's dialogue about love is shattered when one of Charikles' slaves reports that 'Charikles is dead' (1.12; Reardon, p. 185). This introduces an ecphrastic passage resembling Seneca's description of the death of Hippolytus, tangled in his reins and dragged to death behind his chariot. Startled by

---

58 Charikles' desperation at being 'sold for her money' (1.8; Reardon, p. 181) parallels the predicament in which so many of Mary Sidney Wroth's female characters find themselves, in *The Countess of Montgomery's Urania*.

a noise, Charikles' horse bolts and crashes through the woods, dragging and trampling his rider till he is mutilated beyond recognition.[59] In a paradox typical of Achilles Tatius's style, at Charikles' funeral, in Hodges's words, 'the father and the friend strived to out-vie one another in their griefes' (C3v), the father publicly, Kleinias privately (1.14).[60] Kleitophon's dream, followed by Kleinias's loss, anticipates the pattern of abrupt and tragic separations that remains unresolved until the final moments of the novel.

Kleitophon's garden

Achilles Tatius uses this emotional Kleinias-Charikles episode as a prelude to Kleitophon's courtship of Leukippe. Hodges, as do Belleforest and Burton, translates 'Posteaquam funeri iusta soluta sunt, ad Leucippem, quae nostro in hortulo tu[m] morabatur, conuolaui' (B6v) literally: 'After wee had dispatcht his funerall rites, I ranne straightway to *Leucippe*, who was then in our garden' (C4). It is no coincidence that Kleitophon's garden (1.15) bears a strong resemblance to the one in the painting of Europa, described in the traveller's narrative (1.1). For once again the author assures readers of the rhetorical control he exercises to ensure the satisfactory outcome of his artfully unified plot.

These two gardens are connected through the unusual use of chiaroscuro in the painting, and the light and shade of this natural counterpart. In the painted garden, 'the artist had sketched the shadows cast below the leaves, and sunshine filtered in soft splashes onto the meadow through fissures left by the artificer in the leaves above' (1.1; Reardon, p. 176). In Kleitophon's, 'when the highest, sunlit leaves fluttered in the wind, the earth took on a dappled look, with yellow patches in the shade' (1.15; Reardon, p. 187). Their similarity draws attention to their differences. In the painting, the branches intertwine to form a shade. In the garden, the natural relationship of the plants sets the tone for Kleitophon's following speech on attraction between males and females, by which he intends to arouse Leukippe's amorous interest.

Like many other passages, the ecphrasis on Kleitophon's garden becomes the victim of willful translators. Kleitophon describes a substantial delightful garden surrounded on four sides by a high wall, lined with

---

59 *Hippolytus*, in *Seneca's Tragedies*, trans. by F. J. Miller, 2 vols (London: William Heinemann, 1907), 1093–104.
60 'Clinia vero contra (lugendo enim pater, atque amator certabant) secum ipse solus' (B6v).

columned cloisters.⁶¹ Burton, who expands the garden in the painting, severely reduces the scale of this walled area: 'within the Gardain there was a little arbour compassed round with a little wall, at euery corner was a piller which did beare vp the worke in the toppe' (C8v).

The wall encompasses an elaborately described network of shade trees and plants, and a spring. The layout therefore bears a structural resemblance to Dionysophanes' garden in *Daphnis and Chloe*. Achilles Tatius invokes the image of a mirror to represent a microcosmic Platonic universe through a mimetic process, by which an artistic representation of an ideal form is itself reproduced in a reflection: 'Among the flowers, a spring bubbled up within a rectangular pool constructed to contain the flow. The flowers were reflected in the water as in a mirror, so that the entire grove was doubled – the realm of truth confronting its shadowy other' (1.15; Reardon, p. 187). This reflection is the key to the novel's rhetorical artifice, and an invitation to read it on more than one level.

The intermediary between Achilles Tatius and Burton, della Croce's Latin version, is relatively free from ambiguity: 'in florum medio scaturiens fons quadratro alueo, riuoque manufacto excipiebatur, speculique instar efficiebat, horti vt illic duo, alter re, alter vmbra esse videtentur' (B7v). Following his usual practice of introducing variant, though parallel, information, Belleforest captures the image well: 'Au milieu de ces fleurs & fueillages y auoit vne fontaine quarrée, qui surgeoit à gros bouillons, & s'escouloit par vn canal comme vn ruisseau: & faisoit tout ainsi que vn miroir & on apperceuoit là deux iardins, l'vn en effet & l'autre par ombre & representation de la glace' (B7v). But Burton removes the rectangular pool, conflating it with the immediately preceding image of a sea-coloured violet. Inexplicably, the spring and its retaining pond are reduced to a single drop of water: 'there were also Violets, whose colour was like to the colour of a calme sea, on the toppe of which stood, a drop of pure water, as it were a faire spring rising from the roote, and cast the reflexe like vnto a glasse, there seemed to be two Gardaines, one in deed, the other but a shadow' (C4v).

Burton's translation closely echoes Sidney's borrowing from Achilles Tatius for Kalander's garden in the opening sequence of the *New Arcadia*. Sidney emphasises this textual interrelationship through his choice of names. Kalander's son is called Clitophon, Leucippe is a noble woman jilted by Pamphilus, and Clinias, Cecropia's pawn, is a former tragedian,

---

61 'nemus illic creuerat aspectu iucundissimo, maceriaque iustae altitudinis circumcinge[n]te; cuius latera quatuor, (tot enim omnino erant,) tecto colu[m]nis imminente operta visebantur' (B6v–B7).

catalyst, and reporter (*NA*, pp. 19, 96, 260, 288). Sidney's garden, as in *Leukippe and Kleitophon*, signals a narrative schema of illusory doubles: 'In the middest of all the place was a fair pond whose shaking crystal was a perfect mirror to all the other beauties, so that it bare show of two gardens, one indeed, the other in shadows' (*NA*, 14). Hodges, however, loses this mirror imagery entirely. His reduction barely touches on the spring, which 'was first received in a fouresquare bason, and running from thence it fed a little rivulet' (C4v). This failure to understand the symbolism of the reflections, through which Achilles Tatius indicates the integrated rhetorical and philosophical structure of the novel, represents a misinterpretation of cataclysmic proportions. If Hodges could neither read the symbolism of *Leukippe and Kleitophon* nor understand its artistic integrity, then it is certain that the similarly interwoven rhetorical patterns in Sidney's *Arcadia*, which link its various themes through recurrent phrases and images, remained utterly beyond him and his readers.

Pantheia's dream

Hodges misinterprets Kleitophon's dream about the separation of conjoined twins as foreshadowing an episode of *coitus interruptus* in the second Book. This occurs when Kleitophon flees after Leukippe's mother, Pantheia, bursts in on their first (and only) attempt to have sex (2.23). Hodges likewise misrepresents Kleitophon's description of Pantheia's dream, which impels her to rush to check on Leukippe's safety.

Pantheia is awakened by a nightmare, another rhetorical tool to create suspense while its ambiguities are resolved. In it, 'she saw a bandit with a naked sword seize her daughter [...] and slice her in two all the way up from her stomach, making his first insertion' at her groin (2.23; Reardon, p. 201). Della Croce retains the innuendo of sexual penetration (along with the glancing allusion in Europa's white tunic, covering her 'pectus ad pudenda'): 'vteru[m] eius facto a pudendis initio gladio secaret' – 'he slices her womb, having made an entrance by sword at her pudendum' (D5v). As in his description of Kleitophon's dream, Belleforest, and in line with the prevailing mood of the church, attaches shame to female genitalia: 'fendoit le ventre comme[n]çant aux parties honteuses' (D8v). But while Burton retains a hint of genital mutilation in 'ripped her from the lower part of the belly to the brest' (F3), Hodges's simplistic 'ript up her bowels' (E3v) reduces the symbolism to a mere expression of action. Hodges trivialises the detail with which Achilles Tatius enriches the rhetorical texture of his romance.

Pantheia dashes into Leukippe's room, frightening Kleitophon, who had 'then scant layde downe in the bed' with Leukippe (2.23; Burton, F3). She fails to identify him as he rushes out, but grows hysterical and accuses her daughter of stupidly collaborating in the loss of her virginity. To Pantheia, consensual pre-marital sex is a social blight that ruins her daughter's prospects. It would have been preferable had she been raped by a warrior.

Pantheia alludes to her dream's symbolic overtones: 'That incision in your stomach is much more serious: he pricked you deeper than a sword could have' (2.24; Reardon, p. 201). This is clear in della Croce's 'nu[n]c certe crudele[m] in modu[m] dissectus tibi vterus fuit, atq[ue]: adeo, vt ne ferro quidem crudelius diuidi potuerit' (D6), and finds its way successfully into Belleforest's 'Car c'est à la verité que l'on t'a cruelleme[n]t fendu le ventre, & tellement que le fer ne l'eust sceu partir, ou diuiser auec plus d'inhumanité' (E1–E1v), and Burton's 'now I see thy belly is cut vp in most cruell maner: and so much moreouer, that no sword can diuide it alike' (F3). Once again, the proper Hodges continues to exclude references to anatomical parts, removing the metaphorical qualities from Pantheia's speech: 'better thou hadst been ript up alive, then that this bloudy massacre should have been committed upon thine honour' (E4).

Tempers are frayed by morning, when Leukippe brazenly challenges her mother (and anticipates the denouement): 'If there is a virginity test, I'll take it' (2.28; Reardon, p. 202). As early as this second Book, Achilles Tatius is preparing for the concluding eighth, where Leukippe's ability to pass a virginity test saves her from being condemned to a wretched existence as a sex-slave (8.14; Reardon, p. 281). After this episode, Kleitophon only once again pursues Leukippe to consummate their relationship. But by then they will have endured the living hells of 'shipwreck, pirates, human sacrifice, ritual murder' (4.1; Reardon, p. 222).

Debate on erotic love

Through the ruse of Pantheia's dream, the undesirable complication of sexual intercourse between hero and heroine is avoided. But Achilles Tatius, ever one to whet the reader's appetite and not then to disappoint, creates yet another digression to afford himself the opportunity for further rhetorical display. Near the end of Book 2, Kleitophon and Leukippe elope. They are accompanied by Kleitophon's cousin, Kleinias, who masterminds the plan; by Kleitophon's slave, Satyros; and by two servants. They travel by carriage to Sidon, and then Beirut, where they board a ship for Alexandria (2.31; Reardon, p. 203). Menelaos, a passenger, invites them to join him for breakfast.

Menelaos's circumstances are similar to Kleinias's, in that he is grieving for his dead lover, a boy whom he accidentally impaled with a javelin while hunting. To divert them from their sorrows, Kleitophon provokes a debate on erotic love. Its parodic and chauvinistic nature is signalled by the contrived exclusion of Leukippe, who 'was asleep in a corner of the ship'. Kleitophon begins with the inflammatory ironic jibe, 'It does look as if male-directed love is becoming the norm' (2.35; Reardon, p. 205).

Della Croce's literal interpretation lacks impact: 'Quid autem in causa sit, quam ob rem tam multi puerorum amoribus delectentur, ipse sane non video' (E2). Belleforest's adjustment from 'boys' to 'children', albeit implying males, is less harsh: 'Or quant à moy ie ne voy iuste raison aucune qui occassio[n]ne que ta[n]t d'hommes que ie voy s'amusent à la poursuite de l'Amour des enfans' (E6). Burton alters the syntax, separating the problem from its frame: 'what is the cause why so many are in loue with boyes? Surely I my selfe cannot tell, neither see any cause why?' (G2). But as announced in 'The Translator to the Reader', Hodges omits this dialogue from Kleitophon's narrative:

> seeing *Menelaus* weeping for his friend, & *Clinias* making moane for his *Caricles*, to put them out of their dumps, I began to tell love stories, and merry tales, at length to talke much in commendation of women, but *Menelaus* who had alwayes been their enemie spake as much against them, so at last wee fel in a large discourse concerning the dignity of their sex, which I list not here to set down. (E7v)

Expurgating the text of what Caroline taste condemned as vulgar, Hodges deprives his readers of the debate between Kleitophon and Menelaos. This rhetorical *tour de force* takes the form of an exaggerated sexual fantasy, illustrated by a host of Greek mythological episodes. Kleitophon provocatively suggests he is a false witness of 'that true pleasure which is conceived in women', because, he claims, his knowledge of lovemaking is limited: 'I have only had the society of women whose favourite haunt is Love' (Gaselee, 2.37). The translations are flexible. Gaselee's 'Love' translates 'Aphrodite', but eliminates the concept of prostitution in Ἀφροδίτην πωλουμέναις, retained by Garnaud in 'celles qui se vendent pour Aphrodite',[62] by Morales in 'those who put Aphrodite up for sale',[63]

62 Achille Tatius d'Alexandrie, *Le Roman de Leucippé et Clitophon*, ed. and trans. by J.-P. Garnaud (Paris: Les Belles Lettres, 1991), II.xxxvii.5.
63 H. Morales, *Vision and Narrative in Achilles Tatius' Leucippe and Clitophon*, p. 153.

and paraphrased by Winkler as 'commercial transactions with women of the street' (2.37; Reardon, p. 207). Della Croce similarly elides the allusion into 'quantu[m] quide[m] cum iis quae precio prostant' (E3v), which Belleforest represents as 'moy aiant premierement fait l'experie[n]ce auec celles qui s'abando[n]nent pour de large[n]t' (E7v). By contrast, Burton's Elizabethan Kleitophon represents himself as a morally superior virgin, in keeping with the exemplary characterisation of the hero of European erotic romance: 'although herein I haue not bin much conuersant [...] neither hath there bene any vse or delight, wherewith I haue enured my selfe' (G3).

Kleitophon's detailed description of sexual intercourse comprises an amalgam of idealised erotic observations. His ecphrasis expresses voyeuristic delight in visual and tactile detail. The text presents translators with difficulties, principally because its frank exploration of sex is highly condensed and filled with innuendo. Winkler's interpretive translation treats the words more conceptually: 'A woman's body is well lubricated in the clinch, and her lips are tender and soft for kissing. Therefore she holds a man's body wholly and congenially wedged into her embraces, into her very flesh; and her partner is totally encompassed with pleasure' (2.37; Reardon, p. 207). Della Croce's translation, 'corpus amplexatu tenerum, labra basiatu mollia esse. atq[ue]; hac de causa mulier cum vlnas, tum carnem ad id omnino apte co[n]formata sortita est. sane qui ad mulierem sese applicat, is vere voluptate[m] amplectitur' (E3v), is not far removed from Gaselee's, 'during lovers' embraces her body is supple and her lips are soft for kisses [...] she holds the man's body completely fitted in; and he who is within is surrounded with pleasure' (Gaselee, 2.37).

Belleforest's less detailed, and therefore less erotic, interpretation removes the expression of female desire through holding her lover's body. The chauvinistic and repetitive Belleforest restricts himself simply to reiterating that the arms and flesh of a woman are suited to pleasure: 'le corps des femmes est agreable à l'embrassement & les leures molles & douces pour le baiser. & que pour cest effet la fe[m]me a eu les bras & la chair co[n]formes a ce plaisir' (E7–E8). Burton is hardly able to cope. The anodyne indirectness of Burton's expansive opening barely indicates the self-censoring paraphrase that leads him to reduce della Croce's forthright text by nearly half: 'their bodies are tender to imbrace, their lippes soft for to kisse, whose whole proportion of the bodie, is onely made to moue delight: and he which doth enioy a bewtifull woman, hath the true felicitie of all pleasure' (G3). Southampton and his philhellene Protestant circle were not going to accept a literal translation.

Unlike Belleforest, who provides quite a full description of the female ecstatic kiss, with its spiritual and physiological relationship to the heart and to the gasps of orgasm, Burton carefully omits this long discussion. He shrinks della Croce's full and sensuous rendering into an evasive minia-ture: 'In touching of her tender breasts, what great delight there is, I leaue to them whom experience hath made perfect herein; and euen in their naturall actions, shee doth so delight, as that he might thinke himselfe in another world' (G3). He also exercises discretion when representing Kleitophon's challenge to Menelaos, in della Croce, 'Pueroru[m] oscula rudia sunt, co[m]plexus indocti, venus languida, omniq[ue], prorsus iucunditate destituta' (E4) – 'Schoolboys are hardly so well educated in kissing; their embraces are awkward; their lovemaking is lazy and devoid of pleasure' (2.37, Reardon, p. 207). Belleforest's version is extended by doubling information through the creative use of tautology for emphasis: 'La où les baisers des enfans sont rudes, les ambrasseme[n]s sans art, le plaisir flestry & la[n]guissant & leq[ue]l est priué de toute volupté & lyesse' (E8v). Burton, however, introduces the concept of the 'vnnaturall', turning this passage into a denunciation of homoeroticism: 'The kisses of boyes are rude, their imbracings vnapt, and vnnaturall: whose delight doth languish, and is voyd of all true pleasure indeed' (G3).

Menelaos replies that 'young men have the privilege, before wrestling under Aphrodite's rules, of grappling on the mat, publicly locking bodies in the gym; and no one says these embraces are immodest' (2.38; Reardon, p. 208). In Belleforest, della Croce's faithful 'iam vero etiam ante venereos congressus palaestra cum iis decertare, palamque ac sine rubore amplecti licet' (E4v) loses its sense of location to focus on the erotic and tactile: '& aua[n]t que acointer, on se peut iouer, & embrasser sans honte de personne & n'y a aucune te[n]dreur de chair q[ue] cede à l'attoucher des embrasseme[n]s' (E8v–F1). Burton cautiously reports only the general substance in a limp rendering, 'a man may openly talke and play with them and neuer bee ashamed: neither is there any tendernesse of flesh which is like to them' (G3v).

In 'the very image and picture of their kisses are so sweete and pleasant, that you might very wel thinke, that heauenly Nectar to bee betweene your lippes' (G3v), Burton offers a rhythmic approximation of 'Here is a meta-phor for a boy's kiss: take nectar; crystallise it; form it into a pair of lips – these would yield a boy's kisses' (2.38; Reardon, p. 208) – 'basii puerilis imago eiusmodi est, vt si quis concretum atq[ue]; in labra com[m]utatem nectar oscularetur' (E4v). But then he omits Menelaos's concluding argu-ment, that 'you could not pull your mouth away until the very excess of pleasure frightened you into escaping' – 'neq[ue]; os inde abstrahere possis, donec prae voluptate basia ipse refugias'. Belleforest is not so coy. His nectar is the nectar of the gods, and the madness produced by pleasure and which causes one to flee, and to refuse kisses and embraces, is more emphatic: 'les baisers […] sont tout tels en leur image comme q[ue] auroit sur ces leures le Nectar des dieux caillé & co[n]uerti en nos leures, […] & ne peux tirer ta bouche de là, iusques à ce gra[n]d plaisir, & en follatra[n]t tu fuyes & refuses les baisers & accollades' (F1).

Burton represses Achilles Tatius's ecphrases of both female and male erotic arousal, casting Kleitophon in the role of an inexperienced and somewhat homophobic naif. This Elizabethan gloss, and Hodges's more extensive Caroline self censorship, distort the representation of erotic love in the narrative, throwing the author's rhetorical artistry into disarray. England surpassed France in prudishness.

Sexual predation

The sexual gratification that Kleitophon and Menelaos convey through their 'merry tales' introduces, and contrasts with, the relationships in which the disorientated travellers become embroiled. As Leukippe and Kleitophon encounter characters whose values differ from theirs, their beliefs about fidelity in love, personal integrity and sexual morality are thoroughly tested. The fourth day after they set sail, their ship is wrecked in a storm (3.1–2; Reardon, pp. 210–11). Kleitophon and Leukippe 'float to shore at Pelousion' (3.5; Reardon, p. 211). Two days later, they hire an Egyptian boat to sail 'along the Nile to Alexandria' (3.9; Reardon, p. 213), where Egyptian bandits capture them. Leukippe is hauled off as the token virgin, to be offered 'to the god as a purification sacrifice for the group' (3.12; Reardon, p. 214).

Achilles Tatius fills this scene with dramatic irony. Kleitophon, newly escaped to the Egyptian army, from a distance watches Leukippe being ritually disembowelled. Like the bandits – and readers of the text – he has no means of distinguishing this convincing piece of theatre from real life.

The executioner 'raised a sword and plunged it into her heart and then sawed all the way down to her abdomen' (3.15; Reardon, p. 216), in della Croce, 'gladiumque iuxta cor infixum ad ima ventris vsque traxit' (F5), and Belleforest, 'plantant son glaiue dans le coeur la fe[n]dit iusques au pl[us] bas du ve[n]tre' (G3v). This incision, although a reversal of the symbolic one in Pantheia's dream, is no less menacing. But where Burton reconstructs this passage to imitate the earlier configuration, 'thrusting in his sworde at the lower end of her belly, ript her vp to ye heart' (I1v), Hodges merely paraphrases, 'ript her downewards till hee came to the paunch' (F8v).

Kleitophon's summarising lament, 'I do not mourn [...], but rather the farce your murderers made of your misfortune [...], they slit you (alas!) alive, witnessing your own incision' (3.16; Reardon, pp. 216–17), becomes della Croce's 'non quod tam saeui de te ludi facti sint, fleo: sed [...] quod ii te viuam (me miserum) gladiis que mucronem in te defigi videntem dissecuerint' (F5v–F6). Belleforest adds elegant balancing, and refocuses the passage towards Leukippe's virginity by removing any notion of theatrical nonsense: 'ie ne pleure point [...], & ne me tourmente point, de ce qu'on a dressé de si cruels spectacles de ta virginité: [...] ce sont eux (moy miserable!) qui moy voya[n]t tout fendre de leurs glaiues touteviue' (G4). But the Elizabethan expectation of repetitive linkage in poetic fiction, encouraged by Sidney's practice,[64] leads Burton to reiterate his interpretive translation of the disembowelment scene: 'I do not lament thy death, [...] but [...] because thou wast a sacrifice for so vncleane theeues; whom being aliue, they did not only rent out thy verie bowels, but ripping thee vp most butcherly from the lower end of thy belly to thy very heart' (I2). Hodges, consistently oblivious to the narrative function of symbolism, simplifies: 'I grieve not so much [...] that those salvage villaines made such a May-game of thy murther; but [...] that they should rippe thee up alive' (G1v).

At the moment the suicidal Kleitophon is plunging his sword down his throat, Satyros and Menelaos stop him. Appointed Leukippe's executioners, they tell how they used a trick sword and other props a professional actor had brought on board (3.20–2; Reardon, pp. 218–19). Leukippe's theatrical death contains elements of a symbolic conversion. It coincides with a change in the sexual politics of the plot, accentuating her chastity as she becomes the long-suffering victim of aggressive and violent men. But these subtleties remained hidden from English readers.

Leukippe's trials begin when she is reunited with Kleitophon, and an Egyptian general named Charmides gives them a house. Kleitophon experiences a strong desire 'to ravish her' (4.1; Reardon, p. 222) – as Hodges puts it, 'would have done the office of a husband' (G7v). But Leukippe's gentle rebuff, reporting divine intervention, marks a turning-point:

> But it would still be wrong to do that. The day before yesterday, when I was crying because I was going to be butchered, Artemis appeared, standing

---

64 See the section on 'Form' in *NA*, pp. xxv–xxxviii.

above me in my sleep, and said, 'Do not be sad, you shall not die, for I will
stand by you and help you. You will remain a virgin until I myself give you
away as a bride. No one but Kleitophon will marry you'. (4.1; Reardon,
p. 222)[65]

Della Croce's translation offers less protection. Leukippe will not die and
she will marry Kleitophon, but the responsibility for keeping her virginity
is hers alone: 'tu virginitatem tuam tandiu serua, quoad ego te deducam'
(G4). This alteration, from a prophetic remark to a condition (or a
command),[66] colours Belleforest, 'Ce pendant garde ta virginité iusqu'à
ce que ie te conduise aux nopces' (H3v), and both English texts. Burton
reads, 'keepe thou as yet thy virginitie, vntil I shall otherwise appoint thee'
(K1v), and Hodges, 'onely keepe thy selfe chaste, till I shall commend a
husband to thee, who doubtlesse shall bee no other than Clitophon' (G8).
In Hodges's version, erotic romance becomes fairytale.

It may, or may not, be the knowledge of Artemis's divine reassurance
that sustains Leukippe through the series of harrowing experiences that
now befalls her. She does not, like Heliodorus's Charikleia, have divine
associations as both princess and practising priestess, but she does
possess the necessary strength to resist male predators. Leukippe's vision
is, nonetheless, a rhetorical ploy that reassures readers of her superhuman
power to endure suffering. Whether the following comment, 'Of course
I was upset at the postponement but very glad of our expectations' (4.1;
Reardon, p. 222), is attributed to Clitophon, as is usual, or to a sexually
liberated but externally restrained Leukippe,[67] does not alter the vision's
prefiguring her surviving with her virginity intact.

Holding Leukippe prisoner, Charmides burns for hedonistic sex.
Menelaos holds him at bay, extemporising: 'She had her period just
yesterday, and it is not decent for her to be that close to a man' (4.7;
Reardon, p. 225). Charmides will wait, satisfied with touching. Bellefo-
rest gives this sensitive passage a euphemistic rendering of della Croce's
'puella in menstruis heri esse coepit. quamobrem a viro abstinendu[m]

---

65 'Tum Leucippe: Atqui fieri hoc, inquit, nondum licet. Nam cum arae victimae loco desti-
    nata lugerem, visa mihi per somnium Diana, Ne nunc, inquit, luge: non enim moriere.
    ipsa tibi opem feram. tu virginitatem tuam tandiu serua, quoad ego te deducam: tu certe
    non nisi Clitophonti nubes' (G4).
66 As in H. Morales, *Vision and Narrative in Achilles Tatius' Leucippe and Clitophon*, p.
    206.
67 Cf. H. Morales, *Vision and Narrative in Achilles Tatius' Leucippe and Clitophon*, pp. 125,
    206. Cf. della Croce, 'ego vero quanquam moram hanc aegre ferebam, futuri tamen spe
    laetabar' (G4); Burton, 'I although I did greeuously take this delay, yet I reioyced with
    the hope of the thing to come' (K1v); Hodges, 'For this ensuing joy I was not a little glad,
    thogh this delay cut me to the heart' (G8).

est' (G7v) in, 'Ceste fille dés hier commença sentir la maladie co[m]mune des femmes, & pource faut que pour quelques iours elle s'abstienne de l'homme' (H7v). But Burton's brilliantly colloquial Menelaos objects, 'the Mayde beganne yesternight to bee in her flowers, wherefore then shee must abstaine from a man' (K4). True to form, the intimidated Hodges resorts to evasive compression when writing about the female anatomy: 'I wil tell you, she is sick' (H3v).

Achilles Tatius builds these degrading events into a crescendo. Chaireas, a mercenary from Pharos, reveals that an Egyptian soldier named Gorgias 'persuaded your Egyptian valet to mingle' an aphrodisiac 'in Leukippe's cup' (4.15; Reardon, p. 230), bringing on a ten-day-long madness. Chaireas invites Leukippe, Kleitophon and their friends to a party on Pharos. A swallow pursued by a hawk strikes Leukippe on the head. She turns around and sees an artist's studio with a painting of the rape of Philomela, who, held captive in an isolated forest, provides a fore-taste of Leukippe's trials. Achilles Tatius reinforces the symbolic signifi-cance of this and other ecphrases by having Menelaos read the omens: 'just look at the disasters proliferating in this scene: lawless sex, adultery without shame, women degraded!' (5.4; Reardon, p. 234).

Kleitophon is wounded when Chaireas has Leukippe kidnapped by pirates. Hotly pursued by the marshal of Pharos, one of the pirates 'cried out in a loud voice, "Here's your prize!" and so saying, he cut off her head and toppled the rest of the body into the sea' (5.7; Reardon, p. 236). Here Achilles Tatius uses the theatrical trick of the unidentifiable, head-less torso to separate the protagonists, allow them to establish individual identities and further complicate the plot.

Melite and Thersandros

Leukippe and Kleitophon differs from *Daphnis and Chloe* and *An Ethio-pian Story* by using a character chiasmus, so to speak, as the catalyst for the resolution of the plot. Melite falls in love with Kleitophon, and her husband Thersandros with Leukippe. This crossing of partners is compli-cated by the contrast between the gentle Melite's genuine affection and the brutal Thersandros's volcanic lust for his unkempt slave.

'Six months' after Kleitophon buries the headless torso, Kleinias locates him in Alexandria (5.8; Reardon, 237). He brings news that Kleitophon's father is 'on his way here' to deliver news that 'he found a letter from Leukippe's father which had arrived the day after our departure, and in which Sostratos announced Leukippe's engagement to you' (5.10;

Reardon, p. 238). Menelaos, Satyros and Kleinias propose that the incon-solable Kleitophon accept an offer of marriage from the beautiful wealthy Ephesian, Melite, whose 'husband just recently died at sea' (5.11; Reardon, p. 238). He agrees, but insists on keeping his 'vow never to copulate in this part of the world, where I lost Leukippe' (5.12; Reardon, p. 239). It is a promise that takes idiomatic form in della Croce, 'iuraui enim nemini me vnquam hic mei copiam facturum, vbi Leucippen amisi' (I7); bland modesty in Belleforest, 'ie suis de serme[n]t de ne me mesler, ou ioindre à femme qui viue ta[n]t que ie seray au lieu, où i'ay perdu ma chere Leucippe' (L3); compact directness in Burton, 'I sware when I lost *Leucippe*, that heere neuer any shoulde haue my Uirginitie' (N1v); and social decorum in Hodges, 'I have solemnly vowed not to marry any other in that place where I have lost my Leucippe' (K5).

Just as Kleitophon begins to enjoy Melite's affection, Leukippe is abruptly reintroduced. Kleitophon and Melite tour the estates, when 'suddenly a woman threw herself at our feet! She had heavy irons bound around her ankles, a workman's hoe in her hands, her head was shaved, her body was all grimy, her miserable clothing was hitched up for work [...] her back cruelly striped with welts' (5.17; Reardon, pp. 241–2). Unrecognisable, Leukippe is known as Lakaina, the name she was given by the pirates and which she retained when Melite's lecherous bailiff, Sosthenes, bought her from a merchant. She sends Kleitophon a note begging him to purchase her freedom. Their letters are quoted verbatim to heighten a sense of historicity and add dramatic irony. For Kleitophon's reassurance that he has 'imitated your virginity' (5.20; Reardon, 244) is about to be compromised.

Kleitophon's chance encounter with Leukippe occurs on the day he has agreed to marry Melite. One surprise follows another. The brutal Ther-sandros returns, and beats and shackles Kleitophon. Melite finds Leukip-pe's letter. Chagrined at being accused as an adulteress, Meilite promises to free both Leukippe and Kleitophon, provided he fulfills the rites of love (5.26).

Quite apart from purchasing freedom, Kleitophon gives two reasons for consenting to have sex with Melite. The first is that 'I was genuinely afraid that the god Love might exact a terrible vengeance' – in della Croce, 'atque, vt ingenue fatear, ne mihi Amor irasceretur, extimui' (L3). Secondly, he pitiably sees it as 'a remedy for an ailing soul. So when she embraced me, I did not hold back; when our limbs drew close, I did not refuse to touch. Everything happened as Love willed' (5.27; Reardon, p. 249).

The narrator-rhetor Kleitophon's perception of being physically encapsulated by Melite is emphasised through the figure polyptoton, in a series of lengthy words starting with 'περι' – 'around' or 'about'. The music of 'περιβαλλούσης [...] περιπλελομένης [...] περιπλολὰς' is represented in Gaselee's 'I made no attempt therefore to escape from her *encircling* arms, and when she *embraced* me closer I did not resist her *embraces*' (Gaselee, 5.27). Della Croce's close rendering reinforces their physical intertwining through complex verbal repetition: 'sed ta[n]tum aegrotantis animi quasi medicina quaedam. amplexantem igitur deosculantemq[ue]; pari amplexu, deosculationeque accepi' (L3) – but he omits the final reference to the influence of Eros's dominant will.

Belleforest emphasises by variation that what happens between Kleitophon and Melite is strictly a curative for her soul: 'vne medecine q[ue] ie luy donnoy pour alleger son ame co[m]me si elle eut esté languissante, & malade' (N2), a metaphor that Burton drops. Belleforest's triplet version of the embrace contains a courtly, stylised element of internal rhythm, assonance, consonance and rhyme: 'Elle donc m'e[m]brassant ie la tenoy estroiteme[n]t serrée sans resister à ses baisers, embrassements, ny caresses' (N2). Burton simplifies the sustained erotica: 'wherefore I embraced and kissed her againe' (P1). But for all his evasiveness, Burton returns word for word to della Croce's 'haud ita multo post desiderii eius expectationem omnem expleui' (L3) for his closing remark, 'and not long after, I fulfilled all the expectation of her long desire'. By contrast, Belleforest's rendering makes Kleitophon seem far more clinically detached: '& feis tout ce qu'il pleut à l'amour que i'executasse pour son seruice' (N2).

Hodges engages in radical truncation of the erotic, but changes the tone by introducing a note of cavalier libertinism. No trace of Kleitophon's moral dilemma remains in his anodyne précis: 'Beeing set at libertie, and well weighing with my selfe, that I was not to marrie her, but bee her Physitian as it were. I was afraid that CUPID should bee offended with mee, and therefore consented' (M1v–M2). Hodges even omits Achilles Tatius's playful ending, consisting of light-hearted clichés: 'We had no need of bedding or of any of Aphrodite's accoutrements' (5.27; Reardon, p. 249). Della Croce's concise representation, 'neque alium vllum ad venerem apparatum requirentibus' (L3), is partially paraphrased in Belleforest's extended version, 'sans qu'elle ny moy eussions soucy de chercher lict, ny autre lieu proper pour le deduit & plaisir de Venus' (N2), and in Burton's 'we neither had bed, nor any other such preparation which is required for such matter' (P1).

His debt paid, Kleitophon blurts out, 'Now grant me a safe escape and keep your promises about Leukippe' (6.1). As he bolts down the crowd-filled streets thinly disguised in Melite's clothes, he runs straight into Thersandros. Sosthenes has been cultivating Thersandros's passion for Leukippe, and he is about to erupt into violence.

Both principal and secondary characters now experience such abruptly changing circumstances that at times their personalities more closely resemble Theophrastan archetypes than psychologically developing humans: 'Charm, elegance, and utter diversity are the goals: the story and characters, though consistently developed, are just an occasion'.[68] The hope of reunion that Leukippe and Kleitophon repeatedly enunciate, and to which they cling, is suspended until the very end of the story. Only at that moment is Leukippe, by now a symbol of virtue, reprieved from a sentence of sexual slavery by passing a virginity test. At last, Kleitophon reports with relief, they are free to marry, the intention from the outset of their long and varied journey.

The trial and conclusion

The trial scene in Books 7 and 8, the final quarter of the novel, knits together the strands of the story. It brings to fruition the allegories of the divinely approved benefits of virtuous behaviour and chastity, and the humiliation of brutal male tyrants. Predictably positive in its outcome, suspense is achieved through the convincing manner in which the complications unfold. Della Croce's full version, well represented by Hodges, suffers from omissions in Burton that simplify the moral perspective.

Thersandros has Kleitophon imprisoned, accuses Kleitophon and Melite of Leukippe's murder, and Kleitophon of killing Sosthenes. Kleinias defends Kleitophon, alluding to his rejection of Melite's marriage proposals (and reiterating Kleitophon's vow of chaste fidelity at 5.12): 'Kleitophon had no such feeling and strongly rejected the marriage' (7.9; Reardon, p. 264). Della Croce is clear about the futility of Melite's appeals, and makes Kleinias emphasise Kleitophon's revulsion: 'Hic vero non modo impotenti mulieris amori non respondebat, sed etiam a nuptiis quam longissime abhorrebat' (N4v–N5). The expansive Bellefo-rest adds reinforcing innuendo and variations in 'cest adolescent, ne se plaisant de telle acointance, & moins de la rage amoureuse de ceste dame, refusa tout à plat, & hardime[n]t de se marier, & faire nopces auec elle' (P8–P8v). As a prelude to his simplification of Book 8, Burton reduces both complexity and exemplary rhetorical sophistication by omitting this particular statement (R8). Hodges's genteel version softens Kleitophon's rebuffs. Consistent with his condemnation of female sexuality, young Hodges gives Melite the aura of a harlot: 'but this young man was so farre from consenting to her unchaste love, that he would by no meanes bee inticed to marry her' (P1).

Kleitophon is convicted, but 'At the moment when my arms had been tied and the clothes had been stripped from my body and I was hanging in the air on ropes and the torturers were bringing on the whips and fire and rack' (7.12; Reardon, p. 267), proceedings unexpectedly halt for a ceremony honouring Artemis. Kleitophon, narrating, recalls how Leukippe's father, Sostratos, leads 'an embassy to the goddess'. In a vision, Artemis 'indicated that he would find his daughter in Ephesos and his brother's son as well' (7.12; Reardon, p. 267). This completes Artemis's first intervention, where she encouraged Leukippe to 'remain a virgin until I myself give you away as a bride', and promised that 'No one but Kleitophon will marry you' (4.1; Reardon, p. 222). Leukippe now escapes and finds sanctuary in the temple of Artemis, the icon of virginity for which Ephesus was renowned. There she is reunited with Kleitophon and her father.

In Book 8, the last in the novel, Kleitophon provides Sostratos with an almost full account of their adventures – a summary for readers that begins with the formulaic verification of identity: 'Sostratus is my name, Byzantine by birth, uncle to this man, father to this woman' (8.4; Reardon, p. 271). He acknowledges to the traveller that he 'omitted only one scene from my synopsis, the fact that I subsequently discharged my obligation to Melite' (8.5; Reardon, p. 271). By this admission, Achilles Tatius validates the historical accuracy of Kleitophon's narrative, which, because the action of the plot remains incomplete, is chronologically the latest action of the novel.

Achilles Tatius accentuates the unfairness of Egyptian society's indiscriminate privileging of powerful males. But Burton omits from 8.5 Della Croce's 'sed ipsi potius quae inter piratas etiam integram se castamque seruauit, & piratarum omnium maximi Thersandri scilicet inuerecundi, atque audacis violentiae restitit' (O4v). This is not inappropriately translated by Hodges, 'but her, who kept her selfe chast amongst pirates, and withstood the violence of that impudent and immodest slave *Thersander*, whose assaults were worse then any shee received from them' (Q2). And it is expanded and exaggerated in Belleforest's semi-tautological variants and additions, 'mais c'est à elle qu'en est deu l'auantage, qui a gardé sa virginité au milieu des pirates & corsaires, & a resisté à la violence de Thersandre plus effronté, sale & audacieux & iniurieux que pas vn de ceux qui escume[n]t la marine' (R2). By reducing this portrayal of Leukippe's emotional and rhetorical strengths under conditions of the worst possible adversity, Burton dilutes the impact of social criticism in the novel.

The priest describes the legendary virginity test of the temple of Artemis. If a wrongly accused virgin enters the temple, 'a delicate, ethereal melody is heard', and 'the doors of the cave open of their own accord' (8.6; Reardon, p. 273). If she is lying, there is a scream, she is locked in the cave, and after three days will be found to have disappeared. The priest, underestimating Leukippe's stamina, offers no hope: 'a girl trapped in such toils, no matter how she resists, is all too likely to have been –' (8.6; Reardon, p. 273).

Leukippe, since her conversion from a lusting teenager to the epitome of chastity, has become the model erotic romance heroine. She finds the priest's negative stereotyping overbearing, and intervenes: 'Well *I* think you can stop right there! I'm quite prepared to walk into the cave of the syrinx and to be shut up in it' (8.7; Reardon, p. 273). The strength of her personality varies from one translator to the other. Belleforest's version of Della Croce's 'Atqui quod ad me, inquit, attinet, ne sollicitus sis, ego enim fistulae antrum prompte ingrediar' (O7) retains essential detail and also conveys the feisty tone of Leukippe's riposte: 'Ne soyez point en soucy de ce qui me touche, car i'entreray en la grotte auec asseurance' (R4v). Her venom, however, is suppressed in Burton's 'Doo not you (said she) take care for me, for I will very willingly descend therein' (T2v). Hodges, while also reducing, borrows della Croce's diction. As a contrast to the priest's formal register, he devises a simpler naive response that accentuates Leukippe's self-assurance and uncorrupted youth: 'Be not so sollicitous for me, Sir, let me alone, I will gladly enter the cave' (Q4–Q4v).

The archetypal bully, Thersandros, accuses Kleitophon of murder, Leukippe of lying about retaining her virginity, and Melite of adultery. Their trials take place in the last few pages. Burton hastens his readers towards the conclusion, editing out substantial passages of Thersandros's forensic oratory, including his attacks on the priest, Melite and Leukippe.[69] But where, it could be argued, these deletions focus attention on the social and moral significance of chastity, Burton's extraordinary

---

69 The omissions correspond with the following passages in Reardon: 'when such people can determine the trial date [...] presidents and their counselors'; 'She alone has the right to rescue [...] yourself superior to Artemis;' and '"And with him an immoral woman [...]" With these words, he stopped' (8.8; Reardon, pp. 274–6).

addition to the text consciously injects a political message of considerable urgency: 'O most mightie prince, it behooueth you now to looke about you, and to suppresse these manifolde vices, which lately are growen vp in this common wealth' (T3v). Here Burton may be alluding to Edward Squire's plot to assassinate the Virgin Queen, Elizabeth I, in 1596.

During the course of his long narration, virtually the entire novel, Kleitophon has never questioned Leukippe's purity. Yet he and the readers know that, as Pan cannot be trusted, the virginity test may falsely condemn her. The pipes are heard in the midst of his prayer to Pan: 'As Leukippe ran out, the people gave a loud cry of joy and started abusing Thersandros' (8.14; Reardon, p. 281). By comparison, proving Melite's innocence is almost trivialised. Melite will be acquitted only if she 'has not celebrated the communion rites of Aphrodite with this stranger during the period of my absence' (8.11; Reardon, p. 279). Here Achilles Tatius reiterates his theme of the proximity of reality to illusion. For Melite and the readers already know that Thersandros returns before she has sex with Kleitophon. Nonethelesss, her emerging from the Styx reinforces the sudden reversal in her husband's fortunes: 'Thersandros had lost the second round', and is 'condemned to banishment *in absentia*' (8.15; Reardon, p. 281).

The stage finally set for the denouement, Leukippe describes her adventures. Her father, Sostratos, announces that the wild youth Kallisthenes, now a general, has won Kalligone through respect for her chastity. Kallisthenes has secured his support for their marriage.[70] Thersandros abandons his lawsuit and runs away.[71] Leukippe and Kleitophon marry in Byzantium, and then attend Kallisthenes and Kalligone's wedding in Tyre, where they spend the winter. This completes the narrative cycle. Kleitophon never explains why he is alone in a Sidon looking at a votive painting of Europa, and the narrator never asks.

Kleitophon finishes his story and, with it, the interweaving of two structural forms. For despite Kleitophon beginning *ab ovo*, the end of the narrative catches up with its beginning, in imitation of the cyclic first half of an epic structure. Throughout his novel, Achilles Tatius takes an overtly witty approach to theme and form. So deliberately to signal through this structure that his theme is sophisticated, but not of such epic proportions as to require a second half, is typical of his exquisitely crafted rhetorical legerdemain.

---

70 Burton omits Sostratus's 'I shall read you the statement [...] our acquittal' (8.18; Reardon, p. 284.)

71 Burton omits 'he had appealed the case [...] for his crimes'.(8.19; Reardon, p. 284.)

Conclusion

In this rhetorical exhibition-piece, with its overt penchant for ecphrasis and paradox, Achilles Tatius wears his sophist's skills lightly. Early modern translators into Latin, French and English just manage to preserve a semblance of the characteristic bitter sweetness unique to his tragicomic romance. Della Croce's conservatism, which becomes a Greco-Roman stylistic extravaganza in Belleforest's elegant French, is represented in a reserved and bowdlerised fashion by Burton, and softened into a naive love story by Hodges. But while admiring those areas of Achilles Tatius's rhetorical artistry that the limits of their training permit, these translators retain his lightly allegorised denunciation of domestic tyranny, while preferring to suppress his robust approach to sex and sexuality.

Achilles Tatius's *Leukippe and Kleitophon* presented Renaissance translators with an embarrassingly erotic romance, replete with issues of morality and social conscience. That they made such a determined effort to adjust the text into an idealisation of loyalty and chastity reveals the wide cultural influence of Amyot's translation of Heliodorus.

The Greek novel best suited to the Renaissance neoplatonic temperament, Heliodorus's *An Ethiopian Story*, offers a heightened sense of moral and political allegory coupled with idealised Plutarchan characterisation. While sharing Achilles Tatius's obsession with sensual and chaste affection, Heliodorus studiously elevates erotic love on to a neoplatonic plane of heroic adoration. His examples of tyrannical behaviour, more readily than those invented by Achilles Tatius, lend themselves to interpretation as metaphors for the state. And he demonstrates his higher seriousness by fully adopting an epic form.

4

Heliodorus's *An Ethiopian Story* – Theagenes and Charikleia

Charikliea: Royal Foundling

Heliodorus's complex account of the love, separation, loss and reunion of Theagenes and Charikleia may well be 'the longest comic plot in history'[1] (except, perhaps, Mary Sidney Wroth's). It underpins the themes of restoring usurped political and personal rights, of succession and civilising legal reform.

As in *Daphnis and Chloe* and *Leukippe and Kleitophon*, the denouement of *An Ethiopian Story* depends on delayed identification, followed by restitution of social status. Theagenes is a Greek prince and a priest; Charikleia a castaway foundling fostered by Charikles in Delphi, but really the daughter of the King and Queen of Ethiopia, and a priestess. In a novel where extra-marital sex drives much of the action, and moralistic characterisation is in the holistic Plutarchan mode, Theagenes and Charikleia's chaste, neoplatonic love sets them apart. Their intellectual and moral fibre is tested as they respond to a broad range of threatening experiences.

An Ethiopian Story contains Charikleia's biography from the moment of conception, literally *ab ovo*. In a work that begins *in medias res*, it is told through 'nine different sequences, at four different levels of narration, in five different voices besides the narrator's.'[2] Charikleia's life of alienation begins at birth. Ethiopia is a black society; Charikleia, a descendant of Perseus and Andromeda, is white. 'Convinced that your colour would lead to my being accused of adultery', her mother, Queen Persinna, tells King Hydaspes his baby has died. She abandons her nameless child 'by the roadside' (4.8; Reardon, p. 433). Persinna leaves tokens of recognition: distinctively jewelled necklaces, her engagement ring and a waistband on

---

1 N. J. Lowe, *The Classical Plot and the Invention of Western Narrative* (Cambridge: Cambridge University Press, 2000), p. 258.
2 N. J. Lowe, *The Classical Plot and the Invention of Western Narrative*, p. 254.

which she has embroidered the story of Charikleia's origins. This is in an esoteric 'Ethiopian script' of the 'royal kind' (4.8; Reardon, p. 432).

Sisimithres, who finds and fosters the baby, belongs to a select group of King Hydaspes' advisers, the 'all-wise' gymnosophists. His ability to read Persinna's script becomes significant in the final stages of the romance when, aged seventeen, Charikleia is reunited with her parents (10.13–14; cf. 10.9). Sisimithres gives his unnamed foundling a pastoral upbringing, but her beauty begins to attract attention. When she is seven, he takes her on an embassy to Egypt, setting off the romance process of displacement and defamiliarisation.

In Egypt, Sisimithres strikes up an acquaintance with Charikles, 'the priest of Pythian Apollo' (2.29; Reardon, p. 401) at Delphi, to whom he hands over Charikleia and Persinna's tokens. His political mission intervenes, and he is abruptly expelled before he can explain further, 'Because he told the satrap to keep his hands off the emerald mines, claiming that they belong to Ethiopia' (2.32; Reardon, p. 405). Under the care of Charikles at Delphi, Charikleia adopts her second foster-father's name, and becomes a priestess. She falls in love with Theagenes, a descendant of Achilles and leader of a sacred mission (3.5; Reardon, p. 414). They survive many dangerous interventions, marry and succeed to the throne of Ethiopia. White leaders of a black society, they revive the pre-historic myth of the Greek and Ethiopian dynasty of Perseus and Andromeda.

An Ethiopian Story is, indirectly, a political allegory. By allying Ethiopia to Greece through Chariklea's marriage to Theagenes, Heliodorus promotes the rehellenising of the Roman colonies. But he takes care to distinguish between the restoration of social, political and cultural values and futile rebellion. In the conclusion, a colonised Ethiopia wins a military victory over the Persians, and Ethiopia regains possession of its emerald mines. But once he has freed Ethiopia from foreign tyanny and restored regional independence, Charikleia's father, King Hydaspes, diplomatically concedes continuing payment of tribute to the superior power of Persia.

Writing in Greek under Roman rule, Heliodorus uses his plot to promote the philhellene aspiration of restoring Greek social, cultural and political values to the occupied colonies. His principal weapon as a sophist is his controlled rhetorical style. He couches his tragicomic erotic romance in an elegant artistic prose. The narrative is characterised by lengthy periodic sentences, in 'an intricate pattern of balance and rhyme. The style is florid and artificial, but exuberant and alive, employed with a zest and love of words […] The vocabulary is wide and highly nuanced'.[3]

3 J. R. Morgan, in Reardon, p. 351.

During the 1930s, when Greco-Roman rhetorical sophistication was held in low esteem, Maillon roundly condemned Heliodorus's writing as static and mechanical. Nonetheless, his criticisms reveal areas that pose difficulties for translators. Compared with 'the divine simplicity' of his Homeric model, Heliodorus reflects 'the bad taste of an epoch of decadence'. This dictates the use of 'over-subtle phrases with laborious symmetry, […] far-fetched expressions, a difficult syntax'. The restrained narrative style is praiseworthy, but when 'Heliodorus launches into lyrical monologue or discourse, the tone becomes pompous. He appears to caricature the beautiful and noble monodies of the Greek theatre'.[4]

Such criticism is not entirely unjustified. Theagenes' lament over Thisbe's corpse, which he believes to be Charikleia's, opens with a punning allusion to the dramatic style he adopts to summarise the past: 'Theagenes cried aloud in tragic sorrow' ('τραγικόν τι καὶ γοερὸν ὁ Θεαγένης') –

> Pain beyond enduring! Horror wrought by heaven's curse! […] exile from our homeland, exposing us to peril on the sea, peril in pirate lairs, throwing us upon the tender mercies of brigands, and more than once robbing us of all we had? […] Charikleia is dead; my beloved has fallen victim to an enemy's hand […] protecting her chastity and keeping herself for me. For me! (2.4; Reardon, pp. 380–1)

In their sincerity, Theagenes' histrionics differ from Achilles Tatius's brief parody of stage drama in Kleitophon's outpouring of grief over Leukippe's bier (3.16). Nonetheless, both romance heroes open with an exclamatory apostrophe, followed by a list of clauses summarising past action. Sidney reproduces this formula in Amphialus's anaphora-filled self-condemnation in the *New Arcadia*:

> O Amphialus! Wretched Amphialus! Thou has lived to be the death of thy most dear companion and friend, Philoxenus, and of his father, thy most careful foster-father. Thou hast lived to kill a lady with thine own hands – and so excellent and virtuous a lady as the fair Parthenia was. Thou hast lived to see thy faithful Ismenus slain in succouring thee – and thou not able to defend him. Thou hast lived to show thyself such a coward […].[5]

4 J. Maillon, Préface de Traducteur, in Héliodore, *Les Éthiopiques*, ed. by R. M. Rattenbury and T. W. Lumb, trans. by J. Maillon, 3 vols., 2nd edn (Paris: Société d'Édition 'Les Belles Lettres', 1960), i.xcii: 'la divine simplicité de son modèle. Le mauvais goût d'une époque de décadence lui dicte des phrases alambiquées, d'une symétrie laborieuse, lui impose des locutions recherchées, une syntaxe difficile […] Mais, toutes les fois qu'Héliodore se lance dans le monologue lyrique ou le discours, le ton devient pompeux. Il a l'air de faire la caricature des belles et nobles monodies du théâtre grec'. The first edition was published in Paris: Budé, 1935–43.
5 Sir P. Sidney, *The Countess of Pembroke's Arcadia (The New Arcadia)*, ed. by V. Skretkowicz (Oxford: Clarendon Press, 1987), p. 441, hereafter referred to as *NA*.

It is worth noting how easily Maillon's denunciation of Heliodorus's stylistic 'bad taste' and 'affectation' could also describe stylistic features in the sophistic erotic romances of Sidney, Shakespeare and Sidney Wroth.

Renaissance continental translations and philhellene politics

To Renaissance translators, the devotion, self-governance, ethics and morality of Theagenes and Chariklea, coupled with the exemplary kingship of Hydaspes, epitomise the qualities of the ideal representative monarch. Read as a parable illustrating good and evil behaviour, in France *An Ethiopian Story* was presented as a courtesy book and handbook of rhetorical style. In England, first published as a personal compliment to the young Earl of Oxford, it subsequently took the form of an admonition to Charles I, who suspended Parliament from 1629 to 1640.

Known in Eastern Europe in manuscript, the full Greek text of *An Ethiopian Story* was edited by Vincentus Obsopoeus or Opsopaeus from an early fifteenth-century manuscript.[6] The first edition was published in 1534 at Basel, Switzerland, by Johannes Herwagen, whose press would publish della Croce's translation of Achilles Tatius in 1554. In 1534, Basel, which espoused Protestantism in 1529, adopted the reformist Confession of Basel.

Obsopaeus's dedication of 26 June 1531 is addressed from Ansbach to the senators of the Republic of Nuremberg, 25 miles to the north-east in Protestant Bavaria. Anticipating Amyot, he initiates a tradition of praising Heliodorus's artistic complexity and model characters. In this work, readers will find that 'omnium humanorum affectuum absolutissimam quandam imaginem [...] & co[n]iugalis amoris ac fidei, & constantiae pulcherrimum exemplar in Theagene & Chariclia adu[m]brauit'[7] – translated in Nahum Tate's edition as 'the most absolute Image of all humane Affections; a perfect Example of Conjugal Love, Truth and Constancy being wonderfully drawn in the Characters of *Theagenes* and *Chariclea*'.[8]

6 Bayerische Staatsbibliothek, Munich, MS Monacensis Greaca 157.
7 *Heliodori Historiae Aethiopicae libri decem, nunquam antea in lucem editi. Basileae ex officina Hervagiana an. M.D.XXX IIII Mense Februario*, a2. See V. Skretkowicz, 'Sidney and Amyot: Heliodorus in the Structure and Ethos of the *New Arcadia*', *Review of English Studies*, n.s., xxvii (1976), 170–4, and M. A. Doody, *The True Story of the Novel* (New Brunswick, NJ: Rutgers University Press, 1996; repr. London: Fontana Press, 1998), pp. 234–5, and notes. Original texts can be viewed on the Internet via The Kadmos Project, University of Basel (www.ub.unibas.ch/kadmos).
8 *The Aethiopian History Of Heliodorus. In Ten Books. The First Five Translated by a Person of Quality, The Last Five by N. Tate*. (1685), a1v; reprinted as *The Triumphs Of Love And Constancy: A Romance. Containing the Heroick Amours of Theagenes and Chariclea* (1687), a1v.

In an implied comparison with other fictional narratives, Obsopaeus brings to the senators' attention that this story is of greater value to all. It sets out not only seeming antiquity for us, but the entire life of most of us: 'Atqui ijs omnibus multo pretiosior est historia, quae non unam aliquam nobis antiquitatem uidendam exhibet, sed maiorum nostrorum uitam omnem'. His examples of Heliodorus's social and political observations, 'multoru[m] populoru[m] mores, ritus, instituta, ciuitates, uarias Reipublicae formas [...]' (a3v) – 'the customs, rites, institutions, cities, various forms of republics of many nations', provide models of both good and tyrannical governance.

Obsopaeus's tribute to the philhellene principles of Swiss and German Protestant republicanism initiated the Renaissance European convention of interpreting erotic romance as an allegory of political harmony. His observations are cited in Stanislaus Warschewiczki's conservative Latin translation from the Greek, *Heliodori Aethiopicae Historiae libri decem*. Like Obsopoeus's edition, Warschewiczki's volume emanated from Basel, where it was published by Johann Oporin in January 1552 (colophon).

Warschewiczki, a young Polish nobleman, addressed his dedication of 21 July 1551 to King Sigismund II Augustus of Poland, who ruled from 1548 to 1572.[9] During 1551–52, Sigismund was steering his way through a conflict between the Catholic bishops; the Catholic upper house of parliament (which he supported); the lower house of democratising Protestant gentry; and the substantial Greek Orthodox community. Much more than Obsopaeus, Warschewiczki thoroughly politicises Heliodorus, using his model of kingship as a propagandist icon. Hoping Sigismund will exercise tolerance towards his enemies, Warschewiczki emphasises King Hydaspes' courage, justice, clemency and compassion towards his subjects – 'laus fortitudinis, sed etiam iustitiae, clementi[a]e, & pietatis erga subditos tribuiter' (a3v).[10]

Warschewiczki's translation is further politicised through Philip Melanchthon's prefatory epistle to his dearest friend, Oporin, dated 20 April 1551 (a4).[11] Once Luther's assistant in Wittenberg, Melanchthon (1497–1560) advocated tolerance and good works, inspired by faith. Among his students were Philip Sidney's friend in Padua, Matthäus Delius of Wittenberg; and, from the previous generation, Sidney's correspon-

---

9 Warschewiczki's dedication is reproduced at www.ub.unibas.ch/kadmos/gg/pic/gg0253 _002_vor.htm.
10 This translation differs from that in M. A. Doody, *The True Story of the Novel*, p. 239.
11 Melanchthon's epistle is reproduced at www.ub.unibas.ch/kadmos/gg/pic/gg0253_006_ vor.htm.

dents Johannes Crato von Crafftheim (physician to the imperial court in Vienna); Charles de L'Ecluse (the imperial botanist); Andreas Paull, counsellor to the elector of Saxony; the theologian Zacharias Ursinus of Heidelberg; and Sidney's mentor, Hubert Languet.[12]

Melanchthon's blessing increased the significance of Warschewiczki's edition, and *An Ethiopian Story*, to generations of philhellene Protestants. It may have helped persuade Sigismund and the Polish Diet to grant Protestants freedom of worship in 1555, rescinded by the end of the century as Poland succumbed to Jesuit-led control.[13] Further editions appeared in Calvinist enclaves in Belgium, Antwerp (1556) and Ursel (1601). It became the European standard text and the preferred vehicle for rendering Heliodorus into the vernacular.

In 1596, the Heidelberg publisher Hieronymus Commelinus, who died before completing his edition of Achilles Tatius, published Warschewiczki's Latin alongside his own improved Greek text of Heliodorus. Commelinus emends the 1534 Obsopoeus–Herwagen transcription from four manuscripts.[14] Continuing the Protestant tradition of politicising this text, he dedicates it to Georgio Michaeli Lingelshemio, 'Serenissimi Principis Palat. Electoris Consiliario Intimo' – personal counsellor of the most serene Prince, the Elector Palatine. The dedication is followed by a verse tribute to Heliodorus, 'In Heliodorum', by Janus Gruter (¶3), to whom the 1601 Commelinus *Leukippe and Kleitophon* was dedicated. Then comes the critique cited by William Burton, 'De Heliodoro Iudicium' (¶3v–¶6), by Martin Kraus (Martinus Crusius), author of the Greek teaching text, *Martini Crusii Aethiopicae Heliodori Historiae Epitome* (Francofurti: Johann Wechel, 1584).

Commelinus's often reprinted parallel Greek and Latin edition set the textual standard until the end of the eighteenth century, and made Heliodorus a permanent fixture in philhellene Protestant culture. Further emendations to the Greek were introduced by Johannes Bourdelotius in

12 Further details, and translations of Sidney's correspondence, are in J. M. Osborn, *Young Philip Sidney 1572–1577* (New Haven: Yale University Press, 1972), and B. Nicollier-de Weck, *Hubert Languet 1518–1581: un réseau politique international de Melancthon à Guillaume d'Orange* (Geneva: Droz, 1995). See also J. Buxton, *Sir Philip Sidney and the English Renaissance*, 2nd edn (London: Macmillan, 1964), p. 60.

13 R. S. Dunn, *The Age of Religious Wars, 1559–1715*, 2nd edn (New York: W. W. Norton, 1979), p. 74.

14 ¶2v, principally Biblioteca Apostolica Vaticana MS Palatinus Graecus 125, indicated on the title-page: Ἡλιοδώρου Αἰθιωπικων Βιβλια δεκα. *Heliodori Aethiopicorum libri X. Collatione MSS. Bibliothecae Palatinae & aliorum, emendati & multis in locis aucti*, Hieronymi *Commelini opera* (Heidelberg, 1596); cf. Héliodore, *Les Éthiopiques*, ed. by R. M. Rattenbury and T. W. Lumb, trans. by J. Maillon, i.xxv, xlvii–xlviii.

the 1619 Paris edition,[15] with commentary, from which Warschewiczki is cited in this study. Bourdelotius, who held high office in the court of Marie de Médicis, second wife and widow of Henri IV of France, and mother of Louis XIII, associates himself with Huguenot sympathisers by dedicating this volume in March 1619 to Louis XIII's Treasurer, Thomas Morand, Duc du Mesnil-Garnier (a2).

Jacques Amyot also based his edition on Obsopoeus's text.[16] He published this anonymously as *L'histoire aethiopique de Heliodorus, contenant dix livres traitant des loyales et pudiques amours de Theagenes thessalien et Chariclea aethiopie[n]ne, nouuellement traduite de grec en françoys* [trans. by Jacques Amyot] (Paris: [par Estienne Groulleau,] 1547 [i.e., 1548]) – 'Heliodorus's Ethiopian Story, containing ten books treating the loyal and chaste loves of Theagenes of Thessalia, and Charikleia of Ethiopia'. Adopting Heliodorus as royalist propaganda, this volume was published in Paris on 15 February 1548. This was just under a year after Henri II's accession, on 31 March 1547, brought his Italian-speaking queen, Catherine de Médicis, to the centre of power.

Amyot's Heliodorus, representing Perseus's rescue of Andromeda through the characters of Theagenes and Charikleia, parallels other politicised compliments to Catherine's family. Piero di Cosimo's painting of Perseus freeing Andromeda (1513) allegorises the liberation of Florence from the republicans in 1512 by Catherine's great uncle, Giuliano de Médicis (1479–1516).[17] At the banquet celebrating the royal entry into Paris in 1571, Catherine's son, the new king, Charles IX, was represented as Perseus in a sugar sculpture.[18] And in 1582, a pageant in Antwerp welcomed Catherine's fourth son, François Hercule, Duc d'Anjou (1554–84), as Perseus come 'to deliver that country from all tyranny, and afterward govern it by Justice and Reason'.[19]

In 1559 Amyot issued a corrected revision of Heliodorus, *L'histoire aethiopique de Heliodorus, contenant dix livres, traitant des loyales et pudi-*

15 Heliodorus, Ἡλιοδώρου Αἰθιωπικῶν Βιβλία δεκα. *Heliodori Aethiopicorum libri X. Io.Bourdelotius emendauit suppleuit, ac libros decem Animaduersionum adiecit* (Paris, 1619).

16 See L. Plazenet, 'Jacques Amyot and the Greek Novel: The Invention of the French Novel', in *The Classical Heritage in France*, ed. by G. N. Sandy (Leiden: E. J. Brill, 2002), p. 244.

17 Catalogue of the Uffizi Gallery, Florence, at www.arca.net/uffizi1/artista1.asp.

18 F. A. Yates, *Astraea: The Imperial Theme in the Sixteenth Century* (London: Routledge and Kegan Paul, 1975; rev. edn, Harmondsworth: Penguin Books, 1977), p. 144.

19 G. Kipling, *The Triumph of Honour: Burgundian Origins of the Elizabethan Renaissance* (Leiden: Leiden University Press, 1977), p. 166, citing R. Holinshed, *Chronicles*, ed. by H. Ellis, 6 vols (London, 1807–8), iv.471.

*ques amours de Theagenes Thessalien, & Chariclea Aethiopienne. Traduite
de Grec en François, & de nouueau reueüe et corrigée sur un ancien exem-
plaire escript à la main, par le translateur, ou est declaré au vray qui en a esté
le premier autheur* (Paris: Vincent Sertenas, 1559).[20] This often reprinted
edition was licensed on 9 September,[21] two months after 10 July, when
the fifteen-year-old minor, François II, succeeded his father. Catherine's
Florentine court[22] began its thirty-year domination of France, and prob-
ably derived greater enjoyment from Leonardo Ghini's 1556 translation
of Heliodorus from Greek into Tuscan Italian. This volume was dedi-
cated to Conte Michele de la Torre, Vescovo di Ceneda, and reprinted in
1559/60.[23] In 1559, Amyot also published Plutarch's *Les vies des hommes
illustres Grecs, & Romains* and (anonymously) *Les amours pastorales de
Daphnis et Chloe.*

A committed royalist, Amyot uses Heliodorus's text to represent his
nationalist, linguistic and rhetorical aspirations for the French court. He
reinvents Heliodorus's style to satisfy his readership's expectations of neo-
classicism, overlaying it with the rhythmic elegance that permeates his
translations from Greek, and which characterises his *'style royal'*. Amyot's
expansive neo-classical rendering was not universally applauded. In
Historia de los dos leales amantes Theagenes y Chariclea (Alcala, 1587),
Fernando de Mena, who translated Warschewiczki's Latin, criticises the

20 Quotations are from this edition, for which Amyot used MS Vaticanus Graecus 157 and
    Venutus (Venice) Marcianus MS Graecus 409, which contains *Leukippe and Kleitophon*
    and Books 1–3 of *An Ethiopian Story* (cf. *Achilles Tatius. Leucippe and Clitophon*, ed. by
    E. Vilborg (Stockholm: Almquist and Wiksell, 1955), pp. xx–xxi). Amyot's annotations
    are also in Bibliothèque Sainte-Geneviève, Paris, MS Y. 4o. 573, a copy of Marcianus MS
    Graecus 409; cf. Héliodore, *Les Éthiopiques*, ed. by R. M. Rattenbury and T. W. Lumb,
    trans. by J. Maillon, i.xxiv, xxvi, lxvi–lxviii. Evidence that Amyot did not authorise the
    1549 edition is in L. Plazenet, 'Jacques Amyot and the Greek Novel: The Invention of the
    French Novel', pp. 242–3.
21 L. Plazenet, 'Jacques Amyot and the Greek Novel: The Invention of the French Novel',
    pp. 239, 243–5; T. Hägg, *The Novel in Antiquity* (Oxford: Basil Blackwell, 1983), p. 192;
    R. Aulotte, *Amyot et Plutarque: La tradition des Moralia au XVIe siècle* (Geneva: Librairie
    Droz, 1965), p. 157. M. A. Doody, *The True Story of the Novel*, pp. 233–43, and notes,
    provides an account of 'Heliodorus in Print' with extracts from the translators' prefaces.
    G. N. Sandy, 'Jacques Amyot and the Manuscript Tradition of Heliodorus' *Aethiopica*',
    Revue d'Histoire des Textes, xiv–xv (1984–85), 1–22, discusses textual variants added
    by Amyot to his personal copy of Obsopaeus from an unidentifiable manuscript. An
    edition of Amyot's translation is being prepared by L. Plazenet.
22 See De L. Jensen, 'Catherine de Medici and Her Florentine Friends', *Sixteenth Century
    Journal*, ix (1978), 57–74.
23 *Historia di Heliodoro delle cose Ethiopiche. Nella quale fra diuersi, compassioneuoli aueni-
    menti di due Amanti, si contengono abbattimenti, discrittioni di paesi, e molte altre cose
    utile e diletteuoli a leggere. Tradotta dalla lingua Greca nella Thoscana da Messer Leon-
    ardo Ghini. In Vinegia appresso Gabriele Giolito De' Ferrari, 1556.*

anonymous translator of *Historia Ethiopica* (Anvers [Antwerp], 1554) for following Amyot's ornate style, thereby corrupting the natural beauty of Spanish.[24]

Despite the misgivings of purists, in 1548 Amyot was in the vanguard of a complex debate about plain and ornate style. This raged within the French court, the judiciary and the various interest groups of the Catholic Church well into the seventeenth century.[25] But so successful were Amyot's efforts at rhetorical reform that he not only established the orientation of courtly language – 'l'orientation du "langage de Cour"'.[26] He also, through his translations of Plutarch, remained the principal teacher of parliamentary style – 'le principal maître du "style de Parlement"' – from around 1570 till at least 1630.

Sanford's *Historie of Chariclia and Theagenes*

The first English appearance of *An Ethiopian Story* was in James Sanford[27] or Sandford's *The Amorous and Tragicall Tales of Plutarch. Wherevnto is annexed the Hystorie of Cariclea & Theagenes, and the sayings of the Greeke Philosophers* (1567). Sanford dedicated this volume to the philhellene Protestant Huguenot supporter Sir Hugh Paulet.[28] In 1562, Paulet became adviser to Philip Sidney's uncle, Ambrose Dudley, Earl of Warwick, in his command of Le Havre. Sanford identifies Sir Hugh as one who measures faith by good works, and absence of faith by idleness and lust, which he associates with pastoral existence:

> thys particular vice Lawlesse lust, […] the which aryseth and taketh hys begynning of Idlenesse […] There is nothyng which causeth a ma[n] more to degenerate from his kind than this, for it doth make him rather to resemble Beastes, than creatures endowed with reason. Wherfore the Poets

24 The 1554 Antwerp *Historia Ethiopica* from Amyot's French claims to have been corrected from the Greek: 'Trasladada de Frances en vulgar Castellano por un segreto amigo de su patria corrigida segun el Griego'. De Mena's 1587 translation is reprinted in Heliodorus, *Historia Etiópica de los Amores de Téagenes y Cariclea*, traducida por Fernando de Mena, Edicion y Prologo de F. Lopez Estrada, Biblioteca Selecta de Clássicos Españoles, ser. II, xiv (Madrid: Real Academia Española, 1954), pp. xi–xiii. See also L. Plazenet, 'Jacques Amyot and the Greek Novel: The Invention of the French Novel', p. 251.

25 See M. Fumaroli, *L'âge de l'éloquence: Rhétorique et 'res literaria' de la Renaissance au seuil de l'époque classique* (Geneva: Librairie Droz, 1980).

26 M. Fumaroli, *L'âge de l'éloquence: Rhétorique et 'res literaria' de la Renaissance au seuil de l'époque classique*, p. 444.

27 See V. Salmon, 'Sanford, James (*fl.* 1567–1582)', *Oxford Dictionary of National Biography* (Oxford: Oxford University Press, 2004).

28 See C. S. L. Davies, 'Paulet, Sir Hugh (*b.* before 1510, *d.* 1573)', *Oxford Dictionary of National Biography* (Oxford: Oxford University Press, 2004).

not without a cause haue painted out & described Loue like a Shephierde,
signifying therby, that whoso followeth sensualitie, and inordinate desire of
the flesh, are more like beasts than men. (A2–A2v)

Sanford advertises that his tales deal with the tragic 'fruites which spring
of hote Loue and fleshly lust' (A3v), including murder and revenge. But
one story in particular overtly exemplifies the Huguenot virtues of polit-
ical consciousness, self-sacrifice and stoicism. This is encapsulated in its
title, 'Of a man who was iniustly exiled, and how his wife bicause she was
destitute of all helpe and succour, slewe both hir selfe and hir daughters'
(B5v).

Alcippus, a maligned altruist, who 'had very greate consideration and
regarde to the Citie, and did such things, as hee perceiued to be profit-
able for the common wealth, moued all mens hatred towards him, which
maintained and nourished all naughtinesse & wyckednesse in the weale
publike' (B5v). He is banished, his wife Damocrita left penniless, and his
daughters forbidden to marry. The night before a sacrificial ceremony,
Damocrita sets fire to the assembly hall, killing herself and her daugh-
ters, thereby depriving the nobles of the targets of 'their wrath and anger'
(B6v). In an echo of Melanchthon, Sanford advises Paulet, 'We oughte
to take ALCIPPVS as a true paterne and example to imitate, […] but
alwayes perseuer in goodnesse, seeking after such things as are auaileable
for the common Weale, in so doing we liuing shall not onely haue great
honor, […] but dying shall merite and obtayne immortall fame' (Aiiii).

The bulk of Sanford's little book consists of 'The Historie of Chari-
clia and Theagenes Gathered for the most part out of Heliodorus a
Greeke Authour' (B7). Working from Warschewiczki's Latin, Sanford
paraphrases Book 4, in which Kalasiris, an exiled Egyptian priest, tells
Knemon how Theagenes and Charikleia fall in love. Charikleia becomes
seriously ill when her foster-father, Charikles, arranges her marriage
to his nephew, Alkamenes. Sanford bypasses critical essentials, such as
Kalasiris persuading Charikles to lend him 'the band that you said was
abandoned with the child' (4.7; Reardon, p. 431), and his interpretation of
Charikleia's embroidered tokens of identification. By omitting Charikleia's
early history, and replacing dialogue with third-person narrative, Sanford
alters this episode into a tale of exemplary love.

Underdowne's *An Aethiopian Historie*

In 1569, Sanford dedicated *Henrie Cornelius Agrippa, of the Vanitie and
vncertaintie of Artes and Sciences* to Leicester's powerful colleague, Thomas

Howard (1536–72), fourth Duke of Norfolk. In the same year, Thomas
Underdowne published his full translation of Warschewiczki's Latin, *An
Aethiopian Historie written in Greeke by Heliodorus: very wittie and pleas-
aunt* (1569).[29] Describing himself as 'not knowen to your Honour' (¶2v),
Underdowne dedicates his work to Edward de Vere (1550–1604), seven-
teenth Earl of Oxford. Oxford had succeeded his father, John, sixteenth
Earl, to the post of Lord Great Chamberlain in 1562. Accompanied by his
Calvinist uncle, Arthur Golding, Oxford became a royal ward in William
Cecil's moderate Protestant household, and on 19 December 1571 disas-
trously married Cecil's daughter, Anne. Under Cecil, Oxford grew to
oppose militant Protestants, including the Earls of Leicester, Pembroke,
Essex, and the Sidneys, with whom his uncle, Golding, aligned himself.
In 1567, Golding dedicated his translation of Ovid's *Metamorphoses* to
Cecil's rival, Robert Dudley, Earl of Leicester. It may be this Leicester–
Cecil opposition that Underdowne represents in his dedication to Oxford,
where he associates administrative weakness with scholarly philhellenes,
and political astuteness with 'Romans':

> The Greekes in all manner of knowledge, and Learninge, did farre
> surmounte the Romanes, but the Romanes in administringe their state,
> in warlike factes, and in common sense were muche their Superiours: for
> the Greekes were wedded to theire learninge alone, the Romanes content
> with a mediocritie [that is, 'a middle way'], applied them selues to greater
> thinges. (¶2–¶2v)

Underdowne takes the prevalent Renaissance view that the subject best
suited to the acquisition of balanced learning is history. And this, in
his opinion, is the genre to which *An Ethiopian Story* belongs: 'Now of
all knowledge fitte for a Noble Gentelman, I suppose the knowledge of
Histories is moste seeminge. For furtheringe wherof, I haue Englished a
passing fine, and wittie Historie, written in Greeke by *Heliodorus*' (¶2v).

In praising King Hydaspes in a marginal note at the end of Book 9,
Underdowne particularly commends the work's quasi-allegorical, Plutar-
chan characterisation: 'Hidaspes his equal minde and great clemencie to
Oroondates, and he is also a perfitte paterne of all virtues whiche beseme
a Kinge' (Kk3). A further note, added in 1577 and subsequently reprinted,
designates 'Hidaspes the most iust man in the worlde, by testimonie of
his enimies' (R4). Other marginal comments in the 1577 edition show *An
Ethiopian Story* being used as a manual of Christian probity, as suggested
by the new address 'To the gentle reader'. Anticipating Cervantes' *Don

---

29 Unless otherwise stated, this is the edition cited.

Quixote (1605) in condemning chivalric romance, Underdowne names
'*Mort Darthure*, *Arthur* of little *Britaine*, yea, and *Amadis* of *Gaule*' as
being morally flawed. Such works

> accompt violente murder, or murder for no cause manhoode: and fornica-
> tion and all vnlawfull luste, friendely loue. This booke punisheth the faultes
> of euill doers, and rewardeth the well liuers. What a king is *Hidaspes*? What
> a patterne of a good prince? What happie successe had he? Contrarie wise,
> what a lewde woman was *Arsace*? What a patterne of euill behauiour? What
> an euill end had shee? (¶3–¶3v)[30]

Underdowne's annotations, pronouncements, the closeness with which
he adheres to the Latin text, together with his de-emphasising references
to the theatre, identify his translation with the spirit of the more Calvinist
inspired philhellene Protestants.

Fraunce, L'Isle and Gough

Heliodorus first appears in English verse in 1591, tucked into the end of
Abraham Fraunce's volume of trademark hexameter verse, *The Countess
of Pembroke's Ivychurch*. Fraunce's 235 lines in Greek hexameter, 'The
beginning of Heliodorus his Aethiopical History', openly advertise his
philhellene leanings and political connections. Once Philip Sidney's
protégé, Fraunce dedicates this work to Sidney's sister, Mary Sidney
Herbert, Countess of Pembroke, the philhellene Protestant mother of
Shakespeare's patrons, William and Philip Herbert, and aunt of Mary
Sidney Wroth.

Working from the English translation, Fraunce consciously embeds
Underdowne's characteristic diction within a parodic adaptation of
Heliodorus's opening passage. Fraunce's description of the Nile marshes,
for example, enhances the poetic qualities of Underdowne's slightly allit-
erative prose by recombining images and inserting freshly invented mate-
rial. In Underdowne, the marshes are regarded as 'a sufficient defence, for
the saftie of Theeues. And for that cause all suche people come thether
very faste, for they all doo vse the water in steede of a wall. Moreouer
the great plenty of Reede that groweth there in the moorie grounde, is
in manner as good as a Bulwarke vnto them' (A4). During the process
of hellenising his verse, Fraunce reassembles elements of this narrative,
ending his passage with a tightly patterned chiasmus:

---

30 M. A. Doody, *The True Story of the Novel*, p. 242, interprets these criticisms as 'defenses
    intended to shield the "new" Heliodorus from Puritan hostility'.

This makes wandryng squyres that lyue by the spoyle of an other,
Shyfters, nyght-walkers, rouers, and all the detested
Pack of rogues to the poole, tag, rag, to be dayly repayring,
As Lords and Ladies of a lake, securely triumphing.
For this marsh with reedes, this poole with water abounding,
Water seru's as a wall, and reedes insteede of a bullwarck.

(M3v)

The first full rendering of Heliodorus into English verse is William L'Isle's translation, based mainly on Warschewiczki, into heroic couplets: *The Faire Aethiopian. Dedicated to the King and Queene. By their Maiesties most humble Subiect and Seruant, William L'Isle* (1631). The royal compliment was dropped in the posthumous reprint of 1638, *The Famous Historie of Heliodorus. Amplified, augmented, and delivered paraphrastically in verse* (1638).[31]

L'Isle (1569?–1637),[32] who enjoyed a long association with Cambridge and the courts of James I and Charles I, first manifested his philhellene Protestant sympathies under Elizabeth. In 1595, he published *Babilon*, and in 1598, *The colonies of Bartas*, translations of sections of the Huguenot Guillaume de Saluste du Bartas's *Les Semaines*. L'Isle included the commentaries of the Genevan Calvinist leader Simon Goulart, successor to Calvin and de Bèze. Both books are dedicated to Charles Howard, later Earl of Nottingham, the Queen's host for the 1587 Accession Day tilts when *The Shepheards Holidaie*, reported by Angel Day in *Daphnis and Chloe*, was probably performed.

An ardent nationalist and pioneer in the study and editing of Anglo-Saxon texts, L'Isle dedicated his edition and translation of Aelfric Grammaticus's Christian commentary, *A Saxon Treatise* (1623), to Prince Charles as a 'Welcome-Home' (¶1).[33] In 1613, Charles's sister Elizabeth married the Bohemian Calvinist, Frederick V, Elector Palatine (an Elector held an inherited vote in the election of the Holy Roman Emperor). Frederick was elected king of Bohemia on 26 August 1619. Unsupported by James, he was defeated on 8 November 1620 at the Battle of the White

---

31 See B. Dickens, 'William L'Isle the Saxonist and Three XVIIth Century Remainder-Issues', *English and Germanic Studies*, i (1947–48), 53–5.

32 See M. Steggle, 'Lisle, William (*c.* 1569–1637)', *Oxford Dictionary of National Biography* (Oxford: Oxford University Press, 2004).

33 See P. Pulsiano, 'William L'Isle and the Editing of Old English', in *The Recovery of Old English: Anglo-Saxon Studies in the Sixteenth and Seventeenth Centuries*, ed. by T. Graham, Publications of the Richard Rawlinson Center (Kalamazoo, MI: Medieval Institute Publications, Western Michigan University, 2000), pp. 173–206, and S. Lee, 'Oxford, Bodleian Library, MS Laud Misc. 381: William L'Isle, Aelfric, and the *Ancrene Wisse*', in *The Recovery of Old English*, pp. 207–42.

Mountain, where Ferdinand of Tirol's star-shaped hunting lodge, the model for Basilius's lodge in the *New Arcadia*, is located.[34]

Pinning his hopes on gaining Philip IV's support for restitution of the Palatinate to Frederick, during 1623 Charles courted Maria Anna, the Infanta of Spain.[35] L'Isle celebrates Charles's return, and his success in regaining the 'ancient throne' of '*Brute*', to 'ioyne the foure great Nations all in one: / The *Norman*, th'*English*, and *Dardaniane* [...] ioyned by thy Sire', together with 'bloud of *Dane*' on his mother's side (¶1v-¶2r). Only a dangerous winter voyage prevents his bride from accompanying him (a3). As things turned out, L'Isle's panegyric was premature. Charles failed, and by 10 November 1624 he became engaged to Henriette-Marie (Henrietta Maria) (1609–69), daughter of Henri IV of France, and sister of Louis XIII. Charles succeeded to the throne on 27 March 1625; they married on 1 May.

L'Isle's *The Faire Aethiopian* (1631), dedicated to Charles and Henri-ette-Marie, barely masks the reformist agenda of a philhellene Protes-tant constitutional monarchist in the late Elizabethan and early Jacobean mould. His closing lines insist he is not translating for reward, but so 'That after-commers know, when I am dead, / I some good thing in life endevoured' (Bb2). Lacking personal wealth to fund public works, L'Isle recommends that the king and other wealthy patrons undertake a programme of public-spirited projects. These include constructing bridges, drains and causeways; taking on poor boys as bound appren-tices and endowing 'vndowred maids'; restoring tithes to churches; and building walls, forts, hospitals and schools. He encourages readers to engage in philanthropic activities, as opposed to self-glorification in building and furnishing enormous houses. His own humble contribution to posterity will be his writings:

> Yet will I labour what I can with pen
> To profit my succeeding Countrey-men:
> *In vaine (may seeme) is wealthe or learning lent*
> *To man that leaues thereof no monument.*
>
> (Bb2)

L'Isle relocates the English court in Ethiopia, exhibiting a propensity towards prudish moralisation and misogynism. His lyricism and comic vein undermine Heliodorus's seriousness, but his plain pentameter

---

34 See V. Skretkowicz, 'Symbolic Architecture in Sidney's *New Arcadia*', *Review of English Studies*, n.s., xxxiii (1982), 175–80.

35 Cf. *The Spanish Match: Prince Charles's Journey to Madrid, 1623*, ed. by A. Samson (Aldershot: Ashgate, 2006).

couplets reflect a puritanical and nationalistic view of poetic function. L'Isle's remarks on the polyglot orgins of English in his Preface become the rationale for embedding unusual and indigenous vocabulary into his translation:

> About the Tongues when diuers with me wrangle,
> And count our English but a mingle mangle,
> I tell them, all are such; and in conclusion
> Will grow so more by curse of first Confusion.
> The Latine, Greeke, and Hebrew are not free;
> Though what their borrow'd words are know not wee;
> Because their neighbour tongues we neuer knew;
> Nor what they keepe of old; nor what haue new.
>
> (B1)

L'Isle freely cuts and embellishes Heliodorus's 'Romant', combining pane-gyric with political critique:

> Yet sometime tell I lesse, and often more,
> Then read is in Greeke Prose of *Heliodore:*
> That Poetrie may shorten Oratorie,
> And with a Muses vaine improue the Storie.
>
> (B1v)

These 'improvements' introduce political and environmental issues, such as Charles I's commitment to drain the east-coast fens. Commer-cial exploitation of this ecologically sensitive area threatens a territory that L'Isle equates with the marshes near the mouth of the Nile, where Heliodorus sets his opening scene.

L'Isle associates the self-sufficient English fen-dwellers with Heliodo-rus's Herdsmen. These Herdsmen are outlaws fleeing the tyrannical Great King of Persia. Their life style conforms with natural, though not civil, law. Thyamis, a priest usurped by his younger brother, Petosiris, finds sanctuary in the marshes and, as leader of the Herdsmen, brings political order to their disorganised community (1.19). After the opening scene on the beach, Thyamis takes Theagenes and Charikleia to this hideout, where the Herdsmen practise a primitive form of popular government:

> Here all th'Aegyptian Robbers make their Fort,
> And bastard Common-wealth hold aft'r a sort.
> Some euer fishing seldome come off hatches [i.e., 'hecks, fish traps'],
> Some walke the pasture six foot high on skatches [i.e., 'stilts'].
> If Islet any aboue the water peepe,
> Some build a Lodge there [...]
> [...]

> Though Kings of Aegypt would this Fen haue drain'd,
> These would not suffert't, thinking better gain'd,
> With ease, some fish, or fowle, or flag, or reed,
> Than with due care the grazing herds to feed.
> Where now a Pike, well might they feed an Oxe;
> Yea, meat, drinke, cloth, haue from their bleating flocks.
> Yet some they graze, and Herdmen are they call'd,
> Though from all hand of Iustice water-wall'd.
>
> (B4–B4v)

The Herdsmen's lawlessness does not prevent L'Isle admiring their self-sufficiency, or their natural resources. Imitating du Bartas's 'Fifth Day of the First Week', he introduces a catalogue of marsh birds found in England. His deeper purpose is to pillory the ineffectiveness of the law to contain, not the local equivalent of the Herdsmen, but the rich and powerful:

> The Swan both swimming there, and flying freely,
> The loftie Sternet [i.e., 'tern'] crying t'Ely, t'Ely,
> Th'Ibis, Halcyon, Crane with tufted rump,
> Storke, Shov'ler [i.e., 'spoonbill'], Herneshaw [i.e., 'heron'], Bittour [i.e., 'bittern] sounding Bumpe,
> Coot, Red-shanke, Sea-mew [i.e., 'gull'], Teale, Di-dapping-Chucke [i.e., 'dapchick, little grebe'],
> Goose, Sea-pie [i.e., 'oyster-catcher'], Moore-hen, Osprey, Widgen, Ducke:
> I had almost forgot that most of all
> Remarkabl'is, the bird that here we call
> The Cormorant, Embleme of Penall Law,
> With long, sharpe, hooked bill, edg'd like a saw,
> To hold an Eele, but great one seldome takes,
> These are the fowle that haunt the fenny Lakes.
>
> (B4v)

In the context of L'Isle's *The Faire Aethiopian*, Thyamis's restoration to the priesthood (7.8), and King Hydaspes' forgiving nature, may be an indirect plea for the toleration of suppressed English Protestants.

John Gough's *The Strange Discovery* (1640), a drama in blank verse, intermingles original text with passages substantially word for word from Underdowne. Gough reconfigures the plot to focus on moral and legal dilemmas. The play opens with a freshly invented dialogue between Charikles and his servant, Nebulo, as they plan to return from Egypt to Delphi. Sisimithres enters. After some wooden exchanges, which improve in proportion to the amount of Underdowne they contain, Charikles accepts Sisimithres' bag of jewels and his young Ethiopian charge. With major characters such as Thyamis missing, Chariklea's story is interwoven with only two highly eroticised sub-plots. One concerns Cnemon, his father Aristippos, his stepmother Demainete and her maid Thisbe. The other, inevitably, depicts Arsake's vain attempts to seduce Theagenes; the death of Arsake's 'Chamberlaine, nurse, and bawd', Kybele (A1v); Hydaspes' triumph over Arsake's husband, Oroondates, who governs Egypt on behalf of the Persian king; and the gods' 'strange discoverie' (L4v) that will convince Hydaspes that Charikleia is his daughter. It seems unlikely that Gough, in a climate distrustful of Charles I's assumption of power, would not carefully have gauged the impact of Kybele's reminding Arsake not blatantly to murder Charikleia (I4). Nor is it insignificant that, when Charikleia chastises Hydaspes, declaring that a king 'must / Be subject to the law aswell [*sic*] as others' (L4v), there is no direct precedent in Underdowne's 'you youre selfe are iudged nowe and doo not iudge, nor determine' (Mm1).

Exemplary characters and moral lessons

In his 1531 Epistola Dedicatoria, Obsopoeus points out Heliodorus's remarkable achievement in representing 'all humane Affections', including 'a perfect Example of Conjugal Love, Truth and Constancy' in Theagenes and Charikleia. Obsopoeus's perspective derives from familiarity with the portrayal of archetypal abstracts in medieval and Renaissance Christian allegory. Amyot, a French nationalist, translator of Plutarch, and about to become 'the Gallic version of the representative type of the Catholic Reformation bishop',[36] presents a much more complex view in his extensive 'Pröesme du Translateur'. Influenced by the philhellene idealism associated with the Catholic Reformation, Amyot places far greater emphasis on Heliodorus's exemplary characterisation. He links moral purpose to verisimilitude, and to the carefully planned structure of *An Ethiopian Story*. This outline of the qualities desired in the 'reformed' French Christian novel was construed as a vilification of the popular *Amadis de Gaule*, prompting a defence of chivalric romance by Jacques Gohory.[37]

---

36 M. Fumaroli, 'Jacques Amyot and the Clerical Polemic Against the Chivalric Novel', *Renaissance Quarterly*, xxxviii (1985), 22–40 (p. 27). On the 'central role' of *An Ethiopian Story* 'in the post-tridentine debate about the norms of Christian epic and Christian romance', Fumaroli, p. 31, n.21, cites M. Bataillon, *Erasmo y España. Estudios sobre la historia espiritual del siglo XVI*, 2nd edn (Mexico City: Fondo de Cultura Económica, 1966), ch. 13; and A. K. Forcione, *Cervantes' Christian Romance: A Study of Persiles y Sigismonda* (Princeton: Princeton University Press, 1972), pp. 13–29.
37 See M. Fumaroli, 'Jacques Amyot and the Clerical Polemic Against the Chivalric Novel', pp. 30–4. Gohory's response is noted below, in the closing chapter.

The following literal translations of passages from Amyot's 'Prōesme du Translateur' attempt to represent the expansive, figured and balanced rhythmic style he superimposes over Heliodorus's.[38] Echoing Plutarchan ideas about the moral value of literature, Amyot praises the novel for joining profit to pleasure, the richness of its language, and for representing nature and truth. It is therefore

> contrary to the majority of books of this kind, which in the past have been written in our language, in which there is no learnng, no knowledge of the past, nor anything (to put it briefly) from which one could draw some use, in addition, they are most often so badly stitched together and so far from every appearance of verisimilitude, that it seems that they are more often dreams of some sick person sweating in a hot fever, than inventions of any man of reason, and of judgement.[39]

Amyot then relates *An Ethiopian Story* to the spiritually uplifting benefits of mental exercise through recreative reading. Once again, he focuses on utility and the divine property, the faculty of judgement:

> But as among exercises for the body, that one takes for pleasure, the most laudable are those that in addition to the pleasure one receives, are those which address the body, strengthen the limbs, and profit the soul: so among games, and pastimes of the spirit, the most valuable are those which, in addition to the enjoyment that they bring us, also serve to polish (in a manner of speaking) and refine the judgment more and more, in such a way that the pleasure is not at all without use. Which is I hope what one would in this sort find in this imaginary history of the loves of Charikleia, and of Theagenes, in which, in addition to the ingenious fiction, there are in several places fine discourses drawn from natural and moral philosophy: a great number of notable sayings, and sententious discourse.[40]

---

38 Quotations are from *L'histoire aethiopique de Heliodorus, contenant dix livres, traitant des loyales et pudiques amours de Theagenes Thessalien, & Chariclea Aethiopienne. Traduite de Grec en François, & de nouueau reueüe et corrigée sur un ancien exemplaire escript à la main, par le translateur, ou est declaré au vray qui en a esté le premier autheur* (Paris: Vincent Sertenas, 1559).

39 'au contraire la plus grande partie des liures de ceste sorte, qui ont ancienneme[n]t esté escritz en nostre langue, oultre ce qu'il n'y a nulle erudition, nulle cognoissance de l'antiquité, ne chose aucune (à brief parler) dont on peust tirer quelque vtilité, encore sont ilz le plus souue[n]t si mal cousuz & si esloignez de toute vraysemblable apparence, qu'il semble que ce soyent plus tost songes de quelque malade resuant en fieure chaude, qu'inuentions d'aucun homme d'esprit, & de iugement' (¶2v).

40 'Mais tout ainsi qu'entre les exercises du corps, que lon prend par esbatement, les plus recommandables sont ceux qui oultre le plaisir que lon en reçoit, adressent le corps, enforcissent les membres, & profitent à la santé: aussi entre les ieux, & passetemps de l'esprit, les plus loüables sont ceux qui oultre la resiouyssance qu'ilz nous apportent, seruent encore à limer (par maniere de dire) & affiner de plus en plus le iugement, de

Moving on towards characterisation, Amyot draws attention to the bene-
fits of 'several beautiful speeches in which artifice of eloquence is very
well used' – 'plusieurs belles hare[n]gues, ou l'artifice d'eloque[n]ce est
tresbien employé. 'And everywhere human passions are painted from life'
– '& par tout les passions humaines paintes au vif' – 'with such great
decorum' – 'auecques si grande honesteté' – 'that a person would not
know how to derive the opportunity or example of doing evil from it' –
'que lon n'en sçauroit tirer occasion, ou exemple de mal faire' (¶2v). This is
'because, for all unlawful and evil passions, he has fashioned an unhappy
outcome; and conversely, for good and honest ones, a desirable and happy
ending' – 'Pource que de toutes affections illicites, & mauuaises, il a fait
l'yssue malheureuse: & au contraire des bonnes, & honnestes, la fin desir-
able & heureuse' (¶2v–¶3). This is not far from Underdowne's praise of
Hydaspes in 1577 as 'a patterne of a good prince', and his noting that
Arsake, 'a patterne of euill behauiour', met 'an euill end' (¶3–¶3v).

Heliodorus understands human frailty. While his characters range
from the exceptionally good to the egregiously bad, they possess very
human traits of strength and weakness. The principal characters' flex-
ibility, in repressing their personalities and adopting disguises, is empha-
sised through encounters with strongly drawn secondary characters, some
of whom are exemplary Theophrastan archetypes. In addition to filling
set roles, many of these lesser figures have complex histories. A degree
of this nuancing is lost to Renaissance readers because Warschewiczki's
tendency to flatten characters' individuality, followed by Underdowne,
eradicates much of this subtlety. Warschewiczki obscures Heliodorus's
morality-based characterisation in the Plutarchan mode, encouraging
Underdowne to interpret individual episodes as miniature Christian
allegories with a Calvinist message.

Heliodorus's political romance

Heliodorus's pro-Athenian and pro-Ethiopian politics appealed to
Renaissance philhellene republicans and limited monarchists. Persians
and their Egyptian subjects, ruled by the tyrannical Great King of Persia,
are described as cowards, tyrants, or as morally flawed. By contrast, the
good King Hydaspes, in dispute with the Great King over emerald mines

---

sorte que le plaisir n'est point du tout ocieux. Ce que i'espere que lon pourra aucune-
ment trouuer en ceste fabuleuse histoire des amours de Chariclea, & de Theagenes, en
laquelle, oultre l'ingenieuse fiction, il y a en quelques lieux de beaux discours tirez de la
Philosophie Naturelle, & Morale: force dictz notables, & propos sente[n]cieux' (¶2v).

near the second cataract of the Nile, governs Ethiopia by consultative monarchy.

Heliodorus establishes pre-historic religious, political and marital links between Greece and Ethiopia through Persinna's explanation of the waist-band she embroidered for her daughter's tokens: 'Our line descends from the Sun and Dionysus among gods and from Perseus and Andromeda and from Memnon too among heroes' (4.8; Reardon, p. 432). According to this legendary genealogy, Andromeda's father, the King of Ethiopia, imprisons her on a rocky sea-coast as a sacrificial appeasement to a vora-cious sea-monster. Perseus, son of Danae and Zeus, flies overhead on winged sandals, carrying the head of Medusa. Medusa's gaze turns the sea-monster to stone, Perseus rescues Andromeda, and they marry.

Bedrooms in the Ethiopian palace, decorated with scenes depicting the history of Perseus and Andromeda, commemorate this historical union, which Heliodorus's plot replicates. Drawing on the theory of 'maternal impression', Persinna explains how Charikleia has matured into the 'exact likeness' of her ancestor: 'during your father's intimacy with me the painting had presented me with the image of Andromeda, who was depicted stark naked, for Perseus was in the very act of releasing her from the rocks' (4.8; Reardon, p. 433 and note). Heliodorus fudges logical imponderables to force this familial resemblance. When the painting is produced to verify Persinna's claim, no-one contests how accurately it represents Andromeda, nor is the modest Charikleia required to reveal more than the birthmark on her arm (10.15–16).

Persinna's reference to King Memnon of Ethiopia prefigures the new Greco-Ethiopian concord with which the novel ends. In the war between the Greeks and Trojans, Memnon assists his uncle, King Priam of Troy. Priam is killed by Achilles' son, Neoptolemos; Memnon by Achilles himself.[41] These heroic connections relate to Theagenes' pedigree. He descends from Achilles, of the noble Thessalian race of the Ainianes, 'Hellenes in the truest sense of the word, for they trace their descent from Hellen, the son of Deukalion' (2.34; Reardon, p. 407).

This ancestry provides the rationale for Theagenes' sacred mission to Delphi, where he falls in love with Charikleia. Every four years, at the time of the Pythian Games in Delphi, the Ainianes sacrifice to Neop-tolemos, 'treacherously murdered by Orestes, the son of Agamemnon, at the very altar of Pythian Apollo' (2.34; Reardon, p. 407). To reinforce the interrelationship between the Hellenes and Ethiopians, Theagenes, as if he were the victorious Perseus about to rescue Andromeda, wears

41 Cf. Ovid, *Metamorphoses*, 13.580 ff.

a 'clasp with, at its center, an amber figure of Athene with her Gorgon's head talisman on her breastplate' (3.3; Reardon, pp. 411–12). He exhibits legendary Thessalian horsemanship when he stops a runaway bull (10.29). And he accentuates this equine connection through his ceremonial garb, 'a flowing crimson mantle with gold embroidery depicting the battle of Lapiths and Centaurs' (3.3; Reardon, p. 411). This allusion to Books 21 and 22 of Homer's *Odyssey* reminds readers of the wedding-party battle of the Centaurs and Lapiths, and Odysseus's slaughter of the princes on his return to Ithaca.

Homeric beginnings

The battle of Lapiths and Centaurs lies behind the aborted wedding celebrations and slaughter that precede Heliodorus's ecphrastic opening scene, and which are described at the mid-point, the conclusion of Book 5 (5.32). Wine bowls have been used 'like stones', 'drinking vessels as missiles', but 'most were the victims of arrows and archery' (1.1; Reardon, pp. 353–4). By beginning *in medias res* in the manner of Homeric epic, Heliodorus signals the philhellene nature of his invented Ethiopian history. Background information is gradually offered until, by the middle of the novel, at the end of Book 5, events leading up to the beginning are fully explained. The first half contains a complete cycle of largely reported narrative; the second progresses chronologically, picking up threads of preceding plot lines as characters resurface from the past.

An Ethiopian Story begins – like Sidney's *New Arcadia* – with a periphrastic description based on a personification: "Ἡμέρας ἄρτι διαγελώσης' – literally, 'Le jour commençait à sourire'[42] or 'The day began to smile'. This unusual figurative usage provides a brief but illuminating indication that the work is an idealised fantasy, a romance with a happy conclusion. The rhetorical impact is increased by reading an implied zeugma in 'διαγελώσης', compounding the verb with its more usual transferred idiomatic sense of 'brightening', as in 'The smile of daybreak was just beginning to brighten the sky' (1.1; Reardon, p. 353).

Heliodorus shifts immediately from metaphoric expression to the historical authenticity of reported fact:[43] 'the sunlight to catch the hilltops'

42 Héliodore, *Les Éthiopiques*, ed. by R. M. Rattenbury and T. W. Lumb, trans. by J. Maillon, I.1.1.

43 J. R. Morgan, 'History, Romance and Realism in The *Aithiopika* Of Heliodoros', *Classical Antiquity*, I (1982), 221–65, examines the rhetorical tricks used by Heliodorus to convince readers that they are being presented with the truth.

(1.1; Reardon, p. 353). This paradoxical shift in tone was lost to Renaissance readers. The optimism implicit in 'smile' disappears in Warschewiczki's flat 'Cum primum dies illucesceret, & sol cacumina montium illustraret' (A1), reiterated in Underdowne's 'As soone as the daye appeared, and the Sunne began to shine on the toppes of the Hilles' (A1). Amyot independently opts for 'brighten', finding irresistible the invitation to expand the first clause to balance the rhythms of the second: 'Le iour ne faisoit gueres que comme[n]cer à poindre, & le Soleil à rayer sur les cimes des montaignes' (A1). Nor does L'Isle's extravagant versification, 47 lines into his poem, bear any trace of smiling:

> Blacke-winged night flew to th'*Antipodes*
> At sight of Morning Starre, and the Easterne seas
> With-held the rising Beame, vntill it guilt
> The top of trees, and turrets highest built.
>
> (B1v)

From their vantage point above the Heracleotic, westernmost, mouth of the Nile, a band of ten robbers looks out to sea. Heliodorus alternates their perspectives, from distant to close-up. Finding nothing on the horizon, they observe a heavily laden ship near land. The beach is covered with bodies, 'some of them quite dead, others half-alive and still twitching' (1.1; Reardon, p. 353), amidst the residue of 'a sacrifice of thanksgiving – thanksgiving indeed! – to Poseidon' (5.27; Reardon, p. 466).

The narrator in this opening passage is Heliodorus's equivalent to the traveller in *Leukippe and Kleitophon*. Instead of a painting, the narrator describes the bandits coming across a scene that approximates a stage-set, an ecphrastic introduction to a mysterious tale. Heliodorus's stage-related metaphors highlight the dramatic nature of his dialogues.[44] He briefly suspends the action as the robbers become viewers, and then participants, in a dramatic performance: 'In that small space the deity had contrived an infinitely varied spectacle, [...] staging this tragic show for the Egyptian bandits. They stood on the mountainside [...][45] unable to comprehend the scene' (1.1; Reardon, p. 354).

Amyot compresses these disparate dramatic allusions, simultaneously expanding the text. He begins with a relative clause, reflecting Heliodor-

---

44 Héliodore, *Les Éthiopiques*, ed. by R. M. Rattenbury and T. W. Lumb, trans. by J. Maillon, I.1.7, 'ils contemplaient cette scène', and note, 'Le vocabulaire d'Héliodore contient beaucoup de métaphores empruntées au théâtre'. Cf. J. W. H. Walden, 'Stage-Terms in Heliodorus's *Aethiopica*', *Harvard Studies in Classical Philology*, v (1894), 1–43.

45 J. R. Morgan emphasises the point by adding 'like the audience in a theatre' (1.1; Reardon, p. 354).

us's compilation of events: 'lequel spectacle elle [i.e., 'la fortune', trans-
lating 'δαίμων'] presenta aux yeux de ces brigans d'Aegypte qui estoyent
sur la montaigne' – 'which spectacle she presented to the eyes of these
Egyptian robbers who were on the mountain'. He gratuitously adds a
complementary rhythmic clause, perhaps instructing the novice reader
in the significance of visual detail: '& voyoyent bien deuant eux tout ce
que nous auons recité' – 'and seeing right before them everything that
we have described'. He then completes the stage metaphor: 'mais ilz ne
pouoient entendre quel estoit le subiect, & la cause d'vne si merueilleuse
tragedie' – 'but they could not understand what was the subject and the
cause of so marvellous a tragedy' (A1v).

Warschewiczki's rendering preserves the theatrical imagery: 'Denique
multiplice[m] speciem paruo in spacio numen exhibuerat […] & tale
theatru[m] praedonibus Aegyptiis instruens. Hi enim cum se in monte
spectatores harum rerum praebuissent spectaculu[m] intelligere neuti-
quam potuerunt' (A2). Underdowne's suppression of these allusions in
1569, during the formation of professional theatre in London, appears
to stem from his Calvinism. He nonetheless deprives readers of Heliodo-
rus's introduction to the dramatic nature of his work: 'To be briefe, God
shewed, a wonderfull sight in so shorte time … prouidinge suche a sight
for the Theeues of *Egypte* to pause at. For they when they had geuen these
thinges the lookinge on a good while from the Hill, coulde not vnder-
stande what that sight meante' (A1v).

Fraunce's decision to follow Underdowne, rather than to work from
Warschewiczki, perpetuates this non-dramatic perspective:

> Soe blood brewd with wyne, soe buffets ioyn'd to the banquets,
> Killing with swilling and beating vnto the eating,
> Caused a strange wonder to the theeues, whoe saw fro the hil-top
> Men kyld, noe killers; many dead, noe conqueror extant,
> Victory, noe spoyling, shipp fraughted, yet not a shipman.
>   But, notwithstanding for a time they stood thus amazed,
> Yet for greedy desire of gaine they hastened onward
> And drew nere to the place, where men lay all to bemangled,
> And ship-full-fraughted; thinking themselues to bee victors.
>   But, good God, what a sight, what a strange sight, yea, what a sweet fight,
> And yet a woeful sight, to the theeues vnlookt-for apeared?
>
>   (M1v)

By the time the text passes through L'Isle's hands, every vestige of dramatic
reference has disappeared: 'Th'Aegyptian theeues beheld this from the
Mount; / But knew not how it came' (B2). In England, the rhetorical

significance of Heliodorus's metaphorical allusions was completely lost.

Descending the hill, the robbers see a beautiful girl in priestess's attire. She sits on a rock, a badly wounded young man at her feet. The narrator focuses on this couple. As Theagenes regains consciousness, they exchange remarks about life and death. Charikleia catches sight of the bandits, and leaps up to hide. The bandits think she might be a goddess. Physical distance closes and Charikleia addresses them, but the initial disjunctions and mutual incomprehension remain. Charikleia, educated as a priestess in Delphi, speaks Greek, which the Egyptian thieves cannot understand.

The principal characters undergo further disorientation as the opening sequence closes. The robbers flee before another Egyptian-speaking gang, 'three times that number' (1.3; Reardon, p. 356), including two horsemen. These 'Herdsmen', led by Thyamis, imprison Theagenes and Charikleia in a hut on the Nile delta. Thyamis appoints Knemon, 'a young Greek who had been captured not long before' (1.7; Reardon, p. 358), as their guard. Much later, Heliodorus contextualises this philhellene fraternity: Thyamis is a Greek-speaking high priest from Memphis (1.19).

Heliodorus does not identify any character before Knemon overhears Charikleia and Theagenes mention one another's names (1.8). At this point narrative description ceases and communication begins. Names suddenly gain significance, as Heliodorus develops new philhellene strands of the plot through dramatic dialogue and changing narrators. Characters introduce themselves with a factual simplicity reminiscent, though without the starkness, of Achilles Tatius. Underdowne's translation closely represents the text:

> I haue the more compassion on you for that you be *Grecians*, because also I my selfe am a *Grecian* borne [...] But what must wee calle you, saide *Theagenes? Cnemon* answeared he. Of what parte of *Greece* saide *Theagenes?* Of *Athens* answeared he. And howe came you here, saide *Theagenes?* Peace I praie you (q[uoth] he) & aske me that questio[n] no more, let vs leaue that to such as write Tragedies. (B1–B1v)

Underdowne expands Warschewiczki's 'tragoedis' (A8), from Heliodorus's 'τραγῳδῶν' (1.8), an image glossed over by Amyot in 'ne me le demandez point, & ne remuez point ce propoz là' – 'do not ask me this, and do not move this proposition' (A4v).

An Ethiopian Story contains a feast of overt and covert allusions to ancient Greek literature, 'especially the Homeric epics and Euripidean tragedy'.[46] Knemon's request not to be interrogated further is reminiscent

---

46 J. R. Morgan, in Reardon, p. 351.

of Euripides' *Medea*, 1317, which Morgan incorporates into the text as 'Why do you batter and prise open these doors?' (1.8; Reardon, p. 359).

As much of the narrative is developed in retrospect, this kind of dramatic dialogue facilitates articulation of theatrical qualities. Tales are interwoven as if they were scenes. To convey a sense of simultaneity in Homeric manner, Knemon's history, interspersed with those of others, is delivered piecemeal to different audiences. His reply to Theagenes

> beganne in this sorte.
>   My Fathers name was *Aristippus*, he was borne in *Athens*, one of the vpper Senate, as riche as any Comoner in the Cittie, he, after the decease of my Mother […] dothe therefore bringe home a little woman somewhat fine, but passinge malicious, named *Demeneta*. (B1v)

The insatiable Demainete

Knemon lives in exile, the price for rejecting his stepmother Demainete's attempts to seduce him. To disgrace Knemon to Aristippos, she orders her slave, Thisbe, to fall in love with Knemon. Thisbe is to convince him that he can catch Demainete in bed with a lover. In fact, Demainete is in bed with Aristippos, so when Knemon charges in, dagger drawn, Aristippos banishes Knemon as a parricide.

Insatiable, Demainete threatens Thisbe, who tells her that Knemon is having an affair with Arsinoe, a flute-player. Thisbe sets a trap for Demainete in which, under cover of darkness, Demainete will substitute herself for Arsinoe and enjoy Knemon. (Compare Sidney's bed-trick in the *Old Arcadia*, and Shakespeare's in *All's Well that Ends Well* and *Measure for Measure*.) Thisbe toys with Demainete, arguing, 'If you get what you want, it is more than likely that your passion will abate; for most women one consummation is enough to dowse the fires of their desire; performance of the act slakes lust. If (which heaven forfend) your desires persist, we must think again: if at first you don't succeed, [there will be a second setting sail]' (1.15; Reardon, p. 366).

As the following comparisons demonstrate, Heliodorus's forthright approach to the erotic provides a touchstone against which to test his translators' intentions. Amyot's expansive version predictably contains elegantly balanced rhythms and assonance:

> Et lors si vous iouyssez de ce que vous desirez, il est grandement vraysemblable que vostre amour en diminuera: Car il y en a beaucoup à qui le desir passe, & s'estaint en la premiere iouyssance, pource l'accomplissement de l'oeuure est l'assouuissement de l'amour. Mais si d'auenture l'amour vous

demeure encore apres la iouyssance, nous aurons recours aux rames quand
nous ne nous pourrons ayder de la voile, comme lon dict en commun
prouerbe, & prendrons autre aduis. (B2)

And then if you should enjoy what you desire, it is highly plausible that
your love for it will diminish: for there are many for whom the desire passes
and extinguishes itself during the first pleasure, because accomplishing the
task is the satisfaction of love. But if by chance the passion remains in you
even after pleasure, we shall have recourse to the oars when we can get no
help for ourselves from the sail, as one says in the common proverb, and
we shall take another course.

Amyot cannot resist a naughty pun on 'la voile' – 'the sail', but also
connoting 'the sheet'. In contrast, Warschewiczki represents Heliodorus's
style as extremely simple: 'Si igitur adepta fueris id quod cupis, maxime
tum conuenit vacare amori […]' (B8). Underdowne translates Warsche-
wiczki literally:

and if you gette that you desire, then shall it be beste for you to geeue
ouer your loue. For in many the firste experimente hathe quenched suche
earnest desire, for the seede of loue, wherewith wee prosecute any thinge,
is to haue ynough thereof, but if this desire shall then also remaine (whiche
God forbidde) then shall wee make (as the Prouerbe saithe) a newe viage,
and speake ['seeke' in 1577 (B2v)] a newe waie. (C2v)

L'Isle's sense of decorum, encouraged by strict censorship under Charles
I, leads him to exclude this passage.

Thisbe tells Aristippos he can catch Demainete in the act of being
unfaithful. Aristippo enters the darkened room – Thisbe has taken the
lamp. When he accuses Demainete, Thisbe 'slammed the doors as loudly
as she could and exclaimed: "Calamity! Her lover has got away! Be careful
not to lose them both, master"' (1.17; Reardon, p. 368). Demainete is
arrested, but breaks away and hurls herself to her death in 'the Pit in
the Akademia' (1.17; Reardon, p. 368), ironically, a place of sacrifice
honouring the tyrannicides buried there.[47]

After Demainete's death, Thisbe works as an entertainer in Athens,
where Nausikles, an Egyptian merchant, falls in love with her. He rejects
Arsinoe and takes Thisbe to Egypt. In revenge, Arsinoe reveals Thisbe's
plot against Demainete to her family. The family accuses Aristippos of
conspiracy to murder, and demands Thisbe's interrogation. Aristippos
fails to produce Thisbe, is exiled from Athens and has his property confis-
cated. It is to find Thisbe and clear his father's name that Knemon travels

47 J. R. Morgan, in Reardon, p. 368, note 21.

to Egypt, where he is captured by Thyamis before the time sequence in Book 1 begins.

Thyamis's erotic dream

Knemon's experience of the consequences of misplaced passion (1.9–18) serves as a prelude to Thaymis's erotic dream. Thyamis dreams he is home in Memphis. The temple of Isis is 'all ablaze with torchlight; the altars and sacred hearths were drenched with the blood of all kinds of animals'. The gates and colonnades are heaving with people making 'a confused babble of chatter'. Inside the shrine, Isis approaches with Charikleia, and pronounces with oracular ambiguity, 'Thyamis, this maiden I deliver to you; you shall have her and not have her; you shall do wrong and slay her, but she shall not be slain' (1.18; Reardon, p. 369).

Thyamis's vision is sandwiched between Knemon's account of Demainete's repugnant lust and Thyamis's disclosure that he is the eldest son of Kalasiris, the high priest of Memphis. Deeply troubled by Charikleia, he treats his dream as if it were exclusively erotic: 'in desperation he forced the interpretation to conform with his own desires' (1.18; Reardon, p. 369). Thyamis's self-justification is problematic: 'The words "you shall have her and not have her" he took to mean as a wife and no longer a virgin; "you shall slay her" he guessed was a reference to the wounds of defloration, from which Charikleia would not die' (1.18; Reardon, p. 369).

Thyamis's euphemistic metaphor is not easily translatable. Amyot remains coyly evasive, but increases the amount of direct speech: 'Tu l'auras femme, & si ne l'auras pas vierge. Quant à ce mot tu occiras, il l'exposa: Tu blesseras sa virginité, de laquelle besseure [*sic*, for 'blesseure'] Chariclea ne mourroit pas' (B3v) – 'You will have a wife, and thus will not have a virgin. As for the word "you shall kill," he construed it, "You will wound her virginity," from which wound Charikleia would not die'. Underdowne, who follows Warschewiczki closely,[48] is more physically direct: 'Thou hauinge, shalte not haue her, that is a wife, not a mayde, any longer. By that thou shalte kill, he coniectured to be meante, thou shalte breake her limmes, whereof for all that *Cariclea* shoulde not die' (C4v). While 'thou shalte breake her limmes', for Warschewiczki's 'hymene[m] vulnerabis', finds a parallel in Caxton's 'lymmes of generacion' (*O.E.D.*

---

48 'Habebis, & non habebis, vxorem scilicet, non amplius virgine[m], arbitrabatur. At id, Occides, hymene[m] vulnerabis, significare co[n]iectabatur: vnde non morituram esse Charicliam' (C3).

1), 'her limmes' is replaced with 'Hymen' in the corrected 1577 edition
(B4v), and may have originated in an error. Nonetheless, Underdowne's
moral stand undermines Heliodorus's subtle ambiguities. Underdowne's
Thyamis is less complex, and his interpretation driven by 'his own luste',
as well as by desire.

While L'Isle scrambles the ideas, perhaps drawing on a combination
of Amyot, Warschewiczki and Underdowne, his simplistic account is the
clearest of all. Sometimes prefixing names with English chivalric titles,
as in 'sir *Thyam*' (E6v), his debt to Spenser's *Faerie Queene* and Sir John
Harington's *Orlando Furioso* extends to playful use of antiquated and
innovative diction, dramatisation of character, and clarity of expression:

> He seem'd at *Memphis* entring *Isis* Fane,
> That all th'rowout with fire-brands it shane,
> [...]
> That, comming neere the shrine, the Goddesse met him
> With his faire prise in hand, and thus she gret him;
> This Maid (O *Thyam*) I command thee saue her
> From hurt;

a phrase that originates in Warschewiczki's 'Thyami, hanc virginem tuae
commendo fidei' (C3) – Underdowne's 'I committe this Maide vnto thy
fidelitie' (C4)

>   but know, thou hauing shalt not haue her.
> Thou shalt a guest kill, though against my Law,
> But she shall liue: this when he heard and saw,
> His minde was troubled how to conster it;
> And thus he made all for his purpose fit.
> *Haue and not haue*, a wife, no more a maid:
> But how then kill? O *Hymen* stab he said:
> For many a virgin her virginitie
> May wounded haue, and of the wound not die.

>   (C4v–D1)

Thyamis's priestly family

Because he has to argue his claim for taking Charikleia as his bride,
Thyamis's address to the Herdsmen contains more than a degree of
rhetorical posturing. Having shown Thyamis in action as a brave leader,
Heliodorus uses this speech to have him introduce himself, and the key
Kalasiris–Thyamis–Petosiris plot, to the reader. He begins by recapitu-
lating his origins for his audience:

As you know, I was born the son of the high priest ['προφήτου'] at Memphis, but I did not succeed to the priesthood after my father's disappearance, since my younger brother illegally usurped the office. I took refuge with you [...] You chose me to be your leader. (1.19; Reardon, pp. 369–70)

This carefully interpolated report of Kalasiris's disappearance, 'πατρὸς ὑπαναχώρησιν', Warschewiczki's 'post patris discessum' (C3v), is omitted by Underdowne. Underdowne may prefer to simplify the plot, sacrificing Heliodorus's foreshadowing of as yet undisclosed events:

For I (as you can beare me witnes) as though I were the Sonne of the *Prieste* of *Memphis*, frustrate of the Priestely honour, for that my yonger brother by crafte beguiled me of the same, when I fledde to you [...] by all your voices, made youre Captaine. (C4v)

By contrast, Amyot embeds Kalasiris's disappearance within terms that associate the Egyptian church at Memphis with the Roman Catholic hierarchy, familiarising the text for his courtly readership. The effect is multiplied by Amyot rhythmically doubling the major terms:

car estant (comme vous sçauez) filz du grand Pontife, & prestre de Memphis, & ayant esté priué de ceste dignité du Pontificat, laquelle m'estoit affectée, & deuë, comme à l'aisné apres le departement de nostre pere, par les trames iniques & iniustes menées de mo[n] frere puisné [...] (B4)

for being (as you know) son of the head of the church, and priest of Memphis, and having been deprived of this dignity of the leadership of the church, which was destined and due to me as to the eldest after the departure of our father, by the evil wiles and unjust conspiracies of my younger brother ...

Thyamis's structured, logical argument demonstrates his sensitivity and his intellectual superiority over the uneducated Herdsmen. It also displays his hellenism in governing by consensus, discrediting force as a means of persuasion:

I could present her to myself, but I think it better to take her with the consent of you all; [...] but we must also ask the young lady what her feelings are in this matter. If this were simply a case of exercising authority, my will would be quite sufficient: for those with power to compel, polite inquiry is superfluous. But in the case of marriage the consent of both parties is needed. (1.19–21; Reardon, p. 370)

This passage highlights the distinctions drawn by Heliodorus and other writers of erotic romance between tyranny and consensus, in both civil and domestic governance. It contrasts with the pirate Trachinos in

Book 5, whose insistence on the right to marry Charikleia by virtue of rank causes the fracas that precedes the opening of the novel.

With utmost clarity, Thyamis lays down the terms of an Egyptian priest's relationship with a woman: 'As the priestly caste despises common sex ['πάνδημον Ἀφροδίτην'], it is not for bodily pleasure that I have decided she should be mine, but for the continuation of my line' (1.19; Reardon, p. 370). This is effectively how Warschewiczki translates, in 'Cum enim vulgarem Venerem despiciat propheticum genus, non ad voluptatis vsum, sed ad propogatione[m] sobolis hanc mihi adiu[n]gere constitui' (C4v). Underdowne represents this quite closely: 'for seeinge the Prophetical sorte of men, despiseth the common sorte of wemen, I haue decreed to make her my companion, not for pleasure so muche, as to haue issue by her' (D1).

Amyot, both pandering to and establishing French courtly taste, stretches the text to nearly double its length. He introduces rhythmic, parallel, relative clauses and paraphrases, incorporating elegantly sounding assonances and diction:

> Mais pourauta[n]t que nous qui sommes de race prophetique tenons à grand reproche & ofence de se mesler indiferemment auecques toutes femmes, i'ay auisé de prendre ceste pucelle, non pour en abuser à accomplir mon plaisir, mais pour en auoir lignée qui soit apte à me succeder en la dignité pontificale. (B4–B4v)

> But in so far as we who are of the prophetic race hold it a great reproach and offence to mix indifferently with all women, I have decided to take this virgin, not to abuse her in accomplishing my pleasure, but to have appropriate issue to succeed me in the pontifical dignity.

By adding 'pontificale', Amyot magnifies Thyamis's rationale for having sex from simple procreation into the survival of his line of inherited priesthood. At the other extreme, L'Isle's consciousness of the sensitivities of the king and queen, and probably also of the censor, causes him to omit this material altogether (D1v).

Heliodorus's forte is dramatic irony. In this instance, Thyamis reinterprets his dream in the light of changing events. In Book 1, as a prelude to Book 7, the robbers who peer over the mountain in the opening passage return to attack the Herdsmen. Their enlarged force is in the pay of Thyamis's younger brother, the usurper Petosiris. Knemon moves Charikleia into the safety of a cave. Sensing defeat, and 'Unable to bear the thought of Charikleia becoming the property of another man [...]' (1.30; Reardon, p. 376), Thyamis rushes to kill her.

In this instance, the three sixteenth-century translators are remarkably close. Amyot's rhythmic 'qu'ayant Chariclea, il ne l'auroit pas, par ce que ceste guerre la luy osteroit, & qu'il l'occiroit, & non pas seulement la bleceroit, & que ce seroit auecq[ue] vn glaiue, & non pas selon l'vsage de Venus' (C2) is only slightly less direct than Warschewiczki's 'quod habens non habiturus esset Charicliam, vtpote bello ereptam: & quod interfecturus esset, & non vulneraturus: gladio scilicet, & non Venerea lege' (D4). Underdowne alone places a literal interpretation on the closing euphemism: 'that hauinge, thou shalt not haue *Cariclia*, as taken a waie by Warre, and that he shoulde kill, and not wounde her, that is, with his sworde, & not with Carnall copulation' (E2). But L'Isle clearly has no intention of revisiting this subject:

> *Haue, and not haue*; she should be from him tane
> By force of Armes; and yet by him be slaine
> With sword indeed, not as he thought before.
>   (D3v)

In the darkness, Thyamis hears a woman speak Greek, and stabs her. The bandits take him prisoner. When Theagenes and Knemon return to the cave for Charikleia, they come across the dead woman. By torchlight, Knemon recognises Thisbe.[49] Thyamis's companion, Thermouthis, had kidnapped her from the merchant Nausikles ten days earlier (2.10–12).

They leave the camp in pairs, planning to rendezvous at the village of Chemmis, eleven miles away. Theagenes and Charikleia disguise themselves as beggars. Knemon escapes Thermouthis's watchful eye (2.19). On the banks of the Nile, Knemon encounters an aged Egyptian dressed in Greek clothing. It is Kalasiris, the absent high priest of Memphis and father of Thyamis and Petosiris. Kalasiris takes Knemon to Chemmis, 'to the home of a good man who has given me sanctuary' (2.21; Reardon, p. 394), Nausikles, but who is absent. It is there that we find Knemon and Kalasiris at the beginning of Book 5.

Rhodopis: Kalasiris's nightmare

Heliodorus interrelates Kalasiris's and Knemon's experiences. The plot leaves them alone and free to speak, as Nausikles has paid the satrap, Oroondates, to give him troops to search for Thisbe (2.24; cf. 5.8). Kalasiris

---

49 N. J. Lowe, *The Classical Plot and the Invention of Western Narrative*, p. 254, remarks, 'If we do not think of her, it is because we have not yet grasped the sheer classical tightness of Heliodorus' way of playing the novelistic game'.

laments the loss of Theagenes and Charikleia to Thyamis's bandits, the Herdsmen, 'just a few days ago' (2.22; Reardon, p. 395), when the novel begins. He supplies his background, beginning in the factual manner used to validate the truth of the following narrative: 'My home is Memphis. My name is Kalasiris, as was my father's before me' (2.24; Reardon, p. 398). He is a priest of Isis, a widower, and father of two sons. The scene is replete with dramatic irony. Knemon, the insatiable Demainete's victim, listens as Kalasiris relates his tale of unbridled lust for a wealthy courtesan, Rhodopis.

Kalasiris's is a cautionary tale in which a roundly developed character falls prey to a narrow character type. Kalasiris is disgusted by his own emotions, and humiliated by his mere ordinariness. Hindsight colours his opinion of Rhodopis: 'she brought evil to all she met' (2.25; Reardon, p. 398). He recollects with horror the disarray of his feelings: 'It shames me to tell you this […] the self-control I had practised all my life fell before her assault' (2.25; Reardon, p. 399).

Renaissance opinion of Rhodopis varies. Heliodorus describes her as 'A Thracian woman, in the full bloom of youth, second in beauty only to Charikleia' (2.25; Reardon, p. 398); in Amyot, 'vne ieune femme du païs de Thrace, estant en fleur d'aage' (E2). There is no suggestion that she shares Cleopatra's sophistication, rendered in Amyot's version of Plutarch's 'Antony' as 'en l'aage ou les fe[m]mes sont en la fleur de leur beauté, & en la uigueur de leur entendement' – in North's translation, 'at the age when a womans beawtie is at the prime, and she also of best judgement'.[50] Yet maturity is precisely what Rhodopis gains in Warschewiczki's version, 'Muliercula Thracica, maturo aetatis flore' (G4), 'A young woman of Thrace, in the ripe flower of her age'. And, as Underdowne reduces this to 'A woman of *Thrace*, of ripe yeeres' (H3v), Elizabethan and Jacobean readers encounter a malignant Rhodopis who is certainly old enough to know what she is doing.

Underdowne's bleak translation reflects the negative gloss added by Kalasiris: 'She was fully equipped for the sexual hunt: any man who crossed her path was trapped, for there was no escaping or resisting the net of sensuality that she trailed from her eyes' (2.25; Reardon, p. 398).

50 *Les vies des hommes illustres Grecs, & Romains, comparées l'vne auec l'autre par Plutarque de Cheronee, Translatees … par Maistre Iacques Amyot*, 2nd edn (Paris: M. Vascosan, 1565), QQq2; *The Lives of the Noble Grecians and Romanes, compared together by that graue learned Philosopher and Historiographer, Plutarke of Chaeronea: Translated out of Greeke into French by Iames Amyot, Abbot of Bellozane, Bishop of Auxerre, one of the Kings priuy counsel, and great Amner of Fraunce, and out of French into Englishe, by Thomas North* (1579), NNNN5.

Here Amyot exercises his penchant for exaggerating sexual innuendo. He trebles Rhodopis's erotic skills, trebles the parallel clausal structure and extends the fishing metaphor into three concepts:

> Elle estoit si bien exercitée & aprise en toutes caresses, alecheme[n]tz, & atraitz d'amour, qu'on n'eust sceu se garder d'en estre espris en la hantant, tant estoit ineuitable & malaise à s'en depestrer le fillé, & la seinne qu'elle te[n]doit & tiroit de ses yeux. (E2)

> She was so well practised and learned in every caress, allurement, and attraction of love, that one could not know how to protect oneself against being smitten while keeping her company, so much that it was unavoidable and difficult to extricate oneself from the netting, and the seine-net that she set and trawled with her eyes.

Warschewiczki's 'omnibus Venereis illecebris atque lasciuia exacte instructa' (G4), which Underdowne satisfactorily translates as 'very perfitly instructed in all *venerious* entisementes, and wanton behauiour' (H4), has none of Amyot's gentle, courtly allure. Warschewiczki omits the metaphor whereby Rhodopis's eyes become an inescapable net, accentuating the danger of associating with this type of character: 'ineuitabilem que[m] dam & inuictum fascinum meretricium ex illius oculis attrahebat' (G4v) – the 'unavoidable and irresistable fascination of a courtesan, drawing by force of her eyes'. Underdowne goes even further, reinforcing his marginal note, 'Rhodopis, a Harlot' (H3v), with a damning rendering, 'of suche an vnauoidable force, was the Whoorishe allurement, that proceeded from her eies' (H4).

Equally guilty of reducing Rhodopis to a common prostitute, in a travesty of the grief-stricken atmosphere of the original, L'Isle too exaggerates character type. L'Isle accentuates Kalasiris's loss of self-control through a brief dialogue, in which his hubris, exhibited through an inflated tone of superiority, ensures his downfall:

> Here came from *Thrace* (to me may seeme from hell)
> A wanton Peece, nor ouer young nor old,
> Of woman kinde, so tising and so bold;
> That she to Temple came, and at her heeles,
> A traine of seeming Maids as smug as Eeles.
> Thus once she told me, from Philosophee
> I can your schollers draw; you none fro mee:
> And I reply'd, 'tis easier to spill,
> Than make the man: your draught is downe the hill,
> A broad and easie way to vice; but I
> Them vpward driue to vertue lodg'd on high. (G1)

Focusing on the social and political implications of the erotic, Heliodorus emphasises the impact of Kalasiris's moral lapse. He flees the country: 'I referred my case to the court of reason and imposed upon myself a penalty that befitted the sins I had committed not in fact (heaven forfend!) but merely in inclination. Exile was the sentence I pronounced on my concupiscence, and so [...] I left the land of my birth' (2.25; Reardon, p. 399). Warschewiczki retains this rhythmic conclusion in a similarly smooth series of clauses, 'non ob rem ipsam (quod absit) sed sola animi co[n]stitutione co[n]uenienti mihi mulcta imposita, & ratione in iudicium adhibita, exilio punio cupiditatem, & ex patria discessi infelix' (G4v–G5). Underdowne somewhat expands, representing the Latin in an awkward, jolting manner: 'not for dooinge the deede (whiche God forebid) but to pounishe my desire with conuenient pounishment, as in my minde I determined, whiche by reason rulinge in that Iudgemente, I bannished my selfe, and vnhappy name ['man' in 1577 (D8v)] foresooke my Countrie' (H4).

Creating his own parallel moral parable out of this scene, Underdowne adds a further stern marginal note in 1577, advising churchmen to mend their ways: 'God graunt that the honestie of this heathe[n] Priest, condemne not some of our miuisters [*sic*] which professe the Gospell' (D8). L'Isle then turns Underdowne's implied criticism into social reality. L'Isle's Kalasiris does not protest his innocence, and leaves the country only because bishops are not allowed to remarry:

> Though long resisting that entising ill,
> I faint at length, and left I place profane,
> (Twice marrie may not Metropolitane)
> I rather chose obseruing holy Lawes
> My selfe t'absent, pretending other cause.
> (G1)

Amyot, about to become a working Roman Catholic bishop and reformer, conscientiously uses his translation to correct the misdemeanours of priests. Throughout this passage, he provides pairs of variant verbs, as in 'i'estably & constituay la raison iuge de mon faict' – 'I established and constituted reason judge of my action'. But when commenting on Kalasiris's sexual urge, 'la forfaiture [...] que ie co[m]mis, no[n] de faict' – 'the ... violation that I committed, not in fact', Amyot, like the messenger in a morality play, interjects, '(ia à Dieu ne plaise)' – '(it would not please God)'. And by doubling the verb, he increases Kalasiris's contrition: 'mais seulement de volunté, ie puny & chastiay ma concupisce[n]ce par exil voluntaire' (E2v) – 'but solely out of willingness, I punished and chastised my concupiscence by voluntary exile'.

Heliodorus's cyclic tales

Kalasiris's narrative takes place in Nausikles' house in Chemmis. It is framed by the departure and return of Nausikles, and links the Thyamis under-plot to the story of Charikleia. Rhodopis may be the catalyst, but Kalasiris's principal reason for leaving Memphis is to avoid seeing the outcome of a prediction, that his two sons 'would take up swords and fight one another' (2.25; Reardon, p. 399). His public excuse is that he is going to visit his elder son, Thyamis, ostensibly living with his grandfather at Great Thebes. Not until he is reunited with Thyamis and Petosiris in Book 7, and is about to die, do readers learn that Kalasiris's self-imposed exile lasts for ten years (7.8).

Kalasiris travels to the Ethiopian court, promises Queen Persinna that he will find her abandoned daughter, and then moves to Delphi. In 3.5, at Knemon's insistence, Kalasiris describes the ceremony where the priests Theagenes and Charikleia fall in love. Continuing his narrative, Kalasiris tells Knemon how he interprets the characters embroidered on Charikleia's waistband, then puts into effect his plans for their elopement (4.8). He arranges passage with 'Phoenicians from Tyre, merchants by trade, sailing to Carthage in Libya' (4.16; Reardon, p. 439), and describes how Theagenes and Charikleia stage her abduction (4.17), 'in pursuance of our preconcerted plan' (4.18; Reardon, p. 441).

Kalasiris's long report ends with the three of them setting sail and making rapid progress to the point where 'the Sea of Zakynthos came into view' (5.1; Reardon, p. 445), shortly before the events reported at the beginning of Book 1. The timescale shortens abruptly when Nausikles returns, announcing he has found Thisbe (5.2). Dramatic irony governs this scene as Heliodorus permits Nausikles no knowledge of Thisbe's relationship with Knemon, who identified her corpse in the cave, or of Knemon's friendship with Charikleia. In disbelief, Knemon stumbles about Nausikles' house in the dark, eventually overhearing a woman who calls herself 'Thisbe' summarising her capture by robbers, her imprisonment in a cave, the belief that she is dead and her separation from her beloved.

Heliodorus moves rapidly to tie together the various parallel and intertwining strands of the cyclic structure of the first five books. The author-narrator interjects, 'the woman he had heard lamenting was not

Thisbe, but Charikleia!' (5.4; Reardon, p. 448). Charikleia's reintroduction into the main plot remains suspended until 5.11, while, through reported and direct speech, Heliodorus reveals the background to her arrival in Chemmis. Hired by Nausikles, Oroondates' commander, Mitranes, arrives at the Herdsman's island immediately after Petosiris and his bandits fire the marshes and capture Thyamis. Mitranes arrests Theagenes and Charikleia, who are disguised as beggars. Nausikles, hoping to sell Charikleia, convinces Mitranes she is Thisbe, and takes her home. Mitranes sends Theagenes to the Persian satrap, Oroondates (5.8–9). Kalasiris and Charikleia rejoice in their reunion, pretending they are father and daughter, and Nausikles prevails upon Kalasiris to tell his story.

Heliodorus calls attention to the rhetorical and artistic heritage of his erotic romance by openly adapting the narrative transition in *Odyssey*, 8.499–501, 'He spoke, and the singer, stirred by the goddess, began, and showed them / his song, beginning from where the Argives boarded their well-benched / ships, and sailed away'.[51] In similar fashion, Heliodorus's author-narrator intervenes to advance Kalasiris's tale:

> He told the whole story; the first part, that Knemon had already heard, he told briefly and, as it were, in outline, deliberately omitting some details that he deemed it best Nausikles should not know. Then he went on with the sequel, as yet untold, to his earlier narration. (5.16; Reardon, p. 457)

Kalasiris picks up the threads of Theagenes and Charikleia's elopement, and continues his narration until near the end of Book 5, the mid-point of *An Ethiopian Story*. His tale rounds off the cyclic first half that began *in medias res*, explaining the opening paragraphs of Book 1, and anticipating the ending of Book 10.

Leadership and the law

By the end of Book 5, the pirates' leader, Trachinos (cf. τραχύς, 'rough', 'savage', 'cruel'),[52] has fallen 'madly in love' (5.20; Reardon, p. 460). with Charikleia at Zakynthos. Rather than describe Trachinos's personality, Heliodorus creates a dramatic scene to demonstrate his determination,

---

51 *The Odyssey of Homer*, trans. by R. Lattimore (New York: Harper & Row, 1967). *Cf.* Héliodore, *Les Éthiopiques*, ed. by R. M. Rattenbury and T. W. Lumb, trans. by J. Maillon, ii.57, note. Sidney's more complex version in the revised *Arcadia*, cited in the next chapter, involves both the narrator and Philoclea. See *NA*, p. 233.

52 Reardon, p. 460, note; in French, 'le Rude', as in Héliodore, *Les Éthiopiques*, ed. by R. M. Rattenbury and T. W. Lumb, trans. by J. Maillon, ii.77, note.

opportunism, greed and brutality. Kalasiris persuades the Phoenicians
to set sail, but they become becalmed and Trachinos captures them
(5.26). Surprised by a storm, and his pirates unskilled in managing such
a substantial ship, Trachinos abandons his own smaller vessel, gambling
everything in order to keep his prize. They are finally driven ashore near
the Heracleotic mouth of the Nile (5.27). Trachinos decides to combine
the pirates' sacrifice to Poseidon with a feast celebrating his marriage to
Charikleia. He orders Kalasiris to 'secure my bride's compliance', telling
'her beforehand that she is to be married' (5.28; Reardon, p. 467).

Heliodorus uses this episode to create implicit comparisons with Kala-
siris's philhellene son, Thyamis, who in Book 1 demonstrates his popular
leadership of the Herdsman, and proposes a consensual marriage to
Charikleia. Creating dissension, Kalasiris tells Trachinos's deputy, Peloros
(πέλωρος, 'monstrous'),[53] that he is Charikleia's choice. Peloros predict-
ably claims Charikleia by right of pirate law: 'So Trachinos will either
stand aside of his own choice and grant me this bride as the prize to
which I am entitled as the first to have boarded the merchantman, or
else he will find his wedding has a bitter taste, and my right arm will
inflict on him the death he so richly deserves!' (5.30; Reardon, pp. 468–9).
Amyot provides a typically rhythmic, though atypically close, translation
in 'Ie vous auise, que ou Trachinus voluntairement ne cedera & quitera
la pucelle qui m'est iustement deuë, pource que ie me suis ieté le premier
dedans la nauire, ou que ie luy feray sentir de bien ameres noces, en luy
bailla[n]t de ceste main ce qui luy appartient' (L2).

Throughout this passage, as if accentuating the importance of correct
and fair judicial process to his republican-minded dedicatees, Warsche-
wiczki upholds the sanctity of civil law in maintaining order. He begins
by purging Trachinos's summary of the pirate law – at best, a crim-
inal convention rather than a law: 'Itaque aut sua sponte mihi sponsa
Trachinus cedet, aut acerbas sentiet nuptias, ab hac dextra quae conuenit
passus' (Q7v). This deliberate omission is reflected both by Underdowne,
'Wherefore *Trachinus* shal suffer me to marry her of his owne free wil, or
els he shal haue but a soary Marriage, by sufferinge that at my hande, that
he hathe wel deserued' (T3v), and by L'Isle:

> *Trachinus* neuer shall her from me part.
> I haue a reason will our fellowes charme;
> A sword as good as his, as strong an arme.
>
> (M2)

53 Reardon, p. 468, note; in French, 'le Géant', as in Héliodore, *Les Éthiopiques*, ed. by R. M.
Rattenbury and T. W. Lumb, trans. by J. Maillon, ii.77, note.

Peloros accuses Trachinos of violating pirate law, once again summarising its terms (5.31). In a work whose ending depends entirely on the interpretation, reasoned discussion and rescinding of a state law that requires the sacrifice of first-taken prisoners, this debate over so called legislative process within a criminal subculture parodies the main plot. Amyot finds no benefit in beautifying the vulgarity of the dialogue: 'tu veux doncq[ue] enfraindre la loy des coursaires' (L2). Warschewiczki, emphasising the accusation, expands '$Καταλύεις$' into two verbs, 'Dissoluis igitur, & abrogas piratarum legem' (Q8v), carried into Underdowne's translation, 'then doo you disanull and abrogate the Lawe of Pyrates' (T4), but simplified in L'Isle's 'Then breake y'our Law' (M2v).

Trachinos evades the issue by claiming priority of 'another rule which says that subordinates must give way to their superiors' (5.31; Reardon pp. 469–70). Amyot typically doubles the verb, accentuating what the law requires: 'vne autre loy, qui comma[n]de de ceder, & obtemperer au vouloir de ses seigneurs' (L2v) – 'another law, that requires to yield and submit to the will of superiors'. Warschewiczki stresses the grounds of Trachinos's justification within the terms of legal process. This is, after all, the law upon which every properly constituted state government depends: 'alterius legis authoritate & patrocinio nitor, quae vt praefectis cedatur imperat' –'I depend on the authority and defence of another law that demands that a superior is given way to' (Q8v). More anodyne representations appear in Underdowne, 'I leaue [i.e., 'commit'] to another whiche willeth that place be geuen to the Captaines' (T4), and L'Isle, 'But on the ground of other Law I go, / Which giues the Captaine choyce' (M2v).

Heliodorus implicitly compares Trachinos with Thyamis as leaders of outlaw sub-cultures. Where, in Book 1, Thyamis seeks consensus, Trachinos threatens physical violence: 'if you do not do as you are told [' $μὴ τὸ κελευόμενον$'], you will soon regret it – I shall smash your head in with this wine bowl!' and Peloros denounces the law as '$τυραννικοῦ$', 'autocratic' (5.31; Reardon, pp. 470). Amyot represents this closely in 'si tu ne fais ce que ie commande, ie t'en feray bien tost repentir: car ie te rompray la teste de ceste coupe' and 'ceste ordonna[n]ce tyrannique' (L2v) – 'if you do not do what I order, I will immediately make you repent, for I will smash your head with this cup' and 'this tyrannical law'. Once again, Warschewiczki alters the text. Rather than issuing a personal order, his Trachinos takes refuge behind the law: 'Tu vero nisi id quod lex imperat feceris, non multo post plorabis, percussus hoc poculo' (Q8v), and his Peloros makes no comment on its tyrannical nature. These changes affect Underdowne, 'if you doo not as the Lawe willes you, you shall repent it with a blowe of this potte' (T4v), and L'Isle: 'And rest content, or this (and vp he rose / With massie pot in hand) shall crosse your nose' (M2v).

When a drunken and bloody affray breaks out between those 'defending their captain' and those 'championing [...] the cause of right' (5.32; Reardon p. 470), Kalasiris retreats to a hillside. Charikleia, dressed in her sacred Delphic robes, aims her deadly arrows at everyone who crosses her path. Armed with a sword, Theagenes engages in combat with the only remaining pirate, Peloros, 'a man of enormous courage and a practised killer, who had butchered victims beyond number' (5.32; Reardon, p. 470). This bleak description of Peloros, appropriately represented in Renaissance translations, establishes Theagenes' heroic stature in preparation for his trials during the denouement. For Theagenes cuts off Peloros's arm at the elbow, and pursues him into the night. Dawn breaks with Theagenes lying at Charikleia's feet, 'like a dead man' (5.33; Reardon, p. 471). This is what the bandits observe from their hillside in the novel's opening scene.

With the end of Kalasiris's story, Book 5 – and the first cycle – is all but complete. Heliodorus brings the action to a pause with consummate theatricality. Kalasiris sees the bandits defeated, and watches Thyamis's Herdsmen capture his friends. He has no way of knowing that their leader is his eldest son.

Although the past interweaves with the present throughout Books 6 to 10, a sustained narrative, buoyed up with dialogue, relentlessly pushes the plot forward. In Book 6, Nausikles, Kalasiris and Knemon leave Charikleia in Chemmis while they pursue their search for Theagenes. The bandit Herdsmen from the village of Bessa, who have now chosen Thyamis as their leader, capture Theagenes as he is being taken to Oroondates (6.1). At this point, Knemon and Nausikles have fulfilled their narrative functions. Knemon is betrothed to Nausikles' daughter Nausikleia, and dropped from the action (6.8). Kalasiris and Charikleia disguise themselves as beggars, and set out for 'the village of Bessa, where they hoped to find Theagenes and Thyamis. But it was not to be' (6.12; Reardon, p. 483). The Persian Mitranes mounts an unsuccessful attack against Thyamis, in retaliation for kidnapping Theagenes. Thyamis decides to take Memphis, kill Oroondates if he is there and reinstall himself as high priest (6.13).

Heliodorus halts these dizzying scenic switches abrupty, introducing an other worldly, masque-like episode. While Kalasiris and Charikleia look on, an Egyptian woman experienced in the black arts raises her son from the dead. The corpse scolds her for performing before witnesses, but nonetheless foretells their future. Kalasiris, it prophesies, will separate his

sons (Thyamis and Petosiris) just as they are about 'to fight to the death'
(6.15; Reardon, p. 487). Charikleia will find her 'loved one; but after hard-
ships and dangers beyond counting, at earth's farthest boundaries, she
will pass her life at his side in glorious and royal estate' (6.15; Reardon, p.
487). Heliodorus does not deny his readers the reassurances they crave.
The harrowing sequence of adventures that follows will end in married
bliss, in Ethiopia. But first, Theagenes and Charikleia have to survive the
ordeal of imprisonment and torture at the hands of Oroondates' wife,
Arsake.

Thyamis justified

The action of Book 7 turns on the results of Arsake's passionate self-
indulgence: 'Her crimes included being in part responsible for Thyamis's
banishment from Memphis' (7.2; Reardon, p. 488). The narrator dips
briefly into the past, providing the background to Thyamis's leader-
ship of the Herdsman. Thyamis, elevated to high priest in Memphis on
Kalasiris's disappearance, ignores Arsake's lustful advances. Petosiris
ingratiates himself to Oroondates by alleging an affair between Thyamis
and Arsake. Restrained from accusing his wife by 'the awe and respect in
which he held the royal house' of her brother, the Persian tyrant, Oroon-
dates banishes Thyamis, creating 'Petosiris high priest in his stead' (7.2;
Reardon, p. 489).

Heliodorus synchronises Thyamis's return with the king of Ethiopia's
challenge to Oroondates over the emerald mines. These events precipi-
tate Theagenes and Charikleia's reunion in Memphis, their capture by the
Ethiopians en route to Oroondates in Syene and the final identification
scene in the Ethiopian court.

Thyamis presents his case for reinstatement, exposing Petosiris's
treachery. But as Arsake, true to type, 'looked upon Thyamis and then
upon Theagenes, her heart was rent in two, torn asunder by the desire she
felt for each of them' (7.4; Reardon, p. 490). Arsake commands Thyamis
and Petosiris to settle their dispute in single combat (7.4). Heliodorus
couches their chase around Memphis in theatrical terminology. The
inhabitants look on,

> with the entire population of the city lining the walls, watching like the
> presiding judges in a theatre ['θεάτρου'] – at that very moment either some
> divine power or some fortune that arbitrates over human destiny made the
> drama take a new and tragic twist ['καινὸν ἐπεισόδιον ἐπετραγῴδει'], almost
> as if bringing a second drama on stage to compete with the one already in

progress ['ὅσπερ εἰς ἀνταγώνισμα δράματος ἀρχὴν ἄλλου παρεισφέρουσα'].
(7.6; Reardon, pp. 492–3)

This is a key passage in determining the difference between Continental
and English attitudes towards the stage, as opposed to drama as a literary
genre. Where Amyot and Warschewiczki make valiant attempts to render
the spirit of the text, Underdowne's Calvinist interpretation leads him to
exorcise references to the theatre and theatrical audiences.

Amyot adds detail and duplicates most of the original concepts. He
begins with the entire population in Memphis stretched on the walls of
the city, specifically in the crenellations: 'tout le peuple de Nemphis [*sic*]
espandu sur les murailles de la ville aux creneaux'. They situate themselves
'neither more nor less than within a theatre to see this spectacle' – 'ne plus
ne moins que dedans vn theatre, pour voir ce spectacle'. What happens
next is still directed by the inevitable destiny of the gods, or even fortune.
But Amyot concludes by suggesting that this power, 'whichever it is that
governs and directs human affairs', is inaptly described: 'alors la fatale
destinée des dieux, ou bien la fortune, qui que soit celle qui gouuerne &
dirige les choses humaines'. This governing force 'instigates the beginning
of a new tragedy, as if it had wanted to place in the forefront the begin-
ning and argument of another second one, to make it play in comparison
with the first' – 'va susciter vne entrée de nouuelle tragedie, comme si elle
eust voulu mettre en auant le co[m]mencement & argument d'vne autre
seco[n]de, pour la faire iouer au parangon de la premiere' (N2v).

While Warschewiczki represents Heliodorus's essentials far more
compactly,[54] his Latin provides no precedent for Underdowne's
suppressing theatrical allusions in this awkward rendering:

> in the sight of the whole Cittie who looked vpon them, and was iudge of
> that controuersie, either a God, or some manner of Fortune whiche gouer-
> neth humayne affayres, by a newe deuise augmented that, that was donne,
> and in a manner beganne a newe Tragedy like the other. (Z2v)

There is no equivalent passage in L'Isle's *Faire Aethiopian*.

The new drama is the entry of Kalasiris in pursuit of his sons. Still
disguised as a beggar, Kalasiris cannot be recognised will until he doffs
his disguise and 'untied his priest's mane of hair' (7.7; Reardon, p. 493)
– Warschewiczki's '& sacra[m] comam cum non esset religata prom-

---

54 'ciuitate autem, tanquam ex theatro, iudice & arbitra spectaculi constituta: tunc sane seu
   numen, seu fortuna quaedam, gubernans res humanas, noua accessione tanquam in
   tragoedia auxit ea quae agebantur, quasi aemulatione quadam initium alterius fabule[m]
   afferens' (V3).

isit' (V3v), Amyot's 'laissa pendre en la denouant sa bla[n]che perruque sacrée' (N2v) – a detail omitted by Underdowne. L'Isle's rendering is freer, perhaps derived from Amyot, and clearly more Episcopalian: 'And grauely stood before them face to face; / With long white haire, and old Arch-Bishops grace' (O4). When Charikleia then identifies herself to Theagenes through her coded question – 'O Pythian, [...] have your forgotten the torch?' – the principal characters are reunited (7.7).

The wanton Arsake

Leading up to the denouement, Arsake's extended role through Books 7 and 8 provides a catalyst to bring the action full circle. As sister of the Great King in Persia, and wife of his satrap in Egypt, Oroondates, she is portrayed as a born tyrant, brought down by an overwhelming craving for sexual dominance. Her failure to break Theagenes leads to her psychological disintegration.

Describing Arsake as a flawed ideal, Heliodorus combines holistic Plutarchan characterisation with Theophrastan archetype in a sustained moral parable: 'a tall, handsome woman, highly intelligent and arrogant and proud by reason of her noble birth [...] But the life she led was disreputable: in particular she was a slave to perverted and dissipated pleasure' (7.2; Reardon, p. 488). Renaissance translators impose their own characteristics. The reforming Amyot insists that she is accomplished in the arts of rhetoric, criticising her for choosing to be dissolute in spite of her courtly education:

> Ceste dame Arsacé estoit belle, & grande, bien aduisée, & emparlée, pour entretenir toutes gens, & auoit le cueur grand, com[m]e celle qui estoit extraite de treshaulte noblesse [...] mais au demourant de vie reprochable, & qui se laissoit aller & vaincre à volupté impudique, & lasciue. (M6)

> This lady Arsake was beautiful and tall, highly intelligent and eloquent enough to converse with everyone, and had great spirit, for she was descended from very great nobility [...] but nevertheless of a blameworthy life, and one who let herself go, and gave way to lewd and lascivious pleasure.

Amyot doubles Heliodorus's single adjectives and verbs into reinforcing couples. An already balanced structure stretches into a series of short, punctuated, individually pronounced outbursts, building to a crescendo of condemnation.

Warschewiczki evokes a similar rhythmic quality: 'Arsace autem erat alioqui formosa & procera, & singulari industria in rebus administrandis praedita, atque animo elato propter ortus sui nobilitatem […] caeterum propter voluptatem illicitam ac dissolutam in vita, culpa & reprehensione non carebat' (T6). With careful attention to the sequence of co-ordinate conjunctive links in '& […] & […] atque', Underdowne comes close to replicating this in 'Arsace was a bewtifull woman, and of tale stature, & singuler wisedome to doo any thinge, and of a stoute stomake for the Noblenesse of her birthe, […] yet for her vnlawful and dissolute luste shee was not without reprehension and blame' (Y4). But all such attempts at fidelity come to naught in L'Isle's *The Faire Aethiopian*. Modelling his description on Sidney's mock encomium on Mopsa, 'like fair Venus, chaste', and 'as Juno, mild' (*NA*, p. 18), L'Isle describes Arsake through a series of similarly ironic comparisons:

> She was a Faire-one of *Diana's* size,
> And chaste as *Venus*, and as *Pallas* wise,
> And minded-high as *Iuno*, for her birth.
> (O2)

Heliodorus, in the manner of Plutarch, censures Arsake's failings of political and emotional character. He does this by demonstrating the effects of her uncontrollable sexual appetite, aroused by her passion for Theagenes:

> All night she lay there, ceaselessly tossing from side to side, ceaselessly sighing from the depths of her being: one moment she would sit bolt upright, the next slump back on the bedclothes; she would remove part of her clothing and then suddenly collapse back on her bed […]. In short, her desire was degenerating imperceptibly into insanity. (7.9; Reardon, p. 496)

L'Isle alone truncates this indelicacy, adding a comic twist: 'Then downe againe halfe naked tumbled shee, / And wisht *Theagenes* were there to see' (P1).

This prolonged depiction of Arsake's moral failings emphasises Theagenes' and Chariclea's exemplary composure. Arsake, who enjoys the fruits of tyranny from birth, now 'lay on her bed, clawing at herself' (7.22, Reardon, p. 509) in self-mutilation, out of frustration, not guilt. While Underdowne reflects this in 'vexed her selfe cruelly on her Bedde' (Cc1), Amyot's refined readers find her turning her venom against her clothes: 'se iecta sur son lict, & dessira tous ses habillemens de despit quelle eut' (O5) – 'she threw herself on her bed and in spite tore all her clothes that she could'. Arsake's behaviour parodies Charikleia's genuine despair, when, believing Theagenes to be dead, she pulls out chunks of her hair and tears her clothes (6.8). L'Isle conflates these two episodes,

his rhymed exaggerations resulting in ironic comedy in the manner of
Ariosto or Spenser:

> Now like to burst with griefe, rowles on her bed;
> And all to teares her cloths, her haire, her brest;
> Nor all that day could take a minutes rest.
>
> (Q2v)

Heliodorus increases the dramatic irony by making Kybele, the Persian
Arsake's old nurse and bawd, describe Arsake as a philhellene. She is 'a
lover of refinement and all things Greek' (7.12; Reardon, p. 500), 'fond
to a fault of Greek ways and the company of Greeks' (7.14; Reardon, p.
501). Kybele puts it to Theagenes that young men have found it attractive,
even financially rewarding, to accommodate older women who are in a
commanding situation. Underdowne disagrees. His damning marginal
gloss demonstrates his determination to adapt *An Ethiopian Story* into a
cautionary tale. For because the chaste and devoted Theagenes 'woulde
not vnderstande the same shee was forced plainely to tell the same with
a shamelesse Oration, wherein she declareth the properties of suche like
Lasciuious woome[n] passinge finely' (Bb3v).

The wicked Kybele

Heliodorus uses Arsake's passion for Theagenes to complicate, and begin
to unravel, the action. Comparison of the translations shows that the
episode was variably conveyed to Renaissance readers. Charikleia recom-
mends feigning acquiescence to Arsake (7.21), but, when it becomes
evident that Kybele fails to persuade Theagenes, Arsake 'had the old
woman thrown out on her ear' (7.22; Reardon, pp. 508–9). Idiomatic
usage colours Amyot's 'elle co[m]manda que lon iectast par les espaules
hors de sa cha[m]bre ceste vieille' (O5) – 'she ordered that this hag be
thrown out of her room by her shoulders'. Warschewiczki's literal 'Arsace
anu in caput praecipitari iussa' – 'Arsake ordered the old woman to be
thrown out on her head' (Y5) – yields an unexpected result when Under-
downe redirects Arsake's wrath towards Theagenes: '*Arsace* commaunded
to breake his necke' (Cc1). L'Isle embellishes to Kybele's detriment: 'The
Lady gaue her checke / In such a sort, as neere had broke her necke /
Thrown down the staires' (Q2v).

Arsake's head steward is Kybele's son, Achaimenes, who failed to
deliver Theagenes from Mitranes to Oroondates. He informs Arsake that
Theagenes, already her slave, is obliged to obey her wishes. As a reward,

Arsake engages Achaimenes to Charikleia (7.24). Theagenes uses the figure zeugma to produce two meanings in 'unions', as he asks the resourceful Charikleia, 'What plan can we devise to frustrate these abhorrent unions between Arsake and me and Achaimenes and you?' (7.25; Reardon, p. 512). Amyot exaggerates these rhythmic coordinate conjunctions. He expands Heliodorus's compressed zeugma, and produces an affected doubling of meanings throughout: 'quelle inue[n]tio[n] pourrio[n]s nous trouuer pour ro[m]pre, & empescher ceste odieuse co[n]iunction & assemblée d'Arsacé & de moy, & d'Achemenes & de vous?' (O6v) – 'what contrivance can we find to break off and prevent this hateful coupling and union of Arsace and me, and of Achaimenes and you?'

Such courtly elegance is eschewed by Warschewiczki, who emulates Heliodorus by doubling 'detestandus congressus', which means both 'detested intercourse' and 'abominated union': 'aut quam excogitare mochinam, qua & meus cum Arsace & tuus cum Achaemene detestandus congressus discuti possit?' (Y8v). Underdowne separates the meanings to make the point more obvious and exemplary: 'Or what waie shall wee deuise to breake of my abominable facte with *Arsace*, and youre shameful marriage with *Achemenes*?' (Cc3). L'Isle omits the question.

In Book 8, Heliodorus uses the Arsake-Kybele complication to return to the opening plots. The final crises and denouement revolve around Hydaspes' capture of the border city of Philai, and the disputed emerald mines. The essential identifiers are provided by Sisimithres, who took Charikleia with him on his embassy to Egypt, and Charikles who fostered her.

As Oroondates learns of Hydaspes' military success, Achaimenes arrives at Thebes to reveal Arsake's plans for Theagenes (7.27–9, 8.1). Achaimenes emphasises Charikleia's beauty, 'hoping that if Oroondates bedded' her, 'it would not be long thereafter before he could request her hand as the reward' (8.2; Reardon, p. 518). The contextual implication of a sexual association in Heliodorus's 'προσομίλησειεν' elicits euphemisms. Even Amyot's 'espera[n]t encore qu'Oroondates fist le premier son plaisir de Chariclea' (P3v) – 'hoping once that Oroondates took his first plea-sure with Charikleia' – is far more explicit than Warschewiczki's vague 'etiamsi rem habuisset Oroondates cum Chariclia' (Z7), which results in Underdowne's 'trustinge that although *Oroondates* had to doo with *Cari-clia*' (Dd2v). L'Isle eradicates Achaimenes' intention of marriage, openly describing the relationship as one based on lust and slavery: 'hoping, when his Lord / Had done, he might her get to bed and bord; / For iust reward' (R3).

While Oroondates dispatches his eunuch, Bagoas, to bring Theagenes and Charikleia to Thebes, Arsake continues to torture Theagenes. Kybele suggests poisoning Charikleia. A maid accidentally switches the cups. Kybele dies: 'violent convulsions and paroxysms racked her body [...] The old woman's eyes bulged, and, as the convulsions ceased, her limbs became paralyzed and rigid, and her skin took on a blackish hue' (8.7–8; Reardon, p. 524). In her death throes, Kybele accuses Charikleia of murder. Sentenced to burn at the stake, Charikleia survives unscathed as the flames turn away from her. She later recalls a dream in which Kalasiris has prophesied that she will be protected from flame by the 'jewel called pantarbe' (8.11; Reardon, p. 529), which she wears in her mother's engagement ring. Theagenes experiences a corresponding vision of Kalasiris, foretelling their imminent journey into Ethiopia.

Book 9, the penultimate, provides a dramatic suspension of the action. Its prolonged ecphrasis on military armour and tactics is designed to develop Hydaspes' profile as strategist, leader and exemplary archetype. Heliodorus uses this pause to thin out redundant characters and bring together the principals for his complex, drawn-out conclusion. En route to Oroondates, Bagoas with his prisoners is ambushed by Ethiopians. Theagenes and Charikliea are handed over to Hydaspes, then taken to be sacrificed in the Ethiopian royal city, Meroe (9.1). Oroondates is no sooner captured by Hydaspes than Achaimenes, knowing that Arsake has committed suicide, tries to assassinate his master. He is killed by an Ethiopian (9.20).

Heliodorus continues to reduce the outstanding business. In an act of diplomacy that Shakespeare emulates in *Cymbeline*, Hydaspes spares Oroondates and returns all his conquests, excepting 'Philai and the emerald mines' (9.26; Reardon, p. 557). Underdowne's remarks on Hydaspes' exceptional qualities as a ruler derive from the text, where Oroondates (9.27) pronounces him 'τὸν ἐννομώτατον ἀνθρώπον' – Amyot's emphatic 'le plus droict & le plus iuste de tous les hommes' (S6v), Warschewiczki's restrained 'aequissimo omnium hominu[m]' (Ff3v), and Underdowne's 'the tustest [corrected to 'iustest' in 1577 (R4)] man in the worlde'. (Kk3). L'Isle adapts this in 'such a gracious King' (X4v).

Oroondates repays Hydaspes by promising 'unbroken peace and ever-lasting friendship between Ethiopia and Persia', and praying that, in the event he should sufferer misfortune, 'the gods may reward Hydaspes, his house, and his nation' (9.27; Reardon, pp. 557–8), or race ('γένος'). Hydaspes' understanding of international affairs will be tested on the domestic level as he faces the ethical, moral, political and legal dilemmas that await his return from war. To resolve these issues, Theagenes and Charikliea are made to face the prospect of sacrificial execution, a custom used 'to celebrate victories over foreign foes' (10.7; Reardon, p. 562). For Ethiopian law requires Hydaspes to sacrifice an unmarried female and an unmarried male, neither of whom has had sexual intercourse, from among the captives.

Recognising Charikleia

Heliodorus concludes with 'a tight, drama-like endgame on a single set', constituting 'by far the most elaborate' recognition scene 'in ancient literature'.[55] This hinges on a number of legal and constitutional issues, including the relationship between the king, his council of gymnoso-phists, and his subjects. Sisimithres conducts his debate with Hydaspes in Greek, 'so that the people should not understand what he was saying' (10.9; Reardon, p. 564). He expresses the gymnosophists' disgust with both human and animal sacrifice, noting however that 'a king must serve the wishes of his people, misguided though they sometimes are' (10.9; Reardon, p. 565). Warschewiczki and Underdowne omit Sisimithres' condemnation of popular opinion in 'rex teditionem vulgi sedet' (Gg3), 'the King must needes be there to appease the people' (Ll3v). The Gallican Amyot makes the king's responsibility conditional rather than an impera-tive, 'vn Roy est quelque fois contraint' – 'a king is sometimes required' – 'd'obtemperer, & seruir à l'impetueux vouloir de son peuple, quoy qu'il soit desordo[n]né' (T4) – 'to obey and serve the impetuous will of the people, however misguided it may be'.

Under threat of death, Charikleia establishes her identity by producing the waistband and other articles with which she was abandoned, but remains too shy to mention her relationship with Theagenes (10.13). The lengthy debate about her identity, and the comparative status of judge and advocate, concludes when Sisimithres insists that Charikleia exhibit her distinctive birthmark. This is the final, clinching revelation in the recog-nition scene, as Persinna, overwhelmingly convinced, rushes to embrace her daughter.

Sisimithres' statement falls into two sections, political and genealogical issues alternating with two descriptions of Charikleia's birthmark:

'There is one point remaining, [...] for we are talking about the throne and its legitimate line of succession – and, most important, about truth itself.

55 N. J. Lowe, *The Classical Plot and the Invention of Western Narrative*, p. 255.

Bare your arm, girl: she had a black birthmark ['μέλανι συνθήματι'] on her upper arm. There is nothing indecent in laying bare that which will confirm your parentage and descent'.

Straightway Charikleia bared her left arm, and there was a mark, like a ring of ebony staining the ivory ['ἐλέφαντα'] of her arm! (10.15–16; Reardon, p. 569)

Renaissance readers encounter this key passage in a variety of forms. Amyot's enormously expanded version emphasises politics, action and emotional appeal while reducing Sisimithres' observations. Amyot also restructures, conflating both references to the birthmark, and framing them with the remarks on succession:

> Il reste [...] encore vn seul poinct: car puis qu'il est question de la coronne d'Aethiopie, & de la vraye & naturelle heritiere d'icelle, & deuant toutes choses de la verité, il ne fault rien omettre à enquerir, & decider. Monstrez vostre bras nud, ma fille. Ce qu'elle fist, & se trouua qu'elle auoit au dessus du coude vn sein [i.e., 'signe'] noir, qui estoit comme vne petite piece d'Hebene toute ronde, tachant son bras blanc & poly comme Yuoire. En quoy elle ne faisoit rien qui ne fust honneste, descouura[n]t la marque & le tesmoignage de sa parenté & de sa race. (T6v)[56]

True to form, Warschewiczki gives a literal rendering that clearly represents Heliodorus's interlaced pattern of topics.[57] Underdowne, however, depoliticises his text, and alters its rhetorical design by leaving out the opening reference to succession to the throne. He passes directly to the birthmark, which, instead of providing a complementary colour contrast between ebony and Charikleia's ivory skin, becomes an identifying blotch on an elephant's hide:

> Yet ... wee wante one pointe, strippe vp your sleeue Mayde, for there was a blacke spotte aboue your Elbowe: it is no shame to be stripped for triall of your parentes & kinred. *Cariclia* vncouered her lefte arme, & aboute it there was in a manner a mole, muche like to the strakes, that Elephantes haue. (Mm2v)[58]

56 'There still remains one point alone: for as it is a question of the crown of Ethiopia, and of the true and natural heiress of it, and above all else the truth, one must omit nothing in examining and judging. Show your bare arm, my girl. Which she did, and discovered that she had, above the elbow, a black mark, that was like a small piece of perfectly round ebony, staining her arm, white and polished as ivory. In this she did nothing that was not modest, uncovering the mark and the witness of her parentage and of her race'.

57 'Vnum adhuc desideratur, inquit. De regno enim, & illius legitima successione agitur, & ante omnia de veritate ipsa. Nuda brachium virgo, nigra nota pars supra cubitum maculata fuerat. Nihil dedecoris affert, nudatum parentem & generis testimonium. Nudauit illis Chariclia sinistram, & erat quasi ebenus quaedam in circuitu brachium tanquam elephantem macula[n]s' (G8).

58 Cf. *O.E.D.*, streak, *n*.1, 2bα, citing J. Maplet, *A greene Forest, or a naturall Historie* (1567),

That L' Isle's patriotic version of Heliodorus is a panegyric to Charles I
and Henriette-Marie may govern his alterations to this passage. In the
manner of Amyot, he inserts emphatic synonyms to denote the crown
and legitimate succession: 'Royall Descent, / And Crowne, and Scept'r
is waightie consequent: / And truth most waightie of all'. For the initial
description of Charikleia's birthmark, which, as in Amyot, is amalgam-
ated with the second, he substitutes an symbolic signifier: 'another signe
/ I know, may best th'Imperiall cause define'. L' Isle purposefully changes
ebony to azure, possibly associating Henriette-Marie – as did others –
with the Virgin Mary,[59] and coincidentally with the Scottish flag, 'Azure
a saltire Argent'. The heart of the matter is that, in L' Isle, the birthmark
possesses particular significance for the king who, in Heliodorus, has
never before known of it, and accepts Charikleia only after seeing Pers-
inna's emotional display:

> Your left arme (Lady) shew; 'tis no disgrace
> To shew a naked arme in such a case,
> If you be that same royall childe I knew,
> Aboue your elbow a marke there is of blue,
> She shew'd, and so it was; like azure ring
> On pollisht Iu'rie; this when saw the King,
> He was perswaded.
>
> (Z2v)

Language and nationalism

Heliodorus stops the plot to establish Theagenes as a hero in the eyes of
the Ethiopian court. His fortunes change when a sacrificial bull breaks
loose. He leaps from his horse to the neck of the bull, bringing it to
ground (10.30). He then defeats the Ethiopian wrestling champion, a
giant given to King Hydaspes by his brother's handsome son, Meroebos.
Reading Theagenes' victory as a parable, Heliodorus illustrates how brute
power as a means of governing gives way to combined strength, intellect
and force of personality.

In the old-fashioned way that her foster-father, Charikles, promised
her to Alkamenes in Book 4, Hydaspes engages Charikleia without her
consent (10.23–4). Prepared to be sacrificed, Theagenes' final request is
that his executioner should be Hydaspes' 'newly discovered daughter' (10.

K6v, 'beset with black spots or strikes'.
59 Cf. E. Veevers, *Images of Love and Religion: Queen Henrietta Maria and Court Entertain-
ments* (Cambridge: Cambridge University Press, 1989), pp. 103–9.

32; Reardon, p. 582). This moves the plot one stage closer towards resolution, for Ethiopian law demands that 'she who wields the sacrificial knife should be a married woman, not a virgin' (10.33; Reardon, p. 582).

Charikleia explains her relationship with Theagenes to her mother, continuing out of hearing as Heliodorus interrupts the action to bring on an embassy from Syene. This static scene produces a jarring complication. Through an ambassador, Oroondates requests Charikleia's return, so she might be restored 'to her father' (10.34; Reardon, p. 584), whom he believes to be Charikles. Charikles recognises Theagenes, accuses him of kidnapping his daughter from Delphi, and demands her return. When Hydaspes intervenes, Theagenes enigmatically and ironically challenges him: 'It is [...] the man who has the proceeds of the crime in his possession who should do the giving back. That man is you!' (10.37; Reardon, p. 586).

Heliodorus constructs a rapid denouement. After Sisimithres assures Charikles that Charikleia is safe, she throws herself at Charikles' feet, begging forgiveness. In this way, Heliodorus reunites Charikleia with both of her foster-fathers, Sisimithres and Charikles. He then legitimises her marriage to Theagenes. Persinna holds Hydaspes in her arms and explains, 'It is all true, my husband [...] this young Greek is truly to be our daughter's husband. She has just confessed as much to me' (10.38; Reardon, p. 586). Through this complex plot, Heliodorus creates a conundrum that can be resolved only by radical social and political reform. For although by this point Theagenes is Hydaspes' son-in-law in all but ceremony, the law of human sacrifice still requires his death.

The changes required to enable the marriage and crowning of Heliodorus's idealised exemplars of Greco-Roman governance, ethics and morality – the reincarnated Andromeda and the descendant of Achilles – allegorise the evolution of a barbarous state into a modern one. The first step towards social and political inclusion is taken by Sisimithres who, 'speaking Greek no longer, but Ethiopian for the whole assembly to understand' (10.39; Reardon, p. 587), breaks down the linguistic barrier between the king's privileged councilors and the less educated populace.

Warschewiczki, Underdowne and Amyot all agree in why Sisimithres speaks in the vernacular: 'Sisimithres non Graeca lingua, sed vt omnes exaudire possent, Aethiopica' (Kk2v); '*Sisimithres* answeared not in *Greeke*, but in the *Aethiopian* tongue, that all might vnderstande him' (Oo4v); 'Sysimethres [*sic*] luy respondit, non en langage Grec, mais en Aethiopien, afin que tout le monde l'ente[n]dist' (X3). But these translators immediately assert their individuality. Sisimithres argues that the gods have engineered this series of events, and that 'as a theatrical climax ['λαμπάδιον δράματος'] they have revealed that this young stranger is betrothed to the maiden' (10.39; Reardon, p. 587). Warschewiczki reports the theatrical metaphor as 'facem fabulae' (Kk3) – literally 'the torch of a drama', figuratively 'the climax'. This is changed by Underdowne to a literary genre, 'whiche may be the ende and conclusion of this Comedie' (Oo4v); but L'Isle continues to suppress theatrical metaphor. By contrast, Amyot's interpretation consciously emphasises the Christian marriage ceremony's evolution from ancient to modern. Amyot's 'pour la conclusion de tout ce mistere' (X3) – 'for the end of this sacred drama' – endows the passage with Christian overtones. *Mystère*, which more properly translates as 'miracle play', heralds the ritual pageantry surrounding Theagenes and Charikleia's imminent marriage.

Sisimithres' plea to 'abolish human sacrifice' (10.39; Reardon, p. 587) is taken up by Hydaspes, who now also 'spoke in the native tongue' (10.40; Reardon, p. 587). Always a patriotic nationalist, he now exhibits characteristics of a popular monarch. His use of the Ethiopian vernacular instead of Greek allegorises the philhellene rejection of Roman tyranny and the Latin tongue, imposed during the Roman occupation of Ethiopia.

This issue of a national language was particularly meaningful to Amyot, who tried to entice the Italianate monarchy and court to use his French adaptation of Second Sophistic Greek. Of the three Renaissance translators, Amyot seems most to emphasise the political significance of Hydaspes breaking tradition to communicate directly with his subjects. Contrast 'Hydaspes, cum & ipse linguam genti vernacula[m] intelligeret, [...] dicebat' (Kk3); '*Hidaspes* who vnderstoode also the tonge wherein he spake, [...] sayde' (Oo4v); with Amyot's 'Hydaspes, qui sçauoit aussi la langue vulgaire, [...] dist' (X3) – 'Hydaspes, who also knew the common language, [...] said'.

Heliodorus uses the *deus ex machina*, the offstage God, to manipulate the events of his socio-political strategy, which includes resolving the problem of the law. Hydaspes describes his dilemma: 'To refuse the gods their due sacrifice would be irreverent; to put those who are the gods' gifts to the knife would be sacrilegious' (10.39; Reardon, pp. 586–7).

The inevitability of altering the law is decreed by divine will. Hydaspes defers to Sisimithres, who interprets the thrust of events: 'Let us not be blind to the miracles the gods have wrought; let us not thwart their purpose; let us abolish human sacrifice forevermore and hold to purer forms of offering!' (10.39; Reardon, p. 587). Hydaspes and Persinna become the first to practise the reformed law. They hand over the insignia of the priests of the sun and the moon to Theagenes and Charikleia. This marks a further step towards modernisation: 'the absorption of rational, civilised Greeks into their community redeems the culturally ambivalent Ethiopians from the savage excesses of their old religion.'[60]

Theagenes and Charikleia's marriage becomes a benchmark in Ethiopian enlightenment, symbolising a new political and cultural order. But what was attractive to Renaissance believers in the divine right of kings was the notion of Theagenes' inherited divinity. For although Theagenes, alone among the principal characters, chooses to make 'a one-way trip to a new life at the other end of the earth',[61] his return to Ethiopia as Perseus, a national saviour and father of the race, completes a timeless historical and political cycle that heralds spiritual hope and national renewal.

L'Isle's political panegyric

Warschewiczki and Underdowne see in *An Ethiopian Story* a parable teaching exemplary behaviour, the defeat of tyranny and restored succession. Amyot accentuates its model characterization and uses it as royalist propaganda. Collectively, these notions inspire Heliodorus's most significant English follower, Sir Philip Sidney, whose *Arcadia* demonstrates the adoption of erotic romance to express philhellene Protestant ideals. But William L'Isle, who suppresses much of Heliodorus's detail, adds a complimentary conclusion in *The Faire Aethiopian* that takes his narrative into the realm of panegric.

An Ethiopian Story ends with a cursory account in which the wedding party, after performing the rites of sacrifice, returns to the city for 'the more mystic parts of the wedding ritual' (10.41; Reardon, p. 588). L'Isle opens his addition with the wedding feast, introducing a black entertainer, a court slave from the island of Zanzibar:

> A curle-head blacke-boy (taught by *Zanzibar*,
> Who, th'Art to learne, had trauelled as far
> As th'Isle of *Britain*) sung to th'Irish harp
> How Sun and Moone about the Center warp.
>   (Bb1v)

Whether or not L'Isle's allegory is based on Portugal's control of Zanzibar as well as Abyssinia, which included Ethiopia, he uses this slave to represent British rule of Ireland, which Charles was cultivating as a source of

---

60 N. J. Lowe, *The Classical Plot and the Invention of Western Narrative*, p. 237.
61 N. J. Lowe, *The Classical Plot and the Invention of Western Narrative*, p. 239.

revenue. (Ironically, L'Isle published in 1631, and Portuguese influence in Abyssinia ended in 1632–33.)

L'Isle's black singer contributes a synopsis of Theagenes' Greek ancestry, from Achilles and Memnon, and Charikleia's Ethiopian heritage through Perseus and Andromeda, 'Whose picture faire, in black Kings chamber seene, / That Faire-one made be borne of Blackmore Queene' (Bb1v).

In *The Faire Aethiopian*, L'Isle represents Charles I as a heroic Theagenes, and Henriette-Marie as the chaste, fair-skinned Charikleia. As both the French and English monarchs were ritually sanctified by anointing,[62] Charles and Henriette-Marie only differ in status from Heliodorus's characters by not being practising priests. Their wedding in 1625 served as the catalyst for a new understanding between England and France. As L'Isle put it in 1625, in 'A Pastorall Dedication to the King', Charles I, of the English–French teaching text he based on du Bartas's second 'Week', 'While earth stands Cent'r, and Heau'n in circle goes / Together spring French Lillie and English Rose' (¶¶2v).[63] He reiterates this in the epigraph to *The Faire Aethiopian* (1631), 'Dum rotat astra polus, dum fixa est terra, Britannis / Gallica florescant Lilia juncta Rosis' – 'While the pole rotates the stars, while the earth remains still, the lilies of France will flourish joined with the roses of Britain' (A2v). And he revisits this imagery in his dedicatory apostrophe, which begins with a metonym for the golden fleur-de-lis of France:

> O Branch of flowring Gold the best that growes
> On face of Earth, consorted now with Rose
> Both white and red; Sith *Helicon* is thine,
> Me grant a sip of liquor *Castaline*;
> That I in verse this Romant so endight,
> As may thee and thy daintie Buds delight:
> Thy rare endowments euer will I sing;
> For Queene is Patronesse where Patron King.
>
> (B1v)

The King and Queen lost a premature son in May 1629. L'Isle's allusion to their 'daintie Buds', in a work published in 1631 'at the Authors charge', more probably refers to the birth of Prince Charles on 29 May 1630.

L'Isle's nationalisation of *An Ethiopian Story* shows how European

62 F. A. Yates, *Astraea: The Imperial Theme in the Sixteenth Century*, p. 121.
63 G. de Saluste du Bartas, *Part of Du Bartas, English and French, and in his owne kinde of Verse, so neare the French Englished, as may teach an English-man French, or a French-man English.* […] *With the commentary of S.G.S.* [i.e., Simon Goulart, Senlisien] *By William L'Isle of Wilburgham, Esquier for the Kings body.*

erotic romance, however debased from its Greco-Roman model, could be used by a political reformer in seventeenth-century England. His philhellene leanings encourage him to promote a commonwealth, or republican, consciousness for the good of the greater nation-state, and, tacitly, for the Huguenots of La Rochelle, fiercely besieged by Henriette-Marie's own brother, Louis XIII of France. L'Isle is an altruist, not writing for reward, but

> With more effect to serue my Sou'raigne Lord;
> To write, read, giue, keepe hospitalitee,
> As heretofore haue done mine Ancestree:
> That after-commers know, when I am dead,
> I some good thing in life endeavoured.
> [...]
> *In vaine (may seeme) is wealth or learning lent*
> *To man that leaues therof no monument.*
>
> (Bb2)

L'Isle's concern for his reputation, answering Sidney's challenge to poet-haters that 'when you die, your memory die from the earth for want of an epitaph',[64] replaces Heliodorus's valedictory signature at the end of *An Ethiopian Story*: 'So concludes the *Aithiopika*, the story of Theagenes and Charikleia, the work of a Phoenician from the city of Emesa, one of the clan of Descendants of the Sun, Theodosius's son, Heliodoros' (10.41; Reardon, p. 588).

Conclusion

Heliodorus's (and Kleitophon's) Phoenician origins held particular significance for French nationalist philhellenes such as Amyot and Estienne, and for Underdowne, Sidney and L'Isle in England. For according to the historical fragments of pseudo-Berosus, first published in Annius of Viterbo's *Commentaria* (1498),[65] and widely disseminated during the sixteenth and seventeenth centuries, Phoenicia, which occupies the Syrian coast, gave western Europe its first king and its first structured language. As

64 Sir P. Sidney, *A Defence of Poetry*, in *Miscellaneous Prose of Sir Philip Sidney*, ed. by K. Duncan-Jones and J. van Dorsten (Oxford: Clarendon Press, 1973), p. 121.
65 The French tradition is extensively explored in R. E. Asher, *National Myths in Renaissance France: Francus, Samothes and the Druids* (Edinburgh: Edinburgh University Press, 1993), p. 47; the English tradition is summarised in T. D. Kendrick, *British Antiquity* (London: Methuen, 1950), pp. 69–76. See also R. T. John, *Fictive Ancient History and National Consequences in Early Europe: The Influence of Annius of Viterbo's 'Antiquitates'* (London: University of London Press, 1994).

described in Holinshed's 'The Historie of England', this Phoenician king was Samothes, son of Japhet, grandson of Noah.

Samothes became 'founder of the kingdom of Celtica, which co[n]teined in it [...] a great parte of Europe, but specially those cou[n]treys, which now are knowne by ye names of Gallia & Britannia'.[66] Roman authors, who testified that 'Britaine was sometimes ioined to the continent of France',[67] lent weight to Annius's vision of a unified Celtica, or Samothea. This was a pre-Hellenic state that exported its language and culture. For when Samothes taught the Celts astronomy, natural history, and moral and political philosophy, he 'deliuered the same in the Phenician letters: out of which the Grekes [...] deuised & deriued the greke characters'.[68]

A Gallic nationalist, in 1547 Jacques Amyot might well have regarded translating Heliodorus and other Greek texts into Greco-Roman French as an act of cultural repatriation. Warschewiczki in 1551–52, and Underdowne in 1569, employ *An Ethiopian Story* to express philhellene Protestant political modelling. Decades later, in 1630, William L'Isle could find no better literary example to continue to remind Charles and Henriette-Marie of their political and social responsibilities. One of the works that L'Isle acknowledges by citation, the subject of the next chapter, is Sir Philip Sidney's *Arcadia*.

---

66 R. Holinshed, *The Firste volume of the Chronicles of England, Scotlande, and Irelande* (1577), a1.
67 J. Speed, *The History of Great Britaine* (1611), Oo1.
68 R. Holinshed, *The Firste volume of the Chronicles of England, Scotlande, and Irelande* (1577), a1v.

Part two

Philhellene erotic romance

5

National romance and Sidney's *Arcadia*

Political outlines

The preceding chapters demonstrate how, during the sixteenth and seventeenth centuries, the erotic romances of Longus, Achilles Tatius and Heliodorus take on various political inflections. Editors and translators manifest the amalgam of their political, religious, moral and ethical leanings through their dedications, additions, omissions, alterations and rhetorical styles. Part One closes with examples of Heliodorus's *An Ethiopian Story* being adopted by European and English nationalists to promote consultative monarchy within a sovereign state. All would have been aware of, and perhaps even believed, Annius of Viterbo's influential but forged history of kingship in Europe after Noah, in which Samothes ruled over a unified kingdom that included France and Britain.

In using Annius's pseudo-Berosus legend of Samothes to politicise his *Old Arcadia*, Sir Philip Sidney (1554–86) appears to be unique among creative writers of the European Renaissance. Sidney wrote the bulk of the *Old Arcadia* in June 1577,[1] shortly after returning from an embassy to Germany that included a reunion with his mentor, the Burgundian-born Protestant statesman, Hubert Languet (1518–81).[2] On 18 October 1580, Sidney wrote to his brother Robert (1563–1626) that he hoped to send his 'toyfull' book or books,[3] seemingly the completed first version of the *Old Arcadia*, by the following February. Languet, Melanchthon's student, had begun to supervise Robert Sidney's European education in

---

1 The date and composition are discussed in Sir P. Sidney, *The Countess of Pembroke's Arcadia (The Old Arcadia)*, ed. by J. Robertson (Oxford: Clarendon Press, 1973), pp. xv–xvi, hereafter referred to as *OA*, and H. R. Woudhuysen, *Sir Philip Sidney and the Circulation of Manuscripts 1558–1640* (Oxford: Clarendon Press, 1996).

2 M. N. Raitiere, *Faire Bitts: Philip Sidney and Renaissance Political Theory* (Pittsburgh: Duquesne University Press, 1984), p. 10.

3 In *OA*, p. xvi, J. Robertson reads 'book(s)', indicating lack of clarity in the handwriting.

1579.[4] Given Languet's role in the formation of Philip and Robert Sidney's political ideas, it comes as no surprise to find Philip's evolving adaptation of European erotic romance representing a continuum of Protestant monarchomachist thought.

In the *Old Arcadia*, Sidney goes further than Heliodorus in emphasising the dramatic qualities of his work, replicating the form of a play in five movements.[5] Five Books or Acts are separated by Eclogues, passages in prose and verse. While only the First and Second Eclogues provide extensive background information, all four perform a kind of choric function, loosely reflecting the concerns of the main plot. The opening of the *Old Arcadia* represents the work as a combination of history and folklore: 'Arcadia among all the provinces of Greece [...] In this place some time there dwelled a mighty duke named Basilius' ('king' or 'ruler') (*OA*, p. 4). After briefly introducing his characters, whose pseudo-Greek and Latin names emulate those of erotic romance, Sidney reveals the contents of an oracle. It threatens Basilius, his wife, Gynecia,[6] his daughters Philoclea and Pamela, and his state, all within 'this fatal year' (*OA*, p. 5).

Sidney uses erotic romance to demonstrate how all sense of political and social responsibility can be eroded by passion. Basilius's retreat with his family to the countryside is complicated by the contrived chance arrival of Pyrocles and Musidorus: 'Now, newly after that the duke had begun this solitary life, there came [...] into this country two young princes' (*OA*, p. 9). Pyrocles falls in love with a painting of Philoclea in Kerxenus's gallery. Musidorus, not yet introduced to Pamela, taunts him for shamelessly abandoning a virtuous life of chivalric heroism and monarchomachist activity (*OA*, p. 11), as reported in the First and Second Eclogues (*OA*, pp. 67–9, 153–8). Musidorus nonetheless accepts the rationale Pyrocles concocts for adopting the disguise of an Amazon warrior, succumbs to love himself, and serves as assistant to Basilius's 'principal herdman', Pamela's guardian, Dametas (*OA*, p. 6).

---

4 A synopsis of Languet's tutelage of Robert Sidney is in M. V. Hay, *The Life of Robert Sidney, Earl of Leicester (1563–1626)* (Washington: Folger Shakespeare Library, 1984), p. 32.

5 See V. Skretkowicz, 'Sidney and Amyot: Heliodorus in the Structure and Ethos of the *New Arcadia*', *Review of English Studies*, n.s., xxvii (1976), 170–4.

6 Cf. Plutarch, 'Life of Julius Caesar', in *The Lives of the Noble Grecians and Romanes, compared together by that graue learned Philosopher and Historiographer, Plutarke of Chaeronea: Translated out of Greeke into French by Iames Amyot, Abbot of Bellozane, Bishop of Auxerre, one of the Kings priuy counsel, and great Amner of Fraunce, and out of French into Englishe, by Thomas North* (1579), SSS6: 'The ROMANES doe vse to honor a goddesse which they call the good goddesse, as the GRAECIANS haue her whom they call *Gynaecia*, to wit, the goddesse of wemen. Her, the PHRYGIANS doe claime to be peculiar vnto them, saying: that she is king *Midas* mother'.

Playing on a Greek and Latin composite of his name, later changed to a Greek compound in *Astrophil and Stella*, Sidney wrote himself into the *Old Arcadia* as the melancholy Philisides ('lover of a star'). Samothean-born and therefore by Annius's definition fluent in Greek, Philisides is well-educated, accomplished in Renaissance martial arts and well-travelled. A poem in the Fourth Eclogues describes his falling in love with Mira. He emphasises his sincerity by adapting Petrarch's description of his first glimpse of Laura, thereby increasing the significance of the politically charged location where this occurred, 'in fairest wood / Of Samothea land; a land which whilom stood / An honour to the world' (*OA*, p. 336). Rejected by Mira, Philisides abandons Samothea, hoping 'by perpetual absence to choke mine own ill fortunes' (*OA*, p. 341). He finds solace in Arcadia, where 'in that thrifty [i.e., 'prosperous'] world the substantiallest of men would employ their whole care upon' the sheep they owned (*OA*, p. 56).

Sidney's pastoral self-portrait and his affection for Mira relate closely to three poems and a device (Sidney freely interchanges the terms 'device', 'impresa' and 'imprese')[7] he prepared for a tiltyard masque.[8] The first poem refers to 'the chief of cupids Sabboth dayes / the wake of those that honour Samos Ile', when 'Philisides the Sheapheard good and true' visits the husbandman Menalca, and praises his beloved 'Mirrha'. He encourages Menalca to stop work and join him, rather than defile 'this holy time'. Sidney glosses this poem, 'This was to be said by one of the Plowmen after that I had passed the Tilt with my rusticall musick[,] & this freemans songe that followeth' – a 'freeman's song' is a lively one. The preterite conditional verb in the next note also suggests that Sidney's masque was not performed: 'The Imprese to this shuld have ben a harrowe & this word, *Nec habent occulta sepulchra*' – 'Graves do not hold secrets', that is, because they can be ploughed up.

The second, and openly politicised, of these tiltyard poems portrays Elizabeth I as a Protestant icon, 'a roiall saynt', and exhorts celebration of 'her day on which she entred', Accession Day, 17 November. It shares its chorus, 'good lord delyver us', with Sidney's erotic poem, 'Ring out your bells [...] for love is dead', both being secular parodies of the Christian church's Litany, as 'prescribed for use every Sunday, Wednesday and

---

7 V. Skretkowicz, 'Sir Philip Sidney and the Elizabethan Literary Device', *Emblematica*, iii (1988), 171–9 (p. 171).

8 First reported by B. M. Wagner, 'New Poems by Sir Philip Sidney', *Publications of the Modern Language Association of America*, liii (1938), 118–24; see the extensive discussion and transcriptions of the texts, cited here, in H. R. Woudhuysen, *Sir Philip Sidney and the Circulation of Manuscripts 1558–1640*, pp. 266–78, 413–15.

Friday'.[9] The third poem, recited by 'a desert knighte' and addressed 'To her that is [...] Saint of the saboath', adopts the hagiographical tone of the poems in the 1587 *Daphnis and Chloe* jousts, when the shepherds' – or courtiers' – 'holy day' fell on Friday. Such flexible use of religious terms may not fix these poems to 1577, when 17 November fell on Sunday. But they clearly belong to the period when Sidney still felt comfortable about interrelating the Christian allegorisation of the Queen with his autobiographical representation of Philisides as a Samothean.

In the Third Eclogues of the *Old Arcadia*, Philisides is the only one of the 'stranger' or foreign shepherds in Basilius's court to attend the pastoral wedding of Lalus and Kala. Unwilling to reveal his subjection to love, he contributes to the festivities by reciting a song by 'old Languet [...] / Languet, the shepherd best swift Ister knew' (*OA*, p. 255). Specifically naming the Ister, or Danube, anticipates Sidney's direct connection between Philisides and Samothea. For in the pseudo-Berosus fragment in Annius of Viterbo's *Commentaria* (1498), Noah ('father Janus') 'made Tuscon king of Sarmatia from the Don to the Rhine: and all the sons of Istr and of Mesa with their brothers were next to him'. Their dominion extended 'from Mount Adula', at the source of the Danube in the Swiss Alps, eastwards 'to Pontic Mesembria', near the Mouths of the Danube on the Black Sea. 'Under them ruled Tyras, Arcadius, Emathius: Comerus Gallus held Italy. Samotus possessed the Celts; and Jubal took over the Celtiberians'.[10]

For several years Sidney joined the rest of Europe in believing in Annius's construction of the biblical origins of European monarchical history. For like-minded militant Protestants, this provided the political impetus towards re-creating a united Christian Europe, as it was imagined to be prior to the divisive religious wars in France and the Low Countries that, in 1586, drew Sidney to his death.[11]

Annius's impact on the growth of Celtic nationalism was spread through Jean Lemaire de Belges's *Illustrations de Gaule et singularités*

9 K. Duncan-Jones, *Sir Philip Sidney, Courtier Poet* (London: Hamish Hamilton, 1991), p. 145; *The Poems of Sir Philip Sidney*, ed. by W. A. Ringler, Jr (Oxford: Clarendon Press, 1962), CS 30, AT 19, AT 21.

10 R. E. Asher, *National Myths in Renaissance France: Francus, Samothes and the Druids* (Edinburgh: Edinburgh University Press, 1993), pp. 47, 202–3, 'In Europa regem Sarmatiae fecit Tuysconum a Tanai ad Rhenum: iunctique sunt illi omnes filii Istri et Mesae cum fratribus suis ab Adula monte usque in Mesemberiam ponticam. Sub his tenuerunt Tyras: Archadius: Emathius. Italiam tenuit Comerus Gallus. Samotus possedit Celtas: et Iubal occupauit Celtiberos.'

11 See V. Skretkowicz, '"O pugnam infaustam": Sidney's Transformations and The Last of the Samotheans', *Sidney Journal*, xxii (2004 [published 2006]), 1–24.

de Troie (1510–13). In 1561, the Portuguese scholar Gaspar Barreiros ('Varreiro' in the 1565 Latin edition) discredited the fake pseudo-Berosus fragments.[12] Although this exposé was frequently reprinted, the legend persisted for many generations.[13] William Harrison included Annius's material in his 'Historie of Englande', published in the 1577 edition of Raphael Holinshed's *The Firste volume of the Chronicles of England, Scotlande, and Irelande* (1577) (a1–a1v).[14] But in the 1587 edition, *The First and second volumes of Chronicles*, Harrison would warn readers,

> Neuerthelesse, I thinke good to aduertise the reader that these stories of Samothes, Magus, Sarron, Druis, and Bardus, doo relie onelie vpon the authoritie of *Berosus,* whom most diligent antiquaries doo reiect as a fabulous and counterfet author, and *Vacerius* [i.e., Barreiros/Varreirus] hath laboured to prooue the same by a speciall treatise latelie published at Rome. (A3v)

Harrison may have been led by Sidney's Huguenot friend Philippe de Mornay, Seigneur du Plessis-Marly, commonly known as Du Plessis-Mornay, whose *De la Verité de la Religion Chrestienne* (Antwerp, 1581) was dedicated to Henri III of Navarre. The translation of 1587, which Sidney began and Arthur Golding completed and dedicated to Leicester, represents Du Plessis-Mornay's denunciation of Annius's evidence in colloquial English: '*Berosus* and others of the lyke stampe […] I hold them for fabling and forged authors.'[15] Growing condemnation of Annius's fabrication may lie behind Sidney's disassociating Philisides from Samothea in the revision and expansion of *Arcadia* that he undertook during 1582–84.

12 *Chorographia de alguns lugares que stam em hum caminho* (Coimbra, 1561); *Censura in quendam auctorem, qui sub falsa inscriptione Berosi Chaldaei circunfertur* (Rome, 1565).
13 The European dissemination of Annius's text and Barreiros's exposure are described in W. Stephens, 'When Pope Noah Ruled the Etruscans: Annius of Viterbo and His Forged Antiquities', in 'Studia Humanitatis: Essays in Honor of Salvatore Camporeale', *Modern Language Notes*, cxix, no.1 (2004), S201–S223; cf. R. E. Asher, *National Myths in Renaissance France: Francus, Samothes and the Druids*, pp. 46, 77–8, and V. Skretkowicz, '"O pugnam infaustam": Sidney's Transformations and the Last of the Samotheans', pp. 13–14.
14 See K. Duncan-Jones, 'Sidney in Samothea: A Forgotten National Myth', *Review of English Studies*, n.s., xxv (1974), 174–7, and W. L. Godschalk, 'Correspondence', *Review of English Studies*, n.s., xxix (1978), 325–6, and W. L. Godschalk, 'Correspondence', *Review of English Studies*, n.s., xxxi (1980), 192, all supplementing T. D. Kendrick, *British Antiquity* (London: Methuen, 1950), pp. 69–76.
15 *A Woorke concerning the trewnesse of the Christian religion, written in French: against atheists, Epicures, Paynims, Iewes, Mahumetists, and other infidels. By Philip of Mornay Lord of Plessie Marlie. Begunne to be translated into English by Sir Philip Sidney Knight, and at his request finished by Arthur Golding* (1587), G8.

The single remaining reference to 'Samothea land' falls in the new portion of Book 3, where Philisides' otherworldly poem on Mira, Venus and Diana is re-used. Here, because it describes Amphialus's dream 'which he had seen the night before he fell in love with' Philoclea,[16] it assumes an otherworldly nature.

In the style of Annius's pseudo-Berosus, in the *Old Arcadia* Sidney locates Languet's lyric fable in a vague pre-historical moment: 'Such manner time there was (what time I not)' (*OA*, p. 256). During this timeless era before the creation of man, the 'beasts' live in a harmonious hierarchy ruled by those 'with courage clad' (not the meek and cowardly) who, 'Like senators a harmless empire had'. The creatures, 'in language theirs [...] / (For then their language was a perfect speech)', decide to appeal to Jove 'to have a king'. 'Only the owl', possessor of wisdom, 'warned them not to seech', and fled 'to deserts' (*OA*, p. 256), emulating the flight of Astraea, goddess of Justice, from the unjust world. At the same time, the linguistic homogeneity of the beasts' 'perfect speech' dissolves in the narrative into the incomprehensible, species-specific sounds audible to humans, 'neighing, bleating, braying, and barking, / Roaring, and howling, for to have a king' (*OA*, p. 256). Languet's description uses linguistic difference to reveal conflicting self-interests, and the vulnerability of the beasts' sociopolitical union. Instead of deterring their ambitions, Jove's caveat that 'Rulers will think all things made them to please' (*OA*, p. 257) seems to promise rewards to individuals seeking personal benefit, rather than advancement of the commonwealth.

Once Jove contributes a 'naked sprite' (*OA*, p. 257), and each of the creatures gives a characteristic quality, their newly created and compositely endowed generic 'man' gains political superiority. Able to identify factional and interest driven divisions among the beasts, the King disempowers the 'nobler beasts' by overtly assisting the 'weaker sort'. In a pique, the unwitting 'tigers, leopards, bears, and lions' seed' willingly withdraw. They begin to starve, and live outside the law through 'ravin'. Employing political guile, the aspiring tyrant has 'craftily [...] forced them to do ill', creating the justification for their executions. This leaves under human control the easily exploited creatures, those of 'not great, but gentle blood': 'horse and dog', 'the commons, cattle of the field' (*OA*, p. 258). The 'gentle birds' fare no better once the falcon and goshawk have been caged 'in mew' (*OA*, p. 259).

Sidney's mythic Languet closes with caveats. He cautions, 'O man, rage

16 Sir P. Sidney, *The Countess of Pembroke's Arcadia (The New Arcadia)*, ed. by V. Skretkowicz (Oxford: Clarendon Press, 1987), p. 346, hereafter referred to as *NA*.

not beyond thy need; / Deem it no gloire to swell in tyranny. / [...] A plaint of guiltless hurt doth pierce the sky'. Turning to the beasts, he outlines a stark choice: either 'in patience bide your hell, / Or know your strengths, and then you shall do well' (*OA*, p. 259).[17] Deprived from the outset of the owl's wisdom, kings can and will become self-interested tyrants – even benign tyrants like Sidney's Basilius. Subjects may either suffer in abject slavery, or resist. But not having wisdom, as several instances in *Arcadia* illustrate, it proves well nigh impossible for individuals and nations to set aside self-interest to form a collective resistance to tyranny.

Selective monarchomachia

Sidney uses the Philisides–Languet song to signal his association with the philhellene Protestant political reformation, encouraged by Languet's mentor, Philip Melanchthon. The self-assertion with which Languet's fable closes represents a muted version of Melanchthon's defence of 'Whether it is lefull for priuat persons to kyll tyrants, that is cruell officers', available in English since roughly 1550.[18] Given Melanchthon's patronage in 1551 of Warschewiczki's translation of Heliodorus, which Sidney must have known, Sidney had good reason for alluding to monarchomachism in his depiction of a king who strayed from the paths of 'wisdom and virtue [...] the only destinies appointed to man to follow' (*OA*, p. 7).

The Old Testament foundation text for Renaissance disputes on monarchy and tyranny, adapted in Languet's allegory, is 1 Samuel 8.[19] It is paraphrased in *Court Maxims*, written in 1664–65 by Sidney's grand-nephew, the regicide Algernon Sidney (1623–83), the son of Mary Sidney Wroth's brother, Robert:

> God had separated them [i.e., the Israelites] from all other nations, was himself their king and lawgiver, placing over them a government that

17 See M. N. Raitiere, *Faire Bitts: Philip Sidney and Renaissance Political Theory*, especially pp. 68–70, where 'king' becomes synonymous with 'tyrant'; R. Kuin, 'Elective Affinities: Sidney and the New Languet Biography', *Sidney Newsletter and Journal*, xv, no. 1 (1997), 61–77, on B. Nicollier-de Weck, *Hubert Languet 1518–1581: Un réseau politique international de Melanchthon à Guillaume d'Orange* (Geneva: Droz, 1995); and A. Stewart, *Philip Sidney: A Double Life* (London: Chatto & Windus, 2000).

18 P. Melanchthon, *A ciuile nosgay wherin is contayned not onelye the offyce and dewty of all magestrates and iudges but also of all subiectes with a preface concernynge the lyberty of iustice in this our tyme newly collected and gethered out of latyn and so translated in to the Inglyshe tonge by I.G.* [i.e., John Goodale] ([1550?]), (D4v).

19 See M. N. Raitiere, *Faire Bitts: Philip Sidney and Renaissance Political Theory*, pp. 73–6; B. Worden, *The Sound of Virtue: Philip Sidney's Arcadia and Elizabethan Politics* (New Haven: Yale University Press, 1996), p. 270, and V. Skretkowicz, 'Algernon Sidney and Philip Sidney: A Continuity of Rebellion', *Sidney Journal*, xvii, no. 2 (1999), 3–18.

ought to have been an example to all other nations [...] But as they left the true worship of God to follow those nations in their beastly idolatry, they reject[ed] also the civil government of God's own institution, and so the government of God himself also, renouncing the liberty of being subject to him only, to make themselves slaves unto a king. And God had not granted their desires unless he had given them such a king. In mercy he warned them by Samuel what such a king would do [...]: this shall be your misery under him, but if you will have him, you shall; but when he oppresses you and you cry to me, I will not hear you; you have rejected me, I will reject you.[20]

The same biblical passage was used by the monarchomachist and Marian exile Christopher Goodman (1520?–1603) in his condemnation of Mary Tudor and defence of Wyatt's Rebellion, in *How superior powers oght to be obeyd of their subiects: and Wherin they may lawfully by Gods Worde be disobeyed and resisted. Wherin also is declared the cause of all this present miserie in England, and the onely way to remedy the same* (Geneva, 1558).[21] Contrariwise, James VI of Scotland invoked it in *The Trew Law of Free Monarchies* (1598) as confirmation of God's role in the appointment of kings.

Languet's circle took care to anonymise their more controversial publications, such as *Vindiciae, contra tyrannos* (Edimburgi [i.e., Basel], 1579).[22] Written about 1576, the *Vindiciae* demonstrates the extent to which the possible authors – Henri Estienne and Philippe Du Plessis-Mornay, less probably Languet, all of them Sidney's friends – justified resistance to tyrants.[23] The final element of the pseudonym under which it was published, Stephano Iunio Bruto Celta, shows the authors identifying themselves with Annius's unified nation of Celts under Samotus. The 1648 English edition, published in advance of Charles I's execution, includes the original table of contents on its title-page:

> *Vindiciae contra Tyrannos: A Defence of Liberty against Tyrants. OR, Of the lawfull power of the Prince over the people, and of the people over the Prince.*

20 A. Sidney, *Court Maxims*, ed. by H. W. Blom, E. H. Mulier, and R. Janse (Cambridge: Cambridge University Press, 1996), pp. 47–8; see also A. Hecox, 'A Dutch Perspective on Sidney's Eclogues', *Sidney Journal*, xvii, no. 2 (1999), 31–40.
21 On Mary Tudor, see d2v–d3 and f8v–g2; on 1 Samuel 8, see k3v–k4; on Wyatt, see n5v–o2v; and on Goodman, who during 1566–67 secured Sir Henry Sidney's patronage in Ireland, see B. Worden, *The Sound of Virtue: Philip Sidney's Arcadia and Elizabethan Politics*, p. 187.
22 M. N. Raitiere, *Faire Bitts: Philip Sidney and Renaissance Political Theory*, pp. 10, 117–22.
23 The question of authorship is discussed in B. Nicollier-de Weck, *Hubert Languet (1518–1581), Un réseau politique international de Melanchthon à Guillaume d'Orange*, pp. 465–87.

BEING A Treatise written in Latin and French by Junius Brutus, and trans-lated out of both into ENGLISH. Questions discussed in this Treatise.

I. Whether Subjects are bound, and ought to obey Princes, if they command that which is against the Law of God.

II. Whether it be lawfull to resist a Prince which doth infringe the Law of God, or ruine the Church, by whom, how, and how farre it is lawfull.

III. Whether it be lawfull to resist a Prince which doth oppresse or ruine a publique State, and how farre such resistance may be extended, by whom, how, and by what right, or law it is permitted.

IV. Whether neighbour Princes or States may be, or are bound by Law, to give succours to the Subjects of other Princes, afflicted for the cause of true Religion, or oppressed by manifest tyranny.

In the event of monarchic transgression against the 'double covenant', the first, a 'spiritual' contract between the king and God, and the king and people; the second, a 'political' covenant between the king and the people, the *Vindiciae* licenses tyrannicide as being divinely justified.[24]

Despite the relatively wide dissemination of this subversive text, Gabriel Harvey's remark 'that Melancton could traine Iunius Brutus',[25] and William Prynne's many citations of Iunius Brutus and the *Vindiciae* in *The soveraigne power of parliaments and kingdoms* (1643), confirm that the encoded authorship remained safely concealed. In 1578 Estienne had successfully disguised himself as 'Celtophile' in his anonymously published Lucianic satire, *Deux dialogues du nouveau langage françois, italianizé et autrement desguizé, principalement entre les courtisans de ce temps* – 'two dialogues on the new French language, Italianized and otherwise defaced, principally among the courtiers of this era'.[26] New editions of this work were published in 1579 and 1583 in Antwerp, from which the more aggressive 'Romish' Catholics (Carmelites, Augustin-ians, Jacubines and the Minories, along with the Bogards) were expelled by the ninth article of *Antwerpes Vnitye. An Accord or Peace in Religion, and Gouernment, concluded by his Highnes, and the members of the Citie, to the common weale and quietnes thereof there lately proclaymed the 12.*

---

24 R. Mousnier, *The Assassination of Henry IV*, trans. by J. Spencer (London: Faber and Faber, 1973), pp. 94, 109, cited in V. Skretkowicz, 'Shakespeare, Henri IV, and the Tyranny of Royal Style', in *Challenging Humanism: Essays in Honor of Dominic Baker-Smith*, ed. by T. Hoenselaars and A. F. Kinney (Newark: University of Delaware Press, 2005), pp. 179–208 (p. 188).

25 G. Harvey, *Pierce's Supererogation* (1593), O1v.

26 H. Estienne, *Deux dialogues du nouveau langage françois*, ed. and introduced by P.-M. Smith (Geneva: Editions Slatkine, 1980).

of Iune Anno. 1579. Printed in French, and Dutch, by the Kinges printer, and Englished by the Printer hereof. At London. Printed by Richard Daye, dwelling at Aldersgate. An. 1579. Cum Priuilegio Regiae Maiestatis. This proclamation, modelled on the Union of Utrecht, 23 January 1579, led to Antwerp becoming a Genevan-style Calvinist republic,[27] where on 30 September 1581 Hubert Languet died in the arms of Charlotte Arbaleste, Madame Du Plessis-Mornay.[28]

Sidney and Languet were selective monarchomachists. While neither was motivated by Tsar Ivan IV the Terrible's savagery in Russia, both shared William of Orange's objection to Spanish Catholic tyranny, brutally enforced in the Netherlands. The moderate, tolerant Calvinist, William of Orange (1533–84) clearly expressed this in print in *A declaration and publication of the most worthy Prince of Orange, contaynyng the cause of his necessary defence against the Duke of Alba*. His pamphlet was 'Translated out of French into English, and co[m]pared by other copies in diuers languages', and published in London by John Day.

Orange's *declaration* is dated 20 July 1568 (B3v), the day before the disastrous Battle of Jemmingen and only weeks after Alba or Alva executed, in Brussels on 5 June, Orange's fellow rebel leaders, Lamoral, Count of Egmont (1522–68), and Philip de Montmorency, Count of Hoorn or Horn (1518?–68). All three were knights of the Spanish Catholic Order of the Golden Fleece. Orange insists that he is not in rebellion against his king, Philip II of Spain, but rather that he is defending the principles of an agreement guaranteeing the Reformed Church the right to practise unhindered in the Low Countries:

> such crueltyes and tyrannies vsed by the sayde Duke of *Alba* and his adherentes, couetous and bloud-thirsty persons, doe wholy repugne the co[n]tractes […] betwene his said royall Maiesty, and those of the low Countrey […] For although that heeretofore the Duchesse of Parma. &c. at that time Gouernesse for his Maiesty in the low countreis, hath expresly permitted and agreed to the preaching of the word of God, (to the end to auoid such imminent perils and daungers, as at that time threatned the said cou[n]trey,) with promise that none should atte[m]pt any euil against such as had heard the said preaching, or hereafter wold heare them: which

---

27 H. Pirenne, *Histoire de Belgique des origines à nos jours*, 4 vols (Brussels: Renaissance du livre, [1948–52]), cited in B. Nicollier-de Weck, *Hubert Languet (1518–1581), Un réseau politique international de Melanchthon à Guillaume d'Orange*, p. 419. See also A. Hecox, 'A Dutch Perspective on Sidney's Eclogues'.

28 On the dispersal of Languet's estate, and particularly his portrait of Sidney, see R. Kuin, 'New Light on the Veronese Portrait of Sir Philip Sidney', *Sidney Newsletter & Journal*, xv, no. 1 (1997), 19–47.

at commau[n]dement of her highnes we caused to be published through
all the Countreys vnder our gouernement, binding vs and our person, that
the aforesayd shoulde bene inuiolably obserued towards the subiects of his
sayd Maiesty. (A4–A4v)

In the face of continuing tyrannical behaviour by Spanish governors, in
1581 Orange laid down the principles of his rebellion in *The Apologie
or Defence, of the most noble Prince William*, […] *Prince of Orange*.[29]
Attributed to Orange's courtier Pierre Loyseleur, Sieur de Villiers, and
revised by Hubert Languet, *The Apologie* circulated widely in Europe. It
was reissued in London in 1584, seemingly before Orange's assassination
on 10 July.

As anticipated by both Sidney and Languet, the Gallican French
Parliament similarly published a defence of military action against the
tyrannical Catholic Holy League, *A declaration exhibited to the French
king, by hys Court of Parlyament concerning the holy League* (1587). Fulke
Greville in his *Dedication to Sir Philip Sidney*, published as *The Life of
Sir Philip Sidney* (1652),[30] noted that Sidney was deeply concerned about
the economic impact of the religious and political threat posed by Spain
and its allies in the Holy League. Self-interest became conflated with
national interest, as Sidney belonged to only the second generation of
English Protestants following the redistribution of wealth and political
power accompanying the dissolution of the monasteries. Like Languet, he
saw the urgency of forming a counterbalancing Protestant League amid a
European political landscape that was precariously at war with itself.

Languet's pedagogical method informs the entirety of Sidney's romance,
which, like Philisides' song, uses stories to advocate both constitutional
monarchy and subversive stoicism. In the 1590 edition of the *New Arcadia*,
the Philisides–Languet song is printed in the First Eclogues, where it was
placed by Fulke Greville, who shared Sidney's disposition for parable as

---

29 *The Apologie or Defence, of the most noble Prince William, by the grace of God, Prince
of Orange, Countie of Nassau, of Catzenellenboghen, Dietz, Vianden, &c. Burgmaister of
Antwerp, and Vicou[n]t of Bezanson, Baron of Breda, Diest, Grimberg, of Arlay, Nozeroy,
&c. Lord of Chastel-bellin, &c. Lieutenaunt generall in the lowe Countries, and Gouernour
of Brabant, Holland, Zeelande, Vtrecht and Frise, & Admiral, &c. Against the Proclama-
tion and Edict, published by the King of Spaine, by which he proscribeth the saide Lorde
Prince, whereby shall appeare the sclaunders, and false accusations, conteined in the said
Proscription, which is annexed to the end of this Apologie. Presented to my lords the Estates
generall of the lowe Countrie. Together with the said Proclamation or Proscription. Printed
in French and in all other languages. At Delft. 1581.*
30 An inscription on the title-page of the British Library copy (HMNTS E.1288.(1.)) reads
'Nouemb. 24th. 1651'.

method of teaching.[31] The poem, given little narrative context, is sung by an unnamed melancholy 'young shepherd' who is 'a stranger in that country' and is unknown to Basilius (*NA*, p. 478). In this position, the poem foreshadows the examples of opposition to tyranny which Sidney adds to Book 2, in which Philisides is an inexperienced jouster in Andromana's court. In the 1593 'complete' *Arcadia*, the Philisides-Languet poem is relocated by the editors in the Third Eclogues (Kk5v–Ll1v).

Sidney's fictional recipe for how to achieve regional stability represents the Protestant League's desire to build a dynastic hegemony of monarchomachist, anti-papal states.

The *New Arcadia* especially provides glaring instances of tyranny defeated, or at least compromised, by self-righteous, self-sacrificing heroes who install popularly supported monarchs. But most of all, as illustrated by the Languet–Philisides lament for the loss of the mythical Celtic union, *Arcadia* demonstrates the relationship between the absence of wisdom and the dissolution of political and moral responsibility. Basilius, a decent monarch subject to superstition, emotional frailty and lust, jeopardises his family and state, exposing Arcadia to internal strife and foreign domination. Musidorus, sole heir to Thessalia, and Pyrocles, successor to the powerful kingdom of Macedonia, put the future of their homelands at risk. It is only through the formulaic tragicomic accidents of erotic romance that the degrading chaos of the plot results in political stability. Pamela, next in line to the Arcadian Crown, will marry Musidorus and have a daughter who combines their names, Melidora. Philoclea will marry Pyrocles, and have a son, Pyrophilus (*OA*, p. 417). The principal characters, wrong-headed though they be, conform to Sidney's political doctrines in spite of themselves.

Evolution of *Arcadia*

In November 1586, weeks after Sidney died, the publisher William Ponsonby (whose father-in-law, Francis Coldock, published Underdowne's *Heliodorus*) told Fulke Greville that plans were afoot for a pirated edition of 'sr philip sydneys old arcadia'. Greville informed Sidney's father-in-law, Sir Francis Walsingham, that Sidney had left him the unique 'correction of that old one', and that it was 'fitter to be printed'.[32] In 1590 Ponsonby

31 V. Skretkowicz, 'Greville, Politics, and the Rhetorics of *A Dedication to Sir Philip Sidney*', in *Fulke Greville: A Special Double Number*, ed. by M. C. Hansen and M. Woodcock, *Sidney Journal*, xix (2001 [published 2002]), 97–123.
32 Public Record Office, SP12/195, reproduced in V. Skretkowicz, 'Building Sidney's

published Greville's edition of the long, substantially revised first section of Sidney's working papers, now referred to as the *New Arcadia*. The unpublished remains of these papers, mainly the partially revised second half of the original version, were added in the Countess of Pembroke's 1593 edition.[33] Often referred to as the 'composite' *Arcadia*, this volume contains as complete as possible a representation of the form in which the author left his text.

After the *New Arcadia* was printed, but especially after the extended 'complete' version of 1593, Sidney's literary impact was considerable.[34] In 1598, *The Countess of Pembroke's Arcadia* became an anthology of Sidney's creative writing and theory. Reprints kept the dedicatory title, with its overt political affiliations, in the minds of generations of writers and political commentators. But its influence in Europe, where English was not widely spoken or read, was negligible. By the time translations were published in French (1624–25), German (1629), Dutch (1639) and Italian (1659), both English and European literary and political taste had changed.

Sidney's revision incorporates background information into Books 1 and 2, where it is developed and integrated into the plot. The princes' altruism is complicated by newly invented enemies such as Plexirtus, whose attempt to assassinate them on shipboard results in their separation, unexpected reunion in Laconia, and transformation in Arcadia into self-centred, love-smitten heroes. The tyranny of erotic dementia, comically suffered by Basilius and Gynecia in their enchantment with Pyrocles, is given a hardened political edge in the princesses' first cousin, Amphialus, a potentially heroic character psychologically devastated by unrequited love for Philoclea. In an extended addition, Book 3 in the *New Arcadia*, Amphialus's mother Cecropia (Basilius's sister-in-law) kidnaps the princesses and their Amazonian guest in an attempt to secure Philoclea and the throne for her son. The princesses, as their personalities dictate, exhibit tenacity under torture in parallel with Leukippe and Charikleia. Through dangerous single combat, Musidorus outside the castle, and Pyrocles within, demonstrate their chivalric superiority and devotion.

Reputation: Texts and Editors of the *Arcadia*', in *Sir Philip Sidney: 1586 and the Creation of a Legend*, ed. by J. van Dorsten, D. Baker-Smith and A. F. Kinney (Leiden: E. J. Brill, 1986), pp. 111–24 (pp. 114–15); see also H. R. Woudhuysen, *Sir Philip Sidney and the Circulation of Manuscripts 1558–1640*, p. 416.

33 See V. Skretkowicz, 'Textual Criticism and the 1593 "Complete" *Arcadia*', *Sidney Journal*, xviii (2000 [published 2002]), 37–70.

34 See G. Alexander, *Writing After Sidney: The Literary Response to Sir Philip Sidney, 1586–1640* (Oxford: Oxford University Press, 2006).

Where the *New Arcadia* of 1590 ends in mid-sentence, the 'complete' 1593 *Arcadia* appends the lightly modified material that remained in Sidney's working papers. Sidney's revisions to the original Books 3, 4 and 5 seem to have left the editors little to do, apart from synchronising names and reconstructing the Eclogues.[35] Neither Sidney nor his editors would claim that this text represents a sustained artistic entity. The abrupt transition, from the heat of Pyrocles' combat with Anaxius to Musidorus's conversational disclosure of Pamela's agreement to elope to Thessalia, lacks thematic and stylistic cohesion (*NA*, p. 465; *OA*, p. 172 var.).

Despite this unfinished state, Sidney had so raised the political stakes in the new Books 1, 2 and 3 that the intimate relationships between the princes and princesses, Basilius's betrayal of Gynecia and the lengthy trial scene are substantially recontextualised. The narrator's observations on 'how great dissipations monarchal governments are subject unto' (*OA*, p. 320), following Basilius's apparent death, becomes doubly significant after the princesses' kidnapping by Cecropia. Likewise, Philoclea's eloquence and Pamela's withering denunciation of their aunt during their captivity increase awareness of their vulnerability during the trial. The princesses' new enemy, the state, is less well defined, and issues relating to monarchic succession clash with political, ethical, moral and personal interests.

Unfolding the epic cycle

Vast, complex, and displaying a masterful command of textured Greco-Roman styles, the 'complete' 1593 *Arcadia* exudes reminiscences of Renaissance European representations of erotic romance. In 1599, the year Isaac Casaubon published his enlarged Lyon edition of Theophrastus, Ben Jonson's friend John Hoskyns observed in *Directions for Speech and Style* that 'Sir Philip Sidney had much help out of *Theophrasti Imagines*'.[36] Hoskyns identifies 'Heliodorus in Greek' as one of Sidney's models 'for the web' of his romance, along with Sannazaro's *Arcadia* and Montemayor's *Diana*. He should have added Achilles Tatius, whom Sidney follows in placing character types in dilemmas that demonstrate their inflexibility, and in stopping the action to analyse motives.

---

35 Some of the resulting inconsistencies are discussed in V. Skretkowicz, 'From Alpha-Text to Meta-Text: Sidney's Arcadia', in *The Author as Reader: Textual Visons and Revisions*, ed. by S. Coelsch-Foisner and W. Görtschacher, Salzburg Studies in English Literature and Culture 2 (Frankfurt am Main: Peter Lang, 2005), pp. 23–32.

36 J. Hoskins [i.e., Hoskyns], *Directions for Speech and Style*, ed. by H. H. Hudson (Princeton: Princeton University Press, 1935), p. 41; see J. Buxton, 'Sidney and Theophrastus', *English Literary Renaissance*, ii (1972), 79–82.

Because it had fallen into disrepute during the second half of the sixteenth century, not all of Sidney's readers would know that Hoskyns's greatest omission was the multi-volume composite *Amadis de Gaule*. This once internationally revered, anonymously published work hearkened back to a unified kingdom of Great Britain and France through the marriage in Book IV of Amadis and Oriana.[37] Sidney openly mirrors a number of plot lines and names in the often 'antichivalric' *Amadis de Gaule*, and reshapes and considerably develops elements of its action, character and Greco-Roman rhetorical styles.[38]

Owing to its multiplicity of authors, Sidney found a variety of rhetorical models in this work. A wide range of speeches, including challenges, threats, exhortations and emotional outpourings, had been collected in the popular *Le thresor des douze livres d'Amadis de Gaule* (Paris, 1559). The English translation by Thomas Paynell was published in 1567.[39] The posthumously published 1572 edition follows the 1571 Lyon edition in containing material from Book XIII.[40] In dedicating this volume to Sir Thomas Gresham, Thomas Hacket emphasises the rhetorical virtues of this exceptionally popular chivalric romance:

> this booke which I present vnto you, is stufte with pleasant orations, fine epistles, singular complaintes, with matter mixt so fitly and aptly to serue the turne of all persons, not curious nor filled full of obscure and darke sense, but playne and pleasant, depending and answering one an other, with most delectable matter for all causes, as well incouraging the bashfull person and cowarde to bee valiant, as the worthie ladies and damselles in their amorous Epistles, feruente complaintes of iniuries handled moste excellently. (¶2v-¶3)

Sidney draws particularly on Juan Diaz's Book VIII; on Feliciano de Silva's rhetorically stylised Books VII and IX–XI; and on Book XII, attributed

---

37 On anonymous authorship and the pseudo-history of chivalric romance, see D. Eisenberg, *Romances of Chivalry in the Spanish Golden Age* (Newark, DE: Juan de la Cuesta, 1982). For the Internet edition (Alicante: Biblioteca Virtual Miguel de Cervantes, 2003), see www.cervantesvirtual.com/servlet/SirveObras/01159841877587238327702/.

38 See J. J. O'Connor, *Amadis de Gaule and Its Influence on Elizabethan Literature* (New Brunswick, NJ: Rutgers University Press, 1970), pp. 192, 196.

39 See G. Eatough, 'Paynell, Thomas (*d.* 1564?)', *Oxford Dictionary of National Biography* (Oxford: Oxford University Press, 2004).

40 *The moste excellent and pleasaunt Booke, entituled: The treasurie of Amadis of Fraunce: Conteyning eloquente orations, pythie Epistles, learned Letters, and feruent Complayntes, seruing for sundrie purposes*, trans. by T. Paynell (1567). References are to the 1572 edition. See H. Thomas, 'English Translations of Portuguese Books before 1640', *The Library*, 4th ser., i (1926), 1–30 (p. 23), and V. Benhaïm, 'Les Thresors d'Amadis', in *Les Amadis en France au XVIe siècle*, ed. by N. Cazauran and M. Bideaux, Cahiers Saulniers, no. 17 (Paris: Éditions Rue d'Ulm, 2000), pp. 157–81 (p. 158).

to Pedro de Luján.[41] Published in 1546, Book XII is characterised by balanced rhythms, verbal repetitions and apostrophe.

Whereas the influence of the *Amadis de Gaule* is strongly felt in many plot lines and dramatic dialogues of the *New Arcadia*, Hoskyns correctly observes that the overall structure of Sidney's revison emulates that of *An Ethiopian Story*. Unlike the straightforward opening of the *Old Arcadia*, which Hoskyns may not have read, the *New Arcadia* begins in the middle of the action and shifts from one narrator to another. This structure cultivates a sense of dramatic irony, often linking distant passages through verbal and symbolic repetition. Subtle echoic qualities gradually manifest themselves through several readings, a characteristic of Heliodorus's rhetorical artistry. But where *An Ethiopian Story* contains a single, complex series of events that comes full circle at the mid-point, Sidney ambitiously creates a double cycle of virtually independent plots revolving around Pyrocles and Musidorus. Contrasting their past chivalric, monarchomachist interventions with their present erotic obsessions, Sidney integrates both plots at the end of Book 2. With the background to the opening scene finally revealed, as it is at the end of Book 5 of *An Ethiopian Story*, Sidney moves the action forward, but leaves his great work uncompleted.

Despite its thematic and stylistic hiatus, Sidney's shadowing of Heliodorus's structure becomes even more apparent in the 1593 'complete' edition. By locating his mid-point at the end of Book 2, Sidney signals his unfulfilled aim of producing a finished work in four long Books, each separated by a few thematically relevant poems or Eclogues. Taking the Clarendon Press editions as a guide, the first half – Books 1 and 2 of the *New Arcadia* – occupies 305 pages. In its unfinished form, the second half has 352 pages. It contains the new portion of Book 3 (157 pages), plus adjusted versions of the earlier Book 3 (68 pages), Book 4 (61 pages) and Book 5 (66 pages).

In addition to modelling his structure, along with elements of plot and character, on Heliodorus, Sidney goes out of his way to identify his revised work with sophistic erotic romance. His artificial opening passage, replete with artfully stylised sentences, concludes with a parallel to Europa's setting out from the shore of Sidon for Crete, in the beginning of *Leukippe and* Kleitophon (1.1).

The *New Arcadia* opens with a sequence of metaphors. This associates the arrival of spring, the season of love, with change of costume and identity, with a chivalric contest between rivals, and with a resolution of

41 J. J. O'Connor, *Amadis de Gaule and its Influence on Elizabethan Literature*, pp. 6, 183–201.

conflict based on unbiased judgement: 'It was in the time that the earth
begins to put on her new apparel against the approach of her lover, and
that the sun, running a most even course, becomes an indifferent arbiter
between the night and the day' (*NA*, p. 3). This sums up the entire plot.
Immediately, Strephon and Claius reminisce on the elevating influence of
their shared love for Urania. They are on a beach in Laconia, at the spot
where Urania set sail for the island of Cythera, birthplace of Venus:

> yonder did she put her foot into the boat, at that instant, as it were, dividing
> her heavenly beauty between the earth and the sea. But when she was
> embarked did you not mark how the winds whistled and the seas danced
> for joy, how the sails did swell with pride, and all because they had Urania?
> O Urania, blessed be thou, Urania, the sweetest fairness and fairest sweet-
> ness. (*NA*, p. 4)

As Strephon breaks off in tears, Claius observes their paradoxical circum-
stances, in which 'love-fellowship maintained friendship between rivals,
and beauty taught the beholders chastity' (*NA*, p. 5). Sidney uses these
stylistic excesses to reveal the effect of intense strain on stoic self-control.
And his structure encourages comparison between characters, for this is
the first of many exemplary parables exploring the nature and effects of
highly charged erotic relationships.

Like Heliodorus's brigands, Strephon and Claius witness the aftermath
of a tragedy. In *An Ethiopian Story*, this takes the first half of the work to
explain; in the *New Arcadia*, the whole of Books 1 and 2. Where Longus
and Achilles Tatius open with symbolic pictures, Sidney delays intro-
ducing mythological paintings with narrative significance until he brings
Musidorus into Kalander's gallery (*NA*, p. 15). But Strephon's reflecting
on Urania's departure for Cythera invokes two literary parallels. The first,
with *Leukippe and Kleitophon*, is the painting of Zeus, a swimming bull,
carrying Europa,[42] watched from the beach by her distraught maidens
(1.1). This is coupled, when the unconscious Musidorus floats ashore and
he attempts to drown himself, with Ovid's story of Alcyone and Ceyx.[43]
Such prophecy-laden imagery foreshadows the consequences of Basilius's
belief in oracles. It also introduces the notions of metamorphic identity
and personality change that form the basis of Sidney's serio-comic central
plot.

---

42 While she is not mentioned in the *New Arcadia*, in the *Old Arcadia* Pyrocles alludes
    to 'the rape of Europe' (*OA*, p. 163), and Euarchus in his sentencing to 'the example of
    Phoenician Europa' (*OA*, p. 406).
43 On Ovid's contribution to the story, see A. H. F. Griffin, 'The Ceyx Legend in Ovid,
    Metamorphoses, Book XI', *Classical Quarterly*, xxxi, no. 1 (1981), 147–54.

Because the opening scene both introduces and develops events that occur at the end of Book 2, the pseudonyms that Musidorus and Pyrocles adopt on separation – Musidorus 'called himself Palladius and his friend Daiphantus' (*NA*, p. 12) – anticipate a much delayed narrative. Insight into this choice of names is curtailed by the heroes' falling in love and assuming their third identities, Dorus and Zelmane (Cleophila in the *Old Arcadia*). Musidorus's failure to maintain his unattainable ideal as Dorus, 'if we will be men, the reasonable part of our soul is to have absolute commandment' (*OA*, p. 19; *NA*, p. 70), is satirised in his railing against love. This begins with a summary of Musidorus's metamorphoses, and concludes with a rhetorically sophisticated example of love's slackening of mental rigour into sophism: 'Thou changest name upon name; thou disguisest our bodies and disfigurest our minds; but indeed thou hast reason, for though the ways be foul, the journey's end is most fair and honourable' (*NA*, p. 109).

This notion of erotic metamorphosis is supported through Ovidian allusions, and linked to the ambiguous perspectives inherent in monarchomachia through the aphoristic 'love to a yielding heart is a king, but to a resisting is a tyrant' (*NA*, p. 108). The tyranny of love, dramatised by the central anti-romance of Basilius and Gynecia, is counterbalanced by the epyllion of Argalus and Parthenia. Their idealised love, which follows the formulaic separation, reunion and marriage of erotic romance, has the appearance of one of the subordinate digressions in *Leukippe and Kleitophon* or *An Ethiopian Story*. Sidney exploits this similarity to subvert his readers' expectations of erotic fulfilment, using the tragic deaths of Argalus and Parthenia to emphasise the selfish folly of his principal characters.

Sub-plot and exemplary character

Sidney introduces many characters in plain descriptive passages, following Plutarch's holistic method. But he also invests each one with a predominant trait, imitating Theophrastus's exaggerated types. In the *New Arcadia*, Argalus's, Amphialus's and Anaxius's brief introductory biographies disclose their character types, foreshadowing the outcome of the action (*NA*, pp. 27, 61, 390). Argalus and Parthenia illustrate faithful devotion, behaving true to form in their heroic deaths in Book 3. The contrast between the unquestionably heroic Argalus and the emotionally compromised trio of Musidorus, Pyrocles, and Amphialus (*NA*, p. 27) reveals the extent of their wrong-headedness. Such comparisons enhance the irony in Helen's formulaic description, 'the courteous Amphialus', a parody of Virgil's 'pius Aeneas'. For Cecropia's inordinate ambition transforms her son into Pyrocles' anti-heroic rival for Philoclea.

Phalantus's character is both Plutarchan and Theophrastan. A narrow caricature of a playboy courtier, Phalantus serves as a mechanism to introduce threads of the complex sub-plot. The 'bastard brother to the fair Helen, queen of Corinth' (*NA*, p. 91), he meets Artesia in the court of Laconia,[44] and 'for tongue-delight' – lip-service – 'made himself her servant' (*NA*, p. 92). In Greek mythology, Phalantus is the son of Helen of Troy's half-sister, Clytemnestra. But as Phalandria is the Latin place-name for Flanders, and Sidney fashions Phalantus's tournament in defence of Artesia's beauty in the Burgundian style,[45] he may be part of the Languet-related political allegory.

Sidney has Phalantus display portraits of women whose champions he has defeated, introducing female characters of varying significance: Andromana, Queen of Iberia; the Princess of Elis; Artaxia, Queen of Armenia; Erona, Queen of Lycia; Baccha and Leucippe; and the Queen of Laconia. Pamphilus's wife, Baccha, and his jilted fiancée, Leucippe, anticipate Pamphilus's rescue by Pyrocles from Dido (*NA*, p. 236), and interrelate the first and second narrative cycles. The Princess of Elis and the Queen of Laconia, Artesia's relative, have no narrative function. Those who come after – Helen,[46] Parthenia and Urania – all virtuous women, provide a contrast with Andromana, Artaxia and Erona. These problematic personalities connect many of the episodes in Book 2.

The second narrative cycle, centring on Zelmane's father, Plexirtus, and his half-sister, Andromana, begins about one-third into Book 2. Here, in contrast with the opening of the novel, Sidney's plain style and change of season presage tragedy: 'It was in the kingdom of Galatia, the season being (as in the depth of winter) very cold' (*NA*, p. 179). The last of Phalantus's portraits is of Plexirtus's daughter, Zelmane, who falls in love with Pyrocles in Andromana's court. Disguised as Daiphantus, she dies while serving him as a page. Pyrocles adopts both of her names. Musidorus similarly assumes the name of Andromana's son, Palladius, killed helping the princes escape from his lascivious mother (*NA*, pp. 257, 267–8).

44 Artesia is the Latin place-name for Artois, one of the south-eastern Walloon provinces of Belgium.

45 G. Kipling, *The Triumph of Honour: Burgundian Origins of the Elizabethan Renaissance* (Leiden: Leiden University Press, 1977), pp. 118–21, 130, 134–9.

46 On the Italian background to the chastity symbolism of Helen's ermine device, see C. H. Clough, 'Federico da Montefeltro and the Kings of Naples: A Study in Fifteenth-century Survival', *Renaissance Studies*, vi (1992), 113–72 (pp. 158–60).

The two exemplary political stories in this cycle focus on Plexirtus, amalgamating Heliodorus's tales of Knemon, Thyamis and Theagenes. Together they explain the opening beach scene, and anticipate Euarchus's arrival in Arcadia in Book 5 (*OA*, pp. 355–7). The first, about usurpation, is narrated by Musidorus to Pamela; the second, which continues the first, by Pyrocles to Philoclea. Both are completed in Basilius's tale at the end of Book 2.

Musidorus and Pyrocles listen to the King of Galatia (Paphlagonia) tell how Plexirtus has deposed him. Andromana's mother, now the king's concubine, insists that Plexirtus is his child. She persuades the king to execute his natural son, Leonatus. Spared by his murderers, Leonatus returns to support his father, whom Plexirtus has blinded and reduced to beggary. Plexirtus, who 'will not let slip any advantage to make away him whose just title, ennobled by courage and goodness, may one day shake the seat of a never secure tyranny' (*NA*, pp. 182–3), pursues Leonatus but is confronted and defeated by Musidorus, Pyrocles and their allies from Pontus. The forgiving Leonatus sends Plexirtus on a mission to recapture, and keep for himself, the city of Trebizond (*NA*, pp. 262–3).

This second tale is about Plexirtus's half-sister, the tyrannical Andromana ('man-mad'), her stepson Plangus, and the headstrong Erona, queen of Lycia. Sidney introduces this by means of Philoclea's book, which is stolen by Amphialus's spaniel. It contains a copy of Basilius's dialogue-poem, *The Complaint of Plangus* (*NA*, pp. 195–205). Sidney initially develops the character of Andromana in the Second Eclogues of the *Old Arcadia*. A 'great lady' of Palestina, she is 'a heart-burning woman' who falls pregnant and is abandoned by 'a young prince of Arabia who had promised her marriage' (*OA*, p. 154). Like Heliodorus's Arsake in *An Ethiopian Story*, whose heart was 'torn asunder by the desire she felt for each of' (7.4; Reardon, p. 490) Thyamis and Theagenes, Andromana becomes infatuated with both Musidorus and Pyrocles.

In the revised *Arcadia*, Andromana is a major figure, in whom Sidney combines Heliodorus's Arsake with Knemon's wicked stepmother, Demainete. Andromana, demonized by her 'exceeding red hair' and 'small eyes' (*NA*, p. 95), is 'a private man's wife' (*NA*, p. 215) whom young Prince Plangus takes as his mistress. His widower father, the king of Iberia, disguises himself to catch them 'in her house together'. Being of a gullible nature, he believes his son's 'sophistry' in praise of Andromana's 'chastity', becomes besotted with her and, to 'avoid the odious comparison of a young rival', sends Plangus 'to the subduing of a province [...] (which he knew could not be a less work than of three or four years)' (*NA*, p. 216).

The king marries Andromana on the death of her husband. By the time Plangus returns, he has acquired a young half-brother, Palladius, and an unnamed half-sister.

In Andromana and Plangus, Sidney follows Heliodorus's episode of Demainete and Knemon, a cautionary study of the relationship between a female predator and her willing victims. But Sidney additionally interweaves this with didactic parable, as Andromana's successful use of reverse psychology on Plangus is a textbook guide to political manipulation. Like Heliodorus's Demainete, Andromana becomes a sexually aggressive stepmother whom Plangus spurns. She employs 'cunning of malice' to 'overthrow him [...] in the favour of his father' (*NA*, p. 218). She arouses the king's suspicions and jealousy by praising Plangus's kingly qualities and suggesting his desire to rule. She astutely identifies one of her husband's ambitious servants, one who 'would make a ladder of any mischief' (*NA*, p. 219), employing him to suggest that Plangus has enough popular support to stage a coup.

There is no danger of any reader missing the political message. Sidney carefully embeds an allegorical interpretation into the text, preceding it by noting how sharply Andromana, a pragmatic opportunist, seizes upon 'a mere trifle' to advance her interests. The king, chancing upon a 'vine-labourer', asks why he takes a small branch to bind together a broken 'bough'. He then relates to Andromana his anxieties about the labourer's inauspicious reply, 'I make the son bind the father' (*NA*, p. 220). This inspires her to persuade a willing parliament to give Plangus a formal role in the kingship, an honour against which, the more he protests, the more he inflames his father's suspicions.

In the end, Andromana engineers Plagus's banishment as an attempted parricide by playing on his righteous indignation and 'credulity'. Andromana correctly anticipates Plangus's reaction to being warned that she and 'certain of the noble men' (*NA*, p. 220) are plotting against him. His instinct is not to escape, but rather to catch the guilty parties in the act. Carrying a sword 'because of his late-going' (*NA*, p. 221), Plangus is brought secretly and ostensibly to listen to the conspirators. In fact, the theatrical Andromana, alone with the king, convinces him that 'Plangus, soliciting her in the old affection between them, had besought her to put her helping hand to the death of the king, assuring her that [...] he would marry her when he were king' (*NA*, p. 221). Staging an emergency, Andromana's parasite warns the king about 'a man with sword drawn in the next room'. Sidney carefully points out that Plangus's sword is 'not naked' (*NA*, p. 221). This emphasises the extent to which Andromana has warped the king's judgement, who 'thinking he had put up his sword because of the noise, never took leisure to hear his answer' (*NA*, p. 221).

Having completed this lesson in how to manipulate personalities and situations to serve one's political interests, Sidney moves the plot forward. Plangus is rescued from execution by 'a little army' of friends, and spends the next 'eleven or twelve years' with Tiridates, King of Armenia, and his sister Artaxia. They are his cousins, the children of 'his father's sister' (*NA*, p. 222).

The link between these stories is Plangus's desperate love for Erona, an example of the disastrous results of passionate misjudgement. In the First Eclogues of the *Old Arcadia*, Erona is the fourteen-year-old Princess of Lydia, 'stricken' with love of Antiphilus (*OA*, p. 67). In the revised version, Erona of Lycia is nineteen and Antiphilus, modelled on Kybele's son Achaimenes in *An Ethiopian Story*, 'a young man [...] so mean as that he was but the son of her nurse' (*NA*, p. 205). Erona's tyrannical father engages her to the powerful King Tiridates of Armenia (in the *Old Arcadia*, 'Otanes, king of Persia'), whose sister is Artaxia. Erona resists the engagement, and, when her father dies, Tiridates besieges her. Tiridates chooses to settle the issue by means of a challenge, three against three. Pyrocles kills Euardes of Bithynia and Musidorus kills Barzanes of Hyrcania. But Tiridates' general of horse, Plangus, captures Antiphilus (*NA*, p. 207).

Pyrocles' killing of Euardes results in the anti-heroic misogynist, Anaxius (a pun on 'royal' and 'unworthy'), pursuing Pyrocles, seeking to avenge the death of his uncle (*NA*, pp. 234–35). Sidney delays their critical battle till the closing stages of the siege of Cecropia's castle, after Pyrocles, still posturing as Zelmane, has killed Anaxius's brothers, Lycurgus and Zoilus (*NA*, p. 390).

In finally rescuing Antiphilus, Pyrocles kills Tiridates of Armenia. Erona marries the selfish, untrustworthy Antiphilus (*NA*, p. 209), who legalises polygamy and forces Erona to write to Artaxia 'that she was content for the public good to be a second wife' (*NA*, p. 300). When they meet, Artaxia captures both Erona and Antiphilus, whose blind affection has been misplaced. Artaxia has already been wooed by Plexirtus, and promises to reward him with marriage on receipt of 'sure proof that by his means we [i.e., Musidorus and Pyrocles] were destroyed' (*NA*, p. 270).

In the simpler *Old Arcadia*, Artaxia has Antiphilus killed but holds Erona until Musidorus and Pyrocles fight four of Otanes' men. Meanwhile, Artaxia's cousin Plangus falls in love with Erona, and travels through Persia, Egypt and Greece searching for the princes (*OA*, pp. 69–71). In the developed story, the loving Plangus tries to rescue Antiphilus, who instead betrays him in hope of gaining a pardon. Artaxia, however, rewards Antiphilus with his death. She gives in to 'the humble suit of all the women of that city', who 'after many tortures forced him to throw himself from a high pyramis which was built over Tiridates' tomb' (*NA*, p. 303). Erona, Plangus's concern, remains in captivity.

At the end of Book 2, Plexirtus tries to have Musidorus and Pyrocles murdered as they sail for Greece. The resulting fight leaves the princes' ship burning off the coast of Laconia, and, as seen in the opening passage of Book 1, Pyrocles picked up on the open sea, and Musidorus floating ashore. Believing that Plexirtus has fulfilled his contract with Artaxia, Plangus pins his hopes of rescuing Erona on Euarchus, the monarcho-machist King of Macedonia (*NA*, p. 306).

Philisides and tiltyard masquing

Elaborating on Heliodorus's adaptation at 5.16 of the narrative transition in Homer's *Odyssey*, 8.499, Sidney similarly avoids repetition between speakers by having Philoclea explain to Pyrocles which part of the narrative she (and the reader) has already heard. Accordingly, Pyrocles/Zelmane

> told her the story of her life from the time of their departing from Erona, for the rest she had already understood of her sister: 'For', said she, 'I have understood how you first in the company of your noble cousin, Musidorus, parted from Thessalia, and of divers adventures [...] till your coming to the succour of the Queen Erona; and the end of that war [...] I had understood of the Prince Plangus. But what since was the course of your doings [...] I know not'. (*NA*, p. 233)

Pyrocles tells Philoclea how, as he sets out to accept Anaxius's challenge, he first comes across Dido and nine other 'gentlewomen' sexually molesting Pamphilus (*NA*, p. 236). Dido's story provides the means to introduce Philisides into the text.

Phalantus's unexplained portraits of the over-familiar Baccha and gullible Leucippe (*NA*, pp. 95–6) do not prepare readers for Dido's caricature of the philandering Pamphilus. Exemplifying cruel victimisation by an arrogant chauvinist, Dido tells the princes how the inconstant, tyrannical Pamphilus has abused her and her fellow assailants. Pyrocles rescues Pamphilus, but is immediately forced to abandon his fight with Anaxius to save Dido. For Pamphilus and his like-minded friends kill her escort and take her captive, intending to 'kill her in the sight of her own father', Chremes (*NA*, p. 243).

The self-interested Chremes leads Pyrocles and Musidorus into an ambush by Artaxia's soldiers. They are rescued by the king of Iberia, who has vested control of the state in his wife, Andromana, 'whom the Princess Pamela did in so lively colours describe the last day' (*NA*, p. 248). Andromana, like Arsake in *An Ethiopian Story*, simultaneously 'affected' both Pyrocles and Musidorus 'with equal ardour' (*NA*, p. 249). When they refuse her, she has them charged with subversion, and imprisoned.

The princes' enforced stay in Iberia coincides with the annual, week-long 'justs both with sword and lance' (*NA*, p. 253), held to mark Andromana's wedding anniversary. On this occasion, the Iberian knights are challenged by knights sent from the court of Helen, Queen of Corinth. Sidney overlays this passage with contemporary allusions through a series of brief ecphrases interrelating costumes, armour, imprese and oblique biographical references.

In the first justs or jousts, the Iberians' champion is Philisides. Unlike the Philisides of the Eclogues in the *Old Arcadia*, who participates in the present time, this episode takes place before the main plot begins. Here Philisides, a shepherd unexpectedly changed into 'a man-of-arms', enters the tiltyard in jewelled armour 'dressed over with [wool … His] impresa was a sheep marked with pitch, with this word: "Spotted to be known".' Among the ladies present 'was one, they say, that was the "star" whereby his course was only directed' (*NA*, p. 255). Philisides is opposed by the Corinthian Lelius, 'whose device was to come in all chained, with a nymph leading him'. Lelius, 'second to none in the perfection of that art' and identifiable as Elizabeth I's champion, Sir Henry Lee, claims to be 'tied' (*NA*, p. 256) by some mischievous lady to embarrass Philisides by aiming his lance over his head.

Of the two Iberians who are described, one is a writer who enters as 'a wild man' in a costume of 'withered leaves', and the other is the 'Frozen Knight (frozen in despair)', whose armour simulates ice. Lelius's Corinthian companions include 'a great nobleman […] all in white like a new knight (as indeed he was)', another whose mechanical bird flew from his tent to deliver a message 'among the ladies', and a third dressed as a phoenix (*NA*, p. 256).

For three days the Corinthians dominate in the jousts. For the tourney, a sword-fight on horseback, Andromana's son Palladius, who 'had never used arms' (*NA*, p. 254), persuades his mother to release Pyrocles and Musidorus to join the Iberians.

The presence of Philisides suggests a historical basis to Andromana's festivities which, as the Iberians fight in a threesome, may relate to the only known period that Sidney, Edward Dyer, and Fulke Greville ('one Minde in Bodies three')[47] were together with Lee. This was during Sidney's mission to convey the Queen's condolences to Emperor Rudolf II in Prague, from March to mid-June 1577.[48] Earlier in the *New Arcadia*, Sidney's fortnight in Prague provides the model for Basilius's comet-shaped lodge and gardens, symbolic adaptations of Ferdinand of Tirol's unique star-shaped lodge on the nearby White Mountain.[49] While returning from Prague, Sidney's party was diverted to the Middelburg court of William of Orange. They arrived on Monday 27 or Tuesday 28 May, and stayed for about a week.[50] On 30 May, Sidney stood proxy for Leicester as godfather to Orange's daughter, Elisabeth. In March, Orange had written to Marie of Nassau (1556–1616), his daughter with his first wife, Anne of Egmont and Buren (1533–58), urging her to join him. Along with his third wife, Charlotte de Bourbon-Montpensier (1546?–82), Orange was planning Marie's engagement to Sidney.[51]

Orange's court, or one related to it, is one of the few venues where a celebratory tournament, symbolic of the nationalistic Burgundian revival, might have been held, and where Sidney's devotion to a 'star' could be satirised. Musidorus's two assistants in his battle against Amphialus, in Book 3, wear armour that suggests the partnership between Sidney and the House of Orange. One has white or plain steel armour, 'his attiring else all cut in stars [...] of cloth of silver and silver spangles'. His device is 'the very pole itself, about which many stars stirring, but the place itself left void. The word was "The best place yet reserved"' (*NA*, p. 412). This is very like Sidney's personal device in sonnet 104 of *Astrophil and Stella*, where the 'stars upon mine armour [...] prove that I / Do *Stella* love'.[52] Musidorus's other assistant is The Knight of the Sheep, whose green costume 'seemed a pleasant garden wherein grew orange-trees'. Golden oranges are beaten into his armour and embroidered on to his costume, and on 'his shield was a sheep feeding in a pleasant field, with this word, "Without fear or envy"' (*NA*, pp. 411–12). This design closely approximates one in the combined

47 *The Poems of Sir Philip Sidney*, ed. by W. A. Ringler, Jr, OP 6.
48 J. M. Osborn, *Young Philip Sidney 1572–1577* (New Haven: Yale University Press, 1972), pp. 450, 525–8.
49 V. Skretkowicz, 'Symbolic Architecture in Sidney's New Arcadia', *Review of English Studies*, n.s., xxxiii (1982), 175–180.
50 J. M. Osborn, *Young Philip Sidney 1572–1577*, pp. 479–92; R. Kuin, 'The Middelburg Weekend: More Light on the Proposed Marriage Between Philip Sidney and Marie of Nassau', *Sidney Newsletter and Journal*, xii, no. 2 (1993), 3–12.
51 R. Kuin, 'The Middelburg Weekend: More Light on the Proposed Marriage Between Philip Sidney and Marie of Nassau', pp. 5–8.
52 *The Poems of Sir Philip Sidney*, ed. by W. A. Ringler, Jr, AS 104.

1593 edition of *Symbolorum et Emblematum* by Sidney's friend Joachim Camerarius, the younger, whom he visited in Nuremberg between 1 and 4 April 1577. The motto 'Undique Inermis' – 'Everywhere Unarmed' – implies that innocence is its own defence, reflecting the stoic spirit of the Dutch Protestants. Finally, Sidney's 'Orange' sheep contrasts with and perhaps parodies the device, a sheepskin strung up by its middle, of that most noble of the Catholic orders, the Golden Fleece, which William of Orange joined in 1555 while in the service of its head, Philip II of Spain.

Lee's joust against Sidney in the guise of Philisides remains otherwise undocumented. The last time they met in ceremonial combat was on Accession Day, 17 November 1584, when both broke all six lances on one another.[53] Part of Sidney's education, like the baby Gargantua's,[54] consisted of riding and tilting. He must have excelled in these long before attempting the international standard of the court. In the beginning of *A Defence of Poetry*, he reminisces on the instruction he received in the Spanish Riding School in Vienna, in 1572.

Sidney applies his expertise in horsemanship to his creation of Musidorus as a Thessalian, connecting him by nationality to Theagenes and the Centaurs. In *An Ethiopian Story*, Kalasiris describes Theagenes riding between two groups of twenty-five horsemen, in the parade that precedes his sacrifice to Achilles' son, Neoptolemos. He is dressed in a crimson mantle, embroidered with the picture of the battle of the Lapiths and Centaurs:

> The very horse seemed to understand what a fine thing it was to carry such a fine rider on his back, so proudly he flexed his neck and carried his head high with ears aprick; [...] he obeyed the rein's every command, and with each pace he paused for an instant in perfect balance with one leg uplifted, gently clipping the ground with the tip of his hoof so as to give a smooth and gentle rhythm to his gait. (3.3; Reardon, p. 412)

Musidorus displays comparably exquisite horsemanship in a private exhibition for Pamela. Demonstrating this known quality of the Thessalian royal house helps him convince Pamela of his identity: 'who think you is my Dorus fallen out to be? Even the Prince Musidorus'. Pamela also provides the association with the Centaurs:

> you might see him come towards me, beating the ground in so due time as no dancer can observe better measure [...] as if centaur-like he had been

---

53 The scored jousting cheque is reproduced in R. C. Strong, 'Elizabethan Jousting Cheques in the Possession of the College of Arms – II', *The Coat of Arms*, v (1958–59), 63–8 (p. 64), and A. Young, *Tudor and Jacobean Tournaments* (London: George Philip, 1987), p. 49.
54 F. Rabelais, *Gargantua*, i.23.

one piece with the horse [...] he ever going so just with the horse, either forthright or turning, that it seemed, as he borrowed the horse's body, so he lent the horse his mind. (*NA*, p. 153)

The genre of commemorative paintings of battles, real, fictive and combined, first came into its own during the Renaissance Greco-Roman revival. It is perfectly apt, therefore, that Musidorus should strike off the hands of the artist who, armed with a pike, foolishly involves himself in the rebellion against Basilius to study for his 'skirmishing between the Centaurs and Lapiths' (*NA*, p. 282).

Sidney assumes the role of war artist himself. His ecphrases in the *New Arcadia* on armed combat are far more detailed than any Renaissance manuals on the subject.[55] He covers training for war in exhibitions and the hunt; warfare on horseback, fighting individually and in teams with lance and sword; and fighting dismounted either with swords or hand to hand.

The consequences of these expertly described martial encounters are illustrated in many grisly examples of injury and death. Horses are maimed killed or run 'scattered about the field, abashed with the madness of mankind' (*NA*, p. 340). A lance shatters in Agenor's face (*NA*, p. 339); Parthenia bleeds to death from a sword injury to her neck (*NA*, p. 397); Amphialus's guts protrude through a slash in his belly (*NA*, p. 411). To emphasise the macabre effects of war, Sidney switches from plain style to balanced, rhythmic clauses replete with metaphors, personifications and puns in a macabre Senecan manner:

> In one place lay disinherited heads, dispossessed of their natural seigniories; in another, whole bodies to see to, but that their hearts, wont to be bound all over so close, were now with deadly violence opened; in others, fouler deaths had uglily displayed their trailing guts. There lay arms whose fingers yet moved, as if they would feel for him that made them feel, and legs which, contrary to common nature, by being discharged of their burden were grown heavier. (*NA*, pp. 340–1)

There is little room in Sidney's displays of Christian stoic heroism for guns. The author-narrator reports 'divers sorts of shot from corners of streets and house windows' (*NA*, p. 36) when Musidorus enters the Helots' stronghold, Cardamyla, in Book 1, but no one of significance is injured. Sidney's preferred mode of measuring right from wrong – with a hint of Calvinist 'election' – remains single combat, either in isolation or in the

---

55 E. M. Parkinson, 'Sidney's Portrayal of Mounted Combat with Lances', *Spenser Studies*, v (1985), 231–51.

midst of battle, or even in the tiltyard. These scenes of Homeric stature
depend on Sidney's emulation of literary models, supplemented by first-
hand experience gained through many years of practice and observation.
Solidly in the tradition of literary impressionism, Sidney avoids describing
in realistic detail the impact of warfare on the wounded. Fantasy slaughter
abounds, and is regarded as perfectly legal, provided it accords with the
principles of monarchomachia, and reinforces the status of the principal
characters as heroes of erotic romance.

Costume, device and narrative strategy

The need for combatants to be able to identify one another by costume or
device becomes self-evident when Musidorus and Pyrocles unwittingly
fight one another in the battle between the Arcadians and the helots
(*NA*, p. 38). But Sidney's exemplary knights are participants in masque-
like entertainments rather than realistic war, and decorate their shields
with personal rather than heraldic devices. These feature in Phalantus's
tournament in Book 1, in the annual week-long tournament celebrating
Andromana's wedding anniversary in Book 2, and in Book 3 in the bloody
encounters in front of Cecropia's castle.

Heliodorus provides Sidney with his precedent for giving costume a
sophisticated role in the narrative structure of a novel. Theagenes' embroi-
dered picture of the battle between the Lapiths and Centaurs reflects the
pirates' pitched battle on the beach in the opening scene, and anticipates
the end of Book 5, the mid-point, where the battle is described. Heliodorus
also foreshadows his optimistic erotic romance ending through Theagenes'
clasp, which depicts Athene wearing the Gorgon's head on her armour.
This identifies Theagenes with the Greek prince, Perseus, who slays the
Gorgon, then rescues and marries the Ethiopian princess, Andromeda. It
prognosticates Theagenes' survival and marriage to Charikleia, a descen-
dant of Perseus and Andromeda (3.3).

Sidney similarly endows devices and symbolic costume with narra-
tive significance in both the *Old Arcadia* and *New Arcadia*. The degree
to which he makes these esoteric visual arts inform the plot is without
literary precedent, and places an enormous semiotic and interpreta-
tive burden on the reader.[56] Sidney's experience in designing costumes,
and performing in chivalric competitions for which he writes scripts,

56 V. Skretkowicz, 'Devices and Their Narrative Function in Sidney's *Arcadia*', *Emblem-
    atica*, i (1986), 267–92; and see M. Bath, *Speaking Pictures: English Emblem Books and
    Renaissance Culture* (London: Longman, 1994).

exhibits itself in the way he integrates symbolic pictorial motifs into his narrative. In the *Old Arcadia*, but particularly in the *New Arcadia*, the younger generation of characters articulates passions and emotions through complex symbolic costumes that represent their feelings or state of mind. These are based on the same principles as those used in tiltyard masques, which in the early 1580s, and largely under Sidney's influence, become associated with philhellene Protestant politics. In contrast to the rudimentary, literal functions given to devices by Marlowe, Shakespeare and others, a few examples culled from Sidney's wide-ranging repertoire demonstrate his understanding of their narrative potential.

Borrowing a motif and the name 'Cléophile' from the *Amadis de Gaule*, in the *Old Arcadia* Sidney has Pyrocles disguised as an Amazon named Cleophila.[57] (The spelling 'Cleofila' in extracts from Books X and XI in Paynell's *The treasurie of Amadis of Fraunce* (1572) is common in the *Arcadia* manuscripts.) Pyrocles' device on the jewel fastening his mantle symbolises regal superiority, albeit disguised and willingly submitting to love: 'an eagle covered with the feathers of a dove, and yet lying under another dove, in such sort as it seemed the dove preyed upon the eagle, the eagle casting up such a look as though the state he was in liked him, though the pain grieved him' (*OA*, p. 27).

Pyrocles' device in the *New Arcadia* performs a different narrative function. Imitating Heliodorus's use of perspective, Sidney presents this scene from Musidorus's point of view. Resting in a wood during his search for Pyrocles, Musidorus sees an elaborately costumed Amazon who wears a pictorial clasp. It consists of 'a very rich jewel, the device whereof (as he after saw) was this: a Hercules made in little form, but set with a distaff in his hand (as he once was by Omphale's commandment), with a word in Greek, but thus to be interpreted: "Never more valiant"' (*NA*, p. 69). Pyrocles' reflexive statement confirms the superficiality of his metamorphosis. Like Hercules, who retains his essential manliness, Pyrocles only temporarily jettisons his heroic masculinity.[58]

Sidney also alters Pamela's device. Being housed with Basilius's 'principal herdman', Dametas, Pamela's clothes resemble 'a shepherdish apparel', but are made of soft expensive cloth. Her dress is of 'russet velvet, cut after their fashion, with a straight body [i.e., 'a narrow bodice'], open breasted, the nether part full of pleats, with wide open sleeves, hanging down very low; her hair at the full length' (*OA*, p. 37). Her chosen device represents her enforced restraint:

---

57 See J. J. O'Connor, *Amadis de Gaule and Its Influence on Elizabethan Literature*, p. 187.
58 See V. Skretkowicz, 'Hercules in Sidney and Spenser', *Notes and Queries*, n.s., xxvii (1980), 306–10.

betwixt her breasts, which sweetly rase up like two fair mountainets in the pleasant vale of Tempe, there hanged down a jewel which she had devised as a picture of her own estate. It was a perfect white lamb tied at a stake with a great number of chains, as it had been feared lest the silly creature should do some great harm. (*OA*, p. 37)

Representing stoic compliance to her father's demands, she abstains from adding a 'word' or motto, 'but even took silence as the word of the poor lamb'. By connecting Pamela with Tempe, the author-narrator relates her to Musidorus. For, when castigating Pyrocles, Musidorus compares this beautiful deep river valley in his homeland with Arcadia: 'Tempe, in my Thessalia, where you and I (to my great happiness) were brought up together, is nothing inferior unto it' (*OA*, pp. 16–17; cf. *NA*, p. 52).

Sidney adapts this scene in the *New Arcadia*, where the description of Pamela's device is reassigned to Pyrocles. Already in love with Philoclea, he tempts Musidorus to stay in Arcadia. Pamela, he reports, wears a symbolic pendant 'betwixt her breasts, which sweetly rase up like two fair mountainets in the pleasant vale of Tempe', which is in the kingdom over which Musidorus is destined to rule. This pendant, which contains Pamela's device, portrays her as perfect, modest, steadfast and indestructible: 'a very rich diamond set but in a black horn'. But Pyrocles teasingly boasts of his ability to peer voyeuristically at Pamela's 'open breasted' torso when he describes her motto – 'the word, I have since read, is this: "Yet still myself"' (*NA*, pp. 83–4)[59]

Sidney employs an entirely different approach for Philoclea, whose frame of mind he represents through costume alone. Her 'nymphlike apparel' (*OA*, p. 37) associates her with the chaste Diana and her acolytes, whose dress Sidney describes as worn 'tucked up, as nymphs in woods do range, / Tucked up e'en with the knees […] / Her right arm naked was, discovered was her breast' (*OA*, p. 337). Certainly the extent of exposed flesh around and through the slashes of Philoclea's expensive, lustrous lightweight taffeta overwhelms Pyrocles, as she is

so near nakedness as one might well discern part of her perfections, and yet so apparelled as did show she kept the best store of her beauties to herself; her excellent fair hair drawn up […]; her body covered with a light taffeta garment, so cut as the wrought smock came through it in many places (enough to have made a very restrained imagination have thought what was under it). (*OA*, p. 37)

59 On this interpretation, see R. Parker, 'Pamela's Breasts and Related Problems: A Note on Sidney's "Devices"', *Emblematica*, iii (1988), 163–70; V. Skretkowicz, 'Sir Philip Sidney and the Elizabethan Literary Device', *Emblematica*, iii (1988), 171–9.

Philoclea's Diana costume changes radically after she fails to keep the oath she inscribes on 'a fair white marble stone' only 'a few days before Cleophila's coming': 'This vow receive, this vow O gods maintain: / My virgin life no spotted thought shall stain' (*OA*, p. 109). Philoclea reads this stone-plus-motto as a personal device, though it is an unstable signifier. For the narrator is less than certain about its original purpose, using the cautious subjunctive to suggest that Philoclea naively endows it with religious significance: 'it was a fair white marble stone that should seem had been dedicated in ancient time to the sylvan gods' (*OA*, p. 109). Becoming conscious of craving an erotic relationship, 'her memory served as an accuser of her change, and that her own hand-writing was there to bear testimony of her fall'. Symbolically, the medium in which she has written has no more permanence than her teenage promise: 'the ink was already foreworn and in many places blotted' (*OA*, p. 110).

Sidney exceeds the social boundaries within Greco-Roman erotic romance. Longus and Achilles Tatius represent male, though not female, homoerotic relationships. By contrast, Philoclea reluctantly succumbs to what she believes to be a lesbian relationship with Cleophila: 'impossible desires are plagued in the desire itself' (*OA*, p. 111). In the *New Arcadia*, Sidney delicately develops the interplay between Philoclea's emotions. Aware of her mother's passion for Pyrocles, she takes stock of herself, deciding that the integrity of her love alone should determine her commitment: 'And should I be wiser than my mother? Either she sees a possibility in that which I think impossible, or else impossible loves need not misbecome me' (*NA*, p. 149). But Sidney is also careful to express Philoclea's heterosexuality when Pyrocles finally identifies himself: 'her pleasure was fully made up with the manifesting of his being – which was such as in hope did overcome hope' (*NA*, p. 231).

In the *Old Arcadia*, and in the additions in the 1593 'complete' edition, Sidney represents Philoclea's response to Pyrocles through her night attire. The author-narrator describes Philoclea from Pyrocles' perspective as he enters her room: 'upon the top of her bed, having her beauties eclipsed with nothing but with a fair smock (wrought all in flames[,] of ash-colour [i.e., 'silver' or 'grey'] silk and gold), lying so upon her right side that the left thigh down to the foot yielded his delightful proportion to the full view' (*OA*, p. 231). Sidney's earliest readers would probably understand that Philoclea's passion burns with, paradoxically, cold and hot flames, a foretaste of the rejection and reconciliation that follow. For her costume bears a resemblance to that adopted by the Earl of Essex on

May Day 1581, entirely in 'forsaken' tawny, but the cloak 'laid on with flames of fiery gold'.[60]

Philoclea's bed

The symbolism of Philoclea's smock is both self-referential and directed at the reader. Although Philoclea's night attire reflects her dilemma over Pyrocles, she has no expectation that anyone might see her wearing it, and certainly does not expect his invasion of her privacy. Pyrocles is transfixed by Philoclea's thigh and appears to not to understand her personal device which, in a different way, accords with his own position. Beset both by Basilius and Gynecia, Pyrocles' mind is charged with their sexual fantasies as well as his own. He approaches Philoclea's chamber, 'rapt from himself with the excessive forefeeling of his near coming contentment' (*OA*, p. 228), sees Philoclea in her bed, hears her express hatred towards him, and losing the power of speech, 'referred her understanding to his eyes' language' (*OA*, p. 232). Philoclea spurns Pyrocles, claiming that all she wants is a good night's rest: 'Dost thou not think the day torments thou has given me sufficient, but that thou dost envy me the night's quiet?' (*OA*, pp. 232–3). She is shocked, retreats into her bed and chastises him so severely that he faints.

While 'a sexual encounter between lovers who intend to wed is standard procedure throughout *Amadis*',[61] and occurs in the *Old Arcadia*, such activity boldly departs from Greco-Roman erotic romance. The genre requires that the destiny of the principal characters is to marry. But, to achieve suspense and the resulting climax, the desideratum, implicit in *Daphnis and Chloe*, and explicit in *Leukippe and Kleitophon* and *An Ethiopian Story*, is to maintain pre-marital chastity. In a dream, Artemis requires Leukippe to remain chaste, but foretells her marriage to Kleitophon. Kleitophon's dream incorporates erotic architectural symbolism, and curtails his 'stirrings of manly energy' (4.1; Reardon, 221–2). The doors of the temple of Aphrodite slam shut in his face, but a woman, 'who looked just like the statue in the temple', assures him that she will not only open the doors but will also make him 'a high priest of the goddess of love' (4.2; Reardon, p. 222). Heliodorus is even more forthright. As a condition of ever being left alone with Theagenes, Charikleia demands

---

60 P. E. J. Hammer, *The Polarisation of Elizabethan Politics: The Political Career of Robert Devereux, 2nd Earl of Essex, 1585–1597* (Cambridge: Cambridge University Press, 1999), p. 30.

61 J. J. O'Connor, *Amadis de Gaule and Its Influence on Elizabethan Literature*, p. 191.

that he honour her virginity: 'Let him swear that he will have no carnal knowledge of me before I regain my home and people' (4.18; Reardon, p. 441). Mutual respect, and trust in the strength of their love, carry them through the horror of their experiences with pirates and bandits. Alone, captured, deep in a cave,

> they hugged and kissed to their heart's content with nothing to restrain or distract them. They instantly forgot their plight and clasped one another in a prolonged embrace so tight that they seemed to be of one flesh. But the love they consummated was sinless and undefiled; their union was one of moist, warm tears; their only intercourse was one of chaste lips. For if ever Charikleia found Theagenes becoming too ardent in the arousal of his manhood, a reminder of his oath was enough to restrain him. (5.4; Reardon, p. 448)

Heliodorus's description fulfils an anticipatory function, foreshadowing marriage. Sidney adopts this in Pamela's insistence on pre-marital sexual restraint: 'Let not our joys, which ought ever to last, be stained in our own consciences. Let no shadow of repentance steal into the sweet consideration of our mutual happiness. I have yielded to be your wife; stay then till the time that I may rightly be so. Let no other defiled name burden my heart' (*OA*, p. 197). This pleading is to little avail when she falls asleep, and Musidorus tries to rape her (*OA*, p. 202).

Sidney writes the antithesis of this scene in Philoclea's rushing to console the unconscious Pyrocles. The author-narrator describes her spontaneous act of unfettered compassion. 'Starting out of her bed', Philoclea resembles the naked goddess of love, 'Venus rising from her mother the sea'. Laying 'her fair body over his breast' (*OA*, p. 235) she smothers him with kisses, and believing him to be dead, considers 'Thisbe's punishment of my rash unwariness' – suicide (*OA*, p. 236).

Pyrocles revives and carries Philoclea back to bed, where he views, admires and caresses her. Sidney adopts Longus's technique to indicate the passage of time, suspending forward action through a tedious interlude: 'there came into his mind a song the shepherd Philisides had in his hearing sung of the beauties of his unkind mistress', Mira (*OA*, p. 238). Mira's body serves as Philoclea's proxy. The momentum grinds to a halt during this erotic *blazon anatomique*, which adapts a French poetic convention of praising the female nude.

Philisides' 'What tongue can her perfections tell / In whose each part all pens may dwell?' (*OA*, p. 238) is couched in the static, formulaic listing of the encomium tradition. Beginning with Mira's hair, forehead, eyebrows, eyelids and eyes, his view descends to her breasts, nipples, waist, ribs, navel, belly, Cupid's hill (mons veneris), thighs and feet. His description consists of exaggerated comparisons with the moon, stars, sun and sky; with gold, silver, rubies, pearls, sapphires, amethysts, alabaster, porphyry and marble; foamy seas, snow and ivory; milk, wine, spices, sugar and marzipan; apples, cherries, roses and lilies; ermine, doves and swans. Philisides' narrating tongue accompanies his eyes upwards to her back, shoulders, shoulder blades, arms and hands, eventually arriving at her soul, the 'fairer guest which dwells within' (*OA*, p. 242). The process of following the poem signifies the trail of Pyrocles' eyes, perhaps equating them with his tongue, across parts of Philoclea's body.[62]

The calculated diminution of sensuousness throughout this passage dissolves into abstraction, and opting out by the author-narrator: 'beginning now to envy Argus's thousand eyes, and Briareus's hundred hands, fighting against a weak resistance, which did strive to be overcome, he gives me occasion to leave him in so happy a plight […]' (*OA*, p. 243). While the author-narrator denies the reader direct experience of Philoclea's body, Pyrocles freely traverses beyond the limitations of Philisides' fantasy.

Eroticising renaissance romance

Sidney's portrayal of this episode, at the end of Book 3 in the *Old Arcadia*, legitimises consensual intercourse in a love relationship. Philoclea and Pyrocles long since 'passed the promise of marriage' after 'many such embracings as it seemed their souls desired to meet and their hearts to kiss as their mouths did' (*OA*, p. 122). There are, however, immediate political repercussions to be faced.

Sidney offers alternative explanations as to why Philoclea and Pyrocles are asleep when Dametas finds them. The list opens in disapproval and ends in praise. First, God arranged this scenario in order to expose 'their fault' of fornication: 'whether it were they were so divinely surprised to bring their fault to open punishment' (*OA*, p. 273). Second, achieving perfect joy made them faint – revisiting the debate between Musidorus and Pyrocles over the selfish and virtuous meanings of 'enjoying' (*OA*, p. 23; *NA*, p. 75): 'or that the too high degree of their joys had overthrown the wakeful use of their senses'. And third, an argument developed by John Donne in 'The Ecstasy', they are temporarily lifeless during the union of their souls: 'or that their souls, lifted up with extremity of love after

---

62 M. E. Lamb, 'Exhibiting Class and Displaying the Body in Sidney's *Countess of Pembroke's Arcadia*', *Studies in English Literature*, xxxvii (1997), 55–72.

mutual satisfaction, had left their bodies dearly joined to unite themselves together so much more freely as they were freer of that earthly prison; or whatsoever other cause may be imagined of it [...]' (*OA*, p. 273).

Sidney entirely rejects the restraint on physical contact advocated by strict Renaissance Christian neoplatonists, such as Cardinal Bembo in Baldassare Castiglione's *Il Libro del Cortegiano* (1528). In Castiglione, lovers' souls mingle during the kiss.[63] The reformed, openly erotic *Old Arcadia* presents a much more naturalistic view of sex. Pyrocles and Philoclea's souls are not liberated to 'unite themselves' until after 'mutual satisfaction' is achieved through orgasm. Setting himself against reactionary disapproval of the passions,[64] Sidney explores the perfections, flaws and fetishes of human behaviour more fully than the Greco-Roman erotic romances endeavoured to do.[65] Nonetheless, his text has a striking resemblance to Kleitophon's academic description of female orgasm:

> When a woman reaches the very goal of Aphrodite's action, she instinctively gasps with that burning delight, and her gasp rises quickly to the lips with a love breath, and there it meets a lost kiss, wandering about and looking for a way down: this kiss mingles with the love breath and returns with it to strike the heart. The heart then is kissed, confused, throbbing. If it were not firmly fastened in the chest, it would follow along, drawing itself upwards to the place of kisses. (2.37; Reardon, p. 207)

In the revisions that by 1584 constituted his 'complete' *Arcadia*, Sidney removed the details of Philoclea and Pyrocles' sexual relationship. As first published in 1593, when Dametas finds them asleep it is either because 'they were so diuinely surprised, to bring this whole matter to be [emended in 1598 to 'the' (Kk6)] destinied conclusion, or that the vnresistable force of their sorrowes, had ouerthrowne the wakefull vse of their senses' (Ll5v). That is, they either are under the influence of the oracle or have simply fallen asleep. Gone are ideas of punishment, the conflated meanings of joy and their sexual-spiritual ecstasy. Sidney's change of direction reflects an increasing rejection of informal marriage, particularly among politi-

---

63 On this convention, see E. R. Curtius, *European Literature and the Latin Middle Ages*, trans. by W. R. Trask (Princeton: Princeton University Press, 1953; repr. London: Routledge and Kegan Paul, 1979), p. 292, citing S. Gaselee, 'The Soul in the Kiss', *The Criterion*, ii (1924), 349–59.

64 See A. J. Smith, *Literary Love: The Role of Passion in English Poems and Plays of the Seventeenth Century* (London: Edward Arnold, 1983).

65 Cf. R. H. F. Carver, '"Sugared Invention" or "Mongrel Tragi-comedy": Sir Philip Sidney and the Ancient Novel', in *Groningen Colloquia on the Novel*, ed. by H. Hofmann and M. Zimmerman (Groningen: Egbert Forsten, 1997), pp. 197–226, exploring the ancient origins of Sidney's concepts of the novel.

cally and financially significant households. This was legislated against in France, and led to the condemnation of *Amadis de Gaule*.[66]

In the *New Arcadia*, Sidney dignifies the characters of Philoclea and Pamela with considerable fortitude. Their stoicism and rhetorical prowess during their imprisonment, abuse and torture at their aunt Cecropia's hands echo the positive descriptions of Leukippe by Achilles Tatius, and of Charikleia by Heliodorus. Pamela's self-control, however, extends far beyond Charikleia's. In *An Ethiopian Story*, Theagenes' display of horsemanship serves as the prelude to love: 'at the moment when they set eyes on one another, the young pair fell in love, as if the soul recognised its kin at the very first encounter and sped to meet that which was worthily its own' (3.5; Reardon, p. 414). In the *New Arcadia*, when Musidorus performs his exquisite feats of dressage, Pamela proudly reports how she maintains a stern exhibition of self-control and stoic denial: 'But how delightful soever it was, my delight might well be in my soul, but it never went to look out of the window to do him any comfort; but how much more I found reason to like him, the more I set all the strength of mind to suppress it – or at least to conceal it' (*NA*, p. 154).

Pamela's control of her feelings reveals the extent to Pyrocles, compared with Argalus, parodies the hero of erotic romance. Pamela and Philoclea invite Pyrocles, disguised as Zelmane, to join them as they bathe in the river. He lies about 'having taken a late cold' as he witnesses a literary striptease, imbued with lesbian overtones: 'they began by piecemeal to take away the eclipsing of their apparel. Zelmane would have put to her helping hand, but she was taken with such a quivering that she thought it more wisdom to lean herself to a tree and look on'. Pyrocles/Zelmane, who 'could not choose but run to touch, embrace, and kiss her' (*NA*, p. 189), experiences sexual arousal: 'all her parts grudged that her eyes should do more homage than they to the princess of them' (*NA*, p. 190). Sidney undermines Pamela's caution by transforming Pyrocles' mischievous eroticism into an elevating religious experience: Zelmane's 'wit began to be with a divine fury inspired [...] her soul the queen which should be delighted' (*NA*, p. 190). As Zelmane becomes overwhelmed by 'invention' or imagination, she begins to extemporise. Her personality becomes temporarily annihilated as 'she, but as an organ [i.e., 'a tool of her mind'], did only lend utterance'. She breaks into song, which 'was to this purpose: "What tongue can her perfections tell / In whose each part all pens may dwell?"' (*NA*, p. 190).

66 M. Rothstein, 'Clandestine Marriage and *Amadis de Gaule*: The Text, the World, and the Reader', *Sixteenth Century Journal*, xxv (1994), 873–86.

In the *Old Arcadia*, the author-narrator uses Philisides' monotonous poem to screen Philoclea's body from the reader during the sexual act: 'do not think, fair ladies, his thoughts had such leisure as to run over so long a ditty' (*OA*, p. 242). In the *New Arcadia*, the poem reflects what Pyrocles sees from a divinely inspired perspective. Sidney's new prose ending to Book 3 of the 'complete' 1593 *Arcadia* represents Pyrocles sharing an intimate, but sexually innocent, relationship with Philoclea, and they agree to elope (Ii5v; cf. *OA*, p. 237). These particular changes may relate to the period prior to Sidney's marriage to Frances Walsingham, on 21 September 1583, when he was twenty-nine and she sixteen.[67]

In the *Old Arcadia*, Musidorus and Pyrocles are accused of complicity, with Gynecia, in a plot to murder Basilius. Pyrocles admits he 'offered force to' Philoclea (*OA*, p. 394), and is to be 'thrown out of a high tower' (*OA*, p. 408). Musidorus is also guilty of 'ravishment': 'although he ravished her not from herself, yet he ravished her from him that owed [i.e., 'owned'] her, which was her father. This kind is chastised by the loss of the head' (*OA*, p. 406). But in the revised 'complete' *Arcadia* of 1593, Pyrocles takes pride in the innocence of his relationship. His statement contains conditionals and qualifications, and he confesses to nothing. Nonetheless, Sidney adapts the wording of Musidorus's sentence, and Euarchus finds both princes guilty, 'For though they rauished them not from themselues, yet they rauished them from him that owed them, which was their father. An acte punished by all the *Graecian* lawes, by the losse of the head' (Rr6).

In making these revisions, Sidney neglected to change Pyrocles' sentence from being 'thrown out of a high tower' to beheading. But this is of slight importance in an erotic romance in which the outcome is predicated, not on the chastity of the principal couples, as in *Leukippe and Kleitophon* and *An Ethiopian Story*, but rather on the fulfilment of oracles. The oracle in the *Old Arcadia* that impels Basilius to move his court to the countryside, and fixes the action to 'this fatal year', is ominous and ambiguous: 'Thy elder care shall [...] / By princely mean be stolen and yet not lost; / Thy younger shall [...] embrace / An uncouth love [...] / Thou with thy wife adult'ry shalt commit, / And in thy throne a foreign state shall sit' (*OA*, p. 5).

Guided in the *New Arcadia* by Heliodorus's epic structure, in which piecemeal and non-sequential revelation creates suspense, Sidney conceals the words of Basilius's oracle until late in Book 2. The lines he

67 C. Read, *Mr Secretary Walsingham and the Policy of Queen Elizabeth*, 3 vols (Oxford: Clarendon Press, 1925; repr. New York: AMS, 1978), iii.423.

adds predetermine an erotic romance conclusion, in the marriages of Pamela to Musidorus, and Philoclea to Pyrocles:

> Both they themselves unto such two shall wed,
> Who at thy bier, as at a bar, shall plead
> Why thee (a living man) they had made dead.
>   (*NA*, p. 296)

Sidney reinforces this outcome in the new portion of Book 3, ruling out alternatives. Obsession with sex nullifies both Basilius's and Gynecia's sense of responsibility for the state. Cecropia and Amphialus hold the princesses captive. Argalus and Parthenia are slaughtered, Cecropia dies, and Amphialus attempts suicide. Only the oracle suggests that Arcadia is redeemable.

The second-last vignette of Book 3 of the *New Arcadia* leads into the fight between Pyrocles/Zelmane and Anaxius. When Anaxius demands Pamela as his wife, Basilius sends Philanax back to the oracle of Apollo, which has foreknowledge of Philanax's question. It states unambiguously that Basilius's daughters 'were reserved for such as were better beloved of the gods', that 'they should return unto him safely and speedily; and that he should keep on his solitary course till both Philanax and Basilius fully agreed in the understanding of the former prophecy'. This oracle also instructs Philanax, a clear-headed, rational soldier, 'to give tribute, but not oblation, to human wisdom' (*NA*, p. 457).

Sidney uses this second oracle to accentuate the importance to philhellene Protestants of patience, stoicism and faith. The imprisoned Pamela prays that God will enable her to sustain her faith: 'that thou wilt suffer some beam of thy majesty so to shine into my mind that it may still depend confidently upon thee' (*NA*, p. 336). She demonstrates dedication to philhellene Protestantism in her educated response to Cecropia's atheism, as does Philoclea in her patient stoicism under torture and threat of death (*NA*, pp. 358–63; 420–4). In an adaptation of Heliodorus, Pyrocles/Zelmane advocates that Philoclea pretend to comply with Amphialus's desires, echoing Charikleia's advice to Theagenes (6.21; *NA*, 429). In this scene, Sidney casts the misguided Amphialus as a male version of Arsake, and Cecropia in the part of Kybele, her procuress, destined to meet a violent death. The faith that binds Pamela to Musidorus, and Philoclea to Pyrocles, during their captivity informs the rest of the romance.

In the 'complete' *Arcadia*, Pamela and Philoclea agree to elope with their lovers who, out of mutual respect, maintain chaste relationships. These provide a stark contrast to Cecropia advising Amphialus that raping

Philoclea would constitute a successful beginning to marriage (*NA*, p. 402), and Basilius's and Gynecia's misguided love-making (*OA*, p. 227).

Erotic romance and erotic sex

In the *Old Arcadia*, Philisides' bland encomium displaces Philoclea and Pyrocles' heated exertions as they commit themselves to one another, body and soul (*OA*, pp. 238–42). Its paraphrastic vagueness functions like the ending of *Daphnis and Chloe*, where 'Daphnis did some of the things Lycaenion taught him' (4.40; Reardon, p. 348), referring back to the scene in which Lycaenion 'guided him [Daphnis] skilfully on the road he had been searching for' (3.18; Reardon, p. 325). Amyot suppressed this passage in Longus, but Sidney had access to rare manuscript copies of *Daphnis and Chloe*, such as those owned by his friend, Henri Estienne (1528–98). This prolific Huguenot scholar and publisher collected, and had copies made, of Greek manuscripts, including Achilles Tatius.[68] Estienne met Sidney during 1573–74 in Heidelberg, Strassburg and Vienna, and dedicated the first of his own editions of the New Testament in Greek ([Geneva,] 1576) to Sidney. This contains a textual commentary and thirty-six-page essay, 'De stylo Novi Testamenti' – 'on the style of the New Testament'. About the time Sidney was completing the *Old Arcadia*, Estienne edited *Herodiani Historiarum Libri VIII* (Geneva, 1581). In dedicating the second part to Sidney, he maintained that 'Sidney was so learned in reading Greek that translations were superfluous for him'.[69]

Estienne noted in his edition of Appian's *De rebus Hispanicis* (1557) that he had seen two manuscripts of Longus. This was probably between 1547 and 1555 during one of his three visits to Italy, on the first of which (1547–49) he met Annibale Caro, who by 1538 had translated Longus into Italian.[70] Both manuscripts would have included Lycaenion's teaching Daphnis about sex. At least one, not necessarily the manuscript found by Courier in Florence in 1807,[71] also contained the section missing from all other known manuscripts, including Amyot's, 'the great

68 *Achilles Tatius. Leucippe and Clitophon*, ed. by E. Vilborg (Stockholm: Almquist and Wiksell, 1955), p. lxxv.
69 J. M. Osborn, *Young Philip Sidney 1572–1577*, p. 89.
70 M. D. Reeve, 'Fulvio Orsini and Longus', *The Journal of Hellenic Studies*, xcix (1979), 165–7 (p. 167).
71 Biblioteca Laurenziana MS Laurentianus conv. sopp. 627; cf. Longus, *Pastorales (Daphnis et Chloé)*, ed. and trans. by G. Dalmeyda, 2nd edn (Paris: Société D'Édition 'Les Belles Lettres', 1960), pp. xlvii–xlviii and *Achilles Tatius. Leucippe and Clitophon*, ed. by E. Vilborg, p. xix.

lacuna'. This describes Chloe helping Daphnis bathe, her first notions of sexual love, and the brief flyting between Daphnis and Dorcon that leads to Chloe jumping up to kiss Daphnis (1.12–17). Estienne paraphrased these episodes in two Latin poems, 'Eclogue I' ('Chloris') and 'Eclogue II' ('Rivals'), printing them in his edition of Greek lyric poets, *Moschi, Bionis, Theocriti* […] *ab H. Stephano latine facta* (Venice, 1555).[72] Three related incidents in the *New Arcadia* suggest that Estienne may have discussed 'the great lacuna' with Sidney: Pyrocles/Zelmane's watching the princesses bathing, his rushing to touch Philoclea and the increased complexities of Philoclea's sexual awakening (*NA*, pp. 149, 189–90).

In the way Lycaenion's lesson informs the ending of *Daphnis and Chloe*, Sidney uses an anticipatory structure in the *Old Arcadia*, placing three parallel episodes in close proximity. Each escalates sexual and sensual activity. Musidorus's thoughts about raping Pamela grow into Gynecia and Basilius's extensive awareness of one another as they have sexual intercourse, and culminate in the author-narrator's discourse on Pyrocles and Philoclea making love.

The sequence begins when Musidorus convinces Pamela to elope. In a series of poems and songs, they express their respectful, idealistic love for one another. As Pamela sinks into sleep, Musidorus's 'virtuous wantonness' graduates in a rhetorically measured progress from mental towards physical rape. He recites a poem invoking the protection of the god of sleep: 'Let no strange dream make her fair body start' (*OA*, p. 200). But he quickly prefers that she should experience an erotic dream with himself as her lover:

> Then take my shape, and play a lover's part:
> Kiss her from me, and say unto her sprite,
> Till her eyes shine, I live in darkest night.
>
> (*OA*, p. 201)

As if a prelude to Philisides' poem, this scene builds towards a cresendo. Musidorus begins by admiring Pamela's face: 'her fair forehead', her hair, eyelids, eyes, cheeks, lips and perfect teeth, 'those armed ranks, all armed in most pure white, and keeping the most precise order of military discipline' (*OA*, p. 201). Pamela's open mouth focuses attention on her 'soft breath, carrying good testimony of her inward sweetness'. Her breath

---

72 A. Hulubei, 'Henri Estienne et le roman de Longus, *Daphnis et Chloé*', *Revue du Seizième Siècle*, xviii (1931), 324–40, and G. Dalmeyda, 'Henri Estienne et Longus', *Revue de Philologie*, 3rd ser., viii (1934), 169–81; revisited by L. Plazenet, 'Jacques Amyot and the Greek Novel: The Invention of the French Novel', in *The Classical Heritage in France*, ed. by G. N. Sandy (Leiden: E. J. Brill, 2002), pp. 253–4.

'came out as it seemed loath to leave [...], but that it hoped to be drawn in again'. While neither she nor her soul has any desire to enter Musidorus's body, nonetheless, he 'put his face as low to hers as he could, sucking the breath with such joy' (*OA*, p. 201).

Musidorus's inhaling Pamela's soul, a preamble to raping her body, tellingly reverses the imagery of the 'love breath' in *Kleitophon and Leukippe*. It leads ominously towards an erotic anticipation that Sidney, for the moment, curtails. For 'rising softly from her, overmastered with the fury of delight', as Musidorus begins 'to make his approaches', 'a dozen clownish villains' take them hostage, and Pamela remains none the wiser (*OA*, p. 202). (Sidney excised the few lines of this 'rape' scene from the 'complete' *Arcadia*, which in the sequence of events follows Pamela's horror at Musidorus's attempt to kiss her (*NA*, p. 309).) Only long after Pyrocles and Philoclea's love-making does Sidney offer Musidorus and Pamela a more idealised expression of love: 'who, delicately wound up one in another's arms, laid a plot in that picture of death how gladly, if death came, their souls would go together' (*OA*, p. 314).

Gynecia's relationship with Pyrocles and Basilius impacts even more strongly on the scene in Philoclea's bedroom. Gynecia, who is thirty-five (*OA*, p. 384) and ignored by her older husband, forces the disguised Pyrocles to admit his masculinity and agree to a tryst (*OA*, p. 204). Arsake in *An Ethiopian Story* abuses her political status and power, using threats and torture to secure sexual pleasure. Just thinking about the reluctant Theagenes, she madly tears off her clothes in the privacy of her bed (7.9). No less determined, though clearly squeamish, Gynecia apologetically confronts Pyrocles/Cleophila in the cave: 'Let not the abasing of myself make me more base in your eyes, [...] let my errors be made excusable by the immortal name of love!' And as a clinching gesture, to prove her passionate love, 'she discovered some parts of her fair body' (*OA*, p. 205). But Sidney takes care to distinguish her from the sexually insatiable Arsake. His narrator emphasises in the opening of the *Old Arcadia* that she is only acting out of character. Gynecia is not a lascivious tyrant, but 'a lady worthy enough to have had her name in continual remembrance if her latter time had not blotted her well governed youth, although the wound fell more to her own conscience than to the knowledge of the world' (*OA*, p. 4).

Sidney distinguishes Pyrocles from Theagenes, who is disgusted by Arsake, and from Kleitophon, who capitulates to Melite's sincere ardour as they part: 'she unfastened my bonds and kissed my hands and touched them to her eyes and heart, saying: "You see how it beats, how it is pounding under the pressures of agony and hope: may it soon throb with pleasure too!" [...] So when she embraced me, I did not hold back' (5.27; Reardon, p. 249). Because Gynecia, unlike Melite or Arsake, is genuinely appealing, she becomes a standard against which to measure Pyrocles' adoration of Philoclea: 'if Cleophila's heart had not been so fully possessed as there was no place left for any new guest, no doubt it would have yielded to that gallant assault' (*OA*, p. 205).

Pyrocles deceives Gynecia, and takes evasive action: 'remembering she [i.e., 'Cleophila'] must wade betwixt constancy and courtesy, embracing Gynecia and once or twice kissing her' (*OA*, p. 205), he/she makes false promises, 'for well she saw the boiling mind of Gynecia did easily apprehend the fitness of that lonely place' (*OA*, p. 206). Basilius, a figure Sidney bases on Basilique in the *Amadis de Gaule*,[73] which also draws on Heliodorus, is equally aroused by Pyrocles/Cleophila. Pyrocles promises to meet each of them in the cave, freeing himself to visit Philoclea's bedroom. Fusing comedy with horror, the author-narrator presents a voyeuristic account of Basilius and Gynecia's bizarre sexual encounter, as husband and wife commit adultery with one another.

In the *New Arcadia*, Sidney alludes to *Leukippe and Kleitophon* through his description of Kalander's garden. In Kleitophon's reflecting fountain, it is difficult to distinguish between appearance and reality, 'the realm of truth confronting its shadowy other' (1.15; Reardon, p. 187). Kalander's pond likewise 'bare show of two gardens, one indeed, the other in shadows' (*NA*, p. 14). A parallel dualism, between expectation and achievement, is implicit in Gynecia's predicament. Her forwardness with Pyrocles suggests that she anticipates, 'by imagination' (*OA*, p. 227), holding him within her body, as described by Kleitophon in his discourse on women's sexuality (2.37). But everything goes awry for Gynecia, who is completely disoriented. Someone gets into bed with her, though not Pyrocles: 'In what case poor Gynecia was when she knew the voice and felt the body of her husband, fair ladies, it is better to know by imagination than experience' (*OA*, p. 227). Gynecia, a victim of her own adulterous aspirations, does not have to suffer long. Basilius, 'more happy in contemplation than action' (*OA*, p. 274).

> Like a right old beaten soldier that knew well enough the greatest captains do never use long orations when it comes to the very point of execution, [...] leapt into that side preserved for a more welcome guest; and laying his lovingest hold upon Gynecia: 'O Cleophila', said he, 'embrace in your

favour this humble servant of yours! Hold within me my heart which pants
to leave his master to come unto you!' (*OA*, pp. 226–7)

Basilius's panting, gasping, and desperate pleading parodies Achilles
Tatius's sensuous interpretation of the spirituality of orgasm. The exchange
of souls that Pyrocles and Philoclea achieve only a few pages later fails to
take place here.

Substitution of one bed partner for another under cover of dark-
ness lies behind Thisbe's plan to ensnare Demainete in Heliodorus's
An Ethiopian Story (1.15–17). Shakespeare uses a similar ruse, albeit
in differing circumstances, in *All's Well that Ends Well* (III.vii.32) and
Measure for Measure (III.i.242), as does George Attowell in *Frauncis newe
Iigge*. Sidney, however, inventively subverts the adulterous expectations of
both partners, and describes them awakening to the truth of their self-
deception.

During Basilius's unwelcome penetration, Sidney focuses on Gynecia's
anguish and wandering thoughts. Contemplating the circumstances
leading to this unexpected change of partner, she decides she had better
'frame herself, not truly with a sugared joy, but with a determinate
patience, to let her husband think he had found a very gentle and supple-
minded Cleophila' (*OA*, p. 227). She is sustained by the hope of future
sexual fulfilment with Pyrocles, and he in turn depends on this as he
makes his way towards Philoclea's bedroom. All will be well 'so long as
Gynecia bewrayed not the matter (which he thought she would not do,
as well for her own honour and safety as for the hope she might still have
of him [...])' (*OA*, p. 228).

The structural formalism and psychological insight in this erotic
sequence carry into Book 4, where these sexual unions are addressed
in reverse order. At dawn, Basilius makes his way 'to the mouth of the
cave, there to apparel himself' (*OA*, p. 274). There Gynecia overhears her
husband's discourse on the imaginary Cleophila whom he believes he has
just had sex with:

> O who would have thought there could have been such difference betwixt
> women? Be not jealous no more, good Gynecia, but yield to the pre-eminence
> of more excellent gifts; support thyself upon such marble pillars as she doth;
> deck thy breast with those alabaster bowls that Cleophila doth; then [...]
> perhaps thou mayst recover the possession of my otherwise-inclined love.
> But alas, Gynecia, thou canst not show such evidence. (*OA*, p. 275)

This sterile, generic metaphorical diction echoes Musidorus's fantasy
on the sleeping Pamela, and foreshadows Philisides' extravagant poem

on female anatomy. But once Basilius drinks the contents of Gynecia's diamond-studded gold chalice, and collapses (*OA*, p. 278), any significance attached to Pyrocles and Philoclea's sexual encounter diminishes in the light of the immediately ensuing political complications. For during his thirty-hour sleep, the governance of Arcadia is challenged.

Interest theory, philhellene politics, and erotic romance

Sidney's innovative method of characterisation combines ethopoeia and prosopopoeia, as recommended by Aphthonius, Theophrastan type, Plutarchan moral allegory and analysis of personal interests. His plot, which progresses through the juxtaposition of conflicting interests, represents a broad spectrum of these, from the erotically to the politically driven, and from the Machiavellian egocentric to the altruistic. In this respect, he anticipates both the comedy of humours and revenge tragedy.

Pyrocles relies on Gynecia's self-interest preventing her disclosure of his masculinity. Musidorus similarly divides the rebels who capture him and Pamela by playing on their incompatible interests, which he identifies with purposes, or ends:

> 'My masters', said he, 'there is no man that is wise but hath in whatsoever he doth some purpose [...] till he see that either that purpose is not worth the pains or that another doing carries with it a better purpose [...] that makes me desire you to tell me what is your end in carrying the princess and me back again unto her father [...] Thus then you may see that in your own purpose rests great uncertainty; but I will grant that by this your deed you shall obtain your double purpose'. (*OA*, p. 315)

Sidney's focus on personal and political interest prefigures the formal development of 'interest theory' in a number of seventeenth-century political treatises. These characteristically contain the word 'interest' in their titles, as in *De l'Interest des Princes et des Estats de la Chrestienté* (Paris, 1638) by the Huguenot military hero Henri, duc de Rohan (1579–1638).[74] Following publication in Paris (1640) and London (1641) of Henry Hunt's translation, *A treatise of the interest of the princes and states of Christendome. Written in French by the most noble and illustrious Prince, the Duke of Rohan,* 'interest' became a code for Presbyterian polemic. It dominates the nationalistic titles of Sir William Constantine's *The Interest of England*

---

74 J. Scott, *Algernon Sidney and the English Republic, 1623–1677* (Cambridge: Cambridge University Press, 1988), pp. 207–11; V. Skretkowicz, 'Algernon Sidney and Philip Sidney: A Continuity of Rebellion', *Sidney Journal*, xvii, no. 2 (1999), 3–18.

(1642)[75] and *The Second Part of The Interest of England* (1645),[76] and of an anonymous Parliamentary pamphlet of 1646, *The Interest of England Maintained*.[77] Then, following the conclusion of the third Civil War, and unmistakably to associate his publication with others of liberal tendency, either the editor 'P.B.' or the publisher Henry Seile inventively applied it to Fulke Greville's *Dedication to Sir Philip Sidney*:

> *The Life of the Renowned Sr Philip Sidney. With the true Interest of England as it then stood in relation to all Forrain Princes: And particularly for suppressing the power of Spain Stated by Him. His principall Actions, Counsels, Designes, and Death. Together with a short Account of the Maximes and Policies used by Queen Elizabeth in her Government. Written by Sir Fulke Grevil Knight, Lord Brook, a Servant to Queen Elizabeth, and his Companion & Friend (1652).*[78]

Analysing the 'interests' of political leaders and their states facilitated strategic planning. To this end, in the *New Arcadia* Sidney adds a passage to the description of the Arcadians' rebellion in Book 2. United by a common concern about Basilius's absence, their initial aim is to create a responsible government in which, as in monarchomachist treatises, a magistrate's power lies in the support of the people: 'we only are not astonished with vain titles, which have their force but in our force' (*NA*, p. 292; cf. *OA*, p. 127). Sidney illustrates how identifying the rebels' divided interests, as among the tyrannised creatures of Languet's song, exposes the weakness of their coalition and simplifies the task of managing them:

> never bees made such a confused humming, the town-dwellers demanding putting down of imposts; the country fellows, laying out of commons […]

75 Sir William Constantine, *The Interest of England How it Consists in Vnity of the Protestant Religion. With Expedients moderate and effectuall to establish it by the extirpation of the papacy. By a Member of the House of Commons* (1642).

76 Sir William Constantine, *The Second Part of The Interest of England Considered As it relates to the Government of the Church. In three Divisions: wherein is demonstrated, 1. How Church-Government by the Hierarchy of Bishops is destructive to the Interest of this Kingdome. 2. How the Presbyteriall Discipline will conduce to the Interest thereof. 3. Of Tender Consciences, what sort may and ought to bee permitted, what not* […] (1645).

77 Anon., *The Interest of England Maintained: The Honour of the Parliament vindicated; The Malignants Plott upon the Presbyters, to make them doe their worke Discovered. The Designe to destroy Common Freedome, and all just Government, is under the specious pretence of rooting out Sectaries, and Hereticks, evidenced: In Certaine Observations upon a Dangerous Remonstrance lately presented by the Lord Major, and Common Counsell of London, to the Honourable, the Commons of England, in Parliament Assembled* (1646).

78 On the circumstances surrounding publication, see G. Alexander, 'Fulke Greville and the Afterlife', *Huntington Library Quarterly*, lxii (2000), 203–31 (p. 218), and V. Skretkowicz, 'Greville, Politics, and the Rhetorics of *A Dedication to Sir Philip* Sidney', in *Fulke Greville: A Special Double Number*, ed. by M. C. Hansen and M. Woodcock, *Sidney Journal*, xix (2001 [i.e., 2002]), 97–123 (pp. 100–7).

At length, they fell to direct contrarieties: for the artisans, they would have corn and wine set at a lower price [...]; the ploughmen, vine-labourers, and farmers would none of that. The countrymen demanded that every man might be free in the chief towns – that could not the burgesses like of. The peasants would have the gentlemen destroyed; the citizens (especially such as cooks, barbers, and those other that lived most on gentlemen) would but have them reformed [...]

But no confusion was greater than of particular men's likings and dislikings. (*NA*, p. 284)

Philanax similarly analyses Cecropia's interests when she threatens to behead her hostages: 'a prince of judgement ought not to consider what his enemies promise or threaten, but what the promisers and threateners in reason will do; and the nearest conjecture thereunto is what is best, for their own behoof, to do' (*NA*, p. 417). He concludes it would be unwise to lift the siege.

In the 'complete' *Arcadia*, this analysis of interest serves as a preamble to the end of Book 4. This explores the flaws of monarchy, and contrasts alternative forms of government, from responsible monarchy to democracy. Arcadia is an absolute dukedom or monarchy with direct succession. Basilius's elder daughter, Pamela, is under twenty-one and unmarried. It is significant that the laws of Arcadia do not recognise her *de praesanti* marriage to Musidorus. Owing to the centralisation of a monarch's power, on the death of Basilius no one in Arcadia is left who is practised in the science of governing: 'for now their prince and guide had left them, they had not experience to rule, and had not whom to obey. Public matters had ever been privately governed, so that they had no lively taste what was good for themselves' (*OA*, p. 320).

In the absence of a leader to whom power is delegated, the detached perspective required to enhance the *res publica* is paralysed by 'an extreme medley of diversified thoughts' (*OA*, p. 320). Conflicting self-interests of democracy, where individuals have an equal voice, result in disagreement among 'the great men', the gentlemen, the soldiers, 'all the needy sort', the rich, and the wise. The upshot is that 'nobody well knew against whom chiefly to oppose themselves'. Even those favouring a republican form of government cannot agree. Some prefer (as in Languet's song) 'the Lacedemonian government of few chosen senators; others the Athenian, where the people's voice held the chief authority' (*OA*, pp. 320–1). Some royalists promote Pamela's claim, others, the younger Philoclea's. Some want Gynecia to become regent; others, to elect Philanax as 'lieutenant of the state' (*OA*, p. 321).

Intolerant of the abuse of monarchy, but not an anti-monarchist, Sidney is a cautious advocate of monarchomachism and, if necessary, regicide. He expresses a strong preference for maintaining popular, limited monarchy, and 'natural' succession over sudden promotion from an inexperienced bloodline. Such an appointment would only incur 'the tyrannous yoke of your fellow subject, in whom the innate meanness will bring forth ravenous covetousness, and the newness of his estate suspectful cruelty' (*OA*, p. 130; *NA*, p. 286). The 'tyrannically minded' Timautus distinguishes himself by proposing a mixed government that best suits his own interests. He tries to bribe Philanax to make him king of half of Arcadia, offering Philanax 'the choice in marriage of either the sisters, so he would likewise help him to the other, and make such [i.e., 'by that means'] a partition of the Arcadian state' (*OA*, pp. 322).

Readers of the 1593 'complete' *Arcadia* would encounter Timautus's proposal knowing that Sidney's monarchomachist policy is to exterminate tyrannical blood-lines. Precedents are in the expanded Book 2, where style of government relates to character type. The melancholy King of Phrygia is an envious, suspicious, and greedy tyrant, intent on executing Musidorus in a ceremonious 'triumph of tyranny' (*NA*, p. 172). Pyrocles poses as the executioner's assistant, and the king is believed to have been killed in the ensuing mêlée. Before anarchy sets in, 'some of the wisest, seeing that a popular licence is indeed the many-headed tyranny, prevailed with the rest to make Musidorus their chief […], and by him to be ruled' (*NA*, p. 174). However, realising the king is alive, armed, and vindictive, Musidorus leads a force against him and kills the tyrant. Pyrocles necessarily exterminates the immediately heritable blood-line by killing 'his only son, a prince of great courage and beauty, but fostered in blood by his naughty father' (*NA*, p. 174). Refusing the kingship, Musidorus installs 'an aged gentleman of approved goodness' who is 'of the blood royal, and next to the succession', on condition 'that not only that governor, […] but the nature of the government, should be no way apt to decline to tyranny' (*NA*, p. 175).

Similarly eradicating tyranny in Pontus by killing the king, 'a near kinsman to this prince of Pontus' (*NA*, p. 176), 'all the desire of that people' is that Pyrocles become their king (*NA*, p. 177). Pyrocles prefers to create a stable monarchy by arranging a marriage between 'a sister of the late king's' and a 'nobleman, his father's old friend', endowing 'them with the crown of that kingdom' (*NA*, p. 177). As in Mary Sidney Wroth's *Urania*, building a philhellene Protestant league depends on uncompromising belief, utter ruthlessness and the intermarriage of political allies.

Sidney transforms erotic romance into an exemplary political novel with more sophistication than any writer before him – ancient, European or English. An astute analyst, he creates a fiction illustrating the evolutionary nature of government. By the time he opens the final Book in the *Old Arcadia*, and the 'complete' *Arcadia*, the personal interests of the heroes, heroines and divided Arcadians contrast sharply with those of the imperiled state: 'The dangerous division of men's minds, the ruinous renting of all estates, had now brought Arcadia to feel the pangs of uttermost peril (such convulsions never coming but that the life of that government [i.e., 'system of governing'] draws near his necessary period)' (*OA*, p. 351).

The novel as theatre

In Book 3 of the *New Arcadia*, and consequently in the 'complete' text, Sidney prefigures the political chaos that reigns in the fifth Book through the tragic parable of Argalus and Parthenia. Loyal, obedient servants of the state, they become the innocent victims of Cecropia's political, and Basilius's erotic, interests. Their tragic ends have no impact on the plot, other than to exemplify the rapid deterioration of Arcadian society. Yet Sidney focuses so closely on the manner and moment of their unexpected deaths that, as in the digressions in *Daphnis and Chloe*, the action stops for this well-choreographed drama to unfold.

When Gynecia marries Basilius 'even in his more than decaying years' (*NA*, p. 27), her heroic cousin Argalus accompanies her to the Arcadian court. Two years prior to Musidorus's and Pyrocles' arrival in Arcadia, when Parthenia's 'obedient mind had not yet taken upon it to make choice' (*NA*, p. 28), her mother, Kalandar's sister, engages her to Demagoras. In contrast with the well rounded characterisation of Argalus, Demagoras, from neighbouring, war-torn Laconia, is a caricature of 'a great nobleman' who loves 'nobody but himself' (*NA*, p. 28). When Parthenia falls in love with Argalus and refuses Demagoras, both her mother and Demagoras pursue their own interests. The mother dies, and Demagoras applies such a venomous poison to Parthenia's face 'that never leper looked more ugly than she did' (*NA*, p. 30). Argalus kills Demagoras, Parthenia is cured by Queen Helen's physician, and Argalus and Parthenia marry at Kalandar's house (*NA*, p. 48).

Argalus and Parthenia's pre-marital chastity and fidelity anticipates their married bliss. Being a perfect match, like Charikleia and Theagenes they fall in love immediately: 'these perfections meeting could not choose but find one another and delight in that they found, for likeness of manners is likely, in reason, to draw liking with affection' (*NA*, p. 28). Sidney applauds the spiritual benefits of this compatibility, implicitly comparing the nature of their love with that based primarily on enjoying, as earlier proposed by Pyrocles: 'a happy couple, he joying in her, she joying in herself (but in herself because she enjoyed him) [...] each making one life double because they made a double life one' (*NA*, pp. 371–2). Ominously, Sidney reserves his description of their souls' inter-action until they prepare for their final union in a Christian afterlife.

In the lengthy new part of Book 3, Basilius calls on Argalus to kill Amphialus in single combat. The theatrical spectacle of their costumes, and its effect on the reader, is compromised by the knowledge that this is a fight to the death. Torn from Parthenia by civic duty, Argalus rides in dressed as a gigantic eagle which, 'as the horse stirred, the bird seemed to fly' (*NA*, p. 374). The force implied by this symbol is mitigated through Parthenia's love token, a jousting sleeve 'full of bleeding hearts, though never intended to any bloody enterprise'. She made it for him long ago, 'in the time that success was ungrateful to their well-deserved love'. This reflection on the obstacles they overcame to marry casts an ominous over-tone on to Argalus's impresa: 'In this shield, as his own device, he had two palm trees near one another, with a word signifying, "In that sort flour-ishing"' (*NA*, p. 374). His defeat by Amphialus destroys the life-giving relationship between male and female palms. But Argalus's dying words, 'since so it pleaseth him whose wisdom and goodness guideth all, put thy confidence in him, and one day we shall blessedly meet again, never to depart' (*NA*, p. 378), confirms their Christian faith in the survival of love beyond the natural world.

According to ancient custom, Parthenia inhales Argalus's departing soul to preserve it in her own body: 'she with her kisses made him happy, for his last breath was delivered into her mouth' (*NA*, p. 378). His soul becomes the presiding spirit of her life, and the architect of the two-headed child device she adopts when, as the unidentified Knight of the Tomb, she challenges Amphialus. Parthenia's masque-like entry, which Sidney's ecphrasis represents as if it were on to the artificial stage set of a festive Accession Day tiltyard, gains immense impact from dramatic irony. The Knight of the Tomb enters, preceded and followed by four mounted 'damosels [...] apparelled in mourning weeds', each with simi-larly attired servants on either side; 'himself in an armour' painted to represent 'a gaping sepulchre'. His horse was dressed in 'cypress branches, wherewith in old time they were wont to dress graves. His bases [...] were embrodered only with black worms, which seemed […] ready already to devour him' (*NA*, p. 395). Neither the spectators in the plot nor Sidney's readers are given any indication of Parthenia's identity till after she has been wounded by Amphialus, and fulfilled the death-wish anticipated by her costume.

Like Heliodorus, who reinforces the literary pedigree of his work through quotation from his models, Sidney depends on his reader's knowledge of *Leukippe and Kleitophon* to break Parthenia's encrypted cipher. Kleitophon's nightmare depicts the end of his arranged marriage to Kalligone: 'I saw my sister's body and mine grown together into a single body […] a huge, fearsome woman […] severed the girl from me' (1.3; Reardon, p. 178). In Parthenia's parallel impresa, the death of one joined body inevitably results in the death of the other: 'In his shield for impresa he had a beautiful child, but having two heads – whereon, the one showed that it was already dead; the other alive, but in that case necessarily looking for death. The word was "No way to be rid from death, but by death"' (*NA*, pp. 395–6).

Parthenia's stratagem to be killed by Amphialus is her final act of twinning with Argalus. Her brave challenge of Amphialus should not be equated with suicide, despite her foreknowledge that she will die. Unlike the wicked Andromana, who kills herself with her dead son Palladius's dagger (*NA*, p. 258), and the desperate Amphialus who attempts suicide with Philoclea's knives (*NA*, p. 442), Parthenia selflessly and actively lives her life out in service to an ideal. Behind her decisive action lies stoicism, made bearable by Christian hope. Compare Philoclea's stoic reply to Pyrocles when he believes suicide will protect her from accusations of having extra-marital sex. There she insists that suicide indicates lack of Christian faith, 'that since it hath not his ground in an assured virtue, it proceeds rather of some other disguised passion' (*OA*, pp. 298), and that it may 'in the mean time deprive me of the help God may send me' (*OA*, pp. 299).

Parthenia's death fulfils the formula of dying in God's service, advocated by Du Plessis-Mornay in *A Discourse of Life and Death*. Mary Sidney Herbert translates:

> We must seeke to mortifie our flesh in vs, and to cast the world out of vs: but to cast our selues out of the world is in no sort permitted vs. The Christian ought willingly to depart out of this life but not cowardly to runne away. The Christian is ordained by God to fight therein: and cannot leaue his place without incurring reproch and infamie. (E2)

Parthenia's wish, 'to be rid from death' by dying, fulfils the Christian paradox, where death brings new life. Sidney emphasises the dramatic instant of dying through aposiopesis, cutting her off in mid-sentence:[79]

> 'O sweet life! Welcome! [...] I come, my Argalus! I come! And, O God, hide my faults in thy mercies; and grant, as I feel thou doost grant, that, in thy eternal love, we may love each other eternally. And this, O Lord –' [...] with that, casting up both eyes and hands to the skies, the noble soul departed – one might well assure himself to heaven, which left the body in so heavenly a demeanour. (*NA*, p. 398)

Parthenia's masque-like entry and death precede Pyrocles' attempt, in a fit of depression, to brain himself. This is initiated by an extraordinary piece of theatre. As Amphialus's prisoners, Pamela, Philoclea and Pyrocles/Zelmane are housed in vaulted stone chambers, each of which 'had a little window to look into the hall' (*NA*, p. 425). Cecropia believes she can terrify Philoclea into marrying Amphialus, forcing Philoclea to watch as she stages Pamela's execution: 'she bad her prepare her eyes for a new play [...] in the hall of that castle' (*NA*, p. 425). Sidney couches this episode in drama-related metaphors: 'when the hour came that the tragedy should begin', the curtains are 'withdrawn'. Philoclea and Pyrocles/Zelmane watch as a lady wearing Pamela's clothes, covered 'from above her eyes to her lips', is led on to a scaffold 'covered with crimson velvet' (*NA*, p. 425). Her head is hacked off. Only much later do Pyrocles and readers of *Arcadia* simultaneously learn that the victim was Artesia (*NA*, p. 436).

Pyrocles, like Charikleia when advising Theagenes, tries to persuade Philoclea to feign acquiescence to Cecropia's demand. One day, Pyrocles awakens to a noise in the hall, where 'nothing was to be seen thereupon but a basin of gold, pitifully enamelled with blood; and in the midst of it, the head of the most beautiful Philoclea' (*NA*, p. 431). Neither he nor the reader knows that this is another ruse. When Theagenes believes that the corpse he finds in the cave is Charikleia, Heliodorus employs the exaggerated rhetorical styles of Greek tragedy (2.4). Sidney's narrator describes what Pyrocles sees, then portrays his outburst of grief in a similarly artificial, mannered style:

> O tyrant heaven! Traitor earth! Blind providence! No justice? How is this done? How is this suffered? Hath this world a government? If it have, let it pour out all his mischiefs upon me, and see whether it have power to make me more wretched than I am. Did she excel for this? Have I prayed for this?

---

79 On Sidney's use of aposiopesis, see G. Alexander, 'Sidney's Interruptions', *Studies in Philology*, xcviii (2001), 184–204.

Abominable hand that did it! Detestable devil that commanded it! Cursed light that beheld it! (*NA*, p. 431)

Pyrocles' foot slips and his bid to commit suicide fails. He regains consciousness with a Christian stoic purposefulness akin to Parthenia's and Du Plessis-Mornay's: 'I live to die continually, till thy revenge do give me leave to die. And then die I will' (*NA*, p. 433).

In tune with the artistic prose of Achilles Tatius, Heliodorus and Book XII of *Amadis de Gaule*,[80] Sidney's clusters of word repetition are couched in rhythmic, not quite balanced clauses. The narrator's paraphrase of Zelmane's guard, who reports her prisoner to be 'exceedingly sorry for Pamela, but exceedingly exceeding that exceedingness in fear for Philoclea' (*NA*, p. 427), finds a parallel in the excess of Strephon's 'sweetest fairness and fairest sweetness' (*NA*, p. 4). In Pyrocles' reaction to Philoclea's decapitation, extremes of rhetorical artifice inject the horror of Senecan tragedy: 'Alas! why should they divide such a head from such a body? No other body is worthy of that head; no other head is worthy of that body. Oh, yet if I had taken my last leave! If I might have taken a holy kiss from that dying mouth! […] Philoclea is dead […] Philoclea is dead […] Philoclea is dead! O deadly word' (*NA*, p. 433). One spectacle succeeds another, and Philoclea is eventually allowed to reveal the stage-craft behind the illusion. She has been forced to stand beneath a scaffold, her head poking through, a dish of blood around her neck (*NA*, p. 436).

Legal and political process as drama

Like *An Ethiopian Story*, Sidney's dramatised romance reverberates with allusions to the stage. When Musidorus chastises Pyrocles for renouncing the heroic life, he asks insultingly whether he, 'like an ill player should mar the last act of his tragedy' (*OA*, p. 19; cf. *NA*, p. 70). In the last Book or Act of the *Old Arcadia*, Gynecia uses 'tragical phrases' (*OA*, p. 382), and Philanax refers to the stage in accusing Pyrocles of conspiracy to murder Basilius: 'Was all this play for nothing? Or if it had an end, what end but the end of my dear master?' (*OA*, p. 389). But Sidney also writes almost the whole of Book 5 in a static, declamatory dramatic form.

Sidney's intensely theatrical trial scene, to which he made only minor adjustments, loosely resembles the trial with which *Leukippe and*

---

80 J. J. O'Connor, *Amadis de Gaule and Its Influence on Elizabethan Literature*, p. 200, cites two examples from Pedro de Luján's Book XII.lxxvii. See also *The moste excellent and pleasaunt Booke, entituled: The treasurie of Amadis of Fraunce*, trans. by T. Paynell (1572), extracts from XII.xiv, xxi and xxii.

Kleitophon ends. King Euarchus of Macedonia is Basilius's 'old friend and confederate' (*OA*, p. 351). In other words, they are parties to a formal league of mutual support. Euarchus no sooner arrives for a diplomatic visit to Basilius than the desperate Arcadians choose him as their 'elected protector' (*OA*, p. 361). (In the 'complete' *Arcadia*, he sets out to help Plangus, but is forced ashore in Laconia.) He insists that he will 'depose' himself, 'as soon as the judgement is passed, the duke buried, and his lawful successor appointed' (*OA*, pp. 365–6).

Recognising the role of 'exterior shows' (*OA*, p. 375) in persuasion, Euarchus literally sets a stage for himself, leaving 'nothing which might be either an armour or ornament unto him; and in these pompous ceremonies he well knew a secret of government much to consist' (*OA*, p. 375). He orders Basilius's 'throne of judgement seat' to be set up 'in the midst of the green' in front of 'the chief lodge' (*OA*, p. 374). Euarchus takes his place, 'all clothed in black', selectively surrounding himself for visual effect 'with the principal men who could in that suddenness provide themselves of such mourning raiments' (*OA*, p. 375). Basilius's body is 'laid upon a table just before Euarchus, and all covered over with black' (*OA*, p. 375).

Euarchus is Musidorus's uncle, and Pyrocles' father. Pyrocles was six when Euarchus last saw him (*OA*, p. 10). The princes delay disclosure of their identities until after Euarchus has passed sentence. The dilemma this causes is abruptly resolved when Basilius awakens. The trial is a rhetorical *tour de force*. Through considered use of ethopoeia and prosopopoeia, Sidney invents speeches to display the self-representation of the defendants. As if he were a teacher of rhetoric, the author-narrator punctuates his descriptive account with remarks on the tactics of delivery. Musidorus challenges the crowds not to abandon Pamela, using a 'broken manner of questions and speeches [...] to move the people to tender Pamela's fortune' (*OA*, p. 379). Pyrocles bursts into speech before he is invited, a calculated way of scoring the first point.

Pyrocles and Philanax carry on their debate under extremes of emotional and intellectual pressure. Each exhibits a range of styles, shifting abruptly with the nature of the topic and the effect he wants to create. Philanax is prone to a convoluted style, Pyrocles to a plainer form, insisting, in the manner of a European Protestant rhetor, that the virtue of his defence will shine through the clarity of its presentation. In this, as we see at the end of the next chapter, Sidney anticipates James I.

Philanax has prepared his speech; Pyrocles claims he has to compose his defence on the spot, speaking *extempore*. His exceptional abilities of analysis, defence and attack are set in contrast with the uncontrolled emotions that reveal themselves in Pamela's and Philoclea's written submissions: 'Many blots had the tears of these sweet ladies made in their letters, which many times they had altered, many times torn, and written anew, ever thinking something either wanted or were too much, or would offend, or (which was worst) would breed denial' (OA, p. 398). While Philanax suppresses these letters, Sidney gives the full text, and follows them with Philanax's speech against Musidorus. But by this time, Philanax is upset and out of control, 'being so overgone with rage that he forgat in this oration his precise method of oratory' (OA, p. 399).

This sophistic theatre builds towards a climax in Musidorus's vitriolic and sustained counter-attack, 'O gods, [...] and have you spared my life to bear these injuries of such a drivel? Is this the justice of this place, to have such men as we are submitted not only to apparent falsehood but most shameful reviling?' (*OA*, p. 400). Sidney uses Musidorus's defence as the vehicle through which to summarise the action. In Book 1, the princes 'killed the wild beasts which otherwise had killed the princesses' (*OA*, pp. 400–1). In Book 2, they shielded Basilius's life 'against hundreds of armed men' (*OA*, p. 401). In the old Book 3, Musidorus 'conveyed away the princess of this country' to free her 'from the thraldom, by such fellows' counsel as you, she was kept in' (*OA*, pp. 401–2). His addition for the 'complete' *Arcadia* of 1593 reminds Philanax of 'our seruices done to *Basilius* in the late warre with *Amphialus* importing no lesse then his daughters liues, and his states preseruation' (Rr4v), referring to the action in the new section of Book 3.

Erotic romance looks forward to the marriage of young lovers, as predicted by Basilius's oracle. Nor does Sidney ignore the requisite insuperable obstacles. As knights errant, the princes have become private citizens, renouncing any protection offered to foreign royalty, 'and so by making themselves private deprived themselves of respect due to their public calling' (*OA*, p. 404).

Pyrocles and Musidorus are tried separately. Pyrocles is charged with violating Philoclea's chastity (*OA*, p. 405). In Euarchus's opinion, extramarital sex is subversive. It is the 'unnatural' exploitation of 'that which, being holily used, is the root of humanity, the beginning and maintaining of living creatures, whereof the confusion must needs be a general ruin' (*OA*, p. 406). This passage is replaced in the 1593 'complete' *Arcadia* with another that alters both charges to 'ravishment'. Musidorus is convicted of abducting the heir to the throne: 'and if our lawes haue it so in the priuate persons, much more forcible are they to bee in Princes children, where one steales as it were the whole state, and well being of that people, being tyed by the secret of a long vse, to be gouerned by none but the next of that bloud' (Rr6).

Sidney's readers would know that, in *An Ethiopian Story*, Theagenes and Charikleia avoid being sacrificed because Ethiopian law accepts their *de praesanti*, or verbal, marriage contract. Tension builds as Euarchus rejects the princes' claims of marriage: 'Governors of justice' must not 'measure the foot of the law by a show of conveniency'. If they did, they would subject society to the interests of the privileged: 'The marriage perchance might be fit for them, but very unfit were it to the state to allow a pattern of such procurations of marriage' (*OA*, p. 407). Euarchus puts the interests of the state before the individual, as did Elizabeth in preventing Sidney's marriage to Marie of Nassau.

The end of romance

The decorum observed in Greek erotic romance places Sidney under a contract with his readers not to kill his lovers. Euarchus's severe sentences maintain suspense until the closing. No clue is given about how the princes or Gynecia will escape death, or Philoclea her life-sentence 'among certain women [...] observing a strict profession of chastity' (*OA*, p. 381). In Heliodorus's *An Ethiopian Story*, where a law stands between the death of the central characters and their happy survival, the recognition scenes that establish their identities lead to a change in the law. But when Musidorus's servant Kalodoulus reveals the princes' true identity (*OA*, p. 410), Sidney once again rejects Heliodorus's precedent. He keeps readers in suspense, Euarchus issuing a stern rebuke:

> I prefer you much before my life, but I prefer justice as far before you [...] I cannot keep you from the effects of your own doing. Nay, I cannot in this case acknowledge you for mine; for never had I shepherd to my nephew, nor never had woman to my son. Your vices have degraded you from being princes, and have disannulled your birthright. (*OA*, pp. 411–12)

Sidney thwarts his readers' expectations. They do not find the reprieve provided by recognition in *Daphnis and Chloe*, by the chastity test in *Leukippe and Kleitophon* or by the change of law in *An Ethiopian Story*. Instead, Sidney's conclusion comes from the realm of folklore, and contains an ironic critique of historical documentation: 'thus the ancient records of Arcadia say it fell out' (*OA*, p. 51).[81] Without warning, the

---

81 On the narrative use of the 'historiographical pose', see J. R. Morgan, 'History, Romance, and Realism in the *Aithiopika* of Heliodoros', *Classical Antiquity*, i (1982), 221–65.

sleeping potion that Gynecia believed to be an aphrodisiac wears off, Basilius wakes up, and Euarchus's ethically based sentences are revoked (*OA*, p. 415).

Sidney now undermines Euarchus's punitively narrow concept of universal order. Whereas Pamela is able to exercise self-control, Philoclea seems to suffer from a genetic disposition towards erotic love, through her mother and her maternal great-grandmother. On the first page of the *Old Arcadia*, Sidney writes that Gynecia is 'the daughter of the king of Cyprus', but refrains from associating Cyprus with Aphrodite or Venus. At this late stage, the author-narrator explains the forgotten and distorted history of Gynecia's sleeping potion, and why she associates it with an aphrodisiac.

Gynecia's Cypriot grandmother, 'being notably learned (and yet not able with all her learning to answer the objections of Cupid), did furiously love a young nobleman of her father's court' (*OA*, p. 415). When the nobleman resists, 'fearing the king's rage', she makes 'that sleeping drink'. Her servant drugs him, and carries him

> into a pleasant chamber in the midst of a garden she had of purpose provided for this enterprise [...] when the time came of the drink's end of working [...] she bade him choose either then to marry her, and to promise to fly away with her in a bark she had made ready, or else she would presently cry out [...] with oath he was come thither to ravish her. (*OA*, p. 415)

Gynecia's sophisticated grandmother is transformed by love into a self-interested, ruthless schemer. The outcome is predictably positive: 'he married her and escaped the realm with her, and after many strange adventures were reconciled to the king, her father, after whose death they reigned' (*OA*, pp. 415–16).

In Sidney's Arcadian romance, erotic passion leading to a good marriage justifies the use of drugs, kidnapping, blackmail and elopement. Well-intentioned laws, protecting the interests of the state from individuals with wealth and power, are as difficult to adhere to in Arcadia as in Cyprus. Gynecia has her grandmother's determination to succeed, threatening to expose Pyrocles if he refuses her, though the best she can hope to achieve is adultery (*OA*, p. 184). Philoclea is slow to express her Cypriot passion, but in the *Old Arcadia*, the moment her emotions are liberated, she and Pyrocles challenge Euarchus's interpretation, universally accepted throughout Greece, of what constitutes 'holily used' (*OA*, p. 406) sex. In the 'complete' *Arcadia*, they are more of Euarchus's opinion. The revised novel closes, like Heliodorus's *Ethiopian Story*, with marriage, much strengthened monarchic alliances, and an anticipation of mutual erotic pleasure within married love.

Conclusion

In *The Countess of Pembroke's Arcadia*, Sidney draws heavily on the Renaissance representation of ancient erotic romance to create a parable. Through the outcome of its many interwoven episodes, he illustrates a coherent monarchomachist policy intolerant of political and domestic tyranny. He explores and demystifies erotic love, connecting emotional self-governance with political stability. He uses Theophrastan archetypes as foils in the development of a selective range of more rounded, albeit exemplary, central characters in the Plutarchan mode. Most significantly, he uses interest theory, analysing both personal and political interests to illustrate the interaction of individuals, interest groups and the state. In this way, sex and the expression of sexuality are equated with, or given the same value as, fulfilment of political desires, be they mutually agreeable or tyrannically imposed.

Sidney blends factual and fictive history in *Arcadia,*. He synthesises recognisable borrowings from Greco-Roman erotic romance with chivalric fiction, particularly *Amadis de Gaule*. Extensive use of ecphrasis, coupled with the selective application of various Greco-Roman styles favoured by the French court, suggests that Sidney is striving to emulate and surpass French nationalist courtly discourse.

Sidney died on 17 October 1586. He had, during the previous seven years, privately and informally created himself as the literary spokesperson of the English left-of-centre monarchomachist nationalists of Norman stock. Almost immediately following his death, highly placed associates of this group became patrons of the newly formed professional acting companies, and found a fresh public platform for the dissemination of their ideas. Shakespeare's politicisation of erotic romance, and his development of an exaggerated stage '*style royal*' for particularly difficult or tyrannical leaders, connect his work with this generation of philhellene Protestants, who continued the policies of Sidney, Walsingham and Leicester into the 1590s and beyond.

6

Shakespeare and philhellene erotic romance

Shakespeare, Amyot and North's *Plutarch*

In his *Defence of Poetry*, Sidney differentiates between fictive representation and affirmation of fact, asking, 'What child is there, that, coming to a play, and seeing *Thebes* written in great letters upon an old door, doth believe that it is Thebes?'[1] Nonetheless, Shakespeare and his fellow playwrights could confidently expect audiences to read 'Thebes' as a signifier of a forthcoming political allegory on usurpation, tyranny and heroic resistance.

While Sidney's work on *Arcadia* is compressed between 1577 and 1584, Shakespeare's response to European erotic romance manifests itself over roughly twenty-five years, from the mid-1580s until 1611. Shakespeare, like Sidney, traps his characters in circumstances that expose the frailty of totalitarian monarchy, revealing how it undermines the best interests of society and the state. Nor is it entirely coincidental that Shakespeare employs the plots and styles associated with Continental editions of Greco-Roman texts to represent monarchomachist views consistent with the nationalist politics of the tolerant philhellene Protestants.

Shakespeare's allusion to, and absorption of, the Greco-Roman romances is so varied that it has been described as 'vague and elusive, even in his recognition scenes a matter of general similarities of incident and situation.'[2] This chapter places Shakespeare's adaptations of Greco-

---

1 Sir P. Sidney, *A Defence of Poetry*, in *Miscellaneous Prose of Sir Philip Sidney*, ed. by K. Duncan-Jones and J. van Dorsten (Oxford: Clarendon Press, 1973), p. 103.

2 H. Felperin, *Shakespearean Romance* (Princeton: Princeton University Press, 1972), p. 11. Felperin's aesthetic consideration of what constitutes 'Shakespearean romance' exposes the limitations of tracking borrowings and analogues, as in the pioneering work of S. L. Wolff, *The Greek Romances in Elizabethan Fiction* (New York: Columbia University Press, 1912), the basis of C. Gesner, *Shakespeare and the Greek Romance: A Study of Origins* (Lexington: University Press of Kentucky, 1970). A summary of scholarship is in S. Gillespie, 'Shakespeare and Greek Romance: "Like an old tale still"', in *Shakespeare*

Roman material within an English philhellene rhetorical, cultural and political context, not incompatible with his Catholic origins.

Shakespeare's perception of the Greek erotic romances, and of Plutarch's *Lives* and *Morals*, was coloured by the editions and translations available to him. In addition to *Henry V*, the Roman plays – particularly *Julius Caesar, Antony and Cleopatra* and *Coriolanus* – draw directly on Thomas North's 1579 translation of the *Lives*. North's title-page contains a complimentary acknowledgment to Amyot's *Les vies des hommes illustres Grecs, & Romains* as his source: *The Lives of the Noble Grecians and Romanes, compared together by that graue learned Philosopher and Historiographer, Plutarke of Chaeronea: Translated out of Greeke into French by Iames Amyot, Abbot of Bellozane, Bishop of Auxerre, one of the Kings priuy counsel, and great Amner of Fraunce, and out of French into Englishe, by Thomas North*.

North did not base his translation on Amyot's 1559 edition. North's volume closes with a translation by 'Charles de la Sluce' of the 'Lives' of Hannibal and Scipio. Written in Latin by the Florentine Donato Acciaiuoli (1429–78), these were published in *Vitae Parallelae* (Rome, 1470?), and reprinted during the sixteenth century.[3] The publication of the French translation by the Protestant botanist Charles de L'Ecluse (1526–1609) speaks volumes for the combined commercial, political and religious rivalry between France, Spain and Geneva under Calvin's successor, Théodore de Bèze (1519–1605). L'Ecluse's text was first licensed for print, not in Paris, but in Antwerp, by a privilege granted to Guillaume Silvius, printer to King Philip II, on 2 December 1562. Silvius would reprint Amyot's 1559 edition and add 'Les deux vies d'Ha[n]nibal et de Scipion l'Africain'.[4] Silvius, formerly tutor to the sons of William of Orange and a colleague of Christopher Plantin, published his edition in 1564.[5]

Amyot's publisher, Michel de Vascosan, printer to the King of France, ensured that it was noted in the privilege in his second edition (Paris:

---

and the Classics, ed. by C. Martindale and A. B. Taylor (Cambridge: Cambridge University Press, 2004), pp. 225–37. H. Cooper, *The English Romance in Time: Transforming Motifs from Geoffrey of Monmouth to the Death of Shakespeare* (Oxford: Oxford University Press, 2004), excludes all relationships between Shakespeare and the Renaissance revival of Greco-Roman erotic romance.

3 On Acciaiuoli's translations of Plutarch, see M. A. Ganz, 'A Florentine Friendship: Donato Acciaiuoli and Vespasiano da Bisticci', *Renaissance Quarterly*, xliii (1990), 372–83 (p. 375, n.10).

4 P. Sharratt, 'A Rare Edition of Amyot's Plutarch', *Forum for Modern Language Studies*, vii, no. 4 (1971), 409–12 (p. 412).

5 On Silvius's relationship with Plantin, Janus Dousa, William Cecil and Francis Walsingham, see C. Clair, 'Willem Silvius', *The Library*, 5th ser., xiv, no. 3 (1959), 192–205.

Michel de Vasconsan, 1565) that the Antwerp publication was unauthorised.[6] This could not protect Vascosan's second edition which, along with L'Ecluse's 'Hannibal' and 'Scipio', was 're-pirated' in the edition published by François Perrin ([Geneva,] 1567). Vascosan quickly set his rivals a fresh challenge. For his third edition (Paris, 1567), Amyot revised his text. Vascosan added Antonio de Guevara's *Decade, contenant les vies des empereurs*, translated by Antoine Allègre, which he had published in 1556, and counter-pirated 'Hannibal' and 'Scipio'. North, whose publisher was the Huguenot Thomas Vautrollier, does not include Guevara's *Decade*.

In 1559, Amyot gives his name and title, 'Abbot of Bellozane', in the superscription at the head of his dedication to Henri II, rather than on his title-page where the translator's name is not mentioned.[7] (The attribution, 'par Iacques Amyot Abbé de Bellozane', is, however, added to the title-page of Guillaume Silvius's Antwerp, 1564, edition.) While the 1565 and 1567 title-pages of the Paris editions, and those in later reprints, reflect Amyot's promotion, 'lors Abbé de Bellozane […] maintenant Abbé de Saincte Corneille de Compiegne, Conseiller du Roy, & grand Aumosnier de France' – 'formerly Abbot of Bellozane […] now Abbot of Saint-Corneille de Compiègne', his 1559 dedication is reprinted unchanged.[8] But North also adds the title conferred on Amyot in 1570, 'Bishop of Auxerre'. This appears on the title-page of Amyot's 1572 translation of *Les Oeuvres morales & meslees de Plutarque* and, if not earlier, the Paris, 1579, edition of *Les vies des hommes illustres*.

North may also have known about Amyot's promotion from his visit to the Italian-speaking French court. Thomas North (1535–1603?)[9] was the younger brother of Roger, second Baron North (1531–1600),[10] who moved in the circles of the active, philhellene Protestants, and served with Leicester in the Netherlands. Shot in the leg the previous day, Roger North fought at Zutphen where Sidney received his fatal wound, on 2 October 1586. Both Roger and Thomas were fluent in Italian. On 30 May 1574, Amyot's pupil Charles IX of France died and was succeeded by his

---

6 P. Sharratt, 'A Rare Edition of Amyot's Plutarch', p. 409.

7 The title-page reads, *Les vies des hommes illustres Grecs, & Romains, comparees l'vne auec l'autre par Plutarque de Chaeronee, translatees de grec en francois. A Paris: De l'imprimerie de Michel de Vasconsan, MDLVIIII, avec privilege du Roy*.

8 R. Sturel, *Jacques Amyot, traducteur des Vies Parallèles de Plutarque* (Paris: H. Champion, 1908), pp. 615–19, traces the relationships of the printed editions from 1559 to 1619.

9 T. Lockwood, 'North, Sir Thomas (1535–1603?)', *Oxford Dictionary of National Biography* (Oxford: Oxford University Press, 2004).

10 See J. Craig, 'North, Roger, Second Baron North (1531–1600)', *Oxford Dictionary of National Biography* (Oxford: Oxford University Press, 2004).

brother, Henri III. Between October and December, Roger was in the French court as Ambassador Extraordinary. Thomas accompanied him, returning in November.

It is not impossible that North met Amyot in the French court, for, even though Amyot lived in Auxerre, he presided over important functions in Paris. On Sunday 15 June 1572, when Philip Sidney was present, he officiated at the service to mark the signing of the Treaty of Blois, by which the sovereigns of England and France promised to assist one another when attacked.[11] One aspect of Roger North's 1574 mission was to secure the ratification of this treaty.

In 1579, Thomas North published his translation of Amyot's version of Plutarch, dedicated to Queen Elizabeth, who 'can better vnderstand it in Greeke, than any man can make it Englishe' (*2). The 'Lives' of Epaminondas and of Philip of Macedon, first published separately in 1602, were included in the 1603 edition. North's alterations and additions to Amyot's rendering are characterised by diction and rhythms that bring a fresh vitality to the *Lives*. The last reason to which these changes can be attributed is inattention to detail, for North was exceptionally well versed in the Romance languages. In 1557, he published a translation of Antonio de Guevara's *The Diall of Princes* 'Englysshed oute of the Frenche', with additions from the original Spanish.[12] It is a text often named as a stylistic ancestor to euphuism, though in his 'Epistle' before the fourth book, added in 1568, North advances simplicity of style as evidence of the translation being his own:

> the basenes of my style, the playn and humble woords couched in the same, the mean, rude, and yll contryued sentences layd beefore thee, togeether with the simple handelyng of the whole: playnly sheweth to thee whence they are, and easely acquainteth thee with the curious translator. (R1v)

This publication was followed by *The Morall Philosophie of Doni* (1570), 'first compiled in the Indian tongue, [...] and now lastly englished out of Italian'. North uses his dedication to Leicester to confirm his and his brother Roger's allegiance to the philhellene Protestants.

Amyot–North diction and style in *Coriolanus* (1608)

Coriolanus, a critique of Jacobean representative government, provides a rare glimpse into the way Shakespeare exhibits his normally obscured

11 J. M. Osborn, *Young Philip Sidney 1572–1577* (New Haven: Yale University Press, 1972), pp. 39–40.
12 T. Lockwood, 'North, Sir Thomas (1535–1603?)'.

links with the Amyot–North Plutarch. The clearest example survives in Coriolanus's address to Aufidius:

> My name is Caius Martius, who hath done
> To thee particularly, and to all the Volsces,
> Great hurt and mischief. Thereto witness may
> My surname Coriolanus. The painful service,
> The extreme dangers, and the drops of blood
> Shed for my thankless country, are requited
> But with that surname – a good memory
> And witness of the malice and displeasure
> Which thou shouldst bear me.
>
> (IV.v.64–72)[13]

Plutarch is typically compact, straightforward, and virtually devoid of metaphor: 'I am Caius Marcius, he who has wrought thee and the Volscians most harm, and the surname of Coriolanus which I bear permits no denial of this. I have won no other prize for all the toils and perils which I have undergone than the name which is a badge of my enmity to your people' (XXIII).[14]

Amyot, responding to the Italianate tastes of the French court, emulates the rhythmically balanced air of his translation of Heliodorus's *An Ethiopian Story*. Plutarch's plainness now resembles an elegant '*style royal*', broadly derived from Heliodorus and Cicero:

> Ie suis Gaius Martius, qui ay fait & à toy en particulier, & à tous les Volsques en general, beaucoup de maulx, lesquelz ie ne puis nier pour le surno[m] de Coriolanus que i'en porte: car ie n'ay recueilly autre fruict, ny autre recompense de tant de trauaux que i'ay endurez, ny de tant de dangers ausquelz ie me suis exposé, que ce surnom, lequel tesmoigne la malueuillance que uous deuez auoir encontre moy.[15]

Amyot changes 'thee and the Volscians' into the balanced '& à toy en particulier, & à tous les Volsques en general' – 'both to you in particular and to all the Volsces in general'. He creates a rhythmic doublet, pref-

---

13 Unless otherwise stated, I cite *The Norton Shakespeare*, ed. by S. Greenblatt (New York: W. W. Norton, 1997); however, I use Roman numerals to denote acts and scenes.

14 'Caius Marcius Coriolanus', in *Plutarch's Lives*, trans. by B. Perrin, 11 vols (London: William Heinemann, 1914–26), iv.173. For a transcription of this text, see: http://penelope.uchicago.edu/Thayer/E/Roman/Texts/Plutarch/Lives/Coriolanus*.html

15 *Les vies des hommes illustres, Grecs & Romains, comparées l'vne auec l'autre par Plutarque de Cheronee, Translatees* […] *par Maistre Iacques Amyot*, 2nd edn (Paris: M. Vascosan, 1565), D5. See http://web2.bium.univ-paris5.fr/livanc/?cote=01344&do=pages for an Internet facsimile and for this page, http://web2.bium.univ-paris5.fr/livanc/?p=324&cote=01344&do=page.

acing Coriolanus's 'no other prize' with 'autre fruict' – 'I have not received other benefit, nor other reward'. He expands 'for all the toils and perils which I have undergone' into the parallel doublet, 'de tant de trauaux que i'ay endurez, ny de tant de dangers ausquelz ie me suis exposé' – 'for such great toils that I have endured, nor for such great dangers to which I exposed myself'. And Plutarch's 'than the name which is a badge of my enmity to your people' receives a distinctive nuancing in 'lequel tesmoigne la malueuillance que uous deuez auoir encontre moy' – 'which witnesses the ill-will that you must [*or* 'ought to'] hold against me'. Amyot redirects the general hatred of the Volsci towards Coriolanus into Aufidius's personal hatred of him, transmitted into Shakespeare through North's stately, neo-classical rendering:

> I am *Caius Martius*, who hath done to thy self particularly, and to all the VOLSCES generally, great hurte and mischief, which I cannot denie for my surname of *Coriolanus* that I beare. For I neuer had other benefit nor recompence, of all the true and paynefull seruice I haue done, and the extreme daungers I haue bene in, but this only surname: a good memorie and witnes, of the malice and displeasure thou showldest beare me.[16]

Volumnia's colourful language provides an insight into North's method. In Shakespeare, Volumnia explains to Coriolanus the options facing his 'mother, wife, and child': 'Alack, or must we lose / The country, our dear nurse, or else thy person' (V.iii.110–11). This 'nurse' metaphor is neither in Plutarch nor in Amyot's 'pource qu'il est force à ta femme & à tes enfans qu'ilz soient priuez de l'un des deux, ou de toy, ou de leur païs' (E3–E3v) – 'because it is necessary that your wife and your children be deprived of one of two things, either of you or of their country'. It does, however, crop up in Amyot's 'Agesilaus': 'faisant ueoir aux femmes & aux petits enfans les hommes Lacedaemoniens, qui payoient à leur païs un beau & honorable loyer de leur naissance & nourriture' (DD5v). Here North condenses 'place of their birth and upbringing' into two simple nouns: 'making the women and children of SPARTA to see the LACEDAEMONIANS how honorablie they rewarded their nurse and contrie for their good education'

---

16 Plutarch, *Lives*, trans. by North (1579), X5. Amyot is accused of mistranslating in W. Shakespeare, *Coriolanus*, ed. by P. Brockbank (London: Methuen, 1976; repr. 1980), p. 320, n.12, commenting on I.i.216: 'North and Shakespeare follow Amyot's error for *Bellutus*'. Amyot reads 'Vellutus' (C4v), North '*Vellutus*' (V6v), and the 1623 Folio '*Velutus*' (aa2). But the substitution may be phonetic – cf. H. G. Liddell and R. Scott, *A Greek-English Lexicon*, 4th edn (Oxford: Oxford University Press, 1855), introducing 'B […] second letter of the Gr. alphabet […]. The pronunc. was softer than our B: Polyb[ius] and other late authors used it for the Roman V […] and in modern Greek it is pronounced like our V'.

(LLL1v). It is this doublet that recurs in North's expansion of 'leur païs' in 'Coriolanus', and which finds its way into Shakespeare's 'The country, our dear nurse': 'For the bitter soppe of most harde choyce is offered thy wife & children, to forgoe the one of the two: either to lose the persone of thy selfe, or the nurse of their natiue contrie' (Y2v).

This imagery of children and motherhood recurs within a few lines, in Volumnia's concluding summary:

> [...] thou shalt no sooner
> March to assault thy country than to tread -
> Trust to't, thou shalt not – on thy mother's womb
> That brought thee to this world.
> (V.iii.123–6)[17]

Such a physical act of treachery is lacking in Plutarch, and even in Amyot's version, 'tu n'iras iamais assaillir ny combattre ton païs, que premiereme[n]t tu ne passes par dessus le corps de celle qui t'a mis en ce monde' (E3v) – 'you will never assail nor fight your country, except you first pass over the body of her who brought you into this world'. In the process of expanding Amyot, North interprets 'corps', from Plutarch's 'νεκρὰν' (XXXV.3)[18] – 'corpse' – not as a dead body, but, as in common Elizabethan parlance, a live one:[19] 'thou shalt no soner marche forward to assault thy countrie, but thy foote shall treade vpon thy mothers wombe, that brought thee first into this world' (Y3). Having already introduced 'nurse', North's associated shift to the metonym 'wombe' provides Shakespeare with his sustained maternal metaphor.

North's *Lives* both grows out of and bolsters the nationalistic programme of linguistic and rhetorical reform promoted by the philhellene Protestants. His technique of doubling up information in parallel phrases creates an artful Ciceronian expansiveness that mimics Amyot. But North also makes the *Lives* far more metaphorical and lively, creating an intimate conversational and dramatic effect. By eliminating relative clauses, he reduces Amyot's extended phrasing into curt expressions, his long sentences into several short ones.[20] Where Heliodorus's style lies behind Amyot's, Amyot's style serves as North's catalyst for transmuting

17 Cf. G. Braden, 'Plutarch, Shakespeare, and the Alpha Males', in *Shakespeare and the Classics*, ed. by C. Martindale and A. B. Taylor (Cambridge: Cambridge University Press, 2004), pp. 188–206 (pp. 190–1).
18 'Caius Marcius Coriolanus', in *Plutarch's Lives*, trans. by B. Perrin, iv.206.
19 Cf. *O.E.D.*, corpse, *n*.1.
20 See V. Worth, 'Les fortunes de Jacques Amyot en Angleterre: une traduction de Sir Thomas North', in *Fortunes de Jacques Amyot: Actes du colloque international (Melun 18–20 avril 1985)*, ed. by M. Balard (Paris: A.-G. Nizet, 1986), pp. 285–95, esp. 292–3.

his interpretation of Plutarch into the enjoyable styles of erotic romance. By translating in this creative manner, North produces a major contribution to the Renaissance philhellene canon, and assists in Shakespeare's rhetorical development.

Julius Caesar (1599), political identifiers and the rhetorics of erotic romance

Nine years before writing *Coriolanus*, in *Julius Caesar* (1599), Shakespeare is as much concerned as any translator with the stylistic elegance of Greco-Roman historians, including Plutarch. Shakespeare's purpose is to employ rhetorical style as a signifier of political difference. For he uses this play to mirror distinctions between the political aspirations of both the reactionary and reformist groups among the late Elizabethan philhellene Protestants, who challenged the centralist hegemony of the Cecils.

To achieve this goal, Shakespeare re-creates the political divisions in Rome at the time of Caesar's assassination. Julius Caesar was killed on the Ides of March, 44 BC. Four years earlier he defeated Pompey at Pharsalus. Pompey was murdered, and republican Rome, a highly structured adaptation of Athenian democracy, was threatened by the onset of Caesar's tyranny. In *Julius Caesar*, Shakespeare dramatises the political death of the reactionary philhellene Pompeyists at the moment that Caesar, the nation's hero, returns to Rome.

In order to represent the Pompeyists' loss of influence, Shakespeare bestows semiotic value on the linguistic and stylistic differences that separate their political view from that of Caesar and his supporters. Shakespeare achieves this by developing the political and associated Greek–Latin linguistic divide that Plutarch signals in two descriptions of Casca's attack on Caesar:

> *Casca* behinde him strake him in the necke with his sword, [...] and they both cried out, *Caesar* in Latin: O vile traitor *Casca*, what doest thou? And *Casca* in Greeke to his brother, brother, helpe me. (XXX1v)

> *Caesar* feeling him selfe hurt, [...] cried out in Latin: O traitor, *Casca*, what doest thou? *Casca* on thother side cried in Graeke, and called his brother to helpe him. (VVVV3v)

Following Caesar's murder, Brutus and Cassius recruit forces from Roman armies and navies stationed in the Greek-speaking states. Many are Greeks. Cassius takes Messala aside on the eve of the battle at Philippi, and 'tolde him in Greeke' (XXXX3) of his doubts about the outcome.

Later, defeated in the second battle at Philippi, Brutus searches for a friend to help him commit suicide:

> at length he came to *Volumnius* him selfe, & speaking to him in Graeke, prayed him for the studies sake which brought them acquainted together, that he woulde helpe him to put his hande to his sword, to thrust it in him to kill him. *Volumnius* denied his request, and so did many others. (XXXX6)

The sword Brutus fell on was Strato's. Brutus knew Strato through his 'studie of Rethoricke'. After Philippi, when the political divisions were healed, Strato served Octavius as faithfully 'as any GRAECIAN els he had about him, vntill the battell of ACTIUM' (XXXX6v).

In *Julius Caesar*, Shakespeare squeezes the Pompeyists' use of Greek into Cicero's unheard speech, and Caesar's Latin into his dying words, '*Et tu, Bruté?*' (III.i.76) – slightly more accentuated in the 1623 Folio's typography, '*Et Tu Brutè?*' (kk6). He likewise distinguishes the larger political groupings, and divisions within them, through stylistic differences. The decline of the Pompeyists is manifested in Cicero's miscalculated use of Greek, familiar to the bilingual educated elite, but not to the less privileged masses. Depicted as a linguistic and therefore political reactionary, one of the most articulate of all Roman rhetoricians is incomprehensible even to his allies. By changing Casca into a non-Greek speaker whose style consists of colloquialisms and disjointed rhythms, Shakespeare depicts the intellectual and philosophical waning of Pompeyist philhellenism. Questioned about Cicero's speech by Cassius, Casca reports, 'Ay, he spoke Greek', and that 'those that understood him smiled at one another, and shook their heads. But for mine own part, it was Greek to me' (I.ii.274, 277–8).

Casca does not need to understand Cicero to be a Pompeyist. For the Romans, and especially for Shakespeare's Pompeyists, the Greek language that contributed to the cohesion of the empire provided a kind of alter-ego. In his *Lives of the Sophists*, Flavius Philostratus records how the Roman emperor Trajan took the Greek orator Dion of Prusa into his golden triumphal chariot, 'and often he would turn to Dio and say: "I do not understand what you are saying, but I love you as I love myself"'.[21] The anecdote illustrates the extent to which Romans felt their power incomplete unless they associated it with the Greek rhetoric that they endowed with Athenian democratic values.

---

21 *Philostratus and Eunapius*, trans. by W. C. Wright (London: William Heinemann, 1922), I.488 (p. 21); cited in L. Pernot, 'La rhétorique de l'Empire ou comment la rhétorique grecque a inventé l'Empire romain', *Rhetorica*, xvi (1998), 131–48 (p. 146).

Cicero's use of Greek places him in opposition to Caesar's party. Historically, he did not speak out against the monarchists until after the assassination, when he venomously attacked Antony. He was proscribed the following year, 43 BC, by the triumvirs Octavius, Lepidus and Antony, and executed. His death is reported in *Julius Caesar* in the letters of intelligence that Messala delivers to Brutus at Philippi: 'Mine speak of seventy senators that died / By their proscriptions, Cicero being one' (IV. ii.229–30).

Cassius Dio (*c*.AD 150–235), a Bithynian who went to Rome in AD 180, reports a long oration by Cicero that preceded Antony's eulogy (xliv. 23–33).[22] Cicero exhorts the crowd to 'learn at last to know one another, since you are countrymen and fellow-citizens and relatives, and so live in harmony' (xliv.32). While Shakespeare silences Cicero and does not draw on Cassius Dio for Anthony's speech, he may have appropriated this triplet for Brutus's 'Romans, countrymen, and lovers' (III.ii.13). The further adaptation in Antony's 'Friends, Romans, countrymen' (III.ii.70) resounds with rhythmic repetition of cadence, sound and metaphor in the manner of Amyot, North and Sidney.

The elegant styles of European erotic romance implicitly carry with them resonances of the themes of loss, separation, reunion and future happiness. Shakespeare's adopting this for Antony's address foreshadows the triumph of the new Roman nationalist order. By contrast, the failure of the philhellene Pompeyists is guaranteed by associating them with the esoteric use of Greek. The rhetorical nail in the Pompeyists' coffin is Brutus's controlled, but comparatively less rousing, performance in the forum. Brutus, another brilliant rhetorician, falters in the prosaic, complex and unmemorable delivery of the most important speech of his life.

The differences between Brutus's and Antony's styles confirms the opposition, not only of their politics, but also of their characters. Shakespeare's model may be Appian's *Civil Wars*, where their speeches, delivered on consecutive days, are set in opposition. That Appian lived in Alexandria until the Jewish uprising of AD 116, when he moved to Rome, may explain his overt empathy with Antony. Brutus's relatively plain, repetitive style is devoid of metaphor: 'Here, citizens, we meet you, we who yesterday met together with you in the forum' (II.xix.137).[23] His artifice

---

23 *The Civil Wars*, in *Appian's Roman History*, trans. by H. White, 4 vols (London: William Heinemann, 1912–13), iii.479.

lies in a series of accusing questions, followed by an imaginary poetic dialogue:

> What has become of the public tribute during his supremacy? What of the accounts? Who opened the public treasury without our consent? Who laid hands upon part of the consecrated money? Who threatened with death another tribune who opposed him?
>
> 'But what kind of oath after this will be a guarantee of peace?' they ask. If there is no tyrant there will be no need of oaths. Our fathers never needed any. If anybody else seeks to establish tyranny, no faith, no oath, will ever bind Romans to the tyrant. (II.xix.138–9)

By contrast, Appian attributes to Antony a flamboyant, dramatic delivery. The style is similar to his own, for Appian's rhythmic triplets and drama-related metaphors resemble those of the Greek erotic novelists:

> Antony, […] as a consul for a consul, a friend for a friend, a relative for a relative […] spoke as follows: 'It is not fitting, citizens, that the funeral oration of so great a man should be pronounced by me alone, but rather by his whole country […]' Then he began to read with a severe and gloomy countenance, […] dwelling especially on those decrees which declared Caesar to be superhuman, sacred, and, inviolable, and which named him the father, or the benefactor, or the peerless protector of his country. (II. xx.143–4).

Appian accentuates the ease with which Antony manipulates his audience through gestures, describing his delivery in terms of a stage production:

> he gathered up his garments like one inspired, girded himself so that he might have the free use of his hands, took his position in front of the bier as in a play, […] he uncovered the body of Caesar, lifted his robe on the point of a spear and shook it aloft, pierced with dagger-thrusts and red with the dictator's blood. Whereupon the people, like a chorus in a play, mourned with him. (II. xx. 146)[24]

Shakespeare similarly creates theatrical effects as part of Antony's rhetorical programme. As Antony holds up the gown and points at the holes stabbed through the cloth into Caesar's body, he pretends to identify those made by the chief conspirators: 'Look, in this place ran Cassius' dagger

---

24 G. Bullough, ed., *Narrative and Dramatic Sources of Shakespeare*, 7 vols (London: Routledge and Kegan Paul, 1961–73), v.158, suggests that Shakespeare took his Appian from *An auncient Historie and exquisite Chronicle of the Romanes Warres, both Ciuile and Foren*, trans. by W. B. [Barker?] (1578). He would not, however, have found this theatrical metaphor. Barker adapts 'as in a play' to read 'as from a Tabernacle' and reduces 'like a chorus in a play, mourned with him' to 'lyke a Quire, did sing lame[n]tation vnto him' (X3v).

through. / See what a rent the envious Casca made. / Through this the well-belovèd Brutus stabbed' (III.ii.168–70). Then, through a metonymic reference, he conjures up the spectre of Caesar himself: 'Look you here. / Here is himself, marred, as you see, with traitors' (III.ii.190–91). Antony appeals to his audience's emotions, soothing them, exciting them, riling them, denying any political motive. The comforting rhythmic cadence of his verse, in iambic pentameter, distinctively opposes the unmeasured rise and fall of Brutus's Greek-based accentual prose. Brutus is made to sound like a civic official, Antony an intimate companion: 'I am no orator as Brutus is, / But, as you know me all, a plain blunt man / That love my friend' (III.ii.208–10):

> For I have neither wit, nor words, nor worth,
> Action, nor utterance, nor the power of speech,
> To stir men's blood. I only speak right on.
> I tell you that which you yourselves do know,
> Show you sweet Caesar's wounds, poor poor dumb mouths,
> And bid them speak for me.
>
> (III.ii.212–17)

The theatre audience hears Brutus's comparatively unattractive, stiflingly figured style give way to Antony's consciously affected spontaneity. It watches the crowd shift its allegiance, as in Appian, from the first speaker to the much more rousing and convincing second.

Casca's report that 'Murellus and Flavius, for pulling scarves off Caesar's images, are put to silence' (I.ii.279–80) is concrete evidence of the importance Shakespeare gives to signs and symbols. He gives Antony free rein to shift their values when, in the context of the assassination, he links Pompey's and Caesar's legitimate authority in opposition to the heinous crime of the monarchomachists:

> Even at the base of Pompey's statue,
> Which all the while ran blood, great Caesar fell.
> O, what a fall was there, my countrymen!
> Then I, and you, and all of us fell down,
> Whilst bloody treason flourished over us.
>
> (III.ii.182–6)

Shakespeare is able to manipulate the rhetorical presentation of these speeches only because the lyrical prose styles of the Greek romances have taken on a positive significance in the ears and minds of literary London.

When Shakespeare was writing *Julius Caesar*, Thomas North was sixty-four. Most of the first generation of philhellene Protestants, and Philip

Sidney, on whom they pinned their hopes, were dead. If North attended a performance of *Julius Caesar*, he would have observed in Shakespeare's opposition of old-style Pompeyists and new-style nationalists an ambiguous representation of Sidney's ideal of limited monarchy, as expressed in the *Arcadia*. While equating the political chaos of the democratic mob with the danger of tyranny – every mob has its leaders – Sidney favours popular monarchy following established blood-lines. Shakespeare challenges this opposition through his uncompromising refusal to bestow a sense of moral superiority either on the conspiring Pompeyists or on Caesar and his supporters. The Pompeyists abuse their powers of government to oppose an equally opprobrious 'fascist state [...] where mob-rule is the ultimate source of power'.[25]

The prolonged opposition of self-interested parties creates an oppressive atmosphere that leaves Shakespeare's audience, along with the Romans, welcoming the emergence of an untainted leader. The relief at hearing Octavius speak of Brutus with refreshing lack of artificiality is immediate: 'According to his virtue let us use him, / With all respect and rites of burial' (V.v.75–6). This positive portrayal of Octavius as the only effective saviour of Roman values reverses the menacing political connotations attached to his name by Sidney. In *A Dedication to Sir Philip Sidney*, Fulke Greville recalls how Sidney compared Henri III's submission to Philip II with Antony's defeat by Octavius (Augustus), with Elizabeth I holding the balance of power:

> the undertaking of this Antony single – I mean France – would prove a begetting of brave occasions jointly to disturb this Spanish [Augustus] in all his ways of crafty or forcible conquests, especially since Queen Elizabeth, the standard of this conjunction, would infallibly incline to unite with the better part.[26]

And of Philip II of Spain's motive in reinstating captured French territory, Sidney asks 'whether this provident Philip did frame these specious charities of a conqueror, Augustus-like, aspiring to live after death greater than his successor'.[27]

---

25 E. A. J. Honigmann, *Myriad-Minded Shakespeare*, 2nd edn (Basingstoke: Macmillan, 1998), p. 35.

26 *A Dedication to Sir Philip Sidney*, in *The Prose Works of Fulke Greville, Lord Brooke*, ed. by J. Gouws (Oxford: Clarendon Press, 1986), p. 62; text emended from 'Octavian' to 'Augustus' in the light of V. Skretkowicz, 'Greville's *Life of Sidney*: The Hertford Manuscript', *English Manuscript Studies, 1100–1700*, iii (1992), 102–36.

27 *A Dedication to Sir Philip Sidney*, in *The Prose Works of Fulke Greville, Lord Brooke*, ed. by J. Gouws, p. 63.

Antony, Cleopatra, Octavius and the Huguenots

Sidney and Greville allegorise Anglo-Franco-Hispanic relationships through Plutarch's characterisations of Antony, Cleopatra and Octavius. Precisely what combination of political events Shakespeare alludes to in *Julius Caesar* does not readily manifest itself. But in 1599, he had every reason to introduce Caesar's assassination and Octavius's succession into the established dramatic convention of allegorising the French Wars of Religion.

In France, Robert Garnier adapted the political and personal conflicts surrounding Antony and Cleopatra to criticise the needless destruction of war in *Marc-Antoine* (1578). In England, Mary Sidney Herbert's translation, *Antonius* (1592), preceded Samuel Daniel's innovative adaptation, *The Tragedie of Cleopatra* (1594). Like these, Fulke Greville's unpublished *Antony and Cleopatra*, which he destroyed, was also a nationalistic allegory replete with political commentary.

Garnier (1545–90), a lawyer and senior magistrate, published eight plays – seven tragedies and one tragicomedy – written in verbally ornate Senecan declamatory style.[28] *Marc-Antoine*, first published in 1578, appeared in collections of Garnier's tragedies in 1580, 1582, 1585 and 1588. It continues Garnier's exploitation of Plutarch to develop allegorical links between the Roman civil wars and the wasteful horrors of the Wars of Religion. *Porcie* (1568) dramatises the despair of the newly widowed Portia, Brutus's wife, who commits suicide by eating burning coals.

Cornélie (1574) depicts Cornelia struggling against Caesar and Antony's tyranny, closing with her vow to lay to rest the remains of her two husbands, Crassus and Pompey, and her father, Scipio. After fulfilling her responsibilities to these victims of war, she looks forward to an honourable suicide. She exemplifies the plight of women widowed by civil war, and the bravery of those who resist tyrannical dictators to remain in their homes under oppressive regimes. Dedicating *Cornélie* to Nicolas d'Angenne, Seigneur de Rambouillet, Henri III's viceroy in Poland, Garnier regrets that his 'poème' is 'trop propre aux malheurs de nostre siècle' – 'all too appropriate to the miseries of our century'.[29]

In 1578, Garnier emphasises the political allegory of *Marc-Antoine*

---

28 See J. Holyoake, *A Critical Study of the Tragedies of Robert Garnier (1545–90)* (New York: P. Lang, 1987) and G. Jondorf, *Robert Garnier and the Themes of Political Tragedy in the Sixteenth Century* (Cambridge: Cambridge University Press, 1969).

29 *Oeuvres complètes (théatre et poésies) de Robert Garnier*, ed. by L. Pinvert, 2 vols (Paris: Librairie Garnier Frères, 1923), i.90.

through his dedication to the poet Guy de Faur, Seigneur de Pibrac, Privy
Counsellor to Henri III:

> to whom better than you ought the tragic representations of the civil wars
> of Rome be addressed, who hold in such horror our domestic dissensions
> and the unfortunate troubles of this kingdom, spoiled today of its ancient
> splendour and of the reverent majesty of our kings, prophaned by tumul-
> tuous rebellions?[30]

Pibrac, like Garnier, was a Catholic moderate swept up in the tide of
hardening policy. Later in 1578, he became Chancellor to Marguerite
de Valois, Henri III's sister. It was her marriage on 18 August 1572 to
the Huguenot leader, Henri de Bourbon – Henri III of Navarre[31] – that
prompted the St Bartholomew Day's Massacre. Pibrac, whom Sidney
met in Paris in 1572, fell out of favour with philhellene Protestants by
justifying the massacre in *Apologie de la Saint-Barthélemy* (1573). But as
Hubert Languet explained to Sidney, Pibrac had been sheltering Protes-
tant intellectuals, and 'was compelled to ransom his life with that letter
for which you so grievously reproach him; and I by no means approve of
his action.'[32]

Garnier died aged forty-five at Le Mans, 20 September 1590.[33]
Two months barely passed before Mary Sidney Herbert (1561–1621)
completed her translation of *Marc-Antoine*. It was published in 1592 as
the second part of *A Discourse of Life and Death. Written in French by Ph.
Mornay. Antonius, A Tragoedie written also in French by Ro. Garnier. Both
done in English by the Countesse of Pembroke.* Sidney Herbert subscribes
Du Plessis-Mornay's treatise 'The 13. of May 1590. At Wilton' (E3) and
Garnier's drama 'At Ramsburie. 26. of Nouember. 1590' (O2v).[34] Naming
Wilton and Ramsbury signals the political interest of her translations:

30 *Oeuvres complètes (théatre et poésies) de Robert Garnier*, ed. by L. Pinvert, i.165: 'à qui
   mieux qu'à vous se doivent addresser les représentations tragiques des guerres civiles de
   Rome, qui avez en telle horreur nos dissentions domestiques et les malheureux troubles
   de ce Royaume, aujourd'huy despouillé de son ancienne splendeur et de la révérable
   majesté de nos Rois, prophanée par tumultueuses rébellions?' Cf. R. Garnier, *Two Trag-
   edies: 'Hippolyte' and 'Marc-Antoine'*, edited by C. M. Hill and M. Morrison (London:
   Athlone Press, 1975), p. 105.
31 On Navarre, see N. M. Sutherland, *Henry IV of France and the Politics of Religion 1572–
   1596*, 2 vols (Exeter: Intellect Books, 2002).
32 J. M. Osborn, *Young Philip Sidney: 1572–1577*, pp. 215, 227–8.
33 *Oeuvres complètes (théatre et poésies) de Robert Garnier*, ed. by L. Pinvert, i.xlvii.
34 See *The Collected Works of Mary Sidney Herbert*, ed. by M. P. Hannay, N. J. Kinnamon
   and M. G. Brennan, 2 vols (Oxford: Clarendon Press, 1998), i.139–254; and V. Skret-
   kowicz, 'Mary Sidney Herbert's *Antonius*, English Philhellenism and the Protestant
   Cause', *Women's Writing*, vi (1999), 7–25.

these estates belonged to her husband, Henry Herbert, second Earl of Pembroke (*c*. 1534–19 January 1601), an active Huguenot supporter since the 1570s.

Between the time that Garnier published *Marc-Antoine* in 1578 and Sidney Herbert translated it 1590, Amyot's Plutarch became a principal weapon in the Huguenot armoury. In 1583 the Huguenot political commentator Simon Goulart (1543–1628), who in 1607 became the third successive leader of the Genevan Protestants, after Jean Calvin and Théodore de Bèze, published a popular annotated edition of Amyot's *Les vies des hommes illustres*, the *Lives*. In his prefatory note to the reader, Goulart urges the Huguenots to seek inspiration in Plutarch:

> whenever (and it is often) I see and hear these Greeks and Romans brought back onto the theatre of the world by the wise Plutarch, I feel wonderfully moved within myself, as much to condemn my shortcomings in approaching these illustrious persons, illuminated by the only light of nature [...].[35]

Goulart accentuates the relevance of *Les vies des hommes illustres* to contemporary politics. The moral and ethical examples of civil and personal behaviour among Plutarch's Greeks and Romans lead him 'detester les malheurs de ce dernier siecle, où l'impieté & l'iniustice se desbordent & semblent vouloir couurir toute la terre' – 'to detest the misfortunes of this last century where impiety and injustice overflow and seem to want to cover the entire world' (**ii). And he encourages readers to share his allegorical reading.

Goulart fills his margins with summaries of the events that Plutarch describes, adding subversive Huguenot interpretations of their moral and political impact. Protestant leaders, chosen by God, will take heart from the example of Theseus: 'Ceux que le Souuerain Seigneur du monde veut esleuer surmontent en peu d'heure tous empeschemens, & montent au degré que la prouidence leur apreste' – 'Those whom the Sovereign leader of the world wishes to raise surmount in no time at all all impediments, and climb to the degree that providence has prepared for them' (a3v–a4). Lycurgus, 'se resoluant à vne si haute entreprise que le changement de

---

35 Plutarch, *Les vies des hommes illustres grecs et romains* [...] *sommaires et annotations par SGS* [i.e., *Simon Goulart, Senlisien*], trans. by J. Amyot (Colognt [i.e., Cologny or Geneva]: J. Stoer, [1616–]1617), **ii: 'toutesfois quand il m'auient (& c'est assez souue[n]t) de voir & d'ouïr ces Grecs & Romains ramenez sur le theatre du mo[n]de par le sage Plutarque, ie me sens merueilleusement esmeu en moi-mesme, tant pour condamner mes imperfections en m'aprochant de ces illustres personnages esclairez de la seule lumiere de nature'.

tout l'estat de Sparte, monstre rien n'estre impossible au bo[n]s esprits qui desirent le bien public, & qui l'auancent par moyens legitimes sans auoir esgard à leur particulier' – 'resolving on such a great enterprise as changing the entire state of Sparta, shows that nothing is impossible to good spirits who desire the public good, and who advance it by legitimate means without regard to their own interest' (e2v).

Huguenot principles of stoicism and monarchomachia are clearly identifiable in Goulart's comment on Publicola. Although 'Les tyrans ne se retirent pas sur leur premiere perte […] Mais […] le iuste iuge du monde n'ayant pas faute de moye[n]s pour co[n]seruer aux peuples leur liberté, & fauoriser les armes iustes d'heureuses issues, à l'aide mesmes de ceux qui du commencement se monstrent tres-aspres ennemis' – 'tyrants do not give up at their first loss […] But […] the just judge of the world does not lack means to conserve liberty for the people, and to favour just wars with happy outcomes, to the aid especially of those who from the outset show themselves to be bitterest foes' (l4).

Goulart's commentaries publicise Huguenot stoicism, and belief in the triumph of good over evil. They reflect the Calvinist leaders' determination to establish their brand of Christianity in France, reinforced by faith. 'La guerre est vn theatre de gloire aux hommes courageux' – 'War is a theatre of glory to courageous men' (z6v), he remarks in the 'Life' of Coriolanus. And through war, 'Par moyens de peu d'aparence & fort eslongnez de ce que desire le sens humain Dieu besongne & tire de danger ceux qu'il lui plaist maintenir' – 'By barely perceptible means, and far removed from what human reason expects, God works, and draws from danger those whom it pleases him to support' (B3). The Huguenots will be sustained through their struggle by the God who chose their brilliant thinkers and military leaders to act on his behalf.

Sidney Herbert's volume is closely associated with events in France. Du Plessis-Mornay distinguished himself in the Huguenot victory at the Battle of Coutras, 20 October 1587, which Greville sneaked over either to watch or participate in.[36] After Philip II's Spanish Armada failed, Henri III reduced the militant demonising of Protestantism by arranging the execution, on 23 December 1588, of the extremist Catholics, Henri, Duc de Guise, and his brother Louis II de Lorraine, second Cardinal de Guise. In April 1589, Henri III flouted the Council of Trent by working for peaceful reconciliation with the anti-Christ, the Huguenot Henri of

---

36 *The Prose Works of Fulke Greville, Lord Brooke*, ed. by J. Gouws, p. 219; cf. V. Skretkowicz, 'Greville and Sidney: Biographical Addenda', *Notes and Queries*, n.s., xxi (1974), 408–10.

Navarre.[37] The Catholic League vilified Henri III, accusing him of heresy in pamphlets such as *Histoire veritable de la plus saine partie de la vie de Henry de Valois* (Paris, 1589).[38] Now viewed as a heretic and tyrant, he was assassinated on 1 August 1589.

During 1589, Navarre, the king-in-waiting, sent Du Plessis-Mornay's older brother Pierre, Seigneur de Buhy, to seek support from Elizabeth.[39] In October 1590, Navarre, now known as Henri IV, sent the Viscount of Turenne. Henri asked his friend Essex to assist Turenne, who stayed with him at York House.[40] In July 1591, Essex set out on his ill-fated expedition to help the Huguenot forces besiege the ancient Norman capital of Rouen, a key Catholic stronghold. Half of his four thousand men fell ill. On 8 September, his young brother Walter was killed.[41] The shattered Essex returned to Court. On 18 October, he penned an excessively stylised letter to Elizabeth:

> For the 2 windowes of *your* privy chamber shallbe the poles of my sphere wher, as long as *your Majestie* will please to have me, I am fixed and unmoveable: when you thinke thatt heaven to good for me, I will nott fall like a starr, butt be consumed like a vapor by the sun thatt drew me up to such a heyght.[42]

The next day he was apparently in Dieppe.[43] On 9 November he challenged the governor of Rouen, André de Brancas, sieur de Villars, to single combat.[44] He was back in the Court from 19 November to 10 December, and then returned to France from which he was finally recalled.

On 1 January 1592, Henri IV sent Du Plessis-Mornay to England. Arriving with his wife and biographer Charlotte Arbaleste directly from Rouen, he came to persuade Elizabeth to replenish Essex's forces. She instead secured Du Plessis-Mornay's agreement to get Henri IV's

---

37 R. Mousnier, *The Assassination of Henry IV*, trans. by J. Spencer (London: Faber and Faber, 1973), p. 111.

38 See D. A. Bell, 'Unmasking a King: The Political Uses of Popular Literature under the French Catholic League, 1588–89', *Sixteenth Century Journal*, xx (1989), 371–86, and F. A. Yates, *Astraea: The Imperial Theme in the Sixteenth Century* (London: Routledge & Kegan Paul, 1975; repr. Harmondsworth: Peregrine Books, 1977), p. 208n.

39 C. Read, *Lord Burghley and Queen Elizabeth* (London: Jonathan Cape, 1965), p. 456.

40 C. Read, *Lord Burghley and Queen Elizabeth*, p. 456; P. E. J. Hammer, *The Polarisation of Elizabethan Politics: The Political Career of Robert Devereux, 2nd Earl of Essex, 1585–1597* (Cambridge: Cambridge University Press, 1999), pp. 96–7, 105.

41 H. A. Lloyd, *The Rouen Campaign 1590–1592* (Oxford: Clarendon Press, 1973), p. 116.

42 Cited in S. May, *The Elizabethan Courtier Poets* (Columbia: University of Missouri Press, 1991), p. 118.

43 P. E. J. Hammer, *The Polarisation of Elizabethan Politics*, p. 106.

44 H. A. Lloyd, *The Rouen Campaign 1590–1592*, p. 154.

permission for Essex to return.[45] He was replaced on 8 January 1592 and back in court on 14 January 1592.[46] The Du Plessis-Mornays were in England for six weeks, the final three socialising with old friends – 'ses anciens amys'[47] – as they waited for the wind at Dover.

No work more directly prompts Elizabeth for further military and financial support for Henri IV of France than Marlowe's *The Massacre at Paris: With the Death of the Duke of Guise*. Mortally wounded on 2 August 1589, Henry III orders the English Agent to inform Elizabeth of his determination to overthrow 'the Papall Monarck':

> *Nauarre*, giue me thy hand, I heere do sweare,
> To ruinate that wicked Church of Rome,
> That hatcheth vp such bloudy practises.
> And heere protest eternall loue to thee,
> And to the Queene of England specially,
> Whom God hath blest for hating Papestry.
>
> (D5v)

He asks Navarre to revenge his death, and reiterates his monarchical allegiance with Elizabeth: 'Salute the Queene of England in my name, / And tell her *Henry* dyes her faithfull freend' (D6v).

Performed by Lord Strange's Men from 26 January 1593 (Henslowe records it as the 30th),[48] the play celebrates Navarre's ambassadors. 'Bartus', Guillaume de Saluste, Seigneur du Bartas (born 1544; killed in action July 1590) had been Navarre's ambassador to Scotland and England in 1587. 'Pleshe', Philippe Du Plessis-Mornay, had represented his interests in the English court in 1576 and 1577–78, returning in 1592.

Anticipating *Julius Caesar*, but self-consciously associating elegant plainness with the Huguenots and their Elizabethan supporters, political opposition is distinguished by style. The only character to be given a lengthy declamation in the Senecan style is the ambitious, self-interested Guise as he plans to kill Henri III and usurp the throne: 'For this, this earth sustaines my bodies waight, / And with this wiat [*sic*] Ile counterpoise a Crowne' (A5). Marlowe identifies this affected type of royal style with Roman Catholic treachery: 'For this, from Spaine the stately Catholickes, / Sends Indian golde to coyne me French ecues: / For this haue I a largesse from the Pope, / A pension and a dispensation too' (A5v).

45 C. Arbaleste, *Mémoires de Charlotte Arbaleste, sur la Vie de Duplessis-Mornay* (Paris, 1824), pp. 207–8.
46 P. E. J. Hammer, *The Polarisation of Elizabethan Politics*, p. 111.
47 C. Arbaleste, *Mémoires de Charlotte Arbaleste, sur la Vie de Duplessis-Mornay*, p. 207.
48 N. Carson, *A Companion to Henslowe's Diary* (Cambridge: Cambridge University Press, 1988), pp. 75, 85–90, 118.

By contrast, following the Guise's assassination, Henri III, newly liberated from his Papal enemies, announces in plain style,

> I nere was King of France vntill this houre:
> This is the traitor that hath spent my golde,
> In making forraine warres and ciuile broiles.
> Did he not draw a sorte of English priestes,
> From Doway to the Seminary at Remes,
> To hatch forth treason gainst their naturall Queene?
> Did he not cause the King of Spaines huge fleete,
> To threaten England and to menace me?
>
> (D1)

In addition to this compliment in *The Massacre at Paris*, Du Plessis-Mornay's visit in 1592 prompted publication of the second edition of his *Woorke concerning the trewnesse of the christian religion* (1587). Philip Sidney had begun this translation which, shortly after his death, was completed by Arthur Golding. Mary Sidney Herbert's contribution to mustering Huguenot support was to publish her own volume of translations. It is more than fortuitous that this opens with Du Plessis-Mornay's *Excellent discours de la mort et de la vie* (1576), the universally admired Christian stoical essay written in 1575 at Charlotte's 'requeste'.[49] In *Antonius*, Garnier's political allegory is transposed to reflect the precarious plight of the Huguenots. Read in Philip Sidney's terms, Antony is Protestant France led by Henri IV, abandoned by a regretful Cleopatra – Elizabeth – to Octavius, the hardened Roman Catholicism of Philip II of Spain.

Constricting the flowing, sonorous grandeur of Garnier's twelve-syllable alexandrine couplets into predominantly blank verse, Sidney Herbert's line-for-line translation Calvinises the Latinate–Italianate fashion of Henri III's court. Yet it consciously retains an air of English philhellene literary practice through an imaginative adaptation of Garnier's rhythmic, patterned repetitions of word and sound. The stylistic distance that Sidney Herbert puts between her text and Garnier's parallels Marlowe's distinction between the Guise's ornate style and the plainness used by those with Huguenot sympathies. Shakespeare's adaptation of this politics of rhetoric resurfaces in Brutus's impotent complex style, Antony's powerful but deceptive style, and Octavius's liberating plainness.

Registered in the Stationers' Register on 3 May 1592, Sidney Herbert's volume would have been published around the time her brother Robert

---

49 C. Arbaleste, *Mémoires de Charlotte Arbaleste, sur la Vie de Duplessis-Mornay*, p. 89.

Sidney and the Earl of Oxford's nephews, Francis and Horace Vere, were injured at the seige of Steenwyck (June–July 1592).[50] (Sidney's secretary, Rowland Whyte,[51] described how their victory at the Battle of Turnhout, 24 January 1598, was celebrated in a now lost play: 'Sir Robert Sidney and Sir Francis Vere upon the stage, killing, slaying, and overthrowing the Spaniard'.)[52] In advance of Henri IV's renouncing Protestantism on 25 July 1593, Essex was appointed to the Privy Council on 25 February.[53] He may have influenced the Queen's personally instructing Robert Sidney, in October, to ascertain Henri's relationship with the Huguenot church, and to impress upon him Elizabeth's commitment to its survival.[54] Delayed by storms, Sidney caught up with the King at Chartres, meeting with him on 8 February 1594, the day he was crowned. Sidney's detailed reports persuaded Elizabeth to extend his assignment, and on 12 March he accompanied Henri into a welcoming Paris.[55]

Sidney Herbert had already requested her protégé, Samuel Daniel, to produce a companion piece: her 'well grac'd *Anthony*' now 'Requir'd his *Cleopatras* company' (H5). Daniel's *Cleopatra*, the first original English tragedy based on Plutarch's *Lives*, cryptically adapts Amyot's 'Antony'. It illustrates the vulnerability of a state when its suicidal queen renounces politics for self-absorption. While not published till 1594, it was entered in the Stationers' Register on 19 October 1593, the day that Robert Sidney wrote apologetically to his wife about his forthcoming trip to France.[56]

Daniel's Senecan drama adapts Garnier's form. His prefatory 'Argument' (H8–I1) consists of translations and paraphrases of excerpts from Amyot. He uses rhyme, predominantly in a ten-syllable *abab* quatrain. And like Garnier's, his play consists of five Acts, commented on by a Chorus with its own distinctive rhyme scheme. Unlike Garnier, Daniel splits the third and fifth Acts into two scenes, adds a Chorus to the fifth, and reduces the overall length. *Cleopatra* is shorter by 250 lines in the

50 M. V. Hay, *The Life of Robert Sidney, Earl of Leicester (1563–1626)* (Washington: Folger Shakespeare Library, 1984), p. 102.

51 See M. G. Brennan, '"Your Lordship's to Do You All Humble Service": Rowland Whyte's Correspondence with Robert Sidney, Viscount Lisle and First Earl of Leicester', *Sidney Journal*, xxi, no. 2 (2003), 1–37.

52 M. V. Hay, *The Life of Robert Sidney*, p. 105; E. K. Chambers, *The Elizabethan Stage*, 4 vols (Oxford: Clarendon Press, 1923), i.322.

53 P. E. J. Hammer, *The Polarisation of Elizabethan Politics*, pp. 118–19, 128.

54 M. V. Hay, *The Life of Robert Sidney*, pp. 144–5.

55 M. V. Hay, *The Life of Robert Sidney*, pp. 150–1.

56 M. V. Hay, *The Life of Robert Sidney*, pp. 144 and 167, n.2; *Domestic Politics and Family Absence: the Correspondence (1588–1621) of Robert Sidney, First Earl of Leicester, and Barbara Gamage Sidney*, ed. by M. P. Hannay, N. J. Kinnamon and M. G. Brennan (Aldershot: Ashgate, 2005), p. 36.

version published in 1594, 1599, 1601, 1602 and 1605; and by 150 lines in the revision of 1607 and 1611. But Daniel's principled avoidance of verbal patterning and metaphor radically disassociates his work from Garnier's. This radical departure may well reflect philhellene Protestant concern that the Huguenots had now ostensibly been abandoned by Henri IV, and would be annihilated if Elizabeth changed her policy.

Spenser's portrayal of Navarre as Sir Burbon in Book V of *The Faerie Queene* (published 1596)[57] and Shakespeare's Navarre in *Love's Labour's Lost* (1594–95) likewise dramatise immediate concerns about the Huguenot leader's apparent lack of commitment.[58] Henri's reconversion to Catholicism in July 1593 strengthened the monarchomachist debate about the responsibilities of sovereigns in exchange for the loyalty of their subjects. Not until the Edict of Nantes in 1598, closely preceding Shakespeare's *Julius Caesar*, did Henri IV regain heroic status among the English philhellene Protestants by bringing the Wars of Religion to an end, and negotiating legal protection for the beleaguered Huguenots. But if Shakespeare's Octavius portrays Henri IV's peacemaking, his connection with Henri's supporter, Essex, cannot entirely be dismissed.

Greville's *Antony and Cleopatra*: politics and anti-romance

Literary representations of monarchomachist concerns in works associated with the Huguenot crisis blossomed after Fulke Greville published Sidney's *The Countess of Pembroke's Arcadia* in 1590, prefaced by Sidney's dedicatory letter to Mary Sidney Herbert. Greville's terse description of his *Antony and Cleopatra* reveals his recognition of the association between Antony's tragedy and the demise of his close friend Essex, prone to passionate affairs and executed as a traitor in 1601: 'seeing the like instance not poetically, but really, fashioned in the Earl of Essex then falling'.[59] Greville destroyed *Antony and Cleopatra*, possibly to avoid being implicated in incitement to rebellion:[60]

57 See A. L. Prescott, 'Foreign Policy in Fairyland: Henri IV and Spenser's Burbon', *Spenser Studies: A Renaissance Poetry Annual*, xiv (2000), 189–214.
58 See M. Wolfe, 'Piety and Political Allegiance: the Duc de Nevers and the Protestant Henri IV, 1589–93', *French History*, ii (1988), 1–21.
59 *A Dedication to Sir Philip Sidney*, in *The Prose Works of Fulke Greville, Lord Brooke*, ed. by J. Gouws, p. 93; see V. Skretkowicz, 'Greville, Politics, and the Rhetorics of *A Dedication to Sir Philip Sidney*', in *Fulke Greville: A Special Double Number*, ed. by M. C. Hansen and M. Woodcock, *Sidney Journal*, xix (2001 [published 2002]), 97–123.
60 R. A. Rebholz, *The Life of Fulke Greville, First Lord Brooke* (Oxford: Clarendon Press, 1971), p. 131.

Antony and Cleopatra, according to their irregular passions in foresaking empire to follow sensuality, were sacrificed in the fire; the executioner, the author himself, […] many members in that creature (by the opinion of those few eyes which saw it) […] apt enough to be construed or strained to a personating of vices in the present governors and government.[61]

The destabilising effect of passion on the state, the theme of Sidney's *Arcadia*, dominates Greville's *Mustapha* (written 1594–96, revised 1607– 10) and *Alaham* (1599, altered after Essex's fall in February 1601).[62] The political allegory was made more cryptic in response to the Essex debacle,[63] though material deleted from the Choruses of *Mustapha*, and probably also *Alaham*, reappears in *A Treatise of Monarchy*.[64] But Greville's special innovation in *Antony and Cleopatra* (1599–1600) was to create a new kind of drama, an erotic political anti-romance, in which mature and passionate world leaders fall in love, are torn apart and are destroyed. Like Daphnis and Chloe, Kleitophon and Leukippe, and Theagenes and Charikleia, Plutarch's Antony and Cleopatra are of relatively equal social status. But they are the antithesis of the chaste heroes and heroines of Greek erotic romance, whose stories end in happiness. Their relationship begins with competitive displays of wealth, is built on mutual sexual expectation, and ends with their downfall and death.

Into this formula Greville introduces the romance element of erotic voyeurism. While this accords with discussions of the passions and erotic love in the sonnets and longer poems of *Caelica*, his model is almost certainly Plutarch. Plutarch's Octavia is an unruffled administrator, but his Cleopatra reveals an admiring fascination for the sensuous and exotic. Plutarch foregrounds Cleopatra's intellect, her use of position and wealth to bait Antony with entertainments, and her provocative, enervating histrionics. But Greville's blaming both Antony and Cleopatra for ignoring their political responsibilities goes well beyond Plutarch, whose criticism of sensual excess and dereliction of duty is aimed particularly at Antony.

Elizabeth I died on 24 March 1603. Greville wrote *A Dedication*, which he wisely kept out of print, between 1604 and 1610 while enemies kept him out of office. In this Protestantised Plutarchan 'Life', Greville creates a demanding, rambling style. He combines Plutarch's plainness with Ciceronian rhythmic sentences, eliding recurrent metaphors, Donne-like, into one another. As Mary Sidney Wroth would do in *Urania*, Greville

61 *A Dedication to Sir Philip Sidney*, in *The Prose Works of Fulke Greville, Lord Brooke*, ed. by J. Gouws, p. 93.
62 R. A. Rebholz, *The Life of Fulke Greville*, pp. 99, 123, 131, 325–40.
63 R. A. Rebholz, *The Life of Fulke Greville*, pp. 102–3, 132–4.
64 R. A. Rebholz, *The Life of Fulke Greville*, p. 336.

veils personal criticisms in an evasive layer of rhetorical obfuscation.[65]

Greville describes Elizabeth–Cleopatra as being seduced by tyrannical counsellors, particularly Lord Cobham, Robert Cecil and Sir Walter Ralegh:[66]

> I discerned my gracious sovereign to be every way so environed with these, not Jupiter's, but Pluto's, thunder-workers as it was impossible for her to see any light that might lead to grace or mercy, but many encouraging meteors of severity as against an unthankful favourite and traitorous subject.[67]

Essex–Antony, foolishly believing he would be rewarded for ridding Elizabeth of their influence, is a naive altruist. His treason is selfless: 'let his heart be (as in my conscience it was) free from this unnatural crime'.[68] And it is consistent with philhellene Protestant aims of establishing a representative form of monarchy:

> yet (I say) that active heart of his freely chose to hazard himself upon their censures without any other provisional rampire against the envious and suppressing crafts of that party than his own hope and resolution to deserve well.[69]

Greville's report of Sidney assigning Franco-Anglo-Hispanic allegorical values to the characters of Antony, Cleopatra and Octavius differs from Garnier's, Sidney Herbert's and Daniel's commentaries on the French Wars of Religion.

Shakespeare composed *Julius Caesar* in 1599 on the back of celebrating the union of England and France in his Plutarchan biography, *Henry V*,[70] and virtually in conjunction with his play about French reform and reconciliation, *As You Like It*. He needed no invitation to exploit the potential of covert allegorical ambiguity for panegyric. Henri IV's iconic status found a parallel in Essex, a hero of the philhellene Protestant George Carey, second Lord Hunsdon (1547–1603), patron of Shakespeare's company, the Lord Chamberlain's Men.

---

65 Cf. V. Skretkowicz, 'Greville, Politics, and the Rhetorics of *A Dedication to Sir Philip Sidney*'.
66 *The Prose Works of Fulke Greville, Lord Brooke*, ed. by J. Gouws, p. 222.
67 *A Dedication to Sir Philip Sidney*, in *The Prose Works of Fulke Greville, Lord Brooke*, ed. by J. Gouws, p. 94.
68 *A Dedication to Sir Philip Sidney*, in *The Prose Works of Fulke Greville, Lord Brooke*, ed. by J. Gouws, p. 94.
69 *A Dedication to Sir Philip Sidney*, in *The Prose Works of Fulke Greville, Lord Brooke*, ed. by J. Gouws, p. 96.
70 J. Mossman, 'Henry V and Plutarch's Alexander', *Shakespeare Quarterly*, xlv (1994), 57–73.

Philhellene Protestants, as did Essex's secretary Henry Wotton in 1595, took pleasure in reinforcing the monarchomachist warning to monarchs that 'the people and peers of the realm are their makers next unto God'.[71] In *Julius Caesar*, Essex's supporters may have celebrated a short-lived promise of reform. Political and personal allies delighted in Essex's appointment as Lord Lieutenant of Ireland, 30 December 1598, for which he left on 27 March 1599. But by 2 October 1599, when Essex was arrested for leaving his post to confront the Queen,[72] and especially after his execution for treason on 25 February 1601, the play would have invited quite a different construction. Essex's military authority, powerful allies and popular status had become as threatening to the Queen's Privy Council as Caesar's was to the Pompeyists.

Panegyric in *Antony and Cleopatra* (1606): the rewards of patronage

The title of Shakespeare's Jacobean *Antony and Cleopatra* (1606), with its coupling of hero and heroine, signals its conformity with Greville's Elizabethan erotic anti-romance model. The play emphasises the failure of the protagonists to maintain political responsibility over personal obsession. Their inevitable defeat by the level-headed Octavius results in their suicides, Antony for loss of aspiration and honour, Cleopatra to preserve her reputation. But there is national relief at their deaths, as the Roman Empire comes to order under Augustus Caesar.

England and Protestant Europe experienced a parallel emotion on the death of Elizabeth, and the unchallenged accession of James I on 24 March 1603. In *B. Ion: his part of King James his Royall and Magnificent Entertainement through his Honorable Cittie of London*, the pageant partly designed by Ben Jonson for the official entry into London on 15 March 1604, James was hailed as 'Augusto Novo' and 'Caesar Aug' (D3–D3v). Implying relatively consultative, non-tyrannical government, 'Augustus' was the title conferred on Octavius Caesar on 16 January in 27 BC, after he reinstated the republic by demitting control of the state to the Senate. Philip II having died in 1598, in a European context, James shared this honour with Henri of Navarre. In 1592, among those who unofficially proclaimed him Henri IV of France, François de Clary referred to Navarre as Augustus in *Philippiques contre les bulles et autres pratiques de la faction*

---

71   P. E. J. Hammer, *The Polarisation of Elizabethan Politics*, p. 338, citing Wotton's treatise from G. Ungerer, *A Spaniard in Elizabethan England: The Correspondence of Antonio Perez's Exile*, 2 vols (London: Tamesis Books, 1974–76), ii.280–321.
72   M. V. Hay, *The Life of Robert Sidney*, p. 165.

d'Espagne (Tours, 1592),[73] while the Calvinist Johannes Wilhelm Stucki compared him with Charlemagne in *Carolus Magnus Redivivus* (Zurich, 1592).[74] By 1606, when *Antony and Cleopatra* was written, the contemporary identities assigned by Sidney and Greville had radically changed.

Long before Essex's treason in 1601, a third way, the consultative route to compromise through Octavius–Augustus–James, had been well established. In 1587, Leicester's role had been to persuade James that acquiescence to his mother's execution would ensure his unimpeded succession.[75] In 1588, Essex; his sister, Penelope Devereux Rich; and his pro-Catholic adviser, Lord Henry Howard (1540–1614), all exchanged letters with James.[76] In 1579, Howard, second son of the executed poet, Henry Howard, Earl of Surrey, regarded Leicester as 'a would-be usurper of the throne'. By contrast, extreme Protestants viewed Howard as representing a Catholic revolution to undermine the Protestant nobility.[77] Now varied interests were working together. After Essex was executed in 1601, Howard became an intermediary between James and Robert Cecil (1563?–1612), who also corresponded with the King.

Henry Howard overcame the factionalism that separated Essex and Cecil. Well aware of the Cecil circle's dominance, James took pains to reward all those who prepared his way. By 1606, when *Antony and Cleopatra* was written, his liberality among his favourites seemed unbounded. On receiving news of Elizabeth's death, James sent Howard a jewel. On 1 January 1604, Howard became Lord Warden of the Cinque Ports; on 13 March, Baron Howard of Marnhull and Dorset, and Earl of Northampton; on 24 February 1605, Knight of the Garter; and on 29 April 1608, Lord Privy Seal.[78] In April 1603, James released Essex's protégé and convicted

73 J. Powis, 'Gallican Liberties and the Politics of Later Sixteenth-Century France', *The Historical Journal*, xxvi (1983), 515–30 (pp. 516–17), citing p. 64.

74 See V. Skretkowicz, 'Shakespeare, Henri IV, and the Tyranny of Royal Style', in *Challenging Humanism: Essays in Honor of Dominic Baker-Smith*, ed. by T. Hoenselaars and A. F. Kinney (Newark: University of Delaware Press, 2005), pp. 179–208 (pp. 187–9).

75 S. Adams, 'Dudley, Robert, Earl of Leicester (1532/3–1588)', *Oxford Dictionary of National Biography* (Oxford: Oxford University Press, 2004).

76 M. V. Hay, *The Life of Robert Sidney*, p. 210; P. E. J. Hammer, *The Polarisation of Elizabethan Politics*, pp. 91, 168–70. On Howard, see L. L. Peck, 'The Mentality of a Jacobean Grandee', in *The Mental World of the Jacobean Court*, ed. by L. L. Peck (Cambridge: Cambridge University Press, 1991), pp. 148–68; H. R. Woudhuysen, *Sir Philip Sidney and the Circulation of Manuscripts, 1558–1640* (Oxford: Clarendon Press, 1996), pp. 99–103; and P. Croft, 'Howard, Henry, Earl of Northampton (1540–1614)', *Oxford Dictionary of National Biography* (Oxford: Oxford University Press, 2004).

77 B. Worden, *The Sound of Virtue: Philip Sidney's Arcadia and Elizabethan Politics* (New Haven: Yale University Press, 1996), p. 95.

78 M. V. Hay, *The Life of Robert Sidney*, p. 210; P. Croft, 'Howard, Henry, Earl of Northampton (1540–1614)'.

co-conspirator, Henry Lord Wriothesley, formerly third Earl of Southampton, kept alive through Robert Cecil's intervention. Pardoned 16 May, released 5 April, on 2 July Wriothesley became a Knight of the Garter. On 21 July he was re-created Earl of Southampton, and on 18 April 1604 was restored to his title by Parliament.[79]

On 13 May 1603, Robert Cecil was created Baron Cecil of Essendon. James used this occasion to correct the Cecil-inspired imbalance of Elizabeth's final years, similarly advancing four philhellene Protestants. Coincidentally, without this meteoric promotion of those belonging to the Sidney–Devereux–Essex circle, Mary Sidney Wroth's erotic romance, *The Countess of Montgomery's Urania* (1621), would never have been written. Sir William Knollys, Essex's uncle and one of his hostages in 1601, was created Baron Knollys of Greys.[80] Sir Edward Wotton, one of Elizabeth's special ambassadors to James, was created Baron Wotton of Marley.[81] He was half-brother to Essex's secretary, Henry Wotton.[82]

In 1598, Wotton had been put forward for a baronage by Robert Cecil, and Robert Sidney by Essex. Both were blocked.[83] Now Robert Sidney, ambassador to James in August 1588, was created Baron Sidney of Penshurst. On 14 July 1603, he became Anne of Denmark's Lord High Chamberlain; on 9 August, Steward of her Kentish manors and a Member of Council; on 10 November, her Surveyor-General. Sidney was outranked in the Queen's court only by his own supporter, Robert Cecil, Anne's Lord High Steward. On 20 August 1604, Cecil became Viscount Cranborne. On 4 May 1605, 'at the christening of [...] Prncess Mary',[84] when Philip Herbert was created Earl of Montgomery, Sidney received the title of Viscount Lisle and Cecil became Earl of Salisbury. On 20 May 1606, Cecil was installed Knight of the Garter, on 6 May 1608 becoming Lord Treasurer. Sidney waited until 7 July 1616, long after Cecil's death in 1612, to receive the Garter.[85]

---

79 P. Honan, 'Wriothesley, Henry, Third Earl of Southampton (1573–1624)', *Oxford Dictionary of National Biography* (Oxford: Oxford University Press, 2004).
80 See V. Stater, 'Knollys, William, First Earl of Banbury (c. 1545–1632)', *Oxford Dictionary of National Biography* (Oxford: Oxford University Press, 2004).
81 See A. J. Loomie, 'Wotton, Edward, First Baron Wotton (1548–1628)', *Oxford Dictionary of National Biography* (Oxford: Oxford University Press, 2004).
82 See A. J. Loomie, 'Wotton, Sir Henry (1568–1639)', *Oxford Dictionary of National Biography* (Oxford: Oxford University Press, 2004).
83 M. V. Hay, *The Life of Robert Sidney*, p. 159.
84 M. G. Brennan, 'Robert Sidney, King James I and Queen Anna: The Politics of Intimate Service (1588–1607)', *Sidney Journal*, xxv, nos 1–2 (2007), 3–30 (p. 5).
85 See R. Shephard, 'Sidney, Robert, First Earl of Leicester (1563–1626)', *Oxford Dictionary of National Biography* (Oxford: Oxford University Press, 2004).

Mary Sidney Herbert's sons, Philip and William, thrived under James. In May 1603, Philip Herbert was appointed a Gentleman of the Privy Chamber, and on 23 July Knight of the Bath. On 27 December 1604, James played a prominent role in Philip's marriage to Susan de Vere, to whom Mary Sidney Wroth would dedicate *Urania*. From 1605 until James's death in 1625, Philip served as a Gentleman of the Bedchamber. On 4 May 1605, he was created Baron Herbert of Shurland and Earl of Montgomery – the same day on which Robert Sidney became a viscount and Robert Cecil a baron – and, on 23 April 1608, Knight of the Garter.[86]

On 17 May 1603, James appointed William Herbert, third Earl of Pembroke, Keeper of the Forest of Clarendon. On 25 June 1603, he was installed Knight of the Garter. Pembroke played host to King, Queen, and court when they visited Wilton in 1603 while the plague raged in London – probably on 29–30 August, but certainly during October.[87] In 1604, Pembroke represented his mother in seeking a pardon for Cecil's enemy, Sir Walter Ralegh, and maintained the philhellene Protestants' opposition to appeasement with Spain. Despite persistently supporting Parliament against the King, Pembroke continued to collect lucrative honours: 28 January 1604, Lord Warden of the Stanneries and High Steward of the Duchy of Cornwall; 21 May 1604, Lord Lieutenant of Cornwall; January 1608, Warden of the Forest of Dean; 16 October 1609, Captain of Portsmouth; 29 September 1611, Privy Councillor; and 23 December 1615, Lord Chamberlain. He was with the King when he died on 27 March 1625, carried the crown at the coronation of Charles I, and on 18 August 1626 was appointed Lord Steward. On 3 August 1626, he was succeeded as Lord Chamberlain by his brother Philip, his co-dedicatee in the 1623 folio edition of Shakespeare's plays.[88]

The opening of James's reign was not trouble-free. He could never eradicate dissatisfaction about the legitimacy of the Stuart succession, a topic bitterly revived under Charles I by republican monarchomachists

---

86 See D. L. Smith, 'Herbert, Philip, First Earl of Montgomery and Fourth Earl of Pembroke (1584–1650)', *Oxford Dictionary of National Biography* (Oxford: Oxford University Press, 2004).

87 M. P. Hannay, *Philip's Phoenix: Mary Sidney, Countess of Pembroke* (New York: Oxford University Press, 1990), p. 187. See G. Twigg, 'Plague in London: Spatial and Temporal Aspects of Mortality', in *Epidemic Disease in London*, ed. by J. A. I. Champion, University of London Centre for Metropolitan History, Working Papers Series, 1 (London: Centre for Metropolitan History, 1993), pp. 1–17.

88 V. Stater, 'Herbert, William, Third Earl of Pembroke (1580–1630)', *Oxford Dictionary of National Biography* (Oxford: Oxford University Press, 2004).

such as Algernon Sidney.[89] In August 1604, James swept aside philhellene Protestant opposition to conclude the Treaty of London with Philip III, ending the conflict between Britain and Spain. Following the Jesuit-inspired Gunpowder Plot, 5 November 1605, *Macbeth* (1606) provided James with a dramatised genealogical claim to the throne. And it gave Shakespeare an opportunity 'to distance himself from a terrorist group with whom his connections were uncomfortably close'.[90]

Established Renaissance convention requires a politicisation of the Antony and Cleopatra legend. But in the absence of contemporary observation, the range of possible allegorisations remains fluid. A Catholicised contextualisation of *Antony and Cleopatra* (1606) holds that Cleopatra and Egypt represent the Spain that promised, but failed, to support Antony, the English Counter-Reformation. The tragedy of their idealised devotion, the experience of English Catholics, is viewed as preferable to Octavius's pragmatism.[91] But if, following the Gunpowder Plot, Cleopatra represented the seductive chimera of promised religious reconciliation, the play could equally dramatise the continuing philhellene Protestant opposition to James's relationship with Philip III. And it could simultaneously compliment James through the combined attributes of Antony's liberality and Octavius Caesar's political astuteness.

Seven times Antony's followers refer to him – though never to Octavius – as 'emperor'. This complimentary title may designate Antony's responsibility in the East as triumvir; nonetheless, within the play it elevates his status. Lepidus is deposed in 36 BC (III.vi.29), and Antony dies in 30 BC (IV.xvi.64). Shakespeare dramatises the transfer of power to Octavius by linking Cleopatra's visionary eulogy, 'I dreamt there was an Emperor Antony' (V.ii.75), with Octavius Caesar's entry. There Dolabella identifies him as 'the Emperor' (V.ii.110), a title resonating with fulfilment of James's ultimate ambition, to play a unifying role in Europe comparable to the Holy Roman Emperor.

Antony bridges the political, cultural and moral divide between East and West. He alters stylistic register, shifting between the exaggerated hyperbole and grandiose metaphor of the East and the generally elevated

89 Algernon Sidney, *Court Maxims*, ed. by H. W. Blom, E. H. Mulier and R. Janse (Cambridge: Cambridge University Press, 1996), pp. 184, 187, 196–8.
90 C. Asquith, *Shadowplay: The Hidden Beliefs and Coded Politics of William Shakespeare* (New York: PublicAffairs, 2005), p. 216.
91 C. Asquith, *Shadowplay: The Hidden Beliefs and Coded Politics of William Shakespeare*, pp. 228–30, and *Theatre and Religion: Lancastrian Shakespeare*, ed. by R. Dutton, A. Findlay and R. Wilson (Manchester: Manchester University Press, 2003), p. 190.

courtly style of the Romans.[92] Shakespeare achieves these distinctions by exploiting the artful styles invented for Renaissance adaptations of Greco-Roman historiography and erotic romance. His embellishments to the Amyot-North text emulate the stylistic high points of Achilles Tatius, Heliodorus and Sidney.

North's representation of Cleopatra's barge is relatively reserved:

> her barge in the riuer of Cydnus, the poope whereof was of gold, the sailes of purple, and the owers of siluer, which kept stroke in rowing after the sounde of the musicke of flutes, howboyes, citherns, violls, and such other instruments as they played vpon in the barge. (NNNN5)

Shakespeare injects this ecphrastic passage with an exotic artificiality. Clearly audible alliteration, assonance and cadence are balanced by simile and, significantly, prosopopoeia. Personification, a regular feature of Senecan descriptive reporting, is characteristic of European erotic romance, and of such verbal adaptations of the genre as Antony's eulogy in the forum. In *Antony and Cleopatra*, it becomes a vital component in convincing an audience that they are watching not a dramatisation of Plutarch but a variant of emotionally charged erotic romance:

> The barge she sat in, like a burnished throne
> Burned on the water. The poop was beaten gold;
> Purple the sails, and so perfumèd that
> The winds were love-sick with them. The oars were silver,
> Which to the tune of flutes kept stroke, and made
> The water which they beat to follow faster,
> As amorous of their strokes.
>
> (II.ii.197–203)

Antony and Cleopatra forces together disparate episodes from Plutarch's biography of Antony, but, like a Greco-Roman erotic romance, it uses reported narrative and shifts in location to achieve dramatic cohesion. The romance element lies in its idealisation of a joyful and overtly sexual pageant of heroic proportions, displacing the usual Renaissance dramatic representation of Antony and Cleopatra as lamenting, tragic figures. Their uncontrollable emotions overshadow the adulterous nature of their relationship. But their age, their wily worldliness and the breadth of their sexual and political entanglements all add up to impending disaster.

---

92 The range of critical opinion on style in this play is summarised in W. Shakespeare, *Antony and Cleopatra*, ed. by D. Bevington (Cambridge: Cambridge University Press, 1990), pp. 34–40.

The Winter's Tale (1609–10): exemplary rapprochement

In Sidney's *Arcadia*, where fate and family reconciliation avert disaster, divisions between the state ruler and his wife last a matter of weeks. In *The Winter's Tale* (1609–10), sixteen years pass before chance intervenes to bring Leontes and Hermione together in what promises to be genuine marital harmony. This reunion is Shakespeare's most significant addition to Robert Greene's short and much reprinted erotic romance, *Pandosto. The Triumph of Time* (1588), otherwise known by Greene's subtitle, *The Historie of Dorastus and Fawnia*.[93]

Pandosto, a third-person narrative, is artfully punctuated by affected, metaphor-laden soliloquies, much in the manner of Angel Day's euphuistic *Daphnis and Chloe*, published late in 1587. Like Day, Greene combines elements of plot and style from a manuscript copy of Sidney's *Old Arcadia*. And, like Day, Greene asserts his affiliation to an Elizabethan court favourite through his dedication to George Clifford (1558–1605), third Earl of Cumberland, inextricably linked through heritage and marriage to the philhellene Protestants. Clifford, father of Samuel Daniel's pupil Anne Clifford, was the second tilter to face Essex in the 'Daphnis and Chloe' Accession Day jousts of 1587.

Greene's benevolent King Egistus rules Sicilia, his tyrant Pandosto, Bohemia. In *The Winter's Tale*, the tyrant is Leontes, King of Sicilia, while the benign King Polixenes rules Bohemia. Shakespeare mimics Greene's two-part structure and his theme of ethnic and cultural conflict. *The Winter's Tale* opens with Archidamus proclaiming 'difference': 'If you shall chance, Camillo, to visit Bohemia […] you shall see, as I have said, great difference betwixt our Bohemia and your Sicilia' (I.i.1–4). Both Greene and Shakespeare represent the conflict of political practices, the conversion of a tyrant, and resolution in political union through the marriage of the succeeding generation: 'those kingdoms, which through enmity had long time been disservered, should now through perpetual amity be united and reconciled' (p. 224).

When Greene wrote *Pandosto*, Italy, including Sicily, had long been tightly governed by Spanish-Castilian administrators.[94] In fact, the title 'Queen of Sicily' had recently belonged to the Catholic Mary Tudor, as in Thomas North's dedication of Antonio de Guevara's *The Diall of Princes*

---

93 References are to the modernised edition in W. Shakespeare, *The Winter's Tale*, ed. by J. H. P. Pafford, The Arden Shakespeare (London: Methuen, 1963), pp. 181–225.
94 R. S. Dunn, *The Age of Religious Wars, 1559–1715*, 2nd edn (New York: W. W. Norton, 1979), pp. 18–20.

(1557), 'To the Mooste hyghe and vertuouse Princesse, Mary, by the grace of God, Quene of Englande, Spaine, Fraunce, both Sicilles, Ierusalem, and Irelande'. In contrast, following nearly two centuries of Hussite Protestantism, Bohemia's nationalistic nobility continued successfully to resist Rudolf II's attempts to enforce Catholic conversion upon them.[95]

Greene may have won support during the Armada year of 1588 by proposing political and religious rapprochement. But Shakespeare's revival of this well-known story in 1609–10 additionally celebrates, through Leontes and Hermione, the welcome end of civil conflict. Following the Anglo-Hispanic peace of 1604, on 16 June 1608 James entered into a defensive league with the Dutch. On 9 April 1609, he brokered the truce between Philip III and the United Provinces that put a halt to the Dutch civil wars. Shakespeare may parallel this appeasement through the transformation of Leontes from tempestuous Castilian tyrant to loving father and – Shakespeare's addition to Greene – reformed and caring husband. Similarly, Polixenes' tranquil Bohemia could not but reflect the Jacobean court's support for Rudolf II's 1609 Letter of Majesty, 'the fullest guarantee of religious freedom to be found anywhere on the continent'.[96] Nor can the possibility of the play's promoting wider European Christian unity be discounted.[97]

Jealousy, tyranny, and the aggressive 'royal' style

When Pandosto misrepresents the virtuous friendship between his wife, Bellaria, and Egistus, Pandosto orders his cup-bearer, Franion, to poison Egistus (p. 187). Franion's qualified monarchomachism, 'Thou art servant to a king and must obey at command; yet, Franion, against law and conscience it is not good to resist a tyrant with arms, nor to please an unjust king with obedience' (p. 188), leads him to escape with Egistus to Sicilia (p. 189). It is symptomatic of the altered political climate twenty years later under James I that, when Leontes commands Camillo to kill Polixenes, questions of obedience, resisting a tyrant and of conscience, never enter Camillo's head. Instead, he reflects on the Jacobean notion of the divinely appointed monarch: 'If I could find example / Of thousands

95 R. S. Dunn, *The Age of Religious Wars, 1559–1715*, p. 63.
96 R. S. Dunn, *The Age of Religious Wars, 1559–1715*, p. 63.
97 Cf. D. B. Hamilton, '*The Winter's Tale* and the Language of Union, 1604–1610', *Shakespeare Studies*, xxi (1993), 228–50, and J. Ellison, 'The Winter's Tale and the Religious Politics of Europe', in *Shakespeare's Romances*, ed. by A. Thorne (Basingstoke: Palgrave Macmillan, 2003), pp. 171–204, interpreting the play as a Protestant–Catholic allegory.

that had struck anointed kings / And flourished after, I'd not do't [...] I must / Forsake the court' (I.ii.358–63).

Egistus's nocturnal departure with Franion confirms Pandosto's suspicion of Bellaria's adultery. She is arrested, and the daughter she gives birth to set adrift (pp. 192–3). In a parodic shadow of the trial of Mary, Queen of Scots, executed 8 February 1587, Bellaria is arraigned on charges of adultery and treason. Greene portrays Pandosto as a tyrant abusing royal prerogative: 'in this case he might and would dispense with the law, and that the jury [...] should take his word for sufficient evidence; otherwise he would make the proudest of them repent it' (p. 195). He does, however, grant Bellaria's request that he send to Delphos to seek Apollo's verdict:

SUSPICION IS NO PROOF: JEALOUSY IS AN UNEQUAL JUDGE: BELLARIA IS CHASTE: EGISTUS BLAMELESS: FRANION A TRUE SUBJECT: PANDOSTO TREACHEROUS: HIS BABE AN INNOCENT; AND THE KING SHALL LIVE WITHOUT AN HEIR, IF THAT WHICH IS LOST BE NOT FOUND. (p. 196)

Like Gynecia in the five-book versions of Sidney's *Arcadia*, Bellaria is summoned to a public hearing before the judgement seat. Holding the oracle in great reverence, Pandosto has his nobles 'persuade Bellaria to forgive and forget', promises to become 'a loyal and loving husband, but also to reconcile himself to Egistus and Franion' (p. 197), and confesses his guilt. The shock of their son Garinter's death kills Bellaria. Pandosto is prevented from suicide by 'his peers', who argue that 'that the commonwealth consisted on his safety' and that his responsibility is to 'have care of his subjects' (p. 198). But after Dorastus and Fawnia marry, Pandosto is overcome by melancholy and kills himself (p. 225).

Shakespeare eschews Greene's euphuism, shifting Leontes' rhetorical register to an aggressive '*style royal*', built on parallel rhythmic structures but free of metaphor and sound patterns. While, as devised and employed by Amyot, '*style royal*' sets the king on an exalted plane by making him sound admirable, in Shakespeare's intimidating variation this style becomes the political signature of an intelligent and dangerous tyrant.[98] Arrogant and self-righteous, Leontes threatens to dismiss his counsellors: 'Our prerogative / Calls not your counsels, but our natural goodness / Imparts this' (II.i.165–7). He asserts his legal right to alter a consultative monarchy to a tyranny: 'We need no more of your advice. The matter, / The loss, the gain, the ord'ring on't, is all / Properly ours' (II.i.170–2).

---

98 Cf. V. Skretkowicz, 'Shakespeare, Henri IV, and the Tyranny of Royal Style', in *Challenging Humanism: Essays in Honor of Dominic Baker-Smith*, ed. by T. Hoenselaars and A. F. Kinney, pp. 179–208.

He will consult Apollo purely to cast further aspersions on his nobles: 'Though I am satisfied, and need no more / Than what I know, yet shall the oracle / Give rest to th' minds of others such as he, / Whose ignorant credulity will not / Come up to th' truth' (II.i.191–5).

Leontes' tyrannical register, one of the play's stylistic poles, contrasts with the gentle sounds of Polixenes' opening speech. His metaphorical periphrasis, 'Nine changes of the wat'ry star hath been / The shepherd's note since we have left our throne / Without a burden' (I.ii.1–3), reduces to 'I left home nine months ago'. To a Jacobean theatre audience, particularly one familiar with the outlines of *Pandosto*, this contrasting vague, meandering 'royal' style signals an association between Bohemia and the plot expectations of erotic romance.

Plutarch's notion of holistic individual characterisation, where style of speech becomes a symbolic identifier, extends in *Julius Caesar* to distinguish political affiliations and vested interests. In *Antony and Cleopatra*, it signals the cultural, moral and ethical differences between Egypt and Rome. Unlike the historically based plots of *Julius Caesar* and *Antony and Cleopatra*, the schematic artificiality of *The Winter's Tale* allows Shakespeare to reduce the audible symbolism of thematic division by closing the gap between extremes of rhetorical style. It is fitting that he eradicates this stylistic distinction in his conclusion, the genre of European erotic romance being an established signifier of harmonious political and social endings. Relaxed and reconciled, in the final scene Leontes, Paulina, Camillo, Hermione and Polixenes – last heard threatening Perdita (IV. iv.422–9) – become equally comfortable in a quietly elegant and reassuringly controlled third kind of 'royal' style.

Gendering rhetorics: Thucydides and the ermine

Sidney's tyrants have monolithic personalities, experience few or no domestic relationships and exhibit the abstract qualities of Theophrastan types. Shakespeare follows Plutarch's holistic template in characterising Leontes as both a political and domestic tyrant. Leontes paralyses his courtiers with legal definition, but despite his misogynism fails spectacularly to silence the single vestige of monarchomachist principle, in Paulina, that saves his kingdom.

The process of Leontes' reform reflects the philhellene Protestant regard for Plutarch. Plutarch's examples of women opposing male oppression, in 'The vertuous deeds of women', are commended by Goulart, who introduced a prefatory 'Sommaire' before each essay in his Calvinist edition of

Amyot's *Les Oeuvres morales & meslees de Plutarque* ([Geneva:] François Estien[n]e, 1582).[99] Goulart's influential opinions were transmitted to an English readership in one of the first books to be dedicated to James I, *The Philosophie, commonlie called, The Morals written by the learned Philosopher Plutarch of Chaeronea. Translated out of Greeke into English, and conferred with the Latine translations and the French, by Philemon Holland of Coventrie, Doctor in Physicke. Whereunto are annexed the Summaries necessary to be read before every Treatise* (1603).

In the opening of 'The vertuous deeds of women', Plutarch qualifies Thucydides' influential recommendations for female constraint:

> I Am not of *Thucydides* minde [...] touching the vertue of women; for he is of this opinon: That she is the best & most vertuous, of whom there is least speech abroad, aswell to her praise as her dispraise; thinking that the name of a woman of honour, ought to be shut up and kept fast within, like as her bodie, that it never may go forth. *Gorgias* yet (me thinks) was more reasonable, who would have the renowme and fame, but not the face & visage of a woman, to be knowen unto men.[100] (Ss2)

The distinction Plutarch draws approximates the divide between Puritans and Calvinists. Goulart's introductory 'Sommaire', while alluding to women as 'instruments foibles & de peu de monstre' (Q3), 'feeble instruments, and those of small shew' (Ss1v), enunciates what is effectively the philhellene Protestant position. Goulart emphasises that, 'after he had refuted the opinion of *Thucydides*, who would confine women (as it were) into a perpetuall ermitage', Plutarch writes about 'women who for their valour have deserved, that their name and example should continue; to the end that the same might be imitated [...] not onely by other women, but also by the most part of men' (Ss1v).[101]

For Goulart, Plutarch's exemplary women are especially notable for 'an extreame hatred of tyrannie and servitude, an ardent love and affec-

99 On Goulart's 1582 prefaces, see V. Skretkowicz, 'Sidney's *Defence of Poetry*, Henri Estienne, and Huguenot Nationalist Satire', *Sidney Journal*, xvi, no. 1 (1998), 3–24 (pp. 17–23).
100 'Ie n'ay pas mesme opinio[n] que Thucydides [...] touchant la vertu des femmes: pour ce que lui estime, que celle la soit la plus vertueuse, & la meilleure, de qui on parle le moins, autant en bien qu'en mal: pensant que le nom de la femme d'honneur doiue estre tenu re[n]fermé comme le corps, & ne sortir iamais dehors. Et me semble que Gorgias estoit plus raisonnable, qui vouloit que la renommee, non pas le visage, de la femme fust conuë de plusieurs' (Q3v).
101 'apres auoir refuté l'opinion de Thucydide qui veut comme confiner les femmes en vne solitude perpetuelle, [...] celles qui pour leur valeur ont merité que leur nom & exemple demeurast, afin de pouuoir estre ensuiui [...] non seulement par les autres femmes, ains aussi par la pluspart des hommes' (Q3v).

tion toward their countrey, a singular affection to their husbands, rare honestie, pudicitie, chastitie joined with a generous nature, which hath caused them, both to enterprise and also to execute heroique acts'.[102] Their virtuous deeds provide models to emulate, and proof that goodness will triumph through the exercise of stoic patience: 'hold this for certeine, that enterprises lawfull and necessarie, will sooner or later have good issue, to the shame and ruine of the wicked, but to the repose and quietnesse of all persons, who desire, seeke, and procure that which is good (Ss1v).[103]

Neither the figure of Paulina nor the gendered, rhetorically based opposition to tyranny exists in *Pandosto*. Shakespeare's delineation of women in *The Winter's Tale* benefits, as does Sidney's in the expanded *Arcadia*, from the Renaissance redefinition of erotic romance. Achilles Tatius in Leukippe, and Heliodorus in Charikleia, provide examples of eloquent, independent, and strong-willed women whose resourcefulness enables them to survive traumatic abuse. Even Longus endows Chloe with a complex awareness of irony, paradox and logical process, expressed through only apparently unadorned clarity.

The Greek novelists infuse their pairs of central characters with dedication to chastity, patience, tolerance during separation and temptation, and ingenuity and initiative to survive. In *The Winter's Tale*, Paulina's partnership with Antigonus, reminiscent of Parthenia's with Argalus, remains enriched by love even after he disappears. More significant to the process of reconciliation, it is Hermione's other half that, figuratively, has gone missing. 'Chaste' Hermione, a variant spelling of 'ermine', exhibits the ermine's extreme determination to resist contamination, or die.[104] Ubiquitously used during the Renaissance to signify an unsullied person,

---

102 'vne extreme haine de tyrannie & seruitude, vne charité ardante enuers la patrie, vne singuliere affection à leurs maris, l'honnesteté, la pudicité & chasteté coniointes auec vn naturel genereux qui leur ont fait entreprendre & executer des actes heroiques' (Q3v).

103 'tenir pour certain que les entreprises legitimes & necessaires auront bonne issue tost ou tard, à la honte & ruine des meschans, & au repos de toutes personnes qui desirent & procurent le bien' (Q3v).

104 On the names in the play, see W. Shakespeare, *The Winter's Tale*, ed. by J. H. P. Pafford, pp. 163–5, refined by C. B. Hardman, 'Shakespeare's *Winter's Tale* and the Stuart Golden Age', *Review of English Studies*, n.s., xlv (1994), 221–9, especially pp. 225–6, 'Hermione is, according to Renaissance dictionaries, a variant of Harmonia [...] harmony and concord'. On the ermine, see V. Skretkowicz, 'Devices and Their Narrative Function in Sidney's Arcadia', *Emblematica*, i (1986), 267-92; V. Skretkowicz, 'Sir Philip Sidney and the Elizabethan Literary Device', *Emblematica*, iii (1988), 171-9; C. H. Clough, 'Chivalry and Magnificence in the Golden Age of the Italian Renaissance', in *Chivalry in the Renaissance*, ed. by S. Anglo (Woodbridge, Suffolk: The Boydell Press, 1990), pp. 25–47 (p. 32, note 24 and Plate 2); and C. H. Clough, 'Federico da Montefeltro and the Kings of Naples: A Study in Fifteenth-century Survival', *Renaissance Studies*, vi (1992), 113–72 (pp. 158–60).

the motto associating the ermine with integrity and chastity is 'Malo mori quam foedari', translated by Sidney as 'Rather dead than spotted' (*NA*, p. 101).

Hermione's enforced disappearance, assisted by Paulina, is associated with Christian stoicism, patience and fidelity. Even her denunciation of Leontes exudes controlled hostility. The choice of gently sounding maternal imagery, and her inversions and disjointed insertions, studiously contrast with Leontes' acrimonious style:

> My second joy,
> And first fruits of my body, from his presence
> I am barred, like one infectious. My third comfort,
> Starred most unluckily, is from my breast,
> The innocent milk in it most innocent mouth,
> Haled out to murder; myself on every post
> Proclaimed a strumpet, with immodest hatred
> The childbed privilege denied, which 'longs
> To women of all fashion.
>
> (III.ii.94–102)

As his paramount display of Goulart's 'good issue' of women's virtuous enterprise, Shakespeare endows Paulina with outstanding rhetorical prowess. Setting aside Portia in masculine guise, Paulina is one of the earliest female literary advocates. Her exposure of Leontes' injustice illustrates the same Jacobean feminist politics that lie at the heart of Mary Sidney Wroth's *Urania*. Paulina challenges the nobles to exercise the advisory powers Leontes has revoked: 'good my lords, be second to me. / Fear you his tyrannous passion more, alas, / Than the Queen's life?' (II.iii.27–9). The answer is 'yes'. Antigonus slights his wife to avoid confronting Leontes: 'When she will take the rein I let her run, / But she'll not stumble' (II.iii.51–2). Paulina responds to Leontes' threat to burn her at the stake with a vituperative attack, calculatedly hinting at, but withdrawing from, a monarchomachist justification to overthrow him:

> It is an heretic that makes the fire,
> Not she which burns in't. I'll not call you tyrant;
> But this most cruel usage of your queen -
> Not able to produce more accusation
> Than your own weak-hinged fancy – something savours
> Of tyranny, and will ignoble make you,
> Yea, scandalous to the world.
>
> (II.iii.115–21)

At a loss to refute the damning appellation of 'tyrant', Leontes resorts to quibbling: 'Were I a tyrant, / Where were her life? She durst not call me so / If she did know me one' (II.iii.121–3). Shakespeare undermines Leontes' credibility during Hermione's trial, turning the rhythmic beauty of clause-based 'royal' style into a ranting series of run-on lines: 'Let us be cleared / Of being tyrannous since we so openly / Proceed in justice, which shall have due course / Even to the guilt or the purgation' (III.ii.4–7).

Shakespeare asserts the affinity between *The Winter's Tale* and *Pandosto* by retaining the shape and conclusion of Greene's well-known oracle:

> Hermione is chaste, Polixenes blameless, Camillo a true subject, Leontes a jealous tyrant, his innocent babe truly begotten, and the King shall live without an heir if that which is lost be not found. (III.ii.131–4)

'Pandosto treacherous' accepts the oracle's authority. But in a calculated exposure of Leontes' wrong-headedness, he rejects its divine authority: 'There is no truth at all i'th' oracle. / […] This is mere falsehood' (III.ii.138–9).

The loss of belief in oracles figures in philhellene Protestant discussions of the difference between the superstitious religions of ancient Greece and enlightened Christianity. Sidney, in his *Defence of Poetry*, cites Plutarch's 'De defectu oraculorum', 'of the cause why oracles ceased', as evidence that 'the very religion' and 'theology of that nation' included 'dreams' of 'many and many-fashioned gods' and oracles.[105] Goulart's 1582 summary before 'Des Oracles qui ont cessé, & pourquoy' (Ll4v), in an extended version in Holland, warns that 'les Oracles & presentations de certaine idoles' – 'oracles and predictions of certaine idoles' – are among the devil's 'instrumens', used 'tyranniser ses esclaues' – 'to tyrannize over his slaves' (Sssss6v). Sidney echoes Goulart's denunciation of oracles, reiterating that 'all the hurtful belief' in ancient religion was 'taken away' by the advent of Christianity. His main reservation is that, though the ancient poets 'had not the light of Christ', they nonetheless represented religion more faithfully 'than the philosophers, who, shaking off superstition, brought in atheism'.[106]

Like one of Sidney's wrong-headed philosophers, Leontes strikes an atheistic posture. Not until he recants – 'Apollo, pardon / My great profaneness 'gainst thine oracle' (III.ii.151–2) – does he learn from Paulina

---

105 Sir P. Sidney, *A Defence of Poetry*, in *Miscellaneous Prose of Sir Philip Sidney*, ed. by K. Duncan-Jones and J. van Dorsten, p. 108; see V. Skretkowicz, 'Sidney's *Defence of Poetry*, Henri Estienne, and Huguenot Nationalist Satire', pp. 18–19.

106 Sir P. Sidney, *A Defence of Poetry*, in *Miscellaneous Prose of Sir Philip Sidney*, ed. by K. Duncan-Jones and J. van Dorsten, p. 108.

that tyranny, not profanity, is his unpardonable sin. Entering to announce Hermione's death, she asks accusingly, 'What studied torments, tyrant, hast for me?' (III.ii.173). She identifies the flaws in his character, 'Thy tyranny, / Together working with thy jealousies –' (III.ii.177–8), demands that he accept responsibility for his actions, 'O think what they have done' (III.ii.180), and denounces him for what he is: 'O thou tyrant' (III.ii.205). Somewhat schematically, daily repentance on visiting 'the dead bodies of my queen and son' (III.ii.233) purges him of his calamitous ill-judgement.

In the new Sicilian government, Leontes' refashioned monarchy abjures gendered privilege. Shakespeare represents a reformed monarchic constitution on a consultative model, where the king accepts the pre-eminence of divinity and listens to his counsellors. Leontes, transformed into a Jacobean feminist, grants Paulina the role of adviser and custodian of the state. Weighing the advice on remarriage offered by Cleomenes, Dion and Paulina, he concludes, 'My true Paulina, / We shall not marry till thou bidd'st us' (V.i.82–3). Neither ancient erotic romance nor the court of James could boast an equivalent female counsellor.

Erotic closure

In *The Winter's Tale*, Shakespeare condenses many of the prognostications and omens of *Daphnis and Chloe* and *An Ethiopian Story* into a few lines. Like Greene, he hellenises the plot through the Delphic oracle, adding the Mariner's reading of the ominous sky and his warning about 'creatures / Of prey' (III.iii.12). Hermione's ghost appears to Antigonus, names 'Perdita' (III.iii.32) and prognosticates his death: 'thou ne'er shalt see / Thy wife Paulina more' (III.iii.34–5). The storm sets in, Antigonus flees a bear, and a herdsman finds the exposed infant.

Such a mannerist clustering of extraordinary events is compatible with the miniature erotic romance of Florizel and Perdita. Perdita's 'rustic garden' (IV.iv.85), where she is interviewed by Polixenes, differs in its intellectual priorities from Lamon's in *Daphnis and Chloe* (4.2; Reardon, p. 333), and Kleitophon's in *Leukippe and Kleitophon* (1.15; Reardon, p. 186). In these ancient gardens, the relationship between trees, plants and architectural features symbolises an integration between nature, humanity and the divine. Perdita limits her 'rustic garden', to a selection of herbs and non-hybridised flowers (IV.iv.74, 82), and there are no trees, fruit or vines to be propagated by Polixenes' grafting: 'we marry / A gentler scion to the wildest stock, / And make conceive a bark of baser kind / By bud of nobler race' (IV.iv.92–5). Perdita's denouncing 'carnations

and streaked gillyvors, / Which some call nature's bastards' (IV.iv.83–4),
natural hybrids propagated by slips, is a symbolic reminder of Leontes'
denying her a place in his genetic line: 'Shall I live on, to see this bastard
kneel / And call me father?' (II.iii.155–6) – 'carry / This female bastard
hence' (II.iii.174–5). The rhetorical contrast between Leontes' denuncia-
tory silencing of Hermione, and the loving Florizel's, 'When you speak,
sweet, / I'd have you do it ever' (IV.iv.136–7) could not be greater.

Perdita's innate qualities attract Florizel, and her feisty repartee with
Polixenes shows her independent disposition. The erotic romance
of Florizel and Perdita becomes absorbed into the resolution of the
Leontes–Hermione plot. Their anticipated wedding is suspended during
the dramatisation of Leontes' contrition, humility and reconciliation
with Hermione, and is unexpectedly provided with a mature double in
Camillo's marriage to Paulina. In a reversal of the traditional virginity
test, Paulina tests Leontes' reformation, from abuser to adoring partner,
before finally returning his wife to him. During the whole of Act V,
reminded and encouraged by Paulina, Leontes relives the tragedy caused
by his tyranny:

> If one by one you wedded all the world,
> Or from the all that are took something good
> To make a perfect woman, she you killed
> Would be unparalleled.
>
> (V.i.13–16)

The effectiveness of paraphrastically referring to Hermione, on whom she
has secretly attended, as 'she you killed', is measured by Leontes' resigned
echo: 'Killed? / She I killed? I did so' (V.i.16–17). Cured of his misogy-
nism, he endures sixteen years of Paulina's scourging tongue, and accepts
every accusing syllable.

The recognition scene, on which erotic romance endings depend, is
merely reported. To stage it would undermine the impact of the reunion
between Leontes with Hermione. In plain conversational prose, the
Second Gentleman marvels that this outcome is 'so like an old tale that
the verity of it is in strong suspicion' (V.ii.26). This imaginary construc-
tion belies the harsh reality that underlies the separations and emotional
reunions of European erotic romance, with their cryptic and symbolic
tokens of identification. Through 'the Lady Paulina's steward' (V.ii.24),
the Third Gentleman, Shakespeare contrasts the tokens from the Greco-
Roman comic model with those from Senecan tragedy. 'The mantle of
Queen Hermione's, her jewel about the neck of it' (V.ii.30–1) is pitted

against Antigonus's horrifying remains. When he is being eaten by a bear, Antigonus shouts out his name and rank, a desperate message to the Bohemian court: 'he cried to me for help, and said his name was Antigonus, a nobleman!' (III.iii.89–90). All that returns to Sicilia is his letters found with Perdita, 'which they know to be his character' (V.ii.32), and 'a handerkerchief and rings of his, that Paulina knows' (V.ii.59–60). Shakespeare then emphasises the difference between tyranny and responsible kingship by taking Perdita's appearance to be a token, not so much of identification as of his overall symbolic pattern. As if to ensure the stability of the state, she embodies physical evidence of the benefits of grafting the king to the queen: 'the majesty of the creature, in resemblance of the mother' (V.ii.32–3).

As Leontes marvels at the sculptural excellence of Hermione's statue and confronts his guilt, self-recrimination is replaced by silence. Paulina's ecphrastic descriptors follow Philostratus the elder to promote the illusion of figured marble, 'wrinkled' by 'our carver's excellence' (V.iii.28, 30). It looks as if 'it breathed, and that those veins / Did verily bear blood' (V.iii.64–5). The illusion, as Hermione approaches Leontes, resembles Heliodorus's description of a fully armed Persian horseman, 'like a man of steel or a hammer-worked statue come to life' (9.15; Reardon, p. 547).[107] Paralleling Parthenia's masque-like entrance as the Knight of the Tomb, neither the audience nor the fictional onlookers are party to the secret of Hermione's stoicism: 'I, / Knowing by Paulina that the oracle / Gave hope thou wast in being, have preserved / Myself to see the issue' (V.iii.126–9).

With confirmation of Antigonus's death and proof that Hermione is alive, the stylistic register switches to one of calmly dignified elegance.[108] Short phrases, parenthetical afterthoughts, assonance, consonance, alliteration and unusual diction, employed in unexpected order, combine with metaphor to create a new 'royal' resonance, as in Paulina's final speech:

> Go together,
> You precious winners all; your exultation
> Partake to everyone. I, an old turtle,
> Will wing me to some withered bough, and there

---

107 See also L. Barkan, '"Living Sculptures": Ovid, Michelangelo, and *The Winter's Tale*', *English Literary History*, xlviii (1971), 639–67.

108 Compare J. Richards, 'Social Decorum in *The Winter's Tale*', in *Shakespeare's Late Plays: New Readings*, ed. by J. Richards and J. Knowles (Edinburgh: Edinburgh University Press, 1999), pp. 75–91 (esp. pp. 83–8), citing J. D. Cox, *Shakespeare and the Dramaturgy of Power* (Princeton: Princeton University Press, 1989); cf. J. Smith, 'The Language of Leontes', *Shakespeare Quarterly*, xix (1968), 317–27.

My mate, that's never to be found again,
Lament till I am lost.

(V.iii.131–6)

This rhetorical shift prevails in the benevolent 'royal' tones of Leontes' closing speech: 'O peace, Paulina! / Thou shouldst a husband take by my consent, / As I by thine a wife' (V.iii.136–8).

Shakespeare ends this parable of personal and political reconciliation with Leontes celebrating his new political alliance with Polixenes, 'us, a pair of kings' (V.iii.147). Leontes organises the final procession to betoken a new era in gender partnership – 'Good Paulina, / Lead us from hence' (V.iii.152–3). Shakespeare's misogynistic tyrant is repentant, reformed and forgiven, led by a woman to whose wisdom he defers. The philhellene Protestant movement, absorbed into the centre of politics by a relatively benevolent, consultative monarch with an intention to unify Christian Europe, influences European erotic romance to assert the dignity and rights of women.

Cymbeline (1609–10), rhetorical style and the Catholic disjunction

Romantic love brings about political harmony in *An Ethiopian Story*. Renaissance parallels in *Arcadia*, followed by *Pandosto*, reflect the philhellene Protestant policy of encouraging consensual marriage to counter the dynastic power of Catholic Europe.

Cymbeline, King of Britain (1609–10), the last and most ambiguous of the 'histories' in *Mr. William Shakespeares Comedies, Histories, & Tragedies* (1623), represents a conflict between Italian Spain and Rome on one side, and Jacobean Britain on the other. The resolution includes the recognition of royal foundlings, Guiderius and Arviragus, and reunites the disguised and separated couple, Posthumus and Innogen. Their love-marriage precedes the action, defies authority, and catapults the opening *in medias res* into a report on Posthumus, and on his father's place in defending Britain from the Romans. Fate bringing Posthumus and Innogen together is not necessary to the theme of political reconciliation, but it does provide a festive, familial ambience to the closing sequence.

Erotic romance in *Cymbeline* makes palatable the topic of immediately pre-Christian British–Roman political conflict. The plot is virtually contemporaneous with the action of *Julius Caesar* and *Antony and Cleopatra*. Long identified with Augustus and the establishment of the Principate, in *Cymbeline* James also becomes the Belgic king, Cunobelinus or Cymbeline. Cymbeline's association with the ancient culture of the

Netherlands provides a double level of interpretation. In April 1609 James successfully promoted peace between Spain and the rebellious Protestant United Provinces, who broke away in 1567 under Lamoral, Count of Egmont (1522–68) and Philip de Montmorency, Count of Hoorn or Horn (1518?–68). But during the rest of 1609, James asserted, as in *Cymbeline*, Britain's Romano-Christian heritage, and its political independence from Papal authority: 'Although the victor, we submit to Caesar / And to the Roman empire' (V.vi.460–1).[109]

The ending of *Cymbeline* represents harmonious agreement among Christian states. King Cymbeline symbolises a Christianity untainted by dynastic and Papal politics.[110] In this respect, his Britain bears no more affinity to historical fact than does Basilius's Arcadia, which ignores centuries of Turkish domination of Greece. Cymbeline's generosity towards Rome parallels Hydaspes' settlement with Oroondates in *An Ethiopian Story*, but it also reflects a real political issue. On the death of Elizabeth I in 1603, Pope Clement VIII (1592–1605) required Catholics in England to ensure a Catholic succession. In the eyes of Pope Paul V (1605–21), 'James I stood condemned as a tyrant by usurpation'.[111]

Like Henri IV, James I ascended the throne denounced, rather than approved, by the Church of Rome. He used his first speech to Parliament, 19 March 1603, to defend his claim to the English crown,[112] and to associate the political responsibility of the divine monarch with the transparency of plain style:

> it becommeth a King, in my opinion, to vse no other Eloquence then plainenesse and sinceritie. By plainenesse I meane, that his Speeches should be so cleare and voyd of all ambiguitie, that they may not be throwne [i.e., 'twisted'], nor rent asunder in contrary sences like the old Oracles of the Pagan gods … That as farre as a King is in Honour erected aboue any of his Subiects, so farre should he striue in sinceritie to be aboue them all, and that his tongue should be euer the trew Messenger of his heart: and this sort of Eloquence may you euer assuredly looke for at my hands.[113]

James defines the plain style as representing the honesty and responsible government called for by the *Vindiciae, contra tyrannos*. It did nothing to

109 Cf. E. Jones, 'Stuart Cymbeline', *Essays in Criticism*, xi (1961), 84–99; H. Neville Davies, 'Jacobean *Antony and Cleopatra*', *Shakespeare Studies*, xvii (1985), 123–58.

110 Cf. V. Skretkowicz, 'Shakespeare, Henri IV, and the Tyranny of Royal Style', in *Challenging Humanism: Essays in Honor of Dominic Baker-Smith*, ed. by T. Hoenselaars and A. F. Kinney, p. 207.

111 R. Mousnier, *The Assassination of Henry IV*, p. 171.

112 James VI and I, *Political Writings*, ed. by J. P. Sommerville (Cambridge: Cambridge University Press, 1994), pp. 134–5.

113 James VI and I, *Political Writings*, p. 146.

convince Roman Catholics that he should be spared. The papist-inspired monarchomachia of the Gunpowder Plot of 1605 led directly to James's demand for the oath of allegiance as a bulwark against papist threats. His liberal view of Christian Europeanism, however, did not exclude recognition of Rome as the centre of European Christianity. Anne of Denmark's Catholicism, adopted when she was nineteen, four years after their marriage in 1593, posed no threat.[114]

James's objection was to papal insistence on political domination, which he vociferously denounced in *A Premonition to All Most Mighty Monarchies, Kings, Free Princes, and States of Christendom* (1609). There he pressed home the distinction between church and state. Echoing the stance taken by the French king and the nationalist French Catholic Gallican church,[115] on 18 August 1609 James sent a message to Paul V through Henri IV of France's papal ambassador. Here he made it known that he 'was prepared to recognise the Pope as first bishop and head of the Church in spiritual matters provided the Pope would renounce his power to depose kings'. The Pope examined his conscience. It was impossible to agree such a radical change in canon law. To do so would make him a heretic.[116]

James's Protestantism was incompatible with papal practice in both the spiritual and temporal (i.e., political) realms. Doctrinal differences were posited by Cardinal Jacques Davy Du Perron, who as Bishop of Evreux had been instrumental in persuading Henri IV to adopt Catholicism in July 1593. The penultimate paragraph of Du Perron's *A Letter Written From Paris, by the Lord Cardinall of Peron, to Monsr. Casaubon in England* (1612) urges James to reform his heretical ways and become 'a Mediatour for the reconciliation[n] of the Church' (D2v). In a reply subscribed 9 November 1611 (G3), James uses *The Answere of Master Isaac Casaubon to the Epistle of the most illustrious, and most reuerend Cardinall Peron* (1612) to admonish Rome for not acknowledging the doctrinal validity of the Church of England:

114 M. M. Meikle, 'A Meddlesome Princess: Anna of Denmark and Scottish Court Politics, 1589–1603', in *The Reign of James VI*, ed. by J. Goodare and M. Lynch (East Linton: Tuckwell Press, 2000), pp. 126–40 (p. 138).

115 See J. Powis, 'Gallican Liberties and the Politics of Later Sixteenth-century France', *The Historical Journal*, xxvi (1983), 515–30. On the post-tridentine debate about the relative jurisdictions of king and pope, see T. I. Crimando, 'Two French Views of the Council of Trent', *The Sixteenth Century Journal*, xix, no. 2 (1988), 169–86. The *coventional* Gallican Church was not formally established till 1682, when French Catholics, in the Declaration of the Clergy of France, reasserted the rights of the king of France over Papal authority.

116 R. Mousnier, *The Assassination of Henry IV*, p. 176.

the Church of England is so farre from forsaking the ancient Catholike Church […] that she departeth not from the faith of the Church of Rome, in any point wherein that Church agreeth with the ancient Catholike […] His Maiestie grants, that his Church hath departed from many points of that doctrine, and discipline which the Pope of Rome now stifly defendeth: but they doe not thinke this to be a reuolting from the Catholike Church, but rather a returning to the ancient Catholike faith, which in the Romane Church by new deuices hath been manifoldly, and strangely deformed. (C3v–C4)

Casaubon closes with James's firm and definitive rejection of Du Perron's gentle sophistry. His offers of compromise have been spurned by a recalcitrant, aggressive opposition, which he accuses of self-interest:

his Maiestie calling to minde the daily writings and practises of your men, is now […] stedfastly perswaded that through their dealings there remaine no meanes or hope of reconciliation. For they are resolued to defend all; and not to grow better, or by the serious reformation of things depraued to winne the mindes of the godly. In which resolution as long as they persist, and will not yeeld one iot to antiquitie, and truth, his Maiestie professeth once for all that he regardeth them not, neither will hee euer haue any communion with the Church of Rome. (G3)

True to his word, James followed the debate in France, from 1615 working with Pierre Du Moulin, a leader of the Protestant church in France. Educated at Cambridge, where during 1590–93 he served Roger Manners, fifth Earl of Rutland,[117] Du Moulin polishes James's French in his further attack on Du Perron, *Declaration du Serenissime Roy Iaques I. Roy de la Grand' Bretaigne France et Irlande, Defenseur de la Foy. Pour le Droit des Rois & independance de leurs Couronnes, Contre La Harangue De L'Illustrissime Cardinal du Perron prononcée en la chambre du tiers Estat le XV. de Ianuier 1615. A Londres, Par Iehan Bill Imprimeur du Roy. M.DC.XV. Auec priuilege de sa Majesté.*[118]

James maintained the Gallican–Anglican position he enunciated in 1609. During that year, when James was the principal political leader of Protestant Europe, his sparring with the Pope appears to inform the bivalent ending of *Cymbeline*. On 14 May 1610, Henri IV of France (Henri of Navarre) was assassinated, an act justified by the Jesuit interpretation of monarchomachia.[119] James, as sole reigning Protestant monarch, found

117 Brian G. Armstrong and Vivienne Larminie, 'Du Moulin, Pierre (1568–1658)', *Oxford Dictionary of National Biography* (Oxford: Oxford University Press, 2004).
118 Du Moulin describes his role in the 'Advertissement' (Q4) at the end of the volume.
119 See P. Du Coignet, *Anti-Coton, or A Refutation of Cottons Letter Declaratorie: lately*

himself isolated. Even though the polarisation revealed by Du Perron made doctrinal reconciliation impossible, the potential for familial Protestant–Catholic bonding recurs in *The Tempest* (1611). Like Leontes' Sicilia, Alonso's Kingdom of Naples is a Spanish Habsburg state. And, like Polixenes' Bohemia which it borders on to, Prospero's Duchy of Milan is part of the Holy Roman Empire, at one remove from close papal control. Within a decade, Mary Sidney Wroth would reinvent Sicily and Naples as centres of European Protestantism.

Conclusion

Shakespeare's politicised adaptations of European erotic romance identify him with the perpetually evolving and responsive principles of the philhellene Protestants. He parallels their rhetorical distinctions between the high moral and ethical standards of plain speakers, and the tyrannical instincts of those who exercise a pretentious royal style. Determined by tone and register, this does not preclude either simple or complex stylistic elegance, employed with the clarity of Heliodorus and Plutarch, principally through the medium of Amyot and North. Shakespeare combines Plutarch's moralised exemplary characterisation and historical legends in cautionary tales, transposing these into settings more clearly associated with Greco-Roman erotic romance and its Renaissance derivatives. But no English author turns the genre to such extravagantly personal and overtly political use, once again to support the evolving philhellene Protestant movement, as Mary Sidney Wroth does in *The Countess of Montgomery's Urania*.

---

directed to the Queene Regent, for the Apologizing of the Iesuites Doctrine, touching the killing of kings. A booke, in which it is proued that the Iesuites are guiltie, and were the Authors of the late execrable Parricide, commited vpon the Person of the French King, Henry the fourth, of happy memorie. To which is added, A Supplication of the Vniuersitie of Paris, for the preuenting of the Iesuites opening their Schooles among them: in which their King-killing Doctrine is also notably discouered, and confuted. Both translated out of the French, by G. H. Together with the Translators animaduersions vpon Cottons Letter (1611).

7

Mary Sidney Wroth's *Urania*

Philhellene Protestant erotic propaganda

In *Les raisons de la monarchie* (1551), Guillaume Postel argued for the establishment of a universal Christian monarchy. Its spiritual leader would be the Pope, its secular head the King of France, whose title of 'Rex Christianissimus' descended from Clovis through Charlemagne.[1] Work towards this goal of Christian unity, frustrated during Henri III's reign by the Wars of Religion, was revived by Henri IV (Henri III of Navarre). His efforts were undermined by the Guises in France, by Philip II in Spain and by Pope Sixtus V (1585–90), who in 1585 excommunicated Navarre, depriving him of his kingdom and barring him from the throne of France.

Although Navarre was related to Henri III through the male line only in the twenty-second degree,[2] Huguenot propagandist publications defended the legitimacy of his claim. The pictorial title-page of *Carolus Magnus Redivivus* (1592), by Johannes Wilhelm Stucki of Zurich, boasts that 'Charlemagne Lives Again, that is, A Comparison of Charlemagne […] with Henry the great, the most eminent King of France and Navarre'.[3] The subtitle and running-title affirm Henri's role as 'Rex

---

1 Cf. R. E. Asher, *National Myths in Renaissance France: Francus, Samothes and the Druids* (Edinburgh: Edinburgh University Press, 1993), p. 55, and F. A. Yates, *Astraea: The Imperial Theme in the Sixteenth Century* (London: Routledge & Kegan Paul, 1975; repr. Harmondsworth: Peregrine Books, 1977), pp. 121–6 (esp. 'The Idea of the French Monarchy', pp. 122–3).

2 R. Mousnier, *The Assassination of Henry IV*, trans. by J. Spencer (London: Faber and Faber, 1973), p. 106.

3 J. W. Stucki, *Carolus Magnus Redivivus, hoc est, Caroli Magni Germanorum, Gallorum, Italorum, et aliarum gentium monarchae potentissimi, cum Henrico M. Gallorum & Nauarrorum Rege florentissimo comparatio* (1592). The title-page is reproduced in V. Skretkowicz, 'Shakespeare, Henri IV, and the Tyranny of Royal Style', in *Challenging Humanism: Essays in Honor of Dominic Baker-Smith*, ed. by T. Hoenselaars and A. F. Kinney (Newark: University of Delaware Press, 2005), p. 188.

Christianissimus': 'Carolus Magnus Redivivus in Christo, Vivat, Valeat, Vincat' – 'Charlemagne lives again in Christ, he will live, he will be powerful, he will triumph'. In following year, 1593, Navarre achieved a precarious respectability by re-adopting Catholicism. He was crowned in 1594, absolved, officially proclaimed 'Rex Christianissimus' in September 1595, assassinated 14 May 1610 and succeeded by his son, Louis XIII.[4]

Like Henri IV, James I ascended the throne in 1603 denounced, rather than approved, by the Church of Rome. A concerted effort by James ensured that, through intermarriage, familial relationships among high-ranking members of the Protestant League would shortly include the English monarchy. The vehicle for James's success was Frederick V (1596–1632), the son of Stucki's eighteen-year-old dedicatee, Frederick IV (1574–1610), Elector Palatine of the Rhine. In January 1592, on the death of his Calvinist uncle and guardian, John Casimir, Count Palatine of Pfalz-Simmern, Hubert Languet's employer and Philip Sidney's friend, Frederick IV assumed control over the Palatinate. Nurtured in the dynastic politics of Calvinism, Frederick IV married William of Orange's daughter, Louisa Juliana. In 1613, when their son, the Elector Palatine Frederick V, married James I's daughter Elizabeth, Mary Sidney Wroth's father Robert was one of four ambassadors appointed to escort the newlyweds into Bohemia.[5]

In 1625, while Sidney Wroth was still working on *Urania*, James I's son, Charles I, married Henriette-Marie, daughter of Henri IV and sister of Louis XIII. But where real kings toiled in vain to resolve the Christian divide, the fictional politics of Mary Sidney Wroth's *The Countess of Montgomery's Urania* overcomes many of the obstacles to fulfilling the philhellene Protestant aspiration of European integration.[6] The perspective she represents is not unlike that of King James, to whom Protestants were the only true Christians, and Catholics heretical and tyrannical usurpers.

---

4 F. A. Yates, *Astraea: The Imperial Theme in the Sixteenth Century*, pp. 209–11; R. Mousnier, *The Assassination of Henry IV*, pp. 111–15.

5 The others were the Earls of Lennox and Arundel, and Sir John Harrington; see M. V. Hay, *The Life of Robert Sidney, Earl of Leicester (1563–1626)* (Washington: Folger Shakespeare Library, 1984), p. 218.

6 References are to *The First Part of The Countess of Montgomery's Urania*, ed. by J. A. Roberts, medieval and Renaissance Texts and Studies, vol. 140; Renaissance English Text Society, 7th ser., xvii (Binghamton, NY: Center for medieval and Early Renaissance Studies, 1995); and to *The Second Part of The Countess of Montgomery's Urania*, ed. by J. A. Roberts, S. Gossett and J. Mueller, medieval and Renaissance Texts and Studies, vol. 211; Renaissance English Text Society, 7th ser., xxiv (AZ: Arizona Centre for medieval and Renaissance Studies, 1999). References in the text to *The First Part* are preceded by the Roman numeral 'I' and to *The Second Part* by the Roman numeral 'II'.

Sidney Wroth's allegorised political fantasy conjures up a vision of a Protestant Europe coming piecemeal, over three generations, under the control of the Sidney–Herbert families. The eldest of the eleven children of Robert Sidney and Barbara Gamage, Mary Sidney Wroth (18 October 1586/87–1651/53) was born into the complex political military activities of the Sidney–Herbert (Pembroke)–Devereux (Essex) circle. Her intellectual environment dictates her ready acceptance of feudal wealth, dynastic power, and literary, musical and dramatic achievement. An ardent feminist, in *Urania* she represents an influential female presence in each of these spheres. Her heroines celebrate triumphs over a parade of tyrants. Be they heads of state, fathers, suitors or lovers, all of Sidney Wroth's defeated villains have been dedicated to the abuse of women, undermining their sense of personal value and identity.

In *Urania*, Sidney Wroth loosely represents her parents as the King and Queen of Morea, a Greek state in the Peloponnesus that includes both Arcadia and the city of Corinth, where the king keeps his court (I.456, 488, II.406). In portraying the king's determination to restore the crowns of Macedonia and Albania to their rightful claimants (I.116), Sidney Wroth alludes to her father's assisting the beleaguered Protestants of France and the Netherlands, where his military career began in 1585. In 1589, he followed his brother Philip, killed in action in 1586, as Governor of Flushing. Robert Sidney senior instilled a sense of responsibility and leadership in his sons. William, knighted in 1610, died in 1612. Robert (1595–1677)[7] became Knight of the Bath in 1610. Following the return of Flushing to the States of Zealand in 1616, Robert junior took command of the English regiment that remained to serve under the Dutch.

Morea's campaign is led by his 'Nephew' (II.27), Amphilanthus of Naples. This allegorical characterisation forms Sidney Wroth's public endorsement of her cousin, William Herbert, third Earl of Pembroke (1580–1630), during a difficult time in his career. While serving in different royal households, he and his brother Philip enjoyed, and then fell from, the King's favour. William, like Sidney Wroth, held office in the court of Anne of Denmark:

> As she had her *Favourites* in one place, the King had his in another. She loved the elder Brother, the Earl of *Pembroke*; he the younger, whom he made Earl of *Mountgomery*, and Knight of the *Garter:* But either not finding

---

7 See I. Atherton, 'Sidney, Robert, Second Earl of Leicester (1595–1677)', *Oxford Dictionary of National Biography* (Oxford: Oxford University Press, 2004); cf. R. Shephard, 'The Political Commonplace Books of Sir Robert Sidney', *Sidney Journal*, xxi, no.1 (2003), 1–30 (p. 7).

him suitable to his *humour*, or *affections*, or seeing another *object* more delightful, his *fancy* ran with a violent *stream* upon a young Gentleman, who had neither Parts nor Birth to entertain such a current. His name was *Robert Car*, born about *Edenburgh* in *Scotland*, descended from Gentry of that name, a young man about twenty years of Age.[8]

Herbert, who saw little or no military action, maintained his parents' Puritan orientation. He led a spirited campaign, vindicated in the concessions gained in the parliament of 1624, against James I's rapprochement with Spain and his pro-Catholic legislation.[9] During the early 1620s, when the King recruited like-minded pro-Spanish courtiers, the philhellene Protestant programme was regarded as a politically unsustainable anachronism: 'no more was *William* Earl of *Pembroke* [...] a man that merited the highest imployment'.[10]

Sidney Wroth was left financially embarrassed when her husband, Robert Wroth, died on 14 March 1614. Aged twenty-seven or twenty-eight, and mother of one-month-old James (1614–16), she came under Herbert's protection.[11] Their patroness, Queen Anne of Denmark, died on 2 March 1619.[12] Her funeral on 13 May, in which Robert Sidney, William Herbert and Sidney Wroth took an official part, marked the end of many a glittering career.[13] The certainty of redundancy, anticipated by Anne of Denmark's prolonged illness, freed Sidney Wroth to construct her fanciful

8 A. Wilson, *The History of Great Britain, Being the Life and Reign of King James the First, Relating to what passed from his first Access to the Crown, till his Death* (1653), H3v [p. 54], noted by Roberts in I.liii, 777; cf. H. Neville Davies, 'Jacobean Antony and Cleopatra', *Shakespeare Studies*, xvii (1985), 123–58.

9 On Herbert, see I.xlv–xlvii, and V. Stater, 'Herbert, William, Third Earl of Pembroke (1580–1630)', *Oxford Dictionary of National Biography* (Oxford: Oxford University Press, 2004). For the political context, see K. Fincham, 'Abbot, George (1562–1633)', *Oxford Dictionary of National Biography* (Oxford: Oxford University Press, 2004).

10 A. Wilson, *The History of Great Britain, Being the Life and Reign of King James the First* (1653), T4v [p. 144].

11 I.xlv–xlvii, lxxxi, lxxxiv, lxxxviii; *The Poems of Lady Mary Wroth*, ed. by J. A. Roberts (Baton Rouge: Louisiana State University Press, 1992), pp. 23–5. Their relationship is documented in J. A. Roberts, '"The Knott Never to Bee Untide": The Controversy Regarding Marriage in Mary Sidney Wroth's *Urania*', in *Reading Mary Sidney Wroth: Representing Alternatives in Early Modern England*, ed. by N. Miller and G. Waller (Knoxville: University of Tennessee Press, 1991), pp. 109–32, esp. pp. 117–23; G. Waller, *The Sidney Family Romance: Mary Sidney Wroth, William Herbert, and the Early Modern Construction of Gender* (Detroit: Wayne State University Press, 1993); M. G. Brennan, '"A SYDNEY, though un-named": Ben Jonson's Influence in the Manuscript and Print Circulation of Lady Mary Wroth's Writings', *Sidney Journal*, xvii, no. 1 (1999), 31–52 (p. 46).

12 M. M. Meikle and H. Payne, 'Anne (1574–1619)', *Oxford Dictionary of National Biography* (Oxford: Oxford University Press, 2004).

13 *The Poems of Lady Mary Wroth*, ed. by J. A. Roberts, p. 27.

political and social alternatives.[14]

Sidney Wroth seems to have begun the first part of *Urania* in 1618 or 1619, continuing into 1621.[15] The work was entered in the Stationers' Register on 13 July 1621 and published towards the end of the year. By 1626, the year her father Robert Sidney remarried and died,[16] she had made considerable progress on the Second Part, which she left unfinished.[17] Throughout this politically and personally contentious allegory, Sidney Wroth emulates the encoded style of the earlier 'forward' Protestants.[18] Accepting the artful theatricality and role-playing of the court, she understands precisely the degree of obscurity and ambiguity necessary to prick consciences, but also to preserve confidentiality. She avoids libellous reportage by dressing much of the action in an artificial, masque-like ambience, assigning multiple identifications to real people in the manner of Spenser's *Faerie Queene*.[19]

Concealing autobiography and scandal behind a dense multiplicity of improbable plots and magical transformations, *Urania* becomes a cynical prose version of the Jacobean court masque. As in *Cymbeline*, the contrasting settings of court and rugged countryside contain encoded personal allegories, portraying the psychoses, dilemmas and political aspirations of Sidney Wroth's extensive family. Significantly and ahistorically, she elevates them all. Virtually all the positively portrayed characters in *Urania* are kings and queens, or kings and queens in waiting. They reflect the political vision promoted in *Urania* of a blend of responsible monarchies operating within an elected Holy Roman Empire. Their goal is to achieve a mythical social harmony, conjoined with pan-European Protestantism, stoicism and enlightened respect for the education, achievements and rights of women.

There is no reason that Sidney Wroth might not have known the stage version of *Cymbeline*, which represents James I's aspiration to become the foremost Christian leader of Europe.[20] While including ample ambiguous tributes to the royal family's favourites, Sidney Wroth subversively

---

14 Cf. *The Poems of Lady Mary Wroth*, ed. by J. A. Roberts, p. 31.

15 I.xvii.

16 M. V. Hay, *The Life of Robert Sidney*, pp. 228–9.

17 I.xvii–xviii. G. Alexander, *Writing After Sidney: The Literary Response to Sir Philip Sidney, 1586–1640* (Oxford: Oxford University Press, 2006), pp. 318–31, examines the rhetorical effect of Sidney Wroth's studied interruptions and incompletions.

18 See B. Worden, *The Sound of Virtue: Philip Sidney's Arcadia and Elizabethan Politics* (New Haven: Yale University Press, 1996).

19 I.lxix–xcviii, c–ci.

20 I.xlvii; K. Fincham and P. Lake, 'The Ecclesiastical Policy of King James I', *Journal of British Studies*, xxiv (1985), 169–207 (p. 182).

advances Herbert as emperor in opposition to James. Amphilanthus is
unashamedly portrayed as the most powerful, attractive, intelligent and
sensitive nobleman in the old world.[21] His mission is to resolve the polit-
ical embroilments of a fairytale, magic-infested Europe and Middle East,
and to unite their many disparate states. He is awarded the title King
of the Romans 'by the Emperour and the other Princes' for killing the
usurping Duke of Saxony (I.45, 597) while assisting the Pope. He later
achieves universal secular power as the elected Holy Roman Emperor, to
whom, historically, even the Pope deferred.[22]

Sidney Wroth's imaginary construction removes the stranglehold of
the Catholic Austrian Habsburgs on the office of Holy Roman Emperor.
In reality, despite the efforts of Sidney, Herbert and other philhellene
Protestants, following Emperor Mathias's death on 20 March 1619,[23] the
Catholic status quo was bolstered by the election on 28 August 1619 of
Ferdinand II. James I's conciliatory response was to abandon his mili-
tant Protestant son-in-law, Frederick of Bohemia. But, by allegorising
philhellene Protestant propaganda in this way, *Urania*, like Mary Sidney
Herbert's *Antonius*, functions as an encoded call to muster military and
political support for the beleaguered remnants of the Protestant League.

Disjunction at the throne of love

The politics of *Urania* are subsumed within Sidney Wroth's intimate reve-
lations of her unfulfilled devotion to Herbert, and his intermittent but
intense feelings for her. Pamphilia, 'absolute love' (also a female Roman
poet and historian)[24] is the oldest daughter of the king and queen of Morea
– Robert Sidney's fantasy kingdom. She dotes on her inconstant cousin
Amphilanthus, the son of her aunt, the elderly Queen of Naples – Mary
Sidney Herbert. Beginning at the pictorial title-page and ending with a
sequence of 103 sonnets and lyrics, *Pamphilia to Amphilanthus*, the 1621
Urania celebrates Sidney Wroth's adoration of Herbert, and could not
have been published – or possibly even written – without his approval.

The work explores Pamphilia's admiration for Amphilanthus's success
as a single-minded military and political leader, and her emotional devas-

21 I.lxxxvi; cf. M. E. Lamb, *Gender and Authorship in the Sidney Circle* (Madison: Univer-
   sity of Wisconsin Press, 1990), pp. 185–8.
22 I.xlii-xliv, 441, 463.
23 Cf. I.xli–xlii.
24 On Pamphilia as a place-name, see S. T. Cavanagh, *Cherished Torment: The Emotional
   Geography of Lady Mary Wroth's Urania* (Pittsburgh: Duquesne University Press, 2001),
   pp. 22–5.

tation at his inability, or disinclination, to commit to a steadfast relation-
ship. The multiple views of the title-page illustrate one of the high points
of their fictive love, and signals *Urania*'s dependence on masque-like
stage illusion. Readers first view Pamphilia and Amphilanthus through a
baroque four-pillared archway – a proscenium arch – as they walk towards
a triple-arched bridge and triple-arched temple, the spell-binding Palace
or Throne of Love. They progress into a carefully groomed landscape,
described as 'some Magicall work' that 'seem'd as if it hung in the ayre,
the Trees, Fountains, and all sweet delicacies being discerned through it'
(I.48). Pamphilia turns towards Amphilanthus (and the reader). His left
arm is around her waist, his right gestures towards the bridge, a mirror-
image of the text, where Pamphilia's 'left Glove was off, holding the King
by the hand' (I.169). The engraver, Simon van de Passe,[25] may simply have
copied the original sketch without reversing it.

Adapting the 'Arch of Loyal Lovers' in Book IV of *Amadis de Gaule*,[26]
Sidney Wroth idealises constancy and heroism. Pamphilia and Amphilan-
thus approach the bridge with its Towers of Desire (Cupid), Love (Venus),
and Constancy. The Tower of Constancy 'can bee entred by none, till
the valiantest Knight, with the loyallest Lady come together, and open
that gate, when all these Charmes shal have conclusion' (I.48–9). In *The
moste excellent and pleasaunt Booke, entituled: The treasurie of Amadis of
Fraunce*, translated by Thomas Paynell (1567), in an excerpt from Book
XII, Queene Sidonia uses noticeably similar diction in her letter to King
Amadis of France and Oriana:

> *Agesilan,* with my daughter *Diana* for hys spouse, whome hee had woonne
> alreadie by the fayhfulnesse and constancie of his loue, […] set at libertie,
> and out of prison the infant *Dom Rosaran*, and the duchesse of *Bauire,*
> in the inchaunted Towre, whose prisoners they shoulde haue remayned
> without comming forth, vntill they two the most accomplished and perfit
> in fayhfulnesse of loue, may giue them the wayes and meane, and to vs the
> consolation of the heauinesse that we suffer by their absence, the which
> shall endure vntill the excellent King and Queene of *Englande*, be entered
> into the inchaunted Castell, deliuering them out of prison, to the great
> glorie of their fayhfull loues, and to the consolation of vs all.[27]

The conscious overlap of circumstances and superlatives from this
familiar story increases the grandeur of the central characters. For Sidney

---

25 On the relationships between the Sidneys and the de Passe family, see M. G. Brennan,
    'Robert Sidney, King James I and Queen Anna: The Politics of Intimate Service (1588–
    1607)', *Sidney Journal*, xxv, no. 1–2 (2007), 3–30 (pp. 12–14).
26 I.xvii, xxix.
27 Qq4 in the 1572 edition.

Wroth clearly associates Amphilanthus with Amadis, King of Britain, and Pamphilia with his beloved wife, Oriana.

Pictured between the towers, Sidney Wroth's hero and heroine 'passed to the last Tower, where *Constancy* stood holding the keyes, which Pamphilia tooke; at which instant *Constancy* vanished, as metamorphosing her self into her breast' (I.169).[28] Pictorial ellipsis is completed by the text: Pamphilia, embodying constancy, releases the ladies who previously failed the test, Amphilanthus the knights. The throne is dispensed with like a contemporary trick stage prop: 'Then did the musick play againe, and in that time the Pallace and all vanished' (I.170).

Idyllic as this moment seems, the distinctions drawn by this test accentuate the mismatch that dictates virtually every strand of the plot. Unlike Leukippe's and Melite's decisive virginity and lie-detection tests, this Throne is not a touchstone upon which to prove either chastity or fidelity. Pamphilia's 'loyallest', that is, most constant but not at all brave, opposes Amphilanthus's 'valliantest'. For he is rightly accused of being 'matchlesse in all virtues, except thy love; for inconstancy, was, and is the onely touch thou hast [...] thou art constant to love [...] but variety is thy staine' (I.362). The emphatic personality difference dividing them absolutely opposes the instinctive erotic and intellectual compatibility that bonds and drives the characters in Greco-Roman erotic romance, and its derivatives. This is not a perfect love-match, prevented from fulfilment by external forces that test the character of the protagonists, but ending in long anticipated marriage. As if to accentuate that historical considerations rather than literary formulae govern the allegorical relationships between her principal characters, Sidney Wroth converts Urania's false start with Parselius into a fulfilling, long-lasting romantic attachment with Steriamus.[29]

The principal thrust of *Urania* is to analyse Pamphilia's enduring but unsatisfactorily enunciated love for Amphilanthus. This is set against his focus on political leadership and related distractions. His feelings may be genuine when experienced, and his professions of love earnest when expressed. But Sidney Wroth portrays Amphilanthus as a chivalric international superhero rather than a faithful lover, and Pamphilia as laudably, albeit uncontrollably, obsessed. Perspectives on their relationship,

28 Cf. I.lxi, 'From this point onward, Pamphilia is free to redefine constancy'. See E. Beilin, '"The Onely Perfect Vertue": Constancy in Mary Wroth's *Pamphilia to Amphilanthus*', *Spenser Studies: A Renaissance Poetry Annual*, ii (1981), 229–45; M. E. Lamb, *Gender and Authorship in the Sidney Circle*, pp. 163–7; and G. Alexander, *Writing After Sidney: The Literary Response to Sir Philip Sidney, 1586–1640*, pp. 303–5.
29 I.lxxvii–lxxviii.

expressed by various narrators, ensure that the misery wrought by their many failures intensifies moments of happiness beyond due proportion. An injection of realism in the vein of Cervantes' *Don Quixote* (1605, 1615) suggests that such transient pleasures may ultimately be the illusory products of hopeful minds.[30] But such is the sustained impression of grief resulting from unreciprocated, one-sided relationships that any relief experienced by the characters is welcomed by the reader.

Pamphilia and Amphilanthus, like virtually all the lovers in *Urania*, are denied the fictional reassurance afforded the characters in Greco-Roman types of erotic romance. The vows exchanged by Theagenes and Charikleia may be emulated by Amadis and Oriana,[31] and even by Pyrocles and Philoclea. But all hopes of fulfilling Amphilanthus and Pamphilia's *de praesanti* marriage (II.45) are thoroughly undermined by suspicion of inconstancy, reinforced by reports of disloyalty.

A French story

Combining the transient qualities of masque, and doubling (even tripling) her personae through a Heliodoran-style enfolded narrative, Sidney Wroth flags Pamphilia's tale of Lindamira as autobiographical allegory. Pamphilia, 'faigning it to be written in a French Story' (I.499) contained in a 'Booke' she has read, reminds Dorolina that 'what succeeded all this' is 'your fortune, deare Dorolina, and mine' (I.501). And Dorolina rightly concludes that it is 'some thing more exactly related then a fixion' (I.505).

Such cryptic, masque-like allusions to synonymity create a new dimension to European erotic romance. Deciphering what truth may lie behind these names is intended as a provocative challenge to contemporary readers. Lindamira ('behold her beauty') is the eldest daughter of Bersindor, 'a brave young Lord of the Ile of France' and his wife, 'a great Heyre in little Brittany' (I.499). By adding a French dimension to the semi-transparency of this incomplete anagram for Robert Sidney, Lord Lisle, Sidney Wroth incorporates a rare insight into Jacobean racism. The Sidney-Gamage marriage fulfilled the philhellene Protestant commitment to intermarriage among families of French, preferably Norman, origin. As Philip Sidney declared to Languet, he was 'strong in awareness of my French heritage'.[32]

---

30 Cf. I.xxv.
31 I.xxix.
32 J. M. Osborn, *Young Philip Sidney 1572–1577* (New Haven: Yale University Press, 1972), p. 146.

The growth pattern of this Huguenot-supporting community is described in Pamphilia's condensed history. France was once 'divided into severall Kingdomes' and included 'severall Nations'

> which spake different languages, some of these had Kings, the others only Princes; but in successe of time, all came happily under the rule and government of one King, care onely had then by marriages to make a perpetuall union, which onely length of time could doe. (I.499)

In Pamphilia's tale, Lindamira harbours a discreet love for a courtier, 'likewise favoured by the Queene Mother' (I.499), a jealous widow. Anne of Denmark favoured William Herbert, and may have had misgivings about a potential adulterous relationship with Sidney Wroth. However, as is evident from texts as widely ranging as Marlowe's *Massacre at Paris* (1594) and Dudley Digges's *The Compleat Ambasssador* (1655), the term 'Queen Mother' was almost exclusively reserved for the widowed Catherine de Médicis. The passage is reminiscent of earlier philhellene Protestant satires demonising the French court, and contains a spikiness associated with Huguenot treatise, possibly by Henri Estienne, *Discours merveilleux de la vie, actions et deportemens de Catherine de Medicis, Royne mere, Auquel sont recitez les moyens qu'elle a tenu pour usurper le gouvernement de Royaume de France, & ruiner l'estat d'iceluy* (1575) – 'a marvellous discourse on the life, actions and behaviour of Catherine de Médicis, Queen Mother, in which are rehearsed the means she has used for usurping the government of the Kingdom of France, and wrecking the state'.[33] Although the term 'widow', referring to a 'wife separated from or deserted by her husband', is recorded from 1461 but not again until 1725,[34] Sidney Wroth may wish to taint Anne of Denmark through this association with the French queen.

Exposed by an envious courtesan, Lindamira's life in the glittering court evaporates: 'like one in a gay Masque, the night pass'd, they are in their old clothes againe, and no appearance of what was' (I.500). Lindamira, 'that constant woman', admits to having a five-year but unenunciated love for 'The Lord, whom she so much loved, and was accused for' (I.501). The catalyst that finally brings them together is this innocent lord's relating the queen's suspicions. Rumours surrounding Lindamira's rustication, 'her

---

33 It was anonymously published with a false imprint in London as *A meruaylous discourse upon the lyfe, of Katherine de Medicis* (Heydelberge, 1575), and in two Edinburgh editions as *Ane Meruellous discours*, which purport to have been published in Cracow and Paris in 1576.
34 *O.E.D.*, widow, *n.1*, 1.d.

honor not touched, but caste downe' (I.501–2), provoke her husband's jealousy.

At this instant of personal revelation, Sidney Wroth blurs her syntax, alternating pronominal references to 'she' and 'he' to enhance obscurity and ambiguity. The time-frame of her declaration, that 'after fourteen years unchang'd affection, [s]he cast her off contemptuously and scornfully' (I.502),[35] coincides with Sidney Wroth's connection with Anne of Denmark's court, between 1604 and 1618, and the decade of her marriage to Robert Wroth, from 1604 to 1614. Pamphilia's account of Lindamira's mishap ends, like *Urania*, in a sonnet sequence written by Pamphilia, because she 'found her estate so neere agree with mine' (I.502). If the sonnets genuinely represent Lindamira's 'complaint' about her husband's reaction, as they purport to do, then, in an elision of identities, Pamphilia suppresses the conclusion of the French story and supplies her own personal version: 'the complaint is th[is,] divided into seaven Sonnets' (I.502).[36] By constructing the episode to make Pamphilia rather than Lindamira refer to 'ungratefulnesse in him', and then personalise Pamphilia's venom against Lindamira's husband – 'I will with the story conclude my rage against him' (I.502) – Sidney Wroth subsumes Lindamira and Pamphilia within herself as victim, lover and author.[37]

The dispossessed: Urania's misery

Urania is obsessed with romantic attachment, self-interest, political marriage and restitution of status to the dispossessed. Nonetheless, the narrative defies the conventions of both ancient and European erotic romance by concentrating on the author's multiple personae, rather than on the eponymous heroine. Urania's story begins where romances based on *Daphnis and Chloe* usually reach their climax, with the disclosure to her on her sixteenth birthday that she has been fostered (I.22). Almost immediately she learns she is Amphilanthus's sister, 'who in the first weeke after her birth was stolne away' (I.23). This disorientating inversion of the plot sequence is essential to Sidney Wroth's rhetoric of obfuscation. For it is precisely by cultivating uncertainty that she licenses her allusive

35 Sidney Wroth's alternation of gendered pronouns persuades Roberts unnecessarily to emend 'she cast her off' to 'he cast her off', discussed on I.778, having earlier accepted 'she' in *The Poems of Lady Mary Wroth*, ed. by J. A. Roberts, p. 31.
36 Loose syntax and lack of punctuation persuade Roberts unnecessarily to emend 'this' to 'thus'.
37 Cf. M. E. Lamb, *Gender and Authorship in the Sidney Circle*, pp. 185 ff.

narrative of multiple, intertwined erotic plots, punctuated by scenes of loss and recovery, deception and recognition.

Sidney Wroth's dedicatee and model for Urania was Susan de Vere (or 'Vere') Herbert (1587–3 January 1629), the daughter of Edward de Vere, seventeenth Earl of Oxford, and Anne Cecil, daughter of William, Lord Burghley. That Anne Cecil died in June 1588 may lie behind Urania's pained exclamation, 'what torments do I then suffer, which never knew my mother?' (I.19). On 27 December 1604, Susan married Sidney Wroth's cousin, Philip Herbert (1584–1650), created Earl of Montgomery on 4 May 1605. Following Susan's death, on 3 June 1630 Philip married Anne Clifford, the widow of Richard Sackville, third Earl of Dorset.[38]

Making Urania Amphilanthus's sister may also loosely, and allowably, elide 'sister' into its alternative meaning, 'sister-in-law',[39] and implicitly allude to Herbert's deceased sister, Anne (1583–1606). Further biographical allusions are enabled by reducing the distinctions between Urania and Veralinda, who is Amphilanthus's sister-in-law and Leonius's wife.[40] Younger brother of Amphilanthus, and older brother of Urania whom he looks like (I.24), Leonius is transparently associated with Philip Herbert. In the Second Part of *Urania*, their children are Verolindo, Amphilionus, who looks like Amphilanthus and continues Leonius's heroic role, and Lindavera, a shepherdess who compares her foundling circumstances to Urania's (II.103).

Urania opens with a complimentary parody of Sidney's *New Arcadia*. It echoes his tribute to springtime, the season of love, and Claius and Strephon's lament for their departed Urania. Nearly forty years later, Sidney Wroth rejects her uncle's Ciceronian, ecphrastic and periphrastic adornment in favour of a lightly decorative clarity that signals pastoral innocence: 'When the Spring began to appeare like the welcome messenger of Summer, one sweet (and in that more sweet) morning, after Aurora had called all carefull eyes to attend the day, forth came the faire Shepherdesse Urania' (I.1).

Urania's opening soliloquy, where she considers her loss of identity, introduces the work's most frequently reiterated motif, 'misery'. In this

38 See D. L. Smith, 'Herbert, Philip, First Earl of Montgomery and Fourth Earl of Pembroke (1584–1650)', *Oxford Dictionary of National Biography* (Oxford: Oxford University Press, 2004), and R. T. Spence, 'Clifford, Anne, Countess of Pembroke, Dorset, and Montgomery (1590–1676)', *Oxford Dictionary of National Biography* (Oxford: Oxford University Press, 2004).
39 *O.E.D.*, I.1.a.
40 See I.lxxix.

speech, the rhetorical register shifts from the loose meandering of the narrator's opening to a style of cultured simplicity:

> 'Alas Urania', said she, '(the true servant to misfortune); of any miserie that can befall woman, is not this the most and greatest which thou art falne into? Can there be any neare the unhappinesse of being ignorant, and that in the highest kind, not being certaine of mine owne estate or birth? Why was I not stil continued in the beleefe I was, as I appear, a Shepherdes, and Daughter to a Shepherd?' (I.1)

Urania, 'the Prime of Shepherdesses' (I.20) and 'daughter of Italy' (I.25) or Naples, grows up in Pantaleria, an 'unpossest' (I.22) island south of Sicily to which the exiled Lord Pantalerius – 'all-wretched' – has retreated. On her reaching the age of responsibility, Urania's aged foster parents describe finding her with tokens of recognition:

> hard by the sea-side, not farre from these rocks, laid in a cradle with very rich clothes about me, a purse of gold in the cradle, and a little writing in it, which warn'd them that should take me up to looke carefully to me, to call me Urania, and when I came to sixteene yeeres of age to tell this to me, but by no meanes before. (I.22)

Her reflections on the unnaturalness of her predicament, 'Miserable Urania, worse art thou now then these thy Lambs; for they know their dams, while thou dost live unknowne of any' (I.1), initiates a succession of a related dialogues. These touch on the subjects of love, duties to parents, and dynastic heritable rights. Questions of arranged marriage become interrelated with betrayal, subterfuge, crises of identity and heroism. Yet Sidney Wroth's complex feminist agenda makes even Shakespeare's strongest women appear to lack engagement with the realities of female social politics. Women in *Urania* value stoic inner strength, sharing the eloquence and intellectual powers of Sidney's heroines.[41] Urania naturally exudes Christian stoicism in the philhellene Protestant tradition. When captured, she patiently advises Parselius, 'Be satisfied [...] and hazard not your selfe [...] seeking to alter what is ordain'd by Fate, and therefore not to be changed: but rather give us example, as confidently, and mildly to suffer this adversity' (I.29).

Theatres of romance

Emulating Heliodorus's theatricality, Urania's misery provides a scenic change that pays tribute to Inigo Jones's architectural stage sets. This and

---

41 Cf. M. E. Lamb, *Gender and Authorship in the Sidney Circle*, p. 126.

a multitude of comparable surreal masque-like landscapes invite close scrutiny, revealing magical properties and secret messages. They stand in stark contrast to brief passages of natural description devoid of symbolic import, but which demonstrate the extent to which Sidney Wroth has absorbed the early seventeenth-century recognition of the beauty of landscape.

As other shepherds arrive, Urania exits the opening setting, a meadow, reciting a sonnet of her own composition as she seeks the isolation of 'a great rock'. The narrator, reflecting the Renaissance pre-Romantic antiquarian fascination with countrysides characterised by ruins and grottos, focuses on the next scene: 'she saw under some hollow trees the entrie into the rocke [...] shee found a pretty roome [...] not unlike the ancient (or the descriptions of ancient) Hermitages, instead of hangings, covered and lined with Ivie' (I.2).

The technique of opening the narrative with a lamenting speaker, who progresses into an enclosed sacred space containing symbolic iconography, is familiar from Longus and Achilles Tatius. But it is the painstaking description of movement and perspective, as in Heliodorus's opening, filtered through Montemayor's *Diana*, with which the action moves towards a voyeuristic introduction to the second speaker:

> her delicate hands put the naturall ornament aside, discerning a little doore [...] into another roome, like the first in all proportion; but in the midst there was a square stone, like to a prettie table, and on it a wax-candle burning; and by that a paper [...] she discerned in the roome a bed of boughes, and on it a man lying [...] fetching a deepe groane from the profoundest part of his soule, he said: 'Miserable Perissus, canst thou thus live, knowing she that gave thee life is gone? Gone, O me!' (I.2–3)

Perissus – 'extraordinary' – concludes this speech in a lament for Limena, his destined 'harbour'. Using the wooden transitional invitation favoured by neo-classicists, Urania prompts him to 'favour me with the knowledge of your griefe' (I.4), a bridge into the work's principal theme of erotic politics. His response opens with Achilles Tatius's factual autobiographical formula, intended to persuade readers of his credibility: 'my name is Perissus, Nephew I am to the King of Sicilie [...] Heire I am as yet [...] There was in this Country [...] a Lady, or rather a Goddesse [...] called Limena, daughter to a Duke' (I.5).

Believing that Limena has been murdered by her husband, Perissus sets out to avenge her death, and Urania returns to her pastoral duties (I.16–17). There is a moment of stasis when Urania empathises with a lost lamb. An attack by 'a fierce she-wolf' establishes Urania's Christian stoicism: 'O heaven defend me miserable creature if thou please; if not, grant me this blessing' (I.19). That is, if she is ravaged, her parents might be spared the knowledge of her existence.

But immediately the narrative doubles, trebles and then quadruples in complexity. A series of abrupt interventions widens the cast of participants, each contributing fresh plot-lines, as in Heliodorus, through reminiscence. The she-wolf is killed by two youths of seventeen, who live in a cave with their sister and ailing father. Through the father, 'the unfortunate king of Albania' (I.24), Sidney Wroth introduces, but immediately suspends, an inviting transition from pastoral erotic romance to the later-developed monarchomachist theme of annihilating tyranny and usurpation. The deposed king's promise to disclose his secret history is interrupted when 'a mans voice made them stay' (I.21). Outside, Urania discovers the richly dressed Parselius, carrying a sword. Urania tells him (and the reader) where he is, and the little that she knows of herself:

> This Iland is called Pantalaria […] an old man and his wife having bred me up as their owne, till within these few daies they told me that […] I was by them found hard by the sea-side, not farre from these rocks, laid in a cradle with very rich clothes about me, a purse of gold in the cradle, and a little writing in it, […] to call me Urania, and when I came to sixteene yeeres of age to tell this to me. (I.22)

If Urania had been properly educated in Greco-Roman romance and its Renaissance adaptations, she might have taken comfort from the knowledge of the ultimate and inevitable happiness promised to foundlings by the genre.

Parselius establishes the connections between Sicily, Albania, Morea and Naples. As a representation of her elder brother, William (1589/90–1612),[42] Sidney Wroth uses him to interrelate familial and political allegory. He begins with the now familiar series of formulaic identifiers – name, rank, family, background and context: 'My name […] is Parselius, Prince of Morea, being eldest Sonne unto the King thereof, which Countrie I left with a deare friend […] my kinsman, and heire to the Kingdome of Naples, called Amphilanthus' (I.23). The cousins Amphilanthus and Parselius (his 'other part') have been 'bred […] together', and grow up as 'soule and body' (I.23). Their quest is to find Amphilanthus's 'lost Sister', the kidnapped Urania.

Linking them to the opening scene – they travel to Sicily, putting down a rebellion that breaks out 'after the departure of Perissus' – creates a sense

---

42 See M. V. Hay, *The Life of Robert Sidney*, pp. 183–4, 245.

of narrative cohesion. Successfully 'setling the King in his seat' (I.23), they split up to look for Urania. Parselius identifies her because 'you much resemble Leonius, the younger brother to Amphilanthus' (I.23–4), and falls violently but unconstantly in love.

Sidney Wroth forges a strong link between Leonius's courtship of Veralinda, and Parselius's marriage to Dalinea of Achaia,[43] by means of quotations from Sidney's *Astrophil and Stella*. Parselius's *de praesanti* marriage to Dalinea – 'what privately before only three you vow'd in sacred marriage' (I.242) – prompts a nightmare, in which 'my first Love', Urania, 'furiously revild me for my change' (I.243). His remark that 'I waked distracted; shee, deare shee, my wife was grieved with my paine' (I.243), and his later reference to Dalinea as 'she, dearest she' (I.404), reconstruct the second line of the first sonnet in *Astrophil and Stella* (as in the 1598 and subsequent editions), 'That she (deare she) might take some pleasure of my paine' (Xx2). These blatant allusions develop an enigmatic interrelationship between Dalinea and Penelope Devereux Rich – or perhaps one of her daughters.

The vows Parselius makes to Urania return to haunt him late in the Second Part. There Melissea, whose supernatural powers portray Mary Sidney Herbert's awesome matriarchal grip over her family, bars both Parselius's daughter, Candiana, and his son, Trebisound, from the Morean succession: 'for you know the bands you were tyed in to Urania, which must nott by fate ore fortune bee on your parte dissolved [...] one of hers [i.e., Floristello] shall have this throne [i.e., of Achaia] with your daughter [i.e., Candida or Candiana], the true picture of your deerest Dalinea' (II.322). The growing complexity of these relationships reinforces the rhetorical unity of the work by increasing familial and political integration, while carefully obscuring personal and historical allusions.

The dying King of Albania makes Parselius responsible for his three children, Steriamus (possibly meaning 'robbed'), Selarinus ('son of light') and Selarina,[44] whose mother dies when she is seven (I.19–20, 24). Parallels between the Neapolitan and Albanian royal families shift the allegory almost imperceptibly as they begin to integrate. The eldest sons, Amphilanthus and Steriamus; the younger sons, Leonius and Selarinus;

---

43 On Parselius and Dalinea, see S. T. Cavanagh, *Cherished Torment: The Emotional Geography of Lady Mary Wroth's Urania*, pp. 138–46.

44 On signature Iii3v, the variant spelling 'Selerina' (Roberts reads 'Selarina' on I.517; not listed as a press variant on I.708) is the name of the sister of the king of Portugal, wife of Milanor, king of England, and mother of Prince Palladine. See C. Colet, *The Famous, pleasant, and variable Historie, of Palladine of England*, trans. by A[ntony] M[unday] (1588), A1–A1v.

and the daughters, Urania and Selarina, come to resemble one another. Urania accepts Selarina as her 'friend and companion' (I.25) in fulfilment of the king's deathbed wish. After Steriamus is cured of an infatuation for Amphilanthus's beloved Pamphilia (I.68–71, 231), Urania becomes his wife and the new Queen of Albania (I.512). Reflecting the dynastic principles of the Protestant League, royal families join forces to promote their common 'Christian'[45] interest. Selarinus, king of the restored Albanian territory of Epirus, marries the younger sister of Parselius and Pamphilia, Philistella (I.314, 512), and Selarina marries Antissius II of Romania.

Interest theory personalised

Interest theory, applied by Sidney in *Arcadia* to explore personal motive, was developed in the seventeenth century to promote or defend state interests. It worked by states analysing information in an attempt to anticipate interrelationships with the interests of others. Potential benefits could be exploited, and dangers averted. *Urania*, a psychoanalytical novel developing the Plutarchan moralised concept of characterisation, illustrates the importance of adapting this political philosophy to personal relationships. Parselius pursues his self-interest, oblivious of the needs and interests of Urania and Dalinea. The 'valliantest' Amphilanthus suffers from the same lack of insight that plagues Sidney's Amphialus. Both badly fail to appreciate the need to analyse information before taking decisive action in personal and political affairs.

Thematic parallels swirl through the consciously obtuse meta-history of *Urania*, drawing attention to William Herbert's blindness to Sidney Wroth's constancy in love. The allegorised report of Pamphilia and Amphilanthus's exchanging vows (II.45) may be fanciful, or 'a claim of legitimacy on behalf of the two children [William and Katherine] she bore to Pembroke'.[46] Nevertheless, the parallel representation in the Fisher-Lady's love for Laurimello suggests that their 'chast love' (II.368) began after the death of Henry Herbert, second Earl of Pembroke, on 19 January 1601.[47] Sidney Wroth was then fourteen or fifteen, and Herbert twenty-one.

---

45 On the bipolarity of Christian/non-Christian and Western/Eastern, see S. T. Cavanagh, *Cherished Torment: The Emotional Geography of Lady Mary Wroth's Urania*, pp. 27–30.
46 I.lxxiv; cf. I.lxxxviii, and see *The Poems of Lady Mary Wroth*, ed. by J. A. Roberts, pp. 24–5.
47 M. P. Hannay, *Philip's Phoenix: Mary Sidney, Countess of Pembroke* (New York: Oxford University Press, 1990), p. 168. In the 'Index of Characters in Part One', she is called 'Angler Woman' (I.806).

The episode of the Fisher-Lady and Laurimello completes a sequence of studies in the failure to apply interest theory in self-defence. It begins as Amphilanthus and Ollorandus, the young and inexperienced King of Bohemia, enter 'the confines of Bohemia' (I.267). They come across a castle where two knights warn them not to stay, as this is the castle of Ollorandus's father's uncle, Severus, 'the cruelest man that was in all those parts' (I.267). Predictably, as this is a cautionary allegory, they succumb to vanity and poor judgement. Like a Spenserian caricature, Ollorandus, 'The new king imagining this a disgrace [...] to let any such thing passe for feare' (I.267), is portrayed as naive and prone to the folly of bravado. Amphilanthus, guilty of irresponsible irrationality, allows himself to be persuaded to enter. Their taking no heed of Severus's interest in defending the throne he has usurped is a transparent error of judgement. But this localised allegory is also supported by one which credits Mary Sidney Herbert with extraordinary mystical powers of perception and foreknowledge. For in ignoring the sage visionary Melissea's instruction to 'keepe [...] together' (I.142), and accepting separate rooms, they are very nearly assassinated, and endanger the entire Protestant empire (I.285-7).

Chivalric idealism, undermined by the absence of interest analysis, next prompts Amphilanthus and Ollorandus to allow themselves to be deceived and separated. The villainous Terichillus lures his sister Sydelia and her trusting husband, Antonarus of Silesia, into Moravia: 'we believing, went thither, trusting, as not meaning to bee false' (I.281). The magnificent entertainments provided for them are a disarming prelude to Antonarus's execution during a hunt. Amphilanthus agrees to champion Sydelia to avenge Antonarus's murder, heroically kills Terichillus in single combat but remains blind to the inevitable counter-revenge by Terichillus's widow, Orguelea.

Unlike Spenser's proud Orgoglio, Orguelea's name signifies her insight into how to manipulate the most heroic of knights. She preys on their pride in their chivalric interests. Orguelea pretends she has escaped kidnappers, and draws Amphilanthus and Ollorandus into a disused quarry (I.284). Readers familiar with the ominous places of chivalric psychological allegory could anticipate her next deception. She has her maidservant rush by as if fleeing danger, decoying Ollorandus away. An interjection by the narrator draws attention to his unconsidered action, which compounds Amphilanthus's initial error: 'Oh Ollorandus [...] What Witchcraft made thee forget thy vowe, and Melissea's command? [...] how hast thou abandon'd him in greatest neede?' (I.285). Their combined failure to consider the evil intent of others' interests exposes

Amphilanthus to 'the most hazardous and dangerous' victory 'that ever he fell into' (I.286).

Sidney Wroth effects a transition from physical to emotional business by pausing the action to restore Amphilanthus and Ollorandus to health. In contrast with the unnatural, menacing *locus horribilis* of the deserted quarry, their next encounter, in Hungary, is preceded by an idyllic ecphrasis in the exaggerated manner of Achilles Tatius. The narrator focuses on the symbiotic relationship between a river and the 'Osiers' (I.289), or willows, growing in, drooping into and being 'chastly embraced' by it. The beauty and tranquillity of this *locus amoenus* prompt thoughts of love. This transition from chivalric to erotic is problematised for readers, though not for the characters. The willows symbolise unrequited love; [48] while the Fisher-Lady's flesh-exposing 'cut-worke Smock' (I.289), and the 'transparent bridge' (I.289) that she crosses to greet them, indicate an 'easily seen through'[49] set of connections.

Cautionary tales such as these demonstrate the irreconcilable difference between Amphilanthus's 'valiantest' mindset of instinctive reaction, and Pamphilia's considered, stoically patient 'loyallest' (I.48). Sidney Wroth unambiguously demonstrates how Amphilanthus's extreme sense of chivalric duty suspends his analytical powers. An inability to apply interest theory to his personal circumstances leaves him vulnerable to manipulation. Emphasising the implications of this catastrophic flaw is essential to Sidney Wroth's argument, as she relates its tragic consequences to the real business of *Urania*, representing her relationship with William Herbert.

Techniques of elision

Sidney Wroth sets the stage for the blending of Urania into Veralinda in an enigmatic episode. It begins with the King of Morea's decision 'to remove his Court to Corinth' (I.371). In an allegory on 'uncertainty', against her better judgement Pamphilia allows herself to be persuaded to join Urania, Philistella and Selarina on a risky yachting expedition in the Adriatic: 'thus they plotted to deceive themselves, and ranne from safety to apparent danger, for what is the Sea but uncertaintie' (I.371). Sidney Wroth creates an extended metaphor during which a gentle, beguiling sea becomes ferocious as a storm drives them to founder on a

---

48 Cf. *O.E.D.*, 'willow', *n.*, 1.d.
49 Cf. *O.E.D.*, 'transparent', *a.*, 2.*fig.*b.

rocky island.[50] Curiosity leads Pamphilia to explore, and they all become imprisoned in an enchanted theatre. There they remain trapped 'till the man most loving, and most beloved, used his force, who should release them, but himselfe be inclosed till by the freeing of the sweetest and love-liest creature, that poore habits had disguised greatnesse in, he should be redeem'd, and then should all bee finished' (I.373). With a slightly different emphasis from the allegorical Throne of Love, this challenge is structured to compliment Herbert (Amphilanthus) and Susan de Vere Herbert (Urania–Veralinda).

Pamphilia's error in going to sea is glossed by the narrator as a further stage in the development of the allegory: 'Why should Pamphilia, (unlesse on necessity) venture her constant selfe in such a hazard, as if to tempt her enemy?' (I.371). This 'necessity' is designed to illustrate Pamphilia suffering the consequences of being easily persuaded by those she trusts. Amphilanthus fails in his rescue bid, sailing past 'the fatall Rocke' (I.374), and is recalled to quell a civil war in Italy. This blunt but effective narrative instrument facilitates an enormous temporal gap, and a narrator's intervention that predicts a positive conclusion to the Pamphilia–Amphilanthus relationship: 'Alas, unfortunate Lady, […] this is the last time for some moneths, hee shall come so neare, but yeares before his affection bee so much' (I.375).

Sidney Wroth contrives this hiatus in the narrative to introduce the Bellamira episode, an allegorical analogue to the autobiographical tale of the Fisher-Lady and Laurimello. Unlike other writers of erotic romance, Sidney Wroth entices readers to believe in the verisimilitude of *Urania* by incompletely revisiting themes and plots from different perspectives. She uses – perhaps even invents – this demanding narrative process, more montage than collage, simultaneously to insinuate herself and Herbert into these vignettes, and yet distance herself from them. It is as if she possesses an uncanny insight into the disassociated associations of a split personality, at times aware, or not, of its interrelated manifestations.

Selectively sharing confidences between characters with readers, or between the narrator and readers, Sidney Wroth creates an aura of participating in a not quite unravellable mystery, over which only she is in complete control. These semi-transparent, moving narratives rehearse the divisive circumstances that precede her unfulfilling marriage to Robert Wroth, on 27 September 1604; and Herbert's to Mary Talbot, five weeks later, on 4 November.

50 On the narrative function of wind and storms, see S. T. Cavanagh, *Cherished Torment: The Emotional Geography of Lady Mary Wroth's Urania*, pp. 93–113.

The Fisher-Lady's father (Robert Sidney) lives near Buda in Hungary (perhaps alluding to Baynard's Castle) 'by reason of the Courts lying there' (I.291). When her uncle's death (Henry Herbert died on 19 January 1601) brings her cousins Laurimello and his sister (William and Anne Herbert) to join their household, the Fisher-Lady falls in love. Herbert's stay with the Sidneys was intermittent though perhaps frequent, as he was jailed for a month in March 1601 over his affair with Mary Fitton, and remained excluded from Elizabeth's court.[51]

Following a two-year courtship, the Fisher-Lady rejects her suitor, Charimellus, whose 'estate lay in Austria', 'many miles distant' (I.294). Her father then proposes another 'whose estate was greater, and neerer to our dwelling' (I.292), in reality, Robert Wroth. Deceiving herself that she actually can read everyone's interests, the Fisher-Lady spins 'a web to deceive all' (I.293). She will entertain Charimellus again, on condition that Laurimello is his intermediary. To her regret, coyness prevents her declaring her love for Laurimello, 'casting before mine eyes the staine, that justly might be laid on me, a maid, and of so tender yeeres to wooe a man' (I.294). Charimellus's death changes nothing. Her 'childish modesty' so masks her intentions that 'the truth was lost', and Laurimello, 'not once imagining my end, married another Lady' (I.294). Accepting that 'all was lost' (I.294), the Fisher-Lady marries her wealthy neighbour.[52] This self-obsessed, overly shy Lady fails to consider that Laurimello's interests might parallel her own. Even if she had, as the tales of Bellamira and Pamphilia demonstrate, she would not have penetrated the conspiracy to drive her beloved into marriage to another.

The understanding that Amphilanthus (and simultaneously, the reader) will gain from Bellamira's variation on the Fisher-Lady's story enables his necessary transition at the enchanted theatre. Herbert's various personae alter from 'the valliantest' to the 'most loving, and most beloved' (I.373), then later to 'the man most loving, and best beloved' (I.442). His attitude changes from self-pitying and 'forsaken' on learning that the trusting Bellamira–Pamphilia–Sidney Wroth has been betrayed by his servant. Sidney Wroth has taught her readers to recognise that only his well-demonstrated gullibility has duped Herbert into believing her inconstant, and therefore to anticipate his renewed heroic-erotic role.

Critically, the keystone in the political plot anticipates this unravelling

---

51 *The Poems of Lady Mary Wroth*, ed. by J. A. Roberts, p. 24.
52 Despite this allusion to someone who apparently dies around 1604, Charimellus remains unidentified. Roberts proposes an overlap between the two suitors, describing both as Robert Wroth (I.xc).

of the conditions for the prisoners' release, and the metamorphosis of Urania and Veralinda into a single virtual character. Amphilanthus achieves the pinnacle of heroic status, being elected unopposed (I.441) to the exalted position of 'Emperour, who by being King of the Romanes might claime it' (I.454). Before being crowned, he will tackle the enchantment. He does not do this in the manner of an erotic romance hero, out of love for Pamphilia, but rather, as he ironically claims, for 'the desire he had to constant truth in holding vowes', and to liberate 'those famous Princes his friends, and Allies that were there inclosed' (I.442). Their presence at his coronation will glorify his Christian empire.

In fulfilment of the narrator's prediction, Amphilanthus, 'the man most loving, and best beloved' (I.442), becomes entrapped in the theatre. His response to Pamphilia is disappointingly muted: 'He complementally [i.e., 'ceremoniously'] saluted her', initiating 'a worse Charme then the first, because now they perfectly saw and knew, misery' (I.442). Pamphilia is particularly singled out as she returns to her seat, tearful and 'alone, but viewed by all to be so' (I.442). For Amphilanthus has rejected her in favour of 'one of his first Loves' (I.397) who is also enchanted, Musalina, wife of the Duke of Tenedos. The contrasting parallel structure emphasises Pamphilia's desperate isolation: 'yet did hee not imagine, or rather would not consider this was caused by his leaving her, [...] yet did shee not, nor would accuse him, who was altogether so faulty as condemned to be, though more then she deserved[,] unkind' (I.442).

Two interpolated cautionary tales reflect on the action. Ollorandus meets the melancholy or 'sad man' grieving for the death of his first love, who, after he abandons her for a selfish woman, rescues him from hanging, then dies (I.443–8). Next, a young rustic woman cannot decide which of her two lovers, inseparable friends, she would prefer to marry, and loses them both (I.448–54). The implications for Pamphilia and Amphilanthus at the theatre are clear. He will regret leaving her for another; and she, like the Fisher-Lady, will rue the day she hesitated to enunciate her love.

The rhythm changes as the narrator prepares readers for the apocalyptic liberation of the trapped lovers, and the assimilation of Veralinda and Urania, both personae of Susan de Vere Herbert. The shepherd whom Veralinda believes to be her father is directed 'in my sleepe' (I.454) to send her to 'an Iland in the Gulfe of Venice' (I.485), accompanied by 'the Nimph' Leonia – Leonius in disguise (I.454). The formulaic tokens of identification are contained in a 'cabinet' or 'box', only to be opened when 'the adventure you shall see be ended' (I.454). As retrospectively revealed by 'a writing in the Shepherds hand' (I.456), which is in the cabinet, he colludes with the disguised Leonius to escort Veralinda: 'the Nimph', Leonia, 'he knew made to confesse himselfe to him, out of care of her, and then he consented to the journey' (I.457).

Once in the theatre, Apollo commands Veralinda 'to touch them with a rod he threw her down' (I.455). The theatre instantly becomes an allegorical centre of enlightening realisation: Amphilanthus abruptly dislikes Musalina, and Pamphilia separates from Leandrus, previously lying at her feet, gazing 'on her face' (I.421). As their chairs vanish, a pillar of gold appears, to which is attached a book that only Urania can remove. Amphilanthus fails to open it. But at the symbolically poignant moment that Urania, who 'must have Veralindas help to open it' (I.455), succeeds, the 'house' disappears. Together, metaphorically twinned, they read the long-suspended story of Urania's life:

> They found in the Booke the whole story of Urania, and how that after shee was stollen by the Duke as before was confessed by himselfe, and then from him by robbers.
>
> This wise man who had made this inchantment preserved her, tooke her from those robbers, left the purse and mantle with her to be the meanes for those that took her up to cherish her, and then being Lord of this Island, framed this inchantment, whither he knew she should come and give part of the conclusion to it, and so appeare fit to deserve his care, which she might thanke him for; the next story was of Veralinda, which was this. (I.455)

Sidney Wroth significantly deviates from the fictional realism of her literary antecedents by introducing these layers of supernatural intervention. She invokes this technique further to obscure the boundaries between her overlapping caricatures, between historical reality and mythic familial and political destiny.

Like Urania, Veralinda begins life inauspiciously, though she is predestined to enjoy success in her relationship with Leonius. Like Urania, her life is planned by the mysteriously omniscient 'Lord of this Island', Robert Sidney. Her father, the King of Frigia (also 'Phrigia' and 'Phrygia'), 'had many children by his first wife, then married he againe, and by his second onely had one daughter' (I.456), Veralinda, who is destined to 'rule a great people, and weare a Crowne'. Her brothers bribe a servant to murder her, but the servant instead kidnaps her, 'warned in a dreame' to take her 'into Morea, and so into Arcadia', and gives her to the king's shepherd, 'as plainely shewed the divine providence ordained it':

> Hee bred her up untill that time that hee was also in his sleepe appointed to send her thence to the Island, the Lord of this Island a learned man knewe

all this, and made the delicate adventure for her discovery, and the tryall of love. (I.456)

By endowing 'the Lord' with supernatural powers, Sidney Wroth compliments her father, Robert Sidney, putting him on a par with the sage Mellisea, Mary Sidney Herbert. Family connections are sustained by couching Leonius/Philip Herbert's courtship of Veralinda/Susan de Vere in an extended and obvious parody of the *New Arcadia*. Leonius's falling in love with a shepherdess-princess and killing a rampaging bear in Arcadia echoes Sidney's Musidorus (I.426–9). On the advice of an Arcadian shepherd, Leonius disguises himself as Veralinda's maid-servant Leonia (I.429–30), combining Zelmane's (Pyrocles') transvestite disguise and Musidorus's shepherd's costume (I.454–6). It is the Lord's magic that forges the link between Urania and Veralinda, reveals her royal status and brings about Leonius's shedding his disguise in order to declare his love (I.456–7). They become engaged, and soon marry in Morea (I.485).

As an aside, and resembling Pyrocles' rescue of Pamphilus in the *New Arcadia*, Leonius saves Veralinda's philandering father from the vengeful women he has betrayed (I.562–5). Sidney Wroth carefully censors this account, purporting to represent the short and disastrous marriage between Anne Cecil and Susan de Vere's father, Edward, seventeenth Earl of Oxford. Lord Great Chamberlain by birth, Vere enjoyed a profligate life. His second marriage to the Maid of Honour Elizabeth Trentham, gave him an heir, Henry (1593–1625), who succeeded him in 1604.[53] It was to Henry de Vere that Antony Munday, patronised by Oxford from as early as 1579,[54] dedicated his translation of all three Books of *Primaleon of Greece* (1619).[55]

Allegorical parallelism

Munday's translations helped to popularise the early sixteenth-century continental chivalric romances. These generally purport to be historical accounts relating to the monarchies of Greece, France and Britain, including Scotland and England. Consistent with their theme, they

---

53 A. H. Nelson, 'Vere, Edward de, Seventeenth Earl of Oxford (1550–1604)', *Oxford Dictionary of National Biography* (Oxford: Oxford University Press, 2004).

54 See *The Mirrour of Mutabilitie, or Principall part of the Mirrour for Magistrates. Describing the fall of diuers famous Princes, and other memorable Personages. Selected out of the sacred Scriptures by Antony Munday, and dedicated to the Right Honorable the Earle of Oxenford (1579).*

55 Cf. D. M. Bergeron, 'Munday, Anthony (*bap.* 1560, *d.* 1633)', *Oxford Dictionary of National Biography* (Oxford: Oxford University Press, 2004).

contain an abundance of characters with Greek- and Latin-based names. Plot lines, which develop through three or four generations of royalty, include complicated love relationships and heroic action, often influenced by magic and the supernatural. Sidney Wroth conscientiously replicates these features. But the device of revisiting key emotional episodes with different casts of introspective players establishes an allegorical twist and psychological emphasis far more closely related to European erotic romance.

To a far greater extent than *An Ethiopian Story* and *Arcadia*, *Urania* maintains the appearance of random organisation, permitting fragmented and progressive character development. Bellamira's history is told from her father's and her own perspectives. Amphilanthus's proven rashness and gullibility is paralleled, in affairs of the heart, by that of Laurimello and of Bellamira's beloved; and the Fisher-Lady's constraining bashfulness parallels Pamphilia's and Bellamira's. Employing allegorical parallels, Sidney Wroth uses Bellamira's tale to shed light retrospectively on the Fisher-Lady's, and to anticipate Pamphilia's disclosure that the villain behind the deception that divides her from Amphilanthus is Forsandurus, Herbert's tutor Hugh Sanford, who died in May 1607.[56]

In the manner of Achilles Tatius, both histories begin with lists of autobiographical details that establish the veracity of their narrators. Bellamira is introduced by her father, an 'aged and grave' (I.152) hermit: 'heare your poore friend say, his name is Dettareus, borne in Dalmatia, and Lord of Ragusa […] my dearest daughter, (Bellamira by name)' (I.176). And Bellamira adopts the same method: 'my selfe am called Bellamira, my father was called Dettareus […] Steward of the kings house' (I.379) in Dalmatia. It is one of the king's brothers, the ruthlessly self-interested Prince of Istria, who confesses to kidnapping Urania shortly after her birth, when Amphilanthus is just seven – the age difference between William Herbert and Susan de Vere (I.232).

Sidney Wroth skilfully creates tension between narrator and reader by intertwining apparently historical with apparently fictional allegory. Dettareus tells Parselius that, sensing danger to his family because 'the king liked her', he 'hasted to bestow' Bellamira 'on a great heire, who was called Treborius [i.e., Robert Wroth], with whom she happily lived' (I.176). Bellamira will partly corroborate, partly contradict this from her perspective as the victim of others' interests. Dettareus categorically states that 'one day, one instant, and one Planet governd, and gave our

births, onely 24 yeares differing in time' (I.179). Robert Sidney was born
on 19 November 1563, his daughter Mary on 18 October, in either 1586
or 1587.[57] These slight but calculated disparities between fact and fiction
seem to be designed to enshroud autobiographical aspects of the narra-
tive within a halo of doubt.

Sidney Wroth has Dettareus identify himself as an incautious widower
who, in the court of Naples (the Herbert stronghold), pursues a selfish,
one-sided liaison with a married and faithful Lady 'of Apulia' (I.176).
The resulting duel ends with Dettareus giving himself multiple wounds,
believing the husband to be dead, and with the Lady from Apulia commit-
ting suicide. All this is in the distant past, following Bellamira's wedding,
but Dettareus's story ends in the present. After he rejoins the Dalmatian
court, with the king's permission the Lady's husband returns to challenge
and kill Dettareus in a second duel (I.487). Such extraordinary fictions,
allegorical fabrications to illustrate the failure of interest analysis, cast a
long, well-planned narrative shadow over the probity of historical allegory
in *Urania*. Their rhetorical impact is to ensure Sidney Wroth free rein to
disclose and withhold autobiographical information selectively.

The *Urania*'s progressive accretion of implied insights into Sidney
Wroth's and Herbert's unfulfilling marriages advances in Bellamira's
story. The narrator's preamble directs readers to anticipate Bellamira's
personal disaster. And Amphilanthus's inconstancy invites 'plots laid to
destroy' (I.362) him. Through the first part of this rhetorically complex
narrative, Sidney Wroth creates the impression that Bellamira's account
is convincingly candid. She achieves this by separating the identity of
Bellamira's beloved from that of her interlocutor, 'the Lost Man' (I.378).
This is Amphilanthus, but he is disguised by the symbolic tawny armour
he adopts in the mistaken belief that Pamphilia has forsaken him.

Bellamira describes her falling in love, and confesses the shortcomings
of her powers of interest analysis. She admits that she 'fell into a snare [...]
caught by the craft of one, whose wit was too strong for me' (I.379). This
deception, she learns, is perpetrated by her beloved's confidential servant.
He first makes love to her, then becomes the servant of an enemy – she
'who hee perceiveth keeps my love from me' (I.381). The villain betrays
Bellamira's trust, but she assures Amphilanthus that her beloved remains
'Fixed truely in my heart' (I.382), even after 'the death of my husband,
and sonne, by him' (I.380).

This glimpse into Sidney Wroth's post-1614 history defines the moment

57   *The Poems of Lady Mary Wroth*, ed. by J. A. Roberts, p. 6.

when she engages in an oblique form of dramatic irony. Bellamira now recognises the disguised Amphilanthus, but readers are not told for a further ten pages, when she acknowledges this (I.391–2). Only in retrospect does the increased warmth and intimacy of her candour become explicable.

Bellamira's story resonates with echoes of the Fisher-Lady and Pamphilia. It is a hall of distorting mirrors, reflecting variant faces of Herbert as the archetype behind her beloved, Laurimello and Amphilanthus.

The dialogue continues inside a cave housing a monument to her dead son. Bellamira reveals that her beloved's own servant, one who 'had instructed him; from, and in his tender youth' acts as an agent 'to the friends of a great Heire' (I.383) to undermine their relationship. Identified with Amphilanthus through a characteristic 'naturall inconstancy' (I.380), Bellamira's beloved readily believes his servant's lie that she has been 'betrothed to her long loving friend, though not till then beloved of her' (I.383). The servant intercepts Bellamira's declarations of love to his master. The implications of this deception are considerable. Bellamira's beloved contracts himself to 'the mighty Heire of the Forrest' (I.385), and Bellamira accepts Treborius (I.387).

This complex scene reflects on Amphilanthus's hasty decision-making, readiness to believe himself injured and the inconstancy which renders him incapable of understanding steadfastness in others. It is his tragic failing, the entire plot of *Urania* seemingly being designed to illustrate Bellamira's warning, 'Let not feare without assurance […] molest you, lest it make you indeed loose by mistrust, what is yet but mistrusted to be lost' (I.386).

In a thematically overlapping episode, characters who best know Amphilanthus similarly play on his innate mistrust. He succumbs to the conspiracy between the Queen of Slavonia and the salacious Queen of Candia, who would marry Amphilanthus either to 'the Slavonian Kings daughter' (II.131) or 'the Dallmation ore Natolian Lady' (II.132–3). The Queen of Candia's choice is selfish. Either union would facilitate her hoped for clandestine relationship with Amphilanthus: Natolians are enemies of Tartarians and Moreans, and he would be kept apart from the Morean Pamphilia (II.73). The Queen of Candia then works with the Queen of Slavonia, who bribes Amphilanthus's tutor and servant Forsandurus (Hugh Sanford) 'to make the match with' Amphilanthus 'and her eldest daughter' (II.387).

There can be no more trusted statement, and certainly in this novel where reality is blatantly cloaked in multi-layered allegory, than a deathbed confession. So when Pamphilia tells Amphilanthus what Forsandurus has revealed to her as he is dying, her report carries an extra degree of verisimilitude. From Forsandurus, Pamphilia learns the truth of how she and Amphilanthus were duped into their dynastic society marriages. Instead of operating as their trusted intermediary, he admits to keeping Pamphilia and Amphilanthus's love letters.

Amphilanthus, true to his nature, readily believes Forsandurus's lie that Pamphilia 'had left him, and taken the Tar[t]arian' (II.387), Rodomandro. He responds by hastily and disastrously marrying Dalmatia's niece, the Princess of Slavonia, whom he immediately deserts (II.135).

Amphilanthus's failed union with the Princess of Slavonia-Dalmatia represents William Herbert's business-like marriage, portrayed as arranged by Hugh Sanford during 1603–4, to Mary Talbot, daughter of Gilbert Talbot, seventh Earl of Shrewsbury.[58] If the allegory is reliable, the bribing Queen of Slavonia is Gilbert Talbot's wife, Mary Cavendish (died 13 February 1608). Her sister Elizabeth (died 1582) was the wife of Charles Stuart (died 1576) and the mother of Arabella Stuart (1575–1615), James I's cousin and the heir to the throne. It was Arabella who wrote to Gilbert Talbot, 'I heare the marriage betwixt my Lord of Pembroke and my Cousin is broken' – that is, 'brokered' or 'negotiated'[59] rather than 'called off'.

The close relationship between Naples, Slavonia and Dalmatia is paralleled in the Herbert–Talbot–Stuart family ties. On 17 February 1562, William Herbert's father Henry, second Earl of Pembroke, took as his second wife Catherine Talbot, Gilbert Talbot's sister. At the same time, Gilbert's elder brother Francis, Lord Talbot, married Henry Herbert's sister Anne. These were dynastic unions: Henry and Anne Herbert's mother was Anne Parr Herbert, Countess of Pembroke, the sister of Queen Katherine, Henry VIII's sixth wife (II.131–4, 324). Catherine Talbot Herbert died in 1576; in 1577, Henry Herbert married the young Mary Sidney.[60]

Urania as anti-romance

Thus it is that, deep into the Second Part, and driving her cumulative, multiple-perspective personal allegories to their logical conclusion,

---

58 I.lxxxvi–lxxxviii; cf. J. A. Roberts, '"The Knott Never to Bee Untide": The Controversy Regarding Marriage in Mary Wroth's *Urania*', in *Reading Mary Wroth: Representing Alternatives in Early Modern England*, ed. by N. J. Miller and G. Waller, p. 122.

59 *O.E.D.*, broke *v.* 1; cf. I.lxxxvii, citing British Library Sloane MS. 4164, fol. 190v, but Roberts reads 'broken' as 'failed', the opposite of what Arabella is saying.

60 See P. Williams, 'Herbert, Henry, Second Earl of Pembroke (*b.* in or after 1538, *d.* 1601)', *Oxford Dictionary of National Biography* (Oxford: Oxford University Press, 2004).

Sidney Wroth lays bare the secrets of her private life. Her daring and extraordinary exploration of European erotic romance as a purposefully fragmented, intertwining autobiographical diary may be unprecedented in European fiction. Sidney Wroth recognised that writing in English almost exclusively confined her work to a home-bred readership, largely consisting of her prominent socio-political connections. The publication in 1618 of Munday's translation of Books III and IV of Herberay's French *Amadis de Gaule*, and in 1619 of Books I to IV, both dedicated to Philip Herbert, coincides with Sidney Wroth's beginning *Urania*.[61] But its contemporary historical setting, careful structural planning, and sophistication of the political and feminist themes, suggests that *Urania* may contain Sidney Wroth's considered Protestant reply to Cervantes' blatant Catholic propaganda in *Persiles and Sigismunda*. The earliest editions appeared in Spanish (1617), French (1618) and English (1619).[62]

Beginning *in medias res* in an outlaw community, and focusing on the trials of a chaste unmarried couple, *Persiles and Sigismunda* very loosely follows Heliodorus. It conforms to the Greco-Roman romance model. Idealised erotic love, complicated by, but never succumbing to, a rash of seemingly insuperable obstacles, leads at the eleventh hour towards restoration of status, public recognition and marriage. As in Heliodorus, the central figures have royal status. Unlike Heliodorus, their relationship is already well established, they have set out on a pilgrimage and they have been separated. Assisted by supernatural forces, they journey from what is portrayed as an imperfectly Christianised northern Europe to confirm their faith in Rome.

While the far more complex *Urania* bears many generic resemblances to *Persiles and Sigismunda*, ranging from mysterious forces to composite names such as Sigismunda's adopted 'Auristela', it is in no way an imitation. It does, however, use the politics of religion as the running motif of the background action, and comments implicitly on Spain and the Church of Rome. Sidney Wroth challenges the Catholic heartland. She converts the Spanish Habsburg states of Naples and Sicily into strongholds dominated by those tightly integrated (Sidney) families who support the rise of Amphilanthus to the secular post of Holy Roman Emperor. In an

---

61 I.xvii.
62 The principal known English use of *Persiles and Sigismunda*, John Fletcher's *The Custom of the Country* (1619), follows publication of the English translation. See T. L. Darby, 'Resistance to Rape in *Persiles y Sigismunda* and *The Custom of the Country*', *Modern Language Review*, xc (1995), 273–84; and T. L. Darby, 'Cervantes in England: The Influence of Golden-Age Prose Fiction on Jacobean Drama, *c.* 1615–1625', *Bulletin of Hispanic Studies*, lxxiv (1997), 425–41.

almost parodic version of the pilgrimage-quest, she has Pamphilia and Amphilanthus strive to attain personal bliss in Cyprus, 'a strange Country [...] of unchristened creatures' (I.47), at the all-powerful Throne of Love (I.169–70). Christian love drives the ethical, moral and chivalric ideals of Amphilanthus and his followers, demonstrated at state and individual levels in staged set-piece vignettes. But the heart of the work is informed by an erotic love that transcends the limitations of Church and state.

Urania also shares with Sidney's *Arcadia* and Cervantes' *Don Quixote* an innovative approach to Renaissance anti-romance in the chivalric-erotic mode,[63] exploring the consequences of deluded self-interest on personal responsibility. While Sidney pays lip-service to the final outcome of this formula, he emphasises the state over the individual. He gives his work the title of a nation rather than a person or event, and speculates on the incompatibility between good governance and the self-centred focus of characters found in erotic romance.

Don Quixote, which overtly subverts the literary excesses and unrealistic conventions of medieval and Renaissance chivalric romance, nonetheless contains a sustained lament for the decay of ethical and moral ideals in Catholic Spain. These are upheld only by Quixote, the anti-heroic, lonely and demented bachelor whose mental instability and visionary Platonism collide with the realities of a very ordinary, fallen world. *Urania*, whose title disguises the cultural and political significance it has for its central characters, contains an autobiographical allegory representing the devastating effects of self-delusion in matters of chivalry, politics and love.

The great Cham and his dynasty

Whereas the personal misery caused by Forsandurus's ruse pervades *Urania*, he could not be faulted on his awareness of self-interest and political advantage. Mary Sidney's marriage to Robert Wroth (1576–1614) consolidated three generations of the philhellene Protestant Sidney–Wroth–Rich network.[64] Robert Wroth was the grandson of the courtier Thomas Wroth (1518?–73), who in 1538 had married Mary, sister of Robert (1537?–81), second Baron Rich. Their eldest son Robert (c. 1539–27 January 1606) married Susan, the daughter of John Stonard of Loughton. This Robert

---

63 Cf. I.xx–xxv.
64 See *The Poems of Lady Mary Wroth*, ed. by J. A. Roberts, pp. 9–14; S. Lehmberg, 'Wroth, Sir Thomas (1518?–1573)', *Oxford Dictionary of National Biography* (Oxford: Oxford University Press, 2004); and L. L. Ford, 'Wroth, Sir Robert (c. 1539–1606)', *Oxford Dictionary of National Biography* (Oxford: Oxford University Press, 2004).

and Susan were the parents of Robert Wroth (*c.* 1576–1614) who married Mary Sidney, and of Thomas (1584–1672)[65] who married Margaret Rich (died 1635), daughter of Robert, second Baron Rich.

This great and increasingly complex dynasty was not blessed with successful unions or stability for its offspring. In 1580, Margaret Rich's brother Richard died, then before 27 February 1581, she lost her father. On 1 November 1581, her second brother Robert, now third Baron Rich, to Philip Sidney's chagrin married Penelope 'Stella' Devereux, sister of Robert, second Earl of Essex.[66] In 1583, Richard's widow, Katherine Knevet Rich, married the Catholic sympathiser Thomas Howard (1561–1626), the second son of the executed Thomas Howard, Duke of Norfolk (1538–72).[67] In January 1606, their daughter Frances Howard married the thirteen-year-old Robert Devereux, third Earl of Essex. His mother, Frances Walsingham Sidney Devereux, widow first of Philip Sidney and then of the second Earl of Essex, in 1603 married Richard Burke, or de Burgh, fourth Earl of Clanricarde. In 1622, their son Ulrick (1604–57) married Lady Anne Compton, the daughter of Robert Sidney's friend William, Lord Compton, Earl of Northampton, who in 1595 had served as one of young Robert Sidney's godfathers.[68]

On 5–6 January 1606, the ill-fated Howard–Devereux alliance was celebrated at court. Ben Jonson and Inigo Jones staged *Hymenaei: or The Solemnities of Masque, and Barriers*, performed by family and friends. In the absence of Essex, sent to be educated on the Continent, Frances became entangled with Robert Carr. Following their marriage in 1613, both were convicted of murdering Thomas Overbury. In *Urania* the old Duke of Laconia's account of how he turned his back on his wife, allowing

---

65 After Robert Wroth's death in 1614, Thomas Wroth worked closely with Robert Sidney. He dedicated to Sidney his Latin and English (in poulter's measure) parallel text of Book 2 of Virgil's *Aeneid*, entitled *The Destruction of Troy, or the Acts of Aeneas* (1620). The volume also contains *The Abortive of an Idle Houre or a Centurie of Epigrams. And a Motto Vpon the Creede* (1620).

66 See B. Usher, 'Rich, Robert, First Earl of Warwick (1559?-1619)', *Oxford Dictionary of National Biography* (Oxford: Oxford University Press, 2004), A. Wall, 'Rich, Penelope, Lady Rich (1563–1607)', *Oxford Dictionary of National Biography* (Oxford: Oxford University Press, 2004), and S. Kelsey, 'Rich, Robert, Second Earl of Warwick (1587–1658)', *Oxford Dictionary of National Biography* (Oxford: Oxford University Press, 2004).

67 H. Payne, 'Howard, Katherine, Countess of Suffolk (*b.* in or after 1564, *d.*1638)', *Oxford Dictionary of National Biography* (Oxford: Oxford University Press, 2004), A. Wall, 'Rich, Penelope, Lady Rich (1563–1607)', *Oxford Dictionary of National Biography*. Cf. A. Fraser, *Mary Queen of Scots* (London: Weidenfeld and Nicolson, 1969; repr. London: Mandarin, 1990), pp. 506–7.

68 M. V. Hay, *The Life of Robert Sidney*, p. 178.

his dukedom to be usurped by his lover, and of his restoration by the King of Morea and the death of the usurper in close prison, is believed to allude to Carr's homoerotic relationship with Overbury (I.34–37).[69]

Of paramount significance to the revolving saga of Sidney Wroth's relationship with William Herbert is the death in 1614 of Robert Wroth, portrayed in Rodomandro, 'the great Cham' (II.267), 'Chamm' (II.407–8) or khan, King of Tartaria.[70] Following Forsandurus's confession, Pamphilia and Amphilanthus's intimate reunion is disrupted by a series of misfortunes. First, they travel to Tartaria to attend to Rodomandro, by now Amphilanthus's 'true and loyall friend' (II.394). Even in Sidney Wroth's fluid calendar, little time passes between his falling ill (II.394) and the report that

> the King dead, his deerest Pamphilia a widow, yett the mother of a brave boy, who soone after his arivall to that Court also died. Which moved the Queene to leave that Country and goe into Pamphilia, and ther with her father live as contentedly as sad people cowld doe. (II.406)

This passage may have been misplaced in the manuscript, as the next sentence begins, 'Now all funeralls past' (II.406), and leads into Pamphilia, Amphilanthus and the Tartarian's arrival in Cyprus. There Amphilanthus learns that his protégé, the Knight of the Faire Design, is looking for him. The final words in the manuscript signal a further continuation, which Sidney Wroth may not have attempted: 'Amphilanthus wa[s] extreamly [...]' (II.418).

Although *Urania* meanders from one episode to another, it is a carefully structured erotic romance. The brief passage that concludes with Pamphilia's decision to live with her father may be an autobiographical interpolation. Or it may be a first ending rejected in favour of a large-scale inter-referential narrative cycle centred on Cyprus, Venus's birthplace, the enchanted location of 'the Throne and pallace for love' (II.407). Carried by storm to Cyprus, Rodomandro remains likeably comical, much in love with himself and Pamphilia. He is filled with naive goodwill, and sincerely believes that 'I were a most fitt fellowe [...] to finish' (II.407) the enchantments of the Throne of Love. Ironically, he remains light years away from Pamphilia's heart, not knowing that only her constancy and Amphilanthus's valour can make the Throne vanish.

69 I.lxviii.
70 On Rodomandro and Tartaria, see S. T. Cavanagh, *Cherished Torment: The Emotional Geography of Lady Mary Wroth's Urania*, pp. 37–52.

Urania as *roman à clef*

Sidney Wroth's fictional portrait of Herbert promotes him above his rivals, in particular George Villiers, Duke of Buckingham, to whom she mischievously sent a copy of the 1621 *Urania*. When he complained, she sarcastically invited him on 15 December 1621 to return it: 'besids that your Lordship wilbe pleased to lett mee have that which I sent you, the example of which will without question make others the willinger to obay'. Further, she denies that her romance is a *roman à clef*:

> Understanding some of the strang constructions which are made of my booke contrary to my imagination, and as farr from my meaning as is possible for truth to bee from conjecture, my purpose noe way bent to give the least cause of offence, my thoughts free from soe much as thinking of any such thing as I ame censurd for.[71]

Sidney Wroth focuses on the intense emotional experiences of her characters, some more fictitious than others. Such representations resemble the mode of characterisation she uses in the closet drama, *Love's Victory*.[72] And in *Urania*, she explicitly alludes to the principles by which she obfuscates historical allegory, intertwining it with phantom identifiers and misleading signals or signs:

> The Queenes of Naples and Cicely [...] passed the time together, telling stories of themselves, and others, mixed many times with pretty fine fictions [...] Going along the Spring they found many knots, and names ingraven upon the trees, which they understood not perfectly, because when they had decipher'd some of them, they then found they were names fained and so knew them not. But Perissus remembred one of the Ciphers, yet because it was Pamphilias hee would not knowe it. (I.489–90)

To the uninitiated, codes remain encrypted or unshared. Secrets are kept or only partially and strategically divulged. Mistakes are made.

The names of most characters contain obscure allegorical resonances,[73] and several, in addition to having alternative meanings, openly signal concealment. The Greek etymology of the name Amphilanthus signals that he is 'unknown on all sides', but also 'the lover of two' (I.300). His emotional life is paralleled in two characters having Latin and Greek

---

71 *The Poems of Lady Mary Wroth*, ed. by J. A. Roberts, p. 236.

72 *The Poems of Lady Mary Wroth*, ed. by J. A. Roberts, p. 38; see *Lady Mary Wroth's Love's Victory: The Penshurst Manuscript*, ed. by M. G. Brennan (London: Roxburghe Club, 1988).

73 *Urania*, I.lxix–xcviii; cf. H. L. Weidemann, 'Theatricality and Female Identity in Mary Sidney Wroth's Urania', in *Reading Mary Sidney Wroth: Representing Alternatives in Early Modern England*, ed. by N. J. Miller and G. Waller, pp. 191–209, esp. pp. 197–200.

composite names. Emphasising this overlap, Laurimello, 'Apollo's darling', speaks for Charimellus, literally 'whose purpose is to be loved'. Dalinea is an anagram for 'alienda', 'being another', also incorporated into Veralinda, 'true other' and Orilena, 'other'. Similarly, 'alias' or 'other' informs the formation lurking behind Parselius, who fulfils his role as Amphilanthus's 'other part', and Sirelius – 'Sir Other'.

Through Sirelius, the reformed Romanian court of Antissius II and Selarina becomes enmeshed in an obfuscating biographical allegory of the Jacobean court. On their voyage to Romania, they pause on an island where a Romanian 'brave Lord', the king's 'Favourite' (I.514), falls in love with the daughter of a widow. Selarina walks into the countryside, coming across 'two men in Shepheards weeds', aged 'towards forty' (I.514). One is Procatus ('put forward as a pretext') who describes his friend Sirelius's marital breakdown, and the attempt by Sirelius's enraged father-in-law to stab his naively culpable daughter.

Although filled with mutual recriminations, the surviving correspondence from February 1622 between Sidney Wroth and Edward Denny (1565?–1630), [74] Lord Denny, Baron of Waltham, reveals that her self-portrayal as Pamphilia was well known in the court of James I.[75] Denny's poem, 'To Pamphilia from the father-in-law of Seralius', demonstrates how the semi-transparent allegory of *Urania* could prick a guilty conscience, identifying Sirelius as James Hay (*c.* 1580–1636), Gentleman of the King's Bedchamber.[76]

Hay's marriage to Honora Denny lasted from 1607 till her death in 1614 (I.780). The significance of these interrelationships for a political reading of *Urania* must not be underestimated. Honora Denny's maternal grandfather was the militant philhellene Protestant Thomas Cecil (1542–1623). Eldest son of William Cecil, Lord Burghley, Thomas was the brother of Anne Cecil, mother of Sidney Wroth's dedicatee Susan de Vere (Veralinda–Urania). In 1564, Thomas Cecil married Dorothy Neville (1548–1609), daughter and co-heiress of John Neville, fourth Baron Latimer.[77] Their daughter Mary Cecil and her husband Edward Denny were Honora Denny's parents.

The widower Sirelius next courts the daughter of 'a great Duke in

---

74 See N. P. Sil, 'Denny, Sir Anthony (1501–1549)', *Oxford Dictionary of National Biography* (Oxford: Oxford University Press, 2004).

75 Sir Edward Denny, letter of 26 February 1621/22, in *The Poems of Lady Mary Wroth*, ed. by J. A. Roberts, p. 238; cf. pp. 31–5, 237–41.

76 *The Poems of Lady Mary Wroth*, ed. by J. A. Roberts, pp. 31–5, 237; cf. R. E. Schreiber, 'Hay, James, First Earl of Carlisle (*c.*1580–1636)', *Oxford Dictionary of National Biography* (Oxford: Oxford University Press, 2004).

77 Cf. R. Milward, 'Cecil, Thomas, First Earl of Exeter (1542–1623)', *Oxford Dictionary of National Biography* (Oxford: Oxford University Press, 2004).

Romania', who 'was against it vehemently, and shut her up' (I.516–17). Determined to prevent his daughter Lucy's marriage to Hay because he was Scottish, Henry Percy, ninth Earl of Northumberland, kept her with him during his imprisonment in the Tower. Lucy Percy Hay (1599–1660), Sidney Wroth's distant cousin, was the younger sister of Dorothy, whom, after her mother overcame Percy's objections, Robert Sidney junior married in 1616.[78]

James Hay married Lucy Percy on 6 November 1617. After just three years of marriage, Sirelius is taking a break 'to weare this Summer out only in his sorrowes, and then to returne' to his wife (I.517). During 1620, Hay hopelessly advocated support for Frederick of Bohemia, and quarrelled violently with his brother-in-law, Robert Sidney, who apparently never understood the cause.[79]

The background narrative of *Urania* may appear to emulate the direct clarity favoured by Caroline writers of political polemic and its literary representations.[80] But passages of intimate and even scandalous revelation are consciously skewed into obscurity by ambiguous or deceptive diction. At the end of Procatus's story, the narrator instructs the reader to view the Romanian lord and Sirelius as the same person: 'The Queene smiled at this Story thinking how fit it was to be compared to the grave Suter they had left at the Widdowes house [...], so as these storyes may bee called one' (I.517). Such allusive narrative, like Fulke Greville's biography of Philip Sidney, is deliberately designed to obfuscate.[81]

The complexities of Sidney Wroth's extended family and those of her friends inform the genealogies of *Urania*. As in *Love's Victory*, she develops Philip Sidney's technique of building *Arcadia* into a scrapbook of reminiscences.[82] This intensely personal approach to fictional writing parallels the developing fashion for contemporary biography and semi-transparent political romance, notably John Barclay's *Argenis*. This *roman à clef*, in Latin, was published in France late in 1621, and in England in 1622.[83] The

78 See G. R. Batho, 'A Difficult Father-in-Law: The Ninth Earl of Northumberland', *History Today*, vi [November, 1956], 744–51.
79 *The Poems of Lady Mary Wroth*, ed. by J. A. Roberts, p. 32.
80 See D. Norbrook, *Writing the English Republic: Poetry, Rhetoric and Politics, 1627–1660* (Cambridge: Cambridge University Press, 1999).
81 V. Skretkowicz, 'Greville, Politics, and the Rhetorics of *A Dedication to Sir Philip Sidney*', in *Fulke Greville: A Special Double Number*, ed. by M. C. Hansen and M. Woodcock, *Sidney Journal*, xix (2001), 97–123.
82 Cf. V. Skretkowicz, '"A More Lively Monument": Philisides in *Arcadia*', in *Sir Philip Sidney's Achievements*, ed. by M. J. B. Allen, D. Baker-Smith and A. F. Kinney (New York: AMS Press, 1990), pp. 194–200.
83 I.lxx–lxxi; see *The Poems of Lady Mary Wroth*, ed. by J. A. Roberts, pp. 28–9.

English translation, published in 1628 at the King's command, included a key to identification.[84] During the growing monarchomachist republican crisis, readers presented with the obscurities of political romances such as James Howell's *ΔΕΝΔΡΟΛΟΓΙΑ. the Vocall Forrest* (1640) had come to expect dense allegorical commentary. To complicate matters, peculiarities of Anthony Hodges's 1638 translation suggest that inexperience with Elizabethan and early Jacobean symbolism may have rendered readers unable to decipher the encoded imagery of *Leukippe and Kleitophon*, *Arcadia* and perhaps even Shakespeare's romances. Nonetheless, growing antiquarian interests, coupled with experience of quasi-biographical revelation in politically sensitive allegories, prompted requests for keys to both *Arcadia* and *Urania*.[85]

Sidney Wroth committed enormous emotional energy to her eight-year project, using erotic romance to catalogue personal experiences of elation and grief. The opening and closing sections of the Second Part are particularly fraught with family tragedy, presented unchronologically to achieve obfuscation. In September 1620, Sidney Wroth lost her sister Philip or Philippa Sidney Hobart or Hubbard (1594–1620).[86] Philip had processed in Anne of Denmark's funeral four rows behind her mother, Lady Lisle, and one row behind Sidney Wroth.[87] The Second Part opens with a representation of her death, her husband Selarinus (Sir John Hobart or Hubbard) [88] grieving for 'his deerer self [...] who with a feaver in child bed was taken from him', giving birth to young Philistella[89] (II.1).

---

84 *Iohn Barclay His Argenis, Translated Out Of Latine Into English: The Prose Vpon His Maiesties Command: By Sir Robert Le Grys, Knight: and the Verses by Thomas May, Esquire. With a Clauis annexed to it for the satisfaction of the Reader, and helping him to vnderstand, what persons were by the Author intended, vnder the fained Names imposed by him vpon them: And published by his Maiesties Command* (1628).

85 J. Aubrey, '*Brief Lives*', chiefly of Contemporaries, set down by John Aubrey, between the Years 1669 & 1696, ed. by A. Clark, 2 vols (Oxford: Oxford University Press, 1898), ii.250–51, transcribes D. Tyndale's belated 'key' to Arcadia, 18 February 1686/87. W. Dean, 'Henry Oxinden's Key (1628) to *The Countess of Pembroke's Arcadia*: Some Facts and Conjectures', *Sidney Newsletter and Journal*, xii, no. 2 (1993), 14–21, compares Oxinden's key. On 31 May 1640, Sir George Manners, seventh Earl of Rutland wrote to his 'Noble Cosin' asking her 'to interprete unto me the names' in 'your Urania'; cf. *The Poems of Lady Mary Wroth*, ed. by J. A. Roberts, pp. 244–5, and G. Alexander, *Writing After Sidney: The Literary Response to Sir Philip Sidney, 1586–1640*, p. 301.

86 I.xvii, lxxx.

87 J. Nichols, *The Progresses, Processions, and Magnificent Festivities of King James the First*, 4 vols (London, 1828; repr. New York: AMS Press, 1967), iii.541, citing British Library MS. Birch's 4174.

88 R. A. Rebholz, *The Life of Fulke Greville, First Lord Brooke* (Oxford: Clarendon Press, 1971), p. 254.

89 On 30 September 1620, Hobart's father wrote to Robert Sidney expressing his son's extreme grief at his wife's death; see M. V. Hay, *The Life of Robert Sidney*, p. 225.

Sidney Wroth's eldest brother, William, died of smallpox in 1612, aged twenty-two. Similarly, Pamphilia's beloved eldest brother, Parselius, a widower (II.318), dies of 'a disease infectious [...] fatall to all their family' (II.402). Having nursed the dying Parselius, Pamphilia's mother, the Queen of Morea, experiences three years of depression during which she will only see, or take food with, her husband. She finally consents to travel to Corinth, where 'nott longe after she died, and was buried with her deerest sonne and many other of he[r] children who left this world younge' (II.406). Barbara Gamage Sidney, in good health on 12 May 1621, was buried on 26 May.[90]

The metamorphosis of Mary Sidney Herbert

Anomalously, the death of the Queen of Naples is not recorded. Sidney Wroth's aunt and literary mentor, Mary Sidney Herbert, died from smallpox on 25 September 1621.[91] The 1621 title-page includes a memorial notice: *The Countesse of Mountgomeries Urania. Written by the right honorable the Lady Mary Wroath. Daughter to the right Noble Robert Earle of Leicester. And Neece to the ever famous, and renowned Sr. Phillips Sidney knight. And to ye most exele[n]t Lady Mary Countesse of Pembroke late deceased.*[92] Within the cartouche containing this text, the words *Pembroke late deceased* are engraved in reduced size. They are squeezed into a space that would comfortably accommodate *Pembroke* alone, indicating a last-minute adjustment to the plate.

In the political world of *Urania*, Mary Sidney Herbert is 'the widdow Queene of Naples' (I.363), Amphilanthus's mother, and Pamphilia's confidante and emotional ally. She is 'perfect in Poetry, and all other Princely vertues' (I.371), 'rare in Poetry' (I.489) and 'matchles' (I.661). She provides a protective matriarchal centre for the inculcation of philhellene Protestant ideals among her children, grandchildren and their associates. While no reference is made to her until long after her husband sickens and dies (Henry Herbert died in 1601) (I.304), Mary Sidney Herbert's spiritual and psychological manifestations are introduced much earlier. These are the omniscient wizard, Melissea of Delos, and Melissea's sister.

In the First Part, Melissea is 'a grave Ladie, apparreld in a black habit' – the epithet 'grave' is repeated. She dwells in a magnificent alabaster

---

90 M. P. Hannay, *Philip's Phoenix*, pp. 204–5.

91 M. P. Hannay, *Philip's Phoenix*, p. 205; M. P. Hannay, 'Herbert [Sidney] Mary, Countess of Pembroke (1561–1621)', *Oxford Dictionary of National Biography* (Oxford: Oxford University Press, 2004).

92 For a reproduction and discussion, see I.civ–cvi, cxxi.

palace, approachable only through a dark tunnel (I.139, 175, 260). As an astrologer, she possesses special knowledge about Amphilanthus, Pamphilia and their allies. Melissea's prognostications signpost future developments. She sends Steriamus, Dolorindus and Amphilanthus off on political quests that will conclude in erotic fulfilment (I.142). Like the Queen of Naples, Melissea is one of Pamphilia and Amphilanthus's strongest supporters (I.489, 661; II. 175). She also possesses insight into the deceit that drives Amphilanthus and Pamphilia into arranged marriages. She plainly warns Amphilanthus that 'a treacherous servant', coupled with his 'owne rashnesse' (I.140), will cause him to lose Pamphilia. In contrast, she delivers Pamphilia an oracularly enigmatic prophecy: 'I cannot finde that you shall marry yet, nor him you most affect, many afflictions you must undergoe, and all by woman kinde' (I.190).

The Second Part begins with the Queen of Naples greeting her 'deerest sonn', Amphilanthus, now Holy Roman Emperor, and her niece Pamphilia. Sidney Wroth enhances Melissea's other-worldly role in the Second Part, where she appears in visions, or mental constructs. Her prognostications contrast with the action, creating dramatic irony: 'This Lady hath an infinite love to the Morean Court and is their protectress, yett can not alltogether, though help, hinder the Crossnesses of their adventures' (II.61). She acts in concert with the Queen of Naples to create a mystical, protective nursery to nurture and educate many of the offspring of the Morean–Neapolitan alliance (II.22–3, 145).[93] This school is run by Melissea's sister (or sister-in-law), who lives in a 'glorious pallace' (II.4) of white marble, approached only by a dark, narrow passage through a rock – Melissea's palace. She is closely linked to Melissea through a string of consistently shared epithets. The 'aged' (II.112) Melissea is 'wise' (II.3, 225); 'sage' (II.51–3, 112–13, 145, 323, 418); 'grave' (II.112, 174, 233, 321, 353); and 'the sage and most-honored Melissea' (II.401). Her sister, a 'grave Lady', is also described as 'sage, grave, and most carefull' (II.4, 224, 225).

Truth and illusion

Sidney Wroth embeds Selarinus's story within a masque-like mixture of fact and fantasy. While at Melissea's sister's house, Selarinus meets a spiritual manifestation of the daughter of the King of Tartaria, whose mother is 'a Persian' (II.9). This Princess of Tartaria shares her pale complexion and black eyes with Rodomandro (II.7). She looks the same, but is not

---

93 Cf. S. T. Cavanagh, *Cherished Torment: The Emotional Geography of Lady Mary Wroth's Urania*, pp. 198–200.

the same, as 'the King of Tartaria's sister and his onely one', who is 'nott above foreteene' (II.76) when Licandro, Prince of Athens, falls in love with her. The masque-like allegory implies that Hobart, like Selarinus, is driven into an unfortunate affair with an estranged and mad part-sister of Robert Wroth.

Against her father's strongest protest, Rodomandro's sister marries Tolendo of Frigia, 'a younger brother' (II.9), who as second son is not a direct heir. They have a son and a daughter. In Tolendo's family of aspiring tyrants, Frigia's eldest son attempts to seize the throne and Tolendo is killed by his younger brother. Marrying into this political turmoil has cost Rodomandro's sister 'all my freinds […] my owne blood hating mee to death'. She is particularly 'tormented' by 'my brothers hatred to mee' (II.9). Nonetheless, before she retreats 'from all the world' (II.9), she places her children where they are 'safe, and inchanted, wher alsoe many more are' (II.9) – with Melissea's sister.

Rodomandro's sister dismisses her conversation with Selarinus as 'a dreame'. She instructs him to 'beeleeve this butt a fiction' of 'us vaine spiritts heere, who delight in our selves onely in abusing mortalls' (II.10). But Sidney Wroth takes care to ensure this character's veracity. Rodomandro's sister accurately reports that her step-sister, Veralinda, who succeeds as Queen of Frigia when the king's fourth son dies, and is now married to Leonius (Amphilanthus's and Urania's brother), is helping to arm Rodomandro.

Rodomandro is preparing to march on the usurping Sultan of Persia (II.10). This usurper, having murdered his brother and imprisoned young Lindafillia, the 'rightfull Sophie of Persia' and a Christian, demands Rodomandro's fiancée, Pamphilia, as his wife (II.155, 169–70). Rodomandro attacks at the head of the combined forces of the west and the east.

In Persia, the heroes of the younger generation excel themselves. Amphilionus (Veralinda and Leonius's younger son, who resembles Amphilanthus) kills the usurper. Amphilanthus is rescued by his 'Nephew of Albania', Floristello, the son of Urania and Steriamus (II.266). And Amphilanthus's protégé, the Knight of the Faire Design, frees 'his incomparable mistres, Lindafillia, the most rarely lovely and most Vertuously chaste Percian' (II.366).

With disastrous consequences, Rodomandro's real-unreal sister once again appears to Selarinus in a dream-vision. According to the narrator, 'this was the same develish spiritt that hanted him beefor in Melisseas sisters house, and held ther from doing harme many yeers; butt lett loose […] a deadly Hellhound' (II.305). Selarinus remains unaware that her sojourn in the care of Melissea's sister has, like Antissia's, been as a mental patient (II.252). She drugs Selarinus, seduces him, has two children, and after several years abandons him for dead (II.397). Revived by 'a Violl of water' delivered by a disembodied arm with a message from Melissea (II.397), Selarinus is rescued by a Morean widow. He then returns to the Morean court, accompanied by Urania's third son, Stervanius. Once there, Melissea entrusts Selarinus's two 'Fairy babes' to the widow (II.401). By observing that Selarinus's depression makes him prone to 'frenzie' (II.398), and reassuring him that Philistella has 'chosen' Morean widow's home to appear to him in his dreams (II.399), Sidney Wroth hints at a masque-like representation of Hobart's life in the years immediately after he loses his wife.

During the era in which Galileo invites the Vatican censor to give 'these thoughts of mine the labels of chimeras, dreams, paralogisms, and empty images',[94] Sidney Wroth similarly dismisses contentious strands of her densely textured allegory as dreams and visions. Of a parallel nature to the vanishing Throne of Love and enchanted theatre, Melissea's masque for Pamphilia, an allegorical entertainment, is glossed as 'butt a phansie' (II.115). In Melissea's (Mary Sidney Herbert's) illusions, the apocalyptic supernatural elides into the natural: 'ther appeerd a strange darknes, and in that darknes a fearfull fire, which presented a chariott drawne with four firy dragons [...] in the body [...] satt an aged Lady'.

Melissea provides 'many severall shewes and mascoradoes' while she holds a 'privatt conference' with Pamphilia. They return to an allegorical 'show' performed by 'an aged sheapheard and a younge sea-faring lad'. The youth is in love with 'a dainty sea nimph', whom he addresses in a song.[95] In another song, the old man counsels against 'the Idolatry of love'.[96] All three then, singing 'in severall parts, songe the last tow lines [...] and soe vanishte' (II.112–14). When Melissea interprets for Pamphilia, she adds an ominous personal gloss: 'love indeed hath a more steddy place and throne of abiding when in such Royall harts – I doe nott say, your Majesties' (II.115).

94 D. Sobel, *Galileo's Daughter* (New York: Walker & Co., 1999; repr. New York: Penguin Books, 2000), p. 218.
95 *The Poems of Lady Mary Wroth*, ed. by J. A. Roberts, N12.
96 *The Poems of Lady Mary Wroth*, ed. by J. A. Roberts, N13.

Rodomandro's masque

Melissea's aside confirms that Pamphilia's relationship with Amphilanthus is fraught with accusations of lack of constancy (II.110). Their idealised erotic and spiritual union is shattered, and contrasts with the stability of Pamphilia's arranged marriage to the verbally gauche, but thoroughly genuine chivalric hero, Rodomandro. As a record of their tripartite relationship, *Urania* dwells on the erotic emotions that persist when the practice of arranged marriage interrupts love's natural course.

Unlike Lindamira's jealous husband, Rodomandro comes off second best in Amphilanthus's company, but is never portrayed as obstructive, bad tempered or violent. On the contrary, he is an adoring, accomplished courtier who woos Pamphilia through an elaborate masque. Where Sidney Wroth only briefly describes the pre-nuptial masque for the Princess of Cephalonia and the son of the Lord of Zante (i.e., Zakynthos) (I.41–2), Rodomandro's portrayal of Cupid's submission to 'Honor' and Truth, his personal priorities, is a prominent set-piece interpolation into the text (II.46–9).

Rodomandro's masque consists of a flyting between Cupid and 'Honor' in matters of love. If this event has a historical basis, it would have occurred late in 1603, or during the first half of 1604. The narrative records precise details of the performance, but Sidney Wroth's rhetoric of obfuscation ensures that her husband remains only semi-visible. She disguises him within vague, metaphor-laden hyperbole. He is 'neither to high nor of the meanest stature', with 'hands soe white as wowld have beecome a great Lady' (II.42). While his well tanned face 'plainely shewed the sunn had either liked itt to much, and soe had too hard kissed itt', his eyes convey laudable determination: 'His diamound eyes (though attired in black) did soe sparcle gainst his rays as made them in ther owne hardnes knowe strength against his beames' (II.42).

The conflicts within Pamphilia–Sidney Wroth's heart dominate the narrator's interpretation. When the handsome Theagenes, a descendant of Achilles, parades in ceremonial dress on his majestic horse before Charikleia (2.34; Reardon, p. 408), they experience a Platonic recognition of matching souls: 'at the moment when they set eyes on one another, the young pair fell in love, as if the soul recognised its kin at the very first encounter and sped to meet that which was worthily its own. For a brief second full of emotion they stood motionless' (3.4–5; Reardon, pp. 412–14). Shakespeare represents such a moment in *The Tempest*, when Ferdinand and Miranda first meet (I.ii.413ff.). Nothing could be farther from Sidney Wroth's depiction of Pamphilia's sterile, one-way encounter with her husband-to-be.

Rodomandro surrenders himself to Pamphilia: 'the Tartarians black eyes must needs incounter the true heaven of Pamphilias gray eyes and yeeld to them, as to the perfect sky, the rule of his and their thoughts'. In contrast, Pamphilia 'never looked soe much on Rodomandro as to see which way his eyes had beestowed them selves, yett saw Amphilanthus was displeasd' (II.44). For Pamphilia has already given her heart to Amphilanthus, and made herself his subject: 'Commaund when you please, and I obay' (II.45).

Rodomandro enters as one of twelve masquers, elaborately dressed 'after the Tartarian fashion' (II.46). The elegance of display, dance, and rhythmic ecphrasis is interrupted when Cupid objects to the Tartarians abandoning their own women:

> Cupid came in puffing and blowing most pitifully and crying out thes words haulf breathles, and the other part as if distracted: 'O my gallant youthes, whether are you rambled abroad [...] May nott the beauties of Tartaria for ever hate mee, revile my government, scorne my power, to see their deeres thus stray from them to gaze on other faces?' (II.46)

Honor, 'Cupids just borne Kinge' (II.49), intervenes on behalf of the Tartarian ladies:

> leave your bauling, good childe, and knowe that thes most worthy and famous knights have chosen mee ther guide, and I will also bee their guardian, leading them with honor onely to brave attempts [...] I will thus disarme thee and henceforthe charme thee never to meddle wher true honor governs. (II.47)

The masque concludes in Cupid's submission to Honor, in a poem echoing Angel Day's pastoral: 'This is Honors holly day: / Now sheapheard swaines, neatheards play, / Cupid wills itt soe' (II.48).[97] In this way, Sidney Wroth acknowledges Day's literary precedent in incorporating a full masque into European erotic romance. She was subsequently followed by the precocious borrower of others' material Robert Baron, who inserts his masque *Hegio and Agrippa* into *ΕΡΟΤΟΠΑΙΓΝΙΟΝ Or The Cyprian Academy* (1647).

In contrast to her initial response to Rodomandro, Pamphilia's retrospective assessment of him exudes appreciation, if not warmth. He becomes 'an exquisitt man in all things, and a Christian, and grew

97 Cf. *The Poems of Lady Mary Wroth*, ed. by J. A. Roberts, N4, N5.

intimate in freindship with the Emperour', Amphilanthus, 'who esteem'd him above all forraine Princes, except Ollorandus' (II.46), his youthful protégé. (In real life, this may have been Benjamin Rudyerd,[98] or possibly William Sidney and/or young Robert Sidney.) Nonetheless, Pamphilia's relationship with her husband remains, like Rodomandro's masque, enshrouded within the conscientious evasiveness of *Urania*.

Female abuse and martyrdom

The integration of the royal houses of Morea, Naples, Sicily, Achaia, Albania and Macedonia expresses Sidney Wroth's futuristic vision of a united philhelene Protestant Europe. It extends into Asia through a network of partisan political dynasties brought together through the agency of erotic love, and the exercise of free will in marriage. Its combined power under Amphilanthus is unassailable, as it exercises the chivalric code of bringing usurping tyrants to heel, and promotes intellectual, political and emotional liberty for both women and men.

Sidney Wroth's philhelene Protestant policy dictates the perspective in which she places domestic politics. Tyrannical husbands, like tyrannical rulers, are reviled. The ill effects engendered by their repressive practices are illustrated by the kingdom of Dacia. Limandro, Duke of Saxony, describes Dacia as a society institutionalising female subordination. This is based on the conviction that men instinctively know that women are prone to moral turpitude – 'the men having an naturall knowing unworthines about them, which procures too much hatefull Jealousy' (II.14). For women, compulsory attendance at court is little different from structured entrapment, 'butt as if a triall of their fashions, which if in the least amiss, ore if thought soe, itt shalbee for a perpetuall memorie sett up to continuall punnishment, soe as their libertie is butt the forerunner of a lastinger punishment and perpetuall suffring' (II.14).

Through her allegory, Sidney Wroth offers hope to women in analogous situations. In such extremities, the need for love transcends the rules that govern extra-marital relationships. Her message is that women should accept the endearing warmth of human love, as does Celia, whenever it presents itself (II.17).

In addition to associating political with domestic tyranny, Limena's tale connects female abuse with Christian martyrdom. Limena's tyrannical father belongs to an anti-monarchist and anti-populist class of

98 I.xci.

Sicilian 'Gentleman', a group of self-interested usurpers who are defeated by Amphilanthus and Parselius. When civil war breaks out 'betweene the people and the Gentlemen', the people lay siege to the king, wrongly 'imagining he tooke the other part' (I.5) against them. During a lull in the fighting, Perissus 'stole from mine uncle to see my heart' (I.5), only to find that Limena's father has already married her to Philargus – 'lover of money' – a jealous bully and sadist.

As Limena refuses to forfeit her lengthy, loving, and chaste relationship with Perissus, Philargus's abuse escalates from verbal hostility to ritualistic mutilation. He corners Limena in her cabinet or study, draws his sword and threatens her. Her submission to this tyranny reflects the precarious position in which seventeenth-century women were placed by patriarchal regulations of church and state: 'This wretched, and unfortunate body, is I confesse in your hands, to dispose of to death if you will' (I.13).

In his uncle's Kingdom of Naples, Parselius finds Philargus, fully clad in armour, about to whip Limena:

> leading her to a pillar which stood on the sand […] he tied her to it by the haire, which was of great length, […] Then pulled hee off a mantle which she wore, leaving her from the girdle upwards al naked, her soft, daintie white hands hee fastened behind her, with a cord about both wrists, in manner of a crosse, as testimony of her cruellest Martyrdome.
> When shee was thus miserably bound to his unmercifull liking, with whipps hee was about to torment her: but Parselius […]. (I.84)

In Sidney Wroth's Naples, the cradle of philhellene, monarchomachist ideals, Philargus's behaviour is intolerable. Parselius exercises justified killing.

Limena's resignation reflects her legal, though not her moral, position: 'I know, as your wife, I am in your power to dispose of; then use your authority' (I.87). Such acquiescence belongs to less enlightened societies than that to which philhellene Protestants aspired. But the practice prevailed. In 1620, in France, eleven-year-old Henriette-Marie, daughter of the Huguenot leader-turned-Catholic Henri IV and Marie de Médicis, was fully indoctrinated into the reactionary belief that 'a wife ought to have no will but that of her husband'.[99] In 1625, she would marry the would-be tyrant Charles I of England, and change her convictions.

---

99 Sir Edward Herbert, despatch dated 14 August 1620, British Library, Harleian MS 1581, fol. 15, cited in S. R. Gardiner, 'Henrietta Maria (1609–1669)', in *The Compact Edition of the Dictionary of National Biography*, 2 vols (Oxford: Oxford University Press, 1975).

Ancient erotic romance contains stoic heroines, but not Renaissance chivalric solutions. When threatened with rape and physical defilement, Achilles Tatius's Leukippe asserts the inviolability of her personal integrity: 'I am unarmed, alone, a woman. My one weapon is my freedom, which cannot be shredded by lashes, dismembered by sharp blades, or burned away by fire. It is the one thing I shall never part with' (6.22; Reardon, p. 259). The gods intervene to rescue Leukippe and punish Thersandros. In *Urania*, a vehicle promoting philhellene Protestant ideals, evils perpetrated against women are rectified by chivalric heroes like Parselius.

Sidney Wroth demonstrates Philargus's anti-Christian tyranny by associating him with pagan religious sacrifice. He takes Limena '(to my death I hoped)' deep into 'a great Wood, in the midst whereof he made a fire, the place being fit, and I thinke, sure had been used in former time to offer sacrifice unto the Silvan Gods' (I.87). Forced to 'undresse my selfe', she stoically prepares for martyrdom in the cause of Christian–Platonic love, 'the poore offring, but the richest, that richnese of faith in love could offer'.

Philargus's particular pleasure is breast mutilation, associating Limena with the female saints Agathan (breasts cut off), Febronia and Macra (breasts cut off with shears) and Calliopa and Reparata (hot irons applied).[100] But where Limena hides her breasts from her husband, retaining the protection of 'one little Petticote' which he tears away, she happily displays her scars to her beloved Perissus. The narrator's commentary indicates that this token of her trust has a calculated erotic impact:[101] '"he opened my breast, and gave me many wounds, the markes you may here yet discerne" (letting the Mantle fall againe a little lower, to shew the cruell remembrance of his crueltie) which although they were whole, yet made they newe hurts in the loving heart of Perissus' (I.87).

Using a convincing plain style,[102] Limena describes the catalogue of horrors to which her husband subjects her. Philargus 'tooke my clothes, and with them wip'd the bloud off from me [...] taking me by the haire, and dragging me into the Wood among the bushes' (I.88). He ties her to a tree, steals a coat and horse, gags her, arrives at the seaside, procures a boat, and sails from Sicily to Naples. There he applies

---

100 H. Roeder, *Saints and their Attributes* (London: Longmans, Green and Co, 1955), pp. 72–3, 290.

101 Cf. H. Hackett, 'The Torture of Limena: Sex and Violence in Lady Mary Wroth's *Urania*', in *Voicing Women: Gender and Sexuality in Early Modern Writing*, ed. by K. Chedgzoy, M. Hansen and S. Trill (Keele: Keele University Press, 1996), pp. 93–110.

102 Cf. V. Skretkowicz, 'Lady Mary Wroth's *Urania* and the Rhetoric of Female Abuse', in *Challenging Tradition: Women and the History of Rhetoric*, ed. by C. M. Sutherland and R. Sutcliffe (Calgary: University of Calgary Press, 1999), pp. 133–45.

daily whippings, and such other tortures, as pinching with irons, and many more so terrible, as for your sake (seeing your griefe my deerest Lord) I wil omit, declaring only this […] Once every day hee brought mee to this pillar where you found me, and in the like manner bound me, then whipt me, after washing the stripes and blisters with salt water […]. (I.88)

Emulating Heliodorus's historical technique,[103] Sidney Wroth validates the details that Limena presents by having her insist that those omitted are too grisly to record. Her clear, factual account is couched in the plain style of a historian to enhance the impression of truth: 'Thus my Lords have you heard the afflicted life of poore Limena, in whom these tortures wrought no otherwise, then to strengthen her love, and faith to withstand them' (I.88). Her veracity is further attested to by Philargus's confession, as he undergoes the Christian ritual of dying well, or 'holy dying'. Bestowing his estate on Limena, Philargus's last request is that she and Perissus should marry (I.86). They set off for Sicily with a company of Neapolitans, who restore the throne to Perissus (I.89).

Hereditary succession and restoration

Limena's harrowing experience is accentuated by its comic parallel in the allegorical tale of the mad shepherd Alanius's ritual abuse of Nereana.[104] Nereana, Princess of 'Stalamine, anciently Lemnos', rules as a tyrant. She is 'descended from the kings of Romania, absolute Lady of that Iland' (I.192). Expanding the range of monarchomachist satire, Sidney Wroth develops her as a caricature, creating a comic study of Nereana's inter-related psychoses, inflated egocentrism, and erotic obsession for Steriamus. Nereana's 'most ignorantly proud' antics make her the butt of humour among liberally minded Neapolitans and Moreans. Steriamus, harbouring a secret passion for Pamphilia, rejects Nereana's 'profferd love', and castigates her for exhibiting 'impudent pride' and 'vainely over-esteeming your selfe' (I.192). The monarchomachist Sidney Wroth engineers her humiliation, exposing her vanity in an interview with Pamphilia (I.193–5).

Nereana's story opens with Liana's forced engagement. Liana's father, exiled Lord of Provence and chief shepherd of Pantaleria (where Urania spends her childhood), typifies the patriarchal tyranny identified with

103 Cf. J. R. Morgan, 'History, Romance and Realism in the *Aithiopika* of Heliodoros', *Classical Antiquity*, i (1982), 221–65.
104 On Nereana, see S. T. Cavanagh, *Cherished Torment: The Emotional Geography of Lady Mary Wroth's Urania*, pp. 64–8.

states outwith the Morean alliance. Liana loves Alanius, a stranger. But though her father has promised 'never to force me against my will, to marry any' (I.248), he engages her to a countryman 'to breed me too' (I.247). The tyrannical Pantalerian's word is law:

> your Will ought to be no other then obedience [...] you should be rather wilfull in obeying, then question what I appoint; [...] if you like not as I like, and wed where I will you, you shall never from me receive least favour, but be accompted a stranger and a lost childe. (I.248)

Liana catches a shepherd courting a young maid. Not knowing that this impostor has stolen Alanius's clothing, she rejects Alanius, who sinks into a prolonged madness (I.247–52). It still afflicts him when he finds Nereana after her ship has been blown to Sicily, and she is benighted in a forest (I.255–6). Mistaking Nereana for Liana, Alanius folds her in his arms. She wakens, and so haughtily rebukes him that he believes she is 'the Goddesse of those woods' (I.197).

Nereana's degradation into a parodic pre-Christian icon contrasts with Limena's martyrdom. Needing to worship her in woodland garb, Alanius ties Nereana to a tree, 'undress'd her', and pulls her hair down 'full length' (I.197). She is naked 'save onely one little petticoate of carnation tafatie', symbolising desire, and 'her greene silke stockins' (I.197–8), the colour of moral laxity. Alanius rolls her stockings down to approximate buskins, drapes her with field flowers, and places a whittled stick in her hand.

Nereana's misdirected stoicism lacks philhellene Protestant humility. In a self-indulgent apostrophe to herself, she laments her 'luckles chance': 'how art thou lost, abused, neglected and forsaken? [...] thine owne royall spirit shall never leave thee, and if once thou canst but get free [...] thy power reward thy servants disloyalty' (I.198–9). The mad Alanius now believes that Nereana is Arethusa, having 'resumd your naturall body from that *Metamorphosis*' (I.200). But the uneducated anti-humanist, Nereana, 'never having heard of any such thing as a *Metamorphosis*, her wit lying another way' (I.200), displays appalling ignorance of the lessons to be gleaned from Ovid's parables of punished self-love.

Nereana's literary philistinism reflects her moral and ethical failings. During her absence, Lemnos is governed by her younger sister, whom Nereana had kept imprisoned. This sister gains popular support and imprisons Nereana on her return. Nonetheless, despite her history of governing tyrannically, Nereana is restored to preserve the principle of succession (I.335–8, 496). This episode, used to close both the Second and Third Books of the 1621 *Urania*, accentuates the conflict, outlined in the *Vindiciae, contra tyrannos,* between laws governing heredity and the ruler's responsibility to govern well.

If Nereana's allegorical example is matched by the blatant artificiality of her tale, use of the historical plain style gives the story of Corianus's recognition an air of authenticity. The dispossessed Corianus is 'the sunn of the naturall sonn of your father by a great Lady, a widow in this Country' (II.11). Perissus legitimises Corianus, securing the family's income and status by appointing him chief forester. His bride's father, Clominus (Limena's father's younger brother), is made a lord and Household officer, and Corianus's sister enters Limena's household as a Lady of the Queen's Chamber. Corianus is created 'Erle of that Castle, which was a County anciently of itt self' (II.12).

Sidney Wroth uses Corianus to illustrate how the third generation of philhellene Protestants closed ranks in support of fallen worthies. In particular, rather than excluding children born out of wedlock, she argues for legitimacy of birth and hereditary succession, following the sequence of offspring within the 'natural' blood-line. While this was clearly an issue in relation to her two children by Herbert, Corianus's restoration to a 'county' title may be modelled on the earls of Hertford ('cor' = 'heart'). The title of the first Earl, Edward Seymour,[105] bypassed his and Katherine Grey's 'natural' son Edward,[106] Viscount Beauchamp (1561–1612). In the event, Beauchamp's first son, Edward (1587–1618), who on 1 June 1609 married Ann Sackville, one of Anne Clifford's sisters-in-law, predeceased his grandfather, who died in 1621. Corianus's successful appeal for recognition parallels that of Beauchamp's second son, William Seymour (1587–1660).[107] In 1611, William secretly married Arabella Stuart, who died in September 1615. William Seymour subsequently enjoyed a meteoric rise as a late royal favourite. In 1618, the year his elder brother died, Seymour married Frances Devereux, eldest daughter of Robert, second Earl of Essex, and Frances Walsingham Sidney. He succeeded to the earldom of Hertford on the death of his grandfather.

105 See S. Doran, 'Seymour, Edward, First Earl of Hertford (1539?–1621)', *Oxford Dictionary of National Biography* (Oxford: Oxford University Press, 2004).
106 See S. Doran, 'Seymour [Grey], Katherine, Countess of Hertford (1540?–1568)', *Oxford Dictionary of National Biography* (Oxford: Oxford University Press, 2004).
107 D. L. Smith, 'Seymour, William, First Marquess of Hertford and Second Duke of Somerset (1587–1660)', *Oxford Dictionary of National Biography* (Oxford: Oxford University Press, 2004).

Liberation, restoration and marital union

Urania, in which good kings equate with good fathers, and tyrants with oppressive patriarchs, is a Jacobean feminist antidote to Machiavelli's *The Prince*. It serves as a handbook for aspiring or newly ensconced monarchs of uncertain succession, or for their domestic equivalents, the beneficiaries of complex estates. Like Sidney's *Old Arcadia*, and the 'complete' 1593 edition, *Urania* warns of dangerous interests, particularly among blood relatives, that threaten to ensnare any monarchy during its precarious infancy. It also demonstrates emphatically how newly established rulers can benefit from binding themselves to the interests of the Morean–Protestant federation.

The effectiveness of this policy is illustrated when Ollorandus of Bohemia brings Hungary under Morean influence. In conversation with Amphilanthus, 'betweene whom grew so strict a bond of Friendship, as was never to be broken' (I.77), Ollorandus describes a dream in which a beautiful woman exhorts him to 'leave Bohemia, and rescue me from the hands of Rebels' (I.78). When he awakes, he discovers an 'Armour laid with this Shield, and Sword' of the Forest Knight. He and the reader subsequently learn from the supernatural visionary Meilissea that she has planted these arms. That she is 'as carefull, or more of you then any' suggests that, like a *dea ex machina*, she controls Ollorandus's every thought, and that his historical equivalent enjoys a privileged and personal relationship with Mary Sidney Herbert (I.142).

Ollorandus, refused 'the honour of Knight-hoode' by his father 'because my elder Brother, being weake and sickly, had not demanded it' (I.78), has his appeal granted by the Emperor. Armed and of appropriate status, he sets out to rescue Melasinda, the poet and Queen of Hungary. Ollorandus finds her usurped by her cousin, Rodolindus. Melasinda's succession is complex and precarious. She has been crowned 'after the decease of her Uncle' (I.79), the king, and the death of her father, the king's younger brother. But her claim to the throne is challenged by the heavily armed Rodolindus, 'the uncle Kings Bastard sonne', who cleverly and divisively 'claym'd a contract betweene the King and his mother'.

Melasinda takes refuge in 'an ancient Lords Castle, within two leagues of the City of Buda' (I.79).[108] With Ollorandus's intervention, a peaceful accommodation is reached: Rodolindus 'should lay downe all claime to the Crowne, yeelding it wholly to her; but in requitall, shee should

---

108 On Melasinda and Buda, see S. T. Cavanagh, *Cherished Torment: The Emotional Geography of Lady Mary Wroth's Urania*, pp. 55–63.

take him for her Husband [...] but this she must doe, or be left alone, people-lesse, and kingdome-lesse' (I.79). Despite her forced marriage to Rodolindus, love triumphs for Ollorandus and Melasinda. The day after her wedding, overcoming 'a great hate [...] between our Parents' (I.79). and the 'unkindnesse betweene our Parents' (I.80), they begin an enduring relationship in Melasinda's private locked garden. Eventually sensing danger, Ollorandus joins Amphilanthus in Morea, where he is preparing to invade Albania.

Sidney Wroth blends Ollorandus's seemingly innocuous reference to Buda into the illusory *trompe l'oeil* of her quasi-autobiographical fiction. Buda becomes a framing device that creates a carefully blurred synthesis between the closely bonded Ollorandus and Amphilanthus; and between Melasinda and the Fisher-Lady, Bellamira and Pamphilia.

When the now-experienced Ollorandus re-enters Hungary with Amphilanthus, his mind falls under the spell of psychological association: 'knowing, the place where his Mistris most commonly lived at, was seated on this streame [i.e., the Danube], his thoughts were busied on her, and Amphilanthus as passionately contemplated his love' (I.288). Ollorandus's first impression of the Fisher-Lady is that she 'did much resemble his Mistris: but as a true lover thought shee came farre short of her perfections' (I.290). This schematic negation alerts the reader to the implied affinity between them, for the Fisher-Lady (Sidney Wroth herself) lives with her now loving and tolerant husband on a tributary of the Danube (I.295).

This idyllic erotic interlude is divorced from Hungarian politics. Nonetheless, while telling Amphilanthus about her falling in love with her cousin Laurimello, the Fisher-Lady reveals that 'My father had a sister married to one of the noblest and greatest Princes of this Countrie', and that 'my Fathers estate lay neare to the Citie of Buda' (I.291). And it is directly to Buda that Amphilanthus and Ollorandus proceed, the example of the Fisher-Lady's marriage of compromise framed by allusions to Melasinda's (I.296).

Sidney Wroth's history of the developing philhellene Protestant dynasty manifests itself in the Morean–Neapolitan links created around Melasinda. In a self-interested act of bravado, her husband Rodolindus jousts in disguise against the incomparable Amphilanthus. Rodolindus is 'throwne to the ground much brused', and 'within some few months' dies of an infection, leaving Melasinda, a 'perfect and excellent' (I.296) widow.[109]

---

109 Benjamin Rudyerd married Mary Harrington; D. L. Smith, 'Rudyerd, Sir Benjamin (1572–1658)', *Oxford Dictionary of National Biography* (Oxford: Oxford University Press, 2004).

But the loving Melasinda and Ollorandus, whom Amphilanthus appoints his 'Deputy till his arrivall' (I.454) as Emperor in Prague, and 'whom he made his Deputy with the Princesse to governe in his absence' (I.486), continue to fall victim to others' interests.

Melasinda is kidnapped during a revolt of the Bohemians, 'ever the most turbulent, hereticall, and tumultious people' (II.181). Their tyrannical leader has filled his castle with prisoners, including Amphilanthus's 'Chamberlaine of the Empire' (II.181), Polarchos. This wrong is addressed in summary fashion by Antissius II and his master of horse, Allimarlus, one of the select few present at Amphilanthus's *de praesanti* marriage to Pamphilia. A monarchomachist, Melasinda demands that Antissius II behead the tyrant. Accordingly, the tyrant's head, quartered torso and heart are hung on a tree, his bowels left 'in the durt', and his dead servants 'layd round the tree, to serve a fitt guard' (II.179–80). These are grim tokens of the Morean–Neapolitan determination to impose enlightened political dominance through tried and tested means of intimidation. Finally, besieged in Buda, Melasinda is relieved by Amphilanthus, Ollorandus and the young Knight of the Faire Design. After Ollorandus dies (II.366), Melasinda installs her son, Ollorandus junior, as ruler in Bohemia, and retreats to a monastery at Buda. Three years later, she and the widower Parselius flirt with the idea of marriage, but he dies before a legal agreement can be reached (II.401–2).

Meriana and the Macedonian succession

The exemplary nature of Melasinda's political situation becomes blurred through shifting the focus on to her romantic involvements with allegorical representations of the Sidney family. Similarly, the topics of female succession, tyranny and legalised rape, developed in the Meriana episode, gain significance by association with characters in the opening sequence. Intertwining overlapping themes with complex representational characterisation is used with considerable effectiveness by Heliodorus. Here this rhetorical ploy serves the function of signalling personal and familial allegory.

The old Albanian king tells Parselius how, before his children were born, he 'was beaten out of my country' by the Morean–Neapolitan–Macedonian familial alliance for 'taking part with Achaya' during 'the warres between Achaya and Macedon' (I.24). He and his queen are refused hospitality by Parselius's mother, Queen of Morea, who 'being Sister to the Macedonian king then living, would not permit me any favour' (I.24).

Political interests change with the passage of time. Now, because 'your Uncle is dead' (I.24) and the 'Macedonian Usurper' (I.25), Clotorindus, has imprisoned young Queen Meriana, Parselius must take the Albanian royal children into his care.

Meriana ('meriting', or 'deserving her inheritance'), although the 'right heire to the kingdom of Macedon, being only daughter to the last king', has been usurped. Clotorindus, the 'next heire-male, which by the lawes of the country was otherwise, hath got the Crowne' (I.24). To legitimise his claim under Salic law, which excludes females from hereditary succession, he intends to imprison Meriana 'in a strong tower til she be of age, and then to marry her; or if shee refuse, to keep her there stil' (I.24).

Sidney Wroth embeds this exemplary crisis into the mainstream of political interests. She contrives to have Rosindy, Parselius's and Pamphilia's brother, secretly visit, fall in love and exchange vows with Meriana (I.108–10). In Rosindy, Sidney Wroth represents her brother Robert Sidney (1595–1677), later second Earl of Leicester. Their father's two commonplace books, compiled about 1600 and 1613–15 and enlarged by young Robert, 'served as reference works' and the basis of his own seven commonplace books.[110] They may also have coloured Sidney Wroth's depiction of Meriana's predicament.

Robert senior's notes demonstrate that his Protestantism, like his brother Philip's and daughter Mary Sidney Wroth's, 'seems fundamentally more political than theological in nature'.[111] *Urania* also reflects her father's and brother's interest in variant scenarios of succession, by 'heirs who were bastards, fools, women, madmen, foreigners, or children'.[112] Focusing particularly on how 'problems multiply when the new monarch is a woman', Robert senior's observations on 'the constant negotiation or conflict over the extent of the prince's prerogative' that 'takes place in every monarchy'[113] are exemplified by Meriana's plight. In addition, this vignette doubles as a familial satire on the prickly Henry Percy, ninth Earl of Northumberland, Robert senior's friend, whose daughter Dorothy (1598–1659) married Robert junior in July 1616.[114] They were already

---

110 R. Shephard, 'The Political Commonplace Books of Sir Robert Sidney', pp. 6–7; cf. G. Warkentin, 'Humanism in Hard Times: The Second Earl of Leicester (1595–1677) and His Commonplace Books, 1630–60', in *Challenging Humanism: Essays in Honor of Dominic Baker-Smith*, ed. by T. Hoenselaars and A. F. Kinney (Newark: University of Delaware Press, 2005), pp. 229–53.

111 R. Shephard, 'The Political Commonplace Books of Sir Robert Sidney', p. 20.

112 R. Shephard, 'The Political Commonplace Books of Sir Robert Sidney', p. 23.

113 R. Shephard, 'The Political Commonplace Books of Sir Robert Sidney', pp. 21, 23.

114 Cf. G. R. Batho, 'A Difficult Father-in-Law: The Ninth Earl of Northumberland'.

distantly related by marriage. In 1578, Robert's great-uncle Robert Dudley, Earl of Leicester, married the dowager Countess of Essex, Lettice Knollys Devereux. Her daughter, Dorothy Devereux Perrot Percy, sister of Robert Devereux, second Earl of Essex, was Dorothy Percy's mother.

In an extraordinary exhibition of the power of an erotically inclined female adolescent to influence the course of European Protestant political integration, Pamphilia hastens Meriana's restoration. Pamphilia's confidence and assertiveness when intervening on others' behalf contrasts with her own self-doubts. She has no compunction about combining self-interest, erotic romance and international politics to ensure that the Moreans prioritise war against Clotorindus, assuring Rosindy, 'I will order it so, as that shall bee first' (I.111). She knows she can manipulate her mother to persuade the king, because 'the young Queene is her Neece […] and Macedon once quieted, Albania will be the sooner won' (I.116).

To persuade Rosindy to raise his siege of Thessalonica, Clotorindus justifies his claim to the kingdom. He holds Macedon as 'next heire male. And 'now by marriage with Meriana, daughter and heire, as you terme her, to the Crowne' (I.157), he boasts he is related to Rosindy. Rosindy, knowing Meriana's devotion to him, rejects both the marriage and family tie. Questions about the whether this marriage took place, or its legality, are avoided by the defeated Clotorindus's cowardly suicide (I.159). Under attack, he may have decided to murder Meriana, an extension of what Rosindy understands is his original threat, to immure her in a stone cell, 'keeping her thus, with intent to marry her, if he can gaine her consent; if not, so to hold her inclos'd during her life' (I.108). Rosindy and Selarinus search the palace, locating the abandoned Meriana through her barely audible lamentation, 'heere must I consume my dayes unknowne to thee, and wald up with misery, and famine die' (I.159).

Rosindy's rescuing the legitimate heir, now either still unmarried, or illegally married and a widow, has an immediate impact on the state. He and Meriana become 'betroathed […] the Macedonians […] yeelding themselves as her loyall Subjects, and taking oathes to her, and Rosindy of alleageance' (I.160). Having military control, Rosindy ruthlessly extends the grasping tentacles of the Morean royal family's interests. He makes political appointments: 'Then sent hee new Governours and Commanders to all the frontier Townes, and into the cheife strengths within the Land' (I.160). He seizes property, 'requiting the Moreans with the estates of those that were lost in the battaile, and the Towne'. And he encourages pillage to redistribute wealth among the allies or 'strangers', granting them 'the booty, which was infinite' (I.160). Then, by virtue of his marriage and the gift of the newly restored queen, 'who gave precedence in place, and government, to her husband' (I.211), Rosindy becomes King of Macedonia.

Meriana has never seen her Morean family (I.24, 116). She and her cousin Pamphilia are 'but newly acquainted' when they talk about poetry in the company of Meriana's 'younger and halfe Sister' (I.460), Perselina, born after Clotorindus took power. Perselina's father remains shrouded in obscurity, 'having had her by the widdow Queene of Macedon, after whose birth shee soone dyed, hee thought none worthy of her, especially, an Achayan' (I.527). Initially unwilling to 'grow subject to an Husband', Perselina's desire to enhance her wealth and rank encourages her to compromise. She settles for 'such a Husband as she would choose for free living'. In the restructured philhellene Protestant European federation, her father's divisive nationalism is of little relevance. Perselina chooses a reformed Achaian, whose suitability is validated by his 'acquaintance with Rosindy, and service to Parselius' (I.527).

Romania allegorised

It is not politics but self-interest that intervenes when Leandrus of Achaia falls in love with Pamphilia and proposes marriage. In contrast to the many tyrannical patriarchs in *Urania*, the exemplary King of Morea exercises his authority with understanding. Generally, Sidney Wroth's allegory suggests that parents pass on to their children their own tyrannical or benevolent demeanour. This idealised king invites discussion with his daughter, listening carefully as she rejects Leandrus.

Pamphilia clearly benefits from paternal care, but in addition exhibits a mischievous delight in the power she exercises over her father. She conceals her adoration for her cousin Amphilanthus, and implausibly echoes Elizabeth I in arguing that her duty as governor takes precedence over personal interests: 'his Majestie had once married her before, which was to the Kingdome of Pamphilia, from which Husband shee could not bee divorced, nor ever would have other' (I.262). Having already manipulated her mother into persuading her father to liberate Macedonia before Albania, her sophistry reveals the weakness of her argument, but also the strength of her emotions:

> 'Not to Leandrus my Lord', said shee, 'I beseech you, for I cannot love him; nor can I believe he loves in me ought besides my kingdome, and my honour in being your daughter; Antissia better fitteth him, who was appointed for him'.

The King knew she had reason for what she said, and so assuring her, that he would not force her to any thing against her mind, […] they fell into other discourse. (I.262–3)

This disjunction between private erotic feeling and public posturing pervades *Urania*. Pamphilia could have based her rationale for rejecting Leandrus on his father's anti-Morean politics, which allied Achaia, Albania and Romania in a war against the King of Macedonia, Pamphilia's maternal uncle. But she does not. Her father appears to accept her statement, reassures her of his support and lets the subject drop. Leandrus remains her bachelor devotee until he dies suddenly of 'Plurisie, a disease little known then' (I.463). Leandrus's death precipitates his grief-stricken father's suicide. Dalinea succeeds to the throne of Achaia, and in an extension of the Morean-Christian empire, her husband Parselius is made king (I.489).

Pamphilia's remark that 'Antissia […] was appointed for' (I.262)[115] Leandrus reveals her precocious knowledge of international agreements. And the Morean king's respect for her affairs of the heart reflects an enlightened respect for female human rights. By contrast, Antissia's father, the King of Romania, betroths her to Leandrus as a political bargain when they are only children. Leandrus's father, King of Achaia, secures the Romanian throne for Antissia's father, and supports him in defeating the Macedonians. In payment, Antissia travels to Achaia 'to be brought up together' with Leandrus, 'to the end, that conversation (a ready friend to love) might nurse their affections so wel, as she might as contentedly be his daughter' (I.30).

Like Urania, Antissia experiences a displaced childhood. Instead of delivering her to the Achaian court, the Romanian king's servant Sandringal and his greedy wife steal the dowry and set fire to the ship. The plan goes wrong, and only Sandringal and Antissia survive. She is stolen by 'rovers'. Ten years later, Sandringal, himself a pirate, mistakes Urania for Antissia: 'I straight remembered your face' (I.31). Coming under attack, Parselius kills 'the great Pirat of Syracusa' (I.31), but Sandringal is killed by the black knight, Leandrus, whom he regards as one 'with whom few Christian Princes will compare, except the two Cousens Parselius and Amphilanthus' (I.30). Safely in Morea, Antissia becomes Pamphilia's rival for Amphilanthus's attention, as well as her literary protégée.[116]

---

115 On Antissia, see S. T. Cavanagh, *Cherished Torment: The Emotional Geography of Lady Mary Wroth's Urania*, pp. 68–77.
116 On Antissia allegorising female anxieties over literary writing, see M. E. Lamb, *Gender and Authorship in the Sidney Circle*, pp. 159–62, and C. R. Kinney, '"Beleeve this butt

She succumbs to madness, gains a reputation as an insane bad poet, but is cured by a tonic administered by the superhuman family protector, Melissea – Mary Sidney Herbert (II.53).

Following the Morean–Protestant reformation, however, Antissia cements the peace between Morea and its enemies by marrying Dolorindus, son of the King of Negroponte (formerly Euboea). Their wedding is at Constantinople, the seat of the Romanian court, where Antissia is given away by her 'old Uncle' Seleucius, the King of Romania's brother. Ironically, their marriage is celebrated under the aegis of the true object of Antissia's affection, the Neapolitan heir and Emperor-elect, Amphilanthus (I.397).

Sidney Wroth couches her description of the Romanian succession in a complicated condensation of Heliodorus's story of the Athenian, Aristippos; his lecherous wife, Demainete; and his innocent son, Knemon. The King of Romania's promiscuous second wife accuses Seleucius and Antissia's brother, Antissius, of planning a coup (I.54). She assassinates Antissius in an ambush, prompting his wife Lucenia to commit suicide. In a letter, Lucenia begs Seleucius to avenge his usurped great nephew, Antissius II (I.55–8).

Characterisation of the ambitious Romanian queen owes much to Plutarchan moral allegory. Like Heliodorus's Arsake, her irrepressibly salacious personality leads to her own downfall. She has her own son 'made heire apparant', and herself 'Protectresse, till hee came of age' (I.71). She has her husband murdered by her 'favourite' to whom she promises marriage. Her conspiracy unravels when she tries to seduce the son of the Duke of Mantinea, a young member of the King of Morea's embassy of condolence. Precision of detail suggests a contemporary figure: he was 'not of the highest stature, [...] his haire faire, and that beard hee had, something inclind to yellow' (I.73). The Mantinean despises the queen's efforts to ensnare him: 'I love one, whose worth and truth must not be hurt, or blotted in my fault' (I.73). But when the now rejected favourite tries to attack her, 'the Morean' intervenes. Her son, the new king, arrests the favourite, whose confession leads to her execution. Here Sidney Wroth upholds the spirit of responsible monarchy, '(for being a subject, shee was under the law), and so had her head struck off' (I.74).

The queen's death, following her illicit interruption of heritable succession, initiates a conflict between her son – 'the unlawfull king' – and a

---

a fiction": Female Authorship, Narrative Undoing, and the Limits of Romance in *The Second Part of The Countess of Montgomery's Urania', Spenser Studies: A Renaissance Poetry Annual*, xvii (2003), 239–50.

'Rebell', one of the queen's 'antienter favorites', who besieges him (I.75). There is, as is required to install a Morean sympathiser, a public outcry to restore Antissius II (I.75). The usurper gambles his throne in a decisive tourney.

Here Sidney Wroth indulges in the ecphrastic conventions, particularly well developed in the *New Arcadia*, relating to symbolic armorial costume. The usurping king wears green armour, 'floured' (I.76), that is, 'decorated' with gold, both colours of jealousy. There is a shade of triumphalism in his horse's green furniture, 'cut into Garlands of Laurell, and embroidered with Gold'. But the absence of the motto, regarded by Paolo Giovio and his followers as the soul of an impresa,[117] becomes a signifier for his defeat. For though 'In his Shield he had a crowne of Bayes, held up by a Sword; Word he had none, so as it seemd he staid for that, till his hoped for victorie had provided one for him' (I.76). The victory, however, is not his.

Sidney Wroth employs more detailed ecphrases to promote the political group in whose support she has written *Urania*. She focuses particularly on the devices, colour and jewels of the Morean allies. Amphilanthus enters as the Knight of Love, 'with Love painted in his shield'. He is hot and cold, ardent and pure:

> his Armour was white, fillited [i.e., encircled] with Rubies; his furniture to his Horse Crimson, embroydered with Pearle; his Shield with the same device, from which hee tooke his name. Steriamus according to his fortune was in Tawny [i.e., forsaken], wrought all over with blacke (I.76)

Black connotes purity. Because Pamphilia has refused him, 'all the device in his shield' consists of the words, 'The true despis'd' (I.75). Their partner, Ollorandus of Bohemia, identified solely by his device, 'a great and pleasant Forrest', enters in 'a murry [i.e., blood-red] Armour, fillited with Diamonds, his furniture richly wrought with Silver and Gold' (I.76). The Morean side's inevitable victory restores Antissius II, who enters into a loving dynastic marriage with the Albanian princess, Selarina (I.518).

Closing the Sophistic circle

Urania demonstrates how philhellene Protestant interests can achieve European–Asian political stability through intermarriage, based on romantic love. Selarina (Albania) becomes the wife of Antissius II, restored

---

117 *The Worthy tract of Paulus Iovius, contayning a Discourse of rare inuentions, both Militarie and Amorous called Imprese*, trans. by Samuel Daniel (1588), B3v.

King of Romania, whose mad poet aunt Antissia (Romania and Negro-
ponte) loves Amphilanthus (Naples and the Roman empire). Selarinus
(Albania and Epirus) marries Philistella (Morea); Steriamus (Albania)
marries Urania (Naples); Philarchos (Morea) marries Orilena (Metelin
and the Greek islands); Rosindy (Morea) marries Meriana (Macedonia);
Ollorandus (Bohemia) marries Melasinda (Hungary); Leonius (Morea)
marries Veralinda (Frigia); and Parselius (Morea) marries Dalinea
(Achaia).

The notable exceptions to this calculated pattern of intermarriage
are Sidney Wroth's hero and heroine. The arranged marriages between
Amphilanthus (Naples) and the Princess of Slavonia, and between
Pamphilia (Morea) and Rodomandro (Tartaria) suffer from the effects
of forlorn love. Forming the political and erotic centre of *Urania*, like
characters in ancient erotic romance, they are as much victims of hyper-
sensitivity, misunderstanding and others' manipulative interests as of
circumstance.

While their tragedies are those of the heart, Pamphilia and Amphilan-
thus enjoy the protection of Amphilanthus's mother, the Queen of Naples,
and of her caricature, Melissea. If the First Part of *Urania* is dominated
by love originating in chance meetings, the Second Part is governed by
Melissea's planned marriages of the 'sweet younge hopefull budds' of the
next generation (II.23). Many of the military exploits of the Neapolitan–
Morea coalition are taken over by young heroes.

Stylistic plainness takes on a childlike simplicity related to the
visionary masque-like world in which these characters exist. As the chil-
dren sail from Melissea's nursery to be schooled by the Queen of Naples,
they become separated and suffer various 'enchantments'. Clavarindo and
Licandro rescue some of them from Lofturado, the Giant of Engia, and
they are whisked away in 'a faire, white Clowde' (II.73). At least ten chil-
dren are kidnapped and imprisoned by the giant Lamurandus (II.357).
On Melissea's instructions, a self-propelled boat brings Amphilanthus to
their rescue (II.182–8).[118] Such naval enchantments are commonplace.
Leonius and Veralinda's two-year-old daughter, Lindavera, now sixteen, is
carried away in a row-boat from which her nurse has just stepped (II.96).
Like the boat 'without any in her' that Melissea's sister instructs Selarinus
to wait for (II.233), the crewless boat that lures Parselius and Dalinea's son
Trebisound away is guided by 'Majeck', 'Charmed winds' and 'charmed

---

118 On the earlier usage of magic boats, see H. Cooper, *The English Romance in Time:
    Transforming Motifs from Geoffrey of Monmouth to the Death of Shakespeare* (Oxford:
    Oxford University Press, 2004), pp. 106–36.

spirits' (II.218). This is Trebisound's second such experience. He is only five when a boat from an uncrewed, vanishing ship delivers him to Melissea's sister's palace for nurturing (II.5, 224–5), along with the 'new borne' Sultaness of Babylon (II.2). When they grow up, they marry (II.322).

As in the First Part, familial resemblances are used to blur the distinctions between characters.[119] Floristello, the Albanian prince who travels as the Knight of Venus and is destined to marry to Candiana, looks like his mother Urania (II.98). Candiana, aged fifteen, looks like Parselius (II.217); and Trebisound, twenty, 'hath Dalineas face' (II.217). But Candiana also resembles Urania and her brother Leonius – so much so that Leonius and Veralinda's eldest son, Verolindo ('true other'), mistakes Candiana for his lost sister Lindavera (also 'true other') (II.106).

Sidney Wroth extends her strategy of allegorical obfuscation to include rebus-like birthmarks and armorial devices.[120] Candiana 'hath a delicate mole on her left brest resembling a hart, with a dart shott thorough itt' (II.219). This links her to Floristello, the second element of whose birthmark corresponds with hers: 'the figure most perfectly framed of a lyoness in bloody couler, as itt were ramping to pray upon his bleeding hart strooke with loves dart' (II.97). Floristillo's stated belief that his wife bears a different symbol is calculated to undermine readers' certainty: 'she, I am tolde, hath a delicate, curious flower within a starr. And therefor I have my name given mee from this marck, which my wyfe must carry, which is Floristello, and that is my true name though nott knowne' (II.97).

Pictorial birthmarks have graphic parallels. These cryptic written designs have less impact, and Sidney Wroth deleted two of them. Before revision, Floristello and Candiana had their names intertwined: 'his owne name, round with hers hee was to marry in Charecters in the same place the younge princesses name was on her brest which name was also framed with his who showld bee her husband' (II.97). Almost immediately before this, she alters the description given by Floristello, the Albanian, of his missing sister Lindavera. No longer is her name 'written in Charecters naturally under her left breast' (II.428). As the offspring of the allegorical representatives of Philip Herbert and Susan de Vere Herbert, Leonius and Veralinda, the replacement text provides her name with a literal etymology relating her to the earls of Oxford. She is now 'the most

119 Perspectives on genealogy and physical resemblance are in G. Alexander, *Writing After Sidney: The Literary Response to Sir Philip Sidney, 1586–1640* (Oxford: Oxford University Press, 2006), pp. 294–7.
120 Cf. S. T. Cavanagh, *Cherished Torment: The Emotional Geography of Lady Mary Wroth's Urania*, pp. 204–6.

sweete, faire springe [i.e., 'ver'] by the true interpretation and meaning of that name' (I.96).

The most effective of these verbal signs holds the key to identifying Amphilanthus's protégé, the Knight of the Faire Design. He similarly bears 'a sipher on my hart, which is sayd to bee her name whom I must by many hard adventures att last gaine, and knowe her by having a sipher like-wise, which shall discover my name, and then I shalbee knowne' (II.297). Faire Design's cipher remains a secret, even within the inner Morean–Neapolitan circle. When Amphilanthus confers knighthood on Faire Design, a charmed cloud delivers a sword, horse, and armour. The shield has 'the like sipher hee had on his brest' (II.298). The newly rescued King of Denmark identifies Faire Designe as the one destined to reinstall him in his throne, for he is 'the greatest prince by birthe (butt unknowne) that the Christian world hath' (II.329). On the spot, he rewards Faire Design with a sword and sword-proof armour, 'which had in his shield the same devise his other had, butt the couler was a perfect blew for truthe' (II.331). Melissea informs Parselius that this device encodes a family mystery: 'when you are settled in this religious lyfe you intend Hermitt-like to live, examine the lyfe you have lead, and itt may bee you may that way knowe himm as soone as any' (II.323). The identity of the ultimate hero of *Urania*, possibly Sidney Wroth's son William by Herbert,[121] along with his destined wife, remains a concealed enigma.

Urania as Sophistic erotic romance

To a far greater extent than Heliodorus and Sidney, Sidney Wroth compli-cates a cyclical plot structure based on reminiscence. Her intertwining stories repeat themselves in the manner of Spenser and Cervantes, with seemingly endless variation. To achieve such tight structural integration, she may have employed Ramist diagrams, similar to those used by the philhellene Robert Burton to chart the complex argument of his *Anatomy of Melancholy* (1621).

Whether by chance or design, Sidney Wroth's romance has a double ending. An entire era closes when the great Cham dies. But rescuing the sultan, Lindafillia, will bring together both generations of philhel-lene Protestant heroes to resolve the last outstanding political outrage. Rodomandro's intervention to overthrow the Persian usurper leads Rosindy to accept 'all the Monarchy' of Persia, 'till the enchantment'

---

121 I.lxxiv; on his later military career, see *The Poems of Lady Mary Wroth*, ed. by J. A. Roberts, p. 25.

imprisoning Lindafillia 'was ended' (II.274). In one of the latest additions
to the Second Part, Rosindy's third son, Mirasindo – the young soldier
Robert Sidney (1626–68) – describes how he was among the children
enchanted on their way from Naples to Morea. These include Candiana,
the daughter of Parselius and Dalinea; Sellaminda, the daughter of Urania
and Steriamus; and Linderatszo, the son of Antissius II and Selarina. All
are rescued by the Knight of Venus, Floristello, from the lower part of
the same 'charmed house' that holds Sophia. Mirasindo relates how Faire
Design, '(itt is thought) must bee the man to release the Sophia' (II.355).

The closing speaker in the Second Part is Andromarko, whom Amphi-
lanthus presents to Faire Design as his attendant. They 'release the brave
Ta[r]tarian' (II.325), Rodomandro, from a giant, and invite him to
Amphilanthus's wedding. Andromarko is the natural son of Amphilan-
thus's imperial chamberlain, Polarchos, King of Cyprus. As the Emperor's
chamberlain (William Herbert was appointed James's chamberlain in
December 1615), Polarchos 'lives most comunly […] with his Majestie'
(II.407). The Emperor governs *in absentia* on the Welsh model, where
a Council serves under a President, 'and many great lords and delicate
ladyes live heere and grace the Court' (II.407). This idyllic perspective
is not shared by the Cyprian Lady, daughter of the Duke of Sabbro and
Licus, who will become Andromarko's wife. She objects strenuously to
a form of government where the council is 'wholy of men. And wher
woemen hath little Joye of a Court to com to, hath made all great ones
butt the Counsell to stay and keepe att home' (II.411).

Sidney Wroth leaves Faire Design no choice but to seek out his
mentor.[122] In the final speech of the work, Andromarko tells Amphilan-
thus how 'your Faire Designe hath now left all things' to find him, '(beeing
certainly informed by severall wisards, especially the sage Melissea), that
the great Inchantment will nott bee concluded thes many yeeres; nay,
nev[er], if you live nott to assiste in the concluding' (II.418). How this is
achieved remains untold. But Faire Design's being entrusted with the ulti-
mate mission of rescuing the usurped Lindafillia indicates that his future
lies in that direction (II.367).

Unlike the professional rhetoricians who composed the Greco-Roman
erotic romances, Sidney Wroth refuses to bring her work to a climax, fol-
lowed by a denouement. By closing *Urania* with an insight into the heroic
deeds of the third generation of philhellene Protestants, she produces a
tour de force of political propaganda. She employs a complicated rhetorical

122 Cf. II.xxi–xxii.

strategy that deliberately appears to lack form, direction and clarity, yet creates a consistent and coherent entity on a grand scale. Within it, her shifting rhetorical styles consciously signal the didactic intention of a gifted sophistic allegorist.

In opening the Second Part, Sidney Wroth draws particular attention to how the narrator describes the unbounded delight of Amphilanthus's mother, the Queen of Naples, when he arrives with Pamphilia:

> Shall I presume to express the Joye, the wellcome, the all, that rare Queene showed and felt, seeing her dearest sonn and with him her haulf self Pamphilia? Noe, I dare nott; nay, I can nott […] Therfor in plaine relation I say they mett; the Queen blessed them both, as truly hers, and as hers they lived a while with her […]. (II.1)

This overtly transparent style contrasts markedly with the rhetoric of obfuscation with which Sidney Wroth disguises the biographical realities behind her characters. Blending Plutarch's holistic, allegorical approach with Theophrastus's types and an element of historical reality, Sidney Wroth associates the ethical and moral properties of her characters through their rhetorical styles. The Queen of Bulgaria's distant formality is suited to her reputation as the 'Empresse of Pride' (I.399). Her doting but bullied husband, the King of Bulgaria, may be 'the finest speaker in Court language of the World' (I.542), but the narrator dismisses his pompous royal style as 'curious words and phrases', as empty as their sham of a marriage.

In the Talkative Knight, who some believe suffers from 'perpetuall working' (I.631) of the brain, Sidney Wroth portrays a court figure incapable of mastering the rhetorical arts. An exhausting speaker, he blurts out commonplaces in an uncontrolled, arrhythmic series:

> 'Did you ever', said hee, 'see a sweet Lady so much changed as shee is? I knew her, and so did you, a faire, dainty, sweet woman, noble and freely disposed, a delicate Courtier, curious in her habites, danced, rid, did all things fit for a Court, as well as any brave Lady could doe? what can change her thus? they say shee is in love […]. (I.631)

The author-narrator emphasises this rhetorical failure, mimicking the Talkative Knight in relating how he 'talk'd on, and regarded, or not, said Verses, spake Prose, and rime againe, no more heeding answers (so hee heard himself) then if he had rav'd or talk'd in his sleepe' (I.635).

In 'Brittany, anciently called Albion' (I.627), the Duke of Florence misjudges his audience in addressing two arrogant and disrespectful women in what he believes to be an ingratiatingly polite style:

Wee are Travellers and strangers; yet more strangers to the sight of such beauty, as till this instant I never did behold; and which doth so amaze mee with content, as I am rapt into the cloudes of pleasure, not being able to expresse your excellencies but by my infinite admiration; beholding you like so many Sunnes contented to distribute your equall beames to let us be the abler to behold you […]. (I.628)

The two kinswomen give up listening to these excessively copious, rhythmic platitudes and walk away, 'as who would say, by that time the Oration is done, wee will come againe' (I.629). But this same the long-winded Duke of Florence becomes a reformed stylist when he woos the widowed Lady of the Forest Champion, another of Sidney Wroth's personae, who lives in 'the deserts of Brittany' (I.630). The Florentine is particularly attracted to her plain style, 'as made him thinke she was the best spoken woman he had ever heard, and the greatest part of her eloquence was the plainnes, but excellently well plac'd words she deliverd, her speech was as rare and winning, as the Knights troublesome, and most times idle' (I.635). Like her mentor, Mary Sidney Herbert, and her king, James I, Sidney Wroth chooses plainness to convey the essence (or fictional illusion) of truth.

Sidney Wroth's rhetorical awareness identifies *Urania* as one of the great sophistic erotic romances of the Renaissance. The facility with which she alters tone and style to speaker and circumstances, from rustic to oracular pronouncement, corresponds with the complex nature of her semi-translucent, painstaking plot. That this does not make for easy reading may appear to distort the rhetor's goal of clarity and artistry.

Reflecting late nineteenth-century French taste, Jusserand glibly denounced Sidney Wroth for accentuating Sidney's stylistic 'defects'. He clearly disliked the verbal repetition in 'all for others grieved, pittie extended so, as all were carefull, but of themselves most carelesse: yet their mutuall care, made them all cared for' (I.47). But his witty sarcasm, in 'Lady Mary Wroth has a felicity of her own in twisting the idea into the words, screw-wise',[123] is lamentably misguided.

The challenges posed by *Urania* attest to its being written in circumstances unlike those experienced by Sidney Wroth's Greco-Roman and Renaissance precursors. For, through slippery covert allegory and allusive rhetorical obfuscation, she alone felt able to exploit erotic romance to comment extensively on contemporary political events. Rhetorically, this difference in focus manifests itself in the apostrophe for Melasinda. This

123 J. J. Jusserand, *The English Novel in the Time of Shakespeare* [1890], trans. by E. Lee, new edn, intro. by P. Brockbank (London: Ernest Benn Limited, 1966), p. 268.

lament, 'cride out' in unison to Antissius by 'five damoysells', is excep-
tional in prioritising political before personal grief:

> What shall wee wreches doe? Hungaria is lost! Butt most, O most, Melas-
> inda, our Lady and Mistress, and Hungarias Mistress, is lost! Melasinda, O
> Melasinda, the starr of the earthe, the seat of vertu, the Diamond of truthe
> is lost, stolne, caried away, and (wee feare) abused. (II.176)

Jusserand was inattentive to the cultural, political and rhetorical differ-
ences between the late 1570s and early 1580s, when Sidney composed
Arcadia, and the mid-Jacobean period thirty-five years later, when *Urania*
was written. Unsympathetically, Jusserand required Elizabethan balanced
rhythms and neo-classical reserve, albeit in an outstanding exhibition of
asymmetrical Baroque mannerism. Disappointed in his expectation, he
remained oblivious to Sidney Wroth's early Romantic attempt to create,
through intertwining plot-lines, characters and styles, a feeling of mutual
reassurance during an era of religious and political anxiety.

Sidney Wroth's characters, like those in ancient erotic romance, are
never out of danger. But the calculated inversion, in placing the identi-
fication scene at the beginning of *Urania*, emphasises personal, familial
and political reconciliation over loss. It reassures readers from the outset
that, however obscure the organisation of the narrative, the militant Prot-
estantism of the kind espoused by the Sidney–Herbert circle can serve the
political and religious aspirations of erotic love.

Conclusion

Mary Sidney Wroth reshapes Plutarch, Longus, Achilles Tatius, Helio-
dorus, *Amadis de Gaule*, Sidney, Shakespeare and Jonson into a new kind
of European erotic romance, a sophistic prose masque. She challenges
Jacobean court structures, proposing as an antidote to Spanish influ-
ence the militant, philhellene Protestant political structure favoured by
the Sidney–Herbert dynasty. Pamphilia and Amphilanthus's reformed
Europe will perpetuate the Protestant-inspired doctrines of nationalism,
monarchomachism and feminism.

What particularly distinguishes *Urania* from other erotic romances is
its sharp focus on the political, familial and social benefits to be derived
from trans-generation respect, and gender equality. In Sidney Wroth's
Utopian vision, the young are tenderly nurtured, listened to and encour-
aged in self-esteem, freedom of choice and responsibility. Played by
these rules, and fulfilling the aspirations of Renaissance translators and

adapters of the ancient novel, Europe would become a forceful Christian union. It would be founded on exemplary behaviour, good governance, freely negotiated erotic love and dynastic intermarriage among the most worthy philhellene Protestants.

8

The fate of a genre

The semiotics of erotic romance

Despite the centuries of change from the height of the Roman Empire to the Restoration in England, erotic romance retained an other worldly consistency. Its artful structures and rhetorical elegance enhance overtly artificial plots. Its exemplary characterisation provides metonymic representations of idealised behaviour, revealing a didactic purposefulness communicated on more than one level. Its examples of the fortitude and eloquence of heroic young women and men, overcoming the dangers of abandonment, or falling victim to outbursts of oppressive male emotions, exemplify resistance to political, social and familial oppression. And it associates political and domestic harmony, and respect for the rights and feelings of the individual, with the ecstasy of true romantic love.

European erotic romance offered Amyot the opportunity to teach his stylised Greco-Roman language and rhetoric, and, through it, Christian ethics, morality, and personal and political governance. It became the tool of nationalists. More theoretical politicisation of the genre occurred, initially by monarchomachist Protestant publishers and translators of Heliodorus, then by adapters such as Sidney, Shakespeare and Sidney Wroth.

In addition to being associated with political discourse, European erotic romance set the standard by which the social and literary significance of chivalric romance was judged. In the French court, Amyot's enthusiasm in his 1547 (i.e., 1548) preface for Heliodorus's moralistic approach to literature prompted a sophisticated response by Jacques Gohory. Gohory used the dedications in his, and others', translations of *Amadis de Gaule* to identify and defend the literary qualities of chivalric fiction. But his remarks equally identify readers' expectations of erotic romance. In Book X (1552),[1] dedicated to the sister of Henri II, Marguerite de France,

---

1 For publication details, see *Les Amadis en France au XVIe siècle*, ed. by N. Cazauran and M. Bideaux, Cahiers Saulniers, no. 17 (Paris: Éditions Rue d'Ulm, 2000), pp. 210–11.

Gohory remarks on the mystical allegories contained in fiction. In Book XIII (1571), dedicated to the Countesse de Retz, and supported by all the members of the Pléiade, he echoes Amyot in noting that virtue is rewarded and vice condemned, and that a wide range of character types and emotions are described in ornate, plain and flowing style – 'floride, net et coulant'. Here, and in dedicating Antoine Tyron's translation of Book XIV (1575) to Princess Henriette de Clèves, Countesse de Nevers, Gohory proposes that the lies in fiction contain more truth than the lies told by historians.[2]

Sidney's *Defence of Poetry* contains a parallel argument that clearly differentiates between an ideal factual history and a fictional allegory, or exemplary parable:

> If then a man can arrive to that child's age to know that the poet's persons and doings are but pictures what should be, and not stories what have been, they will never give the lie to things not affirmatively but allegorically and figuratively written. And therefore, as in history, looking for truth, they may go away full fraught with falsehood, so in poesy, looking but for fiction, they shall use the narration but as an imaginative ground-plot of a profitable invention.[3]

Works such as Angel Day's adaptation of *Daphnis and Chloe*, which combines these notions of fiction and history, encouraged reading erotic romance as personal allegory. Readers and writers with experience of Sidney's *Arcadia*, Spenser's *Faerie Queene*, court masques and similarly representational poems, plays and fiction expected concealed identities. Sidney Wroth's *Urania* depends for its success on the early seventeenth-century passion for *romans à clef*, which provided a critical model for reading ancient and modern texts. James Hayward, commenting on his 1632 translation of Sir Giovanni Francesco Biondi's *Eromena* (Venice, 1624) from the Tuscan tongue, invokes Heliodorus as a precedent. He emphasises 'that pleasing way of *Helidorian* Poesie (I mean an historicall way of Poetizing, or Poeticall manner of historizing, or displaying of the fained-seeming unfained adventures and actions of persons reall, masked under the vizard of invented names:)'.[4]

---

2 See the transcriptions from Gohory, with commentary, in M. Fumaroli, 'Jacques Amyot and the Clerical Polemic Against the Chivalric Novel', *Renaissance Quarterly*, xxxviii (1985), 22–40 (pp. 36–40).

3 Sir P. Sidney, *A Defence of Poetry*, in *Miscellaneous Prose of Sir Philip Sidney*, ed. by K. Duncan-Jones and J. van Dorsten (Oxford: Clarendon Press, 1973), p. 103.

4 *Eromena, or, Love and Revenge. Written originally in the Thoscan tongue, by Cavalier Gio. Francesco Biondi, Gentleman extraordinary of his Majesties Privie Chamber. Divided into six books. And now faithfully Englished, by Ia. Hayvvard, of Graies-Inne Gent* (1632), A4.

If European erotic romance could contain semi-biographical personae, it was on the understanding that they should be heavily idealised to conform to the model characters created by the ancient sophists. Translators' and publishers' dedications by Protestant monarchomachists connected erotic romance with characters exhibiting political, cultural and intellectual superiority. Among geographically widespread European philhellene Protestants, the genre became synonymous with the high level of principled behaviour that they hoped Christian Europe would adopt. In this passive way, the genre gained a kind of symbolic, or semiotic, value.

Assigning semiotic values in a rhetorical context was a familiar practice during the seventeenth century. The close relationship between quasi-allegorical historical writing and semiotic interpretation is illustrated by the divine Edward Reyner.[5] In *A treatise of the necessity of humane learning for a Gospel-preacher* (1663), Reyner develops notions of parable and style in short chapters entitled 'Of History as useful to know God's works' and 'Of History as useful to know the Examples of men' (K1–K2). Under 'The Usefulness of Rhetoric' (E1), essential to good preaching, Reyner describes 'a *Metonymy* of the *Adjunct*', where 'The *Sign* is put for the *thing signified*', so that '*Bread* and *wine*' stands 'for *Christ's body* and *blood*' (E8).

The posture of historical and biographical authenticity in European erotic romance lends itself to this Anglican kind of Christian reading. Combining a sense of history, allegory, parable and political commentary, the genre took on a kind of flexible semiotic status. In England, it became associated with panegyric, as in Day, and with political reform, as in Sidney, Shakespeare, Sidney Wroth and L'Isle. At times it reflected court policy, as in Burton and Hodges. Even Thornley's translation resonates with the anti-Puritanism of the royalist Cavaliers.

By 1654, Edward Gayton, in *Pleasant Notes Upon Don Quixot*, would claim equal value for romance with philosophical debate, religious discourse and history:

> Let English men write of their owne wits, fancies, subjects, disputes, sermons, Histories; Romancees are as good, vigorous, lasting, and as well worthy the reading, as any in the world. Our *Fairy Queen,* the *Arcadia, Drayton, Beaumont* and *Fletcher, Shakespeare, Iohnson, Rondolph*; and lastly, *Gondibert,* are of eternall fame; But Captaine *Iones,* the only unparallell Romancy, and fit to be the Legend of all Countries, and fit to be translated by forreign Nations, for the reason in the Text.[6]

---

5 C. Cross, 'Reyner, Edward (1600–1660)', *Oxford Dictionary of National Biography* (Oxford: Oxford University Press, 2004).
6 E. Gayton, *Pleasant Notes Upon Don Quixot* (1654), D3. Gayton's final references are to

Gayton's remarks demonstrate how erotic romance became almost iconically revered because it stood for the highest of moral and political principles. But in a nation so divided and at war with itself over what these were, such exaggerated adulation was unsustainable.

Conclusion

More than seventy years lie between Guillaume Postel's *Les raisons de la monarchie* (1551) and the Second Part of *Urania*. During this period, punctuated by wars between Christian and Muslim, Catholic and Protestant, European erotic romance played its part in shaping European politics and nationalist culture. Its strong chivalric element promoted notions of responsible monarchy and intolerance of tyranny, feeding the discontent with bullying and corruption that culminated, in 1649, in the beheading of Charles I.

The Restoration in 1660, followed by the execution of the leading monarchomachists as regicides, and the Glorious Revolution in 1688, took the momentum out of the philhellene Protestant movement. The most crushing blow came in 1685, when the Edict of Fontainebleau revoked the Edict of Nantes. The massive Protestant exodus that had altered the demographics of Thomas Bette's England of the 1560s and 1570s recommenced. With the flux and change of European interests, European erotic romance in the Greco-Roman mould lost its significance as the champion of religious tolerance and limited monarchy. Its complex plots, obscure allegories, supernatural settings, rhetorical sophistication and artificial characters evolved into equally metonymic, but more realistic, reflections of suffering humanity. The taste for European erotic romance declined, having given birth to more modern forms of fiction. In these new novels, formulaic expectations were dropped in favour of a pre-Romantic focus on the individual. Foundlings and paupers continued to be victimised and misunderstood. But it was no longer socially or politically desirable that, in the end, they should turn out to be either wealthy, royal or in love.

Sir William D'Avenant, Gondibert and David Lloyd, *The legend of Captaine Iones* (1631–48); cf. A. Hadfield, 'Lloyd, David (1597–1663)', *Oxford Dictionary of National Biography* (Oxford: Oxford University Press, 2004).

Bibliography

Primary sources

Manuscripts
Bayerische Staatsbibliothek, Munich, MS Monacensis Greaca 157.
Biblioteca Apostolica Vaticana MS Palatinus Graecus 125.
Biblioteca Apostolica Vaticana MS Palatinus Graecus 52.
Biblioteca Laurenziana MS Laurentianus conv. sopp. 627.
Biblioteca Nazionale di San Marco MS Marcianus Graecus 409.
Bibliothèque Nationale MS Parisinus Graecus 2895.
Bibliothèque Nationale MS Parisinus Graecus 2913.
Bibliothèque Sainte-Geneviève, Paris, MS Y. 4o. 573.
British Library MS. Birch's 4174.
British Library Sloane MS. 4164, fol. 190v.
British Library, Harleian MS 1581.
Marcianus MS Graecus 409.
MS Vaticanus Graecus 157.
Public Record Office, SP12/195.
Vaticanus Graeci 114.
Vaticanus Graecus MS 1347.
Venutus (Venice) Marcianus MS Graecus 409.

Printed books

Achilles Tatius, *Narrationis Amatoriae Fragmentum*, trans. by L. A. della Croce (Lyon, 1544).
Les devis amoureux, trans. by 'l'Amoureux de Vertu' [i.e., P. de Vienne] (Paris, 1545).
—— *Amorosi Ragionamente. Dialogo Nel Qvale si Racconta Vn Compassionevole Amore Di Dve Amanti*, trans. by Ludovico Dolce (Venice, 1546).
—— *Dell'amore di Leucippe et di Clitophonte*, trans. by F. A. Coccio (Venice, 1550/51).
—— *Achillis Statii Alexandrini De Clitophontis & Leucippes amorib[us]. Libri VIII. E Graecis Latini facti a L. Annibale Cruceio* (Basel, 1554).

—— *Les quatre derniers livres des propos amoureux contenans le discours des amours et mariage du seigneur Clitophont et de damoiselle Leucippe*, trans. by J. de Roquemaure or Rochemaure (Lyon, 1556).

—— *Les amours de Clitophon et de Leucippe*, trans. by ['B. Comingeois', i.e., François de Belleforest] (Paris, 1568).

—— *Achillis Statii Alexandrini De Clitophontis & Leucippes amorib[us]. Libri VIII. E Graecis Latini facti à L. Annibale Cruceio* (Cambridge, 1589).

—— *The Most Delectable and pleasaunt History of Clitiphon and Leucippe: Written first in Greeke, by Achilles Statius, an Alexandrian: and now newly translated into English, By W.B.* [i.e., William Burton] (1597).

—— *De Clitophontis et Leucippes amoribus lib. VIII. Longi sophistae de Daphnidis et Chloes amoribus lib. IV. Parthenii Nicaeensis de amatoriis affectibus lib. I. Omnia nunc primùm simul edita Graecè ac Latinè* [ed. by J. and N. Bonnvitius] ([Heidelberg,] 1601).

—— *De Clitophontis et Leucippes amoribus lib. VIII. Longi sophistae de Daphnidis et Chloes amoribus lib. IV. Parthenii Nicaeensis de amatoriis affectibus lib. I. Omnia nunc primùm simul edita Graecè ac Latinè* [ed. by J. and N. Bonnvitius] ([Heidelberg,] 1606).

—— *Les Amours de Clytophon, et de Leucippe*, trans. by I[ean] B[audoin] (Paris, 1635).

—— *The Loves of Clitophon and Leucippe. A most elegant History, written in Greeke by Achilles Tatius: And now Englished*, trans. by Anthony Hodges (1638).

—— *The Loves of Clitophon and Leucippe*, ed. by S. Gaselee and H. F. B. Brett-Smith (Oxford: Basil Blackwell, 1923).

—— *The Loves of Clitophon and Leucippe[,] Translated from the Greek of Achilles Tatius by William Burton [,] Reprinted for the first time from a copy now unique printed by Thomas Creede in 1597* (Oxford: Basil Blackwell Publisher to the Shakespeare Head Press of Stratford-upon-Avon, 1923).

—— *Achilles Tatius. Leucippe and Clitophon*, ed. by E. Vilborg (Stockholm: Almquist and Wiksell, 1955).

—— *Achilles Tatius*, with an English translation by S. Gaselee, M.A., rev. by E. H. Warmington (London: William Heinemann, 1969).

—— *Leukippe and Kleitophon*, trans. by J. J. Winkler, in *Collected Ancient Greek Novels*, ed. by B. P. Reardon (Berkeley: University of California Press, 1989).

—— *Le Roman de Leucippé et Clitophon*, ed. and trans. by J.-P. Garnaud (Paris: Les Belles Lettres, 1991).

Amadis de Gaule, *Le Trezieme livre d'Amadis de Gaule*, trans. by I. G. P. [i.e., Jacques Gohory, Parisien] (Paris, 1571).

—— *Le Quatorzieme livre d'Amadis de Gaule*, trans. by A. Tyron (Antwerp, 1574).

—— *Le Thresor des douze liures d'amadis de Gaule, assauoir les Harengues, Concions, Epistres, Complaintes, & autres choses les plus excellentes & dignes du lecteur François* (Paris, 1559).

—— *The moste excellent and pleasaunt Booke, entituled: The treasurie of Amadis of Fraunce: Conteyning eloquente orations, pythie Epistles, learned Letters, and feruent Complayntes, seruing for sundrie purposes*, trans. by T. Paynell (1567; 1572).

Amyot, J., *Projet d'Eloquence Royale*, ed. by P.-J. Salazar (Paris: Les Belles Lettres, 1992).

Anon., *Antwerpes Vnitye. An Accord or Peace in Religion, and Gouernment, concluded by his Highnes, and the members of the Citie, to the common weale and quietnes thereof there lately proclaymed the 12. of Iune Anno. 1579. Printed in French, and Dutch, by the Kinges printer, and Englished by the Printer hereof* (1579).

Anon., *Histoire veritable de la plus saine partie de la vie de Henry de Valois* (Paris, 1589).

Anon., *The Interest of England Maintained: The Honour of the Parliament vindicated; The Malignants Plott upon the Presbyters, to make them doe their worke Discovered. The Designe to destroy Common Freedome, and all just Government, is under the specious pretence of rooting out Sectaries, and Hereticks, evidenced: In Certaine Observations upon a Dangerous Remonstrance lately presented by the Lord Major, and Common Counsell of London, to the Honourable, the Commons of England, in Parliament Assembled* (1646).

Aphthonius, *Aphthonii sophistae praeexercitamenta interprete viro doctissimo* (1520?).

—— *Aphthonii sophistae Progymnasmata, partim a Rodolpho Agricola, partim a Ioanne Maria Catanaeo Latinitate donata: cum luculentis & vtilibus in eadem Scholijs Reinhardi Lorichij Hadamarij. Ad rhetorices candidatos, Tetrastichon eiusdem* (1572).

—— *Progymnasmata*, trans. by G. A. Kennedy, in *Progymnasmata: Greek Textbooks of Prose Composition and Rhetoric*, ed. and trans. by G. A. Kennedy (Atlanta: Society of Biblical Literature, 2003), pp. 96–127.

—— *Progymnasmata*, trans. by M. Heath, published at www.leeds.ac.uk/classics/resources/rhetoric/prog-aph.htm.

Appian, *An auncient Historie and exquisite Chronicle of the Romanes Warres, both Ciuile and Foren*, trans. by W. B. [Barker?] (1578).

—— *Appian's Roman History*, trans. by H. White, 4 vols (London: William Heinemann, 1912–13).

Apuleius, *The Golden Ass [,] Being the Metamorphoses of Lucius Apuleius [,] with an English Translation by W. Adlington (1566)*, rev. by S. Gaselee (London: William Heinemann, 1922).

Arbaleste, C., *Mémoires de Charlotte Arbaleste, sur la Vie de Duplessis-Mornay* (Paris, 1824).

Aristotle, Ἀριστοτέλους πασαν λογικην [...] *Aristotelis omnem logicam, rhetoricam et poeticam disciplinam continens*, ed. by Ioannes Baptista Camotius, 6 vols (Venetiis, 1551–53 [i.e., 1551–52]).

Aubrey, J., *'Brief Lives', chiefly of Contemporaries, set down by John Aubrey, between the Years 1669 & 1696*, ed. by A. Clark, 2 vols (Oxford: Oxford University Press, 1898).

Barclay, J., *Ioannis Barclaii Argenis* (Paris, 1621).

—— *Iohn Barclay His Argenis, Translated Out Of Latine Into English: The Prose Vpon His Maiesties Command: By Sir Robert Le Grys, Knight: and the Verses by Thomas May, Esquire. With a Clauis annexed to it for the satisfaction of the Reader, and helping him to vnderstand, what persons were by the Author intended, vnder the fained Names imposed by him vpon them: And published by his Maiesties Command* (1628).

Baron, R., *ΕΡΟΤΟΠΑΙΓΝΙΟΝ Or The Cyprian Academy* (1647).

Barreiros, G., *Chorographia de alguns lugares que stam em hum caminho* (Coimbra, 1561).

—— *Censura in quendam auctorem, qui sub falsa inscriptione Berosi Chaldaei circunfertur* (Rome, 1565).

Belleforest, F., *L'Histoire des Neuf Rois Charles de France* (1568).

Beroaldo, F., *Commentarii a Philippo Beroaldo conditi in asinum Lucii Apulei* (Bologna, 1500).

Bette, T., *A Newe Ballade Intituled, Agaynst Rebellious and false Rumours. To the newe tune of the Black Almaine, upon Scissillia* (1570).

Biondi, Sir G. F., *Eromena, or, Love and Revenge. Written originally in the Thoscan tongue, by Cavalier Gio. Francesco Biondi, Gentleman extraordinary of his Majesties Privie Chamber. Divided into six books. And now faithfully Englished,* by Ia. Hayvvard [i.e., Hayward], *of Graies-Inne Gent* (1632).

Burton, R., *The Anatomy of Melancholy* (1621).

Camerarius, J., the younger, *Symbolorum et Emblematum* (Nuremberg, 1593).

Casaubon, I., *The Answere of Master Isaac Casaubon to the Epistle of the most illustrious, and most reuerend Cardinall Peron* (1612).

Castiglione, B., *Il Libro del Cortegiano* (Venice, 1528).

—— *Les quatres liures du Courtisan* (Lyon, 1537).

—— *The Book of the Courtier*, trans. by Sir Thomas Hoby (London: J. M. Dent, 1959).

Cervantes Saavedra, M. de, *The Ingenious Hidalgo Don Quixote de la Mancha*, trans. by J. Rutherford (London: Penguin, 2000; repr. 2003).

—— *The Trials of Persiles and Sigismunda, a Northern Story*, trans. by C. R. Weller and C. A. Colahan (Berkeley: University of California Press, 1989).

Cicero, *Brutus*, in *Brutus [and] Orator*, trans. by G. L. Hendrickson and H. M. Hubbell (London: William Heinemann Ltd, 1952).

Clary, F. de, *Philippiques contre les bulles et autres pratiques de la faction d'Espagne* (Tours, 1592).

Colet, C., *The Famous, pleasant, and variable Historie, of Palladine of England*, trans. by A[ntony]. M[unday]. (1588).

Constantine, Sir W., *The Interest of England How it Consists in Vnity of the Protestant Religion. With Expedients moderate and effectuall to establish it by the extirpation of the papacy. By a Member of the House of Commons* (1642).

—— *The Second Part of The Interest of England Considered As it relates to the Government of the Church. In three Divisions: wherein is demonstrated, 1. How*

Church-Government by the Hierarchy of Bishops is destructive to the Interest of this Kingdome. 2. How the Presbyteriall Discipline will conduce to the Interest thereof. 3. Of Tender Consciences, what sort may and ought to bee permitted, what not … (1645).

Daniel, S., *A Defence of Ryme* (1603).

—— *A Panegyrike Congratulatory Deliuered to the Kings most excellent maiesty at Burleigh Harrington in Rutlandshire. By Samuel Daniel. Also certaine Epistles. With a Defence of Ryme, heeretofore written, and now published by the Author* (1603).

Day, A., *The English Secretorie* (1586).

—— *Upon the life and death of the most worthy and thrice renowmed knight, Sir Philip Sidney* (1587).

Digges, D., *The Compleat Ambasssador* (1655).

Dio, C., *Dio's Roman History*, trans. by E. Cary, 9 vols (London: William Heinemann, 1914–27). http://penelope.uchicago.edu/Thayer/E/Roman/Texts/Cassius_Dio/44*.html.

Doni, Anton Francesco, *The Morall Philosophie of Doni: drawne out of the auncient writers. A worke first compiled in the Indian tongue, and afterwardes reduced into diuers other languages: and now lastly englished out of Italian by Thomas North, Brother to the right Honorable Sir Roger North Knight, Lorde North of Kyrtheling* (1570).

Donne, J., *The Complete English Poems*, ed. by A. J. Smith (Harmondsworth: Penguin, 1976).

Du Bartas, Guillaume de Saluste, *Babilon*, trans. by William L'Isle (1595).

—— *The colonies of Bartas*, trans. by William L'Isle (1598).

—— *Part of Du Bartas, English and French, and in his owne kinde of Verse, so neare the French Englished, as may teach an English-man French, or a French-man English.* […] *With the commentary of S.G.S.* [i.e., Simon Goulart, Senlisien] *By William L'Isle of Wilburgham, Esquier for the Kings body* (1625).

Du Coignet, P., *Anti-Coton, or A Refutation of Cottons Letter Declaratorie: lately directed to the Queene Regent, for the Apologizing of the Iesuites Doctrine, touching the killing of kings. A booke, in which it is proued that the Iesuites are guiltie, and were the Authors of the late execrable Parricide, commited vpon the Person of the French King, Henry the fourth, of happy memorie. To which is added, A Supplication of the Vniuersitie of Paris, for the preuenting of the Iesuites opening their Schooles among them: in which their King-killing Doctrine is also notably discouered, and confuted. Both translated out of the French, by G. H. Together with the Translators animaduersions vpon Cottons Letter* (1611).

Du Perron, Jacques Davy, *A Letter Written From Paris, by the Lord Cardinall of Peron, to Monsr. Casaubon in England* (1612).

Du Plessis-Mornay, Philippe, Seigneur du Plessis-Marly, *Excellent discours de la vie et de la mort* (n.p., 1576).

—— *De la Verité de la Religion Chrestienne. Contre les Athées, Épicuriens, Payens, Juifs, Mahumedistes, et autres Infideles* (Antwerp, 1581).

—— *A Woorke concerning the trewnesse of the Christian religion, written in French: against atheists, Epicures, Paynims, Iewes, Mahumetists, and other infidels. By Philip of Mornay Lord of Plessie Marlie. Begunne to be translated into English by Sir Philip Sidney Knight, and at his request finished by Arthur Golding* (1587).

Du Plessis-Mornay, Philippe, Seigneur du Plessis-Marly, and R. Garnier, *A Discourse of Life and Death. Written in French by Ph. Mornay. Antonius, A Tragoedie written also in French by Ro. Garnier. Both done in English by the Countesse of Pembroke* (1592).

Estienne, H (attrib.), *Discours merveilleux de la vie, actions et deportemens de Catherine de Medicis Royne mere. Auquel sont recitez les moyens qu'elle a tenu pour vsurper le gouuernement de royaume de France, & ruiner l'estat d'iceluy* (n.p., 1575).

—— *A meruaylous discourse upon the lyfe, of Katherine de Medicis* (Heydelberge [i.e., London], 1575).

—— *Ane Meruellous discours* (Cracow [i.e., Edinburgh] and Paris [i.e., Edinburgh], 1576).

Estienne, H., *Conformité du Langage Français avec le Grec*, nouvelle ed. par L. Feugère (Paris, 1853; repr. Geneva: Slatkine Reprints, 1970).

—— *Deux dialogues du nouveau langage françois, italianizé et autrement desguizé, principalement entre les courtisans de ce temps* ([Geneva, 1578]).

—— *Deux dialogues du nouveau langage françois*, ed. and introduced by P.-M. Smith (Geneva: Editions Slatkine, 1980).

—— *Projet de l'oeuvre intitulé de la précellence du langage françois*, ed. by E. Huguet (Paris: Armand Colin, 1896).

—— *Traicte de la conformité du language François auec le Grec* ([Geneva], 1565).

Estienne, H., ed., Ἡ Καινη Διαθηκη. *Nouum Testamentum. Obscuriorum vocum & quoru[n]dam loquendi generum accuratas partim suas partim aliorum interpretationes margini adscripsit Henr. Stephanus* ([Geneva], 1576).

—— Ἐκ των Κτησιου, Ἀγαθαρχιδου, Μεμνονος ἱστορικων ἐκλογαι. Ἀππιανου Ἰβηρικη και Ἀννιβαϊκη. *Ex Ctesia, Agatharchide, Memnone excerptae historiae. Appiani Iberica. Item, De gestis Annibalis. Omnia nunc primùm edita. Cum Henrici Stephani castigationibus* (Paris, 1557).

—— Ἡρωδιανου Ἱστοριων βιβλια ή. *Herodiani Histor. lib. VIII. cum Angeli Politiani interpretatione, et hujus partim supplemento, partim examine H. Stephani: utroque margini adscripto. Ejusdem H. Stephani emendationes quorundam Græci contextus locorum* [...] *Historiarum (Zosimi) Herodianicas subsequentium libri duo, nunc primum Graeci editi* ([Geneva], 1581).

—— *Moschi, Bionis, Theocriti* [...] *ab H. Stephano Latina facta. Ejusdem carmina non diversi ab illis argumenti* (Venice, 1555).

Euripides, *Les Troades – Iphigénie en Aulis, Traductions inédites de Jacques Amyot*, ed. by L. de Nardis (Naples: Bibliopolis, 1996).

Faur, Guy de, Seigneur de Pibrac, *Apologie de la Saint-Barthélemy* (1573).

Fletcher, P., *The Purple Island* (1633).

Florio, J., *Queen Anna's New World of Words* (1611).

France, Parliament of, *A declaration exhibited to the French king, by hys Court of Parlyament concerning the holy League* (1587).

Fraunce, A., *The Countess of Pembroke's Ivychurch* (1591).

Garnier, R., *Oeuvres complètes (théatre et poésies) de Robert Garnier*, ed. by L. Pinvert, 2 vols (Paris: Librairie Garnier Frères, 1923).

—— *Two Tragedies: 'Hippolyte' and 'Marc-Antoine'*, ed. by C. M. Hill and M. Morrison (London: Athlone Press, 1975).

Gawdy, P., *Letters of Philip Gawdy of West Harling, Norfolk, and of London to various members of his family 1579–1616*, ed. by I. H. Jeayes (London: Roxburghe Club, 1906).

Gayton, E., *Pleasant Notes Upon Don Quixot* (1654).

Giovio, P., *The Worthy tract of Paulus Iovius, contayning a Discourse of rare inuentions, both Militarie and Amorous called Imprese*, trans. by Samuel Daniel (1588).

Goodman, C., *How superior powers oght to be obeyd of their subiects: and Wherin they may lawfully by Gods Worde be disobeyed and resisted. Wherin also is declared the cause of all this present miserie in England, and the onely way to remedy the same* (Geneva, 1558).

Gough, J., *The Strange Discovery* (1640).

Grammaticus, Aelfric, *A Saxon Treatise*, trans. by William L'Isle (1623).

Greene, R., *Morando* (1584).

—— *Pandosto. The Triumph of Time* (1588).

Greville, F., *The Life of the Renowned Sr Philip Sidney. With the true Interest of England as it then stood in relation to all Forrain Princes: And particularly for suppressing the power of Spain Stated by Him. His principall Actions, Counsels, Designes, and Death. Together with a short Account of the Maximes and Policies used by Queen Elizabeth in her Government. Written by Sir Fulke Grevil Knight, Lord Brook, a Servant to Queen Elizabeth, and his Companion & Friend* (1652).

—— *The Prose Works of Fulke Greville, Lord Brooke*, ed. by J. Gouws (Oxford: Clarendon Press, 1986).

Guevara, Antonio de, *The Diall of Princes. Compiled by the reuerende father in God, Don Anthony of Gueuara, Bysshop of Guadix. Preacher and Cronicler, to Charles the fyft Emperour of Rome. Englysshed oute of the Frenche, by Thomas North, seconde sonne of the Lorde North. Ryght necessary and pleasaunt, to all gentylmen and others whiche are louers of vertue* (1557).

—— *The Dial of Princes, Compiled by the reuerend father in God, Don Antony of Gueuara, Byshop of Guadix, Preacher, and Chronicler to Charles the fifte, late of that name Emperour. Englished out of the Frenche by T. North, sonne of Sir Edvvard North knight, L. North of Kyrtheling. And now newly reuised* […] (1568).

Harvey, G., *Pierce's Supererogation* (1593).

Heliodorus, *Heliodori Historiae Aethiopicae libri decem, nunquam antea in lucem editi*, ed. by Vincentus Obsopoeus or Opsopaeus (Basel, 1534).

—— *L'histoire aethiopique de Heliodorus, contenant dix livres traitant des loyales et pudiques amours de Theagenes thessalien et Chariclea aethiopie[n]ne, nouuellement traduite de grec en françoys* [trans. by Jacques Amyot] (Paris: Vincent Sertenas [par Estienne Groulleau], 1547 [i.e., 1548]).

—— *Heliodori Aethiopicae Historiae libri decem*, trans. by S. Warschewiczki (Basel, 1552).

—— *Historia Ethiopica* (Antwerp, 1554).

—— *Historia di Heliodoro delle cose Ethiopiche. Nella quale fra diuersi, compassioneuoli auenimenti di due Amanti, si contengono abbtattimenti, discrittioni di paesi, e molte altre cose utile e diletteuoli a leggere. Tradotta dalla lingua Greca nella Thoscana da Messer Leonardo Ghini* (Venice, 1556).

—— *L'histoire aethiopique de Heliodorus, contenant dix livres, traitant des loyales et pudiques amours de Theagenes Thessalien, & Chariclea Aethiopienne. Traduite de Grec en François, & de nouueau reueüe et corrigée sur un ancien exemplaire escript à la main, par le translateur, ou est declaré au vray qui en a esté le premier autheur* [trans. by Jacques Amyot] (Paris: Vincent Sertenas, 1559).

—— *An Aethiopian Historie written in Greeke by Heliodorus: very wittie and pleasaunt, Englished by Thomas Vnderdoune. With the Argumente of euery Booke, sette before the whole Woorke* (1569).

—— *An Aethiopian historie, written in Greeke by Heliodorus, no lesse wittie then pleasant: Englished by Thomas Vnderdowne, and newely corrected and augmented, with diuers and sundrie new additions by the saide Authour. Whervnto is also annexed the argument of euery booke, in the beginning of the same, for the better vnderstanding of the storie* (1577).

—— Ἡλιοδώρου Αἰθιωπικων Βιβλια δεκα. *Heliodori Aethiopicorum libri X. Collatione MSS. Bibliothecae Palatinae & aliorum, emendati & multis in locis aucti, Hieronymi Commelini opera* (Heidelberg, 1596).

—— Ἡλιοδώρου Αἰθιωπικων Βιβλια δεκα. *Heliodori Aethiopicorum libri X. Io. Bourdelotius emendauit suppleuit, ac libros decem Animaduersionum adiecit* (Paris, 1619).

—— *The Faire Aethiopian. Dedicated to the King and Queene. By their Maiesties most humble Subiect and Seruant, William L'Isle* (1631).

—— *The famous historie of Heliodorus. Amplified, augmented, and delivered paraphrastically in verse; by their Majesties most humble subject and servant, William Lisle* (1638).

—— *The Aethiopian History Of Heliodorus. In Ten Books. The First Five Translated by a Person of Quality, The Last Five by N. Tate* (1685).

—— *The Triumphs Of Love And Constancy: A Romance. Containing the Heroick Amours of Theagenes and Chariclea* (1687).

—— *Historia Etiópica de los Amores de Téagenes y Cariclea*, traducida por Fernando de Mena, Edicion y Prologo de F. Lopez Estrada, Biblioteca Selecta de Clássicos Españoles, ser. II, xiv (Madrid: Real Academia Española, 1954).

—— *Les Éthiopiques*, ed. by R. M. Rattenbury and T. W. Lumb, trans. by J. Maillon, 3 vols., 2nd edn (Paris: Société d'Édition 'Les Belles Lettres', 1960).

—— *An Ethiopian Story*, trans. by J. R. Morgan, in *Collected Ancient Greek Novels*, ed. by B. P. Reardon (Berkeley: University of California Press, 1989).

Hérembert, J., Sieur de la Rivière, *Les advantureuses et fortunées Amours de Pandion et de Yonice. Tirées des anciens autheurs Grecz* (1599).

Holinshed, R., *Chronicles*, ed. by H. Ellis, 6 vols (London, 1807–8).

—— *The Firste volume of the Chronicles of England, Scotlande, and Irelande. Conteyning, The description and Chronicles of England, from the first inhabiting vnto the conquest. The description and Chronicles of Scotland, from the first originall of the Scottes nation, till the yeare of our Lorde. 1571. The description and Chronicles of Yrelande, likewise from the firste originall of that Nation, vntill the yeare. 1547. Faithfully gathered and set forth, by Raphaell Holinshed* (1577).

—— *The First and second volumes of Chronicles, comprising 1 The description and historie of England, 2 The description and historie of Ireland, 3 The description and historie of Scotland: First collected and published by Raphaell Holinshed, William Harrison, and others: Now newlie augmented and continued (with manifold matters of singular note and worthie memorie) to the yeare 1586. by Iohn Hooker aliàs Vowell Gent and others. With conuenient tables at the end of these volumes* (1587).

Homer, *The Odyssey of Homer*, trans. by R. Lattimore (New York: Harper & Row, 1967).

Hoskins [i.e., Hoskyns], J., *Directions for Speech and Style*, ed. by H. H. Hudson (Princeton: Princeton University Press, 1935).

Howell, J., *ΔΕΝΔΡΟΛΟΓΙΑ. the Vocall Forrest* (1640).

James VI and I, *The Trew Law of Free Monarchies* (1598).

—— *A Premonition to All Most Mighty Monarchies, Kings, Free Princes, and States of Christendom* (1609).

—— *Declaration du Serenissime Roy Iaques I. Roy de la Grand' Bretaigne France et Irlande, Defenseur de la Foy. Pour le Droit des Rois & independance de leurs Couronnes, Contre La Harangue De L'Illustrissime Cardinal du Perron prononcée en la chambre du tiers Estat le XV. de Ianuier 1615. A Londres, Par Iehan Bill Imprimeur du Roy. M.DC.XV.*

—— *Political Writings*, ed. by J. P. Sommerville (Cambridge: Cambridge University Press, 1994).

Jonson, B., *B. Ion: his part of King James his Royall and Magnificent Entertainement through his Honorable Cittie of London* (1604).

—— *Hymenaei: or The Solemnities of Masque, and Barriers, Magnificently performed on the eleventh, and twelfth Nights, from Christmas; At Court: To the auspicious celebrating of the Marriage-vnion, betweene Robert, Earle of Essex, and the Lady Frances, second Daughter to the most noble Earle of Suffolke* (1606).

Kraus, Martin (Martinus Crusius), *Martini Crusii Aethiopicae Heliodori Historiae Epitome* (Francofurti, 1584).

Languet, H (attrib.), *Vindiciae, contra tyrannos* (Edimburgi [i.e., Basle], 1579).

—— *Vindiciae contra Tyrannos: A Defence of Liberty against Tyrants. OR, Of the lawfull power of the Prince over the people, and of the people over the Prince. BEING A Treatise written in Latin and French by Junius Brutus, and translated out of both into ENGLISH* (1648).

Lant, T., *Sequitur celebritas et pompa funeris* […] (1587).

Lemaire de Belges, Jean, *Les Illustrations de Gaule et Singularitez de Troye* (Lyon, 1510–13).

Lloyd, D., *The legend of Captaine Iones* (1631–48).

Longus, *Les amours pastorales de Daphnis et Chloe, escriptes premierement en grec par Longus et puis traduictes en Françoys*, trans. by Jacques Amyot (Paris, 1559).

—— *Daphnis and Chloe Excellently describing the weight of affection, the simplicitie of loue, the purport of honest meaning, the resolution of men, and disposition of Fate, finished in a Pastorall, and interlaced with the praises of a most peerlesse Princesse, wonderfull in Maiestie, and rare in perfection, celebrated within the same Pastorall, and therefore termed by the name of The Shepheards Holidaie. By Angell Daye* (1587).

—— Λόγγου ποιμενικῶν, τῶν κατὰ Δάφνιν καὶ Χλόην βιβλία τέτταρα. *Longi pastoralium, de Daphnide & Chloë libri quatuor* (Florence, 1598).

—— *Gli amore innocenti di Dafni, e della Cloe*, trans. by G. B. Manzini [i.e., trans. by A. Caro] (Bologna, 1643).

—— *Daphnis and Chloe. A Most Sweet, and Pleasant Pastorall Romance for Young Ladies*, trans. by George Thornley (1657).

—— *Gli Amori pastorali di Dafni e di Cloe*, trans. by A. Caro (Parma, 1784; Florence, 1786; London, 1786).

—— *Les pastorales de Longus, ou Daphnis Et Chloé, Traduction de Messire Jacques Amyot, en son vivant Évêque d'Auxerre et Grand-Aumonier de France; Revue, Corrigée, Completée, De Nouveau Refaite en Grande Partie Par Paul-Louis Courier, Vigneron, Membre de la Légion-D'Honneur, Ci-devant Canonnier à Cheval, Aujourd'hui en Prison à Sainte-Pélagie*. Cinquième Édition [first edn Paris, 1803] (Paris, 1821).

—— *Daphnis and Chloe: The Elizabethan Version From Amyot's Translation by Angel Day*, ed. by J. Jacobs (London: David Nutt, 1890).

—— *Daphnis & Chloe by Longus, With the English Translation of George Thornley*, rev. and augmented by J. M. Edmonds; *The Love Romances of Parthenius and Other Fragments*, trans. by S. Gaselee (London: Heinemann, 1916).

—— *Pastorales (Daphnis et Chloé)*, ed. and trans. by G. Dalmeyda, 2nd edn (Paris: Société D'Édition 'Les Belles Lettres', 1960).

—— *Les amours pastorales de Daphnis et Chloé, traduit du grec ancien par Jacques Amyot*, avant-propos de Sabine Wespieser, Les Belles Infidèles (Arles: Actes Sud, 1988).

—— *Daphnis and Chloe*, trans. by C. Gill, in *Collected Ancient Greek Novels*, ed. by B. P. Reardon (Berkeley: University of California Press, 1989).

Loyseleur, P., Sieur de Villiers, *The Apologie or Defence, of the most noble Prince William, by the grace of God, Prince of Orange, Countie of Nassau, of Catzenellen-*

boghen, Dietz, Vianden, &c. Burgmaister of Antwerp, and Vicou[n]t of Bezanson, Baron of Breda, Diest, Grimberg, of Arlay, Nozeroy, &c. Lord of Chastel-bellin, &c. Lieutenaunt generall in the lowe Countries, and Gouernour of Brabant, Holland, Zeelande, Vtrecht and Frise, & Admiral, &c. Against the Proclamation and Edict, published by the King of Spaine, by which he proscribeth the saide Lorde Prince, whereby shall appeare the sclaunders, and false accusations, conteined in the said Proscription, which is annexed to the end of this Apologie. Presented to my lords the Estates generall of the lowe Countrie. Together with the said Proclamation or Proscription. Printed in French and in all other languages (Delft, 1581).

Lyly, J., *Euphues: The Anatomy of Wit* (1578).

Maplet, J., *A greene Forest, or a naturall Historie* (1567).

Marlowe, C., *The Massacre at Paris: With the Death of the Duke of Guise* (1594).

Melanchthon, P., *A ciuile nosgay wherin is contayned not onelye the offyce and dewty of all magestrates and iudges but also of all subiectes with a preface concernynge the lyberty of iustice in this our tyme newly collected and gethered out of latyn and so translated in to the Inglyshe tonge by I.G.* [i.e., Goodale] ([1550?]).

Munday, A., *The Mirrour of Mutabilitie, or Principall part of the Mirrour for Magistrates. Describing the fall of diuers famous Princes, and other memorable Personages* (1579).

Nichols, J., *The Progresses, Processions, and Magnificient Festivities of King James the First*, 4 vols (London, 1828; repr. New York: AMS Press, 1967).

Ovid, *Metamorphoses*, trans. by F. J. Miller, 2 vols (London: Heinemann, 1916).

Orange-Nassau-Dillenburg, Willem I, prince of (William of Orange), *A declaration and publication of the most worthy Prince of Orange, contaynyng the cause of his necessary defence against the Duke of Alba* (1568).

Peele, G., *An eclogue Gratulatorie. Entituled: to the honorable shepherd of Albions arcadia: Robert earle of Essex* (1589).

—— *Polyhymnia* (1590).

Philostratus, the elder, Εἰκόνες, in Lucian of Samosata, Ταδε ἐνεστιν ἐν τῳδε τῳ βιβλιῳ. Λουκιανου. Φιλοστρατου εἰκόνες […] (Venice, 1503).

—— *Icones*, in *Stephani Nigri Elegantissime è graeco authorum subditorum traslationes. uidelicet. Philostrati Icones. Pythagorae Carmen aureum Athenaei Collectanea Musonij philosophi Tyrij De principe optimo Isocratis de regis muneribus orno. & alia multa scitu digniss. & rara inuentu, quae uersa pagina lector bone lubens, & gaudens inuenies* (Milan, 1521).

—— *Les images ou tableaux de platte-peinture de Philostrate Lemnien sophiste grec. Mis en françois par Blaise de Vigenere. Avec des argumens & annotations sur chacun d'iceux* (Paris, 1578).

Philostratus and Eunapius, trans. by W. C. Wright (London: William Heinemann, 1922).

Philostratus, *Imagines*; Callistratus, *Descriptions*, trans. by A. Fairbanks (London: William Heinemann Ltd, 1960).

Photius, *Bibliotheca*, ed. by Andreas Schottus (Augustae Vindelicorum [i.e., Augsburg], 1606).

—— *The Library of Photius*, ed. by J. H. Freese (London: Society for Promoting Christian Knowledge, 1920). www.tertullian.org/fathers/photius_03bibliotheca.htm.

Plutarch, *Του σοφωτατου Πλουταρχου Παραλληλον. Βιοι ῾Ρωμαιων και ῾Ελληνων.* […] *Sapientissimi Plutarchi paralellum. Vitae Romanorum et Græcorum. Quadriginta novem. Ed. pr* (Florence, 1517).

—— *Les Oeuvres morales & meslees de Plutarque. Translatees du Grec en François par Messire Iacques Amyot* (Paris, 1572).

—— *Les Oeuvres morales & meslees de Plutarque, Translatees de Grec en François*, trans. by J. Amyot, 2 vols ([Geneva,] 1582).

—— *The Philosophie, commonlie called, The Morals written by the learned Philosopher Plutarch of Chaeronea. Translated out of Greeke into English, and conferred with the Latine translations and the French, by Philemon Holland of Coventrie, Doctor in Physicke. Whereunto are annexed the Summaries necessary to be read before every Treatise* (1603).

—— *Les vies des hommes illustres Grecs, & Romains, comparees l'vne auec l'autre par Plutarque de Chaeronee, translatees de grec en francois* [trans. by J. Amyot] (Paris, 1559).

—— *Les vies des hommes illustres Grecs, & Romains, comparées l'vne auec l'autre par Plutarque de Cheronee, Translatees … par Maistre Iacques Amyot*, 2nd edn (Paris, 1565). http://web2.bium.univ-paris5.fr/livanc/?cote=01344&do=pages.

—— *The Lives of the Noble Grecians and Romanes, compared together by that graue learned Philosopher and Historiographer, Plutarke of Chaeronea: Translated out of Greeke into French by Iames Amyot, Abbot of Bellozane, Bishop of Auxerre, one of the Kings priuy counsel, and great Amner of Fraunce, and out of French into Englishe, by Thomas North* (1579).

—— *Les vies des hommes illustres grecs et romains* [trans. by J. Amyot …] *sommaires et annotations par SGS* [i.e., Simon Goulart, Senlisien] (Colognt [i.e., Cologny or Geneva,] [1616–]1617).

—— *Plutarch's Lives*, trans. by B. Perrin, 11 vols (London: William Heinemann, 1914–26). http://penelope.uchicago.edu/Thayer/E/Roman/Texts/Plutarch/Lives

Postel, G., *Les raisons de la monarchie* (1551).

Prynne, W., *The soveraigne power of parliaments and kingdoms* (1643).

Rabelais, F., *The Works Of the Famous Mr. Francis Rabelais, Doctor in Physick, Treating of the Lives, Heroick Deeds, and Sayings of Gargantua And his Son Pantagruel*, trans. by Sir T. Urquhart (1664).

Reyner, E., *A treatise of the necessity of humane learning for a Gospel-preacher* (1663).

Rohan, Henri, duc de, *De l'Interest des Princes et des Estats de la Chrestienté* (Paris, 1638).

—— *A treatise of the interest of the princes and states of Christendome. Written in French by the most noble and illustrious Prince, the Duke of Rohan*, trans. by H. Hunt (Paris, 1640; London, 1641).

Sanford, J., *The Amorous and Tragicall Tales of Plutarch. Wherevnto is annexed the Hystorie of Cariclea & Theagenes, and the sayings of the Greeke Philosophers* (1567).

—— *Henrie Cornelius Agrippa, of the Vanitie and vncertaintie of Artes and Sciences* (1569).

Seneca, *Hippolytus*, in *Seneca's Tragedies*, trans. by F. J. Miller, 2 vols (London: William Heinemann, 1907).

Shakespeare, W., *Antony and Cleopatra*, ed. by D. Bevington (Cambridge: Cambridge University Press, 1990).

—— *Coriolanus*, ed. by P. Brockbank (London: Methuen, 1976; repr. 1980).

—— *Mr. William Shakespeares Comedies, Histories, & Tragedies* (1623).

—— *The Norton Shakespeare*, ed. by S. Greenblatt (New York: W. W. Norton, 1997).

—— *The Winter's Tale*, ed. by J. H. P. Pafford, The Arden Shakespeare (London: Methuen, 1963).

Sidney, A., *Court Maxims*, ed. by H. W. Blom, E. H. Mulier and R. Janse (Cambridge: Cambridge University Press, 1996).

Sidney, Sir P., *A Defence of Poetry*, in *Miscellaneous Prose of Sir Philip Sidney*, ed. by K. Duncan-Jones and J. van Dorsten (Oxford: Clarendon Press, 1973).

—— *The Countesse of Pembrokes Arcadia. Written by Sir Philip Sidney Knight. Now since the first edition augmented and ended* (1593).

—— *The Countess of Pembroke's Arcadia (The Old Arcadia)*, ed. by J. Robertson (Oxford: Clarendon Press, 1973).

—— *The Countess of Pembroke's Arcadia (The New Arcadia)*, ed. by V. Skretkowicz (Oxford: Clarendon Press, 1987).

—— *The Poems of Sir Philip Sidney*, ed. by W. A. Ringler, Jr (Oxford: Clarendon Press, 1962).

Silva, Feliciano de, *Le Dixiesme livre d'Amadis de Gaule*, trans. by C. Colet (Paris, 1552).

Speed, J., *The History of Great Britaine* (1611).

Stucki, J. W., *Carolus Magnus Redivivus, hoc est, Caroli Magni Germanorum, Gallorum, Italorum, et aliarum gentium monarchae potentissimi, cum Henrico M. Gallorum & Nauarrorum Rege florentissimo comparatio* (1592).

Theophrastus, Θεοφράστου Χαρακτήρες. *Cum interpretatione Latina, per Bilibaldu[m] Pirkeymheru[m], iam recens aedita* (Norembergae, 1527).

—— *Theophrasti Characteres*, in *Aristotelis opera, tomus sextus*, ed. by Ioannes Baptista Camotius. Venetiis (Venezia, 1552).

—— Θεοφράστου ηθικοι Χαρακτήρες, *sive Descriptiones morum, Graece Isaacus Casaubonus recensuit, in Latinum sermonem vertit, et libro commentario illustravit* (Lugduni [i.e., Lyon], 1599).

—— *Théophraste, Caractères*, ed. by O. Navarre, 2nd edn (Paris, 1931).

—— *Characters*, ed. by J. Diggle, Cambridge Classical Texts and Commentaries, 43 (Cambridge: Cambridge University Press, 2004).

Vienne, P. de, *Les devis amoureux*, trans. by 'l'Amoureux de Vertu' (Paris, 1545).

Virgil, *Aeneid*, trans. by John Studley (1566).

——

The Destruction of Troy, or the Acts of Aeneas, ed. and trans. by T. Wroth (1620).

Viterbo, Annius of, *Commentaria super opera diuersorum auctorum de antiquitatibus* (1498).

Wilson, A., *The History of Great Britain, Being the Life and Reign of King James the First, Relating to what passed from his first Access to the Crown, till his Death* (1653).

Wroth, Lady M., *Lady Mary Wroth's Love's Victory: The Penshurst Manuscript*, ed. by M. G. Brennan (London: Roxburghe Club, 1988).

—— *The Countesse of Mountgomeries Urania. Written by the right honorable the Lady Mary Wroath. Daughter to the right Noble Robert Earle of Leicester. And Neece to the ever famous, and renowned Sr. Phillips Sidney knight. And to ye most exele[n]t Lady Mary Countesse of Pembroke late deceased* (1621).

—— *The First Part of The Countess of Montgomery's Urania*, ed. by J. A. Roberts, Medieval and Renaissance Texts and Studies, vol. 140; Renaissance English Text Society, 7th ser., xvii (Binghamton, NY: Center for Medieval and Early Renaissance Studies, 1995).

—— *The Second Part of The Countess of Montgomery's Urania*, ed. by J. A. Roberts, S. Gossett, and J. Mueller, Medieval and Renaissance Texts and Studies, vol. 211; Renaissance English Text Society, 7th ser., xxiv (Tempe, AZ: Arizona Centre for Medieval and Renaissance Studies, 1999).

—— *The Poems of Lady Mary Wroth*, ed. by J. A. Roberts (Baton Rouge: Louisiana State University Press, 1992).

Wroth, T., *The Abortive of an Idle Houre or a Centurie of Epigrams. And a Motto Vpon the Creede* (1620).

Wycherley, W., *The Plays of William Wycherley*, ed. by A. Friedman (Oxford: Clarendon Press, 1979).

Secondary sources

Adams, S., 'Dudley, Robert, Earl of Leicester (1532/3–1588)', *Oxford Dictionary of National Biography* (Oxford: Oxford University Press, 2004).

—— 'Howard, Katherine, Countess of Nottingham (1545x50–1603)', *Oxford Dictionary of National Biography* (Oxford: Oxford University Press, 2004).

Alexander, G., 'Fulke Greville and the Afterlife', *Huntington Library Quarterly*, lxii (2000), 203–31.

—— 'Sidney's Interruptions', *Studies in Philology*, xcviii (2001), 184–204.

—— *Writing After Sidney: The Literary Response to Sir Philip Sidney, 1586–1640* (Oxford: Oxford University Press, 2006).

Allen, M. J. B., D. Baker-Smith and A. F. Kinney, eds, *Sir Philip Sidney's Achievements* (New York: AMS Press, 1990).

Anderson, G., *The Second Sophistic: A Cultural Phenomenon in the Roman Empire* (London: Routledge, 1993).

Anglo, S., ed., *Chivalry in the Renaissance* (Woodbridge, Suffolk: The Boydell Press, 1990).

Armstrong, Brian G., and Vivienne Larminie, 'Du Moulin, Pierre (1568–1658)',

Oxford Dictionary of National Biography (Oxford: Oxford University Press, 2004).

Asher, R. E., *National Myths in Renaissance France: Francus, Samothes and the Druids* (Edinburgh: Edinburgh University Press, 1993).

Asquith, C., *Shadowplay: The Hidden Beliefs and Coded Politics of William Shakespeare* (New York: PublicAffairs, 2005).

Atherton, I., 'Sidney, Robert, Second Earl of Leicester (1595–1677)', *Oxford Dictionary of National Biography* (Oxford: Oxford University Press, 2004).

Aulotte, R., *Amyot et Plutarque: La tradition des Moralia au XVe siècle* (Geneva: Libraire Droz, 1965).

Balard, M., ed., *Fortunes de Jacques Amyot: Actes du colloque international (Melun 18–20 avril 1985)* (Paris: A.-G. Nizet, 1986).

Baldwin, T. W., *William Shakespeare's Small Latine & Lesse Greeke*, 2 vols (Urbana: University of Illinois Press, 1944).

Barkan, L., '"Living Sculptures": Ovid, Michelangelo, and *The Winter's Tale*', *English Literary History*, xlviii (1971), 639–67.

Bartsch, S., *Decoding the Ancient Novel: The Reader and the Role of Description in Heliodorus and Achilles Tatius* (Princeton: Princeton University Press, 1989).

Bataillon, M., *Erasmo y España*. Estudios sobre la historia espiritual del siglo XVI, 2nd edn (Mexico City: Fondo de Cultura Económica, 1966).

Bath, M., *Speaking Pictures: English Emblem Books and Renaissance Culture* (London: Longman, 1994).

Batho, G. R., 'A Difficult Father-in-Law: The Ninth Earl of Northumberland', *History Today*, vi [November, 1956], 744–51.

Beaton, R., *The Medieval Greek Romance* (Cambridge: Cambridge University Press, 1989).

Beilin, E., '"The Onely Perfect Vertue": Constancy in Mary Wroth's *Pamphilia to Amphilanthus*', *Spenser Studies: A Renaissance Poetry Annual*, ii (1981), 229–45.

Bell, D. A., 'Unmasking a King: The Political Uses of Popular Literature under the French Catholic League, 1588–89', *Sixteenth Century Journal*, xx (1989), 371–86.

Benhaïm, V., 'Les Thresors d'Amadis', in *Les Amadis en France au XVIe siècle*, ed. by N. Cazauran and M. Bideaux, Cahiers Saulniers, no. 17 (Paris: Éditions Rue d'Ulm, 2000), pp. 157–81.

Berger, G., 'Rhetorik und Leserlenkung in der Aithiopika-Epitome des Martin Crusius', in *Acta Conventus Neo-Latini Guelpherbytani. Proceedings of the Sixth International Congress of Neo-Latin Studies*, ed. by S. P. Regard, F. Rädle and M. A. Di Cesare (Binghamton, NY: Medieval and Renaissance Studies, 1988), pp. 481–90.

Bergeron, D. M., 'Munday, Anthony (*bap.* 1560, *d.* 1633)', *Oxford Dictionary of National Biography* (Oxford: Oxford University Press, 2004).

Berry, P., *Of Chastity and Power: Elizabethan Literature and the Unmarried Queen* (London: Routledge, 1989).

Billault, A., 'Plutarch's *Lives*', in *The Classical Heritage in France*, ed. by G. N. Sandy (Leiden: E. J. Brill, 2002), pp. 219–35.

Binns, J. W., *Intellectual Culture in Elizabethan and Jacobean England: The Latin Writings of the Age* (Leeds: Francis Cairns, 1990).

Bos, S., M. Lange-Meyers and J. Six, 'Sidney's Funeral Portrayed', in *Sir Philip Sidney: 1586 and the Creation of a Legend*, ed. by J. van Dorsten, D. Baker-Smith and A. F. Kinney (Leiden: E. J. Brill, 1986), pp. 38–61.

Braden, G., 'Plutarch, Shakespeare, and the Alpha Males', in *Shakespeare and the Classics*, ed. by C. Martindale and A. B. Taylor (Cambridge: Cambridge University Press, 2004), pp. 188–206.

Brennan, M. G., '"A SYDNEY, though un-named": Ben Jonson's Influence in the Manuscript and Print Circulation of Lady Mary Wroth's Writings', *Sidney Journal*, xvii, no. 1 (1999), 31–52.

—— '"Your Lordship's to Do You All Humble Service": Rowland Whyte's Correspondence with Robert Sidney, Viscount Lisle and First Earl of Leicester', *Sidney Journal*, xxi, no. 2 (2003), 1–37.

—— 'Robert Sidney, King James I and Queen Anna: The Politics of Intimate Service (1588–1607)', *Sidney Journal*, xxv, nos 1–2 (2007), 3–30.

Bullough, G., ed., *Narrative and Dramatic Sources of Shakespeare*, 7 vols (London: Routledge and Kegan Paul, 1961–73).

Buxton, J., *Sir Philip Sidney and the English Renaissance*, 2nd edn (London: Macmillan, 1964).

—— 'Sidney and Theophrastus', *English Literary Renaissance*, ii (1972), 79–82.

Carson, N., *A Companion to Henslowe's Diary* (Cambridge: Cambridge University Press, 1988).

Carver, R. H. F., '"Sugared Invention" or "Mongrel Tragi-comedy": Sir Philip Sidney and the Ancient Novel', in *Groningen Colloquia on the Novel*, ed. by H. Hofmann and M. Zimmerman (Groningen: Egbert Forsten, 1997), pp. 197–226.

—— 'The Rediscovery of the Latin Novels', in *Latin Fiction: The Latin Novel in Context*, ed. by H. Hofmann (London: Routledge, 1999), pp. 253–68.

Cavanagh, S. T., *Cherished Torment: The Emotional Geography of Lady Mary Wroth's Urania* (Pittsburgh: Duquesne University Press, 2001).

Cazauran, N., and M. Bideaux, eds, *Les Amadis en France au XVIe siècle*, Cahiers Saulniers, no. 17 (Paris: Éditions Rue d'Ulm, 2000).

Chalk, H. H. O., 'Eros and the Lesbian Pastorals of Longus', *Journal of Hellenic Studies*, lxxx (1960), 32–51.

Chambers, E. K., *The Elizabethan Stage*, 4 vols (Oxford: Clarendon Press, 1923).

—— *Sir Henry Lee: An Elizabethan Portrait* (Oxford: Clarendon Press, 1936).

Chedgzoy, K., M. Hansen and S. Trill, eds, *Voicing Women: Gender and Sexuality in Early Modern Writing* (Keele: Keele University Press, 1996).

Clair, C., 'Willem Silvius', The *Library*, 5th ser., xiv, no. 3 (1959), 192–205.

Clark, D. L., 'The Rise and Fall of Progymnasmata in Sixteenth and Seventeenth Century Grammar Schools', *Speech Monographs*, xix (1952), 259–63.

Clough, C. H., 'Chivalry and Magnificence in the Golden Age of the Italian Renaissance', in *Chivalry in the Renaissance*, ed. by S. Anglo (Woodbridge, Suffolk: The Boydell Press, 1990), pp. 25–47.

—— 'Federico da Montefeltro and the Kings of Naples: A Study in Fifteenth-century Survival', *Renaissance Studies*, vi (1992), 113–72.

Conner, P., *Huguenot Heartland: Montauban and Southern French Calvinism during the Wars of Religion* (Aldershot: Ashgate, 2002).

Cooper, H., *The English Romance in Time: Transforming Motifs from Geoffrey of Monmouth to the Death of Shakespeare* (Oxford: Oxford University Press, 2004).

Cox, J. D., *Shakespeare and the Dramaturgy of Power* (Princeton: Princeton University Press, 1989).

Craig, J., 'North, Roger, Second Baron North (1531–1600)', *Oxford Dictionary of National Biography* (Oxford: Oxford University Press, 2004).

Crimando, T. I., 'Two French Views of the Council of Trent', *The Sixteenth Century Journal*, xix, no. 2 (1988), 169–86.

Croft, P., 'Howard, Henry, Earl of Northampton (1540–1614)', *Oxford Dictionary of National Biography* (Oxford: Oxford University Press, 2004).

Cross, C., 'Reyner, Edward (1600–1660)', *Oxford Dictionary of National Biography* (Oxford: Oxford University Press, 2004).

Curtius, E. R., *European Literature and the Latin Middle Ages*, trans. by W. R. Trask (Princeton: Princeton University Press, 1953; repr. London: Routledge and Kegan Paul, 1979).

Cust, R., 'Burton, William (1575–1645)', *Oxford Dictionary of National Biography* (Oxford: Oxford University Press, 2004).

Dalmeyda, G., 'Henri Estienne et Longus', *Revue de Philologie*, 3rd ser., viii (1934), 169–81.

Darby, T. L., 'Resistance to Rape in *Persiles y Sigismunda* and *The Custom of the Country*', *Modern Language Review*, xc (1995), 273–84.

—— 'Cervantes in England: The Influence of Golden-Age Prose Fiction on Jacobean Drama, c. 1615–1625', *Bulletin of Hispanic Studies*, lxxiv (1997), 425–41.

Davies, C. S. L., 'Paulet, Sir Hugh (*b.* before 1510, *d.* 1573)', *Oxford Dictionary of National Biography* (Oxford: Oxford University Press, 2004).

Davies, H. Neville, 'Jacobean *Antony and Cleopatra*', *Shakespeare Studies*, xvii (1985), 123–58.

Dean, W., 'Henry Oxinden's Key (1628) to *The Countess of Pembroke's Arcadia*: Some Facts and Conjectures', *Sidney Newsletter and Journal*, xii, no. 2 (1993), 14–21.

Denton, J., 'Renaissance Translation Strategies and the Manipulation of a Classical Text. Plutarch from Jacques Amyot to Thomas North', in *Europe et Traduction*, ed. by M. Ballard (Arras: Artois Presses Université, 1998).

Dibden, T. F., *An Introduction to the Knowledge of Rare and Valuable Editions of the Greek and Latin Classics*, 4th ed., 2 vols (1827).

Dickens, B., 'William L'Isle the Saxonist and Three XVIIth Century Remainder-Issues', *English and Germanic Studies*, i (1947–48), 53–5.

Diggle, J., 'A Note on Achilles Tatius', *Classical Review*, xxii, no. 1 (1972), 7.

Doody, M. A., *The True Story of the Novel* (New Brunswick, N.J: Rutgers University Press, 1996; repr. London: Fontana Press, 1998).

Doran, S., 'Seymour [Grey], Katherine, Countess of Hertford (1540?–1568)', *Oxford Dictionary of National Biography* (Oxford: Oxford University Press, 2004).

—— 'Seymour, Edward, First Earl of Hertford (1539?–1621)', *Oxford Dictionary of National Biography* (Oxford: Oxford University Press, 2004).

Dorsten, J. van, *Poets, Patrons, and Professors: Sir Philip Sidney, Daniel Rogers, and the Leiden Humanists* (Leiden: Leiden University Press, 1962).

Dorsten, J. van, D. Baker-Smith and A. F. Kinney, eds, *Sir Philip Sidney: 1586 and the Creation of a Legend* (Leiden: E. J. Brill, 1986).

Duncan-Jones, K., 'Sidney in Samothea: A Forgotten National Myth', *Review of English Studies*, n.s., xxv (1974), 174–7.

—— *Sir Philip Sidney, Courtier Poet* (London: Hamish Hamilton, 1991).

Dunn, R. S., *The Age of Religious Wars, 1559–1715*, 2nd edn (New York: W. W. Norton, 1979).

Dutton, R., A. Findlay and R. Wilson, eds, *Theatre and Religion: Lancastrian Shakespeare* (Manchester: Manchester University Press, 2003).

Eatough, G., 'Paynell, Thomas (*d.* 1564?)', *Oxford Dictionary of National Biography* (Oxford: Oxford University Press, 2004).

Edwards, M. J., *Plutarch: The Lives of Pompey, Caesar and Cicero*[.] *A Companion to the Penguin Translation* (London: Bristol Classical Press, 1991; repr. 2003).

Eisenberg, D., *Romances of Chivalry in the Spanish Golden Age* (Newark, DE: Juan de la Cuesta, 1982). www.cervantesvirtual.com/servlet/SirveObras/ 01159841877587238327702/.

Ellison, J., 'The Winter's Tale and the Religious Politics of Europe', in *Shakespeare's Romances*, ed. by A. Thorne (Basingstoke: Palgrave Macmillan, 2003), pp. 171–204.

Felperin, H., *Shakespearean Romance* (Princeton: Princeton University Press, 1972).

Fernie, E., 'Lee, Sir Henry (1533–1611)', *Oxford Dictionary of National Biography* (Oxford: Oxford University Press, 2004).

Fincham, K., 'Abbot, George (1562–1633)', *Oxford Dictionary of National Biography* (Oxford: Oxford University Press, 2004).

Fincham, K., and P. Lake, 'The Ecclesiastical Policy of King James I', *Journal of British Studies*, xxiv (1985), 169–207.

Forcione, A. K., *Cervantes' Christian Romance: A Study of Persiles y Sigismonda* (Princeton: Princeton University Press, 1972).

Ford, L. L., 'Wroth, Sir Robert (*c.* 1539–1606)', *Oxford Dictionary of National Biography* (Oxford: Oxford University Press, 2004).

Forster, L., *Janus Gruter's English Years: Studies in the Continuity of Dutch Literature in Exile in Elizabethan England* (Leiden: Leiden University Press, 1967).

Fraser, A., *Mary Queen of Scots* (London: Weidenfeld and Nicolson, 1969; repr. London: Mandarin, 1990).

Freeman, A., 'Marlowe, Kyd, and the Dutch Church Libel', *English Literary Renaissance*, iii (1973), 44–52.

Fumaroli, M., *L'âge de l'éloquence: Rhétorique et 'res literaria' de la Renaissance au seuil de l'époque classique* (Geneva: Librairie Droz, 1980).

—— 'Jacques Amyot and the Clerical Polemic Against the Chivalric Novel', *Renaissance Quarterly*, xxxviii (1985), 22–40.

Ganz, M. A., 'A Florentine Friendship: Donato Acciaiuoli and Vespasiano da Bisticci', *Renaissance Quarterly*, xliii (1990), 372–83.

Gardiner, S. R., 'Henrietta Maria (1609–1669)', in *The Compact Edition of the Dictionary of National Biography*, 2 vols (Oxford: Oxford University Press, 1975).

Gaselee, S., 'The Soul in the Kiss', *The Criterion*, ii (1924), 349–59.

Gesner, C., *Shakespeare and the Greek Romance: A Study of Origins* (Lexington: University Press of Kentucky, 1970).

Gillespie, S., 'Shakespeare and Greek Romance: "Like an old tale still"', in *Shakespeare and the Classics*, ed. by C. Martindale and A. B. Taylor (Cambridge: Cambridge University Press, 2004), pp. 225–37.

Godschalk, W. L., 'Correspondence', *Review of English Studies*, n.s., xxix (1978), 325–6.

—— 'Correspondence', *Review of English Studies*, n.s. xxxi (1980), 192.

Goldhill, S., *Who Needs Greek: Contests in the Cultural History of Hellenism* (Cambridge: Cambridge University Press, 2002).

Goodare, J., and M. Lynch, eds, *The Reign of James VI* (East Linton: Tuckwell Press, 2000).

Graham, T., ed., *The Recovery of Old English: Anglo-Saxon Studies in the Sixteenth and Seventeenth Centuries*, Publications of the Richard Rawlinson Center (Kalamazoo, MI.: Medieval Institute Publications, Western Michigan University, 2000).

Green, L. D., 'Reynolds, Richard (*c*.1530–1606)', *Oxford Dictionary of National Biography* (Oxford: Oxford University Press, 2004).

Griffin, A. H. F., 'The Ceyx Legend in Ovid, *Metamorphoses*, Book XI', *Classical Quarterly*, xxxi, no. 1 (1981), 147–54.

Hackett, H., 'The Torture of Limena: Sex and Violence in Lady Mary Wroth's *Urania*', in *Voicing Women: Gender and Sexuality in Early Modern Writing*, ed. by K. Chedgzoy, M. Hansen and S. Trill (Keele: Keele University Press, 1996), pp. 93–110.

Hadfield, A., 'Lloyd, David (1597–1663)', *Oxford Dictionary of National Biography* (Oxford: Oxford University Press, 2004).

Hägg, T., *The Novel in Antiquity* (Oxford: Basil Blackwell, 1983).

Hamilton, D. B., '*The Winter's Tale* and the Language of Union, 1604–1610', *Shakespeare Studies*, xxi (1993), 228–50.

Hammer, P. E. J., *The Polarisation of Elizabethan Politics: The Political Career of Robert Devereux, 2nd Earl of Essex, 1587–1597* (Cambridge: Cambridge University Press, 1999).

—— 'Cuffe, Henry (1562/3–1601)', *Oxford Dictionary of National Bibography* (Oxford: Oxford University Presss, 2004).

Hammond, N. G. L., and H. H. Scullard, eds, *The Oxford Classical Dictionary*, 2nd edn (Oxford: Clarendon Press, 1970).

Hannay, M. P., *Philip's Phoenix: Mary Sidney, Countess of Pembroke* (New York: Oxford University Press, 1990).

—— 'Herbert [Sidney] Mary, Countess of Pembroke (1561–1621)', *Oxford Dictionary of National Biography* (Oxford: Oxford University Press, 2004).

Hannay, M. P., N. J. Kinnamon and M. G. Brennan, eds, *The Collected Works of Mary Sidney Herbert*, 2 vols (Oxford: Clarendon Press, 1998).

—— *Domestic Politics and Family Absence: The Correspondence (1588–1621) of Robert Sidney, First Earl of Leicester, and Barbara Gamage Sidney* (Aldershot: Ashgate, 2005).

Hardin, R. F., 'A Romance for Young Ladies: George Thornley's Translation of *Daphnis and Chloe*', *Classical and Modern Literature*, xv (1994), pp. 45–56.

—— *Love in a Green Shade: Idyllic Romances Ancient to Modern* (Lincoln: University of Nebraska Press, 2000).

Hardman, C. B., 'Shakespeare's *Winter's Tale* and the Stuart Golden Age', *Review of English Studies*, n.s., xlv (1994), 221–9.

Hay, M. V., *The Life of Robert Sidney, Earl of Leicester (1563–1626)* (Washington: Folger Shakespeare Library, 1984).

Haynes, K., *Fashioning the Feminine in the Greek Novel* (London: Routledge, 2003).

Hecox, A., 'A Dutch Perspective on Sidney's Eclogues', *Sidney Journal*, xvii, no. 2 (1999), 31–40.

Heiserman, A., *The Novel Before the Novel* (Chicago: University of Chicago Press, 1977).

Hoenselaars, T., and A. F. Kinney, eds, *Challenging Humanism: Essays in Honor of Dominic Baker-Smith* (Newark: University of Delaware Press, 2005).

Hofmann, H., ed., *Latin Fiction: The Latin Novel in Context* (London: Routledge, 1999).

Hofmann, H., and M. Zimmerman, eds, *Groningen Colloquia on the Novel* (Groningen: Egbert Forsten, 1997).

Holyoake, J., *A Critical Study of the Tragedies of Robert Garnier (1545–90)* (New York: P. Lang, 1987).

Honan, P., 'Wriothesley, Henry, Third Earl of Southampton (1573–1624)', *Oxford Dictionary of National Biography* (Oxford: Oxford University Press, 2004).

Honigmann, E. A. J., *Myriad-Minded Shakespeare*, 2nd edn (Basingstoke: Macmillan, 1998).

Hulubei, A., 'Henri Estienne et le roman de Longus, *Daphnis et Chloé*', *Revue du Seizième Siècle*, xviii (1931), 324–40.

Hunter, R. L., *A Study of Daphnis and Chloe* (Cambridge: Cambridge University Press, 1983).

Hutson, L., *The Usurer's Daughter: Male Friendship and Fictions of Women in Sixteenth-Century England* (London: Routledge, 1994).

Jensen, De L., 'Catherine de Medici and Her Florentine Friends', *Sixteenth Century Journal*, ix (1978), 57–74.

John, R. T., *Fictive Ancient History and National Consequences in Early Europe: The Influence of Annius of Viterbo's 'Antiquitates'* (London: University of London Press, 1994).

Jondorf, G., *Robert Garnier and the Themes of Political Tragedy in the Sixteenth Century* (Cambridge: Cambridge University Press, 1969).

—— 'Drama', in *The Classical Heritage in France*, ed. by G. N. Sandy (Leiden: E. J. Brill, 2002), pp. 453–70.

Jones, E., 'Stuart Cymbeline', *Essays in Criticism*, xi (1961), 84–99.

Jusserand, J. J., *The English Novel in the Time of Shakespeare* [1890], trans. by E. Lee, new edn., intro. by P. Brockbank (London: Ernest Benn Limited, 1966).

Keaney, J. J., 'Theophrastus', in *The Oxford Classical Dictionary*, ed. by N. G. L. Hammond and H. H. Scullard, 2nd edn (Oxford: Clarendon Press, 1970), pp. 1058–9.

Kelsey, S., 'Rich, Robert, Second Earl of Warwick (1587–1658)', *Oxford Dictionary of National Biography* (Oxford: Oxford University Press, 2004).

Kendrick, T. D., *British Antiquity* (London: Methuen, 1950).

Kennedy, G. A., *A New History of Classical Rhetoric* (Princeton: Princeton University Press, 1994), pp. 230–2.

Kinney, C. R., '"Beleeve this butt a fiction": Female Authorship, Narrative Undoing, and the Limits of Romance in *The Second Part of The Countess of Montgomery's Urania*', *Spenser Studies: A Renaissance Poetry Annual*, xvii (2003), 239–50.

Kipling, G., *The Triumph of Honour: Burgundian Origins of the Elizabethan Renaissance* (Leiden: Leiden University Press, 1977).

Kuin, R., 'The Middelburg Weekend: More Light on the Proposed Marriage Between Philip Sidney and Marie of Nassau', *Sidney Newsletter and Journal*, xii, no. 2 (1993), 3–12.

—— 'New Light on the Veronese Portrait of Sir Philip Sidney', *Sidney Newsletter & Journal*, xv, no. 1 (1997), 19–47.

—— 'Elective Affinities: Sidney and the New Languet Biography', *Sidney Newsletter and Journal*, xv, no. 1 (1997), 61–77.

Kuin, R., and A. L. Prescott, 'Versifying Connections: Daniel Rogers and the Sidneys', *Sidney Journal*, xviii, no. 2 (2000), 1–35.

Lamb, M. E., *Gender and Authorship in the Sidney Circle* (Madison: University of Wisconsin Press, 1990).

—— 'Exhibiting Class and Displaying the Body in Sidney's *Countess of Pembroke's Arcadia*', *Studies in English Literature*, xxxvii (1997), 55–72.

Laughton, J. K., 'Leveson, Sir Richard (1570–1605)', in *The Compact Edition of the Dictionary of National Biography*, 2 vols (Oxford: Oxford University Press, 1975).

Lee, S., 'Oxford, Bodleian Library, MS Laud Misc. 381: William L'Isle, Aelfric, and the *Ancrene Wisse*', in *The Recovery of Old English: Anglo-Saxon Studies in the Sixteenth and Seventeenth Centuries*, ed. by T. Graham, Publications of the Richard Rawlinson Center (Kalamazoo, MI: Medieval Institute Publications, Western Michigan University, 2000), pp. 207–42.

Lehmberg, S., 'Wroth, Sir Thomas (1518?–1573)', *Oxford Dictionary of National Biography* (Oxford: Oxford University Press, 2004).

Lestringant, F., 'Les amours pastorales de Daphnis et Chloé: fortunes d'une traduction de J. Amyot', in *Fortunes de Jacques Amyot: Actes du colloque international (Melun 18–20 avril 1985)*, ed. by M. Balard (Paris: A.-G. Nizet, 1986), pp. 237–57.

Liddell, H. G., and R. Scott, *A Greek–English Lexicon*, 4th edn (Oxford: Oxford University Press, 1855).

Lloyd, H. A., *The Rouen Campaign 1590–1592* (Oxford: Clarendon Press, 1973).

Lockwood, T., 'North, Sir Thomas (1535–1603?)', *Oxford Dictionary of National Biography* (Oxford: Oxford University Press, 2004).

Loomie, A. J., 'Wotton, Edward, First Baron Wotton (1548–1628)', *Oxford Dictionary of National Biography* (Oxford: Oxford University Press, 2004).

—— 'Wotton, Sir Henry (1568–1639)', *Oxford Dictionary of National Biography* (Oxford: Oxford University Press, 2004).

Lowe, N. J., *The Classical Plot and the Invention of Western Narrative* (Cambridge: Cambridge University Press, 2000).

McCoy, R. C., '"A dangerous Image": The Earl of Essex and Elizabethan Chivalry', *Journal of Medieval and Renaissance Studies*, xiii (1983), 313–29.

McDermott, J., 'Howard, Charles, Second Baron Howard of Effingham and First Earl of Nottingham (1536–1624)', *Oxford Dictionary of National Biography* (Oxford: Oxford University Press, 2004).

Mack, P., *Elizabethan Rhetoric: Theory and Practice* (Cambridge: Cambridge University Press, 2002).

Martindale, C. and A. B. Taylor, eds, *Shakespeare and the Classics* (Cambridge: Cambridge University Press, 2004).

May, S. W., *The Elizabethan Courtier Poets* (Columbia: University of Missouri Press, 1991).

Meikle, M. M., 'A Meddlesome Princess: Anna of Denmark and Scottish Court Politics, 1589–1603', in *The Reign of James VI*, ed. by J. Goodare and M. Lynch (East Linton: Tuckwell Press, 2000), pp. 126–40.

Meikle, M. M., and H. Payne, 'Anne (1574–1619)', *Oxford Dictionary of National Biography* (Oxford: Oxford University Press, 2004).

Miller, N., and G. Waller, *Reading Mary Sidney Wroth: Representing Alternatives in Early Modern England* (Knoxville: University of Tennessee Press, 1991).

Milward, R., 'Cecil, Thomas, First Earl of Exeter (1542–1623)', *Oxford Dictionary of National Biography* (Oxford: Oxford University Press, 2004).

Morales, H., *Vision and Narrative in Achilles Tatius' Leucippe and Clitophon* (Cambridge: Cambridge University Press, 2004).

Moreschini, C., 'Towards a History of the Exegesis of Apuleius: The Case of the "Tale of Cupid and Psyche"', trans. by C. Stevenson, in *Latin Fiction: The Latin Novel in Context*, ed. by H. Hofmann (London: Routledge, 1999), pp. 215–28.

Morgan, J. R., 'History, Romance and Realism in the *Aithiopika* of Heliodoros', *Classical Antiquity*, i (1982), 221–65.

Bibliography

—— 'Daphnis and Chloe: Love's Own Sweet Story', in *Greek Fiction: The Greek Novel in Context*, ed. by J. R. Morgan and R. Stoneman (London: Routledge, 1994), pp. 64–79.

Morgan, J. R., and R. Stoneman, eds, *Greek Fiction: The Greek Novel in Context* (London: Routledge, 1994).

Mossman, J., 'Henry V and Plutarch's Alexander', *Shakespeare Quarterly*, xlv (1994), 57–73.

Mousnier, R., *The Assassination of Henry IV*, trans. by J. Spencer (London: Faber and Faber, 1973).

Nelson, A. H., 'Vere, Edward de, Seventeenth Earl of Oxford (1550–1604)', *Oxford Dictionary of National Biography* (Oxford: Oxford University Press, 2004).

Nicollier-de Weck, B., *Hubert Languet 1518–1581: Un réseau politique international de Melancthon à Guillaume d'Orange* (Geneva: Droz, 1995).

Norbrook, D., *Writing the English Republic: Poetry, Rhetoric and Politics, 1627–1660* (Cambridge: Cambridge University Press, 1999).

North, J., *The Ambassador's Secret: Holbein and the World of the Renaissance* (London: Hambledon and London, 2002).

Norton, G. P., 'Amyot et la rhétorique: La revalorisation du pouvoir dans le *Projet de l'éloquence royale*', in *Fortunes de Jacques Amyot: Actes du colloque international (Melun 18–20 avril 1985)*, ed. by M. Balard (Paris: A.-G. Nizet, 1986), pp. 191–205.

O'Connor, J. J., *Amadis de Gaule and Its Influence on Elizabethan Literature* (New Brunswick, NJ: Rutgers University Press, 1970).

Orgel, S., '"Counterfeit Presentments": Shakespeare's *Ekphrasis*', in *England and the Continental Renaissance: Essays in Honour of J. B.Trapp*, ed. by E. Chaney and P. Mack (Woodbridge: The Boydell Press, 1990).

Osborn, J. M., *Young Philip Sidney 1572–1577* (New Haven: Yale University Press, 1972).

Oxford English Dictionary (OED Online).

Panayotakis, S., M. Zimmerman and W. Keulen, eds, *The Ancient Novel and Beyond* (Leiden: Brill, 2003).

Parker, R., 'Pamela's Breasts and Related Problems: A Note on Sidney's "Devices"', *Emblematica*, iii (1988), 163–70.

Parkinson, E. M., 'Sidney's Portrayal of Mounted Combat with Lances', *Spenser Studies*, v (1985), 231–51.

Payne, H., 'Howard, Katherine, Countess of Suffolk (*b*. in or after 1564, *d*. 1638)', *Oxford Dictionary of National Biography* (Oxford: Oxford University Press, 2004).

Peck, L. L., 'The Mentality of a Jacobean Grandee', in *The Mental World of the Jacobean Court*, ed. by L. L. Peck (Cambridge: Cambridge University Press, 1991), pp. 148–68.

—— ed., *The Mental World of the Jacobean Court* (Cambridge: Cambridge University Press, 1991).

Pelling, C., *Literary Texts and the Greek Historian* (London: Routledge, 2000).

Pernot, L., 'La rhétorique de l'Empire ou comment la rhétorique grecque a inventé l'Empire romain', *Rhetorica*, xvi (1998), 131–48.

—— *La rhétorique dans l'Antiquité* (Paris: Le Livre de Poche, Librairie Générale Française, 2000).

Perrot, J. de, 'Robert Greene and the Italian Translation of *Achilles Tatius*', *Modern Language Notes*, xxix (1914).

Pirenne, H., *Histoire de Belgique des origines à nos jours*, 4 vols (Brussels: Renaissance du livre, [1948–52]).

Plazenet, L., *L'ébahissement et la délectation. Réception comparée et poétiques du roman grec en France et en Angleterre aux XVIe et XVIIe siècles* (Paris: Honoré Champion Éditeur, 1997).

—— 'Jacques Amyot and the Greek Novel: The Invention of the French Novel', in *The Classical Heritage in France*, ed. by G. N. Sandy (Leiden: Brill, 2002), pp. 237–80.

Powis, J., 'Gallican Liberties and the Politics of Later Sixteenth-century France', *The Historical Journal*, xxvi (1983), 515–30.

Prescott, A. L., 'Foreign Policy in Fairyland: Henri IV and Spenser's Burbon', *Spenser Studies: A Renaissance Poetry Annual*, xiv (2000), 189–214.

Pulsiano, P., 'William L'Isle and the Editing of Old English', in *The Recovery of Old English: Anglo-Saxon Studies in the Sixteenth and Seventeenth Centuries*, ed. by T. Graham, Publications of the Richard Rawlinson Center (Kalamazoo, MI: Medieval Institute Publications, Western Michigan University, 2000), pp. 173–206.

Raitiere, M. N., *Faire Bitts: Philip Sidney and Renaissance Political Theory* (Pittsburgh: Duquesne University Press, 1984).

Read, C., *Mr Secretary Walsingham and the Policy of Queen Elizabeth*, 3 vols (Oxford: Clarendon Press, 1925; repr. New York: AMS Press, 1978).

—— *Lord Burghley and Queen Elizabeth* (London: Jonathan Cape, 1965).

Reardon, B. P., ed., *Collected Ancient Greek Novels* (Berkeley: University of California Press, 1989).

—— 'Achilles Tatius and Ego-Narrative', in *Greek Fiction: The Greek Novel in Context*, ed. by J. R. Morgan and R. Stoneman, eds (London: Routledge, 1994), pp. 80–96.

Rebholz, R. A., *The Life of Fulke Greville, First Lord Brooke* (Oxford: Clarendon Press, 1971).

Reeve, M. D., 'Fulvio Orsini and Longus', *The Journal of Hellenic Studies*, xcix (1979), 165–7.

Richards, J., 'Social Decorum in *The Winter's Tale*', in *Shakespeare's Late Plays: New Readings*, ed. by J. Richards and J. Knowles (Edinburgh: Edinburgh University Press, 1999), pp. 75–91.

Richards, J., and J. Knowles eds, *Shakespeare's Late Plays: New Readings* (Edinburgh: Edinburgh University Press, 1999).

Roberts, J. A., '"The Knott Never to Bee Untide": The Controversy Regarding Marriage in Mary Sidney Wroth's *Urania*', in *Reading Mary Sidney Wroth:*

Representing Alternatives in Early Modern England, ed. by N. Miller and G. Waller (Knoxville: University of Tennessee Press, 1991), pp. 109–32.

Roeder, H., *Saints and Their Attributes* (London: Longmans, Green and Co, 1955).

Rothstein, M., 'Clandestine Marriage and *Amadis de Gaule*: The Text, the World, and the Reader', *Sixteenth Century Journal*, xxv (1994), 873–86.

Rowe, J., 'Gawdy Family (*per. c.* 1500–1723)', *Oxford Dictionary of National Biography* (Oxford: Oxford University Press, 2004).

Salmon, V., 'Sanford, James (*fl.* 1567–1582)', *Oxford Dictionary of National Biography* (Oxford: Oxford University Press, 2004).

Samson, A., ed., *The Spanish Match: Prince Charles's Journey to Madrid, 1623* (Aldershot: Ashgate, 2006).

Sandy, G., 'Classical Forerunners of the Theory and Practice of Prose Romance in France. Studies in the Narrative Form of Minor French Romances of the Sixteenth and Seventeenth Centuries', *Antike und Abendland*, cxviii (1982), 169–91.

—— 'Apuleius's *Golden Ass*: From Miletus to Egypt', in *Latin Fiction: The Latin Novel in Context*, ed. by H. Hofmann (London: Routledge, 1999), pp. 81–102.

Sandy, G. N., 'Jacques Amyot and the Manuscript Tradition of Heliodorus' *Aethiopica*', *Revue d'Histoire des Textes*, xiv–xv (1984–85), 1–22.

—— 'Resources for the Study of Ancient Greek in France', in *The Classical Heritage in France*, ed. by G. N. Sandy (Leiden: E. J. Brill, 2002), pp. 47–78.

——, ed., *The Classical Heritage in France* (Leiden: E. J. Brill, 2002).

Schmeling, G., ed., *The Novel in the Ancient World* (Leiden: E. J. Brill, 1996).

Schreiber, R. E., 'Hay, James, First Earl of Carlisle (*c.*1580–1636)', *Oxford Dictionary of National Biography* (Oxford: Oxford University Press, 2004).

Scott, J., *Algernon Sidney and the English Republic, 1623–1677* (Cambridge: Cambridge University Press, 1988).

Sharratt, P., 'A Rare Edition of Amyot's Plutarch', *Forum for Modern Language Studies*, vii, no. 4 (1971), 409–12.

Shephard, R., 'The Political Commonplace Books of Sir Robert Sidney', *Sidney Journal*, xxi, no. 1 (2003), 1–30.

—— 'Sidney, Robert, First Earl of Leicester (1563–1626)', *Oxford Dictionary of National Biography* (Oxford: Oxford University Press, 2004).

Sil, N. P., 'Denny, Sir Anthony (1501–1549)', *Oxford Dictionary of National Biography* (Oxford: Oxford University Press, 2004).

Simonin, M., *Vivre de sa plume au XVIe siècle ou la carrière de François de Belleforest* (Geneva: Droz, 1992).

Skretkowicz, V., 'Greville and Sidney: Biographical Addenda', *Notes and Queries*, n.s., xxi (1974), 408–10.

—— 'Sidney and Amyot: Heliodorus in the Structure and Ethos of the *New Arcadia*', *Review of English Studies*, n.s., xxvii (1976), 170–4.

—— 'Hercules in Sidney and Spenser', *Notes and Queries*, n.s., xxvii (1980), 306–10.

—— 'Symbolic Architecture in Sidney's *New Arcadia*', *Review of English Studies*, n.s., xxxiii (1982), 175–80.

—— 'Building Sidney's Reputation: Texts and Editors of the *Arcadia*', in *Sir Philip Sidney: 1586 and the Creation of a Legend*, ed. by J. van Dorsten, D. Baker-Smith and A. F. Kinney (Leiden: E. J. Brill, 1986), pp. 111–24.

—— 'Devices and Their Narrative Function in Sidney's *Arcadia*', *Emblematica*, i (1986), 267–92.

—— 'Sir Philip Sidney and the Elizabethan Literary Device', *Emblematica*, iii (1988), 171–9.

—— '"A More Lively Monument": Philisides in *Arcadia*', in *Sir Philip Sidney's Achievements*, ed. by M. J. B. Allen, D. Baker-Smith and A. F. Kinney (New York: AMS Press, 1990), pp. 194–200.

—— 'Greville's *Life of Sidney*: The Hertford Manuscript', *English Manuscript Studies, 1100–1700*, iii (1992), 102–36.

—— 'Sidney's *Defence of Poetry*, Henri Estienne, and Huguenot Nationalist Satire', *Sidney Journal*, xvi, no. 1 (1998), 3–24.

—— 'Lady Mary Wroth's *Urania* and the Rhetoric of Female Abuse', in *Challenging Tradition: Women and the History of Rhetoric*, ed. by C. M. Sutherland and R. Sutcliffe (Calgary: University of Calgary Press, 1999), pp. 133–45.

—— 'Mary Sidney Herbert's *Antonius*, English Philhellenism and the Protestant Cause', *Women's Writing*, vi (1999), 7–25.

—— 'Algernon Sidney and Philip Sidney: A Continuity of Rebellion', *Sidney Journal*, xvii, no. 2 (1999), 3–18.

—— 'Textual Criticism and the 1593 "Complete" *Arcadia*', *Sidney Journal*, xviii (2000 [published 2002]), 37–70.

—— 'Greville, Politics, and the Rhetorics of *A Dedication to Sir Philip Sidney*', in *Fulke Greville: A Special Double Number*, ed. by M. C. Hansen and M. Woodcock, *Sidney Journal*, xix (2001 [published 2002]), 97–123.

—— '"O pugnam infaustam": Sidney's Transformations and the Last of the Samotheans', *Sidney Journal*, xxii (2004 [published 2006]), 1–24.

—— 'From Alpha-Text to Meta-Text: Sidney's Arcadia', in *The Author as Reader: Textual Visons and Revisions*, ed. by S. Coelsch-Foisner and W. Görtschacher, Salzburg Studies in English Literature and Culture 2 (Frankfurt am Main: Peter Lang, 2005), pp. 23–32.

—— 'Shakespeare, Henri IV, and the Tyranny of Royal Style', in *Challenging Humanism: Essays in Honor of Dominic Baker-Smith*, ed. by T. Hoenselaars and A. F. Kinney (Newark: University of Delaware Press, 2005), pp. 179–208.

Smith, A. J., *Literary Love: The Role of Passion in English Poems and Plays of the Seventeenth Century* (London: Edward Arnold, 1983).

Smith, D. L., 'Herbert, Philip, First Earl of Montgomery and Fourth Earl of Pembroke (1584–1650)', *Oxford Dictionary of National Biography* (Oxford: Oxford University Press, 2004).

—— 'Rudyerd, Sir Benjamin (1572–1658)', *Oxford Dictionary of National Biography* (Oxford: Oxford University Press, 2004).

—— 'Seymour, William, First Marquess of Hertford and Second Duke of Somerset (1587–1660)', *Oxford Dictionary of National Biography* (Oxford: Oxford University Press, 2004).

Smith, J., 'The Language of Leontes', *Shakespeare Quarterly*, xix (1968), 317–27.

Sobel, D., *Galileo's Daughter* (New York: Walker & Co., 1999; repr. New York: Penguin Books, 2000).

Spence, R. T., 'Clifford, Anne, Countess of Pembroke, Dorset, and Montgomery (1590–1676)', *Oxford Dictionary of National Biography* (Oxford: Oxford University Press, 2004).

Stater, V., 'Herbert, William, Third Earl of Pembroke (1580–1630)', *Oxford Dictionary of National Biography* (Oxford: Oxford University Press, 2004).

—— 'Knollys, William, First Earl of Banbury (*c.* 1545–1632)', *Oxford Dictionary of National Biography* (Oxford: Oxford University Press, 2004).

Steggle, M., 'Lisle, William (*c.* 1569–1637)', *Oxford Dictionary of National Biography* (Oxford: Oxford University Press, 2004).

Stephens, W., 'When Pope Noah Ruled the Etruscans: Annius of Viterbo and His Forged Antiquities', in 'Studia Humanitatis: Essays in Honor of Salvatore Camporeale', *Modern Language Notes*, cxix, no.1 (2004), S201–S223.

Stewart, A., *Philip Sidney: A Double Life* (London: Chatto & Windus, 2000).

Strong, R., *The Cult of Elizabeth: Elizabethan Portraiture and Pageantry* (London: Thames and Hudson, 1977).

Strong, R. C., 'Elizabethan Jousting Cheques in the Possession of the College of Arms – II', *The Coat of Arms*, v (1958–59), 63–8.

Sturel, R., *Jacques Amyot, Traducteur des Vies Parallèles de Plutarque* (Paris: H. Champion, 1908).

Sutherland, C. M., and R. Sutcliffe, eds, *Challenging Tradition: Women and the History of Rhetoric* (Calgary: University of Calgary Press, 1999).

Sutherland, N. M., *Henry IV of France and the Politics of Religion 1572–1596*, 2 vols (Exeter: Intellect Books, 2002).

Tatum, J., ed., *The Search for the Ancient Novel* (Baltimore: Johns Hopkins University Press, 1994).

Thomas, H., 'English Translations of Portuguese Books before 1640', *The Library*, 4th ser., i (1926), 1–30.

Thorne, A., ed., *Shakespeare's Romances* (Basingstoke: Palgrave Macmillan, 2003).

Todd, F. A., *Some Ancient Novels* (London: Oxford University Press, 1940).

Twigg, G., 'Plague in London: Spatial and Temporal Aspects of Mortality', in *Epidemic Disease in London*, ed. by J. A. I. Champion, University of London Centre for Metropolitan History, Working Papers Series, 1 (London: Centre for Metropolitan History, 1993), pp. 1–17.

Uffizi Gallery, Florence, 'Catalogue', www.arca.net/uffizi1/artista1.asp.

Ungerer, G., *A Spaniard in Elizabethan England: The Correspondence of Antonio Perez's Exile*, 2 vols (London: Tamesis Books, 1974–76).

University of Heidelberg: www.uni-heidelberg.de/presse/news/2210gelehrten.

html.

Usher, B., 'Rich, Robert, First Earl of Warwick (1559?–1619)', *Oxford Dictionary of National Biography* (Oxford: Oxford University Press, 2004).

Veevers, E., *Images of Love and Religion: Queen Henrietta Maria and Court Entertainments* (Cambridge: Cambridge University Press, 1989).

Wagner, B. M., 'New Poems by Sir Philip Sidney', *Publications of the Modern Language Association of America*, liii (1938), 118–24.

Walden, J. W. H., 'Stage-Terms in Heliodorus's *Aethiopica*', *Harvard Studies in Classical Philology*, v (1894), 1–43.

Walker, J., *Rhetoric and Poetics in Antiquity* (Oxford: Oxford University Press, 2000).

Wall, A., 'Rich, Penelope, Lady Rich (1563–1607)', *Oxford Dictionary of National Biography* (Oxford: Oxford University Press, 2004).

Wallace, M. W., *The Life of Sir Philip Sidney* (Cambridge: Cambridge University Press, 1915).

Waller, G., *The Sidney Family Romance: Mary Sidney Wroth, William Herbert, and the Early Modern Construction of Gender* (Detroit: Wayne State University Press, 1993).

Warkentin, G., 'Humanism in Hard Times: The Second Earl of Leicester (1595–1677) and His Commonplace Books, 1630–60', in *Challenging Humanism: Essays in Honor of Dominic Baker-Smith*, ed. by T. Hoenselaars and A. F. Kinney (Newark: University of Delaware Press, 2005), pp. 229–53.

Weidemann, H. L., 'Theatricality and Female Identity in Mary Sidney Wroth's *Urania*', in *Reading Mary Sidney Wroth: Representing Alternatives in Early Modern England*, ed. by N. J. Miller and G. Waller (Knoxville: University of Tennessee Press, 1991), pp. 191–209.

Wilhelmi, T., ed., *Die griechischen Handschriften der Universtätsbibliothek Tübingen: Sonderband Martin Crusius: Handschriftenverzeichnis und Bibliographie* (Wiesbaden: O. Harrassowitz, 2002).

Williams, P., 'Herbert, Henry, Second Earl of Pembroke (*b.* in or after 1538, *d.* 1601)', *Oxford Dictionary of National Biography* (Oxford: Oxford University Press, 2004).

Wisker, R., 'Leveson, Sir Richard (*c.* 1570–1605)', *Oxford Dictionary of National Biography* (Oxford: Oxford University Press, 2004).

Wolfe, M., 'Piety and Political Allegiance: The Duc de Nevers and the Protestant Henri IV, 1589–93', *French History*, ii (1988), 1–21.

Wolff, S. L., *The Greek Romances in Elizabethan Prose Fiction* (New York: Columbia University Press, 1912).

Woodward, A. M., 'Greek History at the Renaissance', *Journal of Hellenic Studies*, lxiii (1943), 1–14.

Worden, B., *The Sound of Virtue: Philip Sidney's Arcadia and Elizabethan Politics* (New Haven: Yale University Press, 1996).

Worth, V., 'Les fortunes de Jacques Amyot en Angleterre: une traduction de Sir Thomas North', in *Fortunes de Jacques Amyot: Actes du colloque international*

(Melun 18–20 avril 1985), ed. by M. Balard (Paris: A.-G. Nizet, 1986), pp. 285–95.

Worth-Stylianou, V., 'Translations from Latin into French in the Renaissance', in *The Classical Heritage in France*, ed. by G. N. Sandy (Leiden: E. J. Brill, 2002), pp. 137–64.

Woudhuysen, H. R., *Sir Philip Sidney and the Circulation of Manuscripts, 1558–1640* (Oxford: Clarendon Press, 1996).

Yates, F. A., 'Accession Day Tilts', *Journal of the Warburg and Courtauld Institutes*, xx (1957), 4–25.

—— *Astraea: The Imperial Theme in the Sixteenth Century* (London: Routledge & Kegan Paul, 1975; repr. Harmondsworth: Peregrine Books, 1977).

Young, A., *Tudor and Jacobean Tournaments* (London: George Philip, 1987).

Index of place-names

General index

In preparing the indices, largely from lemmata supplied by Victor Skretkowicz, I have been greatly assisted by Dr Stefanie Lethbridge of Freiburg University and Ms Pia Prestin of Tübingen University. JBL.